A Companion to
the Anthropology
of Politics

The Blackwell Companions to Anthropology offer a series of comprehensive syntheses of the traditional subdisciplines, primary subjects, and geographic areas of inquiry for the field. Taken together, the series represents both a contemporary survey of anthropology and a cutting-edge guide to the emerging research and intellectual trends in the field as a whole.

1 *A Companion to Linguistic Anthropology*
   edited by Alessandro Duranti
2 *A Companion to the Anthropology of Politics*
   edited by David Nugent and Joan Vincent

## Forthcoming

*A Companion to Psychological Anthropology*
edited by Conerly Casey and Robert B. Edgerton
*A Companion to the Anthropology of Japan*
edited by Jennifer Robertson
*A Companion to the Anthropology of American Indians*
edited by Thomas Biolsi

# A Companion to
# the Anthropology
# of Politics

Edited by David Nugent
and Joan Vincent

**Blackwell**
Publishing

350 Main Street, Malden, MA 02148-5020, USA
108 Cowley Road, Oxford OX4 1JF, UK
550 Swanston Street, Carlton, Victoria 3053, Australia

The right of David Nugent and Joan Vincent to be identified as the Authors of the Editorial Material in this Work has been asserted in accordance with the UK Copyright, Designs, and Patents Act 1988.

First published 2004 by Blackwell Publishing Ltd

Library of Congress Cataloging-in-Publication Data

A companion to the anthropology of politics / edited by David Nugent and Joan Vincent.
      p. cm. – (Blackwell companions to anthropology)
   Includes bibliographical references and index.
   ISBN 0-631-22972-8 (alk. paper)
    1. Political anthropology. I. Nugent, David. II. Vincent, Joan. III.
   Anthropology of politics. IV. Series.

   GN492.C66 2004
   306.2–dc22
                                                                    2003018395
A catalogue record for this title is available from the British Library.

Set in 10/12.5pt Galliard
by Kolam Information Services Pvt. Ltd, Pondicherry, India
Printed and bound in the United Kingdom
by TJ International Ltd, Padstow, Cornwall

For further information on
Blackwell Publishing, visit our website:
http://www.blackwellpublishing.com

# Contents

# Synopsis of Contents

### 1  AFFECTIVE STATES
*Ann Laura Stoler*

In this essay, Stoler challenges the assumption that the mastery of reason, rationality, and the exaggerated claims made for Enlightenment principles have been at the political foundation of nineteenth- and early twentieth-century colonial regimes and should be at the center of critical histories of them. Colonial states and their architects were focused instead on the racially appropriate distribution of sentiments, on racialized assessments of affective dispositions, and their beneficent and dangerous political effects. Analyzing the staging and aftermath of a demonstration of Dutch-born and creole Europeans in Java in May 1848, she examines the strain between parental feelings and political allegiance and what urgent efforts Dutch authorities made to educate the affective habits of both.

### 2  AFTER SOCIALISM
*Katherine Verdery*

A defining characteristic of former socialist societies was their property order, distinctive from that of capitalist societies. This chapter discusses how socialist property was organized, with examples drawn from agriculture, and explores the implications for post-1989 transformations toward private ownership in Eastern Europe and the former Soviet Union.

### 3  AIDS
*Brooke Grundfest Schoepf*

Political and economic interests have shaped response to the AIDS pandemic from the outset. Struggles over meanings and resources, and their effects on prevention and treatment policy, are analyzed with special reference to Africa, where the author has conducted AIDS prevention research since 1985. The results of these struggles have implications for the rest of the world, wherever poverty, violence, and inequality create HIV risk that cannot be overcome by individual actions.

## 4  CITIZENSHIP
*Aihwa Ong*

Against the background of debates that globalization has led to claims for mutlicultural citizenship, this chapter considers how neoliberal techniques are remaking the spatial, social, and moral borders of the nation. The capacity of entrepreneurial figures to manipulate and transform borders into values of trade and production has restructured the value of capital and labor across transnational space, leading to a "splintering" of citizenship. Two alternative interventions to the proliferation of transborder assemblages of human needs are suggested. Strategies can be informed by an ethics of corporate reciprocity on the one hand, or by an informal moral economy on the other, requiring many agents to distribute different kinds of material, technical, and social goods in the interest of achieving a kind of complex equality across the spaces of global capital.

## 5  COSMOPOLITANISM
*Ulf Hannerz*

There is a cosmopolitanism of culture and a cosmopolitanism in politics – is there a connection between them? This chapter explores that issue, and several other questions relating to this complex concept and its place in an interconnected world. Are cosmopolitans always members of the elite, or are the social bases of cosmopolitanism now changing? Can cosmopolitans have roots? Does cosmopolitanism in politics aim at a world government, or are there other alternatives in building an acceptable world order? What are bottom-up and top-down cosmopolitanisms? What is the place of cosmopolitanism in an unequal world?

## 6  DEVELOPMENT
*Marc Edelman and Angelique Haugerud*

"Development" is a slippery concept that has attracted attention from an astonishing array of scholars. This essay explores the Enlightenment roots of debates about development; the clash of radical and mainstream paradigms such as twentieth-century theories of imperialism, modernization, and dependency; and the rise of economic neoliberalism. Anthropology absorbed the seismic changes of the new free-market regime partly by culturalizing and dehistoricizing globalization, and by downplaying its political-economic and legal dimensions.

## 7  DISPLACEMENT
*Elizabeth Colson*

The political implications of the massive population displacements characteristic of the current world are a challenge to those concerned with how people engage with one another in political action. Political anthropologists who study displacement deal with questions of identity, processes of estrangement and stigmatization, definitions of boundaries and citizenship, the strategic resources of diasporas, and how all of this impacts upon evolving definitions of an international political order.

## 8  FEMINISM
### Malathi de Alwis

This chapter revisits the Strathernian formulation of an awkward relationship between anthropology and feminism. It explores the category of the "political" through an ethnography of a Sinhalese women's protest movement, but seen from the perspective of the anthropologist as feminist, who struggles with the contradictions inherent in participant observation.

## 9  GENDER, RACE, AND CLASS
### Micaela di Leonardo

Feminist scholarship on gender, class, and race politics has matured over the last quarter-century. But globalizing neoliberal capitalism and the growth of purblind idealist postmodern scholarship have conjoined to deflect attention from progressive scholarly and popular analyses. An historical and ethnographic consideration of "home" in America illustrates the productiveness of a feminist "culture and political economy" epistemic frame in political analysis.

## 10  GENETIC CITIZENSHIP
### Deborah Heath, Rayna Rapp, and Karen-Sue Taussig

This chapter examines the dispersed power relations and cultural-technical alliances that characterize the geneticization of contemporary science and social life. Illustrated with examples from our multi-site fieldwork on genetic knowledge production, our analysis draws on insights from science studies, feminist scholarship and queer theory, disability studies, and ongoing discussions of emergent forms of citizenship. Within a technically mediated public sphere, identities and alliances are transformed, calling into question the distinction between the subjects and objects of scientific inquiry.

## 11  THE GLOBAL CITY
### Saskia Sassen

The organizing theme of this chapter is that a focus on cities allows us to see a variety of processes as part of globalization in a way that the typical focus on macrolevel cross-border processes does not. What are often barely visible or recognizable localizations of the global assume presence in cities. The global city in particular enables global corporate capital, by providing specialized capabilities and world-class supplies of professional workers. But it also can function as a space of empowerment for disadvantaged groups because it enables forms of politics and types of political actors excluded from the formal national political system.

## 12   GLOBALIZATION
*Jonathan Friedman*

This chapter focuses on the relation between class formation and the dynamics of global process. It suggests that class is an extremely important parameter of analysis that has been overlooked by most of the anthropological literature on globalization. After arguing that class relations have a definite cultural content and are susceptible to ethnographic scrutiny, the chapter locates class as a process in relation to larger global processes, suggesting that class structure in European states represents something of a "structure of the long run." The chapter continues with a comparative historical analysis of the discourses of global elites, and argues that current multicultural/ hybrid discourses about globalization are a rerun of earlier elite discourses. This implies that many of the contemporary assumptions concerning globalization are socially positioned ideological products rather than examples of scientific analysis.

## 13   GOVERNING STATES
*David Nugent*

This chapter develops a critical commentary on Weberian and post-Weberian approaches to the state. Drawing on ethnographic material from the northern Peruvian Andes, it shows the importance of distinguishing state (in the Weberian sense) from governmentality (in the Foucauldian sense). Most scholars have treated the governmental states of Western Europe as normative, and in the process have obscured the broad range of forces that have sought to order national societies in relation to the extraction of wealth and the accumulation of capital.

## 14   HEGEMONY
*Gavin Smith*

A term made important in social science and the humanities by Antonio Gramsci, hegemony refers to the complex way in which power infuses the various levels of the social world: social reproduction, social practices, and the constituting of the social person. Beginning with an understanding of how the term emerges from the historical context and epistemology of Gramsci's writings, the essay then explores the possible usefulness and limitations of the term for current social and political analysis.

## 15   HUMAN RIGHTS
*Richard Ashby Wilson*

Cultural relativism in the Boasian tradition obstructed the anthropological study of human rights in the years immediately after World War II, but the rise of Marxism and opposition to the Vietnam war raised the profile of social justice issues in the discipline. This focus became more explicitly rights-oriented in the 1990s with the rise of globalization literature and global justice institutions such as the UN International Criminal Courts. Anthropological studies during this time have enhanced debates about globalization by emphasizing social agency, context, and history, and the plurality of the global order.

## 16  IDENTITY
*Arturo Escobar*

Identity has become a major topic in the battlefields of theory and of politics. When connected to the study of social movements, identities can be shown to be central to the contestation over meanings and practices of world-making. This chapter features the novel ethnic identities of black groups in the Colombian Pacific rainforest region, showing their contribution to alternative forms of understanding nature, development, globalization, and modernity itself.

## 17  IMAGINING NATIONS
*Akhil Gupta*

This essay revisits theories of nationalism by focusing on questions of time and temporality, in particular, the question of whether the ideas of time central to Anderson's influential work on nationalism may not be usefully rethought from the perspective of Third World nationalism. Accordingly, notions of homogeneous, empty time, the modularity of the nation form, the seriality of the contingent, contested effort to forge a hegemonic nationalism, and the impact of late capitalism on national sovereignty are questioned.

## 18  INFRAPOLITICS
*Steven Gregory*

This chapter examines the impact of neoliberal economic reforms associated with "globalization" on two communities on the southeast coast of the Dominican Republic. It is argued that an ethnographic perspective is critical to understanding how global processes are differentially materialized within the political and historical context of specific nation-states.

## 19  "MAFIAS"
*Jane C. and Peter T. Schneider*

Attempts to analyze "mafias" in general rely on a market model that pays scant attention to differences among groups, or to their respective political and cultural contexts. This approach makes it easy to imagine the coalescence of many organized crime formations into a global criminal network – the underside of capitalist globalization. Anthropological analyses of organized crime point rather to significant differences among criminal traditions, and to the importance of specific processes through which *mafiosi* "condition" and "provision" their respective environments.

## 20  MILITARIZATION
*Catherine Lutz*

This chapter suggests a theoretical account of militarization and its relationship to broader social changes, from the emergence of nation-states to the course of racialization and other inequalities to the convergence of interests in military spending. It gives a terse account of the twentieth-century history of the militarization process and of the distinct modes of warfare that have developed over that time, and suggests how we can connect these global and national histories with specific ethnographically understood places and people.

## 21  NEOLIBERALISM
*John Gledhill*

Starting from debates about whether neoliberalism as originally understood is now behind us, this analysis demonstrates that the neoliberal model of a market society is far more radical than that of classical liberalism and continues to play an important role in shaping the logic of political processes. The chapter concludes with examples of contemporary challenges to this "deep neoliberalization."

## 22  POPULAR JUSTICE
*Robert Gordon*

Increasing disorder in many parts of the world has led to the rise of vigilantism, a phenomenon that raises questions about academic and popular conceptualizations of the state and law. Vigilantism is non-state-sponsored activity that mimics formal judicial processes. Focusing on vigilantism in South Africa, this chapter emphasizes the public spectacularity of its punishments and argues that vigilantes are double agents of law and order: In seeking to create it they undermine it.

## 23  POSTCOLONIALISM
*K. Sivaramakrishnan*

This chapter develops a commentary on the postcolonial condition in India through an analysis of representations of wildness, nature, and civility, and the practices of nature conservation. It also suggests new directions for postcolonial theory grounded in a political anthropology that simultaneously examines questions of interest and identity. It recommends multi-scale analyses of situations like the politics of nature conservation, where colonial oppositions between the wild and the civilized are reinvented in contemporary struggles over recognition and resources.

## 24  POWER TOPOGRAPHIES
*James Ferguson*

"Nation-building" and "state and society" approaches to African politics, while apparently opposed, in fact operate with an identical "topography of power" that imagines the national and the local as distinct "levels," one "above" and the other "below." By questioning this topography, and exploring the role of transnational institutions and processes in constituting and empowering both the national ("state") and the local ("civil society"), it is possible to obtain a different perspective on a range of theoretical and practical issues in the politics of contemporary Africa.

## 25    RACE TECHNOLOGIES
*Thomas Biolsi*

This chapter disaggregates "Race" into the dispersed and strategic practices that produce racial identity and alterity in local settings. Drawing on the examples of White, Black, and Indian race-lines in the United States, four technologies of race are described: Making differentiating statements about the racial self and others, techniques of racial classifying, practices of racial mixing, and regimes of racial spacing, which together produce the apparently stable "races" we live both within and against.

## 26    SOVEREIGNTY
*Caroline Humphrey*

Most theories of sovereignty operate at the level of states and nations. This chapter interrogates these theories by investigating the everyday foundations of sovereign rule in a post-Soviet, Siberian city. The emphasis is on how spontaneous and ad hoc – almost molecular – accretions form into new structures of power, which can be recognized as "sovereign." An ethnography of a non-legal, "Mafia"-run urban domain is used to explore the relation between everyday and state sovereignty.

## 27    TRANSNATIONAL CIVIL SOCIETY
*June Nash*

Indigenous peoples throughout the Western hemisphere are seeking a new relationship with the nations within which they are encompassed. They are calling for full participation in civil society as autonomous subjects. This expansion of civil society is the culmination of earlier challenges to the seventeenth-century vision of a citizens' monitoring body by women and pluriethnic constituents. Indigenous struggles for autonomy thus extend the libertarian values that animated civil society of the eighteenth century to embrace collectivist principles derived from distinct traditions that reject the patriarchal premises of modern nations.

## 28    TRANSNATIONALITY
*Nina Glick Schiller*

Past scholarship that normalized and naturalized the nation-state hindered the emergence of transnational studies and distorted the study of migration. Stimulated by contemporary globalization, a transnational perspective on migration has emerged. The new perspective highlights the significance of transnational social fields, differentiating between *ways of being* and *ways of becoming*. However, the emergence of transnational studies may impede analysis of new global concentrations of imperial power.

# Preface

In the course of completing this book we have accumulated many debts, personal and professional. It is impossible to thank everyone who has helped us, but certain people stand out. First and foremost, we would like to thank our contributors, whose stunningly original and insightful scholarship fills these pages. We have learned a great deal from them, and trust that readers will enjoy and benefit from their work as much as we have.

We would also like to express our gratitude to Blackwell's Jane Huber – the most human of editors. It was she who solicited the volume as a Companion to Blackwell's *Reader in the Anthropology of Politics: Theory, Ethnography, and Critique*, which appeared in November 2002. Jane's warmth, care, and inspiration have been indispensable throughout the long months we have worked on this project, and we will miss her humor and grace. May all authors be so fortunate as to have an editor as concerned and understanding as she. We also thank Jane's assistant editors, Sarah Coleman and Annie Lenth, for their contribution to the volume's final appearance.

Finally, we would like to thank family and friends, whose support and encouragement have been essential to the completion of this book.

The editors would like to dedicate this volume to Elizabeth Colson, in gratitude for her incomparable scholarship and a career of critical engagement with "things political."

David Nugent
Waterville, Maine

Joan Vincent
New York
21 June 2003

# Notes on Contributors

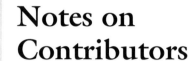

**Thomas Biolsi** teaches Anthropology at Portland State University in Oregon. He has been conducting fieldwork on Rosebud Reservation in South Dakota for 20 years, and his research interests center on the history of United States Indian policy and the politics of Indian–White relations. His most recent book is *"Deadliest Enemies": Law and the Making of Race Relations on and off Rosebud Reservation*.

**Elizabeth Colson** is retired from the Department of Anthropology, University of California, Berkeley. She has also been attached as faculty or research associate to Manchester, Boston, and Brandeis Universities, the University of Zambia, and the Refugee Studies Centre at Oxford University. Much of her research over the past 50 years, especially that in Zambia where she is involved in a longitudinal study of a resettled population, has focused on the consequences of displacement.

**Malathi de Alwis** is a Senior Research Fellow at the International Centre for Ethnic Studies, Colombo, and Visiting Associate Professor of Anthropology at the Graduate Faculty, New School for Social Research, New York. She is the co-author, with Kumari Jayawardena, of *Casting Pearls: The Women's Franchise Movement in Sri Lanka*, the editor of *Cat's Eye: A Feminist Gaze on Current Issues*, and the co-editor (with Kumari Jayawardena) of *Embodied Violence: Communalizing Women's Sexuality in South Asia*.

**Micaela di Leonardo** is the Board of Lady Managers, Chicago Columbian Exposition Chair and Professor of Anthropology, Gender Studies, and Performance Studies at Northwestern University, Evanston, Illinois. She writes both about race/ethnicity, gender/sexuality, and political economy in the United States and the intertwined American histories of scholarly work and popular culture. Her most recent book is *Exotics at Home: Anthropologies, Others, American Modernity*.

**Marc Edelman** teaches anthropology at Hunter College and the City University of New York Graduate Center. He has done research on agrarian history, rural development, social movements, and the nineteenth- and twentieth-century roots of nationalism and contemporary politics in Latin America. In recent years he has been involved in research on transnational peasant and small farmer networks in Latin America, Europe, the United States, and Canada. His books include *The Logic of the Latifundio* and *Peasants Against Globalization*.

**Arturo Escobar** was born and grew up in Colombia. He teaches at the University of North Carolina at Chapel Hill. His main interests are political ecology and the anthropology of development, social movements, and new technologies. He is the author of *Encountering Development: The Making and Unmaking of the Third World*, and co-editor (with Sonia Alvarez and Evelina Dagnino) of *Cultures of Politics/ Politics of Culture: Revisioning Latin American Social Movements*. He is currently completing a book based on ten years of research in the Colombian Pacific.

**James Ferguson** is Professor of Anthropology at Stanford University. He has done research in Lesotho and Zambia, and has written about questions of power and the state; "development"; rural/urban relations and the question of modernity; and the theory and politics of ethnography. His most recent book is *Expectations of Modernity: Myths and Meanings of Urban Life on the Zambian Copperbelt*.

**Jonathan Friedman** is Directeur d'Études at the École des Hautes Études en Sciences Sociales, Paris, and Professor of Social Anthropology at the University of Lund, Sweden. He has done research in Southeast Asia, Oceania and Europe, and written widely on general issues concerning structuralist and Marxist theory, models of social and cultural transformation, global process, cultural formations, and the practices of identity. He is a co-editor of *Social Analysis, Anthropological Theory, Ethnos,* and *Theory,* and the author of *Worlds on the Move: System, Structure and Contradiction in the Evolution of "Asiatic" Social Formations* and (with Kajsa Ekholm-Friedman) *Essays in Global Anthropology.*

**John Gledhill** is Max Gluckman Professor of Social Anthropology at the University of Manchester. His research has focused on rural society, politics, and social movements in Latin America, most recently the ethnography and history of the Nahuatl-speaking communities of the coastal sierras of Michoacán state in Mexico. His most recent book is *Power and Its Disguises: Anthropological Perspectives on Politics.*

**Nina Glick Schiller** is an anthropologist at the University of New Hampshire, Durham. Examining the constructions of categories of identity, she has worked with Haitians, the homeless mentally ill, and people with AIDS. Her most recent research explores the simultaneity of homeland ties and immigrant incorporation in small cities in the United States and Germany. Her latest book, co-authored with Georges Fouron, a Haitian scholar, is *Georges Woke up Laughing: Long Distance Nationalism and the Search for Home.*

**Robert Gordon** professes anthropology at the University of Vermont, Burlington. He has research experience in Papua New Guinea, Lesotho, South Africa, and Namibia. Among his publications are *The Bushman Myth* and *Law and Order in the*

*New Guinea Highlands* (with Mervyn Meggitt). Current research interests range from Tarzan to the history of colonial anthropology to domestic violence.

**Steven Gregory** teaches anthropology and African American studies at Columbia University, New York. He is the author of *Black Corona* and *Santería in New York: A Study in Cultural Resistance*. His most recent research examines the impact of neoliberal economic reforms and global processes in the Dominican Republic.

**Akhil Gupta** is Associate Professor in the Department of Cultural and Social Anthropology at Stanford University, California. He has done ethnographic research on agricultural communities and state bureaucracies in India, and has written extensively on space, place, and fieldwork. He is currently working on a project that looks at the implications of reincarnation for social theory, and another that is attempting to rethink theories of the state from the perspective of everyday practices and representations. He has edited *Caste and Outcast*, the autobiography of the first major Indo-American author, Dhan Gopal Mukerji.

**Ulf Hannerz** is Professor of Social Anthropology, Stockholm University, Sweden. He has taught at several American, European, and Australian universities and is a former Chair of the European Association of Social Anthropologists. His research has been especially in urban anthropology, media anthropology, and transnational cultural processes, and his most recent books in English are *Cultural Complexity*, *Transnational Connections*, and *Foreign News*. He was the anthropology editor for the 2001 edition of the *International Encyclopedia of the Social and Behavioral Sciences*.

**Angelique Haugerud** is on the anthropology faculty at Rutgers University in New Jersey. She has conducted field research in East Africa during the past two decades and is the author of *The Culture of Politics in Modern Kenya*. She is co-editor (with M. Priscilla Stone and Peter D. Little) of *Commodities and Globalization: Anthropological Perspectives*.

**Deborah Heath** is Associate Professor of Anthropology, Lewis and Clark College, in Portland, Oregon. An early advocate of multi-site anthropology of science, her research on genetic knowledge production, including a stint as a full-time DNA sequencing technician, has tracked the translocal links between the lab and its wider worlds. She initiated the collaborative project "Mapping Genetic Knowledge," and is launching a new project on Beauty Science. Recent publications include the co-edited collection *Genetic Nature/Culture*.

**Caroline Humphrey** is Professor of Asian Anthropology at the University of Cambridge and a Fellow of King's College, Cambridge. She has worked since 1966 in Asian parts of Russia, Mongolia, Inner Mongolia (China), India, and Nepal. Among her publications are *Karl Marx Collective: Economy, Society and Religion in a Siberian Collective Farm*; *Marx Went Away but Karl Stayed Behind*, and *The Unmaking of Soviet Life*.

**Catherine Lutz** teaches anthropology at the University of North Carolina at Chapel Hill. She is the author of *Homefront: A Military City and the American Twentieth*

*Century, Reading National Geographic* (with Jane Collins), and *Unnatural Emotions*. She has also conducted studies on militarization and on domestic violence for activist organizations, including the American Friends Service Committee.

**June Nash** has done fieldwork in Chiapas, Mexico, Pathengyi, Burma, the tin-mining communities of Bolivia, and a de-industrializing city in Massachusetts. She returned to her first field site in Chiapas in 1989, where she has worked for the past decade analyzing the rise of the Zapatista rebellion and its impact on highland Mayan Communities as well as the Lacandón rainforest where it began. She recently published *Mayan Visions: The Quest for Autonomy in an Era of Globalization*.

**David Nugent** is Associate Professor of Anthropology and Director of Latin American Studies at Colby College in Maine. He is the author of *Modernity at the Edge of Empire: State, Individual, and Nation in the Northern Peruvian Andes*, and the editor of *Locating Capitalism in Time and Space: Global Restructurings, Politics, and Identity*. He is currently working on a project that examines underground processes of state formation and alternative democracies in twentieth-century Peru.

**Aihwa Ong** is Professor of Anthropology and of Southeast Asian Studies at the University of California, Berkeley. She has conducted field research in Southeast Asia, south China, and California. Her books include the award-winning *Flexible Citizenship* and *Ungrounded Empires*. New works are *Buddha is Hiding: Refugees, Citizenship, the New America* and, with co-editor Stephen J. Collier, *Global Assemblages: Technology, Politics, and Ethics as Anthropological Problems*.

**Rayna Rapp** teaches anthropology at New York University. Her scholarship has its roots in her early work as a founder of US women's studies and as a reproductive rights activist. Numerous publications include *Testing Women, Testing the Fetus: The Social Impact of Amniocentesis in America*. Her two current collaborative projects focus on how new genetic knowledge is made and how it impacts different constituencies; and on the social epidemic of learning disabilities in the USA.

**Saskia Sassen** is the Ralph Lewis Professor of Sociology at the University of Chicago, and Centennial Visiting Professor at the London School of Economics. She is currently completing a forthcoming book, *Denationalization: Territory, Authority, and Rights in a Global, Digital Age* based on her five-year project on governance and accountability in a global economy. Her most recent works are *Guests and Aliens* and her edited book *Global Networks/Linked Cities*.

**Jane C. Schneider** teaches anthropology at the City University of New York Graduate Center. She is the co-editor (with Annette B. Weiner) of *Cloth and Human Experience*, and the author of several essays on cloth and clothing. Her anthropological field research has been in Sicily and has led to three books, co-authored with Peter Schneider: *Culture and Political Economy in Western Sicily*; *Festival of the Poor: Fertility Decline and the Ideology of Class in Sicily*; and *Reversible Destiny: Mafia,*

*Antimafia, and the Struggle for Palermo*. She is the editor of *Italy's Southern Question; Orientalism in One Country.*

**Peter T. Schneider** teaches sociology at Fordham University College at Lincoln Center, New York. He is co-author, with Jane Schneider, of *Culture and Political Economy in Western Sicily, Festival of the Poor: Fertility Decline and the Ideology of Class in Sicily,* and *Reversible Destiny: Mafia, Antimafia, and the Struggle for Palermo.* He is pursuing his interests in organized crime and criminalization through a new section on these issues at the New York Academy of Sciences.

**Brooke Grundfest Schoepf** went to Zaire (now Congo) in 1974–8 to teach economic and medical anthropology. Since that time she has led research and training teams in ten African countries. In 1985–90 she and colleagues conducted multidisciplinary AIDS prevention research in Kinshasa and other cities of Congo. Their work has appeared in books and journals from 1988. Schoepf's forthcoming book is *Women, Sex, and Power: A Multi-Sited Ethnography of AIDS.* She is a senior fellow at the Institute for Health and Social Justice, Department of Social Medicine, Harvard Medical School, Boston.

**K. Sivaramakrishnan** is Associate Professor of Anthropology and International Studies, and Director, South Asia Center, at the University of Washington, Seattle. He is the author of *Modern Forests: Statemaking and Environmental Change in Colonial Eastern India,* and the co-editor (with Arun Agrawal) of *Agrarian Environments: Resources, Representations, and Rule in India,* and *Regional Modernities: The Cultural Politics of Development in India.*

**Gavin Smith** has worked in Latin America and Europe. His book, *Livelihood and Resistance,* was an ethnographic study in Peru of the relationship between people's forms of livelihood and their political expression. His *Confronting the Present* reports on his European research, and also explores issues related to political engagement and scholarship. He has also edited, with Gerald Sider, a book on the selectivity of history – *Silences and Commemorations.*

**Ann Laura Stoler** is Professor of Anthropology and History at the University of Michigan, Ann Arbor. She has worked for some 30 years on race and the politics of colonial cultures in Southeast Asia and on the historical and contemporary face of race in France. Her most recent books include *Carnal Knowledge and Imperial Power: Race and the Intimate in Colonial Rule,* and *Tense and Tender Ties: The Politics of Comparison in Colonial Studies and U.S. Empire.*

**Karen-Sue Taussig** is an Assistant Professor of Anthropology and Medicine at the University of Minnesota. She has conducted ethnographic research on genetics and social life in the Netherlands and the United States since 1993. She is currently completing a book about genetic practices and social life in the Netherlands.

**Katherine Verdery** teaches Anthropology at the University of Michigan. She has conducted both field and archival research in Romania and for the last decade has been working on property restitution, specifically of land, in Transylvania. The results of that work are forthcoming as *The Vanishing Hectare: Property and Value in Postsocialist Transylvania*. Previous books include *What Was Socialism, and What Comes Next?* Her next project concerns the process of collectivizing land in Romania in the 1950s.

**Joan Vincent** is Professor of Anthropology Emerita at Barnard College, Columbia University. She is the author of numerous books and encyclopedia articles on political anthropology. These include *Anthropology and Politics* (1990, reissued 1995) and Blackwell's *The Anthropology of Politics: A Reader in Ethnography, Theory, and Critique*. She has most recently completed *Seeds of Revolution: The Cultural Politics of the Irish Famine* (forthcoming).

**Richard Ashby Wilson** is the Gladstein Chair of Human Rights and the Director of the Human Rights Institute at the University of Connecticut. His most recent books are *The Politics of Truth and Reconciliation in South Africa* and *Human Rights in Global Perspective* (co-edited with Jon P. Mitchell). He is editor of the journal *Anthropological Theory*.

# Introduction

## Joan Vincent

Certain attributes of anthropology make its research into politics an exhilarating if, at times, a dangerous project. Anthropology has its beginnings not, as many suppose, in European colonialism but in the observation and study of the problematic nature of political relations among marginalized populations in the home territory: in the United States, among Native Americans; in Britain along the Celtic fringe of Scotland and Ireland; in continental Europe among the "folk" or "peasant" peoples; and in Asia among minorities, some "enclaved," some religious converts. All had in common rapid, even cataclysmic, change. For some this accompanied conquest or territorial expansion and the uprooting that modernity demanded. For some it meant isolation, assimilation, or under-development. Characteristic of all such peoples among whom anthropologists worked was change in place, change of fortunes, change in their human condition. These are the worldwide conditions that shaped anthropology in its beginnings and continue to do so today.

The anthropology of politics has certain specific characteristics that distinguish it from other disciplines in the social sciences and humanities that study the political realm. First and fundamentally, it is grounded in its practitioners' *field* research and analyses and syntheses derived from the fieldwork of others. Equally important to the anthropology of politics (as, perhaps, this *Companion* documents too profusely) is reading. Anthropologists read in the vernacular language of their respondents and in the language of their discipline. They read the ethnographies and analyses of other anthropologists utilizing iconic comparative frameworks that contribute to, but do not delimit, their own findings – or, better – constructions. And they read politics as written by political scientists and historians, sociologists and literary critics, philosophers, theologians, and medical scientists that project concerns and concepts that cross disciplines and languages. Our *Companion* readers will find all these practitioners within its pages – and veterinarians, police officers, and protesters besides.

And, as anthropologists read, so, surely, do they write. For this dimension of their craft they have retained the somewhat old-fashioned (and not always apt) term "ethnography" (*ethnos*, Greek for nation, used in Aristotle's sense as "public," as in "public domain" or "public health"). It is because anthropology's sense of self is rooted in ethnography that, in this *Companion*, not simply reading but field experience – formative of what is perceived as awareness and knowledge for transmission to others – figures large in some of the chapters that follow. This is not an anecdotal ploy, a colorful interlude in the exegesis; it is a device to empower the reader. God – or the Devil – is in the detail. Ethnography is the anthropologists' pride and joy, the discipline's life-blood on which all else in their craft depends. It empowers the reader and it empowers the critic. It is detailed but principled. It permits the comparisons and contrasts – some, perhaps, unexpected – that move the discipline along to engage with changed forms of political activity, new ideologies. It expands anthropology's horizons. As Richard Fardon has observed, "Anthropologists are at their best when spotting what other commentators have missed, underplayed, or simply not been willing to do. *They go where other researchers do not go, and for longer.*" And, as this quotation indicates, they are *au courant*. That remark (with emphasis added) appeared in the *Times Literary Supplement* on 9 May 2003!

In the most abstract terms, the political anthropologist's goal is to understand, interpret, and transmit the ideologies and circumstances of political structure, political organization, and political action. These relate to each other as choreography does to dance, and as dance does to performance. They may address issues of temporality in discerning political systems and political processes. And, having read across these parallel tracks in the study of politics, placing a new light or providing a new insight, here or there, the palimpsest of "deep politics" is enriched and the nature of universal human politics made less obscure.

There is nothing quite like this in primarily Western-oriented textbooks and training manuals in political science, political sociology, or political philosophy. Political anthropology's depth of field research underpins its critiques of stereotypes and misinterpretations of political systems of oppressed and abused populations from the Colonial to the Cold War era and, alas, today – in the twenty-first millennium's newly flaunted Age of Empire. But anthropology's contribution to political knowledge is necessarily dyadic: the power-full, as well as the power-less, Western corporate capitalist as well as subaltern Third Worlders are integral parts of the fieldwork milieu, although the one may be more spectral, the other more embodied. For anthropologists, irrespective of where they are working in the world, in Silicon Valley or South African township, in post Cold War Russia or postcolonial Dominican Republic, a particularly valued contribution lies in discerning and laying bare the politics below the surface realities they seek to understand – in a word, infrapolitics.

## THE COMPANION

The readers' *Companion* is rich fare. In the pages that follow, you will find that the anthropology of politics is, like anthropology itself, always in crisis. It is poised on thresholds or cusps: postcolonialism; after socialism. Some chapters address what are increasingly seen as global crises: AIDS, refugees, displaced persons, the disappeared, the spread of corporate capitalism, lack of access to neoliberal (purportedly) "free" trade, environmental "disasters." They contribute knowledge of what really happens *on the ground*, in places often far away from those who are politically responsible. They discuss remedies: human rights tribunals, condom distribution programs. They bring a sense of political structures "disturbed," displaced, or disrupted. They report indigenous forms' spread, globally in some cases: "mafias," protection rackets, vigilantes, trade in drugs and arms, refugees, aspiring citizens, body parts.

Other chapters report on changing phenomena, new wine in old bottles: civil society, flexible citizenship, genetic citizenship, the global city, emergent forms of sovereignty, in some cases pushing the old concepts to the limits on ethnographic proving grounds for their earlier adequacy. Many reflect – and reflect on – conceptualizations and theory that have traveled across the humanities and social sciences: governing states, identity, imagined nations. Some adopt new frameworks: power topographies; race technologies. Some make use of the archives in the field and in the metropole, in bureaucratic and medical records, reading other people's correspondence, past and present.

The ethnographic coverage is broad: in time from colonial Java to post 9/11 Fort Bragg; in space from Latin America to the Caribbean; within the United States of America from Silicon Valley, California, to a South Dakota Indian reservation, to New Haven, Connecticut; in Europe from Sicily, through Romania to Russia; from Africa to South Asia (India and Sri Lanka) and thence to China and across the Pacific rim back to Canada and California. No wonder cosmopolitanism, transnationality, and globalization provide political anthropology's contemporary world-views as they do for many of the people among whom they work. And, as if to satisfy the most voracious of this *Companion*'s readers, the index is geared to providing even more "exotic" (from the Greek *exo*, meaning "outside") commonalities and contrasts in the human political condition.

# Affective States

CHAPTER **1**

*Ann Laura Stoler*

Much of colonial studies over the last decade has worked from the shared assumption that the mastery of reason, rationality, and the exaggerated claims made for Enlightenment principles have been at the political foundation of nineteenth- and early twentieth-century colonial regimes and should be at the center of critical histories of them. We have looked at what colonial authorities took to be indices of reasoned judgment and the political effects of policies that defined rationality in culturally narrow and prescribed ways – at the epistemological foundations of received categories as much as the content of them. Students of the colonial consistently have argued that the authority to designate what would count as reason and reasonable was colonialism's most insidious and effective technology of rule – one that, in turn, would profoundly affect the style and strategies of anticolonial, nationalist politics.

Viewed in this frame, colonial states would seem to conform to a Weberian model of rationally minded, bureaucratically driven states, outfitted with a permanent and assured income to maintain them, buttressed by accredited knowledge and scientific persuasion, and backed by a monopoly of weaponed force. Similarly, they have been treated as contained if not containable experimental terrain for efficient scientific management and rational social policy, "laboratories of modernity," information-hungry machines that neither emergent European states nor capitalist enterprises in Europe could yet realize or afford. In either account, it is the conceit of reason and the celebration of rationality on which imperial authority has been seen to rest – and eventually to fail and fall.

It is precisely confidence in this model and the genealogy of that claim that I question here. If a homage to reason was a hallmark of the colonial, it was neither pervasive, persuasive, nor empire's sole guiding force. As striking in the nineteenth-century Dutch archives of colonial Indonesia – in its more public as well as its secret documents, official and private correspondence, commissioned reports, guides to good health, economic reform, household management, primary education, and belles-lettres – is not the rule of reason but what might be (mis)construed as its very opposite: namely, a discursive density around issues of sentiments and their subversive tendencies, around "private" feelings, "public moods," and their political consequences, around the racial distribution of sensibilities, around assessments of affective dispositions and their beneficent and dangerous political effects.

Dutch colonial authorities were troubled by the *distribution* of sentiment, by both its excessive expression and the absence of it; of European fathers too attached to their mixed-blood offspring, of Indies-born European children devoid of attachment to their (Dutch) cultural origins, of European-educated children who, upon return to the Indies, held sympathies and sensibilities out of order and out of place. Administrative debates over social policy were strained over the extent to which the affective attachments colonial agents and subjects held for family, language, and homeland were at odds and whether they should – and could ever – be under the state's control. What states of mind and sentiment might be considered concerns of state were questions revisited by those who governed from up close and afar. It pitted governor-generals against ministers of colonies, local officials against their superiors, and city police charged with enforcing state directives against the colony's most prominent European city fathers. Here, I argue that the "political rationalities" of Dutch colonial authority – that strategically reasoned, administrative common sense that informed policy and practice – were grounded in the management of such affective states, in assessing appropriate sentiments and in fashioning techniques of affective control.

The formal and formulaic styling of the official archives of the nineteenth-century Dutch East Indies may be read as discourses devoted to the supremacy of reason, but in the first part of this essay, I suggest they yield a different sense of the colonial when read for the sensibilities to which they were attuned, through impassioned as well as disinterested stories, through a fuzzier set of conceptual distinctions, through a blurred rather than a sharp Cartesian lens. I outline how sentiment has been situated in colonial studies and why it has been treated as an embellishment to, rather than the substance of, governing projects.

The second part offers a challenge to that analytic convention. It looks at an unprecedented protest on Java, in Batavia – the seat of Dutch authority in the Indies – in May 1848 (not coincidentally a cataclysmic revolutionary moment in European history), a protest remarkably organized and attended by both European-born and creole whites – many of whom were themselves agents of the state. The demonstration, its staging, its aftermath, and the arresting accounts of it that circulated in the colony, the Netherlands, and among empire-watchers beyond opens a set of broader questions: how colonial authorities imagined a shrinking world with global resonance, in which riots in Paris could unseat Dutch rule in Java; what they saw as the relationship between the parental and political sensibilities of their agents and potential adversaries and what urgent efforts they made to educate the affective habits of both. The demonstration and subsequent analyses of it pitted parental sentiments against the security of rule, and in so doing forced civil servants to choose between loyalty to Dutch metropolitan authority and a close-knit family – and ultimately to choose a Netherlands fatherland or an Indies homeland with which they would ally themselves.

## SENSE AND SENSIBILITY IN COLONIAL STUDIES

If a discourse that both speaks of, and expresses, sentiment is everywhere in the colonial archives, why then has that relationship between its management and colonial governance been so easily side-stepped and so awkward to pose? At one level the answer may seem obvious. Critical analyses of colonial authority have often treated the affective as a smokescreen of rule, as a ruse masking the dispassionate calculations that preoccupy states, persuasive histrionics rather than the substance of politics, the moralizing self-presentation of the state as itself a genre of political authority.

One view has described an age of empire in which imperial states and their bourgeois subjects celebrated the story that humanitarian social reform was empire's *raison d'être* and driving force. In empires at home and abroad, "compassion," "pity," and "empathy" – imposed and unsolicited – motivated reformist zealots who swarmed in the underworlds of Amsterdam, London, Paris, and their colonial "Other Worlds" overseas. Echoing Bernard Shaw in his 1907 play *Major Barbara*, students of colonialism have waged a political assault on such moralizing missions and their "do good" bourgeoisies, mocking "uplift" projects and their redemption-seeking advocates. Impatient with benevolent, sentimental imperialisms and their self-serving justifications, we have looked more at the "rational" categories behind panics and the strategic disciplinary social reforms that followed.

Others have turned away from a focus on sentiment altogether, dismissing both the denigrating irrationalities and charged passions attributed to colonized peoples as transparent features of colonialism's reductive racist ideologies. In this view, a more rational actor better captures the nature of agency across the colonial divide: attachments and affections – tender, veiled, violent, or otherwise – get cast as compelling flourishes to historical narratives, but as distractions from the "realpolitik" of empire, its underlying agenda, and its true plot.

Some might (rightly) argue that this caricatures or, at least, overstates the case. Early students of colonialism who have identified the psychic injuries of empire, what Frantz Fanon and Homi Bhabha, following him, referred to as the "weeping wounds" imposed on the colonized. Aimé Cesaire, Albert Memmi, and George Orwell have singled out the anxieties and insecurities of those taught to rule and the violence that followed from the prescriptions imposed on and weakly or fiercely embraced by them. Still, *how* sentiments figured in and mattered to statecraft remains marginal, and what habits of the heart and what *redistribution* of sentiments were produced by colonial states (as distinct from the trauma of postcolonial conditions) and what dissensions existed between the order of families and that of states is barely addressed.

Again colonial print culture points in a different direction: official archives, novels, the press, and epistolary history register "structures of feeling" of political import – emergent critique, inchoate common and unarticulated expectations, what Raymond Williams (in his influential work *Marxism and Literature*) describes as interpretive labor barely within the semantic and political reach of their authors. We might even ask whether affect versus reason, feeling versus thinking, were familiar and current distinctions to which administrative expertise could then be addressed. The categories may have been available and relevant but, as we shall see, confidence in their clarity and content was not.

It is not just that private passions had public consequences, a point that has been made often and well. Nor is it that the metaphors of feeling culled from other intimate, trusted, and well-established communities of sentiments shored up the ties between ruler and ruled, as Lynn Hunt cogently argues in her analysis of the "family romance" of the French Revolution (see her classic work, *The Family Romance of the French Revolution*). Nor is it, as US historian Melvin Yazawa contended, to account for the model of governance in the early American Republic, that "the conception of a polity that combined restraint with affection...[drew on] the traditional familial paradigm of patriarchal authority" (Yazawa l985:19). These analyses focus on the practical power of paternalistic *metaphor* and familial *analogy*, less on the sorts of governing practices that directed and reworked those family affections.

My argument is rather that the Dutch colonial state's concern over sentiment, the state's assessment of the intensity of "feelings," "attachments," and senses of belonging – that prompted loyalties to race over family, or family over state – were not metaphors for something else but instrumental as "dense transfer points of power" in themselves (a term Michel Foucault uses to describe, not "structures of feeling," but the power inherent in discourses of sexuality). Such concerns informed virtually every aspect of social policy, political calibrations, and the tone and tenor of the archives produced about them. The philosopher William Connolly's claim that public reason depends on "a visceral register," "on culturally formed moods, affects, sensibilities," begins to address the issue: management of the agents and subjects of colonial rule depended on reformatting the visceral and mediating the ties that bound families as well (1999:27).

Debates in the Dutch East Indies over educational reform, orphanages for abandoned "mixed-blood" children, citizenship requirements, marriage laws, and the entrance requirements for civil servants were charged with a common tension. Each was riveted on what sorts of institutions, policies, and environment would produce *sensibilities* that were fitting, *aspirations* that were appropriate, *dispositions* that would confirm the explicit and implicit entailments of social membership and the truth-claims that distinguished ruler from ruled.

While evidence of rationality, reason, and progress were invoked to confirm privilege and station, European colonials policed their borders by other criteria, attended to with equal and studied care. As I have long argued, access to European legal status for the Indies born of mixed parentage was accorded on the display of a familiarity and proficiency with European cultural styles that required proofs of estrangement of other kinds – evidence of feeling "distanced" from that "native part of one's being" – of "feeling no longer at home" in a native milieu. That racial membership was as much about the cultivation of cultural competencies, moral virtues, and character as it was about the hue of skin produced a quest for measures of those competencies and how they might be obtained.

Investment in the distribution of sentiment showed up in other registers of governance as well, in the "emotional standards" that policy-makers imagined were needed to rule. Evaluations of internal comportment – evidence of integrity, reserve, and trustworthiness – generated and motivated the density of the colonial state's archival production and bureaucratic labors. In *A Social History of Truth* (1994), Steven Shapin argues that "good character" measured one's degree of civility and respectability in the world of seventeenth-century science – precisely because it appraised one's claims to be convincing and worthy of trust. It economically signaled whether one could speak the truth – and therefore whether one was competent to assess the character and truth statements of others. In the nineteenth-century Indies, assessments of sentiment similarly determined how truth-claims were made and whose accounts were reliable. Appeals to sacrifice, social empathy, family honor, and parental affections guided the rhetorical strategies of bureaucratic reports, both their credibility and the future advancement of their authors.

Entrance exams for the Indies civil service, like those for the British in India, measured character as much as bookkeeping skills – "self-denial, diligence, temperance, and self-control" were coveted bureaucratic traits. Sympathy and compassion may have defined "masculine sensibility" in the eighteenth century, as students of that period argue, but it extended to nineteenth-century political life as well. Thomas Haskell's subtle argument that the market gave rise to "new habits of causal attribution that set the stage for humanitarianism" by making trust and breach of promise central to the character of social relations on which capitalism would rest suggests another (Haskell 1985); namely, that racialized categories of colonial rule depended on an implicit causal argument that affective states (rather than physiology alone) so well measured reliability, morality, and the habituated " invisible bonds" of race, that they could serve as the basis for citizenship as well. "Men of character" *were* by definition men of reasoned feeling – qualities that both indexed social origins and were built into racial grammars. As Amat Rai contends, "the rule of sympathy" both marked and created colonial inequalities of the British empire in India (Rai 2002). But one could go further: it also produced structures of feeling, comportment, and taste that distinguished the quality of citizens from subjects and their disparate entitlements.

Nor were emotional excess and its inappropriate display imagined as confined to the colonized side of the imperial divide, with reason and rational action on other. If sentiments may be taken as "settled dispositions," and reason as "the internalization of public procedure," as various students of the social history of emotions suggest, then both shared a coveted space of governance – for it was through these settled dispositions and practices of European officials and their families that colonial regimes *reordered* relations within those families themselves.

Historian of South Asia, Christopher Bayly, in a thoughtful study of British India's information order, argues that the mastery of "affective knowledge" was an early concern of the colonial state that diminished throughout the nineteenth century as that state became more hierarchical and governing became a matter of routine (1996). Here, I argue the very opposite: that affective knowledge was at the core of political rationality in its *late* colonial form.

The accumulation of affective knowledge was not then a stage out of which colonial states were eventually to pass. Key terms of the debates on how best to support poor whites and alter their child-rearing practices through the 1930s (just before the overthrow of Dutch rule in the 1940s) make that point again and again. When architects of colonial social policy argued against "care by the state" (*staatszorg*) for support of abandoned mixed-blood children and for "mother care" (*moederzorg*) instead, they were putting responsibility for the formative production of sentiment at the heart of their political agendas. When these same high officials disputed how best to secure "strong attachments" to a Dutch homeland among a disaffected and expanding European Indies population, "feeling" was the word that cropped up again. Deliberations over the quality of upbringing and rearing were disquieted reflections on what it took to make someone moved by one set of sensory regimes – of sounds, smells, tastes, and touch – and estranged from another. Dutch authorities never agreed on how to cultivate European sensibilities in their young, nor just how early in a child's development they imagined they needed to do so. But as a broader view of the history of child-rearing would show, these were not idiosyncratic colonial concerns. They were shared by a range of macropolities as well as seventeenth-century philosophers, eighteenth-century medical experts, and nineteenth-century purveyors of domestic science who harped on similar questions: whether affective dispositions were transmitted through a wet nurse's milk, in the moral ecology of an infant's home, through playmates, or in the social comportment of one's mother. In the mid-nineteenth century Indies too, enormous administrative time and energy were expended on devising education and social policy that would provide European-born children and those of their creole counterparts with proper "feelings" and "attachments" to things Dutch and with a "disaffection" for that which was native – or preferably a disinterested sympathy for it.

Preoccupation with the making of virtuous selves prompted recurrent debates over where it should take place and who should be charged with responsibility for it: state institutions or families – isolated rural reformatories or carefully cordoned urban orphanages, European parents (however impoverished or ill-educated) or rather surrogate providers, those in the colonies or instead in Europe, in proximity to parents or removed from the home. Social planners, parents, doctors, and teachers stumbled repeatedly over the same question: whether what it took to be European required the instilling of specific formal knowledge or less tangible ways of being and feeling in the world. For nearly a century, between the 1830s and 1930s, Dutch authorities called on experienced counsel and expert knowledge to determine how to provide European children in the Indies with a sense of national and racial affiliation and to gauge how much an education of the sentiments was critical to both. They understood what anthropologist Janis Jenkins has underscored in a different context: that states do more than control emotional discourse, they attempt to "culturally standardize the organization of feeling" and produce as well as harness emotional discourse within it (1991:139–165).

Such a focus opens another possible premise: that the role of the state is not only as Antonio Gramsci defined it, in the business of "educating consent." More basically, such consent is made possible, not through some abstract process of "internalization," but by shaping appropriate and reasoned affect, by directing affective judgments, by severing some affective bonds and establishing others, by adjudicating what constituted moral sentiments – in short, by educating the proper distribution of sentiments and desires. As a starting point, such a premise anticipates questions that much current literature on state formation dissuades one from exploring. What makes it easier to imagine that millions of people willingly die for nations but not for states (as Benedict Anderson asks in his classic work, *Imagined Communities*)? How is it that a citizenry can accrue virtue by sacrificing their lives for nations, but people are killed not by nations but by states? How is it that states are commonly viewed as institutional machines that squelch and counter passions, while nations are envisaged

as culturally rich producers of them. Why does the pairing of "state" and "sentiment" read as an oxymoron?

It is certainly not because the dissonance of that pairing has always been the case.
Attending to the relationships between affective disposition and political control,
between the art of governance and the passions, between politics and sentiment were
defining concerns of seventeenth- and eighteenth-century statecraft, and of those
moral and political philosophers of the "long" eighteenth century, so deeply intent
on identifying the relationship between the two. The relationship between "private
vices" and "public benefits," between affective life and political life, between individual passions and social welfare was central to the philosophical queries and concrete
agendas of the most familiar figures – Bacon, Spinoza, Locke, and Hume – and
lesser luminaries such as Mandeville, Hutcheson, and Shaftesbury. As students of
seventeenth-century philosophy such as Susan James are increasingly prepared to
argue, not only have the passions been systematically ignored as "a central topic in
the heartland of early modern philosophy" (1997:2). It is precisely the fact that the
passions were seen as directed in the interests of political power that captures a critical
impulse of European society in that period.

It was Francis Bacon (philosopher *cum* civil servant) who argued with such clarity
that the governance of states should be conceived of as something not dissimilar to
"the government within." Both, he claimed, required knowing "how affections are
kindled and incited; how pacified and refrained . . . how they disclose themselves, how
they work, how they vary, how they gather and fortify, how they are enwrapped one
within another" (quoted in Hirschman 1977:16). For Bacon, the role of the state was
clear: namely, to curtail the dangerous and combustible passions of ordinary men.
Statecraft was not opposed to the affective, but about its mastery. Like Foucault's
notion of governmentality – statecraft joined the care and governing of the polity to
the care and governing of the affective self.

These earlier philosophers debated not only the state's responsibility to check
unruly passions but to harness them in the interests of the public good. Albert
Hirschman's observation that the nineteenth-century modern state would later be
"called upon to perform this feat . . . as a civilizing medium" alerts us to a crucial
point: that what is now taken as intuitively incompatible in the heyday of colonialism
– namely, a state devoted to reason *and* defined by its efficacy in dealing with sentiment and affective knowledge – was once not so. We may credit Foucault with
reminding us that all sentiments have their histories, but it was Hirschman's unique
insight that a sentiment's history is an inspired way to trace the changing form and
content of what constitutes the subject and terrain of politics. The seventeenth-
century notion that states should be called upon to harness individual passions, to
transform and civilize the sentiments of their subjects, as Hirschman recognized, was
"to prosper as a major tenet of 19th-century liberalism" (1977:16).

Hirschman's compelling history of the passions suggests another historical frame
for understanding what made up colonial rule; not one that starts with the supremacy
of reason in the nineteenth century and then traces it back to the roots of rationality
in the Enlightenment. Rather one that sets out another genealogy of equal force –
and of as long a *durée*. Such a genealogy might register the incessant flux in political
theory in the seventeenth and eighteenth century over what morality was (either a
"natural sense" or a "cultivated taste" as it was for Shaftesbury). It would look to

that eighteenth-century "culture of sensibility" that tied material power and moral weight to the taste and character of cultivated men. It would register that sustained oscillation between reason and sentiment rather than the final dominance of the one and their definitive severance. It might take up William Reddy's case (in *The Navigation of Feeling*) that modernity's early moments in the "age of reason" could as accurately be characterized as an "age of sentiment." It would register the recurrent attack on what constituted reason in the eighteenth century. Nor would such a genealogy track a rule of reason (veering on or off course) with an undercurrent of emotional strain. Rather it might resituate the art of governance as one modeled after an earlier genre that took as its project the art of knowing oneself as part of the "art of knowing men" (James 1997:2–3). As Alasdair MacIntyre (1984:149) writes, "Virtues are dispositions not only to act in particular ways, but also to *feel* in particular ways. To act virtuously is not to act against inclination; it is to act from inclination formed by the cultivation of the virtues. Moral education is an '*éducation sentimentale*'."

Indies' colonial authorities would have agreed. Placing colonial governance in such a frame makes more sense. A joint commitment to reason and to affective knowledge was central to nineteenth-century imperial polities and a basic tension within them. Gary Wilder refers to "colonial humanism" as a new way of exercising political authority in the early twentieth-century Greater France (1999:33–55). But in the Indies, the fact that men of force were men of feeling intervenes earlier: by the 1830s and 1840s in debates over social projects, public welfare, and in concerns over the viability of Dutch authority.

Thus to return to an earlier question: Why can students of colonialism declare with such conviction that "colonialism became the mode of universalizing the rule of reason" in the nineteenth century? Why have those who study colonial authority and its representations ignored Hirschman's observation? As we shall see, it is not official archives that bracketed sentiment from their cultures of evidence and documentation, but our preemptive readings of them.

## PARENTAL FEELINGS AND TORN HEARTS

Education is used to train members of a class and to divide them from other men as surely as from their own passions.

(Williams 1977:137)

On May 23, on a Monday evening in 1848 when most members of Batavia's European community would otherwise have been just stirring from their late afternoon naps, there was an extraordinary meeting of an extraordinary mix of society, unprecedented in the history of the Dutch Netherlands Indies. From 500 to 600 people (that authorities later identified as "European," "Creoles," and "Colored,") gathered on the steps of the exclusive European Harmonie Club, to register their dissatisfaction with a specific set of government policies and to make a specific set of demands. At the top of their strategic list was growing resentment at a decree of 1842, that produced a monopoly on senior posts in the colonial civil service, exclusively for those who would pass their exams at the Delft Academy in the Netherlands. The many who could not afford to send their sons to Delft (those with too many children to support or who chose not to do so) were barred from the higher administration and confined to minor posts with meager salaries and 50 percent lower pensions.

In practice the ruling sent a confused message about privilege and race for while it blatantly discriminated against the middling Indo-Europeans whose sons were confined to the lowliest civil service jobs, it was also perceived as an unjust assault on those Dutch-born and creole Dutch who were unwilling to send their sons off to Europe for a decade of their lives. Those gathered at the Harmoniehof charged the government with discriminatory pension allocations to civil servants trained in the Indies, and condemned an educational policy that forced estrangement from their sons. Among those gathered were several hundred "colored" who were "well-to-do," but equal numbers of senior Dutch civil servants, high-placed administrators of justice, finance, and religion, and respected "city fathers."

It was an extraordinary event but not a spontaneous one. Not only was the Governor-General informed several days earlier when, why, and where the gathering would take place – after negotiation he grudgingly granted permission for it, in part because the organizers (among whom was the influential, high-placed, religious leader Baron van Hoevell and Vice-President of the High Court Ardesch) persuaded him that "parental feelings" were really "social" rather than political matters, unlike their other shelved demands for parliamentary representation, a reduction of the autocratic power of the Minister of Colonies, and freedom of the press – which he thought were decidedly not.

Still the 15-page petition addressed to the king in the name of the Indies' *inboorlingen* (natives) was uncompromisingly bold in its claim. *Inboorlingen* for them did not refer to the native population but those of European descent with attachments to the Indies, whether or not they were Indies born. The petition called for the dismissal of a virulently anti-creole member of the Indies Advisory Council, abolition of the existing civil service exam (the *Radikaal*) and improved higher education in Java for those of European descent. The gathering took place without incident, ended a few hours later, and was never to be repeated again. In Dutch colonial historiography (that so shies from evidence of white sedition) it has rarely received more than a paragraph.

On the face of it, this was neither a radical nor a particularly revolutionary event. But if the gathering was tempered and contained, the events that surrounded it, the interpretations of what it represented, and the sentiments that motivated and were attributed to those who took part were not. Reports were filed of *liplaps* (those of mixed blood) in the crowd, armed with hidden daggers and walking sticks concealing their swords. Over 1,300 artillery and infantry troops were ordered by the Governor-General to wait on the outskirts of Batavia ready with arms, on the ostensible fear of what such a gathering might encourage among the wider Javanese and Chinese population. The Minister of Colonies Baud urged that the gathering's organizers immediately be dismissed from their posts and banned from ever returning to Java. In subsequent months, thousands of pages of government reports assessed the social make-up of the Indies' European community and its liberal political currents – identifying those already affiliated and which others might potentially join. By the time news of the event reached Minister Baud in The Hague some seven weeks later (the Suez Canal had not yet been opened), secret government missives were steeped in talk of treason, the dangerous threat to peace and order that this backhand stab at metropolitan rule inspired. What was at issue was the sustainability of Java as a Dutch colony – and the jewel of its empire.

But who and what was the threat was not clear, certainly not to Governor-General Rochussen in his letter to Baud four days after the gathering: Was it subversion (led by such liberal "hotheads" as van Hoevell and his cronies) among the European-born, well-to-do city fathers? A creole revolt among the Europeans who were Indies born and bred? Or a bid for total rupture from the Netherlands among the impoverished "coloreds" with nothing to lose? Rochussen reported an "extremely agitated" public mood and his outrage at Van Hoevell's betrayal and audacity in publishing a "disobligingly rude" article from confidential government documents in the most widely read Indies European press. And interspersed with these comments, he would circle back to the rumors in white Batavia, to the stir among educated people in the literate city about revolution in Europe and what the Marseille mailboats would bring to Java.

Why did the gathering generate the fervor it did and what were the stakes? Was it, as some authorities thought, the prelude to a revolutionary overthrow among liberal-minded colonials with a communist bent, influenced by the events in Paris two months earlier, or a refusal to accept the racialized terms of educational policy? Or was the threat more local, immediate, and more threatening still, generated not by an impassioned outburst but by a critique lodged in the sustained distress of parents who refused to allow their sons' careers to be contingent on an education in Europe, on 4,000 miles of distance and at least eight years of separation from their mothers and fathers? Whatever the answer (and it was partly *how to frame the question* that the administrative alarm was about), on the line was the Dutch regime's ability to assess sentiment – to predict and manage its visceral – and what Hume understood so well as its "contagious" quality.

In May 1848 Victor Hugo (2002:552) was to write from Paris, "From February to May, during these four months of anarchy in which the collapse was felt on all sides, the situation of the civilized world has been unparalleled/impossible. Europe feared a people, France; this nation feared a part of it, the Republic; and this part feared a man, [Auguste] Blanqui. The ultimate word for everyone has been fear of something or someone." The revolutionary fervor that swept through France in February 1848 resonated throughout Europe, but as Victor Hugo observed, what was at risk and under attack was not always the same. Demonstrations, petitions, and pamphlets in Vienna, Prague, Milan, in Berlin, Frankfurt, and Dresden, among Italians and Czechs, were about civil rights, representation in parliament, workers' councils, and workers' benefits. What motivated disenfranchised middle classes in February was not what made the working classes take to the streets in May. People talked of revolution and the abolition of slavery in Guadalupe in late April, but at the very proclamation there was, as Hugo snidely observed, a white proclaiming it, a mulatto holding his parasol, and a man of color carrying his hat (Hugo 2002:551).

And what did this have to do with Batavia? Some authorities thought everything; some saw the Harmoniehof demonstration as local and localized with little to do with events in Europe at all. Authorities seemed to have feared less a revolution in the making, inspired by the vibrant and violent French and German models, but rather one of another sort – a creole revolt against a metropolitan hold on power, against what one petition called "the Russian autocracy" of colonial rule, against a bureaucratic system that made advancement contingent on prolonged absence from family; and not least, protest among the respected and "respectable" against a system that assured loyalty to the Dutch state rather than the Indies through a careful design that valorized and required for promotion competence in a removed, Netherlands-filtered knowledge of Java.

If students of the colonial are now more ready to accept the argument that metropole and colony should be treated as one analytic field, there is less consensus on what those contingencies looked like on any specific historical ground. We remain confounded by the direct and indirect ways in which metropolitan practices shaped the face of empire and the other way around. But the conundrum is not ours alone: working out those contingencies of comparison and scale, what made up a "community of sentiment" and what did not, were the very dilemmas of rule and what the tools of statecraft were designed to assess.

Authorities in Batavia spent the next weeks and months after the May demonstration trying to work out whether it was a home-grown colonial liberalism that had seized white Java, parental sentiment that was turning the state's very agents against it, ripples of constitutional reform in the Netherlands reverberating in the archipelago, or revolutionary fervor that traveled with the mailboat from Marseille. Rochussen's report to Baud was confused about what was a risk, and what and who was to blame. When February's overland post arrived in Java on March 23, he reported no mention of the "new popular revolution and the fall of the crown." But by mid-April private French tradesmen came laden with news of increased "communist thinking" spreading among Europe's working poor. Still, that news was almost two months out of synch with the quick-fire shift in political direction in France, where what had been accomplished in February and March "evaporated" by May. By June the workers' national councils were abolished, thousands were killed or arrested, the bourgeoisie was in the ascendancy, and the workers' movement was a shambles. Radicals did sing the *Marseillaise* in Amsterdam like they did in Paris, but revolution in the Netherlands was quickly turned into constitutional reform, the King abdicated, ministers resigned, and although the *burgerij* – the stolid bourgeoisie – came into partial power, over the next 25 years, 80 of the 100 government ministers were still of patrician origin.

Events in Java were clearly part of a global historical moment but the public mood was on a track of its own. In the narrative offered to the Minister of Colonies by the Governor General, generalized disquiet among the European population was evident in early May. By the 14th of the month – only nine days before the demonstration, hundreds of people gathered at the old city's customs house to await the ship from Singapore carrying their subscriptions to the European press. The scene described is so dissonant with current historiography on Java, that it is almost hard to imagine what the Governor-General described as an alarming outburst on the dock, of people cheering, "the boom has fallen, the day of freedom has arrived for the colonies' inhabitants to air their grievances and have their desires heard." Police reports from the night before described something stranger still, a charivaresque cacophony in the colored quarters of the old city, where small groups were heard shouting, "*Samoanja radicaal*," accompanied by music on copper kettles and rowdy groups throwing stones at the house of that high official they labeled "an enemy of the people," while calling for his deportation from Java.

But what was this outcry, "*Samoanja radicaal*," which seems to capture a bilingual *jeu de mots*, a Dutch Malay play on words, embedded in the phrase? The Malay word *samoanja* [semuanja] literally means "they're all," or "everything is," which is clear enough. But *radicaal* in mid-nineteenth-century Indies Dutch had two very different referents: one to "radical," in the more familiar political sense that we know, and second to the "Radicaal/Radikaal," the name for the despised diploma for entry into the elite ranks of the civil service, which spoke of metropolitan privilege and could be granted only if one passed through the academy in Delft. It was, of course, abolition of this very diploma that was the principal demand of the demonstration the next day. Whether "*Samoanja radicaal*," on the streets of Batavia in 1848 meant "everything is about the diploma," or "everyone should be able to get the diploma," or "they're all radical" is impossible to say without more context. But there was no further mention of the phrase. It disappears from the archive as does its rich ambiguity and bivalence from Indonesia's historiography. Nor did the Governor-General bother to explain it to Baud, an ex-colonial himself, who (was it assumed?) knew what it meant.

It is not clear that the Governor-General himself did. His narrative moved from concerns over high officials "liberally expressing themselves in an unseemly manner," to an understanding that more was at issue than a "momentary outburst of feeling." His story jumped from Batavia to Paris and back again, lingering on a thumbnail sketch of the Indies population, so negative in its appraisal that it would suggest that the colony was already on the road to revolt and would not await the independence movement that would come in such a different guise and composition a hundred years later. In his breakdown were "the Javanese without any attachment to us," the Arabs who "hate us," "the Chinese who cherish money and sensual pleasures," and a European population with increasing numbers of liberal thinkers, made up of "the most energetic but not the most moral part of the nation."

But more disturbing to him still were increasing numbers of "coloreds" so reduced to poverty they could only hope for a change and had nothing to lose. Here was a population, he argued, growing in proportion to the number of Europeans, more dangerous in relation to the increased scientific knowledge that had filtered to them, and more discontented with regard to the low-ranking civil-service posts which they had long occupied, considered their own, and now saw threatened by more Dutch youths descending from Java. These "colored," he insisted, were despised by natives and Europeans, but what most marked them, he held, was that they had been devoid in their youth of the language of parental love (*ouderliefde*) and were either nameless or with names that branded them as illegitimate by birth, and with souls full of hate for Europeans, among them those who were accounted their fathers.

Parental love, either too much of it, as among Creole whites, or not enough, as among mixed-bloods, seems to come up at every turn. Parliamentary representation in Holland was a problem, but the "more dangerous grievances" were those perceived as widely shared and broadly spread among Europeans, old-timers and newcomers, Creoles, and the Colored: what they all wanted was an end to the privileges of the Delft monopoly and the Radical certificate denied their offspring.

Worse still was this forced separation, what feelings it engendered, and what it did to people's lives. Rochussen punctuates his narrative with three searing tales that were plastered across the local European press: the case of a Dutch mother who went into shock and then was senseless or mad for several months after her small son's departure for Europe, knowing she would not recognize him, nor he her, upon his return a decade later; a father ruined by debt and broken by his efforts to send his son to school in Holland; and perhaps most poignant of all, the story of a well-groomed young man returning to Java after ten years' leave, poised on the dock as his ship landed, asking, "which of these ladies is my mother?"

Rochussen's defense of his actions, that he had granted permission for the gathering because these "fatherly hearts" (*vaderhart*) were bleeding too badly to be restrained or refused – was not as convincing to the king, who questioned his judgment and took the political bite of those parental sentiments to be what they were – directed against the metropolitan monarchy and the emergent colonial state.

Historians of the Indies have alluded to the "demonstration," but the machinations that surrounded it have been of little interest, and the political threat envisioned at the time is perhaps so unthinkable that it has been rendered irrelevant, minor, and erased. The prominent Dutch historian Cees Fasseur, one of the few to write about it, makes passing mention of the newspaper coverage of the maddened mother and ruined father as evidence that "pathos" was played upon and running high (1993:121). But government authorities at the time took more seriously the political force of affect and undoubtedly dismissed his dismissal and questioned his claim. For debates prompted by the event stayed focused for literally decades on two things: what sorts of domestic and pedagogic environments could instill loyalty to Dutch rule, and what sorts would nurture affective attachments dangerous to it?

In subsequent months, the Dutch administration hardened its conviction that a European education was critical to "the necessity for close ties between the motherland and the colony" and to counter a prevailing trend: namely, "that with European children raised in the Indies those ties had come unbound and European parents too had estranged themselves from the motherland." Family rearing was important but only if mediated by other sorts of apprenticeship defined by the interests of the state. While some proposals were made to establish secondary schools "in healthy highland areas of Java . . . separated from the Indies world" (on a "European footing" and with only European servants), more powerful voices did not agree. The latter argued that the neglectful and indulgent mothering styles of native and Indo-European women were turning their mixed-blood children toward native sensibilities rather than "cultivating" in them the energetic self-discipline that emerged in an authentic Dutch milieu. In the end, European higher education in the Indies was extended to Java but always limited on two foundational grounds: that Indies mothers were incompetent to rear their young as true Europeans; and that prolonged residence in the Netherlands would "awaken love of the fatherland" for those Indies-born children so sorely deprived of it. The Minister of Colonies succinctly made the latter case (AR/KV 1848/ no. 389, 22 September 1848):

> Raising and educating Europeans in the Indies will stand in the way of a desirable civilizing of the native and this upbringing will have the result that these children so frequently suckled with the breast milk of Javanese wet nurses along with their own native children, at a more advanced age, will lack any sense of unity with Europeans. They become haughty, imperious, lazy and lascivious. They will learn from their youth to

mistreat and denigrate servants. They become, in male adulthood, still greater despots than now is the case with the native rulers themselves.

At issue was *not* the insubordinate sentiments of the colonized but rather the inappropriately expressed aspirations of those "out of character" and "out of place": "haughty" referred to those mixed-bloods who refused to do manual labor: "imperious" to those creoles who claimed their right to the status of "full-blooded" Europeans: "lascivious" to those whose sexual interests were seen as misdirected toward those above their racialized standing and class. At issue was an "emotional economy" that not only "mirrored controversies about social status," but tied affective expression to the worth of human kinds.

This fear of contagious emotions prompted another fear: that those who remained too attached to the Indies would see themselves more as "world citizens" (the first time the term appears) than as partisans of Dutch rule. Over the next 70 years, Dutch authorities continued to battle over when and how to intervene in the education of school-age children and in the formative rearing of the very young. Crucial to this understanding was that local knowledge should never be too local and that familial attachments were to be mediated and reworked through concerns of state, filtered through a fine sieve, through the ears of Dutch categories, distilled into a typology, reconfigured as qualified knowledge in a usable form. While that could conceivably be done in Indies schools run on European principles by Europeans, success was easier to assure from a distance in the Netherlands – where racialized categories could be reduced to a number of traits, assuring that the colonial lens would color a world in which family ties between parents and their young would be reconstituted, where moral virtue would be defined by a muted attachment to one's offspring, and where local knowledge would be digested through institutions of learning in Europe and re-served as qualified knowledge that was no longer local at all.

## AFFECTIVE REGISTERS IN THE PUBLIC SPHERE

Colonial scripts prompt us, their distant readers, to imagine that concern with the affective was centered on unbridled passions, irrational outbursts, or at least the unpremeditated affective states their bearers embraced. They make it plausible to imagine that European authorities feared most what the Dutch novelist Louis Couperus referred to in 1900 as the "hidden force" to which the colonized had access and colonials unknowingly could be subject, to a display of sentiments that showed more powerful mystic and mental states. But, as the May 23 demonstration suggests, this may not have been the case. Stronger than extemporaneous passions was the fear of *sustained* sensibilities, and the political standards they called into question. Momentary outbursts were manageable. It was those sentiments – such as those of parental distress – that expressed tacit judgment, "settled dispositions," and expectations with high political stakes. Sentiment mattered not because it was in conflict with reason but because it demanded specific sorts of reason that indicated social knowledge of expectations and a rich evaluative vocabulary of social critique.

What colonial officials feared was not the *economic* costs of educating Europeans in the Indies (undoubtedly cheaper for the state), but the disparate cultural, economic, and political investments of those families that sought to bring up their children in the Indies and dared to think of the Indies as their "fatherland" and make it their home. If postcolonialism produces a fax nationalism as Ben Anderson suggests, colonialism produces its own distorted long-distance variant. Colonialism remains viable as long as the longings are for a European elsewhere, if colonial pleasures were seen as the hardship allowance but never a home. The colonial difference was key: in the colonies freedom of speech, press, and representation were inappropriate, and those Europeans that wanted them were advised to just go home.

Immanuel Kant's reason-based account of moral thinking and practice may have informed imperial policy, but so did John Locke's, that moral thinking was embodied in the dispositions of the everyday, in the habits of comportment that had to be learned. Like Locke, colonial experts debated the sensibilities that endowed certain individuals with the "capabilities" to exercise freedom, to be responsible as citizens capable of progress, to be deemed actors who were "rational men." Those city fathers, government officers, men of class and character who gathered on the streets of Batavia in 1848 were deemed "unseemly," unreasonable, and therefore unsuitable colonial men. To be reasonable was to master one's passions, command one's sensibilities, and abide by proper invocation and dispersal of them.

George Orwell's futuristic fantasy, *1984*, of a thought-police staked out in an interior family space, was undoubtedly based on the specter of totalitarian European states, but it may have been equally motivated by another state Orwell knew more intimately and at least as well, the British imperial one. The colonial state could only be selectively panoptic; directed less on the internal dynamics in domestic space of the colonized than on the minute movements and psychological perturbations of their white and not quite white agents – in their clubs, offices, with their children and at home. Reading Orwell's "Shooting an Elephant" up against *1984* suggests a colonial order of things in which sentiments (nostalgia, humiliation, and rage) were produced by political systems. They were not metaphors for them.

Sentiment is the ground against which the figure of reason is measured and drawn. Colonial documents carve out "structures of feeling" across dry reports that state agents passed among themselves. "Unseemly" sentiments indexed mismanagement of the polity and mismanagement of the self. A genealogy of colonial morality would not be a search for what is moral and what is not but rather a history that would address its changing vocabulary and political coordinates. It might look at imperial interventions in the emotional economy of the everyday, but also at why colonial authorities knew what we are only beginning to grasp, that the viability of colonial regimes depended on middling masters predicting and prescribing what sentiments, in whose hands, would be contagious – and which would not.

## NOTE

Part II of this chapter is based on documents collected at the General State Archives (Algemeen Rijksarchief [AR]) in The Hague, the primary archive for nineteenth-century Dutch colonial state records. This account is based on the following: KV no. 317 (5 August 1848); KV no.158 (25 May 1848); KV no. 391 (8 September 1848), and the documents filed therein. Following the publisher's format, I have not noted each of the specific documents throughout the text.

For detailed references to these documents see my forthcoming book, *Along the Archival Grain: Colonial Archives and their Affective States* (Princeton University Press).

## REFERENCES

Bayly, Christopher A. (1996) *Empire and Information: Intelligence Gathering and Social Communication in India, 1780–1870*. Cambridge: Cambridge University Press.

Connolly, William (1999) *Why I Am Not a Securalist*. Minneapolis: University of Minnesota Press.

Fasseur, Cees (1993) *De Indologen: Ambtenaren voor de Oost, 1825–1950* [The Indologen: Civil Servants for the East, 1825–1950]. Amsterdam: Bakker.

Haskell, Thomas (1985) Capitalism and the Origins of the Humanitarian Sensibility. *American Historical Review* 90:339–361, 547–565.

Hirschman, Albert (1977) *The Passions and the Interests: Political Arguments for Capitalism Before Its Triumph*. Princeton, NJ: Princeton University Press.

Hugo, Victor (2002[1848]) *Choses vues*. Paris: Gallimard.

James, Susan (1997) *Passion and Action: The Emotion in Seventeenth-Century Philosophy*. Oxford: Clarendon Press.

Jenkins, Janis (1991) The State Construction of Affect: Political Ethos and Mental Health Among Salvadoran Refugees. *Culture, Medicine, Psychiatry* 15:139–165.

MacIntyre, Alasdair (1984) *After Virtue: A Study in Moral Theory*. Notre Dame: University of Notre Dame Press.

Rai, Amit (2002) *The Rule of Sympathy: Sentiment, Race and Power, 1750–1850*. New York: Palgrave.

Shapin, Stephen (1994) *A Social History of Truth: Civility and Science in Seventeenth-Century England*. Chicago: University of Chicago Press.

Wilder, Gary (1999) The Politics of Failure: Historicising Popular Front Colonial Policy in French West Africa. In *French Colonial Empire and the Popular Front: Hope and Disillusion*, ed. Tony Chafer and Amanda Sackur, pp. 33–55. Basingstoke: Macmillan.

Williams, Raymond (1977) *Marxism and Literature*. Oxford: Oxford University Press.

## SUGGESTED FURTHER READING

Elias, Norbert (1982) *The Civilizing Process*, trans. Edmund J. Jephcott. New York: Pantheon.

Ellison, Julie (1999) *Cato's Tears and the Making of Anglo-American Emotion*. Chicago: Univesity of Chicago Press.

Fanon, Frantz (1986) *Black Skin, White Masks*, trans. Charles Lam Markmann. London: Pluto.

Hunt, Lynn A. (1992) *The Family Romance of the French Revolution*. Berkeley: University of California Press.

Memmi, Albert (1967) *Colonizer and Colonized*. Boston: Beacon.

Reddy, William (2001) *The Navigation of Feeling: A Framework for the History of Emotions*. New York: Cambridge University Press.

Rosaldo, Michelle Z. (1984) Toward an Anthropology of Self and Feeling. In *Culture Theory: Essays on Mind, Self, and Emotion*, ed. Richard A. Shweder and Robert A. LeVine, pp. 137–157. Cambridge: Cambridge University Press.

Sica, Ala (1988) *Weber, Irrationality, and Social Order*. Berkeley: University of California Press.

Solomon, Robert (1988) On Emotions as Judgement. *American Philosophical Quarterly* 25:183–191.

Stoler, Ann Laura (1995) *Race and the Education of Desire: Foucault's History of Sexuality and the Colonial Order of Things.* Durham, NC: Duke University Press.

Stoler, Ann Laura (2002) *Carnal Knowledge and Imperial Power: Race and the Intimate in Colonial Rule.* Berkeley: University of California Press.

Stoler, Ann Laura (in press) *Along the Archival Grain: Colonial Cultures and their Affective States.* Princeton, NJ: Princeton University Press.

Yazawa, Melvin (1985) *From Colonies to Commonwealth: Familial Ideology and the Beginnings of the American Republic.* Baltimore, MD: Johns Hopkins University Press.

# After Socialism

CHAPTER **2**

## Katherine Verdery

> The socialist economies of Eastern Europe did not have *any* property system ... governing their productive activities.
>
> (Frydman and Rapaczynski 1994:11)

> Ownership is the back-bone of the economic system of Socialist countries.
>
> (Knapp 1975:64)

Anthropological study of "actually existing" socialism was just gathering momentum when the events of 1989 effectively ended its existence in Eastern Europe and the former Soviet Union. Over 20 years of research had produced a variety of writing on processes of socialist planning, rural political economy, kinship, gender, ritual, and ethnic and national identity; collectively, these works were beginning to reveal the lineaments of how socialist societies operated and how they differed from each other. Summarizing one clear result, Ernest Gellner observed that socialism's defining trait was the exhaustive invasion of the economic by the political. Perhaps nowhere else was the phrase "political economy" so apt a description. In this sense, "politics," although manifest in most anthropological writing on socialism, had not been the focus of scholarly argument: rather, it simply permeated that work. To grasp the intertwining of the political with the economic (and with everything else) would prove essential to comprehending trajectories out of socialism after 1989.

One area of which this was particularly true was the transformation of property, in a process usually referred to as "privatization." Because the destruction of private property had been so central an imperative in building up socialism – recall Marx and Engels's dictum in the *Communist Manifesto*, "The distinguishing feature of communism is the abolition of bourgeois property" – the destruction of socialism after 1989 meant almost everywhere the recreation of private property. That process was soon to reveal, however – to scholars, at least – the necessity of better understanding how property functioned in socialism. Not surprisingly, its operation proved quintessentially political.

My task in this essay is to outline the politics of socialist property and to indicate what that meant for property after socialism. This is not a topic with a wide anthropological literature. To be sure, anthropologists have long occupied themselves with describing property forms in various settings. Beginning in the 1990s, a number participated in the resurgence of anthropological interest in property, investigating new property phenomena such as indigenous land claims, cultural and intellectual property, property in body parts, and the property implications of new reproductive technologies. Some of this work raises questions about how we should understand property and whether it is even useful as an analytic concept. But anthropologists had not much investigated property in *socialist* contexts, merely writing about life within socialist property organizations such as collective farms, without investigating them as property forms per se. Most of what we know about socialist property has come from legal scholars (e.g., Knapp 1975 and Butler 1988) and economists (e.g., Kornai 1980, 1992).

The same has been true since 1989: anthropologists have described property transformation, especially the dismantling of socialist agriculture, without systematically exploring the property forms of the period before. Debate (such as that evident in my two epigraphs) comes primarily from lawyers, political scientists, and economists. Unlike many other topics in this volume, then, mine is relatively unencumbered by scholarly debates within anthropology. Instead, we have argued against the simplistic treatment of privatization in those other fields – objecting, for instance, to the ethnocentric assumptions of the "bundle of rights" conception so widely used in economics and legal studies, or to neo-institutionalist analyses aimed at designing market-based property regimes from the top down. A particular target of my own work on the privatization of land (Verdery 2004) is the idea that socialism was a "property vacuum," having no property order, and that as a result its collapse left a *tabula rasa* upon which new forms could be written unproblematically. I hold the view that socialism had a distinctive property order, though its categories and operation differed fundamentally from those of market economies.

To write of "property in socialism" reifies and homogenizes a reality that was much more complex, with variations occurring both across the region and through time. In the space available to me, however, I can offer only a schematic, condensed account, aimed at clarifying the problems of making "private property" from the property relations of socialism in the former Soviet bloc (the literature upon which I draw). In analyzing socialist property, I follow Bronislaw Malinowski's dictum and ask not just about *ownership* but about how socialism's resources were *used*. This strategy enables me to examine socialist property in something like its own terms, instead of as a failed form of Western property.

I should begin by stating how I understand the notion of property. I think of it as a set of political, economic, cultural, and social constructs and relationships through which persons are related to one another by means of things or values. Central to it are cultural idioms by which persons are defined and linked through social relations to one another and to values. Property is about boundary-making: it sets up inclusions and exclusions, "belongings," such as what "belongs" to whom, and who belongs to or has affinities with some larger entity that occupies a relation to specific values or things. Along with this boundary-making, property is about appropriation, and thus about power. Power affects *which* actors and relations are recognized or privileged in a given understanding of property, as well as permeating the wider field of social relations in which persons and values are linked. Moreover, the ways of linking persons and values often require adjudication – a power-laden process. The social relations of property, like all social institutions, are rule-bound; power is inherent in setting and contesting those rules. In short, I see property as simultaneously a cultural system, a set of social relations, and an organization of power, all coming together in social processes.

Using this framework, I shall organize my discussion as follows. First, I look at socialist property as a cultural system: what kinds of *categories* did socialist systems create for property? Here I emphasize the categories as formally constituted in law; I discuss later on how they functioned in practice. Second, I consider it as a system of power and social relations: how did these categories become real, and what kinds of property relations were constituted thereby? How did a system based on ownership by "the whole people" break that entity down into smaller ones interacting with one another to make property rights effective? I examine how resources were transacted within the "unitary fund" of socialist property and explore some of the stratagems by which actors strove to make its rigid constructs workable; my examples come mainly from socialist agriculture. I conclude by discussing some implications of this way of organizing property for its transformation after 1989.

## TYPES OF PROPERTY AND OWNERS UNDER SOCIALISM

The outlines of socialist property as a cultural system emerge from inspecting its legal categories, as evident in legal texts. We should exercise care in reading them, for law did not occupy the same place in socialist societies as in Western ones, and property was no exception. Under socialism it was less a *legal* and more an *administrative* matter; it was governed not by legal procedures aimed at creating regularity and certainty but by administrative measures, regarded as having the *force* of law though not created through a legislative process backed by courts. This said, however, it is worth inspecting the law because the categories employed in a society's laws help to reveal its conceptual foundations, giving a sense of its universe of both power and meaning, as well as of how these differ from those of other property regimes.

Michael Heller observes that whereas the categories of market-based economic and legal systems focus on the scope of individual rights for each of several types of property – such as "real" and "personal" property, "tangible" and "intangible" property, or state, common, and private property – socialist legal categories empha-sized, rather, the *identity of the owners*, the property types associated with each, and the social relations characterizing them (Heller 1998:628). Socialist law recognized three principal kinds of owner: the state, socialist cooperatives, and individual persons or households. These related to four property types: state property, cooperative property, personal property, and private property. "The state" owned state property (though, technically speaking, the owner was not the state but another abstract entity, "the whole people"); "cooperatives" owned cooperative property (technically, the owner was the collective membership of that cooperative, not a larger socialist entity); and "individual" households owned personal and private property, the two types being distinguished from each other in that personal property consisted of items of consumption, private property of means of production (see note on p. 34).

State property/ownership was the most important of these types of property and owners; all other forms were subordinated to it. For example, in agriculture there were two main organizational forms, state and collective farms. In all countries the cooperative property held jointly by members of a collective farm was ostensibly separate from state property. If a state farm were being expanded into the lands of that collective farm, however, state planners had no qualms about annexing the collective's land without acknowledging the joint rights of the farm members over it. Although for both cooperative and state property the property right was absolute, exclusive, inalienable, indivisible, and immune from attachment for debts, nonetheless "the state property right is *more absolute* than other property rights and than all other real rights" in civil law, and also *more exclusive* (Lupan and Reghini 1977:54–55). In the words of a Romanian judge with whom I spoke, "Socialist state property was *more* inalienable, *more* exclusive, *more property* than any other form, and judicial practice was to shore it up, buttressing its status over that of other kinds." This superiority of state property was reflected in the much greater material endowment of state enterprises than of the "lower" cooperative form, which was accorded many fewer resources.

"Cooperative property" consisted of means of production "donated" or pooled by individuals who had formed a cooperative. It most commonly included means of production in various trades' cooperatives, the means of cultivation in collective farms, and land that people were compelled to give them (except that in Albania and the Soviet Union, where all land belonged to the state; collective farm members jointly owned only the means of cultivation). Unlike state property, which belonged to "the whole people," cooperative property belonged *only* to those who had pooled it; their property rights resembled those of shareholders in a capitalist firm. State property coexisted uneasily with this form and was always meant to absorb it. Together, the categories of state and cooperative property made up the supercategory of *socialist property*, which included nearly all society's major means of production. Socialist law linked socialist property closely with a third type – personal property, which (according to plan) was to increase continually as part of projected improvements in the standard of living. This category consisted primarily of objects of consumption – houses, furnishings, automobiles, and so on. Laws constrained their use to keep people from turning them into means of production. For instance, one could own one's car but was prohibited from using it as a taxi to generate revenue, and one could not own more than one house lest the others be used for rental income.

In contrast to personal property, the fourth type – private property – concerned not consumption but means of production owned and used by petty-commodity producers such as uncollectivized peasants and trades-people (e.g., tailors, cobblers, or carpenters); such property was likely to be organized in households rather than in socialist organizations. Seen as a residue of the bourgeois order, private property was slated for eventual elimination and was of minimal importance in all but Poland and Yugoslavia (where private property-owning cultivators formed the large majority of the rural population). This long-term plan to eliminate cooperative and private property underlay the hierarchical relations of property forms: state property was prior to all others and enjoyed the fullest legal protection, followed (in order) by cooperative, personal, and private property.

The three types of owners (the "whole people," cooperatives, and households) were distinguished from other possible actors in that they alone were empowered to *own* and thus to appropriate. It is important to note that these actors were *defined as jural subjects precisely by their property status.* As Butler puts it for the Soviet Union, "Juridical persons are those organizations which possess separate property, [and] may acquire property and personal non-property rights and bear duties in their own name" (1988:179). Thus, jural personhood was a function of property status, and to be a jural person automatically entailed having certain property rights.

## ADMINISTRATIVE RIGHTS AND EXCHANGES OF GOODS

Defined as a jural person, an entity could further allocate rights to specific subunits – for instance, "the state" could parcel out rights to use state property, both to cooperatives and to other lower-level actors, such as state firms, socialist organizations (e.g., the trade unions or the Councils of National Minorities), or lower-level territorial units. Understanding this is crucial to understanding how state ownership worked. To do so requires that we stop asking about ownership and look at the distribution of various kinds of rights and relations, as well as at patterns of actual use.

The state held the dominant property rights, as I noted above. In order for it to be an effective actor, state property was said to form a *unitary fund*, inalienable and indivisible. It contained all means of production, including raw materials and circulating capital. But how did this arrangement work in practice – how could "the state" create production with its "unitary fund"? The most important relationship after the state's ownership prerogatives was based in the so-called *right of direct (or operational) administration* – what I will refer to as "administrative rights" – organized in what I will call, following Max Gluckman, a hierarchy of administrative estates (Gluckman 1943; Humphrey 1983). These rights were not exercised only at the top, but were allocated downward to actors at lower levels; some of their recipients were empowered to allocate them further. Here is Heller's account of how it worked (1998:629):

> Instead of assigning an owner to each object, socialist law created a complex hierarchy of divided and coordinated rights in the objects it defined . . . The law integrated ownership of physical assets within overlapping state structures, often linking upward from a state enterprise, to a group of similar enterprises, to the local and then central offices of a ministry responsible for that branch of industry.

That is, the Communist Party planning mechanism granted administrative rights to ministries, state-owned enterprises, and local authorities, who might further allocate their administrative rights downward, in the name of both the Party and their bureaucratic segment or firm. The same idea appears in a statement by Romanian legal specialists Lupan and Reghini: "In order that the state's property have productive effect, the socialist state institutes with respect to the goods belonging to it a right of direct administration, for its subunits, and a right of use, for cooperative organizations and physical individuals" (1977:54).

Through granting administrative rights, then, the party-state retained its claim to supreme ownership but exercised that ownership by allocating use and administrative rights to lower-level entities, assigning parts of the property of "the whole people" to inferior levels in the bureaucratic hierarchy. Crucially, this system of multiple and overlapping administrative rights permitted myriad transactions to occur without the institutions and forms associated in capitalism with changes in ownership, such as mortgages or sale contracts (Feldbrugge 1993:231). For instance, if one state enterprise made a contract with another to deliver its product – say, a piece of machinery – the machinery was at all times state property. Its owner did not change; all that changed was who held the power of administrative rights over it. Thus, the director of the first firm held the power to dispose of the product to the second firm – a power common to ownership relations – but ownership did not change thereby.

An important result of the patterns I have been describing was that because the units that received administrative rights thus entered as jural persons into direct relation with means of production, their managers could come dangerously close to infringing on the state's property right, even treating the firm and materials as their fief and some of the revenue as their own. The "underground factories" reported in the Soviet Union, for instance, involved managers' employing entire sections of the workforce and the infrastructure of the factory for production entirely on their own, and then keeping the proceeds. Indeed, the inability of the political center to keep these actors in check, and their gradually increased autonomy in consequence, were critical elements in socialism's transformation (e.g., Staniszkis 1989). Especially once central control began to weaken in the mid to late 1980s, these managers arrogated state powers, even selling off state assets – often to themselves. By the time privatization officially commenced, many of socialism's erstwhile directors were well on their way to being private owners, a process that socialism's hierarchy of administrative estates had facilitated. For this reason, it would be inadvisable to see administrative rights as an insignificant form of property relation. Their exercise in practice constituted state firms – particularly their directors – as powerful actors.

Socialist managers would exercise their administrative rights within socialist property in several different ways. One set involved moving around large-scale means of production – such as the machinery mentioned above. In agriculture this took the form of moving control over land among state farms, collectives, and individual households. These practices would have consequences decades later when those farms were disbanded. For example, because the early collectives had to show good results so as to "attract" more members, farm heads consolidated the pieces already donated to make compact fields of good quality that they could cultivate "rationally." That both state and collective farm heads were able to allocate rights to land at will, enjoying priority over private property rights, enabled them to reorganize the landscape for their convenience through numerous land exchanges. These were of three kinds: between collective/state farms and individuals, between collective and state farms, and among collectives or among state farms. That is, the exchanges occurred across three of the four main property types and all three kinds of owners.

In Romania, for example, Decree 151 (1950) enabled collectives in formation to create contiguous parcels by exchanging land with individual private owners who had not yet joined the collectives. Often, the land of villagers who had joined the collective or its precursor did not form contiguous blocks; officials had the right to create these by compelling nonmembers with land in the middle of a good field to exchange it for parcels at the edge. State farms seeking to consolidate their fields had the same prerogative. Individuals could not refuse these exchanges, having to accept parcels much inferior to those they had been compelled to turn over. Indeed, the decree stated that the contracts for such exchanges were valid even *without* the signatures of the owners thus displaced, as long as the local authorities invoked Decree 151 in their records. Technically speaking, farm officials were supposed to make and archive such contracts, but often – from haste, or carelessness, or confidence in the supremacy of their own property form – they did not. Their cavalier treatment of land enabled farm members after 1989 to challenge the jural status of such earlier exchanges so as to recover their better-quality parcels.

In the same spirit of rational cultivation, state and collective farms often exchanged their donated or confiscated lands with each other. Because farm directors administered the property rights to the land (albeit via different mechanisms), they could dispose of it as necessary to pursue their objectives; the wishes of the former owners had no place in such exchanges. Leaders could even enforce exchanges on private owners living in uncollectivized areas, whose private property lay at the bottom of the hierarchy of property forms.

All these exchanges altered the landscape fundamentally, creating large, undivided fields from the intricate patchwork of tiny parcels owned by persons from multiple places. Farm managers could do this, moving parcels formerly owned by myriad individuals like so many pieces on a chessboard, precisely because they enjoyed far-reaching rights to acquire and dispose of landed property, indifferent to the possible rights of the former private owners (and even to whether the land was legally state or cooperative property). Treating all collective lands as a single fund, farm managers could trade them with other units, without having to record a "property transfer" in the land registry books. After 1989, these deedless exchanges would create havoc for reconstituting private ownership.

## APPROPRIATION AND COUNTER-APPROPRIATION

Another way in which socialist managers exercised their administrative rights involved moving around items of smaller scale – not land, for example, but bags of fertilizer or apples. These items might either be allocated to them as raw materials for production (fertilizer) or come from the production process itself (apples), destined for consumption. Managers' right to move these items around at will contributed to one of the hallmarks of socialist political economies: widespread barter and trading of goods, practices necessary for production in socialism's "economies of shortage" (see Kornai 1980; Verdery 1996, chapter 1). Managers' behavior could aggravate this shortage, for they operated within soft rather than hard budget constraints and also within *plans*, which assigned them production targets; therefore enterprises hoarded their materials. In all types of firms, managers struggled to secure extra resources and to hide them from state agents who came expressly to squeeze them back out into the state property funds. Because glitches in socialist planning and distribution could prevent managers from mobilizing the necessary raw materials for the level of pro-duction expected of them, they not only demanded more inputs than they needed but held onto any excess they received or were able to produce themselves. Technic-ally speaking, it was only the managers holding administrative rights to *state* property who could do this with one another, but in practice they were linked in giant trading networks with the managers of *cooperative* enterprises (like collective farms) as well.

If enterprise managers helped to generate shortage by hoarding, however, they also strove to reduce its effects by widespread barter. They traded with other managers whatever they might have in excess supply in exchange for inputs they needed. Although these practices did not fully alleviate the problem of obtaining resources for production, since one could not always count on covering all one's needs through one's network at the necessary times, they became an integral and time-consuming part of socialist production in both agricultural and industrial settings. Reforms introduced in each East European country during the 1960s and 1970s modified economic organization and sought to make managers more accountable for their production costs, without, however, eliminating these horizontal trading networks. After 1989, those networks would prove to be sources of "social capital" – and they would be an effect of the exercise of administrative rights within socialist property.

This far-flung system of exchange rested on the personal relations of enterprise directors. It involved both items necessary for production and also the exchange of favors and gifts that might enable a director to obtain needed goods at a later time. Such exchanges of gifts and favors oiled the joints of the socialist economy and justifies our seeing socialism as a complex form of "gift economy." The gifts often came from the production process itself – especially in agriculture, where directors appropriated immense quantities of apples, vegetables, or grain to send to their cronies and party superiors. The return on such gifts might be looser plan targets, special bonuses, access to raw materials otherwise hard to obtain, or generalized goodwill. Moreover, as Caroline Humphrey has brilliantly shown (1983), participa-tion in such exchanges might be crucial to obtaining effort from those in one's workforce. What made the exchanges possible to begin with, however, was the granting of administrative rights, which entailed managerial discretion over the use of various kinds of socialist property.

Such personalization of items from the socialist property fund was rampant throughout socialist economies. As Martha Lampland has argued (1995:262–266), even to call it "personalization" may misrepresent the reality, for the line separating personal gain from the pursuit of advantage for one's unit was often difficult to draw. Moreover, officials who engaged in such behavior were not protecting only them-selves: they were creating an umbrella for whole retinues of their own – virtually the entire leadership group of the collective, for example, or at least the director's faction within it. And they were helping to make similar umbrellas for their superiors, in vast pyramids of patronage that reached to the top of the system.

A major consequence of these practices was that the boundaries within the unitary fund of property became blurred, and objects might move among numerous persons exercising with respect to them rights that were akin to ownership rights but were not consecrated as such. For example, two firms that regularly traded raw materials for production, such as a shoe factory and a factory that made leather coats, might not have clear boundaries around their "inventory," since the goods in any firm's fund of circulating capital were fungible, enabling timely substitution of materials from other enterprises. Distinctions between state and cooperative property were irrelevant in this huge "unitary fund" of socialist property; means of production and product as well belonged to "everyone," but particularly to those who managed social resources. The "fuzziness" of boundaries around socialist property makes determining both the ownership and the assets of either firm a complex process.

My discussion so far has shown how socialist managers used the official system of administrative rights to accomplish their goals while oiling it with unofficial exchanges so that it would work. I also observed that these exchanges might entail removing from circulation large portions of the goods their units produced. What about the *members* of these enterprises, the people whose land and labor made everything possible? How did they feel about socialist property and all that managerial maneuvering? At the bottom level of the hierarchy of estates, the struggle over conflicting forms of appropriation came to a head. It was here that managers' strategies for making their enterprises produce might set them at odds with their direct producers. We see this especially well with something that occurred in all types of socialist firms: "theft." I will illustrate this with theft from collective farms.

The total product of a collective farm was finite and could support only so many destinations. If farm directors gave priority to delivering on their contracts and to the gift economy, there could be little left for paying members. Indeed, the chronic complaint of collective farm members in nearly every country was that their work was woefully underpaid. This fact led them to leave agriculture for industry, if they could, and, in a "natural" form of counter-appropriation, to take things from the collective. Inspiring this was the example of their superiors, whose behavior made it fairly easy to see the collective product as "ours" for the taking. Although theft of socialist property was punishable by much heavier penalties than theft of personal property, villagers never saw their farm president sanctioned for the uses he made of their collective product. How could one distinguish "theft" from "gifts" in such circumstances?

In this way, when the heads of socialist firms unofficially moved goods into the socialist gift economy, they further blurred the boundaries within socialist property. Their self-interested notion of collective ownership, or at least collective entitlement, generalized downward from those who were not prosecuted for it to those who were, for collective farmers might be prosecuted for stealing just a few potatoes or a sack of corn from their places of work. Even if laws to this effect were rarely applied, abundant anecdotes attest to a climate of constant vigilance by farm officials and to the constant concern of members about being caught. Villagers who engaged in these practices generally presented themselves as having a *right* to take from the collective – indeed, some claimed that it was inappropriate to use the word "theft" for such behavior (e.g., Humphrey 1983:136). They saw their collective property as producing goods that belonged to them and to which they had a right, even if they sometimes had to appropriate those goods on their own. In this respect, theft of CF products was a defense of their *personal property* right against what they saw as illegitimate appropriation by farm officials.

When villagers were prosecuted for theft of collective farm produce, two fundamentally different conceptions of ownership came into conflict, conceptions rooted in one's place in the political hierarchy. "Theft" as a construct presupposes a system of clearly defined persons, objects, and boundaries that separate them; theft is a violation of those boundaries, as one agent takes something from a bounded fund of objects to which another agent lays claim. In the official organization of socialist property, the system of boundaries was three-tiered. The strongest boundary separated the "patrimony" of "the whole people" (the entire country) from that of other countries. Inside that boundary was another one separating socialist from private property; for purposes of this discussion, that boundary was the most consequential. Within socialist property there was yet another boundary, very weak and rarely observed in practice, separating state from cooperative property. Actors could appropriate the socialist product by moving things upward (across the boundaries between private and socialist, or collective and state) or laterally within a given category. What was unacceptable to the authorities was any movement of goods *downward* across the boundary between socialist property and lower types. That was theft. Party officials did plenty of it, but those appropriations often disappeared into the much larger flow of gifts and tribute upward. In equating their own appropriations with those of officials, collective farmers made the mistake of not realizing that what mattered was the *direction* in which their appropriations moved.

## IMPLICATIONS

I have been arguing that contrary to Frydman and Rapaczynski's claim (see the epigraph above) about socialism's "not having *any* property system," it had a very complex one. To grasp that system has required setting aside questions about ownership and looking at patterns of use, administrative rights, and social networks of appropriation, exchange, and reciprocity. Laws and administrative measures defined a specifically socialist property regime encompassing both agricultural and industrial production, in both state and cooperative enterprises. To solve the problem of producing within a system of centralized appropriation, communist parties established hierarchies of administrative and productive estates, held together by delegating administrative rights. These rights (the most important form of property right in socialism) were intended to link the different legal property types and to establish specific relations for values and goods. Translated into practice, however, these ceased to serve as rights over *things* but entered into social relations that privileged rights over *people*. Extended networks of reciprocity moved products upwards, laterally, and downwards, all in the service of collecting people whose goodwill, trades of raw material, protection, patronage, and effort would put socialism's productive means into motion. Those patterns, however, placed multiple demands on the social product and generated an ongoing struggle – more intense in countries such as Romania and Albania than in others – around appropriation at the bottom. Here the politics of appropriation within the hierarchy of estates in socialism's property regime came full circle.

This organization of property had major implications for the post-socialist property order that would take shape after 1989, particularly in agriculture. The policies of *de*collectivization initiated then aimed to undo the system I have described and to create or recreate private property, the form most disdained in socialist planning. How does my discussion here prepare us for the problems this transformation would encounter? I will suggest three general points that I believe are applicable to some extent for all post-socialist countries. They concern the evaluation of socialist assets, the hierarchy of property types, and the relation of administrative to legal regulation.

As a property regime, socialist property instituted an entirely new set of values, based in an ideological opposition between "socialism" and "capitalism." The values I have noted here were (1) administrative rights (rather than market forces) as the basis for moving goods and assessing their worth; (2) a hierarchy of actors and statuses, with the state at the top managing the patrimony of "the whole people," smaller cooperative entities holding common resources, and private property in households at the bottom; and (3) the priority of an administrative over a juridical definition of property. Each of these sets of values would have consequences for post-socialist property transformation.

I begin with the movement of goods by administrative means. Socialism's property regime established among people and goods a set of relations that did not rest mainly on a commodity basis. One goal, of course, was to erect a bulwark between the socialist and capitalist worlds, to protect local resources from being sucked into external capitalist markets. Serving that end were the strictures against any form of alienating socialist property, even by the party-state itself, and the insistence on the integrity of the unitary fund belonging to the whole people and administered by cadres. Thus protected from the market, the resources controlled and appropriated within socialist property relations were subject to evaluative criteria driven not by the market but by politics (e.g., what one's patron wanted, what kinds of production would best fortify the Party's power – rather than how profitable an activity might be). Under these arrangements, it was exceedingly difficult to assess the "book value" of firms being privatized, since the state, as the ultimate holder of financial obligation, had absorbed most of the liabilities of its subordinate firms, and the materials a given firm utilized in production were so often not those the state had allocated to it. After 1989, the problems of evaluating the assets of socialist enterprise, including both state and collective farms, would defeat even the smartest economists. Questions of value, from the most basic (what kind of life do people want to live) to the niggling details of a firm's purchase price, joined with questions of morality to dominate public consciousness. Who ought or ought not to be profiting from the wealth accumulated under socialism – the former managers of state firms, or foreigners, or the general public?

Some answers to these questions came from a second aspect of the socialist property regime: its creation of a ranked hierarchy of forms, with those of the state at the top, cooperative/collective forms second, and individuals/households (especially those with private property) at the bottom. This hierarchy produced a very powerful class of state-enterprise directors benefiting maximally from state resources and from their control of administrative rights over these. Even before 1989 they had begun using these rights to decompose state property from within, thereby weakening the political center (see Staniszkis 1989). As that center grew weaker, the power of these directorial networks intensified. In short, socialism's property regime gave a decisive edge in the post-socialist era to a specific group of actors: state enterprise directors. They were used to manipulating the fuzzy boundaries of socialist property, to moving resources around to maximum advantage. They disposed of large funds of social capital, in the form of their networks, and of cultural capital, in the form of their higher education and more extensive experience with the most modern technology their national economies could support. In agriculture specifically, we see the advantage of state over collective property in the greater cultural and social capital of state than of collective farm heads. State farm directors had wider circles of connections, more complex managerial experience, greater familiarity with new farming technology, better-endowed farms from which to strategize their exit, and so on, all owing to the higher position of state over cooperative property forms. Although international blueprints called for privatizing *ownership* rights, these socialist managers began by privatizing only their *administrative* rights, enabling them to avoid the liabilities of ownership by shucking those off onto the state, while still drawing upon central investments.

In this they were aided by socialism's overlapping estates of administration, which had socialized responsibility so thoroughly that the buck never stopped anywhere but continued to circulate in "gifts." They were aided, as well, by the alliances these circulating gifts entailed. Networks of directors, as Stark (1996) has shown, could use their administrative advantage to resist competitive privatizations – quite successfully, in places like Romania and Ukraine, where local actors worked to keep foreigners out. Indeed, Stark suggests, the unit for privatization ought never to have been made the individual *firm* but, rather, the inter-firm *network*. In some countries these networks would generate viable capitalist firms; in others, they would obstruct the privatization process, even using it to fortify their power by continuing to surround themselves with retinues of petitioners. This resistance would make it difficult to create the property "bundle" so dear to the advocates of private property and would perpetuate use-right arrangements similar to those of the hierarchy of administrative estates. Although it is not surprising that state enterprise directors tended to fare well in the post-socialist period, my purpose here has been to show how their future success was already inscribed in the property regime of socialism, as was the disadvantage of certain others.

Finally, I turn to the party-state's preference for politico-administrative over legal procedures. This preference entailed making decrees and administrative decisions about the use of resources but not necessarily ratifying these decisions by the legal procedures that had governed property transformation in pre-communist times. Across the whole region, 1989 initiated a process of reversing this set of priorities, attempting to create the "law-governed state." The logistical nightmares encountered in that process were legion. To illustrate these, I will discuss an example involving the ownership status of the land held in collective farms (which, as I noted, was not state-owned in most countries but belonged to the members jointly).

During the socialist period, land was administratively moved around more or less at will among collectives, state farms, and households; because who "owned" it was rarely an issue; officials generally did not record the changes by inscription in the land registers when they exchanged parcels or modified land use. But after 1989, ownership suddenly mattered very much. Had the members relinquished ownership rights altogether upon joining the collective, or did those rights maintain some kind of shadow existence throughout? What did the joint ownership of cooperatives actually mean, from a legal point of view? Did membership mean transferring actual title to physical land or, rather, transmuting that into ownership of shares, comparable to the rights of membership in a corporation, as suggested by Linda Miller (personal communication)?

Post-1989 legislators argued these questions at length, and the answers differed by country, as did the ownership status of collective farm land (see Knapp 1975). For Romania, lawyers with whom I discussed the issue gave contradictory accounts, as do Romanian law books. Writing about the status of cooperative land as part of their discussion of decollectivization, two Ministry of Agriculture legal specialists state both that "the cooperative appeared as the titulary of the property right and thus exercised possession, use, and alienation over lands of any kind in its patrimony" and that "the land continued to remain the property of the cooperative member" (Scrieciu and Chercea 1996:524, 534). The matter was crucial, for the answer to it would affect the policy options for property reform. If farm members had in fact retained some ownership rights, then after 1989 a new "law-governed state" could only confirm their ownership, rather than (re)create it. That is, collectives would have to be unmade by *restituting* or *reconstituting* prior ownership rights, rather than by impropriating owners or distributing the land exclusively to people who lived in villages, or by some other kind of land reform. Indeed, restitution would require no separate law, merely the members' joint declaration to dissolve the collective, at which point everything would revert to the status quo ante. – Never mind the complexities of discovering what that was, after so many years of exchanging land, erasing boundaries, and transforming the landscape (see Verdery 1996, chapter 6).

The more significant underlying issue, however, is this: from the vantage point of what mode of regulation – legal or politico-administrative – should the question be answered? Although law did have its place in the socialist system (increasingly so, as time went on), "legality" simply did not have the same status or legitimating function in the socialist property system that it has in market democracies. Property *law* was a supplement to the more active principle, property *administration*. Moving from such a regime to one supposedly grounded in law and judicial process raised innumerable difficulties concerning whether and how to translate administrative decrees into the language of the law in order to formulate policy. Can we select out the "law-governed" aspects of the socialist system and build a new one upon those? Or must we retroactively legalize that system – even though the premise of the 1989 events was its illegitimacy – in order to proceed?

For those who regard the entire communist period as illegitimate, none of its acts has legal status. Hence, trying to determine and reverse the legal effects of an administrative decree is pointless; one need only make new laws. The weaknesses of this position include the following. To declare the acts of the socialist period illegal ignores the judicial maxim of *tempus regit actum*, which posits that the status of an action in its original context should govern how it is regarded now. If an administrative decree "acquired the force of law," as we might translate it, then those effects should be taken seriously in disposing of present ownership claims. Moreover, dismissing the entire socialist period as illegal wreaks havoc on a notion of law-governed practice rooted in predictability and continuity. How can one simply hop over the intervening "illegal" 45 years and assert new ownership, without compromising the principle of a just claim?

The alternative is to recast the acts of that period in terms that permit continuity, even if to do so is to legitimize the system one seeks to displace. That is, restitution builds political legitimacy paradoxically: instead of playing up the *il*legitimacy of the old regime, it may require first *legalizing* the status of property under socialism *so as to* return rights to previous owners. The status of land in Hungary, Transylvania, and

Slovakia offers a particularly clear example. There, the Habsburg-derived system of land registration meant that no transaction could be performed except on the basis of a *previous* legal transaction recorded in the land register. For me to receive back a parcel of land upon which the collective farm built a structure, I must first have the structure and the parcel it stands on written into the register *as belonging to the collective farm* and then re-register it in my name. This procedure effectively legalizes the seizure of my parcel and the new use to which it was then put – that is, the procedure runs directly counter to the premise of *un*lawful seizure upon which restitution is based!

The work involved in retroactively legalizing 45 years of transactions, however, would be unmanageable. The complexities relate not only to the legal status of different kinds of resources but also to the weak or fuzzy boundaries that characterized socialist property. Lacking clear edges, it was held together by social relations that were reticular and rhizomatic, that worked *across* property types. Those uncertain edges could be advantageous, as David Stark (1996) has argued for "recombinant property." In agriculture, they could also produce chaos. All the moving around of resources, the exchanges of parcels, the hiding of land, the erasure of field boundaries; all the uncertainties about the ownership status of collective and state farm land; all the failures to write land transactions into the land register – these would make it extremely difficult to reestablish ownership rights once socialism was ended.

In this essay I have presented property in and after socialism as a quintessentially political matter – as part of a *political* economy. The politics of property resided at many levels: in the new mechanisms of appropriation that socialist property forms enabled; in the political relations of subordination and the administrative rights accompanying them; in the political values determining the hierarchy of owners and of property types; in the appropriations of productive resources by socialist managers helping their allies and currying favor with patrons; and in the counter-appropriations by various kinds of workers. These forms of politics in property shaped the trajectory of ownership that would emerge after 1989, as managers attempted to retain certain features of socialist property so as to drain state subsidies into their newly private firms; as persons well situated in the hierarchy of property types would often find themselves well situated to move into new forms of ownership, at the expense of others less favored; as local officials would manipulate the uncertainty about prior ownership to deny some people's claims in favor of their clients and friends (see Verdery 2004). The extent to which property transformation would be politicized and the means of doing so varied from one country to another. In all, however, its politicization under socialism would shape the outcome, affecting as well the legitimacy of a post-socialist property regime.

## NOTE

I use the term "cooperative" in referring to the category that includes both agricultural and non-agricultural enterprises of non-state type. When I wish to speak of non-state agricultural enterprises, I use the term *collective*, as in "collective farm," rather than speaking of "cooperative farms," since the term "collective farm" is the more widely used in English and bears more appropriate connotations.

# REFERENCES

Butler, William E. (1988) *Soviet Law.* London: Butterworth.

Feldbrugge, Ferdinand J. M. (1993) *Russian Law: The End of the Soviet System and the Role of Law.* Dordrecht: Martinus Nijhoff.

Frydman, Roman, and Andrzej Rapaczynski (1994) *Privatization in Eastern Europe: Is the State Withering Away?* Budapest, London, and New York: Central European University Press.

Gluckman, Max (1943) *Essays on Lozi Land and Royal Property.* Rhodes-Livingston Papers, 10. Livingstone, Northern Rhodesia: Rhodes-Livingstone Institute.

Heller, Michael A. (1998) The Tragedy of the Anticommons: Property in the Transition from Marx to Markets. *Harvard Law Review* 111:621–688.

Humphrey, Caroline (1983) *Karl Marx Collective: Economy, Society and Religion in a Siberian Collective Farm.* Cambridge: Cambridge University Press.

Knapp, Viktor (1975) Socialist Countries. In *International Encyclopedia of Comparative Law*, vol. 6, ed. F. H. Lawson, pp. 35–67. New York: Oceana.

Kornai, Janos (1980) *Economics of Shortage.* Amsterdam: North-Holland Publishers.

Kornai, Janos (1992) *The Socialist System.* Princeton, NJ: Princeton University Press.

Lampland, Martha (1995) *The Object of Labor: Commodification in Socialist Hungary.* Chicago: University of Chicago Press.

Lupan, Ernest, and Ionel Reghini (1977) *Drept civil: Drepturi reale principale.* Cluj: Universitate Babe-Bolyai, Facultate de Drept.

Scrieciu, Florin, and Xenia Chercea (1996) *Legislaţia în agricultură şi industria alimentară.* Bucharest: WEGAFOR.

Staniszkis, Jadwiga (1989) *The Dynamics of the Breakthrough in Eastern Europe.* Berkeley: University of California Press.

Stark, David (1996) Recombinant Property in East European Capitalism. *American Journal of Sociology* 101:993–1027.

Verdery, Katherine (1996) *What Was Socialism, and What Comes Next?* Princeton, NJ: Princeton University Press.

Verdery, Katherine (2004) *The Vanishing Hectare: Property and Value in Postsocialist Transylvania.* Ithaca, NY: Cornell University Press.

# SUGGESTED FURTHER READING

Abrahams, Ray, ed. (1996) *After Socialism: Land Reform and Social Change in Eastern Europe.* Providence, RI: Berghahn.

Armstrong, George M. (1983) *The Soviet Law of Property: The Right To Control Property and the Construction of Communism.* The Hague: Martinus Nijhoff.

Buechler, Hans C., and Judith-Maria Buechler (2002) *Contesting Agriculture: Cooperativism and Privatization in the New Eastern Germany.* Albany: State University of New York Press.

Burawoy, Michael, and Katherine Verdery, eds. (1999) *Uncertain Transition: Ethnographies of Everyday Life in the Postsocialist World.* Boulder, CO: Rowman and Littlefield.

Campeanu, Pavel (1988) *The Genesis of the Stalinist Social Order.* Armonk, NY: M.E. Sharpe.

Creed, Gerald W. (1995) The Politics of Agriculture in Bulgaria. *Slavic Review* 54:843–868.

Creed, Gerald W. (1998) *Domesticating Revolution: From Socialist Reform to Ambivalent Transition in a Bulgarian Village.* University Park, PA: Pennsylvania State University Press.

Eyal, Gil, Iván Szelényi, and Eleanor Townsley, eds. (1998) *Making Capitalism Without Capitalists: Class Formation and Elite Struggles in Post-Communist Central Europe*. New York: Verso.

Hann, Chris M., ed. (1998) *Property Relations: Renewing the Anthropological Tradition*. Cambridge: Cambridge University Press.

Leach, Edmund R. (1961) *Pul Eliya, A Village in Ceylon: A Study of Land Tenure and Kinship*. Cambridge: Cambridge University Press.

Malinowski, Bronislaw (1935) *Coral Gardens and Their Magic*. London: Allen and Unwin.

Rose, Carol M. (1994) *Property and Persuasion: Essays on the History, Theory, and Rhetoric of Ownership*. Boulder, CO: Westview.

Stark, David C., and László Bruszt (1998) *Postsocialist Pathways: Transforming Politics and Property in East Central Europe*. Cambridge: Cambridge University Press.

Strathern, Marilyn (1999) *Property, Substance, and Effect: Anthropological Essays on Persons and Things*. Brunswick, NJ: Athlone Press.

Swinnen, John F. M., Allan Buckwell, and Erik Mathijs, eds. (1997) *Agricultural Privatisation, Land Reform and Farm Restructuring in Central and Eastern Europe*. Aldershot, UK, and Brookfield, USA: Ashgate.

Verdery, Katherine (2002) "Seeing Like a Mayor," or How Local Officials Obstructed Romanian Land Restitution. *Ethnography* 3:5–33.

Verdery, Katherine, and Caroline Humphrey, eds. (in press) *Property in Question: Appropriation, Recognition, and Value Transformation in the Global Economy*. Providence, RI: Berghahn.

# CHAPTER 3  AIDS

*Brooke Grundfest Schoepf*

The dawn of the twenty-first century finds the world beset by the most devastating pandemic known to history. The slow-acting Human Immunodeficiency Virus (HIV) spread silently in the 1970s, and was recognized in the US and Africa in the early 1980s. By the end of 2002 an estimated 25 million people had died of AIDS and more than 42 million people were estimated to be infected worldwide. An estimated 95 percent of new infections occur in the Third World, the majority in young people. Most will die within the next five to ten years because they do not have access to life-extending drugs. The rate of new infections, now occurring at 5 million per year, is expected to accelerate each year.

Anthropologists study disease epidemics as social processes, charting ways that the spread of infection is shaped by history, political economy, and culture. While infection with the HIV virus causes the immune system damage that leads to AIDS, sociocultural processes, including sexual strategies adopted for survival, enhance the vulnerability of the poor and powerless to infection. Anthropological research on AIDS contributes to understanding complex, multi-layered relations between culture, social relations, political economy, and disease. It yields new evidence confirming the importance of quality biomedical health services, and of participatory interventions with respect to condom use among people at risk of sexually transmitted infections (STIs) and HIV.

AIDS research by anthropologists is ever more closely linked to the politics and ethics of social practice, including effective HIV prevention and treatment. Findings on changing popular representations, sexuality, and sexual relationships can help make prevention strategies more "culturally appropriate," and avoid treatment failures. There is still little evidence, however, that public health research and practice make use of ethnographic findings. Most international prevention policy and forecasting continues to focus on individual behavior change rather than on social changes that address the causes of risk. At the same time that sophisticated epidemiology is critical to understanding the course of the epidemic, ethnography is essential to its interpretation. In addition, ethnography reveals the changes that communities need to envision and learn from people struggling with AIDS in order to consider how they might be brought about. New research is needed to understand how people respond to treatment when it becomes available to the 30 million people across the planet who now lack access to it.

This chapter examines the politics of AIDS in Africa. It begins in the mid-1980s and continues into the present. My understanding is grounded in participation in the struggle to discover and reshape meanings of AIDS in Africa and the West. In 1985 I proposed ways to use culturally informed community-based empowerment methods to complement mass-media campaigns. I joined with colleagues to form the trans-disciplinary CONNAISSIDA Project in what was then Zaire (now the Democratic Republic of Congo, or DRC). Formed from the French words *connaissance* (knowledge) and *Sida* (AIDS), CONNAISSIDA means "knowledge of AIDS." All of us were already experienced field researchers with several ongoing ethnographic projects. Dr. Rukarangira and Mme. Walu conducted studies of the informal economy and long-distance trade in Kinshasa and southeastern Zaire. Claude Schoepf and I were writing up earlier fieldwork; Professor Ntsomo Payanzo, later to become Minister of Higher Education and Scientific Research, was a participant-observer of the political system. We investigated popular representations of and responses to AIDS and compared these with what was known in the biomedical research community. Centered on medical and economic anthropology, the project conducted ethnographic action-research in Kinshasa, incorporating understandings from social psychology, public health, and development studies. We acted on the understanding that prevention would require new community-based approaches to empower people with knowledge cast in terms that they could work into their daily lives (Schoepf et al. 1991; Schoepf 1993). In 1991, at the request of anthropologists from other African countries, we trained them in the method. Funding agencies remained unconvinced. A number told us that the method was too labor-intensive, hence too costly. Others believed it unscientific and the results "merely anecdotal." From the outset we feared that AIDS would burgeon into a pandemic of enormous magnitude and far-reaching social impact. Without amelioration of the harsh social inequalities, we foresaw that even imaginative public education would fail to prevent widespread HIV infection.

## SOCIAL EPIDEMIOLOGY

In the US, AIDS was first detected among white, middle-class men having sex with men, and among wealthy heterosexual Africans seeking treatment in Europe. Once informed about the causes and prevention of HIV infection, persons not yet infected could protect themselves and their partners. Although no one has ever been cured of AIDS, when anti-retroviral drugs became available from the mid-1900s, it no longer signified impending death. The vast majority of those infected have not had the good fortune to benefit from these drugs.

This chapter explores why this is so. It situates risk of HIV in the material conditions of existence of much of the world, in the meanings of disease, and in the power relations expressed in sex and gender. Structural violence, a term used to encompass the concatenation of adverse social, economic, and political conditions

in which the world's poor live out their lives, contributes decisively to the dissemination of the Human Immunodeficiency Virus (HIV). AIDS has struck with particular
severity in poor communities beset by grinding poverty, drought, hunger, genocide,
and war.

Sub-Saharan Africa is the world's poorest region and the most affected by AIDS
to date. Half its more than 700 million people live in what the World Bank
terms "absolute poverty," on less than one dollar per day. By the end of 2002, an
estimated 29.4 million Africans, 70 percent of the world total, lived with HIV/
AIDS; another 25 million are believed to have died since the epidemic began. In
2002, some 2 million Africans died of AIDS and 3.5 million acquired HIV infection,
the vast majority through heterosexual intercourse. The highest levels are in southern
Africa, with 39 percent of adults infected in Botswana. Prevalence in three other
countries exceeds 30 percent of adults, while South Africa, with 20 percent of adults
infected, has nearly 5 million people living with HIV and AIDS. Nigeria has even
more, with infection prevalence estimated at just below 6 percent of its more than
165 million population. Ninety percent of AIDS deaths occur in adults aged 20 to
49, the prime working years. In the 16 most affected countries – located chiefly in
southern and eastern Africa – AIDS now is the leading cause of adult deaths. AIDS
has increased mortality in young children by two to three times. More children now
die from AIDS than from either malaria or measles, which formerly were the major
killers. Life expectancy has declined by ten or more years, wiping out any gains made
since independence.

Africa has endured a quarter-century of profound, multiplex crises with roots in the
soil of colonial conquest, harsh exploitation, and authoritarian rule. Many in the
"international community" have been loath to acknowledge the external forces that
contribute to the crisis, focusing instead on mismanagement and corruption. Most
economies remain distorted, dependent on the export of a few tropical products or
minerals to world markets. In the mid-1970s increased fuel prices and declining terms
of trade for major mineral exports sent shock waves across the continent. Governments borrowed heavily to finance infrastructure development and support social
programs. Leaders of authoritarian states, supported by the major Western powers,
took the opportunity to create a class base for themselves by transforming public
resources into private wealth.

These processes continued in the 1980s, while Structural Adjustment Programs
(SAPs) imposed by the institutions of international finance, sacrificed health, education, and social programs to debt reimbursement and the creation of a more favorable
climate for foreign investment. Coupled with the collapse of world markets for
tropical produce and open markets for imports, SAP policies led to deindustrialization and exacerbated poverty. The results included mass unemployment, decline in
the viability of peasant farming systems, increased migration in search of cash, and the
break-up of families. In the 1980s and 1990s low-intensity wars, genocide, and
military occupation brought civilian deaths and flight into forced migration, with
rape and other forms of gender violence used to terrorize populations. These dislocations set the stage for sex with multiple partners and the widespread dissemination of classic STIs through communities with deteriorating health infrastructure
(Schoepf, Schoepf, and Millen 2000).

## GLOBAL SPREAD SINCE 1980

As economic crisis spread across the continent in the late 1970s, the HIV virus silently spread as well. Seemingly unrelated, the two are in fact intimately entwined. The effects of poverty accelerated the spread of STIs, and the increased risk of acquiring HIV; in some regions the new virus was well established by the mid-1980s. By the 1990s deaths from AIDS in turn plunged afflicted regions deeper into economic crisis as the virus spread into new communities. Today, public health and social infrastructures, weakened by two decades of economic crisis and SAPs, are unable to cope with heavy burdens of infectious and parasitic disease. Vaccination programs and other preventive measures have been allowed to lapse. Mass poverty, combined with user fees and privatization of health care, means that millions cannot afford treatment, even for readily curable diseases. The pandemic is more than a series of personal and family tragedies. AIDS deaths, having depleted the workforce and raised dependency ratios, are likely to shred the already torn social fabric of numerous countries. Despite a number of successes registered in slowing the epidemic, infection rates are still rising in most countries across the continent, where the virus spreads at an accelerating pace, posing a threat to many millions of people.

Africa is not the only region to experience high rates of infection. In the urban ghettos of the US, beset by a form of poverty made intractable by racism, deindustrialization, and social policies that increase inequality, AIDS rapidly became the leading cause of death from disease in the 1980s. In Southeast Asia, India, and China, large poverty-stricken populations have swelled the numbers of HIV-infected people, fueled by drugs and traffic in women. The same elements now spread HIV in Eastern Europe and Central Asia, where the collapse of the former Soviet Union demolished public health systems and left millions at the mercy of a "free" market economy in which most are powerless to compete. As in the US and elsewhere, many, especially young people, destitute and without hope for the future, have turned to alcohol, intravenous drugs, and prostitution. AIDS battens on profitable illicit enterprises with global interconnections. Russian gangsters supply drugs and sex workers to Western European markets and arms to Africa. Arms from Eastern Europe are used to control the diggings where young men labor for a pittance to produce diamonds, gold, and coltan sold to US markets. In such conditions, in cities teeming with unemployed, and in rural areas that are home to landless and migrant farm workers, the numbers of persons with HIV are expected to multiply rapidly in coming years. The threat of collapse in these societies is finally drawing attention to AIDS as a global security issue.

## HEALTH KNOWLEDGES: EPISTEMOLOGY AND POWER

AIDS is particularly difficult for lay people, including political leaders, to understand. Relatively few in Africa have had secondary education, let alone training in contemporary biology. With a lengthy and variable period between infection and the onset of disease symptoms, AIDS appears to strike arbitrarily. The multiple disease processes offer a broad cultural field for reinterpretation in keeping with other widespread concepts of disease causation. As a sexually transmitted infection, complex cultural and psychological meanings intervene. Not surprisingly, across the continent, many men think of AIDS as "a disease of women."

As there is neither cure nor vaccine for AIDS, prevention and treatment of HIV are the only means of controlling the pandemic. Yet both prevention and treatment are exceedingly complex. They require considerable resources in money, trained person-nel, and imagination. Above all, they require political commitment to provide public services, and willingness to embark upon sociocultural change, especially to institute changes in power relations that determine how individuals interact with one another sexually and socially. Not least among the power relations that must be changed are inequalities of class, gender, generation, and ethnicity in local, national, and inter-national arenas. The *histoire immédiate* of AIDS and of policies elaborated in the effort to contain it are of more than just scholarly importance. Though it is now described as a "disaster," a "humanitarian catastrophe," even a "holocaust," the international community was slow to recognize the epidemic's potential and slow also to respond to it. The remainder of this chapter will show why this is the case, and examine policy successes and failures.

Public health action takes place on a terrain of unequal power, where different forms of knowledge struggle for control. In the case of AIDS, the defining power lies in the international biomedical arena, but these definitions have encountered endur-ing disease representations and practices from other knowledge systems, especially with respect to contagion and "disordered" sexuality in afflicted societies. Inter-nationally, AIDS is "an epidemic of signification." Response to AIDS is political everywhere, in Africa no less than in the West. Many responses have been moralizing and stigmatizing. Initially recognized among elites in many countries, HIV rapidly spread along the "fault-lines of society" to the poor and disinherited. The contradic-tions between need and response have been particularly sharp.

Knowledge is socially situated and contested, with competing groups claiming the power to define how we know, and to determine what facts shall be considered "real." This can be explained, at least in part, by discourses surrounding the appear-ance and spread of the new virus. As I suggested more than 15 years ago, "AIDS brings forth representations that support and reproduce already constituted gender, color, class, and national hierarchies. Societal responses to AIDS, including disease control policies, are propelled by cultural politics forged in the history of relations between Africa and the West."

The World Health Organization (WHO) began to grapple with AIDS in 1986. The blueprint it followed across the world shunted AIDS control into a new program in which separate bureaucracies were established in WHO and in each participating member country. The new structures were intended to sharpen governments' aware-ness and provide new resources that could not be turned down by health departments perennially short of funds. This had several unintended consequences. Not least, AIDS was viewed as a strictly medical problem to be met by health action, narrowly defined. In many countries AIDS has yet to be appropriated by governments and communities as a general problem to be addressed across the society.

Many policy-makers in the biomedical units of international development funding agencies were also slow to react. They failed to understand how difficult it would be to slow the spread of HIV through a general population of youth and young adults.

Attention focused instead on "prostitutes as a reservoir of infection" and for the rest of the decade policy-makers ignored the tragic fact that by the time HIV was widely recognized in Africa, it had already spread beyond categories of people identified as "risk groups." By 1985, surveys in several Central African cities found that more than 5 percent of the population was seropositive.

International agencies' failure to acknowledge AIDS was not simply a failure of the imagination. It required class and gender blindness of a peculiar sort. Concerned chiefly with birth spacing and reducing mortality in young children, one program officer of a major foundation wrote in response to my request for funds in 1986 that his organization provided funds only for research on women and children, not on AIDS. Yet by 1986, 30 percent of women delivering babies at Kigali's main hospital were seropositive. Most (68 percent) reported a single lifetime partner.

Several spokesmen for donor agencies with dwindling budgets noted that there were more people dying of malaria and measles than of AIDS. This was true enough in 1988, but with an average ten-year period between infection and disease, death rates then current were a misleading gauge of future impact. At the time, major donors were unwilling to allocate more funds to health in Africa. "Cost recovery" was the watchword for public health, and privatization was encouraged, despite deepening poverty that left many unable to pay for health care.

In the US, AIDS appeared to be "an urban disease." Some policy-makers argued that since Africa is overwhelmingly rural, and rural peoples are "traditional," most of the population would not be affected. They held a utopian vision of "merrie Africa," where people lived harmoniously in villages isolated from the wider world – a view long challenged by anthropologists and historians. Social scientists warned against this complacency. They pointed to a century of widespread change in rural social and sexual relations, to trade and labor migration that separated families and led to multiple sex partners, making many vulnerable to infection with STIs and AIDS.

By 1982, highway truck stops and trading towns serving farming and fishing communities in Uganda were reporting "slim disease," the wasting that characterizes the AIDS syndrome in Africa, where gastro-intestinal infections are common. In 1986, studies in trading towns in the Lower Congo and on the Congo–Uganda frontier found traders' wives infected with the virus. CONNAISSIDA co-director Dr. Rukarangira observed that long-distance traders and transporters based in south-eastern Congo had wives and girlfriends at each of their stopovers who facilitated their business (Schoepf et al. 1991). Later studies in other countries produced similar findings (Haour-Knipe, Leshabari, and Lwihula 1997). The inexorable spread of HIV with migrant workers across the continent to southern Africa, and from the West African coast northwards to the Sahel, is testimony to the correctness of the earlier predictions. Historian Shula Marks (in Delius and Walker 2002) observes that in retrospect, AIDS was "an epidemic waiting to happen." So it was, but sociologist Charles Hunt (1989 [1987–88]) warned of the danger in 1987. It gives social scientists no satisfaction to see such predictions come true.

As late as 1991, some development agency physicians continued to assert that the heterosexual epidemic could be contained by modern public health information and condom campaigns directed to "high risk groups." These are sex workers and their clients, and working-class men, such as long-distance truck drivers, fishermen, and migrant workers, who spend long periods away from their families. Designated as "core transmitters" because many have multiple sex partners, they were targeted for education stressing condom protection with casual partners. The economic conditions driving sex work, migrancy, and family separation were not addressed. Nor was it recognized that people tend to redefine their relationships as they come to know one another, so that the categories of "prostitute" and "casual partner" might not apply, even when gifts of cash and goods were made. The responsibility of men who enjoyed the "triptych of masculinity" in full measure, their wealth, power, and renown affording them access to many women, was ignored, while working men and women and the poor were stigmatized as "promiscuous."

Gender inequalities that make many women and girls unable to refuse unsafe sex were officially recognized as a cause of AIDS only in 1990, but remained a given, rather than something to be addressed as an urgent priority. It took much longer for officials to recognize the role of economic crisis in the form of debt and SAPs, while the *causes* of crisis they still avoid. Some acknowledged (or paid lip service to) economic and cultural constraints that prevent many from protecting themselves and their children from AIDS. Most continued to focus on changing the behavior of individuals in special "risk groups," rather than seeking the critical processes of economic empowerment and sociocultural change. Yet those Africans who reflected critically on the issues recognized that the changes required to control the epidemic would affect all levels of social life. The result of this official blindness is now recognized: the effects of AIDS in Africa are in some countries already, and in still others will soon be, nothing short of catastrophic.

Why did it take so long for the potential of the AIDS pandemic to be recognized in the international community? Part of the answer lies in the distribution of power between knowledges. Problems of public concern must be posed by institutions and actors socially authorized to do so. Only members of the research establishment are socially authorized to produce policy knowledge. In the domain of epidemic disease, the principal institution is the World Health Organization (WHO) and its contributors, primarily the US, Japanese, and Western European governments. The actors are the epidemiologists and specialists in public health that the WHO employs and funds. These are generally not social scientists, and above all, not ethnographers, who use qualitative methods to understand culture: social relations, meanings, and their contexts. Merrill Singer (1998) has suggested that anthropologists were left out of the loop because by the time they began to analyze data from their long-term fieldwork, the social and behavioral sciences already dominated the field.

The experience of the CONNAISSIDA Project suggests a more complex, political answer. In Kinshasa in 1984, the government authorized Project SIDA, biomedical research on AIDS, jointly funded by the US and Belgium. In 1985, when I broached the idea of broadening our ongoing ethnographic research to include AIDS prevention, Dr. Jonathan Mann, then Director of Project SIDA, had the US government send me home from Kinshasa (I was a consultant to the Peace Corps' African Food Systems Initiative at the time). I was told that he feared that encouraging people in Kinshasa to talk about AIDS would create difficulties for the biomedical research project. The following year, Dr. Mann departed from Kinshasa for Geneva to organize the WHO Global Program on AIDS (GPA). I returned on another short-term contract and stayed on to write the project paper with colleagues. The Zaire government authorized CONNAISSIDA without difficulty, with its National Security

Agency to keep a weather eye on our activities. The new US director of the biomedical project, however, continued to decline cooperation.

That was 17 years ago, but the public health model that incorporates capitalist microeconomic assumptions about health resulting from individuals' rationally chosen lifestyles still remains dominant. Its focus on individual motivation leaves little scope for understanding how behaviors are related to social conditions, or how communities shape the lives of their members. Responsibility for this particular public health discursive model and the resulting social demobilization cannot be laid solely at the feet of biomedical policy-makers. Its assumptions are embedded in the public culture of late twentieth-century Western societies. But the focus on individual sexual behavior, the claim to exclusive value-neutral objectivity, and the commitment to the survey as the sole method of "science" is very much their responsibility. Given the conservative political climate, they made politically convenient choices (Schoepf 2001).

The political roots of this epistemological failure are underscored by critical traditions in epidemiology and social medicine, which have situated the primary origins of epidemic diseases in economic misery since the nineteenth century. Rudolph Virchow developed a concept of health as what economists today call a "public good." He maintained that governments have a responsibility to preserve the public's health, and conversely, that medicine must intervene in social and political affairs to prevent epidemics.

It took another century for health to be considered a human right, enshrined in the Universal Declaration, although still honored more by rhetorical flourishes than by actual resource allocation. Thus by the mid-1980s, entitlement was no longer part of mainstream discourse in Western development institutions. Donors' health allocations favored population control over primary health care programs. Training in demography was funded in preference to ethnography. Privatization of health care became the watchword in the West, as in SAPs mandated in the South.

Soon, however, struggles over meaning were international and interdisciplinary. Although many African and Western researchers contested the narrow paradigm and its implications, they were ignored. Epidemiologists and health planners joined critical social scientists in recognizing the social forces propelling the HIV epidemic in Africa. These were mainly academics, not employees of governments or the WHO but public health specialists committed to social medicine and community health. They sought to read social patterns from seroprevalence numbers, rather than simply seeing individual "risk factors." They also sought to dispel the racist assumptions and moralizing that accompanied constructions of "African sexuality" and AIDS.

## CULTURAL POLITICS

Several authors note that African governments "under-reacted" to the threat posed by AIDS in the mid-1980s, attributing this to a series of internal cultural factors. They overlook international factors such as the funding "crunch" associated with structural adjustment, and the racism and stigma that accompanied the discovery of heterosexual transmission in Africa. On all sides, African leaders, the US, and international institutions were unwilling to act on the scale and in the ways required.

There were several reasons for this. First, African mistrust at high levels of government was fueled by Western cultural politics that stigmatized Africans, backed by a long history of "missionary medicine" that viewed STIs as shameful. In addition, in Congo and elsewhere, men's validation of their power and masculinity was linked to sex with many women. Some leaders feared that they were infected themselves. Both factors contributed to rejection and disbelief. This made the US and other Western governments leery of getting involved in the prevention of sexual transmission. Fear of losing foreign tourist revenues and desire to attract new investments also contributed to reticence on the part of African government officials who were the major beneficiaries of such ventures (Charles Nzokia, cited in Schoepf 2001). International pressure on African governments to trim their budgets, downsize personnel, and require cost reimbursements or privatize government services exacerbated the "under-reaction." This was not the moment to commit substantial new funds to public health (Schoepf, Schoepf, and Millen 2000).

African leaders were not the only ones to reject the construction of "heterosexual AIDS" as a uniquely African epidemic. In 1980s Kinshasa, popular slogans also reflected an understanding of the racism inherent in such constructions, and expressed resistance to the stigma it entailed. For example, in Kinshasa, SIDA was termed the *Syndrome Imaginaire pour Décourager les Amoureux*, an imaginary syndrome to discourage lovers. Which lovers were being discouraged? African lovers, of course. By whom? By Europeans, of course. Really, they are jealous, people said. One of the first AIDS control campaigns in Africa was launched after a song by Franco (Luambo Makiadi), a widely known popular musician, led people to talk *more* openly about AIDS. Public information and the experience of numerous deaths "from a long and painful illness" among friends, acquaintances, and celebrities got people's attention. Urban popular knowledge grew rapidly.

In Kinshasa, denial lasted longer among government officials than among city-dwellers reeling under the impact of AIDS deaths. AIDS became known as the syndrome of *Salaires Insuffisants Depuis des Années* ["too little salary for too many years"], reflecting a broad understanding of the ways that AIDS is driven by poverty. People in Cameroon a few years later expressed this as the "Acquired Income Deficiency Syndrome" (Paul Nchoji Nkwi, personal communication). In other countries where AIDS deaths came later and governments were not trusted (and particularly in apartheid South Africa) AIDS messages were rejected as "an American Invention to Discourage Sex." Many viewed condom campaigns as instruments of Western-inspired population control.

This legacy continues to fuel conspiracy theories that hamper the prevention of HIV and other diseases. Periodically, rumors that condoms (and vaccines against tetanus or polio) will lead to female sterility cause panics across the continent. Women in Kinshasa explained, "We have heard that condoms can slip off the man, lodge inside the woman, travel up and cause infection." Trusted health workers can dispel such fears with a gesture that mimes removal of the errant condom. But many government health workers are not trusted, for they engage in the same corrupt, exploitative, and oppressive practices as others in authority. Budget reductions and SAPs have made a bad situation worse, as declining wages and a dearth of supplies have created widespread alienation from the service goals of health care (Schoepf, Schoepf, and Millen 2000). Rumors embody mistrust of all governments.

Anthropologist Amy Kaler was puzzled to find that rural Muslim men in the President's home region in Malawi were mistrustful of government condom advice, despite their favored regional and religious status close to the seat of power and patronage. Most had yet to see or know a person with AIDS. To them, condoms signified population control. They linked government population policy, low-key though it was, to economic decline and growing hunger. They reasoned that Malawi could not afford to feed its growing population in the face of drought and reduced international support. The role of SAPS in creating mistrust of Malawi's new elected government seems clear. The World Bank pressured officials to remove fertilizer subsidies on which small farmers depended, but Parliament was understandably reluctant. It held off until immediately after the 1994 elections, then complied. Privatization and liberalization have enabled officials to grow wealthy, while poor farmers are marginalized, impoverished, and mistrustful of those in power.

Elsewhere, intellectuals mistrustful of the international agencies on account of their role in promoting structural adjustment and other repressive policies, view their neglect of effective HIV prevention and treatment as a means of ridding the continent of "surplus people." They reason that a large African labor force is not required in modern capital-intensive extractive industries such as oil and mining, which receive the bulk of new foreign investment. This view also competes with biomedical authority. Both views hamper social mobilization against HIV and thus contribute to the demise of the very people intellectuals seek to defend.

The power and influence of conservative religious leaders, who view AIDS as "the devil's work" or as "divine punishment for sin" also hampers prevention. Some teach that faithful wives will be spared and oppose condom campaigns as encouragement of "immorality." Charismatic evangelical pastor-prophets, not a few of them former politicians, lead "healing churches." Like many "traditional healers," they have gained new adherents in response to social and economic crises. Some actually claim to cure AIDS. Since opportunistic infections may come and go while HIV continues to destroy the immune system, such claims may seem plausible to sufferers, at least for a time. The next sickness may be interpreted as a new attack, or a failure to conform to prescribed rituals. Such "demedicalization" makes it difficult to conduct effective prevention campaigns that stress condom use and changes in gender relations.

## GENDER, SEX, AND POWER: RISK AND PREVENTION

Similarities in cultural constructions of masculinity and femininity across the African continent are underlain by similar patriarchal ideologies of male dominance and female subordination. As in many parts of the world, men's status among peers is enhanced by claims to numerous sexual partners. Yet, conceptually "patriarchy" conflates too many dimensions of women's status relative to men. Research on AIDS must examine, rather, the ways that gender differences are related to other types of social differentiation, using insights from a quarter-century of research on patriarchy and class, and adding age to the equation.

AIDS research physicians in Kinshasa told us that "African men won't use condoms." Indeed, we found that condoms were not popular among men, many of whom enjoyed a double standard with numerous, often younger, sex partners, while wives' sexuality might be strictly controlled. For them, health officials' advice to "avoid prostitutes" (a term with multiple meanings) and to use condoms in "risky" encounters was impractical. Condoms, linked to STDs and prostitution, symbolized mistrust. Men also found condoms difficult to introduce in a stable relationship or a friendly encounter. Women who had multiple partners but did not consider themselves prostitutes rejected condom protection. Even if they suspected that a partner might be infected, few women, married or single, proposed condoms or refused sex with a steady partner without fear of reprisal. As campaigns became more culturally sophisticated and awareness of AIDS deaths grew, these constraints eased. An effective social marketing campaign in Kinshasa even made condoms stylish and popular. Packaged with a picture of a leaping leopard, symbol of the ruler and the national football team, they promoted the brand "Prudence – For the man sure of himself" (Rukarangira and Schoepf 1989).

Problems remain. Condoms are unacceptable to those who adhere to widespread African beliefs about sex and reproduction, since they interfere with procreation and the health benefits believed to accrue from semen. Educated women who earn their own incomes may be able to discuss sexual relations, contraception, and HIV protection with regular partners, but if they reject condoms, women who want to stay married may be powerless to insist. For women with little or no schooling, income rarely brings empowerment in marital relations. In rural Tanzania, for example, where the conservative Protestant ideology of "the Christian family" upholds male dominance, only single women can insist on condom use (Baylies and Bujra 2000). Economic empowerment does not extend to sexual politics in the home, and young women are particularly vulnerable.

Preventing AIDS requires eliminating barriers that deny most women control over sexual decisions, and the impoverished – men, women, and youth – control over their lives. The well-documented role of formal education in sociocultural change renders recent declines in school attendance, consequent upon SAPs, poverty, and AIDS orphan-hood, extremely dangerous, especially for girls. Most of these economic and cultural obstacles were delineated by CONNAISSIDA as early as 1986, and reported in its publications from 1988. Although public health officials dismissed them as "anecdotal," numerous recent studies have replicated the findings in other settings. Yet few replicate CONNAISSIDA's critical problem-solving action research (Schoepf et al. 1991; Schoepf 1993). Instead, they state that their research will contribute to the elaboration of prevention programs. Is this delay ethical or might researchers and others learn better by doing?

The concept of vulnerability is much debated. Are women passive victims or can they act to protect themselves? Reality seldom yields either/or answers. For example, poor prostitutes who have knowledge of AIDS and condoms are not entirely powerless. Their need for income, however, places them at risk when clients offer higher prices for unprotected sex. Most women sex workers are unschooled rural migrants lacking marketable skills, unable to find other employment. Others have fled abusive marriages and drudge labor to go into a hand-to-mouth existence filled with violence, fear, and police harassment. Some are urban women abandoned, widowed, or divorced, with children to support. Clients who reject condoms may threaten to go elsewhere or threaten violence. Those who acquiesce may pay less than the going rate.

Institutional changes can support changes in individual behavior. For example, hotel and brothel owners in some Nigerian towns have been induced to maintain a "condoms only" policy, removing the responsibility from individual women. Broad non-judgmental concern is needed to promote acceptance of sex workers as people whose lives should be protected.

Not all sex is entered into for pleasure; young women are especially subject to coercion and harassment. Historians Delius and Glaser (see Delius and Walker 2002) situate the violence of youth in contemporary South Africa, including sexual violence, within the context of a developing masculinist culture of rebellion against both the apartheid state and the authority of elders. As in the US, gang cultures of un-employed, out-of-school youths enforce demands for sex from young women by threats and beatings. Some researchers adopt varieties of frustration–aggression hypotheses and social learning theory to situate male dominance and violence at the individual level, but fieldwork among survivors of extreme violence in Rwanda and Sierra Leone underscores the evidence that contextual political and cultural explanations are required. Rape and sexual torture were not merely condoned by military commanders, but used by them as instruments of policy to instill terror in civilian populations. Although international agencies are finally recognizing the role violence plays in spreading HIV, they lack the necessary sharp focus on gender and power relations. They issue instead bland statements such as "the presence of soldiers with cash spreads HIV."

Complex and ever-changing relations of power and powerlessness in sexual rela-tionships require ongoing study. Women's agency sometimes leads to increased vulnerability, as when women use multiple partners to obtain cash for survival or for increased consumption, and when men meet requests to use condoms with violence or abandonment. In the presence of HIV and male dominance, women's survival strategies turn into death strategies. In other words, to paraphrase Marx, women may make their own history, but they do so under conditions inherited from the past. The gender discourses of most national and local leaders, and the gendered power relations operating across African societies, have changed little in response to the AIDS pandemic. Irrespective of whether leaders draw on "traditional" or "modern" authority, pervasive male dominance and moralizing hamper HIV/AIDS prevention. Their values, social status, and didactic approach combine with young people's own constructions of masculinity and femininity to undermine any likelihood of practicing safer sex.

## SUCCESS STORIES: GOOD NEWS FROM AFRICA

In Uganda, Tanzania, and Senegal, many religious leaders and community elders resisted condom promotion as "immoral." Even as they emphasized sex only within faithful marriages, alarmed governments also instituted strong safer sex educational campaigns, and some made free STD treatment and condoms widely available. Researchers in Uganda report a decade of declining incidence of new HIV infections in the trading towns of Masaka, Rakai, and other districts, and recent decline in the capital, Kampala. While the magnitude and scope of change in Uganda are unique, declining prevalence has been registered in parts of

Kenya, Zambia, Tanzania, and South Africa, and low and stable prevalence in Senegal. Prevalence in Kinshasa is reported to have remained low (about 5 percent) and stable for more than a decade, despite extremely harsh economic conditions. The good news there is tempered by bad, however. A number of skeptics point to the dearth of surveillance data from 1991, when violence prompted international researchers to flee. In the eastern Congo, a decade of ethnic cleansing and low-intensity warfare is certain to have raised HIV prevalence, as did genocide in Rwanda in 1994, and in the camps on the border controlled by perpetrators of genocide.

Uganda's high-level political commitment and a diverse spectrum of community-based initiatives constituted a broad-based social mobilization that appears to have generated significant behavior change among those at risk of HIV. Institutional and interpersonal supports for regarding AIDS prevention as a political imperative, one of national and cultural survival, were created from the late 1980s. The government has promoted the empowerment of women and youth in government and civil society. One third of Parliament is female by law and four MPs represent youth. Free public primary education is provided for four children per household, and must include at least one girl.

Multiple communication channels and news of deaths supported a climate in which people talked about AIDS. The non-governmental AIDS Support Organization (TASO) linked support for people with AIDS to prevention. Women's groups emphasized the need to protect young girls from older men, and stiff penalties against rape were debated. Openness and involvement by multiple sectors of government and by national and local-level organizations of civil society appear to have reduced stigma and generated significant behavior change. Thus youth began to put off having sex; delayed sexual debut raised the age of exposure in girls. Other changes include reduced numbers of partners, reduced visits by men to sex workers, and markedly increased condom use in casual sex. Sex workers in Kampala reported nearly 100 percent condom use, while use by truckers, traders, and the military was statistically significant. In one study, nearly 60 percent of men and 38 percent of women with "non-regular partners" reported using a condom with their last contact. Changes resulted not only from mass and targeted campaigns that increased knowledge and public discussion. High mortality increased community and personal perception of risks, creating a climate that encouraged action. The challenge worldwide is to achieve similar gains before mortality reaches devastating proportions.

All these changes indicate that Africans are neither locked into risky sexual behaviors nor unable to change their culture. Nevertheless, the epidemic has not ended. Tensions between structure and agency must be confronted in creative ways where young people continue at risk. Girls may delay their sexual debut, but may be married to older men, of whom more than a few may be infected. Thus marriage is likely to pose a continuing source of HIV risk, especially for women, until the condom question within marriage and low-risk reproduction can be addressed by "Voluntary Testing and Counseling" (VTC) or by other means to minimize exposure when children are desired. Keeping all children in school, and teaching the biology of sex and reproduction, are crucial, yet AIDS and economic crisis have taken a heavy toll on educational systems.

## POLICY DEBATES OF THE THIRD AIDS DECADE

The most cost-effective prevention measure would undoubtedly be a therapeutic vaccine. Neither cure nor vaccines, however, are likely to emerge in the near future. Should they become available, access will be limited by the inability of most patients to pay, and by the dilapidated condition of public health systems. In the mid-1990s, effective life-prolonging drugs (highly active retroviral therapies, or HAART) became available in the developed countries. Their high cost has prohibited access in all but a limited number of Third World settings. Official agencies and many mainstream biomedical researchers argued that treatment was too complex and too costly to be applied widely in Third World countries. The argument was based, in part, on cost-benefit analysis calculated per years of healthy life-years saved. Because most Africans earn very little, their lives calculated in terms of economic return are considered cheap.

Health and human rights activists argue that this view is untenable, especially since costs have plummeted in recent years, due to the increased effectiveness and reduced prices of new drugs. They call on pharmaceutical companies to reduce prices still further, and governments to provide access to all those in need of treatment. Drugs that keep the viral load to low levels can limit HIV transmission. In addition to considerations of equity, human rights, and social justice, the relationship between therapy and prevention constitutes a good reason for instituting anti-retroviral therapies as widely as possible.

Dr. Paul Farmer (2001), a physician and medical anthropologist, conducted a demonstration project in a relatively resource-poor setting in Haiti. His rural hospital provides free HAART treatment to 300 poor patients. In the absence of sophisticated laboratory analyses, diagnosis and monitoring are done on the basis of symptoms. An effective primary care system with community outreach workers ensures patients' adherence to difficult treatment regimens. The experiment provides evidence of links between treatment and prevention. The hope of leading healthy lives with the virus reduces stigma and fosters an incentive to protect others.

Drug costs nevertheless remain out of reach of Africa's poor majority. Unless drug companies' patent monopolies can be broken, current inequalities will be magnified, as only those who can afford it are able to obtain treatment. Public health systems must be rebuilt, and extended into rural areas, for without general access to health care, importation of anti-retroviral drugs, even at reduced prices, would block over-stretched health systems from providing even minimal services to people sick with curable diseases.

The International AIDS Conference held in Durban in 2000 marked a sea-change in the views expressed by the international biomedical community, tantamount to a paradigm shift. For the first time, establishment scientists joined Third World researchers and activists to call for universal access to new anti-retroviral therapies, increasingly shown to be feasible in resource-poor environments, for everyone in need.

A new storm gathered when South African President Mbeki asserted that poverty, not a virus, is the cause of AIDS, and that anti-retroviral drugs harm patients, rather than help to prolong their lives. His stance, based on the arguments of a maverick biologist, touched off an international protest by some 15,000 AIDS researchers attending the Durban conference. Mbeki retracted his opposition, and although the South African government won a lawsuit enabling it to import generic low-cost drugs, it declared even these too expensive to be distributed free in the public health system.

Dr. Helen Schneider, who heads the Health Policy Institute at Witwatersrand University in Johannesburg, uses AIDS as a lens through which to view politics in the post-apartheid state, where the struggle for democratic rights is at issue. Activists who helped shape AIDS policy in the Mass Democratic Movement of the 1980s and 1990s have been sidelined as the new state attempts to centralize power. Yet the state's power is not monolithic and its reach is limited, leaving political space for the mobilization of various civil constituencies, including labor unions, HIV/AIDS sufferers and their support groups, gay rights activists, AIDS researchers, health workers, political parties, and even some state officials. Calls upon government to provide jobs, housing, and income support for the poor have become linked to HIV/AIDS issues, as a statement by African women at the Durban Conference clearly shows.

This rich brew of concerned citizenry is unusual, not only in Africa but in the world. There is nothing automatic about the coordination of agency with social change. Contestation is fierce and its outcome is far from predetermined. Schneider (in Delius and Walker 2002) suggests that calling on leaders to take primary responsibility for shaping AIDS policy is unwise. Their political agendas do not always support the most effective policies, nor is their power unchallenged. She refers to the South African situation, but her insight applies to other countries too. In some African countries – as in the US – conservative forces that oppose condom protection have been allowed to set policy, while elsewhere, government leaders willing to promote condoms have faced stiff opposition from religious and self-styled "moralist" groups. The Planned Parenthood Federation recently warned that conservative Christian advisors to President Bush seek to place restrictions on AIDS funds by mandating an abstinence-only policy in international as well as domestic AIDS prevention.

Placing too much responsibility (and external funding) in the hands of politicians serves to increase their political popularity and power, which also may be unwise. At the same time, non-governmental organizations (NGOs) offer no panacea. Unless political mobilization for equality and social justice continues, local actors may be co-opted into self-serving NGO strategies that fail to promote community consciousness-raising (Baylies and Bujra 2000).

Nevertheless, complex dynamics of governmental, donors, and local-level actors' agendas have led to development business as usual, to the detriment of HIV prevention. The bodies of youth and women continue to be sites of struggle. The World Bank, which in 1999 declared AIDS its top health priority in Africa, has yet to acknowledge the role of SAP policies. Conditionalities surrounding Structural Adjustment Programs mandate privatization, export-led growth, user fees, and an end to worker protection. Compliance is the precondition for debt relief. Despite rhetoric and promises by the institutions of international finance and Western heads of state, debt forgiveness has not taken place on a significant scale. Moreover, proposed "poverty alleviation measures" are unlikely to lead to the broadly based development needed to place Africa on the road to recovery. The new United

Nations' Global Fund for Malaria, Tuberculosis, and AIDS is sorely under-funded, and cannot meet the challenge of building health systems.

President Bush announced his intention to act: he will ask Congress for 10 billion dollars to fund US AIDS treatment and prevention in 14 countries of Africa and the Caribbean over the next five years. This money would not go to the UN's Global Fund. What funds will be forthcoming and how they will be earmarked will surely lead to new controversies. They may serve primarily to subsidize pharmaceutical companies that use the World Trade Agreement to protect their patents.

Human rights and governance issues loom large across the continent, but AIDS policy for the most part remains donor-driven. Exceptions are noteworthy. Access to free anti-retroviral therapies is not only a matter of social justice. It is also a way to protect African societies from the increasing devastation wrought by the global pandemic, combined with economic crisis and exacerbated by debt service payments. In 1999, medical anthropologist Dr. Katele Kalumba, Zambian Finance Minister at the time, proposed a plan to link debt relief to AIDS in what became "the Lusaka Declaration," signed by 50 African Health Ministers.

## CONCLUSION

Despite some notable successes in limiting transmission, the virus continues to spread, not only in cities where the epidemic is well-established, but in rural areas and in countries apparently free of HIV in the 1980s. The understandings on which the political economy and culture perspective that informs this critique are based, and the conclusions with respect to the need for global redistribution of power and wealth that follow, have not been readily accepted by policy-makers. Instead, there is a tendency to seek panaceas, limited interventions that appear to offer hope of interrupting the epidemic without threatening vested interests. The epistemological choice is political, for it allows policy-makers to avoid economic and social changes that address causes of risk. Anthropological studies from across the planet link macrolevel political economy to microlevel sociocultural analysis. They situate AIDS within histories of colonialism, under-development, and worsening inequality. Studies of high politics and fine-grained ethnography show how poverty, inequality, ideologies of male dominance, and moralist discourses about sex contribute to HIV risk.

The socioeconomic conditions that drive the pandemic cannot change without international commitment to development to end Africa's deep crisis. At the same time, however, national leaders and civil society must face up to the cultural power politics involved at all levels, "from the boardrooms to the bedrooms," as the saying goes.

## REFERENCES

Baylies, Caroline, and Janet M. Bujra, eds. (2000) *AIDS, Sexuality and Gender in Africa: Collective Strategies and Struggles in Tanzania and Zambia*. London: Routledge.
Bond, George, John Krenski, Ida Susser, and Joan Vincent, eds. (1997) *AIDS in Africa and the Caribbean*. Boulder, CO: Westview.

Delius Peter, and Liz Walker, eds. (2002) AIDS in Context. Theme Issue. *African Studies* 61:5–192.

Farmer, Paul (2001) *Pathologies of Power: Health, Human Rights, and the New War on the Poor.* Berkeley: University of California Press.

Haour-Knipe, Mary, Melkizedec Leshabari, and George Lwihula (1997) Interventions for Workers Away from Their Families. In *Preventing HIV in Developing Countries: Biomedical and Behavioral Approaches,* ed. Laura Gibney, Ralph J. DiClemente, and Sten H. Vermund, pp. 257–282. New York: Kluwer.

Hunt, Charles W. (1989[1987–88]) Migrant Labour and Sexually Transmitted Disease. *Journal of Health and Social Behavior* 30:353–373.

Rukarangira, wa Nkera, and Brooke G. Schoepf (1989) Social Marketing of Condoms in Zaire. *Health Promotion Exchange* 3:2–4.

Schoepf, Brooke Grundfest (1988) Women, AIDS and Economic Crisis in Central Africa. *Canadian Journal of African Studies* 22:625–644.

Schoepf, Brooke Grundfest (1993) Action Research on AIDS with Women in Kinshasa: Community-Based Risk Reduction Support. *Social Science and Medicine* 37:1401–1413.

Schoepf, Brooke Grundfest (2001) International AIDS Research in Anthropology: Taking a Critical Perspective on the Crisis. *Annual Review of Anthropology* 30:335–361.

Schoepf, Brooke G., Claude Schoepf, and Joyce V. Millen (2000) Theoretical Therapies, Remote Remedies: SAPs and the Political Ecology of Health and Disease in Africa. In *Dying for Growth: Global Inequality and the Health of the Poor,* ed. Jim Y. Kim, Joyce V. Millen, Alec Erwin, and John Gershman, pp. 91–126, 440–447. Monroe, ME: Common Courage Press.

Schoepf, Brooke G., Engundu Walu, wa Nkera Rukarangira, Ntsomo Payanzo, and Claude Schoepf (1991) Gender, Power, and Risk of AIDS in Zaire. In *Women and Health in Africa,* ed. Meredeth Turshen, pp.187–205. Trenton, NJ: Africa World Press.

Singer, Merrill, ed. (1998) *The Political Economy of AIDS.* Amityville, NY: Baywood.

## SUGGESTED FURTHER READING

Bond, George C., and Joan Vincent (1990) Living on the Edge: Structural Adjustment in the Context of AIDS. In *Changing Uganda: Dilemmas of Structural Adjustment and Revolutionary Change,* ed. H. Bernt Hansen and Michael Twaddle, pp. 76–99. London: James Currey.

Farmer, Paul E. (1992) *AIDS and Accusation: Haiti and the Geography of Blame.* Berkeley: University of California Press.

Farmer, Paul E., Margaret Connors, and Janie Simmons, eds. (1996) *Women, Poverty, and AIDS: Sex, Drugs, and Structural Violence.* Monroe, ME: Common Courage Press.

Ntozi, James P.M., John K. Anarfi, John C. Caldwell, and S. Jain, eds. (1997) Vulnerability to HIV Infection and Effects of AIDS in Africa and Asia/India. *Health Transition Review* 7 (supplement 1).

Schoepf, Brooke Grundfest (1991) Ethical, Methodological and Political Issues of AIDS Research in Central Africa. *Social Science and Medicine* 33:749–763.

Schoepf, Brooke Grundfest (1992) AIDS, Sex and Condoms: African Healers and the Reinvention of Tradition in Zaire. *Medical Anthropology* 14:225–242.

Schoepf, Brooke Grundfest (1993) Women and AIDS: A Gender and Development Approach. *Women and International Development Annual* 3:55–85.

Schoepf, Brooke Grundfest (2004) *Women, Sex and Power: A Multi-sited Ethnography of AIDS in Africa.* Oxford: Blackwell.

Schoepf, Brooke G., wa Nkera Rukarangira, Claude Schoepf, Engundu Walu, and Ntsomo Payanzo (1988) AIDS and Society in Central Africa. In *AIDS in Africa: Social and Policy Impact*, ed. Norman Miller and Richard Rockwell, pp. 211–235. Lewiston, NY: Edwin Mellen.

Setel, Philip W. (1999) *A Plague of Paradoxes: AIDS, Culture and Demography in Northern Tanzania*. Chicago: University of Chicago Press.

Yamba, C. Bawa (1997) Cosmologies in Turmoil: Witchfinding and AIDS in Chiawa, Zambia. *Africa* 67:200–203.

# Citizenship

CHAPTER 4

## Aihwa Ong

### BEYOND THE MULTICULTURALISM DEBATE?

For some time now, American citizenship has been a subject of intense debate. Great waves of migrations from Latin America and Asia, circulations of business travelers and students, and the ever growing number of individuals with dual citizenship all add to a society of astonishing flux and diversity. More and more people – migrants, refugees, expatriates, and global managers consider themselves part of transnational networks that diffuse the sense of citizenship as a watertight category. Scholars have moved beyond citizenship as a set of legal rights – either you have it or you don't – to an unavoidable consideration of membership that encompasses a range of subjects who include non-citizens. Culture wars since the 1970s have broadened discussion beyond the juridico-legal meanings to the symbolic and social meanings of American citizenship.

Discussion of the changing experience of citizenship has been enriched by anthropological approaches and insights. First, there is the distinguished history of anthropologists grappling with the everyday meaning – the marrow, the soul, and the ethics – of American citizenship. In particular, African American anthropologists have considered their scholarship inseparable from a critique and rumination on the spiritual substance of citizenship in America. Indeed, the African American Civil Rights movement in the 1960s inspired struggles for more democratic inclusion among other minorities and immigrant groupings. As the idea of adherence to a single cultural nation wanes, anthropologists turn their attention to the ways everyday behavior and thinking define the norms of belonging that operate as informal modes of inclusion and exclusion. For instance, many authors note that in daily life, middle-class Americans seek to maintain their "comfort level" by drawing up social rules against those perceived to be culturally deviant. Renato Rosaldo (1997) observes that the enduring exclusions of the color line often deny full citizenship to Latinos and other "persons of color." Rosaldo uses the term cultural citizenship to mean "the right to be different . . . without compromising one's right to belong, in the sense of participating in the nation-state's democratic processes." In the struggle to enfranchise themselves, the demands of poor migrants can range from legal, political, and economic issues to matters of human dignity, well-being, and respect. Ethnographic studies of disciplining regimes, including the use of the labels of immigrant and refugee, have been deployed both to reform poor newcomers and to defer indefinitely the integration of Asian immigrants.

The influx of a wide variety of immigrants and their claims for inclusion have influenced Western political theories. Will Kymlicka (1995) maintains that in Canada liberalism must include the recognition of "multicultural citizenship," since the claims of ethnocultural groups must be protected in order to promote justice between groups, something which is a matter of both justice and self-interest in advanced liberal democracies. Charles Taylor (1994) argues that equal rights are realized only when there is mutual respect for cultural difference, merely putting into practice the promise of liberalism for nurturing of the modern, authentic self.

A later trend in anthropological research, spearheaded by Akhil Gupta and James Ferguson (1992), has questioned the spatial dimensions that long shaped our thinking about culture and citizenship. Anthropologists point out that increased migrations across national borders have ruptured old categories that assumed a homology between nation-states, populations, and cultures. The study of transnationalism initiated by Basch, Glick Schiller, and Blanc (1993) opened up the question of how citizenship may be constructed from abroad by expatriates seeking to remake their homelands. Some anthropologists claim that diasporic communities relocated in new differentiated and mobile spaces now negotiate their positions in the setting of what Arjun Appaduraai (1996) calls "post-national" orders. My own (1999) focus on Asian business emigrants' new transnational practices suggests an emerging "flexible citizenship," a strategy that combines the security of citizenship in a new country with business opportunities in the homeland. At the same time, anthropologists working with displaced populations in their homeland have studied social movements that seek to claim citizenship – basic social rights – in places as far apart as São Paulo and Beijing. These studies show that spaces of citizenship formation have changed radically from the national territory to transnational spaces and globalizing cities.

A convergence of anthropological and political approaches has shaped current discussions of citizenship, highlighting the political significance of cultural difference in liberal democracies, and a rethinking of the spatialities of the making of citizenship. For many, an insistence on cultural difference and a critique of cultural hegemony are the key elements in recasting the substance of citizenship today. Yet an even more radical transformation is being wrought by flows of network capital that unravel the symbols and spaces of citizenship. That is the subject of this chapter. I shall relate how certain space-making technologies of neoliberalism are shattering a legacy of moral gains in splintering citizenship claims in the United States.

## "Latitudes of Citizenship"

Silicon Valley in California is the hub of supply chains that link multiple sites of production and government across the world. Circulations increasingly shaped and dominated by the rationalities of neoliberal capitalism have effectively disembedded rationalities from their local milieus (a process Gilles Deleuze and Felix Guattari (1994) call "deterritorialization") and re-embedded them in new economic spaces. Those people who are technically citizens of the United States and those who are not are intertwined in these entangled flows and yet experience very different rights and privileges. The processes that distribute disparate forms of legal and labor conditions in new geographies of production constitute, in effect, "latitudes of citizenship." Latitude, first of all, defines the *division* of the global North from the South, of the rich from the poor, of those who have gained from global capital flows from those enchained by them. Latitude also describes *transversal* flows of capital that cut into the vertical entities of nation-states, as well as the *conjunctural* intersection of global forces in the articulation of strategic zones such as Silicon Valley. Because the space of production shaped by transnational networks is distinct from the space of adminis-tration, this partial disembeddedness from the nation-state allows a variety of norms and forms governing social relations. Thus latitudes of citizenship also imply freedom from narrow limits (of nation-states and legal regimes), and the scope and flexibility to combine disparate combinations of rights, privileges, and labor conditions in a geography of production. Such ensembles of unequal life chances are shaped by processes that are at one and the same time both trans-border and highly site-specific in constituting particular positions of subjection.

By thus lateralizing and lowering labor value in production along with the flow of network capital, the space-making techniques of neoliberalism are splintering citizen-ship claims. Lines of differentiation by skill and occupation that are continuous across national borders assign managers, techno-migrants, and low-paid migrant workers to different kinds of political fate, depending on their specific locations in geographies of production and of administration. This layering of the conditions of achieving citizenship, and of the possibilities of citizenship claims, underlies the processes of stratification that structure ethno-racial differentiation. Thus, alongside preexisting ethno-racial forms, a lateralization of corporate and labor values across national borders poses the question of what is at stake for Americans as United States citizens? And moreover, it does this in a global ethical way that transcends immediate differ-ences of culture, race, and nation.

## Traversing Spheres of Value

The growth of the American nation has always depended on the image and actuality of the pioneer, a figure celebrated as much for his sense of adventure in taming virgin or savage territories as for his capacity to generate wealth out of his territorial claims. California is a space where the American frontier once ground to a stop, where the Westerner saw an end to his dreams of self-realization. Nevertheless, throughout the twentieth century, the United States (hereafter American) economy has always exceeded the limits of the continent, attracting Asian immigrants for whom Califor-nia was the Old World's New World, the West of the East, a place where the Pacific ended and hyper-modernity (leap-frogging over the older modernities of Europe and the American eastern seaboard) began. Through hard work and social mobility, these immigrants sought ways to sustain and transform their entanglements across the Pacific. Early twentieth-century Asian immigrants became plantation workers, truck farmers, railroad workers, laundrymen, grocers, garment workers, houseboys, and restaurant operators, and many dreamed or schemed that their children would become middle-class.

By the 1980s many new arrivals from Asia were already middle-class, bearing financial, intellectual, and cultural capital that put them in a position to extend the American frontier to the far corners of that continent. These new Westerners deployed and reproduced the logics and asset specificities of the neoliberalism that underpins American economic territorialization in the Asian Pacific region. The strategies they employed in the process have important implications for how we understand the process of globalization.

Much of the literature of globalization assumes a direct internationalization of production and finance, relying on a pure flow of capital, products, and peoples through networks, without giving any attention to how particular kinds of activities make such movements possible and configure them in specific shapes at different scales. I use the term *flexible citizenship* to point to the limitations of this approach – to refer to the assemblage of transnational practices for gaining access to different global sites (for business advantages, real estate deals, enrollment in top universities, or security for the family) as well as for the versatile mobilization of business, legal, and social assets that facilitate a high degree of mobility. I have identified the cultural logics that underpin such accumulation strategies of ethnic Chinese managers as they seek to deploy themselves, their family businesses, and their families in different sites of the Asian Pacific. Such flexible citizenship strategies mesh with the neoliberal dynamic of interactions between capital, markets, and labor that have been spread in new ways. For instance, the Enron Corporation was a spectacular example of neoliberal maneuverings, growing as it did from a Texan pipeline company to a trader of energy across different market zones. Neoliberal entrepreneurialism adds value to commodities by shifting capital among multiple zones of exchange. New assemblages of the state and private actors have come into play in diverse arenas of market competition.

In California, the growth of Silicon Valley industries has fueled a relentless demand for foreign economic and intellectual capital. Asian actors have come to play a crucial role because they possess not only economic and intellectual capital, but also the specific assets – practices and relationships – that shape firm-to-market relations across heterogeneous zones between Asia and America. David Stark has argued that this new entrepreneurial figure is an individual who possesses "asset ambiguity," by which he means the kind of talent that can exploit the blurring of borders between countries, races, skills, and cultural signs. The Asian Pacific is a region where techniques for converting value across various spheres are very challenging, especially for mainstream Americans. But it is also a region where overseas Chinese from different countries have region-specific assets that sustain relations of trust that permit the manipulation of borders between cultures, languages, and nations. They can open doors to new places, translate instructions and values from low to high-end labor markets, and build the institutional bridges necessary for circulating information, capital, goods, and people.

For instance, Asian entrepreneurs are the creators and operators of many kinds of transnational networks central to making regional hubs in Silicon Valley, Vancouver, and Los Angeles. Asian American companies benefit in the high-tech field from cultural practices and rituals that forge links with Taiwanese venture capitalists, thus generating ethnic-specific strands in the industrial-capital circuit. Through these connections, Dell Computer, the world's largest manufacturer of desktop monitors, relies on hundreds of component manufacturers in Taiwan and China. Besides building these global assembly chains, Asian capital is frequently handled by accounting firms that immigrant Chinese have set up in cities like Los Angeles. These firms "baby-sit" newly arrived money through the regulatory channels of the American system. Trans-Pacific connections also circulate Taiwanese capital in the aerospace industry. Because Taiwan is interested in developing its own aerospace industry, Taiwanese venture capitalists have bankrolled ethnic Chinese, formerly employed by Boeing and other aircraft companies, to set up workshops that manufacture avionics components for their previous employers. Thus intra-ethnic ideas and practices bridge transnational zones, reproducing in new spaces the hidden force behind economic territorialization. Many multinational companies throughout the region depend on Asian managers as much as Asian workers to translate across political, social, and cultural lines. Thus ethnic Chinese communities can be found all over the Asian Pacific, having developed over time templates for doing business in different places. Their bilingualism or multilingualism is central to all these maneuvers and border crossings. Many ethnic Chinese activities are carried on entirely in Mandarin or Cantonese, or in local native languages such as Malay, Tagalog, or Vietnamese, with English used only as a technical language and for communicating with mainstream Americans. Asians thus came to personify the twenty-first-century entrepreneur not simply by virtue of their intellectual or financial capital, but also for their capacity to keep in play multiple orders of worth in heterogeneous spheres of production, and for extending their strategic horizons into ever more remote Asian market landscapes.

An Asian circulating managerial class now shapes labor and immigrant policies in the national space of the United States because of its centrality to the growth of the computer industry that dominates Northern California's economy. Santa Clara County, at the heart of Silicon Valley, has a population that is half white, and a quarter each Asian and Hispanic. In 1999, one quarter of the Valley's businesses were run by Asian Americans, accounting for some 17 billion dollars in gross revenue each year. By the end of the century, almost a third of the chief executive officers in Silicon Valley were Asian-born. Many of them, US-educated and formerly employed by the big corporations, have become crucial to the supply chain of the informational industry. Immigrants mainly from Taiwan and Hong Kong operate small companies that constitute the local manufacturing base of the globally oriented corporations. In a similar fashion, South Asian entrepreneurs from the republic of India form trans-Pacific network economies that not only lead to mutual industrial upgrading, but also become supply chains for high-tech professionals recruited by Silicon Valley firms through Indian universities and cyber-cities.

These transnational corporate networks have also brought into being high-tech spaces of labor under the control of an Asian expatriate managerial elite. The information economy is dependent upon a regime of production in which the outsourcing of most mass-production processes to sites in Southeast Asia has been synchronized with manufacturing activities in Silicon Valley, leading to unequal working conditions at both the global and local levels. Boy Luthje (1998) has called this post-Fordist reorganization of global production "systematic rationalization," a mode of labor management in highly flexible and segmented regional production networks that stabilizes working conditions and wages below those established in accordance with union-represented, Fordist norms. Corporate giants such as Intel, Hewlett-Packard, and Sun Microsystems depend on local contract manufacturers to assemble the elements and parts that make up "hot" products (such as personal computers and cell-phones) faster and more conveniently than by offshore manufacturing. Solectron of Milpitas, founded by two IBM engineers originally from Hong Kong, is the largest contract manufacturing business in Silicon Valley. The company has grown to become a manufacturing and design partner to their corporate customers. Manufacturing work is contracted out to smaller companies operated by Asian immigrants, who use their local ethnic networks mainly to employ non-unionized Southeast Asian women and girls as temporary workers hired for 90 days. At the end of that time these workers can be hired back with no improvement in wages, no contract security, and no grievance procedures. The United States is the only liberal democratic country in which employers are not required by law to demonstrate "cause" if they wish to fire an employee (Colker 1998). To meet stepped-up production schedules contract manufacturers turn to smaller subcontractors and even to their own employees, putting out non-automated work to their own shop-floor workers to be assembled at piece rates in their homes.

Most piece-workers are Southeast Asian women working at their kitchen tables. It has been estimated that at any one time, more than a third of the 120,000 Southeast Asian immigrant population in Northern California is hired to assemble printed wire boards. Most are home workers who recruit stay-at-home relatives, even children, to assemble circuit boards and other components. Home workers make 4–5 dollars an hour, or 40–50 dollars per board, at work that involves fusing (often toxic) components and wiring boards. The work is sometimes paid by the piece (a penny a transistor is the going rate) and even with overtime, workers barely earn the state's legally recognized minimum wage. Piecework itself is not illegal, but it is subject to minimum wage and overtime laws. In many cases, workers are already employed by a company at hourly wages and are then sent home and paid as piecework to do assembly work there. In many of these subcontracting take-home arrangements, the labor practices violate industrial laws. A mid-1999 exposé by reporters at the *San Jose Mercury News* triggered an investigation by the Department of Labor of the contract manufacturers who pay Vietnamese women piece-rate wages for work in the home. In another case, Asian lawyers filed suit against Asian-owned companies for owing back wages and overtime compensation to a Cambodian worker, who took home work and assembled components, earning a piece rate of 1–5 dollars. Almost a third of all workers in high-tech manufacturing are now employed on ambiguous terms of contract and contingency.

Local Asian network production systems deploy cultural authority, kinship, personal relations, and language to take advantage of employees working in substandard conditions. Two nonprofit organizations that focus on the plight of Southeast Asian workers in Santa Clara County have tried unsuccessfully to organize unions among workers in electronics workshops and supermarket chains. Their main obstacle was the fact that the immigrant workers viewed their Asian employers (even those of a different ethnicity) as their patrons and protectors from the larger society.

The workers were afraid to complain against their employers for fear of losing their jobs or having their wages reduced. The Santa Clara Center for Occupational Safety and Health (SCCOSH) has used skits and radio dramas to warn workers about the hazards of the chemicals they handle and to instruct them in their legal rights against arbitrary dismissal. One organizer from the United Food and Commercial Workers' Union attributed the problem to Chinese culture. "Employers have the same kind of authority as teachers and parents. If that's the case, you can't get workers to challenge them. Confrontation and conflict are not highly valued." More practically, perhaps, a worker explained that, being in a new country, they did not want to start problems.

The deployment of personal relationships engendered a sense of loyalty among immigrant Southeast Asian workers who, lacking language and skills, were afraid that they would not be able to obtain jobs outside local ethnic networks. At the mercy of volatile market conditions, they shuttle in and out of the electronics, garment, and food industries, their hourly wage less than the cost of a cup of coffee, and are invisible to the cappuccino-sipping internet employee higher up the labor commodity chain. The capacity of transnational managers to move among different sites of production, moving rapidly among different streams of low-skilled workers at home and overseas, has severely degraded work conditions in the United States. Ethno-racial affiliations, once the firm grounding for American labor organization in "communities of adversity" such as these, are here manipulated by employers to control, isolate, and weaken workers, inflicting a symbolic violence that blurs the moral distinction between loyalty and exploitation.

The restructuring occasioned by the high-tech boom is merely the most striking case of globalism and nepotism opening up opportunities for Asian immigrants in United States society either to grow wealthy as expatriate entrepreneurs and techno-migrants at the top, or for migrant piece-workers to make low wages at the bottom. Each stratum has become distinctly gendered and ethnicized: the male Chinese contract manufacturer at the top; the male Indian engineer in the middle; and the Southeast Asian female piece-worker at the bottom. This ethnic ranking is almost identical with that I observed in runaway electronics factories established in Southeast Asia in the 1980s. It is eerily familiar yet temporally disconcerting that the racially segmented industrial system spawned in Asian postcolonial developing countries has been recycled in the United States, becoming a centerpiece of its high-tech economy. The key to the process of Asian immigrant integration into the top and bottom tiers of the transnational networks lies, first, in the increasing number of people having to do piecework or homework rather than being employed in secure jobs, and second, their employment in footloose factories that can slither in and out of national spaces of production, whether in the United States or elsewhere. American law in the age of hyper-capitalism has always opted for undercutting labor rights in favor of flexibility and profitability. But, in recent years, there has also been back-pedaling on union-protected workers' rights and on race-based rights. The narrow space of civil rights that remains is focused on individual freedom, including that of the Asian immigrant entrepreneur, whose flexible business practices promise the greatest profits. It is, perhaps, not surprising that worker-abuse cases exposed by the *San Jose Mercury News* drew angry letters to its website. What is more surprising, perhaps – or not, depending upon one's analytical realism – is that most anger was expressed by long-resident United States citizens. They argued that the main issue was not the legality of uncompensated piecework assembly for the workers, but rather, the opportunities provided to the employers for entrepreneurial opportunity, advancement through hard work, and individual choice. These were the values that lay at the heart of Silicon Valley production. Flexible transnational production systems thus carry in their wake a distinctive moral capital that is unequally distributed – one that plays an important role in shaping actual working conditions on the ground.

## CONTINUITIES AND DISCONTINUITIES IN AMERICAN CITIZENSHIP

The question is thus posed: in what ways have new circulations of labor associated with hyper-capitalism affected American citizenship? Do these new actors – Asian entrepreneurs and low-skilled workers – represent a break with the symbols of American citizenship? What are the implications of the new demographics of entrepreneurship and widespread piece-labor for the substance and meaning of citizenship in the United States? What kind of idealism remains in a moral project of citizenship increasingly governed by mobile, flexible, and supranational forms of capitalism?

From its inception, the American nation was imagined as a racial, class, and gender formation governed by an Anglo-Saxon hegemony that projected (white) racial and class interests as universal for the entire nation. The concept of the American nation as one specific, homogeneous, racial identity has been and continues to be the ideal against which all potential citizens are weighed as being either within or marginal to the nation. Michael Omi and Howard Winant (1986) assert that race is the nation's key organizing principle for social action at the macrolevel of economics, politics, and ideological practices, as well as at the microlevel of individual action. An intertwining of race and economic performance has shaped the ways different immigrant groups have attained status and dignity within a national ideology that projects worthy citizens as inherently "white." Historically, newcomers have been situated along a continuum from black to white and the framing of immigrants in terms of a bipolar racial order persists to this day, as I demonstrate in my forthcoming book, *Buddha is Hiding: Refugees, Citizenship, the New America*.

Racial categories are fundamentally about degrees of deserving and undeserving citizenship. Such relative positioning in the national moral order is part of the political unconscious that variously informs official and unofficial perception and action. As Brackette Williams (1995) has pointed out, there is a black–white continuum of status and dignity, and the relative positioning of a group determines its moral claims to certain areas of privilege and advantage, and conditions fear or threats to these prerogatives from subordinated races. These processes of relative positioning, group status competition, and race envy thus transform cultures into race-based traditions.

Racial bipolarity has historically contributed to a classificatory system that differentiates among successive waves of immigrants, assigning them to different racial way stations along the path to whiteness. By the late nineteenth century, English and German (and a small number of Presbyterian Scots and northern Italians) forged patterns of financial and kinship networks within and beyond the United States. The consolidation of this white American elite with transnational connections is celebrated in the novels of Henry James and Edith Wharton. At the same time, there was a structure of expectation for how things ought to work out, in a just and moral world, of citizenship acquisition for less fortunate immigrants. The original racial bipolarity of that time was of White Anglo-Saxon Protestants (WASPS) vis-à-vis Poles, Italians, Germans, and Slavs (PIGS) who happened to be Roman Catholics. Not until the mid-twentieth century did later non-Christian European immigrants, such as the Jews, ascend to white status through the euphemized process of ethnic succession (Sacks 1994).

The ethnic succession model of European immigrant groups emerged within a nineteenth-century American society in which the most fundamental labor relations were grounded in a legacy of white–black relations under slavery. Emancipation "naturalized" the social order, as Copeland put it (1993), "the Negro" becoming a "contrast conception" or "counter-race" to free labor. The free workingman came to embody republican citizenship, and any immigrant who failed to gain an independent livelihood was in danger of sinking into wage slavery, the antithesis of the independent citizen. In the nineteenth century, this racial classificatory logic situated poor Irish immigrants on the east coast and Chinese immigrants on the west coast near the black end of the continuum, their working conditions being similar to those of unfree black labor (Roediger 1991; Takaki 1990 [1979]). Early Chinese immigrants were subjected to this process of "Negroization" and were also considered heathens and thus a threat to God-and-Country Republicanism. Chinese "coolies," like black slaves, were considered antagonistic to free labor. An image grew of Chinese immigrants as "new barbarians" or as "a depraved class," as money-grubbing, and as a threat to white women, altogether having a cancerous effect on American civil society. In this way American orientalism cast Asians outside the pale of white civilization within the bipolar racial formation, assimilating "primitive" Asians to the "black" half of the model on the side of unfree labor, lacking public status, clearly outside the nation. Only after their gradual attainment of middle-class norms in the period after World War II did the slow whitening of Asian immigrants earn them the label "model minority" as a contrasting category to the now black "underclass."

Currently, in an age of globalized capitalism, the process of conferring honorary whiteness continues, and Asians for the first time attain the status of ideal American citizens who embody qualities such as economic and intellectual capital, as well as the transnational networks and skills so critical to American expansion. Yet, as the new representatives of moral worthiness, Asian entrepreneurs strive not so much to be accepted as whites as to participate more fully in a national space through that combination of nepotism and globalism so necessary to producing wealth and power in the decentralized and dispersed systems of capitalism. When he was asked about being at the top of the ethnic hierarchy in Silicon Valley, a Berkeley-educated Taiwanese owner of an electronic company answered, "We carry our weight. Why shouldn't we be represented at the top?" He is considered a cyber-hero, like Jerry Yang of Yahoo.

The notion of citizenship being tied to work and earnings gains in geometric value when humanity is more and more measured against mobile capital. In *Heaven's Door: Immigration Policy and the American Economy*, Harvard economist George J. Borjas recommends more restrictive immigration policies against poor Hispanic immigrants, while laying out the welcome mat for the possessors of "human capital." In a number of other advanced liberal democracies, immigration laws have already been adjusted to ease the flow of professional and "investor immigrants." The new citizen hero is the *Homo economicus* of high-tech and high finance, a versatile figure that possesses many kinds of capital, redefines the norms of work routines, and transgresses boundaries of time and space. Regardless of whether they are foreign-born, alien residents, permanent residents, or citizens, high-tech managers and knowledge workers in the United States may now possess a kind of transnational citizenship. Advanced education, capital accumulation, hyper-mobility, and flexibility are the passports not only to wealth production but also to the power to rule others. The role of Asian entrepreneurs and knowledge workers in Silicon Valley, against the background of a looming Chinese economy, has recast American thinking about Asians. Transnational skills, not intra-national suffering, have become the moral capital of citizenship, and Asians have increasingly been accorded the racial coding of desirable citizens. Yet, while the variety of capital and the kinds of actors who have come to represent the heights of American bourgeois citizenship have changed, the very process of honorary whiteness has, through the assimilation of such figures, become a force in global racial bipolarity.

Decentralized, dispersed, and flexible forms of capitalism have ruptured ideologies of ethnic succession in the United States, but the structure of belief and expectation that minorities and immigrants could convert their sacrifices and suffering into identity-claims, and contribute to the eventual benefit of the group as a whole, has been a very powerful force in giving a moral character to citizenship. In her book, *American Citizenship: The Quest for Inclusion*, Judith Shklar argues that from the perspective of the historically excluded – racial minorities, women, and immigrants – the struggle for American citizenship has "been overwhelmingly a demand for inclusion in the polity, an effort to break down excluding barriers to recognition, rather than an aspiration to civic participation as a deeply involving activity." This intertwined process – the access to voting and income that is inseparable from attaining social standing worthy of respect and prestige – has been central to the meaning and color of American democratic citizenship. For minorities and poor immigrants, this promise took the form of ethnic succession, whereby exclusions endured by earlier generations of migrant workers encouraged them to lay claim to a communal identity based on adversity and suffering. Ethno-racial mobilization involved making a contribution to the well-being of later generations as well as to that of society as a whole. Thus, the struggles of earlier generations of workers on behalf of their communities resulted in legislation to protect the health, wages, social security, and other benefits contributed to the civil rights of all American workers. Besides fighting for the steady improvement of labor laws, communities of adversity have disrupted the structure of racism and gender bias to improve work conditions. Immigrants, like slaves before them, have not merely broken down barriers to inclusion, but have struggled for the substantive expansion of the meaning of free labor and its link to the promise and substance of democracy.

The chain of inter-generational and ethno-racial class struggles that made the sufferings of past generations visible has been broken with the blurring of borders between nations, production sites, and industrial labor histories. The contemporary working poor lack the ideological and material base to fight for better working conditions, as greater flexibility allows their bosses to hire them as temporary, underpaid, and replaceable workers. A reversal in the demographics of labor distribution in the United States, with a growing majority of workers doing piecework and in-home work, has strengthened the power of corporations to erase or evade the civil-rights gains of the last two centuries. The opportunities in older factory regimes for making a substantial contribution to improvements in the quality of work conditions have become less likely with the fragmentation of workplaces and the movement of labor sites offshore. Floating factories, combined with endless streams of migrant labor, provide the means by which any constructive pressures brought by workers are undermined or simply evaded. Forms of labor exploitation, coercion, and denigration that had disappeared from most workplaces have reemerged, and the state apparatus is experienced even more than before as a system of containment and restriction. Police raids on sweatshops produce a constant source of fear for undocumented workers.

No longer is material capacity and symbolic coinage to be derived from advancing the well-being of others, either one's own ethno-racial group or society as a whole. The diminished likelihood that any substantive accomplishment will be achieved through organized means that call for communal efforts, whether racial or ethnic, means that communal contributions to larger social norms for the overall well-being of all working people are no longer operative. Indeed, in many cases migrants are the worst abusers of their own countrymen. Peter Kwong (1997) has studied the extensive human smuggling networks linking Fuzhou to New York City's Chinatown. Debt peonage forces migrants to work under slave-like conditions in the warrens of Chinese garment, food, and service industries, places American labor inspectors and unions have failed to penetrate. American unions have been severely weakened in their fight to sustain decent working conditions in all industries, but especially in those dominated by immigrants of color. For this reason, some Asian American leaders have expressed a desire to reject the transnational linkages and demands of global capitalism in favor of local community-based politics (Hu-DeHart 1999). Some Asian American scholars have criticized the way the label "immigrant" has been used against Asian workers embedded within the American economy, yet lacking the social protection of the state (Lowe 1996; Volpp 2001). Transnational capitalism is no longer directly responsive to long-term gains in labor norms nor to laws governing the well-being and dignity of free labor as a right of citizenship. Furthermore, the ethical meaning of US citizenship – of Emersonian self-reliance – has now been reduced to an extreme form of market individualism, where all that is left is for workers to endeavor to fight off particular instances of personal discrimination and injustice in a globalized wilderness. Making a contribution to the good of society has become an empty claim, since workers can no longer establish moral borders to protect the next generation. The constant influx of even poorer and more exploitable immigrants has made them more totally replaceable than ever before. Workers do not or cannot hope for higher moral laws governing working standards. The symbols of suffering remain, but it is hard to establish evidence of it and of its alleviation that may inspire future generations of workers claiming it as their legacy. The denigration of idealism in citizenship – the moral worthiness of ensuring that basic working conditions for the poor be upheld and that capitalists pay back society through taxes – means that today's entrepreneurs, whether local or foreign-born, recognize only the necessity of getting rich by maximizing the advantages of transnational mobility and the ties that provide opportunities for evading taxes. In this regard, the Enron scandal may be said to be an emblematic rather than a deviant form of today's corporate capitalism today.

Being a worker in the American national space is no protection against a progressive degradation of labor and civil rights. The relentless manipulation and crossing of borders by capital and people further the conversion of values across multiple economic zones, thus enriching individuals and companies within the American nation. But the floating of values has also undone the meaning of work in America, erasing the older-established morality of labor dignity, while labor values float down to the lowest denominator of labor extraction and denigration. The neoliberal logic of exploiting the ambiguities of economic and social orders has meant erasing hard-won battles for labor rights, and tolerating historically inferior American working conditions for people judged to be socially, morally, and economically inferior, that is, minorities and the latest wave of immigrant workers. Mobile Asians are honorary whites not merely because of their value-adding activities, but because of their space-defying agility in juggling different regimes of worth in an ever-expanding American economy. Such flexible citizenship and leap-frogging of capital markets have ruptured American belief in the succession model, in the right of workers to make a living with dignity, and in the expectation that political representation will improve the working conditions of ordinary people in the nation.

The old meaning of citizenship – based on free labor, the succession model of social mobility, and worker mobilization against undemocratic practices – was first eroded with the deindustrialization of America. It is now further endangered in the post-Fordist era, when temporary piecework and sweatshop workers have proliferated in the shadow of a dominant service economy. Citizenship based on income, the dignity of work, and representation is now mainly achievable only in the service sector, among those workers in office buildings, hotels, and other major institutions, who have secure jobs to fight for. For the low-wage, part-time workers in the shadow of high-tech manufacturing, however, as well as those in the apparel and cannery industries, the expectation of building on the struggles of earlier generations of workers is no longer tenable. In other words, a worker who is technically an American citizen may not enjoy basic rights because her work status and location, rather than formal citizenship, determine her conditions of existence. On the other hand, transnational entrepreneurs often enjoy rights and privileges regardless of their formal citizenship status. This lateralization of economic frontiers has raised questions about the territorial basis of citizenship when different assemblages of individuals/managers/workers enjoy such radically different conditions of citizenship within national space.

The global terrorist attacks of recent years may serve to accentuate the processes outlined above, and to exacerbate the problems of immigrant communities of color. At moments of heightened international crisis, citizenship rights are the first to suffer. There has already been increased surveillance of migrant populations or of individuals suspected of being terrorists. On the one hand, hundreds of Middle Eastern and South Asian nationals have been detained without criminal charges (often in shackles), and prevented from having contact with their families. By violating the human rights of these detainees, the INS has violated its own standards and those of international law. On the other hand, asylum-seekers arriving without proper papers have been detained in degrading conditions, and local police officers are now helping to enforce INS rules in some states along the US–Mexican border. We can expect more INS crackdowns on the migrant poor and less sympathy among the American public for the ethical demands of immigrant labor. But political mechanisms to secure the borders of the homeland against terrorist suspects do not interrupt the ongoing lateralization of economic relations that continue to depend on mobile businessmen, professionals, and migrant labor that enjoy mixed bundles of rights and privileges. We are left with the question: on what basis can the poor working migrant populations make claims for protection in latitudinal structures of production?

## REFERENCES

Appadurai, Arjun (1996) *Modernity at Large: Cultural Dimensions of Globalization.* Minneapolis: University of Minnesota Press.

Basch, Linda, Nina Glick Schiller, and Cristina S. Blanc (1993) *Nations Unbound: Transnational Projects, Postcolonial Predicaments, and Deterritorialized Nation-states.* Langhorne, PA: Gordon and Breach.

Colker, Ruth (1998) *American Law in the Age of Hypercapitalism.* New York: New York University Press.

Copeland, Lewis C. (1993) The Negro as a Contrast Conception. In *Race Relations and the Race Problem: A Definition and an Analysis,* ed. Egar T. Thompson, pp. 152–179. Durham, NC: Duke University Press.

Deleuze, Gilles, and Felix Guattari (1994) *A Thousand Plateaus: Capitalism and Schizophrenia,* trans. Brian Massumi. Minneapolis: University of Minnesota Press.

Gupta, Akhil, and James Ferguson (1992) Beyond "Culture": Space, Identity and the Politics of Difference. *Cultural Anthropology* 7:6–23.

Hu-DeHart, Evelyn (1999) Introduction. In *Across the Pacific: Asian Americans and Globalization,* ed. Evelyn Hu-DeHart, pp. 1–28. Philadelphia: Temple University Press.

Kwong, Peter (1997) *Forbidden Workers: Illegal Chinese Immigrants and American Labor.* New York: New Press.

Kymlicka, Will (1995) *Multicultural Citizenship: A Liberal Theory of Minority Rights.* Oxford: Oxford University Press.

Lowe, Lisa (1996) *Immigrant Acts: On Asian American Cultural Politics.* Durham, NC: Duke University Press.

Luthje, Boy (1998) Race and Ethnicity in "Post-Fordist" Production Networks: Silicon Valley and the Global Information Technology Industry. Unpublished manuscript, Department of Social Sciences, University of Frankfurt.

Omi, Michael, and Howard Winant (1986) *Racial Formation in the United States.* New York: Routledge and Kegan Paul.

Ong, Aihwa (1999) *Flexible Citizenship: The Cultural Logics of Transnationality.* Durham, NC: Duke University Press.

Roediger, David R. (1991) *The Wages of Whiteness: Race and the Making of the American Working Class.* London: Verso.

Rosaldo, Renato (1997) Cultural Citizenship, Inequality, and Multiculturalism. In *Latino Cultural Citizenship: Claiming Identity, Space, and Politics,* ed. William V. Flores and Rina Benmayor, pp. 27–38. Boston: Beacon Press.

Sacks, Karen (1994) How Did Jews Become White Folks? In *Race,* ed. Steven Gregory and Roger Sanjek, pp. 78–102. New Brunswick, NJ: Rutgers University Press.

Takaki, Ronald (1990 [1979]) *Iron Cages: Race and Culture in 19th-century America.* New York: Oxford University Press.

Taylor, Charles (1994) The Politics of Recognition. In *Multiculturalism*, ed. Amy Gutmann, pp. 56–57. Princeton, NJ: Princeton University Press.

Volpp, Leti (2001) Feminism versus Multiculturalism. *Columbia Law Review* 101:1181–1617.

Williams, Brackette (1995) The Symbolics of Ethnic Historical Traditions and "Suffering": Some Implications for the Doctrine of Equal Citizenship in the United States. Unpublished manuscript.

# CHAPTER 5 Cosmopolitanism

## Ulf Hannerz

Looking ahead from the beginning of a new millennium, Richard Shweder has offered a provocative scenario of an emergent, bifurcated, liberal world order (2000:170):

> this system would be two tiered and operating at two levels, global and local. I imagine its personnel will belong to two "castes." There will be the cosmopolitan liberals, who are trained to appreciate value neutrality and cultural diversity and who run the global institutions of the world system. And there will be the local non-liberals, who are dedicated to one form or another of thick ethnicity and are inclined to separate themselves from "others," thereby guaranteeing that there is enough diversity remaining in the world for the cosmopolitan liberals to appreciate. The global elite (those who are cosmopolitan and liberal) will, of course, come from all nationalities. In the new universal cosmopolitan culture of the global tier of the world system, your ancestry and skin color will be far less important than your education, your values, and your travel plans.

Shweder's conceptualization of "cosmopolitanism" allows us to identify a number of the issues that have recently restored this old, multifaceted notion as a key word of culture and politics.

Portraying the world order in terms of two "castes," he chooses perhaps the most dramatic metaphor possible to imply inequality among human beings. One stratum "runs" the overarching institutions of the global system; there is a sense of smooth decision-making and routine operations here. But Shweder's cosmopolitans are not only engaged in power and its management. Combining value neutrality with an appreciation of cultural diversity, they seem to stand both above culture and, with pleasure, in the midst of its assembled complexities and contradictions. And then, in contradiction to the kind of social closure that we otherwise associate with a caste order, Shweder finds theirs notably open in its recruitment patterns. Education counts for more than ancestry; cosmopolitans can be of any nationality or pigmentation. But they evidently travel. Locals, meanwhile, keep their traditions going, watch their boundaries, and largely remain in place.

My aim in this chapter is to sketch some current arguments over cosmopolitanism and their significance for anthropologists as they move back and forth between "the global" and "the local," in the process often blurring that initial, problematic contrast. The anthropology of cosmopolitanism has not yet come very far, but I believe it is a field that will soon engage more scholars, not only in conceptual and theoretical work but in ethnography as well. At this stage, then, it may be useful to identify points of departure and the directions taken thus far.

To begin with, there is the intricate doubleness of concepts of the cosmopolitan that entail both cultural and political referents. There is, furthermore, the question of who may now turn out to be a cosmopolitan. Have old conventions of recognizing cosmopolitanism been too constraining, or have its social bases changed? Where in the landscape of global society is organized cosmopolitan action initiated? And, finally, we must ask whether, in a world shaped by inequality between regions, the meanings and implications of cosmopolitanism can everywhere be the same.

## COSMOPOLITANISM IN CULTURE AND POLITICS

Probably like any work of its kind, *Webster's Third New International Dictionary of the English Language* has much to offer under "cosmopolitanism" and its related entries. Under "cosmopolis," for example, we find "a community of citizens of the world bound by juridical or moral principles"; under "cosmopolitan," "marked by interest in, familiarity with, or knowledge and appreciation of many parts of the world; not provincial, local, limited, or restricted by the attitudes, interests, or loyalties of a single region, section, or sphere of activity; worldwide rather than regional, parochial, or narrow"; and under "cosmopolitanism," "the theory or advocacy of the formation of a world society or cosmopolis" as well as "excessive admiration and imitation of the cultural traits or achievements of others at the expense of the cultural identity or integrity of one's own land or region."

In all their variety, these dictionary definitions lean in two major directions: one has to do with a knowledge and even appreciation of human diversity, and may be broadly termed cultural. The other has to do with community, society, and citizenship at a more or less global level, and can be summarized as political. Are these two clusters of meaning that might seem just accidentally to share a set of labels, or can we discern a relationship between them?

I first became interested in questions of cosmopolitanism in the context of the changing organization of culture in the world and, consequently, I dwelt initially on the intellectual and aesthetic facets of the notion, on cosmopolitanism as a kind of meaning management – a metaculture, although that was not a term I used in my early essay on "Cosmopolitans and Locals in World Culture." I described cosmopol-itanism as an openness toward divergent cultural experiences, a search for contrasts rather than uniformity, but not simply as a matter of appreciation. There was also the matter of competence: at one level a general readiness to make one's way into other cultures; at another level, a cultivated skill in maneuvering more or less expertly with one or more cultures besides one's own.

Since then there has been an accelerated interest in the political aspects of cosmo-politanism. It is easy to see why. The politics of cosmopolitanism go back to the Stoics of Greek antiquity and to Immanuel Kant's "Perpetual Peace," but around the turn of the third millennium they were animated by a new series of conditions and experiences. The end of the Cold War allowed new possibilities in organizing power as well as responsibility. If the term "globalization" had to a remarkable extent been appropriated to refer to the deregulation of markets and the triumphant march of capitalism, "cosmopolitanism" suggested that human beings could relate to the world not only as consumers, or members of a labor force, but also as citizens. This meant that cosmopolitanism might become a critique of at least certain qualities of global capitalism, as well as a search for ways to constrain it. Moreover, the Cold War order did not pass away smoothly everywhere. New wars and conflagrations, such as those of the Balkans, involved atrocities that contributed to placing human rights prominently on a cosmopolitan agenda.

Environmental changes were also seen as matters which required active handling at a level beyond the nation-state, since they could not be contained within its boundaries. "Risk" became a key word that could cover more gradually evolving dangers as well as the threat of seemingly more sudden disasters, such as nuclear-power accidents. And as much as ever, the politics of cosmopolitanism might also stand opposed to nationalism, nativism, and xenophobia, adversary responses to global interconnectedness that might be reactions to the influx of migrant labor and refugees, but also to other social and cultural traffic across borders. In this case it becomes particularly clear that the arena of cosmopolitan engagement is not always in itself necessarily transnational. Often xenophobia has to be opposed primarily in national or local arenas. Yet in virtually all instances the cosmopolitan impulse has tended to be one of favoring more inclusive arrangements of compassion, solidarity, and peacefulness – again, extending shared moral principles to all humanity, in "a community of citizens of the world."

Having focused earlier on cosmopolitanism as a stance in the management of cultural experience, here I want to inquire into the relationship between the culture and the politics of cosmopolitanism. Is there a necessary linkage? Perhaps not. Cosmopolitanism has two faces. In its aesthetic and intellectual dimensions, it can become a kind of consumer cosmopolitanism, a cosmopolitanism with a happy face, enjoying new cuisines, new musics, new literatures. Political cosmopolitanism is often a cosmopolitanism with a worried face, trying to come to grips with very large problems. We may suspect that it is entirely possible for people to be pleased with their experiences and their personal levels of connoisseurship in regard to cultural diversity without having any strong sense of civic and humanitarian responsibility transcending national borders.

Yet, if these two senses of cosmopolitanism must not simply be conflated, there could be at least a kind of elective affinity between them. For an illuminating point of departure, we may turn to a recent American debate, initiated by the philosopher Martha Nussbaum, contrasting cosmopolitanism and patriotism as political and moral notions. While strongly cosmopolitan in her own preferences (yet at the same time seeing no necessary conflict between the two) she recognized a certain weakness in a philosophical or programmatic cosmopolitanism. "Becoming a citizen of the world is often a lonely business," she wrote. "It is . . . a kind of exile – from the comfort of local truths, from the warm, nestling feeling of patriotism, from the absorbing drama of pride in oneself and one's own." And, she continued, cosmopolitanism "offers only reason and the love of humanity, which may seem at times less colorful than other sources of belonging" (1996:15).

Nussbaum's critics mostly agreed with her on this point. Some even felt that she had not made it strongly enough, not least because they felt that cosmopolitanism had dubious viability. The political scientist Benjamin Barber suggested that she understated the "thinness" of cosmopolitanism. It offered nothing for the human psyche to fasten on. In the opinion of Michael McConnell, a law professor, if one taught children to be "citizens of the world," they would, in all likelihood, become neither patriots nor cosmopolitans, but ideologues intolerant of lesser individuals and cultures. The poet Robert Pinsky concluded that most people would not be willing or able to muster the levels of abstraction and disembodiment required by global citizenship.

We should perhaps be aware here that "patriotism" should not simply be understood as synonymous with "nationalism." The philosopher Kwame Anthony Appiah (1996) suggests that cosmopolitanism and patriotism, unlike nationalism, are sentiments rather than ideologies, and consequently there may be conservatives, socialists, and liberals among cosmopolitans as well as patriots. Presumably, if cosmopolitanism has such an umbrella character, not necessarily fully understood, this contributes to keeping it forever debatable, and offers one reason why we may often be better off speaking of cosmopolitanisms in the plural form. Yet at this point, we may still accept that, between notions of patriotism and nationalism, there is in ordinary usage a considerable overlap; and to approach a further understanding of the politics and culture of cosmopolitanism, I believe we can relate what Nussbaum and her interlocutors suggested about the deficiencies of cosmopolitanism to a slightly more elaborate conception of nationalism that has emerged in several disciplines in recent times.

It has become an established practice to distinguish between two basic types of nationalism, one sometimes referred to as "ethnic" or "primordial" and the other as "civic"; the labels vary. The "ethnic" variety is indeed based on ethnicity, or something very like it. Belonging to a nation is then seen to be based on ascription, and an assumption of cultural homogeneity and great historical depth. Consequently such nationalism has great symbolic density, a major resource in contexts where solidarity has to be mobilized. The other side of the coin is that it is often rigid and exclusionist when it comes to membership, and this often generates conflict. Civic nationalism is more strictly political. Membership requires quite simply a commitment to to an overarching political order. In principle, regardless of culture and history, anyone may join. Admirable as such openness and flexibility may be, however, some would argue that there is in civic nationalism a certain cultural deficit. It may be too symbolically narrow and thin to gain full commitment.

Actually, not all the cultural density accumulated in a sense of national identity and nationhood need be of a narrowly ethnic, conflict-oriented character. As the political psychologist Michael Billig has pointed out, there is often in stable, affluent contemporary societies a strong "banal nationalism," based on the recurrent practices and experiences of everyday life that come to define much of what it means to belong to a particular nation-state. Still, we seem to have here two nationalisms, thick and thin – and only a thin cosmopolitanism. Why should there be no thick cosmopolitanism? The kind of cosmopolitanism identified by Nussbaum and her interlocutors bears a strong resemblance to civic nationalism, as understood by political philosophers. Yet it does not seem self-evident, especially in the present era, that ethnic nationalism monopolizes key formative experiences that have enduring consequences for identities and orientations.

For a growing number of people, border-crossing involvements with different places, cultures, and nations may well have such qualities. Such people may encounter what is initially culturally alien through new work experiences, new links of friendship and kinship, or memorable pleasures and challenges. Widespread interest in forms of cultural blending – "hybridity," "creolization," "mestizaje" – is one indication of this. Probably less self-consciously, however, as such encounters become a part of many people's life course and of everyday experience, there may grow what (in line with Billig's terminology) one might describe as "banal cosmopolitanism." To use a somewhat paradoxical but now recurrent formulation, it is a matter of being, or becoming, at home in the world. Rather than merely constituting some kind of individual self-indulgence, the cultural, experiential, sometimes aesthetic cosmopolitanism could perhaps become so intertwined with political cosmopolitanism as to provide it with both an important resource base of affect and a sense of competence: fully developed, a thick cosmopolitanism. And, unlike ethnic nationalism, such cosmopolitanism might be inclusive rather than exclusive or confrontational, emphasizing the achievement rather than the ascription of understandings and social relationships.

The intertwining of the cultures of cosmopolitanism with its politics undoubtedly proceeds along various lines and takes many different shapes. Why should there not be as much scope for variation and complexity here as in nationalism? It may be time for the political philosophers of cosmopolitanism to let more ethnographers in.

## THE SOCIAL BASES OF COSMOPOLITANISM

Some cosmopolitans identify themselves self-consciously as such. Others have the label affixed to them by others, not always with good intentions. Historically, "cosmopolitan" has often served as a term of denunciation, of more or less vicious description of the other. Cosmopolitans, it is implied, are people of doubtful loyalty to the "fatherland" – possibly parasites, potential traitors, and renegades. Typically, in such usage but not only there, cosmopolitans are taken to be "rootless."

Dictionary definitions that refer to an excessive admiration of things foreign point in this direction in a comparatively benign way; being judged perhaps a bit flighty in one's interests and attitudes might not matter so much. But there have also been periods and places where belonging to a people described as cosmopolitan affected one's standing and life chances a great deal. For Russian Jews, to whom the term was applied in a somewhat offhand way under the czars as well as during the Soviet period, it entailed no advantage and might be dangerous. In more open societies, too, where the implications of the term are not so sinister, questions of the social distribution of cosmopolitanism can nonetheless be controversial, depending on what cosmopolitans are held to do with that openness.

As the quotation above from Richard Shweder suggests, cosmopolitanism is often considered an elite characteristic. This is not to say that all elites are in one sense or another cosmopolitan, but historically, at least, it has been assumed that a cosmopolitan orientation has gone with more formal education, travel, and leisure, as well as sufficient material resources to permit the cultivation of knowledge of the diversity of cultural forms. A Bourdieuan perspective suggests that cosmopolitan tastes and knowledge serve as symbolic capital in competitive elite games of distinction. Although largely a matter of an intellectually and aesthetically oriented cosmopolitanism, this might also have a political dimension, drawing on wider horizons and more extended networks.

Even now, cosmopolitanism may continue to be a privilege associated with other privileges. In an increasingly mobile world, I have argued before, not all sheer physical mobility automatically entails cosmopolitanism. Going abroad and encountering otherness might involve not affirmative openness, but a rejection of what is alien, or a narrow, controlled selection from it. Some tourists seek out the particular qualities of a distant place (such as sunshine) rather than embracing it as a whole; others want the distant place to be as much like home as possible. Business travelers may find it convenient and comforting if all the hotels in major chains stretching across the world look and feel much the same. Exiles, having had a foreign haven more or less forced upon them, may prefer to encapsulate themselves as much as possible with other exiles from their homeland. Labor migrants may be in a distant place struggling to earn a living, not for the sake of interesting experiences. Cosmopolitan attitudes can grow under circumstances such as these, but they are hardly inevitable.

Yet now, too, more occupations are practiced transnationally, often by choice and under more or less favorable circumstances. These need not automatically involve cosmopolitanism either, but they may well lend themselves rather better to serving as a springboard for it. When the sociologist Robert Merton first elaborated the cosmopolitan/local distinction a half-century or so ago (a contribution that has mostly been ignored in recent discussion) it was in an American small-town context. There, he noted, locally oriented influentials depended on who they knew, while cosmopolitans built their influence on what they knew – an expertise that they could take along with them when they moved on. Thus cosmopolitans are often people with credentials of knowledge that can be readily decontextualized and recontextualized. Or at least this is the way it may be understood as long as nobody gets around to comparing their credentialized knowledge to the detail and precision of local knowledge.

The linkage between cosmopolitanism and older or more recent elites seems open to at least two unfavorable interpretations. On the one hand, cosmopolitanism may be understood as engaged in creating another burden for ordinary people, a mode of domination even less accessible to control from below than any earlier social order, perhaps a dystopian global cosmopolis. On the other hand, cosmopolitans, footloose, carrying their assets with them, may be suspected of escaping from local or national contexts, avoiding responsibility, and not sharing in a common burden. The metaphor of rootlessness clearly fits in here. A relatively recent, internationally prominent argument of this kind is that of the American scholar-politician Robert Reich, categorizing "symbolic analysts" as footloose, affluent specialists in the global knowledge economy, quick to withdraw from any commitments to the welfare of their compatriots.

In Shweder's scenario, the relationship between elite cosmopolitans and subordinate locals does not immediately appear particularly conflict-ridden, but rather more as a structural division of labor. Yet one can discern that cosmopolitanism may add an element of its own to any climate of distrust found between upper and lower strata in many societies. If things go wrong, is the elite even going to be there to face the music?

Pinsky (1996:87–88), one of Nussbaum's critics in the debate referred to above, offers a dark view of privileged cosmopolitanism in a formulation that, had it not been published several years before, might seem like a comment on Shweder's imagery:

> I have the impression that some of the fiercest nationalisms and ethnocentrisms of the world are fueled in part by resentment toward people like ourselves: happily situated members of large, powerful nations, prosperous and mobile individuals, able to serve on UN commissions, who participate in symposia, who plan the fates of other peoples while flying around the world and staying in splendid hotels.

This, Pinsky suggests, is "the village of the liberal managerial class," whose folk arts are United Nations institute reports, curriculum reform committees, and enlightened social administration.

"Ingratiatingly populist," is literary and cultural critic Bruce Robbins's blunt response to Pinsky's anti-cosmopolitanism. Indeed, there has been a streak of populism and nativism in adverse commentaries on cosmopolitanism, also from academics and intellectuals, who thereby occasionally risk finding themselves in questionable company. Nevertheless, Pinsky's suggestion that cosmopolitanism may at times generate its opposite should not be disregarded. The dramatic, if only relative, success of various anti-immigrant political groupings in Western Europe at the turn of the millennium may not have been simply a reaction against an influx of migrants and refugees. It could be provoked, too, by the manner in which complaints about those everyday nuisances and irritations that flux and diversity bring have frequently been met with a habitual, more or less privileged, cosmopolitan response of politicians, officials, and others, celebrating the aesthetic and intellectual pleasures of diversity. Such celebration often carries the aesthetic element in cosmopolitanism to an extreme, viewing cultural diversity as differing performances to be enjoyed from a good seat in the audience, as it were, but not as a matter of mutual adaptation. Across a certain social divide, in a recognizably schismogenic format, enthusiasms on one side may provoke growing xenophobia on the other. If this occurs, the fault would appear to lie not with cosmopolitanism per se, but with a resort to the wrong kind of cosmopolitanism. I will come back to this.

In his own essay on "The Village of the Liberal Managerial Class," Bruce Robbins discerns an affinity between cosmopolitanism and professionalism. He attributes this to professionalism's peculiar ability to produce bonds among detached, institutionally scattered subjects. Thus an older and more aristocratic cosmopolitanism is replaced by that of "the new class," as the sociologist Alvin Gouldner once called it. Here Robbins thus to a degree agrees with Pinsky about a current social locus of cosmopolitanism, even as he takes a more favorable view of it. Elsewhere, however, Robbins is more inclined to emphasize non-elite modes and sites of cosmopolitanism – among "North Atlantic merchant sailors, Caribbean *au pairs* in the United States, Egyptian guest workers in Iraq, Japanese women who take *gaijin* lovers" (1998:1). He thus contributes to an important tendency that has developed since the 1990s. Although some qualities of cosmopolitanism come more readily and are more affordable for people in relatively privileged positions, they can also appear elsewhere in the social landscape. Several recent writers in anthropology and its environs have paid attention to this possibility. In his much cited essay, "Traveling Cultures," James Clifford identified "discrepant cosmopolitanisms" generated through displacement and transplantation resulting from violent histories of economic, political, and cultural interaction. Because Clifford's essay was principally concerned with the part travel plays in constituting the contemporary world, it had no extended discussion of cosmopolitanism per se. Nevertheless, it effectively dramatized the fact that not for a long time has the world been made up of "haves" who move and "have nots" who stay put.

## ETHNOGRAPHIES OF COSMOPOLITANISM

As anthropologists have begun to turn more often than before to varieties of cosmopolitanism, it has often been the non-elite forms which have attracted their attention. Pnina Werbner (1999) thus finds a kind of piecemeal, collective cosmopolitanism in Pakistani migrants' exploration of the commoditized material culture of Marks and Spencer and other British chain stores. Yet they are also encapsulated within transnational communities that reach out to their districts of origin in Pakistan. Perhaps the person in Werbner's account who comes closest to the conventional image of individual cosmopolitan openness to the world is one Pakistani villager, not particularly well educated, a member of a Sufi cult who was formerly a migrant laborer in the highly mobile, heterogeneous society of the Arabian Gulf. This man had performed the pilgrimage to Mecca and thus bore the honorific of *Haji*. He had picked up Arabic, some English, and a smattering of Japanese (having been employed by a Japanese firm) and could anticipate an assignment in Amsterdam if his cult leader decided to establish a branch there. If so, he would probably find himself working alongside Turks and Arabs as well as other Pakistanis but, after his Gulf experience, he saw no difficulty in that, nor in the prospect of learning Dutch. Here, then, was a man who appeared "at home in the world." Yet, as Werbner notes, his was a cosmopolitanism dependent on and channeled through his cult membership.

Huon Wardle (2000) develops the theme of cosmopolitanism by combining personalized ethnography from among his neighbors and associates in urban Jamaica with philosophical notions from Kant and Simmel. Against the background of the pervasive harshness of Caribbean working-class living conditions and the openness of the region to outside influences, he notes the transnational networks, not least of kinship, in which ordinary Jamaicans are linked throughout the North Atlantic world. But looking beyond their material circumstances and practical adaptations, Wardle finds that a cosmopolitan philosophy and a shared community aesthetic has emerged out of the uncertainty and flux in their way of life.

As James Ferguson finds very different cosmopolitans in the classic ethnographic territory of the urban Zambian Copper Belt, on the other hand, we are among people who are not likely to have traveled much outside their own country. Nevertheless there is a distinct cleavage of cultural styles between cosmopolitans and those more locally oriented, reminding one of older cultural bifurcations described in earlier urban ethnographies from Central and Southern Africa. For cosmopolitans, "style" is an accomplished, cultivated, performance capacity, a matter of seeking worldliness and at the same time distancing oneself from parochial ties and traditions. But there are varieties of cosmopolitanism on the Copper Belt. Some cosmopolitans are "high" and some "low," some reputable and others disreputable. Many of the more conspicuous cosmopolitans are hoodlums and prostitutes.

The Pakistani *haji*, the Copper Belt street sophisticates, and the Jamaican proletarian city-dwellers are not likely to be labeled cosmopolitan by anyone in their own environment. Nor do they probably think of themselves as such. Yet they are all people that anthropologists now place within cosmopolitanism as an analytical category. Their cosmopolitanism is not all of a kind, and two distinctions, at least, need to be made. To begin with, along the lines previously suggested, these are all cultural rather than political cosmopolitans, since all deal more or less capably with human diversity. Second, one may distinguish between a cosmopolitanism that is more instrumental, involving skills and a degree of self-confidence in dealing with a heterogeneous, even alien, environment without necessarily relishing it for its own sake, and a cosmopolitanism where diversity, newness, and wider horizons are sought as being rewarding in themselves. Werbner's Pakistani *haji* is of the first kind; Ferguson's Zambian cultivators of urban chic are of the second.

Calling for further analytical distinctions does not necessarily entail a claim that any one kind of cosmopolitanism is more "real" than any other. It involves only a realization that the notion of cosmopolitanism we began with is broad enough to cover a great many different instances. It may also be the case, however, that in a trend toward finding cosmopolitanism in more places, the concept itself becomes attenuated and barely recognizable. There may be some virtue, after all, in not straying too far from dictionary definitions.

When ethnographers "discover" people who have been cosmopolitans all the time, though not previously recognized as such, this may reflect both the career of the concept and scholars' current inclinations to test its boundaries. But it is also likely that the actual distribution of the social qualities we identify as cosmopolitan has changed during the present era, and that more people outside the elite are now included within that category. Although mobility is not equated with cosmopolitanism, when a great many people are on the move for one reason or another, cosmopolitanism is likely to grow, even if, for some, it is a reluctant cosmopolitanism. For those who travel, cosmopolitanism may involve an increased ability to cope with newness and uncertainty, and faith in the ability to do just that; for those who remain at home it may entail a growing ability to coexist in their habitat with newcomers and strangers.

Moreover, meanings and the forms that carry meanings may travel even when people do not. Consumer habits, and especially media consumption, have greatly changed people's imagined worlds. Much of this openness comes with entertainment and popular culture, but the effect of news reporting on people's sense of involvement has also been intensely debated at least since the Vietnam War – the first televised war – reached into living-rooms across the world. A few years later, television reporting of the Ethiopian famine drew an enormous response from European and American viewers. Bob Geldof's Band Aid campaign and the song "We Are the

World" were clear manifestations of the blending of cosmopolitan humanitarianism with Western popular culture. What do you feel, what do you do, when you see dying children on the television screen, or emaciated bodies behind the barbed wire of a concentration camp, or "terrorists" crashing passenger planes into crowded skyscrapers?

You may feel strongly about it and respond strongly to it – elsewhere I have described this as "electronic empathy" (Hannerz 1996:121) – and it can motivate cosmopolitan politics. Yet empathy and activism do not necessarily follow from such media experiences. The anthropologists Arthur and Joan Kleinman (1996) have argued that suffering, broadcast on a daily basis as "infotainment" can be diluted, distorted, and turned into quite another commodity. If there are different reactions to media experiences, they probably depend on the wider social and cultural contexts within which audiences have them. We could doubtless learn much more about the way people deal with news through ethnographic studies of media reception, but thus far such studies have dealt mostly with responses to works of fiction, not to world news.

It is also true that the growth of new media technologies, and widened access to them, does not always lead to more cosmopolitanism, or to a broadening of its social bases. For migrant populations, video tapes and cable television can increase the chances of staying encapsulated within the culture of one's origins, rather than approaching what is new and unknown in the immediate surroundings. Through media, people can attend not only to what is abroad when they are at home, but also to what is at home when they find themselves abroad. And while several commentators have identified the internet as a tool of cosmopolitanism, one may sense that it is again in large part a tool available especially to the more or less elite – not least in that "village of the liberal managerial class."

## ROOTS AND COSMOPOLITANISM

The idea that cosmopolitans are "rootless" has a long history. "Deterritorialization," in contrast, is a more recent key word, summarizing notions that large-scale migration and the proliferation of media now combine to loosen people's ties to particular limited spaces. But does it follow that rootlessness and cosmopolitanism more than ever belong together and spread together?

It seems entirely possible that some people are less rooted, or have more complex roots, than others. The experiences of migrancy and diaspora may relativize and circumscribe rootedness. If few people are entirely deterritorialized, many may well have the sense of being more or less at home in more than one place. Having "roots" is not necessarily a matter of being forever rooted, but can refer to putting down roots, becoming rooted. But there is no necessary relationship between cosmopolitanism and degrees of rootedness. Writing in *Blood and Belonging* about late twentieth-century nationalist conflicts, and identifying himself as a cosmopolitan, the well-known scholar-journalist Michael Ignatieff suggests that this is the privilege only of someone who can take a secure nation-state for granted. We seem far away here from that scene in which the state declares certain elements in its population cosmopolitans as a first step toward identifying them as traitors.

The African-born, American-based philosopher Kwame Anthony Appiah indeed argues that a "rooted cosmopolitanism" or, alternatively phrased, a "cosmopolitan patriotism," is entirely possible. His father, a well-known Ghanaian politician, identifed firmly with his home region of Ashanti throughout his involvement in the struggle for Ghanaian independence. Yet in an unfinished note found after his death, he reminded his children that they should be citizens of the world. Wherever they chose to live, they should make sure they left that place better than they had found it. "The cosmopolitan patriot," his son writes (Appiah 1996:22), "can entertain the possibility of a world in which everyone is a rooted cosmopolitan, attached to a home of his or her own, with its own cultural particularities, but taking pleasure from the presence of other, different, places that are home to other, different, people." This, one notes, is a different world from that envisaged by Richard Shweder, with its hierarchical caste system of cosmopolitans and locals.

## TOP-DOWN AND BOTTOM-UP

Some forms of cosmopolitanism can be characterized as "top-down," others as "bottom-up" (and sometimes the two meet). Although these may be related to questions of the social bases of cosmopolitanism, they also involve another distinction. There are approaches to cosmopolitanism that start at a macrolevel with the establishment of overarching structures and processes, and there are, on the other hand, approaches that begin at a microlevel, with personal or group experience and orientation, but that may, through aggregation, rise through existing structures or bring into being new and wider structures.

Returning to our earlier distinction between cultural and political cosmopolitanism, one may suspect that in such terms the former is more often "bottom-up," involving a shaping of identity and affect through personal experience. Yet we may also keep in mind attempts at cosmopolitan "cultural engineering." Organizations such as UNESCO can be seen as involved in top-down cosmopolitanism by promoting an appreciation of cultural diversity, somewhat intricately if they are also based on a nation-state logic. Moreover, this is also not just cultural cosmopolitanism, but a politics of it.

In "top-down" political cosmopolitanism, "global governance" has emerged as a central concept. This may sound rather like what cosmopolitans have sometimes been accused of – striving toward a remote, yet omnipresent superstate. Yet governance is not identical with government, and in the global arena the assumption tends to be that it involves ways in which the human community can run its common affairs without an ultimate centralizing institution.

In its well-known report *Our Global Neighborhood* (1995), the Commission on Global Governance – co-chaired by a Swedish prime minister and a long-time secretary-general of the British Commonwealth – emphasizes this point. Were one to travel in the direction of world government, their foreword argues, one could find oneself in an even less democratic world than at present, one "more accommodating to power, more hospitable to hegemonic ambition, and more reinforcing of the roles of states and governments rather than the rights of people." The Commission (1995:2) defines governance as the sum of the many ways individuals and institutions, public and private, manage their common affairs. It is a continuing process through which conflicting or diverse interests may be accommodated and co-operative action may be taken. It includes formal institutions and regimes empowered to enforce compliance, as well as informal arrangements that people and institutions either have agreed to or perceive to be in their interest.

The report acknowledges that global governance has often been taken to involve primarily inter-governmental relationships, but urges that it must be understood to engage non-governmental organizations (NGOs), citizens' movements, multinational corporations, and the global capital market, all interacting through global communications media. Global governance thus moves beyond internationalism to cosmopolitanism.

The Commission on Global Governance, with a mixture of politicians, statesmen, high-ranking public servants, and policy-oriented scholars among its members and on its staff, typifies recent activism in the area of global governance. This is, again, cosmopolitanism with a worried face, working through various organizational forms, identifying problems and setting agendas, trying at the very least to exercise moral pressure, striving to achieve binding agreements and establish powerful new institutions. The creation of the International Criminal Court is a conspicuous twenty-first-century example of an attempt at global governance, but the main public events of political cosmopolitanism have been large and sometimes controversial conferences – in Rio de Janeiro, Mexico City, Beijing, Kyoto, and Durban – on themes such as the environment, poverty, gender, or race.

In scholarship concerned with cosmopolitanism, disciplines tend to focus differently on top-down and bottom-up phenomena. Not surprisingly, political scientists focus on top-down global governance, along with political philosophers and legal scholars. Yet perhaps there is also room for anthropologists here. Along the lines suggested most memorably by Laura Nader (1972), they can "study up," writing ethnographies of contemporary power – not least of those institutions of governance that exercise power by creating and managing knowledge. The ethnography of science has become a leading growth area in sociocultural anthropology, and we can foresee its further expansion into the study of research networks and institutions engaged in the production of theory and policy for global governance. And, insofar as the working of the state is increasingly a focus of anthropological scrutiny, it would be unfortunate if that scrutiny stopped short at state borders. For, again, global governance involves a great deal of international governmental activity.

Beyond this, at a more macro-anthropological level yet, we can envisage a continuation of an old concern with comparative political structures, now involving a broad concern with regions where, as it were, questions of global governance meet "tribes without rulers." When global society becomes more cohesive, when it forms an increasingly dense web of more or less encompassing institutions and procedures, when linkages between different levels and heterogeneous institutional and organizational spheres give shape to heated debates and new ambiguities over goals and means, anthropology's habitual inclination to be curious about "wholes," contextualizations, and syntheses, and somewhat disrespectful of conventional limits of inquiry, could be a scholarly resource worth reinventing.

It seems more probable, however, that most anthropological interest in political cosmopolitanism will be drawn to its bottom-up manifestations, such as the way people come together in civic activities that transcend cultural or political boundaries. In 1998 the German sociologist Ulrich Beck published a *Cosmopolitan Manifesto* which appeared in newspapers and journals in several countries and may be read as a proposal for bottom-up cosmopolitanism. The *Manifesto* proposes that a new dialectic of global and local questions does not fit into politics at the national level. These questions, he noted (Beck 1998:30):

> are already part of the political agenda – in the localities and regions, in governments and public spheres both national and international. But only in a transnational framework can they be properly posed, debated and resolved. For this there has to be a reinvention of politics, a founding and grounding of the new political subject: that is – cosmopolitan parties. These represent transnational interests transnationally, but also work within the arenas of national politics. They thus become possible, both pragmatically and organisationally, only as national-global movements and cosmopolitan parties.

Such groupings, whether parties in the strict sense of the term, or movements, or some other organizational form, may be cosmopolitan in various ways. They may focus on concrete issues that are identifiable at either local or national levels, yet cannot be solved at either. Their solutions pertain to values more associated with the human condition than with either local or national traditions. The effective way of confronting them is likely to include a coalescence of organized action beyond their boundaries.

Questions of gender, environment, human rights, and peace are prominent among those that lead to cosmopolitan mobilization. If, as Appiah suggests, cosmopolitanism is a sentiment rather than an ideology, problems of definitions may vary along with perceived solutions. Working modes differ too, as, for example, between Amnesty International, Greenpeace, and Attac. Mobilization tends to be around single issues and is often reactive. Such defensive cosmopolitanisms are often instrumentalist in their cosmopolitan orientation. Yet because such bottom-up cosmopolitan activity is again and again experienced as an appropriate response, it may prove to be a learning process whereby political cosmopolitanism eventually appears as an ordinary rather than an extraordinary activity.

Bottom-up cosmopolitanism entails different, varied, and often complicated relationships to "the state." There are times when states engaged in top-down intergovernmental relations work well in tandem with cosmopolitan bottom-up activists. Their efforts are largely complementary. There is also a tendency in political cosmopolitanism to operate on a transnational or global scale, for the reasons that states, and the international society formed by states, are found insufficient as machineries or arenas for some given purpose, and state loyalists may find this hard to accept. There are also instances when cosmopolitans come together precisely to put pressure on particular states, as in cases of human rights violations. It is hardly a coincidence that state apparatuses have often been most active in casting a shadow of suspicion over cosmopolitans by labeling them as "rootless."

A kind of cosmopolitan bottom-up civic involvement that often occurs within state boundaries, but which clearly concerns cultural boundaries and cultural cosmopolitanism, has to do with immigration and minority affairs, and thereby also with cultural diversity and multiculturalism. Public usage of the culture concept has been controversial in debates between cosmopolitans and anti-cosmopolitans. I have argued elsewhere that research into varieties of culturespeak, such as popular theories, proto-theories, and quasi-theories of culture and their implications, would definitely have some relevance to policy (Hannerz 1996). This brings us back to the complex relationship between a certain form of celebratory cosmopolitanism and xenophobia.

In arguing for the possibility of a rooted cosmopolitanism, Appiah (1996:25) warns against conflating cosmopolitanism with humanism. Cosmopolitanism focuses on the fact that there are different local human ways of being, whereas humanism, although it can be made compatible with cosmopolitan sentiments, can also live with what Appiah calls "a deadening urge to uniformity." A central question here would seem to be how far one is prepared to take the celebration of difference. In *Works and Lives* (1988), Clifford Geertz urges on anthropologists the necessity of enlarging "the possibility of intelligible discourse between people quite different from one another in interest, outlook, wealth, and power, and yet contained in a world where, tumbled as they are into endless connection, it is increasingly difficult to get out of each other's way." What, then, are the implications of being tumbled into infinite connectedness?

Again, some would simply prefer others to get out of their way. Verena Stolcke (1995) has identified a widespread conception of what she calls "cultural fundamentalism," according to which: (1) human beings are by nature culture bearers; (2) cultures are distinct and incommensurable; (3) relations between bearers of different cultures are intrinsically conflictive; and (4) it is in human nature to be xenophobic. Cultural fundamentalism comes in many varieties and, in part, as Stolcke points out, it has come to replace an older-style racism that has become too historically and intellectually compromised to be effective in public debate. Cultural fundamentalism is often explicitly opposed to agendas of multiculturalism.

Cosmopolitanism, it seems, stands in opposition to three of the four cultural fundamentalist assertions Stolcke discerns. In its positive stance toward cultural diversity, cosmopolitanism appears intrinsically multiculturalist. The difficulty here is that multiculturalism itself has also become not just an affirmation of diversity, but an internally varied, not always coherent, set of -isms that sometimes themselves have a streak of cultural fundamentalism. Some multiculturalists assert cultural closure and incommensurability even as they claim rights of cultural coexistence within a social and political unit. A multiculturalism that would best match a cosmopolitan preference for cultural openness would be one where boundaries between cultural units are relatively permeable, open to choice and dialogue, even critique.

And Geertz's observation on inevitable interconnection is important here. Cultural fundamentalism can be conveniently and comfortably relativist in a way racisms of the past were not. As long as cultures are kept apart, there is no reason to be judgmental or interventionist. But in social contexts where diversity is a fact of life, where people do, indeed, get in each other's way, there has to be an acceptance of at least a minimal overarching shared order, of the common rules of the game which pertain to public life. A cosmopolitanism oriented toward aesthetic experience and cultural consumption may somewhat insouciantly view otherness largely as performance. The citizen cosmopolitan, even one with a soft spot for diversity, has to cope with it in relationships and interactions. Civic, bottom-up cosmopolitanism requires some order, and it is not possible for each way of life and thought to claim sanctuary from external criticism on the grounds of cultural integrity. It requires an ongoing exchange over differences as that shared order is worked out. In such an exchange – where inevitably questions of trust and power will also arise – recognition of and respect for differences may be only a tentative working assumption: an obstacle placed in the way of facile ethnocentrisms, a search for ways to leave large spaces open for diversity and choice. If this formulation has a certain quality of a recipe, it should, nevertheless, be obvious that ethnographies of everyday cosmopolitanisms may well highlight such perhaps rather unspectacular processes of adaptation.

## Conclusion: Cosmopolitan Projects

Cosmopolitanism has to do with a sense of the world as one, but the really existing world is one structured in considerable inequality. If one must always keep in mind the possibility that top-down cosmopolitanism may be a convenient mask for powerful interests, there is particular reason to ask how the network of perspectives toward cosmopolitanism is variously grounded in regions of the world as it is now. An attempt to understand cosmopolitanism as a contemporary global key term must be set in the context of the structure of center and periphery – a structure whose continued existence, it should be observed, is itself being debated.

Is there a tendency to conflate cosmopolitanism and metropolitanism, in such a way that the former is taken to be a manner of seeing the world from the dominant perspective (or one of the competing perspectives) of the center? When the street people of Copper Belt towns choose cosmopolitanism as a lifestyle, it is in large part the cultural flows from affluent countries of the global North that they embrace. Given the asymmetrical relationships of global society, it is perhaps not self-evident that cosmopolitanism is an equally viable and desirable commitment for people everywhere. Is this primarily a noble, compassionate humanitarianism suitable only for "world citizens" at the the privileged centers of the global social order, while the societies and people of peripheral regions may have other priorities? Skeptics may hold that the peripheries of the present world order are poorly served by orientations which could lead to a brain drain of its educated elite, and to "cultural imperialism" for those who remain behind. Yet perhaps even in this order, the patriots of one country will still sometimes find their allies among the cosmopolitans of another.

Somewhat paradoxically, in a field of debate over cosmopolitanism largely populated by scholars and intellectuals from Europe and North America, there is sometimes, not least in generalizing theoretical statements, a rather uncosmopolitan disregard for other parts of the world. As we have seen, anthropologists, with their habitual involvement with all parts of the world, can add usefully to decentering that debate. Yet contributions to a thicker understanding of cosmopolitan orientations and practices can come from many kinds of field sites (and combinations of sites), North and South.

In that argument over cosmopolitanism initiated by Martha Nussbaum, another philosopher, Michael Walzer (1996:125), observed that no one had ever offered him "world citizenship," nor described the naturalization process, nor enlisted him in the world's institutional structures, nor given him an account of its decision procedures, nor provided him with a list of the benefits and obligations of citizenship, nor shown him the world's calendar and the common celebrations and commemorations of its citizens. A skeptical reminder, indeed, that cosmopolis is not yet in existence, and possibly never will be. And cosmopolitanism as a concept is still imprecise, referring to a great variety of personal, collective, political, experiential, and intellectual, but often unfinished, projects.

The anthropology of cosmopolitanism is thus likely to be one of inquiry into emergent experiences, commitments, and relationships; and also a study of its opposites, critics, and adversaries in debate and in life. For the anthropologists of cosmopolitanism, there may be the further ingredient of reflexivity that, as the theoretical issues and ethnographic facts are dealt with, they may be working out their own commitments and identifications. Like the philosophers, that is, they may find that they should take sides.

## REFERENCES

Appiah, Kwame Anthony (1996) Cosmopolitan Patriots. In *For Love of Country*, ed. Joshua Cohen, pp. 21–29. Boston: Beacon Press.

Beck, Ulrich (1998) The Cosmopolitan Manifesto. *New Statesman*, 20 March: 28–30.

Commission on Global Governance (1995) *Our Global Neighborhood*. Oxford: Oxford University Press.

Hannerz, Ulf (1996) *Transnational Connections: Culture, People, Places*. London: Routledge.

Nussbaum, Martha C. (1996) Patriotism and Cosmopolitanism. In *For Love of Country*, ed. Joshua Cohen, pp. 3–17. Boston: Beacon Press.

Kleinman, Arthur, and Joan Kleinman (1996) The Appeal of Experience, the Dismay of Images: Cultural Appropriations of Suffering in Our Times. *Daedalus* 125:1–23.

Pinsky, Robert (1996) Eros against Esperanto. In *For Love of Country*, ed. Joshua Cohen, pp. 85–90. Boston: Beacon Press.

Robbins, Bruce (1998) Actually Existing Cosmopolitanism. In *Cosmopolitics*, ed. Pheng Cheah and Bruce Robbins, pp. 1–19. Minneapolis: University of Minnesota Press.

Shweder, Richard A. (2000) Moral Maps, "First World" Conceits, and the New Evangelists. In *Culture Matters*, ed. Lawrence E. Harrison and Samuel P. Huntington, pp. 158–176. New York: Basic Books.

Stolcke, Verena (1995) Talking Culture: New Boundaries, New Rhetorics of Exclusion in Europe. *Current Anthropology* 36:1–13.

Walzer, Michael (1996) Spheres of Affection. In *For Love of Country*, ed. Joshua Cohen, pp. 125–127. Boston: Beacon Press.

Wardle, Huon (2000) *An Ethnography of Cosmopolitanism in Kingston, Jamaica*. Lampeter: Edwin Mellen.

Werbner, Pnina (1999) Global Pathways: Working Class Cosmopolitans and the Creation of Transnational Ethnic Worlds. *Social Anthropology* 7:17–35.

## SUGGESTED FURTHER READING

Billig, Michael (1995) *Banal Nationalism*. London: Sage.

Beck, Ulrich (2000) The Cosmopolitan Perspective: Sociology of the Second Age of Modernity. *British Journal of Sociology* 51:79–105.

Gouldner, Alvin W. (1979) *The Future of Intellectuals and the Rise of the New Class*. London: Macmillan.

Hannerz, Ulf (2000) Introduction. In *Nationalism and Internationalism in the Post-Cold War Era*, ed. Kjell Goldmann, Ulf Hannerz, and Charles Westin, pp. 1–21. London: Routledge.

Ignatieff, Michael (1994) *Blood and Belonging*. London: Vintage.

Kohn, Hans (1945) *The Idea of Nationalism*. London: Macmillan.

Merton, Robert K. (1957) *Social Theory and Social Structure*. Glencoe, IL: Free Press.

Nader, Laura (1972) Up the Anthropologist: Perspectives Gained from Studying Up. In *Reinventing Anthropology*, ed. Dell Hymes, pp. 284–311. New York: Pantheon.

Reich, Robert (1991) *The Work of Nations*. New York: Knopf.

Robbins, Bruce (2001) The Village of the Liberal Managerial Class. In *Cosmopolitan Geographies*, ed. Vinay Dharwadker, pp. 15–32. New York: Routledge.

Uimonen, Paula (2001) *Transnational_dynamics@development.net*. Stockholm Studies in Social Anthropology 49. Stockholm: Almqvist and Wiksell.

Waldron, Jeremy (1995) Minority Cultures and the Cosmopolitan Alternative. In *The Rights of Minority Cultures*, ed. Will Kymlicka, pp. 93–119. Oxford: Oxford University Press.

## CHAPTER 6

# Development

## Marc Edelman and Angelique Haugerud

"Development" is a slippery concept. Is it an ideal, an imagined future toward which institutions and individuals strive? Or is it a destructive myth, anthropology's "evil twin" (Ferguson 1997), an insidious, failed chapter in the history of Western modernity (Escobar 1995)? Conventionally, "development" may connote improvements in well-being, living standards, and opportunities. It may also refer to processes of commodification, industrialization, modernization, or globalization, and it can be a legitimizing strategy for states. A vision of development as improved well-being, especially in post-colonies, has gradually replaced the one-dimensional economistic measures such as GDP growth, typically favored by neoclassical economists. Influenced by scholars such as Amartya Sen, the United Nations Development Program created a Human Development Index that combines indicators of health, life expectancy, literacy, formal education, political participation, and access to resources. During roughly the same period, a growing coterie of scholars and grass-roots activists, some of them influenced by Michel Foucault's understandings of power, has rejected outright the desirability of "development," which they see as a destructive and self-serving discourse propagated by bureaucrats and aid professionals that permanently entraps the poor in a vicious circle of passivity and misery.

Some scholars and activists in the latter category imagine a "post-development" era in which community and "indigenous" knowledge become a reservoir of creative alternatives to development (as argued by A. Escobar, M. Rahnema, V. Bawtree, and W. Sachs, among others). Others focus on alternatives *in* rather than *to* development and favor reforms within the existing apparatus. An inclination to celebrate the "local" and the "indigenous" figures in larger pendulum shifts during the past 50 years, notably in the differing views of community and "traditional" culture, with these alternately romanticized or demonized in development thought. Nearly all analysts agree that most development projects fail. Nonetheless, a faith in progress (an assumed capacity to improve the conditions of existence) continues among supporters of all three positions – "development," "development alternatives," and "post-development" alike.

In short, as "development" has become an increasingly contentious concept, it has attracted attention from an astonishing array of scholars. Mostly gone are musty oppositions between "applied" and "mainstream" or "academic" anthropology. The formation of anthropology as the "science of 'less developed' peoples" remains relevant to anthropology's place in the academic division of labor, even though the social evolutionist underpinnings of this conception have been eroded during the twentieth century (Ferguson 1997:152). Anthropological discomfort with development, Ferguson argues, does not signal the discipline's critical distance from it but rather an ambivalent intimacy. This essay explores the diverse ways anthropologists and other social scientists have intervened in and been influenced by debates about development.

We begin with the roots of anthropological debates in the works of Smith, Malthus, Marx, and Weber. Next we outline the clash of radical and mainstream paradigms: twentieth-century theories of imperialism, modernization, and dependency, as well as orthodox Marxist and poststructuralist critiques of dependency theory. Critics of modernization theory often ignored its statist dimensions, much as opponents of today's neoliberalism tend to view it as a simple precursor to the free-market "Washington consensus" of the 1980s. Neoliberalism is the focus of the chapter's second half, where we suggest that anthropology has culturalized and dehistoricized globalization, downplaying its political-economic and legal dimensions. Here we review briefly anthropological approaches to NGOs, civil society, gender, the relationship between culture and development, consumption, and environmentalism. Today's fierce debates about globalization confirm that development is still contested on normative as well as instrumental grounds, and that it is still a vital issue for both scholars and those they study. In a world where one half of the population subsists on 2 dollars a day or less, it would seem misleading to speak of "post-development." Yet the search for alternatives to the exhausted paradigms of the recent past and the grim realities of the present is clearly more timely than ever.

## EARLY FOUNDATIONS AND DEBATES

Key theorists from the Enlightenment to the twentieth century have shaped later development debates in powerful ways. It is important to examine such work on its own terms, but also to recognize that ideologically motivated appropriations and simplifications of ideas rooted in other ages and places often reflect contemporary struggles over development doctrine and policies. Smith, Malthus, Marx and Engels, and Weber are worth revisiting, partly to move beyond the association of canonical thinkers with their "one big idea" (Smith and the "invisible hand," for example), and to understand better the ideologically motivated representations of their thought that infuse contemporary development debates.

Adam Smith, almost universally portrayed as an unambivalent and prescient apostle of the free market, never elaborated a coherent theory of development, but he did have strong opinions about the causes of the differences between rich and poor countries. Smith, rather than a timeless prophet, was very much a creature of his epoch. In the eighteenth century, market relations expanded rapidly alongside vestiges of feudal or manorial societies. Smith's ideas about the wealth and poverty of nations mirrored his opinions about capitalists and aristocrats, and rested on his distinction between productive and unproductive labor. The latter did not result in a concrete, vendible commodity, while the former increased the value of raw materials and generated a product that could replace capital stock and materials, pay workers' wages, and provide a profit to the owner and, possibly, the landlord. The difference between rich and poor countries was, for Smith, that in rich countries a large proportion of the total social product was reinvested in production, while in poor countries most of it was consumed in maintaining "unproductive hands" (Smith 1976, Book II:356).

Smith's claim that "great nations" are sometimes impoverished by "public prodigality" could be read as foreshadowing today's neoliberal attacks on "big government" or "unproductive spending" (Smith 1976, Book II:363). One must be cautious, however, in treating Smith's late eighteenth-century work (first published in 1776) as sacred writ, laden with solutions to twentieth- or twenty-first-century dilemmas. Indeed, Smith's famous "invisible hand" of Providence only became the "invisible hand" of the market in later writings of his liberal epigones.

Rather than being a totally convinced champion of market liberalism, Smith questioned development processes observable at the time. In *The Wealth of Nations* he railed against the greed of elites, declaring "All for ourselves, and nothing for other people, seems, in every age of the world, to have been the vile maxim of the masters of mankind." He was not averse, in some circumstances, to maintaining wages above market levels, noting that merchants and master-manufacturers complained that high wages necessitated price increases but said nothing about "the bad effects of high profits" or the "pernicious effects of their own gains." He also cautioned against the "disorder" that could result from premature removal of protectionist tariffs (Smith 1976, Book III:437, Book I:110, Book IV:491). Given Adam Smith's iconic stature today, his works deserve to be reread with an eye for their complexity and contradictions and for how they are situated in the broader sweep of Enlightenment thought.

Population dynamics have long been central to debates about development and under-development. Examples are numerous: how population pressure on resources contributes to the formation of ancient states or the destabilization of contemporary ones, the perennial argument between those who consider population growth a leading cause of poverty and theorists of demand for labor or human capital who emphasize inequality and the incentives that poor people have to reproduce, the role of the demographic transition in improving the status of women, the contentious struggle for safe forms of contraception and abortion, and the ethics of other kinds of natality control (including coerced sterilization, infanticide, sex-selective abortion, and China's one-child policy). The ideas of Thomas Malthus are almost always explicitly invoked or implicitly present in these discussions, even two centuries after their initial formulation.

Malthus is best known for a simple idea in his "first essay," which was published anonymously in 1798, just after one of the earliest arguably capitalist crises. Demographic growth, he argued, will always outstrip increases in food production unless slowed by "preventative" or "positive" checks. Malthus explained poverty in relation to this "law," rather than as an outcome of capitalist development, and he prescribed measures to ameliorate it like those that economic elites still favor today, such as preserving private property and abolishing laws protecting the poor. He had a puritanical and pessimistic outlook on humanity's prospects, which was part of a broader, reactionary political vision. Malthus inveighed against the French Revolution ("one of the most enlightened nations of the world . . . debased by . . . a fermentation of disgusting passions"). He argued that progressive taxation, as proposed by Anglo-American revolutionary Thomas Paine, was "evil," and that man does *not* possess "a right to subsistence when his labour will not fairly purchase it."

Given Malthus's enduring celebrity, it is perhaps surprising that his best-known idea – that population grows geometrically and agricultural production arithmetically – is not widely accepted. Malthus failed to foresee that improved technologies would boost food output and reduce "positive checks" on population growth. Nor did he anticipate the demographic transition from high fertility and high mortality to low fertility and low mortality, which has been observed in country after country.

The pessimism Malthus expressed in the "first essay" diminished during his later lifetime and, in his treatment of public debt and business cycles, he is sometimes said to have anticipated Keynesian thinking. This lesser-known, mature Malthus (see *Principles of Political Economy*, 1820) also argued for at least some state intervention in the economy and lamented how abstract economic doctrine at times bore little relation to reality.

In the nineteenth century, the work that most contributed to gaining Karl Marx's ideas a mass audience is Marx and Engels's *The Communist Manifesto* (1848). The *Economic and Philosophic Manuscripts of 1844* may better describe their view of human agency, and Marx's *Capital* may contain more detailed analyses of commodity fetishism and the capitalist mode of production, but the *Manifesto* contains one of the most succinct outlines of Marx's theory of development, important not just on its own terms but for how it later influenced the political programs of Marxist movements in Russia and the "Third World." It includes attention to key themes such as the ubiquity of class struggle, the social contradictions and historical specificity of each mode of production, the dynamism of capitalism as a force for dissolving tradition and generating technological advances, and the capitalist imperative of seeking new markets.

Marx and Engels's picture of a succession of modes of production has often been read as an evolutionary, Enlightenment-style "master narrative" or as an inexorable, teleological Hegelian process in which history advances toward a predetermined outcome. This is not entirely wrong; Marx's thought was characterized by a tension between the positing of epochal, evolutionary processes and the recognition of contingent, historically specific forces. Marx's dual role as scholar and militant suggests that he gave greater weight to the role of ideas and political struggle in history than is usually acknowledged by commentators who paint him as a crude economic determinist. Nonetheless, Marx and Engels' scheme of a universal succession of modes of production was simplified, first by Stalin, then by pro-Soviet communist parties throughout the world, and eventually by French "structural" Marxists, notably Louis Althusser and his followers, including several prominent cultural anthropologists.

Ironically, Marx increasingly questioned the certainty that slavery, feudalism, capitalism, socialism, and communism would succeed one another in lock-step fashion. For example, unlike later Russian Marxists, Marx in later life tended to support the position that the rural peasant commune (or *mir*) in nineteenth-century Russia could serve as a springboard for a direct transition to socialism, rather than the notion that the proletarianization of the peasantry and the dissolution of the *mir* were part of a necessary capitalist stage that would precede socialism.

The *Manifesto*'s analysis of why the bourgeoisie needs a "constantly expanding market" has recently been linked to the notions that either many features of today's globalization are actually rather old or that Marx and Engels were extraordinarily prescient. The destruction of national industries, the increasingly cosmopolitan character of consumption, the creation of "new wants," and the use of cheap commodities to force "barbarian nations" into "civilization" are – shorn of their mid-nineteenth-century Eurocentric language – central themes in later discussions of development. Fascination with the contemporaneity of the *Manifesto*'s words, however, too easily obscures two crucial elements: first, Marx and Engels saw expanding markets as a means of competition between firms and nations and of resolving inevitable, periodic crises in the capitalist mode of production; and second, their apparent prescience with respect to some dimensions of change existed alongside a certain blindness to the persistence of others, especially nationalism, ethnic intolerance, and religious zealotry.

Max Weber was – like Smith and Marx – concerned with the conditions that gave rise to capitalism in "the modern Occident." Weber posited a variety of capitalisms – commercial, speculative, colonial, financial, and even "political" – characterized by a common profit-making orientation. But his theory of capitalist development is nonetheless frequently represented as limited to "the West" and as giving almost exclusive emphasis to religious factors. In *The Protestant Ethic and the Spirit of Capitalism* (1904), his first major work, he posed "traditionalism" as an obstacle to the spread of market relations. Contemporary scholarship – and punditry – that privileges "cultural" or "ideological" factors in development, as well as neoclassical laments about the intractability of the backward-bending supply curve of labor, may be read as echoing Weber's concern with "rationalizing" institutions in order to transcend the heavy weight of "tradition."

The same could be said of discussions today that try to explain capitalism's development in the West, and its apparent failure almost everywhere else, as a result of cultural predispositions or the entrepreneurial capacities unleashed in societies with legal systems that applied uniform yet minimal bureaucratic standards to the registration and mortgaging of property, the signing and enforcement of contracts, and the accountability of officials. In *The Protestant Ethic*, Weber suggested that Martin Luther's notion of the "calling" – a "life-task" set by God – provided, for the first time in history, a positive ethical framework for justifying individual accumulation through rational self-discipline, the severing of obligations to larger kin groups, and the abandonment of traditional notions about just price and wage levels. This "social ethic of capitalistic culture," which Weber characterized as "the earning of more and more money, combined with the strict avoidance of all spontaneous enjoyment of life," was both cause and effect of the extension of market relations to more and more areas of economic and social life (Weber 1958:53–54). Success on earth, in Calvinist-Protestant doctrine, was evidence of an individual's membership in the predestined "elect," who were bound for heaven. Weber's critics and admirers sometimes interpreted his argument about the spirit of capitalism in causal terms and as an idealist alternative to a competing philosophical materialism derived from Marxism. Yet

Weber's claims about Protestantism were considerably more complex and linked to several of his other central concerns, notably bureaucracy, rationalization, and the nature of the state.

Weber believed that what energized modern capitalism was not religious doctrine per se, but rational social actors, operating within a rationalized legal system that permitted individuals to weigh utility and costs and to feel confident about the security of their capital. The modern state and the enterprise or firm were similar inasmuch as both operated according to formal, bureaucratic criteria rather than the personalistic or familial considerations that governed economic life in traditional societies. The frequently cited (and variously attributed) adage that Weber was arguing with "the ghost of Karl Marx" is only partly accurate. Diverse scholars sympathetic to Marxist approaches – from Georg Lukács to C. Wright Mills, Eric Wolf, and Anthony Giddens – acknowledge major intellectual debts to Weber, especially his analyses of political power and legitimacy. Other Marxists, including literary theorist Raymond Williams and anthropologist William Roseberry, echo key aspects of Weber's thought (though without explicit recognition) in their analyses of how ideas and meanings are themselves material products and forces.

Classical theorists like Smith, Malthus, and Marx, are sometimes relegated to the "prehistory" of development thought, primarily because they concentrated on the economics of Western Europe and North America rather than on the poorer countries. However, their influence, along with that of Weber, on the development debates of the twentieth century, was immediate and profound. Nor was their interest limited to the developed countries of the North. All had significant interests in other parts of the world, especially Asia, as well as comparative sensibilities that are part of what makes their works of continuing relevance even today.

## THE TWENTIETH CENTURY: FROM IMPERIALISM TO DEPENDENCY AND THE WORLD-SYSTEM

Weber's concern with "traditionalism" as an impediment to development, first articulated at the dawn of the twentieth century, combined an Enlightenment notion of progress with a modern understanding of the history of capitalism. Yet Weber accorded little attention to capitalist crises, an issue that had engaged Marx and one that animated development debates in the first half of the twentieth century. The frequent booms and busts that affected Europe and North America, as well as the imperial expansion of the major European states after 1870 and of the United States following the 1898 Spanish-American War, led scholars to scrutinize more closely the functioning of a system that increasingly appeared to contain both extraordinary dynamism and immense destructive powers.

The approach that had the most impact in the West, particularly during the 1930s depression in the United States, was John Maynard Keynes's "pump-priming" policy, which sought to temper the business cycle through government measures to stimulate demand and increase employment. But while demand-side policies might alleviate the worst effects of a major slump, they did little to explain phenomena such as imperialism or uneven development.

Early twentieth-century theories of imperialism converged with the radical analyses of dependency and under-development that came to exercise an outsize influence in anthropology in the 1970s. These radical understandings of dependency engaged mainstream paradigms, especially "modernization" approaches, and dependency in turn became a target for the critiques of orthodox Marxist and poststructuralist theorists.

In 1902, an English liberal and advocate of free trade, John Hobson, noting that the word was "on everybody's lips," published a work which single-handedly re-shaped in economic terms popular and academic understandings of imperialism. Arguing that the "taproot of Imperialism" was the tendency to produce more goods than could be sold at a profit and to accumulate more capital than could be profitably invested, he suggested that "manufacturers, merchants, and financiers . . . are tempted more and more to use their Governments in order to secure for their particular use some distant undeveloped country by annexation and protection" (Hobson 1965:80–81). While Hobson influenced radical foes of capitalism, notably V. I. Lenin and Rosa Luxemburg, he nonetheless believed that measures to increase workers' purchasing power and to tax excess capital could obviate the "need to fight for foreign markets or foreign areas of investment" (Hobson 1965:86).

Various Marxist theories shared the view that imperialism grew out of crises in the capitalist system, even though they differed in the emphasis each accorded to the importance of under-developed regions as sources of cheap or strategic raw materials, markets for manufactured goods, outlets for excess capital, and places where super-profits could be derived from super-exploitation of poorly paid workers. In Latin America, heated polemics during the 1920s and 1930s between Marxist revolution-aries and anti-imperialist reformist populists set the stage for debates in the 1960s between proponents of radical and "structuralist" versions of dependency theory. Both strands of theory – in the 1920s and in the 1960s – viewed under-development and development as products of a single, worldwide process of accumulation that continually reproduced both outcomes. Engagement with the work of Lenin, Lux-emburg, and others was key for neo-Marxists who, in the 1950s and 1960s, sought to explain continuing under-development in the poorer countries. The central innov-ation of these theorists derived from the observation that – contrary to the predic-tions of Hobson and Lenin – capital flows from under-developed to developed areas generally exceeded developed-country exports of surplus capital (Baran and Sweezy 1966:107–108).

This inversion of the classical theories of imperialism became the germ of the circulationist or market-based approaches to dependency, under-development, and the world system that exercised so much influence in anthropology and sociology in the 1960s and 1970s. But while the intellectual genealogy of dependency theory can be traced back to a radical lineage in and around the independent US socialist magazine *Monthly Review* (which published an influential Spanish-language edition), it also originated in the work of individuals and institutions in the mainstream of economic policy-making in Latin America.

Founded in 1948, and directed after 1950 by Argentine economist Raúl Prebisch, the United Nations Economic Commission on Latin America initiated an intellectual revolution that had a profound impact on development policy in the hemisphere and beyond, as well as on a generation of social scientists. ECLA doctrine held that Latin

American countries that relied on primary product exports were negatively affected by the secular decline in terms of trade; in other words, over time a larger quantity of exports (say, bags of coffee or tons of bauxite) was required to purchase the same volume of imports (for example, jeeps or machine tools). This shift occurred primarily because of the monopoly and monopsony powers in what Prebisch called the "center" of the world economy that facilitated the extraction through trade of surplus from the "periphery." Export-led development thus entailed anemic growth, foreign exchange shortages, and vulnerability to market fluctuations – many Latin American countries in the mid-twentieth century earned half or more of their export earnings from one or a handful of commodities. ECLA promoted a "structuralist" approach to economics and a model of inward-looking development based on import substitution industrialization (ISI) and dynamizing domestic markets. While ECLA economists eventually admitted to having misgivings about ISI, industrialization continued to be a sine qua non of "development" for them, as well as for most neoclassical theorists.

In addition to Prebisch, several of Latin America's most influential social scientists were associated with ECLA during the 1960s and early 1970s, including economist Celso Furtado and sociologist Fernando Henrique Cardoso, who in 1994 would be elected president of Brazil on a neoliberal platform and who, together with Enzo Faletto, authored one of the most widely read treatises on dependency and development (Cardoso and Faletto 1979). Cardoso and Faletto's "historical structuralist" study of dependency noted that the larger Latin American countries, initially reliant on primary product exports, had begun to industrialize during the 1930s, when developed-country demand for these commodities contracted. This incipient industrialization brought to the fore a new national, urban-industrial bourgeoisie which, in a "developmentalist alliance" with the expanding working class, wrested power from traditional oligarchies and established a range of populist political experiments and a style of "associated dependent development" ever more reliant on foreign, as opposed to national, capital. Populist class pacts were typically fragile, however, and their rupture tended to produce authoritarian political outcomes, a conclusion Cardoso and Faletto based on the Brazilian experience after 1964, but which would soon be confirmed by the military coups in Chile, Uruguay, and Argentina in the 1970s.

A second influential strain of dependency analysis arose among radical theorists enthused by the 1959 Cuban revolution. The best-known in the English-speaking world was the prolific and peripatetic German-American economist Andre Gunder Frank, although he was but one figure in a large, trans-disciplinary intellectual-political nexus that spanned Latin America. Frank (and others in this group) sought to demolish the "dual society" thesis, the widely held belief – rooted in Weberian and Parsonian sociology and in the work of economist W. A. Lewis – that Latin America (and by extension other poor regions) included a dynamic capitalist sector and a stagnant "traditional" or "feudal" one, which could only be modernized through incorporation into the "advanced" sector. Instead of "dualism," Frank, Mexican anthropologist Rodolfo Stavenhagen, and others proposed a model of "internal colonialism" that saw urban zones as beneficiaries of surpluses extracted from rural – and particularly indigenous – areas. This mirrored the "metropolis–satellite" (or what Prebisch had termed "center–periphery") relations that linked developed and under-developed regions as outcomes of a single historical process and which Frank, at least, defined as "capitalist" since the sixteenth century.

The claim that development and under-development resulted from the same "capitalist" historical process had important implications for development policy and for those seeking radical change. Marxists – particularly the pro-Soviet communist parties – had long argued that Latin American societies were significantly "feudal," a characterization based on the existence in the countryside of coerced, non-waged labor relations and vast, extensively exploited properties owned by traditional elites whose aspirations and sumptuary practices were said to resemble those of medieval European nobles. Progress, according to this analysis, based on Stalin's simplification of Marx, could only occur if "feudalism" were overthrown and replaced by capitalism, as had occurred in Europe; the Left and working class ought, therefore, to align with the "progressive bourgeoisie" to break the back of the landed oligarchy.

If, however, as Frank maintained, Latin America had been "capitalist" since the sixteenth century, and if contemporary under-developed regions, such as northeastern Brazil, were actually erstwhile boom areas now drained of their wealth, it followed that there was not really a "progressive bourgeoisie" opposed to a "feudal" oligarchy and that the political task for radicals was to topple the entire capitalist class through revolutionary struggle. In the context of Latin America in the 1960s and 1970s, the dependency approach's radical variants, which generally asserted the revolutionary potential of the peasantry and denied that elements of the bourgeoisie could be progressive, came to be a theoretical justification for guerrilla movements, most of which were defeated at an immense cost in lives.

Although Frank was trained in the orthodox neoclassical economics department at the University of Chicago, he had early sympathies for Keynesianism and the heterodox, visionary economics of Kenneth Boulding. Even at Chicago, as he later reported in a retrospective intellectual autobiography, he "spent more and more…time studying and associating with the anthropologists," largely because they – like him – assumed "that the determinant factors in economic development were really *social*" (Frank 1991:17). As early as 1959, he participated with Margaret Mead in a session at the American Anthropological Association meetings and, in the early 1960s, Darcy Ribeiro invited him to teach anthropology at the new University of Brasilia (a position followed by a prolonged sojourn in Chile, Mexico, and Germany). In 1968, he issued a passionate call for "liberation anthropology" in *Current Anthropology* and, in another paper, lambasted both "formalist" and "substantivist" economic anthropologists for ignoring the effects of colonialism and imperialism on under-development. Later he wrote appreciatively of Kathleen Gough, Eric Wolf, and June Nash, as well as of Clifford Geertz, whose *Agricultural Involution* he considered an incisive refutation of the "dualism" thesis (Frank 1991).

While Frank (1991:36) remarked that dependency theory "succumbed to the [1973] coup in Chile," the approach took on a second life in 1974 with the appearance of US sociologist Immanuel Wallerstein's *The Modern World-System*, the first part of a multi-volume work on the history of the world economy. Wallerstein drew inspiration from Fernand Braudel's 1972 magnum opus on the sixteenth-century Mediterranean, European debates about the transition from feudalism to capitalism, and an extraordinarily wide and insightful reading of the history of diverse world regions and of development-related theory, ranging from Eric Wolf and

Barrington Moore to Pierre Chaunu and R. H. Tawney. Wallerstein analyzed the emergence in "the long sixteenth century" of a single world economy, larger than any empire, and its functional division into what he called – in an unacknowledged reworking and expansion of Prebisch's categories – "core," "semiperipheral," and "peripheral" regions, characterized respectively by the prevalence of wage labor, tenant farming and sharecropping, and coerced labor.

Despite its deployment of an erudite apparatus of commentary on a vast literature of secondary sources, Wallerstein's work, like that of the dependency group, was not fundamentally historical in the sense of understanding uneven development, labor arrangements, stratification patterns, or political systems as outcomes of struggles between contending social groups located in concrete social formations. Some critics took him to task for not distinguishing sufficiently between relations of production and relations of exchange, and for according the latter explanatory priority in ac-counting for the shape of the world-system. Others maintained that even the history of the world-system had to be understood from the bottom up, not just as an expanding sphere of exchange but as an outcome of diverse local initiatives and local responses, themselves the outcomes of social struggles, that sought distinct kinds of relations to international and other markets.

This critique of world-system theory contributed, particularly in the works of Eric Wolf and Sidney Mintz, to solidifying the position of historically oriented political economy within US anthropology. More broadly, it affected agrarian studies, and eventually, those strains of postcolonial studies that sought to root changing identities in historical processes of nation-state formation and transitions to new kinds of global spaces and governmentality. Thus by the 1970s, a new critical anthropology emerged as the discipline was profoundly reshaped by outside influences, including dependency theory, world-system theory, and neo-Marxist critiques of both modernization and traditional functionalist anthropology. "[H]istory, political economy, and colonialism began to gain new legitimacy as bona-fide anthropological topics" that were central to disciplinary theory, rather than consigned to the "applied" slot. Now the notion of development itself was critiqued, particularly its presumed equation with moral and economic progress (Ferguson, 1997:162–163), and its understanding of the world as a set of individual societies moving independently through history (a conception fam-ously undone by Eric Wolf in *Europe and the Peoples Without History*). In a parallel change, the 1970s move beyond economistic indicators of development created new employment opportunities for anthropologists in development agencies, and contrib-uted to the emergence of a new subfield of development anthropology. Many develop-ment anthropologists straddled (sometimes uneasily) the worlds of academe and development agencies. They brought new critical perspectives to the very institutions charged with implementing the policies that the discipline increasingly questioned.

## THE TWENTIETH CENTURY: FROM MODERNIZATION TO NEOLIBERALISM

The modernization paradigm that the dependency theorists attacked had antecedents in Weber and attracted followers in sociology, psychology, and anthropology. The quintessential statement of the modernization paradigm, however, is W. W. Rostow's

1960 book, *The Stages of Economic Growth*. Subtitled "A Non-Communist Manifesto," Rostow saw his work as "an alternative to Karl Marx's theory of human history" and to Soviet hubris about the superiority of socialism. Rostow played major roles in the Kennedy and Johnson administrations, including service as one of the main architects of US policy in Vietnam.

The most frequently cited of Rostow's claims is that all countries eventually pass through the same stages: (1) "traditional society," characterized by "pre-Newtonian" technology, little or no social mobility, a fatalistic ethos, and strong kin-based ties that limit investment and circumscribe economically rational decision-making; (2) a pre-take-off period in which consolidated nation-states emerge and traditional institutions and values begin to break down and coexist alongside ideas of progress and new types of enterprises; (3) "take-off," when traditional impediments to economic growth are overcome, agriculture modernizes, industry expands, and investment rates rise; (4) "the drive to maturity," marked by ongoing technological innovation and specialization of the industrial base; and (5) "the age of high mass consumption," a period of widespread affluence, growing urbanization, service-sector expansion, and ubiquitous consumer durables, such as automobiles and refrigerators.

Modernization theory – and Rostow in particular – was much criticized for emphasizing economistic measures of progress, such as GNP growth, as well as for a "culturalist" preoccupation with "traditional" values and institutions and a corresponding neglect of structures of exploitation, and for assuming that all societies traveled the same historical trajectory, albeit at different paces. While such objections are largely valid, critics rarely acknowledge that one of the main criteria of development for most modernization theorists was not so much growth per se, but rather increasing structural complexity in the economy. Moreover, from the vantage point of the early twenty-first century, several other dimensions of Rostow's work – and of the modernization paradigm in general – stand out as the antithesis of today's neoliberal version of free-market fundamentalism. First, Rostow stressed the central role of the state in economic development, as a provider of the "social overhead capital" (ports, railways, roads, and so on) necessary for growth and, in the stage of "mass consumption," the state as a guarantor of social welfare and security. Second, he not only considered the state a key agent of development, but saw the nation as the geographical and political space in which progress along the five-stage trajectory would be made or arrested. This focus on individual countries was entirely consonant with how the world economy was then organized and how the Bretton Woods institutions (the World Bank and the International Monetary Fund) envisioned the development of *national* economies, each with its particular resource endowments and forms of protectionism. Finally, Rostow considered that one feature of the "drive to maturity" would be the production at home of goods formerly acquired abroad, an affirmation consistent with those of protectionist advocates of import substitution industrialization, such as his "structuralist" critics in ECLA.

It should hardly be surprising that modernization theory, derided by its critics as a legitimating ideology for capitalism, had a statist dimension. From the end of World War II until the collapse of the Bretton Woods system of capital controls and fixed exchange rates in the early 1970s, the intimate links between state and market were part of the prevailing common sense of the economics profession and policy-makers.

In the post-World War II era in the developed world (and in many "semiperipheral" countries as well), this view underlay the rise of welfare state institutions. The 1944 Bretton Woods Agreement that established the International Monetary Fund created a liberalized trade regime but, influenced by Keynes and his disciples, was distinctly non-liberal in the financial arena, endorsing national controls on capital movements. By the early 1970s, a combination of market pressures (expanding demand for international financial services, "stagflation," OPEC states' accumulation of petro-dollars), technological changes (telecommunications and computer revolutions), and calculated actions by key states (deregulation of US financial markets) contributed to scuttling the Bretton Woods system of fixed exchange rates and controls on capital and to encouraging speculative financial movements that complicated any national defense of the welfare state. Neoliberal economists such as Friedrich von Hayek, whose *Road to Serfdom* appeared in 1944, had been widely viewed as outlandish zealots. But in the recession, stagflation and fiscal crises of the mid-1970s, their ideas began to gain support, part of an epochal shift that helped lay the groundwork for the globalization era. The elections on neoliberal platforms of Margaret Thatcher in Britain in 1979 and Ronald Reagan in the United States in 1980 initiated the ascendance of a new free-market regime that made rapid inroads there and in much of the rest of the world. How did anthropology absorb this seismic change? Partly by culturalizing globalization, and downplaying its political-economic and legal dimensions.

## ANTHROPOLOGY AND DEVELOPMENT IN THE GLOBALIZATION ERA

Globalization, even more so than development, is a protean term, a moving target that is not the same from one day to the next or in different locations or social situations. David Harvey points out that the term globalization was "entirely un-known before the mid-1970s" and that it then "spread like wildfire" when American Express used it to advertise the global reach of its credit card (Harvey 2000:12–13). Globalization, Tsing (2000:332) observes, is "part corporate hype and capitalist regulatory agenda, part cultural excitement, part social commentary and protest." For many anthropologists, globalization signifies accelerated flows or intensified connections – across national and other boundaries – of commodities, people, symbols, technology, images, information, and capital, as well as disconnections, exclusion, marginalization, and dispossession.

A growing literature on anthropology and globalization exhibits three striking limitations: tendencies (a) to dehistoricize globalization and to favor a "giddy pre-sentism" (Graeber's term), (b) to bypass or downplay the nation-state, and (c) to naturalize contemporary neoliberalism by, for example, treating global phenomena as impersonal "flows" (Graeber 2002:1224–1225) or as an inexorable or overly coher-ent set of forces (Cooper 2001; Tsing 2000) and then focusing on how they are culturalized. The most comfortable niche for anthropologists discussing globaliza-tion has been to show how non-elites "creatively resist, appropriat(e), or reinterpret some apparently homogenizing influence imposed from above (e.g., advertising, soap operas, forms of labor discipline, political ideologies, etc.)" (Graeber 2002:1223). It is worth considering what this genre excludes and with what effects. For example, Inda and Rosaldo (2002:27) acknowledge as "important gaps" in their excellent anthology on *The Anthropology of Globalization* "transnational social movements, global religious communities, global cities, and transnational pollution," as well as the work of "precursor theorists" writing about the "political economy of culture" such as Eric Wolf, Sidney Mintz, June Nash, and Michael Taussig. The World Trade Organization (WTO) is not even mentioned in the index of any of the three recent volumes on globalization that Graeber (2002:1226) reviews – or, as he notes, "for that matter, some recent volumes that actually have pictures of the Seattle protests on their cover!"

The WTO, viewed by its detractors as part of an evil troika whose other two members are the World Bank and the International Monetary Fund, inspires social movements and imaginings that are central to understanding globalization, development, social change, and modernity. Anthropology should have much to contribute to the fiery debates about the Bretton Woods institutions and about the WTO's power, secrecy, lack of public accountability, and capacity to override laws passed democratically by sovereign nations. A few scholars (such as Michael Goldman and Richard Harper) have begun to make these institutions objects of ethnographic research, but the linkages between their findings and those of scholars operating at higher levels of abstraction are tenuous. Neither the ethnographers of the economic governance institutions nor the niche grand theorists of transnationalism and hybridity appear to have dwelled on how their respective methodological approaches may limit understanding of globalization. The role of anthropologists – many of whom work within the international financial institutions, particularly the World Bank – has similarly received only cursory attention.

Whether globalization is new or not is the subject of much debate. Deregulated global financial markets linked in real time, declining transport and communications costs, and increasingly significant multilateral institutions and agreements are clearly major changes in the last two decades. Some scholars nonetheless argue that globalization – particularly of commodities markets – has been around at least since 1492, if not longer (Harvey 2000:21). Others see the period from 1870 to 1914 as a prior age of globalization – a time of laissez-faire policies well suited to an era of imperialism. In any case, labor is less mobile today than it was in the 1800s, when passports were unnecessary, and international labor migration peaked during the century after 1815 (Cooper 2001:194). The foreign-born proportion of the US population was 14 percent in 1900 and only 11 percent 100 years later, even after a period of sustained immigration. Whether new or newly recognized, globalization and transnationalism have captivated scholarly imaginations. Yet this infatuation recalls a similar glorification in the 1950s and 1960s of modernization – now widely seen as a failed development paradigm (Cooper 2001; Tsing 2000).

What is historically remarkable is today's celebration of a particular form of globalization – economic neoliberalism – and the increasingly common tendency for tests of market viability to be taken for granted or naturalized in domains as disparate as academia, journalism, and art. An earlier generation of scholars (among them Karl Polanyi and E. P. Thompson) saw the question of how market relations are extended to new domains and then naturalized as a defining feature of major historical transitions. Today again anthropologists can help explain how ideological expressions of the "free market" are naturalized and how they come to seem inevitable (if not necessarily legitimate). Yet anthropologists' attention often turns elsewhere. One might ask if anthropologists' celebrations of the end of the era of totalizing narratives "draw attention away from the current attempt to impose the largest and most totalizing framework in world history – the world market – on just about everything" (Graeber 2002:1224).

Whether one views today's historical moment as market tyranny or market triumph, there is little doubt about the force of one economic model, one conception of economy. Often forgotten is that the reproduction of this model occurs through institutions, processes, and politics. There is nothing inevitable, ethically neutral, or natural about world markets in their current form.

Ours is an era of flexible production, footloose capital and factories, and corporations that demand flexibility of their workers even as they offer those workers fewer guarantees of job security or retirement or health benefits. Underpaid, disposable, perpetually temporary "McWork" jobs proliferate in the service sectors of affluent countries, while corporations engage in two "races" – the "race to the bottom," where labor is cheap and regulations weak or unenforced, and the "race toward weightlessness," to outsource production, keep the fewest employees on the payroll, and produce the most powerful brand images (Klein 2000:4). Neoliberalism has brought declining corporate taxes and a continuing erosion of public-sector health, education, and other services. It has brought expanding informal economies, contract farming, ecotourism, and struggles over environmental protections and access to land and other resources. It has also generated the sharpest economic inequalities the world has ever seen. Do anthropologists who write about globalization, transnationalism, development, and modernity treat too much of this larger economic picture as given?

Economic globalization issues – development issues – fuel highly energized social movements in many parts of the world (more so in Europe, Asia, Latin America, and Canada than in the United States). As globalization hype wears thin and the harm done by garment, coffee, and other industries is publicized, consumers in wealthier nations begin to feel complicit in corporate misdeeds, and consumer boycotts and anti-corporate activism spread. On US college campuses, an earlier political focus on issues of race, gender, sexuality, and identity politics now includes corporate power, labor rights, and environmental justice. Anti-sweatshop campaigns against producers of apparel bearing university logos have evolved into campaigns for living wages for campus workers such as janitors and cooks. The Gap, Shell, Disney, McDonald's, and many other corporations have been targets as well. And protesters at demonstrations against the World Bank and International Monetary Fund demand debt relief for poor nations and shout slogans about controversial economic policies such as water privatization and other structural adjustment programs. Yet anthropology has been slower than other disciplines, such as political science and sociology, to embrace research agendas centered on economic globalization, activist networks, and social movements.

## NGOs, Civil Society, and Gender

During the 1980s, non-governmental organizations came to play a growing role in mainstream and alternative development projects, large and small. The reduction of the neoliberal state's social welfare programs, the dismissal of intellectuals from downsized public universities and government agencies, and the crucial participation of civil society organizations in the democratization of African countries, Latin American military regimes, and formerly socialist countries, all fueled the NGO boom. As the importance of supra-national governance institutions grew in the late 1980s and 1990s, NGOs and other civil society organizations became a constant presence at "parallel summits" held outside meetings of the World Bank and IMF, the WTO, and the G7/G8 heads of state. US and European cooperation policies shifted toward an emphasis on funding citizens' groups that were often held up as scrupulous and efficient alternatives to the corrupt, bloated, and ineffective public sectors that had previously absorbed most foreign aid. NGOs increasingly assumed responsibilities for delivery of services ranging from health care to agricultural extension, and they also became conduits for political demands initially articulated by social movements and other pressure groups.

Contrasting theoretical conceptions of how to bound "civil society" are often tied to distinct development agendas and views of democratization. Many concur that "civil society" is the associational realm between the household and the state, while others emphasize the emergence of a global civil society and transnational advocacy networks. Beyond that, however, two polar positions exist, separated by opposing views on whether to include economic actors – specifically, markets and firms – within "civil society." Those who argue for considering markets and corporations as part of the category typically favor a neoliberal development agenda (an irony, given this position's roots in Hegel and Marx) which sees "civil society" as a domain outside of and morally superior to the state. They posit choice and freedom of association as fundamental characteristics of both the market and "civil society," making support for economic liberalization and "civil society" institutions not only entirely compatible, but complementary strategies for checking state power. In contrast, theorists who exclude the market and firms from "civil society" usually consider it a domain of associational life that attempts to defend autonomous collective institutions from the encroachments of *both* the market and the state. In comparison with neoliberal theorists, they tend to accord much greater analytical importance to how social inequality structures or limits political representation.

During the past two decades, the struggle between these divergent conceptions has played out in academia, bilateral and non-governmental funding agencies, supranational governance institutions, and the countries of the South. Typically, proponents of neoliberal development strategies have favored strengthening legal institutions and elite lobbying groups as a way of facilitating market-driven approaches to growth and to resolving social problems. Supporters of alternative strategies, on the other hand, characteristically have backed organizations with a dual focus on income-generating projects for historically disadvantaged sectors of the population and pressure-group tactics intended to create more profound structural change. The latter line of attack, favored by many European donor NGOs and bilateral cooperation agencies, has given grass-roots organizations a significant impact in reshaping all manner of development-related debates and policies.

Recent shifts in understanding the gendered dimensions of development are emblematic of civil society's growing influence on policy-makers' debates. The "Women in Development" approach that accompanied the United Nations Decade for

Women (1975–1985) sought to address "male bias" by increasing female access to, and participation in, development programs (much as rural development programs had tried to compensate for "urban bias"). By the mid-1990s, however, at the insistence of an increasingly vocal international women's movement, mainstream development institutions recognized that the WID paradigm did little to address key concerns, such as unequal inheritance and property rights for men and women, domestic violence, men's abandonment of their children, or family planning and prevention of sexually transmitted diseases. Addressing these issues not only required male participation within a new "Gender and Development" framework (that largely superseded WID), but also presupposed fundamental modifications of existing practices of masculinity and femininity. Scholars such as Sylvia Chant and Matthew Gutmann, however, note that recent Gender and Development policies have not fundamentally altered WID's emphasis on programs designed by and for women. Thus Chant and Gutmann argue that development programs should incorporate "men as a gendered category in a feminist sense," with attention to unequal relations between men as well as between men and women.

## Culture and Development

Is under-development a state of mind, an artifact of culture or values? Few anthropologists would agree, though many writings about development now reduce the spirit of capitalism to ahistorical cultural essences – a move that divorces culture from politics and economy in ways Weber and other classical theorists did not. Devotees of modernization theory still view "traditional" culture as an obstacle to change, while others have attributed the pre-1997 economic dynamism of the "Asian tigers," for example, to either Confucian values or long-established Asian forms of household organization.

Contemporary anthropology's emphasis on culture as contested, flexible, fragmentary, and contingent is hard to reconcile with mainstream "culturalist" explanations of under-development or Confucian capitalism, which tend to assume that people mechanically enact norms. Thus anthropologists often clash with their development agency employers, as well as with some political scientists and economists, when analyzing cultural aspects of development. Without denying that norms influence behavior, many anthropologists focus on what norms or symbols individuals invoke in particular situations to justify or explain their actions – exploring the rich possibilities of contradictory or contested cultural imperatives, and their situational contingency. Development practitioners, on the other hand, demand simplifying models that travel well across national boundaries.

Supposed cultural conservatism or cultural difference maps onto ethnic identities and hierarchies, and these too figure in representations, whether official or social scientific, of putative differences in receptivity to development. Ethnic or cultural difference becomes an easy alibi for histories of regional economic and social inequalities and deprivation, as in the well-documented case of the San peoples of southern Africa, or among Chinese minorities. Indigenous and minority rights movements complicate earlier assumptions about culture and development, individual and group rights, and what rights accompany indigenous or minority status. Successful claims to local authenticity or indigenous identity in international arenas may confer significant material advantages, and thus encourage people to strategically deploy or reinvent cultural, ethnic, indigenous, or local identities. Cultural symbols are invoked as well by right-wing and conservative movements (such as anti-immigrant movements in Europe or Islamic fundamentalism), though anthropologists have been less likely to theorize movements that promote exclusivity, racism, or intolerance. Ethnographic studies of identity or cultural politics, what it means to be "indigenous," and when essentialism is strategic or romantic, place anthropologists at the center of development politics and practice – whether they claim "development" as their focus or not.

## CONSUMPTION

Anthropology originally drew students to societies marked by the absence of modern consumer goods that signal development. Today, however, expanding ethnographic study of consumption reflects profound changes in the discipline, including a recognition of commodities' embeddedness in social relations in any economy, and a move beyond the gift/commodity dichotomy and its attendant evolutionary assumptions (as scholars such as James Carrier and Daniel Miller have shown). Studies of consumption illuminate new material aspirations and imaginings, and some probe connections between the conditions of production of commodities such as sugar or grapes in poorer nations and changing consumption preferences in wealthier industrialized nations.

What are the implications of such studies for development? Here one finds a split between those who see emancipatory versus destructive forces in commodification and mass consumption, though anthropologists studying these phenomena in the 1990s were moving beyond such oppositions and instead exploring how processes of commodification differ from the assumptions of modernization models. Much critical analysis focused on a different aspect of commodification – namely the effects of neoliberalism and structural adjustment programs, a conventional domain of development. Although scholars have rejected many elements of 1960s modernization theory, that paradigm's traditional/modern binaries are very much alive in everyday language and culture, especially in consumption practices, which can signal newly imagined futures, conformity, creativity, rebellion, subversion, or strategic image-making, among other possibilities. Consumer appearances, for example, are so important that one finds impostors who talk on toy cellular telephones, parade in supermarkets with luxury-filled carts they later abandon as they sneak out the door without buying anything, and people who suffer extreme heat in their cars rather than roll down the windows and reveal that they have no air conditioning (examples Eduardo Galeano discusses in *Upside Down*). Neoliberalism denies to many the consumer paradise it promises.

## ENVIRONMENT AND DEVELOPMENT

The "ecological anthropology" and "cultural ecology" of the 1970s, which frequently rested on functionalist and exaggeratedly localistic assumptions, have ceded ground to "historical ecological" or "political ecology" approaches, the concerns of which often paralleled those of new environmentalist movements and non-governmental organizations working for "sustainable development." Political ecology links environment, development, and social movements, often drawing on poststructuralist theory as well as political-economy critiques of development (as in the 2001 volume edited by Peluso and Watts). The new approaches vary in method and focus, but usually eschew adaptation as a starting premise. Indeed, maladaptive processes have become a key concern, while other analyses contain implicit adaptationist assumptions discussed in an idiom of "sustainable development." Would environmental catastrophe result, for example, if 5 billion people in poor nations were to consume at the level enjoyed by the 1 billion who live in the wealthiest societies? Is "sustainability" possible on a small or large scale, and what role does it imply for market forces, whether local or global? How have differing interpretations of "sustainability" shaped struggles over development policy?

Today's free-market enthusiasts challenge the notion of environmental crisis, sometimes questioning the scientific reality of global warming and ozone depletion, or simply suggesting that market forces can resolve environmental problems. Less orthodox economists, such as Herman Daly, emphasize that the economy cannot expand forever precisely because it is part of a finite and non-growing ecosystem. They propose an unorthodox form of "getting the prices right": counting "externalities" as costs and rejecting the practice of including consumption of natural capital as income. "Sustainable development" was initially defined in Gro Harlem Brundtland's UN-sponsored report *Our Common Future* as practices that satisfy the needs of our generation, without jeopardizing the possibilities for future generations to satisfy their needs. Yet "needs" – left undefined – proved to be one of several contentious aspects of the new paradigm, which the World Bank, multinational corporations, and radical environmental movements all claim as their own.

Anthropological studies of the environment and resource conservation focus less on economic policies or new forms of multilateral governance than on indigenous rights, social constructions of nature, and debates between radical and mainstream environmentalists. Environmental stresses and resource conflicts have become a pressing post-Cold War security issue, sometimes expressed as identity politics. Yet political ecology until recently has been surprisingly silent about geopolitical questions such as regional integration, transnational governance and environmental security, and decentralized politics.

## POST-DEVELOPMENT?

Some scholars urge us to look beyond "development" as the answer to poverty, hunger, and oppression. They employ Foucauldian notions of power, analyzing, for example, how "empowerment" becomes subjection, and why it is that the more "participatory" rural development appraisals are, the more they conceal community power structures. Among the dangers of conventional participatory development approaches is the capacity of the language of "empowerment" to conceal both large-scale inequalities and naive assumptions about local authenticity and participants' sincerity.

Advocates of "post-development" exalt familiar images of the "local," but often they tend to romanticize or essentialize it. In a reversal of modernization theory's assumption that "traditional" communities pose obstacles to change, some scholars and activists now celebrate community as a valuable source of local or indigenous knowledge and critique. Post-development approaches tend to view states as simply the agents of brutal or failed modernization rather than as possible vehicles of democratization and beneficial access to markets. Such approaches raise questions about when "local" people might prefer a state that works for them rather than state withdrawal. As Michael Watts has noted (in a 1998 volume edited by Doreen Massey and John Allen), there is a danger in uncritically privileging "the local," "place," "culture," "the people," or "popular discourse from below" without acknowledging "the potentially deeply conservative, and occasionally reactionary, aspects of such local particularisms."

## Conclusion

Two contradictory claims about the origins of "development" and "under-development" are encountered in the anthropological literature. One locates development squarely in the Enlightenment and the transition from feudalism to capitalism, the first period in history when it became possible to imagine spectacular advances in the productive forces that made progress possible. Another claim, prominent in poststructuralist scholarship, sees "development" as a post-World War II discourse intended to justify the remaking of the "Third World," and suggests that "under-development" – also primarily a discourse – originated in a 1949 speech by Harry Truman. Advocates of the first position see the second as ignoring both intellectual and economic history, overly focused on discourse, and insufficiently attentive to long-standing processes of exploitation. Proponents of the second tendency criticize supporters of the first approach for accepting an old "master narrative" about progress and for not acknowledging the utter failure of most twentieth-century development efforts, whether carried out by states, multilateral institutions, or small NGOs. Some maintain that disillusion with development is so widespread that we have moved into a "post-development era."

Such a claim can only seem far-fetched to citizens of countries where unaccountable World Bank and International Monetary Fund bureaucrats have largely defined economic policies and where levels of poverty and inequality show no signs of diminishing. If not development, then what? Alternatives imagined by post-development enthusiasts often remain just that – imaginary. Proponents of development alternatives or "another development" have put forward a range of proposals, including "localization," "delinking" from the market, "fair trade," participatory budgeting, taxes on volatile capital movements, and a startling number of populist, nationalist, and regional integration efforts to re-embed the economy in society. They generally differ from post-development theorists in their continuing search for practical experiences that prove effective in raising living standards and that have potential for "scaling up." Often development alternatives are part of the practice of social movements and other civil society organizations. As yet, however, apart from some tepid attempts to theorize a "third way" between capitalism and socialism, remarkably few in the development alternatives camp have tried to challenge the macroeconomic premises of neoliberalism or assert a role for a reinvigorated state as a vehicle for democratization, social justice, or even simply improved access to markets.

Meanwhile, modernization theory and its assumptions about supposed cultural obstacles to change remain alive and well among many development practitioners. And assumptions about "development," whether explicit or not, feature in the torrent of contemporary academic studies of "modernity." Yet contemporary anthropology tends to dehistoricize globalization, naturalize neoliberalism, and bypass the state in favor of the "local" or the transnational. Today's debates over globalization confirm that development is still hotly contested. As Graeber (2002:1223) suggests, globalization "has made the political role of anthropology itself problematic, in a way perhaps even more profound than the 'reflexive moment' of the eighties ever did." Development institutions that employ anthropologists typically assign them microinterventions and culture-broker roles, yet a genuine anthropology of development must analyze larger institutional practices and orientations that are more easily critiqued from afar. Writing openly about the international financial and governance institutions while preserving access to small-scale foreign field sites is as much a challenge today as it has ever been.

In short, development continues to perplex anthropologists and others. Though master narratives are in decline, and most development projects fail, dreams of alleviating poverty and suffering endure.

## REFERENCES

Baran, Paul A., and Paul M. Sweezy (1966) *Monopoly Capital: An Essay on the American Economic and Social Order.* New York: Monthly Review Press.

Cardoso, Fernando H., and Enzo Faletto (1979 [1969]) *Dependency and Development in Latin America.* Berkeley: University of California Press.

Cooper, Frederick (2001) What is the Concept of Globalisation Good For? An African Historian's Perspective. *African Affairs* 100:189–213.

Escobar, Arturo (1995) *Encountering Development: The Making and Unmaking of the Third World.* Princeton, NJ: Princeton University Press.

Ferguson, James (1997) Anthropology and its Evil Twin: "Development" in the Constitution of a Discipline. In *International Development and the Social Sciences: Essays on the History and Politics of Knowledge,* ed. F. Cooper and R. Packard, pp. 150–175. Berkeley: University of California Press.

Frank, Andre Gunder (1991) The Underdevelopment of Development. *Scandinavian Journal of Development Alternatives* 10:5–72.

Graeber, David (2002 ) The Anthropology of Globalization (with Notes on Neomedievalism, and the End of the Chinese Model of the State). *American Anthropologist* 104:1222–1227.

Harvey, David (2000) *Spaces of Hope.* Berkeley: University of California Press.

Hobson, John A. (1965 [1902]) *Imperialism: A Study.* Ann Arbor: University of Michigan Press.

Inda, Jonathan Xavier, and Renato Rosaldo, eds. (2002) *The Anthropology of Globalization: A Reader.* Oxford: Blackwell.

Klein, Naomi (2000) *No Logo.* New York: Picador.

Malthus, Thomas R. (1970 [1798]) *An Essay on the Principle of Population and A Summary View of the Principle of Population.* London: Penguin Books.

Marx, Karl, and Friedrich Engels (1968 [1848]) Manifesto of the Community Party. In Marx and Engels, *Selected Works.* New York: International Publishers.

Smith, Adam (1976 [1776]) *An Inquiry into the Nature and Causes of the Wealth of Nations.* Chicago: University of Chicago Press.

Tsing, Anna (2000) The Global Situation. *Cultural Anthropology* 15:327–360.

Weber, Max (1958 [1904/05]) *The Protestant Ethic and the Spirit of Capitalism.* New York: Charles Scribner's Sons.

## SUGGESTED FURTHER READING

Appadurai, Arjun (1996) *Modernity at Large: Cultural Dimensions of Globalization.* Minneapolis: University of Minnesota Press.

Black, Jan K. (1999) *Development in Theory and Practice: Paradigms and Paradoxes.* 2nd edn. Boulder, CO: Westview Press.

Cavanagh, John, Daphne Wysham, and Marcos Arruda, eds. (1994) *Beyond Bretton Woods: Alternatives to the Global Economic Order.* London: Pluto.

Chant, Sylvia, and Matthew C. Gutmann (2001) *Mainstreaming Men into Gender and Development: Debates, Reflections, and Experiences.* London: Oxfam Working Papers.

Cooper, Frederick, and Randall Packard, eds. (1997) *International Development and the Social Sciences: Essays on the History and Politics of Knowledge.* Berkeley: University of California Press.

Cowen, Michael P., and Robert W. Shenton (1996) *Doctrines of Development.* London: Routledge.

Crush, Jonathan S., ed. (1995) *Power of Development.* London: Routledge.

Hoben, Allen (1982) Anthropologists and Development. *Annual Review of Anthropology* 11:349–375.

Kalb, Don, Marco van der Land, Richard Staring, Bart van Steenbergen, and Nico Wilterdink, eds. (2000 ) *The Ends of Globalization: Bringing Society Back In.* Lanham, MD: Rowman and Littlefield.

Larraín, Jorge (1989) *Theories of Development: Capitalism, Colonialism and Dependency.* London: Polity Press.

Leys, Colin (1996) *The Rise and Fall of Development Theory.* Oxford: James Currey.

Nolan, Riall W. (2002) *Development Anthropology: Encounters in the Real World.* Boulder, CO: Westview Press.

Peluso, Nancy L., and Michael Watts (2001) *Violent Environments.* Ithaca, NY: Cornell University Press.

Scott, James C. (1998) *Seeing Like a State: How Certain Schemes to Improve the Human Condition Have Failed.* New Haven: Yale University Press.

Wolf, Eric R. (1982) *Europe and the Peoples Without History.* Berkeley: University of California Press.

# CHAPTER 7 Displacement

## Elizabeth Colson

## THE CHALLENGE OF THE DISPLACED

Anthropologists, like all humans, are political animals. They live in the world as well as study it. What they write about inevitably is a product of the state of that world. From one decade to the next, what seems to be important to understand shifts as political phenomena, which at one moment seem to be permanent features of the social environment, turns out to be a transitory outcome of ongoing political processes.

In some decades anthropologists have been primarily concerned with governance as carried out through offices exercising authority, with the means used to legitimate both offices and their occupants, and with restraints on arbitrary action. At other times they have been more concerned with political strategies used by political actors contending for office and the control of social agendas. In either case, political phenomena have been interpreted as linked to control of territory or to control over people and resources anchored in space, despite the knowledge that humans are migratory and have always moved to escape local difficulties or find new opportunities. During the twentieth century much of the world's population found itself in motion, and political issues associated with displacement may well dominate the twenty-first century if governments continue to be destabilized, struggles over oil and other natural resources intensify, and economic dislocations in conjunction with climate changes and the flooding of low-lying areas send ever more people in search of shelter.

During the 1990s between 90 and 100 million people were displaced by so-called development projects, while countless others fled economic impoverishment. Another 30 million were refugees across international borders or in refugee-like situations within their own countries (Cernea and McDowell 2000:2).

At the beginning of the twenty-first century, large numbers continue to be displaced because they stand in the way of economic enterprises that uproot individuals and communities as land is taken for new urban developments or urban renewal programs, or for road construction, the damming of rivers, the creation of national parks, or mining. Rarely do such enterprises benefit the displaced either economically or socially. Often enough, displacement is associated with a radical reduction in economic and social resources and therefore with increased political vulnerability. Whether they are officially resettled or forced to fend for themselves, those displaced face new political environments even though they remain within their homelands.

Local political leaders typically lose credibility when they are unable to prevent the move. People become highly suspicious of the intentions of central government, knowing that it has been willing to override their claims to land and their right to remain undisturbed. The basic trust on which government must rely if it does not wish to rule through blatant force is compromised. The place of people in the political environment where they settle is in doubt, especially if they come without resources to attract patrons. If they settle as individuals, they are disadvantaged until they learn how the local power structure operates. Those resettled as communities may find themselves in a hostile environment, for previous occupants of the area are rarely compensated for having to share local resources with the newcomers, and the community is seen as a rival political entity operating within the space formerly controlled by local political figures. Resettlement communities are also likely to have peculiar political features that both advantage and disadvantage them in contrast to the long settled. They are usually answerable to a double chain of administration in the years associated with displacement. Given the magnitude of moving large numbers of people and settling them elsewhere, governments typically create agencies with the mandate to supervise the move and administer the resettlement area. These operate outside or alongside the local government and have unusual power to determine where people will live, what kind of housing they will live in, how they may dispose of dwellings and land, what, where, and when they may plant, what kind of livestock they may have, and much else. Local political control is compromised, although usually only for a number of years until the settlement is assumed to stand on its own feet. Those who do not like it can always leave, but they may have no place to go that provides a living.

Those displaced for development purposes differ from refugees and those displaced within their own borders by war or other unrest in that they have no right of appeal to international law against what they see as the arbitrary actions of administering agencies or their national governments. But this may be changing. The World Bank has introduced guidelines to improve the chances of those displaced by projects financed by the World Bank, but governments are not forced to follow the guidelines in their treatment of those who must move, nor does the World Bank always withdraw from projects that disregard its guidelines and adopt policies guaranteed to impoverish those displaced and likely to create social disruption and political unrest (Scudder 1998; Cernea and McDowell 2000).

Recent decades have also seen the emergence of international networks used by those threatened with displacement to publicize what is happening through the media and to form alliances with organizations that bring pressure to bear on transnational firms engaged in building dams or oil lines or other projects that disrupt lives. They have been able to organize boycotts or lobby home governments to intervene on their behalf. The most successful such campaign so far is one that involved an alliance between the James Bay Cree of Canada and conservationist organizations to prevent further hydroelectric development. They were able to lobby effectively among potential users of the power. The decision of the State of New York not to purchase power generated by the project made it uneconomic and it was abandoned, at least for the moment (Scudder 1998). Appeals have also been carried to the United Nations, but with less effect. Some of those threatened with displacement, of course, have turned to guerrilla warfare or sabotage.

However numerous the "development displaced" may be, they do not exist as a legal category. Nor is there any recognition that the international order has any kind of legal duty toward them. So far, they have not been sufficiently organized, despite their numbers, to have any major impact upon the structure of the evolving international political system, which lacks agencies created to serve them and official channels through which to press their claims.

Those defined as refugees have had a much greater impact, although their numbers are much smaller. They are, by definition, people who are outside the jurisdiction of their own countries because of a fear of persecution due to race, ethnicity, religion, or political identity, and as such they are recognized as having a claim for protection and asylum under the 1951 United Nations Convention on Refugees. The 1967 Protocol extended the mandate of UNHCR to include those displaced within their own countries by civil war or other factors that made it impossible for their own governments to protect them.

In 1951 and even in 1967, it was assumed that the world is normally politically stable, and with stability, asylum-seekers should be few in number. Since then we have discovered that stability is an ideal condition that rarely reflects political realities. Each year continues to produce new waves of the displaced who have a claim to status as refugees and therefore a claim on the right to find asylum in other countries. In 2002, Asia alone held 6 million, and 2003 is likely to see an increase in their number. Turkey, for one, was preparing in late 2002 for an expected influx of Iraqi refugees who were to be moved to camps well away from its border with Iraq as insurance that political unrest among its own Kurdish population would not be reinforced by Kurdish militants from Iraq if Iraq were invaded. Africa hosted at least an equal number of refugees. In 2002 some 4 million southern Sudanese were displaced within the Sudan by the ongoing civil war, or were in camps in Ethiopia, Kenya, and Uganda, or were asylum-seekers as far away as the middle west of the US or the Australian outback. Much of northern Uganda was in turmoil, with 500,000 Acholi, one half of the Acholi population, forced into "protected camps," along with other northerners. Perhaps 450,000 Angolans were dispersed in neighboring countries, some in camps and some self-settled, while others were displaced within Angola. The outbreak of civil war in the Ivory Coast in the late months of 2002 led to a massive exodus of some 3 million immigrants, many long settled in the country, when government troops burned their quarters to force them back to countries of origin, while international agencies called for funds to feed and shelter them. Sierra Leone, Liberia, the Democratic Republic of the Congo, Ruanda, Burundi, and Zimbabwe also contribute to the uprooted of Africa. The major flows of refugees from Eastern Europe that aroused international attention in the early 1990s has stopped, but political unrest continues in many regions with a potential for more uprooting. People continue to try to escape political persecution or unrest in various Latin American countries.

Those who watch events within a country may see good reason to fear what will happen if they stay. Those who have left may fear to return. But internationally, the right to become and remain a refugee entitled to asylum depends on the willingness of other countries to classify their homelands as risk areas. If it seems politically expedient to label a country as "safe," those who leave may be refused asylum elsewhere, and those who have already found asylum may be forced to return home even though the future is precarious. Hutu refugees in camps in Tanzania found just how vulnerable they were to redefinition when the Tanzanian government, with UN approval, forced them back into Burundi when it was still torn by civil strife. Vietnamese boat people in camps in Hong Kong were first given a choice to return home. Those who refused were deported to Vietnam when the camps closed.

In the next decade, trouble spots associated with displacement may change. Some of those now displaced may be able to return home. But the number of the displaced is unlikely to fall, nor will the impact upon host countries be less challenging.

The arrival of large numbers of refugees strains resources and can reinforce unrest in the country of asylum. They may upset ethnic balances. They compromise the security of border areas. Their indeterminate legal status may compromise local government, especially if they become the wards of international organizations who administer through their own agents. Refugees, therefore, are more likely to be seen as a threat rather than as a resource in their own right, given the skills they bring with them.

Western Europe braces itself against the influx of people fleeing disorder or oppression and poverty in Asia, Africa, and Eastern Europe and steadily tightens immigration controls. There is talk of "Fortress Europe." An ongoing problem for the European Union is how to harmonize the asylum policies and refugee regimes of its different members. The Australian government refuses to accept shiploads of people escaping wars and oppression in Afghanistan and Iraq, who wind up in prison camps in the Australian desert or on offshore islands, much to the dismay of some Australian citizens. The United States and Canada, like other targets of immigration, try to redefine who can claim refugee status under international law and so have a right of asylum, and to differentiate them from those trying to escape a poverty enhanced by the Western drive to control the world economy to the benefit of its own people.

Whatever their status, from their very number, the displaced are perceived as a threat to the political stability of existing nations. Displaced populations are people displaced from space, outside the normal channels of governance, whether they have been forcibly uprooted and resettled because economic interests are allowed to preempt their land, or outlawed because those in power see them as a threat, or set in motion by invasion or civil war. In Mary Douglas's terms (1966) they have become "matter out of place." requiring special treatment, seen as threatening to those who must host them. They are essentially stateless at a time when crucial rights, including the right to work and the right to move freely, are based on citizenship, and under international law this means citizenship within a state (Shore 2000:71). Displacement is both a crisis of identity for those who move and a challenge to the political order of the current international system conceived as an alliance of nation/states.

The displaced confront us with questions about the role of the state and its exercise of power. Their plight, especially the plight of those who flee persecution or warfare, raises issues of human rights versus citizens' rights. That is, what does the international system owe to the people of the earth? Who has the right and what should be the means used to restrain governments from defining any of their people as belonging to categories to whom legal norms need not apply? Who has the obligation to provide protection to the uprooted who lack protection at home, and in what should this consist?

Since World War II, acceptance that there is an international order, and that this has some kind of responsibility to assist those in distress, has led to the emergence of international organizations whose mandate is assistance but whose role is frequently that of containing and governing the displaced who cannot go home and are unwanted elsewhere. The United Nations High Commissioner for Refugees plays a primary role, supplemented by the United Nations Development Program, the World Health Program, and the World Food Program, but they frequently deputize their responsibility to provide assistance to various non-governmental charitable organizations. These are new political phenomena, which in some places and some circumstances supplant established governments. They are partially funded through charitable donations, but much of their funding comes from international agencies or national agencies, such as USAID, who place greater trust in so called NGOs (non-governmental organizations) with headquarters in Europe and the US, than they do in the governments of states that host the displaced but lack resources of their own to provide for the maintenance of a large number of mostly destitute people. The NGOs provide an alternative government, rivaling that of the state and local authorities. They are answerable primarily to their own donors rather than to the people in their charge or the people of the country hosting the refugees. Their governing has been described as arbitrary, since they have power to make decisions about many aspects of the lives of those in their care and may have a major voice in determining whether people may move on to new countries of permanent asylum. They are caretakers and gatekeepers (Barrows and Jennings 2001).

These are the agencies that govern the lives of many refugees who find themselves in holding camps, where some of them may live out their lives and where new generations born in the camps now reach maturity. Camps for Palestinian refugees have been in existence for 50 years.

The camps have much in common with prisons or other total institutions, but control is not total and a new political order emerges in the camps, frequently enough based on gang rule. Agency employees, often expatriates, are in nominal charge, but they can rarely police large camps, nor are they aware of much happening among the inmates, who in any event usually have to subvert camp rules if they are to survive. They lie about their numbers. They trade rations with people outside the camps to meet other needs. They engage in trade when this is not permitted. They move back and forth across the boundaries of the settlement. If they are near the borders of their home countries, men may slip across to continue the battle or cultivate fields, while women and children remain in the camps to be fed and cared for. Camps become staging grounds for political action. They also provide an environment that intensifies ethnic identities and ethnic hostilities, as leaders elaborate and indoctrinate others with myths emphasizing an ethnic superiority seen against the depravity of rivals who have forced them out. Camps can also be dangerous places. Defined as transit centers, it is difficult to create strong local governments within the camps or to provide people with a sense of community pride attached to their present residence. Conditions are conducive to petty theft and violence, including murder and rape, when even food may be in short supply and people humiliated by defeat and their failure to find acceptance elsewhere assert themselves through attacks on fellow inmates, and especially on women and children.

Refugees who move on to new countries, if they do so legally, become immigrants and eventually may again become citizens. Usually, on arrival, they are defined as needing assistance from sponsoring individuals or agencies that have an obligation both to educate them on how to behave in the new setting and what they can in turn expect. Their initial experience of governance within the new country is therefore through specialized agencies and relationships comparable to those set up for legal minors. To escape these, they turn to earlier arrivals of their own ethnic group to orient them to the new country and the new society. This gives a new importance to ethnic associations in countries of asylum, comparable to that enjoyed by the ethnic associations that formed to ease adjustment during the massive immigrations of the early twentieth century and then became useful political tools in election battles to control the resources of city and state governments.

Refugees are also members of a new diaspora and one that encompasses the world. People may have little choice of where they go, since countries must agree to accept them. Those resettled maintain contact with kin and friends wherever settled, whether in another country, or left behind in camps, or remaining in the homeland. Nuer in Minneapolis phone fellow Nuer resettled in Australia and Britain, or still in camps in Kenya, or even still at home in the Sudan (Holtzman 2000). Videotapes recording celebrations circulate around the world. Increasingly the internet provides a forum spanning the continents. Like other diasporas before them, they engage in politics, collect funds to finance resistance movements and rival militias, and otherwise attempt to affect conditions in their homeland, whether or not they themselves plan to return. Their involvement with the homeland continues to be a major influence on how they identify themselves, and helps to reinforce a pride battered by their loss of status when their previous training goes for nothing and those they encounter have no clue to standards against which they may judge themselves. Attachment to the diaspora also differentiates them from other citizens of the countries where they are settled, and their political allegiance is likely to be to the ethnic bloc.

## ANTHROPOLOGY AND DISPLACEMENT

Displacement is political and it has obvious political consequences, but it is not a neatly defined phenomenon for study by political anthropologists. It is a process through which people go rather than a phenomenon in its own right. It can be studied from many stances, depending upon whether one is looking at people threatened with displacement, in flight, housed in holding camps, becoming immigrants, or involved in diaspora politics, or whether one looks at the institutional arrangements created to meet what is assumed to be a temporary emergency, or the long-term impact on national and international political theories about the nature of the state, political identities, boundaries, and human rights.

When ethnographic work was based on assumptions about stability, it was difficult to consider displacement as involved in what was looked at. People were seen as adapted to their geographical environments, their ways of life as long-term adjustments to local conditions. Moreover, whether ethnographic work relied on the memories of older people or on participant observation in ongoing communities, it concentrated on the normative, usually interpreted as working to maintain the system in place. Displacement, whether it had occurred in the immediate past or was current, was defined as an abnormal disruptive episode unsuitable for study by anthropologists in their role as ethnographers. What happened over time, unless it was seen as cyclical, was left to historians. There are no contemporary anthropological studies of the forceful settlement of Native Americans onto reservations in the nineteenth and early twentieth centuries, of the holocaust, or of the massive transfers of population that took place immediately after World Wars I and II. Here Mooney's study (1896) of the Ghost Dance of the Plains is an honorable exception.

From the 1950s on, a few anthropologists began to direct ethnographic attention to examining the experience of refugees and those displaced by big dams and other such projects. The willingness to focus upon displacement as a phenomenon worthy of study reflects a number of developments within anthropology itself. There was the realization that ethnographies deal with an historical moment, and that what takes place within that moment needs to be put into context by attention paid to what is happening in the larger economic and political environments that structure what people can do and to some extent determine what they can think. The accumulating historical scholarship meant that it was impossible to ignore what came before one's arrival. Displacement turned out to be part of the history of most groups studied by anthropologists, just as it has been the future fate of many. Ethnographic fieldwork was also transformed by jet travel and rapid communication. One no longer went to a place and left and thereafter remained ignorant of what happened next. When people we had worked among were displaced and scattered around the world, anthropology had to change. It had already developed some tools for the study of people in movement through work on labor migration in Africa and Latin America. It had also begun to focus upon processes of change and to look for similarities among the experiences of very different people exposed to the same circumstances of industrialization or political incorporation, and so to move beyond the unique to the general. Each experience of displacement may be bitterly unique, but the processes of displacement and subsequent responses were seen to have much in common.

The first ethnographic studies of forced displacement are probably those carried out on the displacement of the people of Bikini and Enewetok shortly after World War II, when the United States government decided to convert their atolls into atomic-bomb test sites. It was impossible to concentrate on the local politics of the atoll communities when what was happening was being determined by actors usually unknown to local people and always outside local control. The relationships the islanders had with various agencies of the United States government, involved first in their removal and then in servicing the resettlement areas, were determinative of what happened locally.

Other studies of so-called "development displacement" followed, but it was the outpouring of refugees associated with the war in Southeast Asia during the 1960s and 1970s that produced the first major anthropological work dealing with refugees.

By the end of the twentieth century, the ethnography of warfare, violence, and displacement was an established field of research. By then it was evident that displacement is endemic, driven by international developments that create standards for emulation, fuel the drive to obtain resources to maintain such standards, arm the forces of contenders for resources, disenfranchise the weak, and arouse and blunt international compassion. All this is now included under that innocuous term "globalization."

For political anthropologists, displacement is a special challenge, for its causes lie usually with decisions made by political actors who are outside the limited geographical area upon which the anthropologist usually focuses. Those displaced move through space and through time, and in that journey encounter different political institutions and political actors who have their own agendas and their own assumptions about how people should be governed. They form new groups and create networks in an attempt to regain some control over their own lives, and they are in communication with people in their homeland and those who have been given asylum elsewhere. With these they consider how to influence what is happening at home or form alliances to influence political decisions in the place of settlement. Most of what is happening takes place over a considerable period of time and much of it is outside the anthropologist's own range of observation. Many of the actors are known only by name, if at all. All of this belongs in a different universe than that of the village or local-level politics, the focus of the earlier anthropological engagement with political action. Even so, something of the early work remains relevant.

Political anthropology emerged as a distinctive field within anthropology in the 1940s with the publication of *African Political Systems* (Fortes and Evans-Pritchard 1940), a harbinger of an emergent specialization within the discipline. It was the product of a generation deeply disturbed by the discrediting of Western civilization. The atrocities of World War I, the demise of old states, the rise of fascism, and the economic debacle of the Great Depression had shaken earlier beliefs in the idea of progress and the civilizing mission of the West. Earlier studies of law and governance exist, such as Barton's work on the Ifugao of the Philippines (1919) or Rattray's work on the Ashanti of West Africa (1929), carried out by men involved in the governance of newly acquired colonial territories, or Lowie's (1927) work on the political institutions of Plains Indians. But *African Political Systems* initiated a new focus upon the political order.

The implicit working assumptions of the period derived from the seventeenth and eighteenth centuries, and the search for institutions that restrained the rapaciousness of individuals. What force restrained anarchy? What gave legitimacy to law? How was naked power contained? The emphasis was upon government seen as the legitimate channel through which order was maintained (Vincent 1990:225). These remain legitimate questions and may have particular relevance in an era of destabilization of governments and disenfranchisement of vulnerable populations.

Anthropologists had no problem identifying governmental institutions among people like the Ashanti, who had a centralized system based on a hierarchy of office and councils prior to incorporation within the British colonial empire. What aroused intense speculation was the political life of people such as the Nuer of the Sudan, or the Tallensi of northern Ghana, who ordered relationships using the vocabulary of kinship and seemed to live without obvious institutions of government, whom

Hobbes would have seen as living in anarchy. Somehow they settled most disputes and found a basis for alliances transcending the immediate ties of kinship. They were even able to mobilize for warfare. If this were possible, what were the essential tasks by which one could identify some form of political order, discern the boundaries within which it operated, and speak of government? The Nuer, the Tallensi, and for that matter the Ifugao, like Native Americans before them, challenged assumptions about the nature of the state and the reasons for its existence – challenges earlier faced by philosophers of the seventeenth and eighteenth centuries, when the Native Americans confronted them with different forms of order, and still earlier by the Greeks and Romans, who tried to imagine how and when governance emerged and the forms it could take. The subject has remained part of the anthropological agenda, though by the 1990s more among archaeologists than social anthropologists, who by now are probably more concerned with what happens when a state disintegrates than with constructing evolutionary models of political order. What *African Political Systems* established was that it was possible to study political action and forms of social control even in the absence of offices with assigned functions.

By the 1960s, interest in indigenous political schemes waned. Colonial elites were demanding and achieving independence from metropolitan rulers, while at the same time extending Western models of governance to the level of the ward, the village, and the homestead. Even at the local level, people were immersed in political activity premised on a different future as coalitions formed to demand independence and then to compete for power within newly formed postcolonial states. The urgent questions in political anthropology dealt with strategies available to competitors, the formation of informal networks for political action, the playing off of factions against each other, and the creation of patron/client ties linking big men to followers – in other words, party politics rather than governance.

Marxism and the class struggle dominated much of the political theory of the day. European and US political scientists identified economic class as the driving force behind political mobilization. Mobilization based on ethnicity was seen as of minor interest and primarily a thing of the past. Political theory also took as given that the major players were territorial states, that every inch of land was under the jurisdiction of some state, and that every individual must be a citizen of some state. The world order was defined as an assemblage of United Nations, that is, of territorial states.

In the new states, where many anthropologists still worked, governments faced the task of transforming regions, arbitrarily defined and bounded to suit colonial purposes, into nations with territorial boundaries and particular histories worthy of inspiring loyalty. They also had to create a sense of common citizenship among those who might previously have seen themselves as united only in opposition to the colonial order defined as government. Independence achieved, rival leaders needed new slogans around which to mobilize followers and, in the absence of obvious class differences, they did this by emphasizing ethnicity based on language or some other shared attribute. This was risky, for it could raise memories of loyalty to kin and old polities whose territories transcended the boundaries inherited from the colonial order, and the followers so created had to be rewarded through the spoils of office, pitting one ethnic constituency against another.

In the nature of the case, anthropologists, who still drew much of their impetus from research outside the United States and Western Europe, had good reason to emphasize the importance of studying how boundaries, whether they were geographical or ethnic, were constructed and maintained, and the bases of political identities and loyalties. Some saw ethnicity as an inheritance from the past based on primordial sentiment linked to kinship. Others were impressed by a similarity of tactics used to mobilize the demand for independence with those now being used to create what were in fact new ethnic coalitions, as appeals were made to common language or religion, and symbolic rituals were created to dramatize ethnic superiority and solidarity. The greater that solidarity became, the greater became the threat to the stability of the state trying to contain the ambitions set free by independence.

The ethnic mobilization that took place in the former colonial world during the 1970s and 1980s was responding to the same forces that led to the ethnic mobilization that transformed Europe in the nineteenth and early twentieth centuries, when states acquired the resources to extend their control over local communities, and the impact of literacy and industrialization led to a reevaluation of existing cultural and linguistic differences. Education became a criterion for office and education privileged one language and its speakers at the expense of others. They in turn became conscious of discrimination and exclusion, and they were potential recruits for leaders who urged the need for a place of their own, governed by those who spoke their language and shared their assumptions. Given the ethnic intermixture so characteristic of Europe, the success of any one minority could only create new disaffected communities. Self-determination brought the redrawing of territorial boundaries. It also led to the expulsion of millions now defined as ethnic aliens, who were not easily assimilated elsewhere, even when they were assumed to be of the same stock. Seventy years after the expulsions associated with the redrawing of the map of Europe in the 1920s, descendants of the original migrants may still be considered strangers and identify themselves with reference to the lands from which their parents and grandparents were expelled.

Political anthropology's interest in nationalism and the nation or state flourished in the 1980s and 1990s, nurtured by the increased centering of ethnographic work on Europe and the urban US, where ethnic politics acquired new salience. When colonial empires vanished, citizens of metropolitan countries no longer had privileged access to colonial jobs or other benefits of empire. Citizenship in the larger political unit became less compelling. Scottish nationalism, Basque nationalism, Breton nationalism rose to claim local autonomy or independence. In the former Soviet Union and the Eastern bloc, potent nationalisms led to the radical reformation of territorial units, with subsequent large-scale population movements. The Soviet Union, Yugoslavia, and Czechoslovakia have broken up into ethnically defined states, making some of their people into second-class citizens and others into refugees. Cyprus was torn apart as its Turkish-speaking Islamic citizens protested against domination by the Greek-speaking Orthodox majority. The resulting civil war displaced a substantial portion of the population.

When the right to citizenship becomes associated with descent or blood, rather than with allegiance to a government, those outside the dominant group are at risk of expulsion. Immigrants and their descendants become unlikely recruits to the political community, unless they are defined as sharing ethnicity with those to whom the state belongs. Even then they may bear a stigma, as have German-speakers repatriated to Germany from Poland, the Ukraine, and Czechoslovakia.

In Western Europe, the United States, and Canada, multiculturalism, or the rights of ethnic minorities to maintain distinct identities, became more salient, but political action usually focused on attempts to appropriate state resources to the benefit of a particular group. At the same time, the consciousness of ethnic divisiveness played an important role in a new concern with creating strong barriers to immigration, and thus the expansion of the agencies that patrolled the borders and dealt with aliens.

In the late twentieth century, the newly established territorial states of Asia and Africa contended with political rivalries challenging regional control by the center, which sometimes led to a loss of all possibility of governing. Ethnic politics was increasingly important in Europe and the Americas. Political anthropologists may have been slow to recognize the implications of nationalism because disenchantment with the state was characteristic of the politically involved during the late 1960s and early 1970s. The legitimacy of the existing governments was questioned. Some wanted a transfer of power to emergent ethnic polities. Others wanted a transfer of power to some larger international order. The disrepute of colonial government was extrapolated to all government, aided by a suspicion of government fueled by US involvement in the war in Vietnam and the feminist critique that queried all received authority as an illegitimate reflection of patriarchy. From some points of view, those exercising power within a government, along with the state itself, were enemies of the people.

Political anthropology was profoundly affected by the critiques and by the perception that political manipulation was going on via the media and other agencies controlled by those in power. This made it more difficult to think of political life as involving independently reasoning people who acted in terms of their own interests but from different positions of power. Interest shifted to the symbolic domination that created the categories of thought that legitimated those in power and gave them hegemonic control (Foucault 1977). Strategies of symbolic domination included rhetorical devices, conventions of etiquette, spatial layouts, the organization of time, and the organization of ritual occasions, all aimed at making for docility and political subordination. It had to be assumed that hegemony was never complete, and that those subject to domination retained some sense of what they themselves wanted, given an alternative interest in the way individuals and communities circumvented and rebuffed authority. Covert resistance was seen as desirable since personal autonomy was highly valorized.

## THE STUDY OF THE POLITICS OF DISPLACEMENT AND RESETTLEMENT

Political anthropologists who deal with forced displacement find themselves perforce concerned again with governance in various guises, as agents that create conditions under which people become vulnerable to uprooting and as agents that deal with them in passage and in their various places of resettlement or refuge. Equally, governments and political communities are vulnerable to the changing balances of political forces as people are expelled or settle in new countries. Political ideals, including definitions of citizenship and limitations on the intrusion of government, alter in the face of new demands.

Displacement alters the meaning of boundaries. Recent decades have seen the struggle to eliminate boundaries as barriers to the flow of trade, capital, and industrial enterprises, while at the same time governments have noticeably become more concerned to raise barriers to the flow of people across their boundaries as the number of people determined to cross increases.

Fear of potential displacement and a flood of asylum-seekers also lead to new forms of international intervention that interfere with the rights of states to deal with their citizens as they will. What is happening in many parts of the world, especially in Africa but also in the Middle East, bears a strong resemblance to the interventions of the nineteenth and early twentieth centuries that established colonial regimes in much of Africa and Asia. International forces are sent to keep order to prevent further violence and displacement. International agencies undertake the care and governance of those displaced and form extraterritorial political enclaves within the countries where they are at work. Western Europe and North America may be the primary targets of refugees seeking long-term asylum, but they also engage with the uprooted through their predominant control over the international agencies and non-governmental organizations that are the caretakers for the dispossessed.

Political identities are of crucial importance to those who move, and often to those who must receive immigrants. The passport and the identity card emerged as definitions of personhood in the twentieth century, as becomes obvious to all displaced persons. These emphasize that one is a person by virtue of being a citizen of some state, although the growth of diasporas indicates that more and more people have loyalties that transcend state boundaries, while the increasing importance of ethnicity is an appeal to an identity based on other qualities.

Symbolic processes fashion and maintain the new political identities. They are used as a means of degradation, to create categories of people defined as dangerous or expendable and therefore suitable subjects for expulsion or the coercion that leads to flight. They are used to spell out the meaning of the categories that govern life after uprooting: refugee, asylum-seeker, economic migrant, illegal immigrant. And they differentiate those so categorized from others who move across borders freely: tourists, agents of international charitable agencies, corporation employees. They also are used to define appropriate action when people settle in a new country. And they are manifestly at work in the ordering of refugee camps or resettlement schemes, where they ensure that people are reminded that they are subordinates and under the authority of those who have the right to care for them.

But displacement itself is not a form of symbolic domination. The displaced are subject to brute force. Even those who are told to leave because their land is wanted by others for economic reasons, and who are given assistance to resettle elsewhere, know that displacement symbolizes nothing but their weakness. They may be asked to agree to being uprooted but they are unable to prevent it. Those violently uprooted, or who leave because of fear of persecution, are only too conscious that they live in a dangerous world, akin to the pre-state order envisaged by Hobbes, without a citizen's right to pursue redress through legal channels.

They may not share the intellectual's or the libertarian's disillusionment with the state as a political form, however much they wish to change the occupants of office or the political institutions of their home governments, or to alter the laws of countries of asylum to improve their chances. Refugees show a strong preference for settlement with the possibility of becoming citizens over a life in holding camps. They know they continue to be vulnerable until they can reestablish themselves as citizens, whether in their own or in some other state.

With governments becoming increasingly unwilling to grant asylum, and the difficulties faced by those who lack resources if they try to cross territorial boundaries, this is no easy matter. Once uprooted, many remain in limbo, as witness the continued existence of holding camps whose residents are essentially outside the governance of the territorial state where the camp is based, and the increasing throngs of illegal immigrants who live without the protection of the law even though they claim the right of asylum.

In the meantime, though citizenship remains tied to the territorial state, increasingly the uprooted are regarded as a charge upon some larger world order, demonstrated by the attempts to create an agreed ethic of human rights which inhere in the individual as a member of the human species rather than as a citizen of any political unit, the enlarging mandate of the UN High Commissioner for Refugees, and the attempt of the World Bank to intervene in order to lessen the impact on those slated to be uprooted by economic enterprises.

The rise of new forms of international organization subsumed under the term of globalization is preempting powers previously lodged in the state or left to the individual (Harrell-Bond 1986; Shore 2000; Barrows and Jennings 2001). Political actors involved in displacement and its aftermath include such contenders for power as the European Union, NAFTA, various branches of the United Nations, international business corporations that escape state controls, and the proliferating non-governmental aid organizations that have become surrogates for governments too poor or too weak to control what goes on within their borders or to cater for the influx of the dispossessed from across their borders.

## REFERENCES

Barrows, Ondine, and Michael Jennings, eds. (2001) *The Charitable Impulse: NGOs and Development in East and North-East Africa*. Oxford: James Currey.

Barton, Roy F. (1919) *Ifugao Law*. Berkeley: University of California Press.

Cernea, Michael, and Christopher McDowell (2000) Reconstructing Resettlers' and Refugees' Livelihoods. In *Risks and Reconstruction: Experiences of Refugees and Resettlers*, ed. Michael Cernea and Christopher McDowell, pp. 1–8. Washington, DC: World Bank.

Douglas, Mary (1966) *Purity and Danger*. London: Routledge and Kegan Paul.

Fortes, Meyer, and E. E. Evans-Pritchard, eds. (1940) *African Political Systems*. London: Oxford University Press.

Foucault, Michel (1977) *Discipline and Punish: The Birth of the Prison*, trans. Alan Sheridan. London: Penguin Books.

Harrell-Bond, Barbara (1986) *Imposing Aid: Emergency Assistance to Refugees*. Oxford: Oxford University Press.

Holtzman, Jon (2000) *Nuer Journeys, Nuer Lives: Sudanese Refugees in Minnesota*. Boston: Allyn and Bacon.

Lowie, Robert (1927) *The Origin of the State*. New York: Russell and Russell.

Mooney, James (1896) *The Ghost Dance and the Sioux Outbreaks of 1890.* Annual Report of the Bureau of American Ethnology 14. Washington, DC: Smithsonian Institution.

Rattray, R. A. (1929) *Ashanti Law and Constitution.* Oxford: Clarendon Press.

Scudder, Thayer (1998) Development-induced Impoverishment, Resistance and River-Basin Development. In *Understanding Impoverishment: The Consequences of Development-induced Displacement,* ed. C. McDowell, pp. 49–74. Oxford: Berghahn.

Shore, Chris (2000) *Building Europe: The Cultural Politics of European Integration.* London: Routledge.

Vincent, Joan (1990) *Anthropology and Politics: Visions, Traditions, and Trends.* Tucson: University of Arizona Press.

## SUGGESTED FURTHER READING

Black, Richard, and Khalid Koser, eds. (1999) *The End of the Refugee Cycle? Refugee Repatriation and Reconstruction.* Oxford: Berghahn.

Castles, Stephen, and Alastair Davidson, eds. (2000) *Citizenship and Migration: Globalization and the Politics of Belonging.* London: Macmillan.

Daniel, E. Valentine, and John Knudsen, eds. (1995) *Mistrusting Refugees.* Berkeley: University of California Press.

Lieber, Michael, ed. (1977) *Exiles and Migrants in Oceania.* Honolulu: University Press of Hawaii.

Loizos, Peter (1981) *The Heart Grows Bitter.* Cambridge: Cambridge University Press.

Hirschon, Renée (1998) *Heirs of the Greek Catastrophe: The Social Life of Asia Minor Refugees in Piraeus.* Oxford: Berghahn.

Gilad, Lisa (1990) *The Northern Route: An Ethnography of Refugee Experience.* St. Johns: Memorial University of Newfoundland.

Malkki, Liisa (1995) *Purity and Exile: Violence, Memory, and National Cosmology Among Hutu Refugees in Tanzania.* Chicago: University of Chicago Press.

Picciotto, Robert, Warren van Wicklin, and Edward Rice, eds. (2001) *Involuntary Resettlement: Comparative Perspectives.* World Bank Series on Evaluation and Development, 2. New Brunswick, NJ: Transaction Publishers.

Renner, Michael (2002) *The Anatomy of Resource Wars.* Worldwatch Paper 162. Washington, DC: Worldwatch Institute.

Zolberg, Aristide, and Peter Benda (2001) *Global Migrants, Global Refugees: Problems and Solutions.* Oxford: Berghahn.

## CHAPTER 8

# Feminism

## *Malathi de Alwis*

The relationship between anthropology and feminism has been commented upon and analyzed quite extensively over the years. Although foundational texts for "second wave" feminism, such as Simone de Beauvoir's *The Second Sex* and Juliet Mitchell's *Psychoanalysis and Feminism*, drew upon anthropological materials and arguments, the marriage between anthropology and feminism was primarily solemnized through two edited volumes – Rosaldo and Lamphere's *Woman, Culture, and Society*, and Reiter's *Towards an Anthropology of Women* – which had a significant impact not only on feminist scholarship and politics, and the discipline of anthropology, but on social and biological sciences more generally.

Indeed, some of the arguments posed in these volumes, such as Sherry Ortner's gendering of the nature/culture paradigm, Michele Rosaldo's gendering of the domestic/public paradigm, and Gayle Rubin's formulation of a sex/gender paradigm, have been particularly hegemonic and helped frame and extend feminist debates in a variety of disciplines and fields. Although di Leonardo faults these two collections for a certain naïveté in "seeing no contradiction between their scholarship and anthropology's traditional edificatory role in the West" (1991:33), they nevertheless mark an important moment within American anthropology, where a commitment to a particular feminist politics was passionately articulated. This is especially clear in Rayna Reiter's opening comments in *Toward an Anthropology of Women* (1975:11):

> This book has its roots in the women's movement. To explain and describe equality and inequality between the sexes, contemporary feminism has turned to anthropology with many questions in its search for a theory and a body of information. These questions are more than academic: the answers will help feminists in the struggle against sexism in our own society... our political critique must be based on this understanding of the origins and development of sexism.

Rosaldo and Lamphere stated their debt as well as their accountability to the women's movement less explicitly, but they were quite clear that their alliance was with "many women today" who are "trying to understand our position and to change it" (1974:1). This imperative for change, for transformation, is one of the central reasons, one could argue, that "feminist analysis has been one of the primary contexts in which a practice approach has developed in anthropology" (Collier and Yanigisako 1989:27; Ortner 1984).

In the 1980s and 1990s, anthropology's rediscovery of a feminist critique within itself had several outcomes. In 1987, Marilyn Strathern, in an extremely prescient and thought-provoking essay, called attention to the awkward questions that social anthropology poses to feminist theorizing. She pointed out that anthropological and feminist practices are "differently structured in the way they organize knowledge and draw boundaries, in short, in terms of the social relations that define their scholarly communities" (1987:289). Laclau and Mouffe's *Hegemony and Socialist Strategy: Towards a Radical Democratic Politic* is not unrelated to this comment. Most relevant here is their observation that women's recent protest agitations, along with those of racial and sexual minorities and other marginalized groups, have led to a "politicization of the social" more radical than any known previously, because it dissolved the distinction between the private and the public "not in terms of the encroachment on the private by a unified public space, but in terms of a proliferation of radically new and different political spaces" (1985:81).

But it is Pradeep Jeganathan who, in a provocative paper given at the 2001 meeting of the American Anthropological Association, posed the crucial question of the relationship between the knowledge anthropologists produce as disciplinary practitioners and what they constitute in their epistemological projects as "politics." Making forays into Foucault's discussion of "disciplines," with its distinction between scientific discourse and political practice, and placing it alongside Althusser's observation that "everything which touches on politics may be fatal to philosophy, for philosophy lives on politics," she engages with historian and anthropologist Bernard Cohn's famous depiction of "anthropology land" as an "analytical construct that *depends upon the exclusion of what might be called politics from its very constitution*" (2001:7, emphasis added). But, notes Jeganathan, "For the suture of history and anthropology to be always already political, then the yield of that suture must be known, *a priori*" and that is not always possible. "We must know who we are allied with, how we are allied with them in these [epistemological] struggles, what our stakes are in those alliances, that is to say what we will lose if those alliances fail, and more, what we will lose if those struggles fail" (2001:9). In light of this, she suggests, the "play" between history and anthropology may be similar to what philosophy is for Althusser: "a necessary path to tread upon and travel, but then still not be 'politics,' but rather, perhaps, its condition of possibility, which, in turn, may not be located within the epistemological architecture of anthropology, but may, as it were, constitute its limit" (2001:10).

Jeganathan makes explicit the difference between disciplinary formations and political practices that Marilyn Strathern left implicit. Feminism, which one could argue is a product of political struggle and which informs political struggles in turn, cannot share a discipline with anthropology, which is constituted through different rules and protocols that are analytically prior to political practice (Jeganathan [*pace* Foucault] 2001:6). Hence the awkwardness when one seeks to suture seamlessly two dissonant categorical practices within the subdiscipline of "feminist anthropology." This certainly poses a salient issue for "feminist politics" within anthropology, as it does, indeed, for the anthropology of politics.

So where does this leave those feminists who wish to pursue the discipline of anthropology? Can we speak from within the domain of feminist politics rather than about it? Is such a disciplinary positioning possible if politics marks the limit of anthropology? How can anthropologists who are also feminists frame research questions about political struggles in which they are actively participating and intervening?

Let me begin by going back to basics, back to ethnography. The general trend, especially in South Asian feminist studies, has been to an increasing preoccupation with redefining the genre of ethnography rather than exploring what is meant by "feminist" or "feminist politics" in the light of anthropological practice (Visweswaran 1997). This has had crucial consequences for how we conceptualize and engage with the "political." As Laclau and Mouffe have noted, women's contemporary agitations, along with those of racial and sexual minorities (and other marginalized groups) have led to a "politicization of the social" more radical than any known previously because it dissolved the distinction between the private and the public "not in terms of the encroachment on the private by unified public space, but in terms of a proliferation of radically new and different political spaces" (1985:81).

This chapter explores how feminist anthropologists engage with these "new and different political spaces." Does such an engagement in itself constitute a particular form of "feminist politics"? If so, what are its contours and what are its implications for the discipline today? Most important, is it possible for anthropologists to write "not *about* a feminist politics, as if one's words were somehow outside the dynamics and divisions of their referent, but to speak from within that domain" (McClure 1992:343, emphasis added)? I address these questions by describing my own struggles to combine a "feminist politics" with anthropological field research on a contemporary social movement that was not only the single largest women's protest movement of its time, but arguably one of the most effective in the modern history of Sri Lanka.

## THE MOTHERS' FRONT: CALLING THE "POLITICAL" INTO QUESTION FROM OUTSIDE THE FEMINIST DOMAIN

Between 1987 and 1991 Sri Lanka witnessed an uprising by nationalist Sinhala youth (the JVP or Janatha Vimukthi Peramuna) and reprisals by the state that gripped the country in a stranglehold of terror. The militants randomly terrorized or assassinated anyone who criticized them or supposedly collaborated with the state, while the state similarly, but on a much larger scale, murdered or "disappeared" anyone they suspected of being a "subversive." This included thousands of young men, some young women, several left-wing activists, playwrights, lawyers, and journalists who were either monitoring or protesting the state's violation of human rights. Bodies rotting on beaches, smoldering in grotesque heaps by the roadsides, and floating down rivers were a daily sight during the height of state repression from 1988 to 1990.

It was in this context that the Mothers' Front, a grass-roots women's organization with an estimated membership of over 25,000, was formed in July 1990 to protest the "disappearance" of approximately 60,000 young and middle-aged male kin.

Their primary demand, published in a national newspaper sympathetic to the leading opposition party, was for "a climate where we can raise our sons to manhood, have our husbands with us and lead normal women's lives" (*Island,* February 9, 1991). The text made it clear that they were not "political." This claim bears examination. The Front's use of the term "political" was particularly ironic, since it was common knowledge that it was not only founded but was also being funded and supported by the main opposition party, the SLFP (Sri Lanka Freedom Party).

The leader of the SLFP, Mrs. Sirimavo Bandaranaike, was adamant that the Mothers' Front was "not a political movement," that "politics did not come into play," and that her party was not interested in scoring any "political mileage" by supporting it. Sentiments were expressed in one newspaper's editorial column that movements such as the Mothers' Front were an "expression not so much of overtly political movements but of the travails of a most highly valued force in Sri Lankan society – motherhood." It went on to make a distinction between "male-dominated, patriarchally styled political movements" which "indulge in politics ranging from the destructive to the esoterically liberal" and those of women, mothers, who are normally channeled into kitchen activity and only "burst into the political arena" against many odds: "When mothers emerge as a political force," it concluded, "it means that our political institutions and society as a whole have reached a critical moment – the danger to our way of life has surely come closer home."

Both Mrs. Bandaranaike's statement and the editorial mobilized seamlessly the "political" – in the sense of wishing to be involved in governance (i.e., challenging the present government in power) – with "doing politics" – in the sense of a practice that is corrupt, manipulative, and destructive (a common perception in Sri Lanka). However, the editorial went one step further when, in its conclusion, it referred to the Front as "a political force." This implicitly called into question the role of "political institutions" and "society as a whole." Its subsequent use of the word "home" added emotive value and urgency to this characterization, so that "political force" appeared much more positive than the phrase "doing politics" as a description of the activities of patriarchal political movements. The strength of the women or mothers lies in the fact that, while usually limited to the kitchen (the "private" realm), they have gone against great odds to "burst into the political arena." The editorial's conscious delineation of the kitchen as a gendered exclusionary space seeks to legitimize the women's exclusion through a negative reading of "patriarchal politics."

This rhetoric was very much in keeping with that of the Mothers' Front. They asserted that they were not "political," their primary demand being for the return of their male kin so that they could lead "normal women's lives," and they were not "feminist," as their president, Dr. Manorani Saravanamuttu, made clear to me in a personal communication. They were operating under the aegis of the SLFP, she explained, because the Front needed some form of protection during the initial stages of its campaign. She spoke openly of this strategy at the First National Convention of the Mothers' Front on February 21, 1991, as one that women's groups in Latin America had also adopted. The Front's primary role, Dr. Saravanamuttu was quick to stress, was to act as "peaceful watchdogs of whatever government was in power" (*Daily News,* February 20, 1991).

The rhetoric of the Mothers' Front, like that of the newspaper that sought to represent them, raises an interesting conundrum. Both seem to call into question the very parameters of the "political" through asserting and assigning an apparent apoliticality or even an anti-politics to the movement. Yet, despite the Front's protestations that they were not "political," several government ministers used various rhetorical ploys to slander them on this very premise. Their most vociferous critic was Ranjan Wijeratne, the Minister of State for Defense. On several occasions in several newspapers, he denounced the movement as being "subversive," "anti-government," "against the security forces who saved democracy." He threatened to "get at the necks of those using the Mothers' Front" and stepped up police surveillance on its leaders. Both the government-owned media and various government ministers repeatedly accused the SLFP of trying to use the Mothers' Front to further its own power.

The Sri Lankan state's rhetorical responses thus attempted to question the credibility of the Mothers' Front by insinuating that its members were mere puppets of a political party that was using them for its own ends. Its efforts to enforce the boundaries of the political vis-à-vis the Mothers' Front was, in fact, what Butler describes as an anti-political move, a silencing, an "authoritarian ruse" (1992:4). An insistence that the "political" is of necessity constructed through the production of a determining exterior is to be found in the work of several political theorists. This is what Derrida calls "a constitutive outside" that produces and naturalizes the pre- or non-political that determines "the political" (1992:20, note 1). Butler, developing his point, makes a distinction between "the constitution of a political field that produces *and naturalizes* the constitutive outside and a political field that produces and *renders contingent* the specific parameters of that constitutive outside" (1992:20, note 1). Using Connolly's notion of "constitutive antagonisms" (which "finds a parallel expression in the work of Laclau and Mouffe") she suggests "a form of political struggle which puts the parameters of the political itself into question" (1992:20, note 1). This provides a helpful entrée into the politics of the Mothers' Front. It can be read as a movement that, indeed, calls the political into question and thus retains a certain contingent efficacy through that very move. The movement's reclaiming of new political spaces (other than the kitchen) may be located within this epistemological trajectory.

## THE MOTHERS' FRONT: CREATING NEW "POLITICAL" SPACES

The rallies and rituals in which members of the Mothers' Front participated constituted a particular terrain of discourse upon which the Sri Lankan state was forced to operate as well (de Alwis 1997). Yet, even more significant was the Front's ability to constitute a new political space through the skillful use of religious rituals. As Marx has observed, "religious distress is at the same time the expression of real distress and the protest against real distress" (quoted in Comaroff 1985:252). The families of the "disappeared" were intimate with manifestations of religious distress, running the gamut from beseeching gods and goddesses, saints and holy spirits, with special novenas, penances, offerings, and donations, to the chanting of religious verses over a period of months, taking vows, making pilgrimages, and performing *bodhi pujas* (offerings to the bo tree), as well as resorting to sorcery.

The politically savvy SLFP founders of the Front orchestrated genuine displays of distress into public and political spectacles. Most noteworthy was an appeal to the goddess Kali that was organized to follow shortly after the speech-making of the Second National Convention had concluded. Quite oblivious to the presence of police, press, politicians, and curious onlookers, the mothers dashed coconuts on the ground, lit lamps, tore their hair, struck their heads on the ground, and wept and wailed as they beseeched the goddess to find their "disappeared" and punish those who had brought such suffering upon their families. "They didn't just take one of my sons, no, they didn't even stop at two, they had to take all three of my boys," intoned one woman. "My own boys that I carried in my womb, fed with my bloodmilk (*le kiri kala*) and nurtured for the past 20 years . . . Even if these beasts (*thirisan*) are at liberty now, may they suffer the consequences of their actions unto eternity, in all their future lives." Another moaned and muttered, "May they suffer lightning without rain (*vehi nethi hena*), may their families be ground to dust." Others called out the names of perpetrators, including Sri Lanka's President Premadasa, and cursed them. Asilin, a neighbor I accompanied to this protest, was chanting over and over again: "Premadasa, see this coconut all smashed into bits, may your head too be splintered into a hundred bits, so heinous are the crimes you have perpetrated on my child." Another woman wept, saying, "Premadasa, I bore this child in my womb for ten months, may you and your family be cursed not for ten days or ten weeks or ten months or ten years or ten decades but for ten aeons."

To ward off the mothers' curses, President Premadasa – who was extremely superstitious and thus particularly unnerved by the Front's public rituals – sought refuge in an elaborate counter-ritual, the *Kiriammawarungé Dané* (the Feeding of Milk Mothers), an archaic ritual now connected with the goddess Pattini. Though the commonly held belief is that Pattini guards against infectious diseases, she is also the "good mother" and ideal wife who maintains a just and rational society. She thus provided a societal and state counterpoint to the "bad mother," the evil and demonic goddess Kali, who was associated with sorcery and familial conflicts. Ironically, in spite of his adoption of ritual counter-measures, President Premadasa was blown to smithereens by a suicide bomber before the year was out. A few days later, a beaming Asilin came to see me with a gift of plantains. "He died in just the way I cursed him," she said triumphantly.

The Mothers' Front's unprecedented public utterance of curses produced nuanced and complicated responses. Sorcery is not only a public regulatory mechanism where formal institutions for settling disputes are absent or lacking, it is also a private practice conducted in great secrecy. Although a familiar practice resorted to by all classes of Sinhala Buddhists, and even some Sinhala Christians, it is frequently portrayed by the bourgeoisie as a practice of the lower classes, and thus, like public displays of excessive weeping, coded as "unrespectable" (see de Alwis 2000).

The Sinhala press, which had consistently sentimentalized these women's maternity, and thus their suffering, incorporated the Mothers' Front's curses within a continuum of maternalized suffering: "The mothers first wept and wailed at the loss of their children. They sighed and moaned. After a while, those tears and sighs turned to anger. Then these mothers began to curse those who had denied them their children," wrote one observer. Articles that reproduced some of their curses were quick to stress the brittleness and vulnerability of these aged women and the sentimental response they evoked. "Tears welled up in the eyes of the onlookers who heard [one mother's] sorrowful lamentation." This concerted focus on the sincerity and depth of feeling with which the mothers' curses were articulated, and the fact that they were accompanied by much weeping and lamentation, was aimed at evoking empathy, pity, and sadness, never horror at what these women were wishing on the perpetrators of "disappearances."

The SLFP also sought to stress the moral righteousness of the curses. Even while constantly reminding the women that their tears were a sign of weakness and enervation, it enthusiastically promoted their curses as the powerful political weapons of the weak. It was not surprising, then, that Asilin, along with many other members of the Mothers' Front, took credit for the death of President Premadasa. And indeed, the SLFP publicly credited his death to the Mothers' Front as yet one more incident in a long chain of events. Others were a bombing of the motorcade of the Minister of State for Defense, a vociferous critic of the Front; the sudden confessions of a former Deputy Inspector General of Police notorious for his atrocities; and the unnerving of President Premadas who, several months earlier (as Sirimavo Bandaranaike pointed out in her speech at the Front's Second National Convention) had himself bathed by seven virgins to ward off similar curses.

Indeed, for a group of women marginalized by class and gender for much of their lives, such Pyrrhic victories as effecting the death of a president were very precious. It did not concern them that the movement's organized visit to the goddess Kali's shrine was part of a carefully orchestrated political spectacle at which they were to be the chief performers. What mattered most was that they were finally being given a chance to do something concrete for their "disappeared" after a morning during which politicians took turns to spout "hot air" while they listened and wept. Once the women entered the courtyard of Kali's shrine, they felt more confident and purposeful: "We knew what we had to do here . . . not like when we were in the [meeting] hall just sitting and listening. . . . after all we have been doing these *pujas* [rituals] in many other *devales* [Hindu shrines] . . . we were glad that we got an opportunity to come to this famous *devale* and do a *puja* too." It was *their* participation that mattered. When the representative of a party supporting the Mothers' Front's campaign attempted to read out a chant to the goddess Kali, the organizers had great difficulty in getting the women's attention. The chant could barely be heard over their lamentations and cursing. Many of them continued with their own invocations despite a request for silence.

## THE CONUNDRUM OF RELIGIOSITY

The Front's mobilization of a new political space so strongly inflected with religiosity posed a conundrum for those feminist and left activists who perceived it as the introduction of "voodoo" into politics. Yet, as political scientist Jayadeva Uyangoda noted (1992:4), the Mothers' Front was merely valorizing women as the "carriers and bearers of culture," as those who have a "primary and initiating role in religious and magical rituals." The unfolding of such a doubly stereotyped identity was made even more problematic by these women's implicit faith in the efficacy of divine intervention over "rationalist and enlightened traditions of politics" (Uyangoda 1992:5). By personalizing politics and representing President Premadasa as the epitome of evil, the SLFP and the Mothers' Front were not only leaving "counter-democratic forces and structures unidentified and un-critiqued," they were also replicating the government's use of "sinister substitutes" for "open political competition, debate, discussion and electoral mobilization" by exploiting and manipulating the "religious emotions of the people" (1992:5).

While I share these concerns over the increasing authoritarianism of state and counter-state institutions, leading to the debilitation of "secularist foundations of political conduct" (1992:6), I am, nevertheless, troubled by Uyangoda's valorization of the "traditions of political enlightenment" that are posited as "rational" and "democratic" in opposition to the "irrational" and "dark" underworld of demons and sorcerers that had "burst its way into the light" and become "public and acknowledged" (1992:5). Such a formulation replicates Christian and anthropological discourses on demonism, which David Scott (1994) has so brilliantly deconstructed and historicized. Such a formulation enables the argument that those who participate in such "demonic" practices are by extension "less rational and more emotional," a labeling that Uyangoda himself asserted was not applicable to members of the Mothers' Front (1992:4).

The mobilization of maternalized suffering and religiosity by the Mothers' Front marked out a crucial space – both conceptually and materially – within the political landscape of Sri Lanka. Their use of curses as public protest had no precedent in Sri Lanka and threatened to circumvent the state's emergency laws constraining protest demonstrations and rallies. Yet to have banned people's right to religious worship was something even a government that defined itself as one that had the best interests of the populace in mind – even Sri Lanka's autocratic government – would not have dared. And, for a believer such as the president, the presumption that a curse could bring about change through the intercession of a deity complicated efforts to forestall such changes.

The women's curses, accompanied by much weeping and lamentation, enabled a certain sentimentalization of maternalized suffering yet could not mitigate the threat they posed in seeking to effect change through divine intervention. Maternalized curses, unlike maternalized tears, disrupted normative representations of Sinhala "culture" and "tradition" premised upon a sanitized notion of Buddhism that strove to deny and repress demonic beliefs and practices. The curses of the Mothers' Front represented the "dark underworld" that had "burst its way into the light" (Uyangoda 1992:5). Similarly, the Mothers' excessive weeping and cursing could not be circumscribed within a bourgeois norm of conduct. Yet, this unfolding of "unrespectability," I suggest, was circumscribed within a rubric of "motherhood" that both legitimized their protests and evoked sympathy. The women were not only speaking as mothers and wives; they were also calling for a return to "a climate where we can raise our sons to manhood, have our husbands with us and lead normal women's lives," as one woman was quoted as saying.

In a context where left and feminist voices had been silenced by both an autocratic government and a militant nationalist movement, the mobilization of such a fraught maternalism succeeded in winning the support of the Sinhala media and public. Furthermore, in engendering a discourse of human rights, it provided a damning (albeit narrowly formulated) critique of the state. But, most important, it appropriated and defined a new political space and rhetoric that enabled the gestation of a powerful political movement with a much broader, radical agenda, which was able to overthrow by democratic means a repressive government that had clung to power for over 17 years. Its impact during its brief but spectacular appearance upon the public stage cannot be underestimated. Its consequences for feminist politics are equally telling.

The next section provides several alternative readings of the rhetoric and practices of the Mothers' Front from *within* the domain of feminist politics in Sri Lanka.

## FRAMING "FEMINIST POLITICS" OR FEMINISM AS A PATH TO POLITICS

The mobilization of motherhood as a space for protest has been, and continues to be, an issue heatedly debated by feminists all over the world. Every time the specificity of a category is articulated (Butler 1992:15):

> there is resistance and factionalization within the very constituency that is supposed to be unified by the articulation of its common element . . . all women are not mothers; some cannot be, some are too young or too old to be, some choose not to be, and for some who are mothers, that is not necessarily the rallying point of their politicization in feminism.

The presence of the Mothers' Front in the political landscape of the 1990s engendered a great deal of debate among feminists, not in Sri Lanka alone but in the South Asian subcontinent. Everyone had strong opinions on the issue, and this led to both disagreements within some organizations and unusual alliances among others. I participated in many debates as a member of Women for Peace at regional feminist conferences in Sri Lanka, India, and Pakistan, and in informal conversations and meetings with feminists who were members of left parties, religious groups, and/or engaged in the monitoring of human rights. In the account that follows, rather than identifying individual voices, I set out the general positions and concerns that I heard articulated in these debates and conversations. At one level, these might be reduced to two central paradigms: whether motherhood empowers women or whether it produces victims; whether it reduces motherhood to a category or whether it produces actors or agents. At a more abstract level, they might be viewed as bringing these very paradigms into crisis, blunting the acuity of such binary oppositions.

This was the dilemma that my feminist group, Women for Peace, faced in 1989, when it tried to launch a national campaign for peace. We used a "non-threatening" quotation from Bertolt Brecht, which invoked mothers as peace-seekers, in the hope of attracting the signatures of as many women as possible. Although this proved successful, several women refused to sign the petition on the grounds that it was exclusionary and perpetuated a particular heterosexist norm.

For others, the Mothers' Front posed a different dilemma. It was not a question of whether feminists would be willing to unite with it under the category of "motherhood" but whether they were willing to come out publicly in support of women who had openly declared that they were not feminists. Some feminists balked at a public show of support lest their seal of approval undermined the Front's cause; others felt that it was crucial to declare solidarity with such a large movement of grass-roots women in order to honor their courage in speaking out during a time of great repression and violence. This viewpoint engendered further scrutiny, debate, and critique. Although the state's domestication of terror had had a direct effect on the women's familial subject positions, many feminists were uncomfortable that it had chosen to articulate its protest as mothers rather than as women. By banding together as mothers, they observed, the women were essentializing a *particular* feminine identity that was not only tied to very normative and heterosexual notions of family, but was also much valorized and sentimentalized by the Sinhala state (de Alwis 1998).

Yet other feminists insisted that the strategic value of mobilizing a maternal identity lay precisely in the fact that it was so revered and valorized by Sinhala society and the state. Although the Front's members might not perceive it as such, one speaker remarked, "at least we feminists must take into account and try to understand and promote the subversive potential of these mothers." She proffered the counter-example of another group that was protesting "disappearances" – the Organization of Parents and Family Members of the Disappeared (OPFMD) – which was not mobilizing around "motherhood" and was not as successful in getting media attention or public sympathy and support.

Most of the feminists were also concerned about the limited agenda of the Mothers' Front. While an overt proclamation of a non-feminist agenda (such as that of Dr. Saravanamuttu, its president) could be read as a strategy to defuse unnecessary public criticism and secure a narrower focus on the women's demands for the return of their "disappeared," it was seen to be particularly unfortunate that only a rather desultory effort had been made to link the southern women's concerns with those of their Tamil and Muslim counterparts in the north and east of the country, where a civil war had been in progress for almost two decades. The very name Mothers' Front was reminiscent of a Tamil women's grass-roots organization formed in Jaffna in 1984. This erasure was seen by some feminists to be primarily the work of the male organizers of the Sri Lanka Freedom Party (SLFP). Their Sinhala nationalist focus, along with an astute understanding of the emotiveness of Sinhala motherhood, led them to pay no more than lip service to the suffering of minority women, they explained.

Other feminists, however, defended the SLFP organizers, noting that they had internationalized the southern Mothers' Front when they evoked the Madres of Plaza de Mayo, who were renowned the world over for protesting the "disappearance" of their male kin during the "dirty war" in Argentina. This movement had attracted international attention and funds. These feminists also reminded the SLFP's critics that representatives from both the eastern and the southern Mothers' Fronts had been invited to be on the presidium, along with Dr. Manorani Saravanamuttu (a Tamil) at the first National Convention of the Mothers' Front on February 19, 1991. That first convention had focused mainly on procuring international support. It was attended by over 100 foreign guests representing embassies, non-governmental organizations (NGOs), and the press, and (as they noted) the SLFP organizers had used the occasion to express considerable concern over the plight of mothers in the north and east of the country and the need to form branches of the national organization in those regions as well.

Other feminists countered these arguments by noting that the SLFP had only been making token use of the representative from the eastern Mothers' Front in order to create a good image before the international press:

The SLFP wanted to show that the Mothers' Front was being run by women from different ethnic groups and classes, and because it had such a nice, friendly group of women working together, there was no way it could be labeled an anti-government organization ... after all, women are supposed to be pro-peace, right? That's what the international public loves to hear about.

Feminists, myself included, who had attended the Second National Convention in 1992, went further, arguing that, since that time, the SLFP had dispensed with even rhetorical flourishes about the suffering of minority women. Only two out of the 20 speakers at this rally had mentioned the suffering of Tamil mothers, and no Tamils (with the exception of Dr. Saravanamuttu) were given an opportunity to address the gathering. We noted that the absence of Tamil or other minority participation in the Mothers' Front meetings had not only reduced the possibility of launching a more integrated, national campaign that might have benefited from the experiences of Tamil women, but that the SLFP had done even greater damage by appropriating the Tamil group's name, thus erasing their critical activism from the memory of an entire population in southern Sri Lanka. Many feminists who had objected to the Front's mobilization of "motherhood" confessed that they would have been more willing to compromise if it had been used as a space within which women of different ethnic groups could have united and launched a collective critique of the state.

What also disturbed many Sinhala feminists who had had extended interaction with members of the southern Mothers' Front, including me, was that many claimed never to have heard of the Tamil Mothers' Front. The suffering of Tamil and Muslim women in the northern and eastern war zones seemed far removed from their reality – a fact due mainly to a ban on journalists reporting from the war zone. They listened to stories of their suffering in the same way that they listened to my narratives of the Madres of Plaza de Mayo, with blank-faced politeness tinged with a certain impatience as well as weariness. Several of these women also espoused a certain kind of Sinhala nationalism that made it difficult for them to distinguish Tamil civilians from Tamil militants. One woman with several nephews in the army went so far as to tell me that she felt she could not blame Sinhala soldiers for rounding up Tamil boys every time the armed forces were attacked: "I'm only angry that these boys did the same thing to their own brothers ... people of their own blood." Yet there were also several women who wept when they listened to my narratives about the suffering of minority women and criticized the state in a rich and pungent idiom.

Most feminists with whom I talked were greatly concerned over the organizational structure of the Mothers' Front. While the Front identified itself as the largest grass-roots women's movement in the country, it was common knowledge that it was founded, funded, and coordinated by the SLFP whose politburo was predominantly middle-class and male. As members of autonomous women's groups, many feminists felt very uncomfortable about working with a political party that not only did not espouse a feminist ideology but was perceived to be using the Mothers' Front for its own political ends. As one feminist argued, "compared with the autonomous motherist movements in Latin America, particularly the Madres in Argentina, the Front's members have no agency and are trapped in the fists of the SLFP." Feminists who belonged to the women's sections of left-wing parties hotly disputed this. They pointed out that such a facile equation between non-membership in an autonomous group and non-agency was unfair, particularly since the Mothers' Front had an extremely narrow agenda focused exclusively on the women's demands and their needs.

Yet other feminists pointed out that it was an undeniable fact that this narrow agenda fitted in very well with the larger project of the SLFP to topple the government and regain power. And indeed, a close scrutiny of the day-to-day running of the Front, as well as the organization of their rallies and conventions, made it very clear that the Front's members were rarely in control. It was common knowledge, they argued, that both at an everyday level and in organizing rallies and rituals, the financial backing and infrastructural support of the SLFP was crucial. The members of the Mothers' Front elected their own office-bearers and ran their regional offices relatively autonomously, but they remained under the control of their SLFP members of parliament, who provided much of their funding and office space. The SLFP coordinators of the Front set the agenda for rallies planned in Colombo, handled the advertising, sent out invitations, and hired buses to transport women from various regions of the country. Mangala Samaraweera, a member of parliament who had been a professional dress designer before he embarked on a political career, also designed the Mothers' Front logo, the Sinhala letter "M" surroounding a woman cradling a baby. He also openly acknowledged that he was instrumental in choosing the Front's color – yellow – as it was not identified with any Sri Lankan political party and because it echoed the yellow ribbons that symbolized hopes for the return of the US hostages held in Iran in the 1970s. His office drafted petitions for the Front – demanding the appointment of an independent commission to inquire into "disappearances," calling for the state to issue death certificates and to compensate the families of the "disappeared" – and organized the lobbying of key government departments to bring these demands into effect.

In the end, none of the autonomous feminist groups came out publicly in support of the Mothers' Front, though this did not preclude their members from attending its public rallies as individuals, and offering their advice to the two male founders of the group. Many feminist groups also extended the mandates of their organizations by setting up self-employment schemes and trauma centers for counseling the families of the "disappeared" in the southern, central, and eastern parts of the island.

## CONCLUSION

In this last section, I have tried to delineate the production of a particular "feminist politics" in Sri Lanka, provoked by the oppositional practices and rhetoric of the Mothers' Front which, as I have argued above, was practicing a specific form of "politics" that sought to question the very notion of the "political." Forms of political protest such as this, that are at once maternalized, racialized, and classed, present feminists with a conundrum, especially in a politico-historical context where alternative forms of critique are vilified and delegitimized. In 1992, Butler made a plea, timely then, for releasing the term feminism, "into a future of multiple significations, to emancipate it from the maternal or racialist ontologies to which it has been restricted, and to give it play as a site where unanticipated meanings might come to bear" (1992:16). Only then, she argues, will something like agency come into play. It worries me that in Sri Lanka an increasing number of women's organizations are resorting to "motherhood" as a space of protest following the relative success of the Mothers' Front in winning the sympathy of the public, gendering discourses of human rights, and placing a government on the defensive. Even the Women's Action Committee, a feminist coalition made up of representatives from autonomous feminist groups as well as women's sections of left-parties, has now regrouped as the Mothers and Daughters of Lanka. This is a particularly troubling trend.

This seemingly expedient move to appropriate the mother as a stable subject for feminist politics (i.e., one that cannot be easily adjusted or altered) evokes Butler's caution (1992:4) that "To claim that politics requires a stable subject is to claim that there can be no *political* opposition to that claim. Indeed, that claim implies that a critique of the subject cannot be a politically informed critique but, rather, an act which puts into jeopardy politics as such." Thus, it is imperative that feminists rethink the way debates about motherist movements are formulated. We need to interrogate how the very mobilization of "motherhood" as a space of protest is enabled within our societies while alternative forms of protest are being increasingly disabled.

As an anthropologist, my research into the Mothers' Front was framed by and engaged feminist politics. This engagement led me to inquire into the complex and contradictory aspects of a movement such as the Mothers' Front. Further, it led me to appreciate the importance of exploring not only its conditions of possibility but also its implications for feminist praxis in Sri Lanka and South Asia generally. I have thus produced a contingent reading of the political efficacy of the Mothers' Front in an attempt to circumvent unproductive binary readings of such movements as either essentializing or empowering, victimized or agentive. Yet the question still remains whether, despite feminist anthropology's attempt to select research questions and write from within the domain of "feminist politics," it is not still caught on the cusp of an uneasy relationship between anthropology and feminism: disciplines brought to a crisis by politics.

## REFERENCES

Butler, Judith (1992) Contingent Foundations: Feminism and the Question of Postmodernism. In *Feminists Theorize the Political*, ed. Judith Butler and Joan W. Scott, pp. 3–21. New York and London: Routledge.

Collier, Jane, and Sylvia Yanagisako (1989) Theory in Anthropology Since Feminist Practice. *Critique of Anthropology* 9:27–37.

Comaroff, Jean (1985) *Body of Power, Spirit of Resistance*. Chicago: University of Chicago Press.

de Alwis, Malathi (1997) Motherhood as a Space of Protest: Women's Political Participation in Contemporary Sri Lanka. In *Appropriating Gender: Women's Activism and the Politicization of Religion in South Asia*, ed. Amrita Basu and Patricia Jeffrey, pp. 185–201. London: Routledge.

de Alwis, Malathi (1998) Maternalist Politics in Sri Lanka: A Historical Anthropology of its Conditions of Possibility. Ph.D. dissertation, University of Chicago.

de Alwis, Malathi (2000) The "Language of the Organs": The Political Purchase of Tears in Sri Lanka. *In Haunting Violations: Feminist Criticisms and the Crisis of the* "Real," ed. Wendy Hesford and Wendy Kozol, pp. 195–216. Champagne: University of Illinois Press.

di Leonardo, Micaela (1991) Introduction: Gender, Culture and Political Economy: Feminist Anthropology in Historical Perspective. In *Gender at the Crossroads of Knowledge: Feminist Anthropology in the Postmodern Era*, ed. Micaela di Leonardo, pp. 1–50. Berkeley: University of California Press.

Jeganathan, Pradeep (2001) Cohn and Anthropological History. Paper presented at the Annual Meeting of the American Anthropological Association, Washington, DC, November 18.

Laclau, Ernesto, and Chantal Mouffe (1985) *Hegemony and Socialist Strategy: Towards a Radical Democratic Politics.* London: Verso.

McClure, Kirstie (1992) The Issue of Foundations: Scientized Politics, Politicized Science, and Feminist Critical Practice. In *Feminists Theorize the Political*, ed. Judith Butler and Joan W. Scott, pp. 341–368. New York: Routledge.

Ortner, Sherry (1984) Theory in Anthropology Since the Sixties. *Comparative Studies in Society and History* 26:126–166.

Reiter, Rayna (1975) Introduction. In *Toward an Anthropology of Women*, ed. Rayna Reiter, pp. 11–19. New York: Monthly Review Press.

Rosaldo, Michele, and Louise Lamphere (1974) Introduction. In *Woman, Culture, and Society*, ed. M. Rosaldo and L. Lamphere, pp. 1–15. Stanford, CA: Stanford University Press.

Scott, David (1994) *Formations of Ritual: Colonial and Anthropological Discourses on the Sinhala Yaktovil.* Minneapolis: University of Minnesota Press.

Strathern, Marilyn (1987) An Awkward Relationship: The Case of Feminism and Anthropology. *Signs* 12:276–292.

Uyangoda, Jayadeva (1992) Tears and Curses and Voodoo in Politics. *Pravada* 1:4–6.

Visweswaran, Kamala (1997) Histories of Feminist Ethnography. *Annual Review of Anthropology* 26:591–621.

## SUGGESTED FURTHER READING

Atkinson, Jane (1982) Anthropology: Review Essay. *Signs* 8:236–258.

Beauvoir, Simone de (1949) *The Second Sex: The Manifesto of the Liberated Woman*, trans. E. M. Parshley. New York: Vintage.

Gordon, Deborah (1993) The Unhappy Relationship of Feminism and Post-Modernism in Anthropology. *Anthropology Quarterly* 66:109–117.

John, Mary (1996) *Discrepant Dislocations.* Berkeley: University of California Press.

Mitchell, Juliet (1974) *Psychoanalysis and Feminism.* New York: Vintage.

Moore, Henrietta (1988) *Feminism and Anthropology.* Minneapolis: University of Minnesota Press.

Rapp, Rayna (1977) The Search for Origins: Unravelling the Threads of Gender Hierarchy. *Critique of Anthropology* 9–10:5–24.

Rapp, Rayna (1979) Anthropology: Review Essay. *Signs* 4:497–513.

Rosaldo, Michele (1980) The Use and Abuse of Anthropology: Reflections on Feminism and Cross-Cultural Understanding. *Signs* 5:389–417.

Schirmer, Jennifer G. (1993) The Seeking of Truth and the Gendering of Consciousness: The CoMadres of El Salvador and the CONAVIGUA Widows of Guatamela. *In VIVA: Women and Popular Protest in Latin America*, ed. Sarah Radcliffe and Sallie Westwood, pp. 30–64. London: Routledge.

# Gender, Race, and Class

## CHAPTER 9

*Micaela di Leonardo*

> When land is gone and money spent
> Then learning is most excellent.
>                         (Medieval lyric)

Over the past quarter-century, scholarship on gender, race, and class politics has matured in an extraordinary way – feminist scholarship, in particular, has literally come into existence as a result of the second wave of global feminism. But the same period has also witnessed the triumphant spread of capitalism concurrent with the fall of the Soviet sphere and China's capitalist turn. Whatever we may think of the economic problems and lack of civil liberties in the former communist states, it is now the case that, globally, we no longer have any ongoing state alternatives to the capitalist mode of production, and that we face a worldwide disappearance of middle-class sectors as extreme wealth and poverty increase rapidly.

Neoliberal ideology, which rationalizes trade "liberalization" and thus the decline of poorer states' abilities to plan their economies, the widespread commodification and selling off of formerly public resources, as well as stigmatizing all welfare-state amelioration of capitalist exploitation, has gained enormous purchase worldwide through both its celebration of individualized consumption and its novel joining of neoclassical economic theory with an identity-politics reading of civil liberties. Thus politicians, North and South, can claim to stand for the rights of women, racial and religious minorities, even homosexuals, while blandly observing the growing immiseration which disproportionately affects most of those populations. Neoliberalism, we might say, paraphrasing Anatole France, in its majestic equality, forbids both rich and poor women, non-whites, non-heterosexuals, and non-citizens from sleeping under bridges. And it recommends that, while they are at it, they decorate themselves and their living spaces with the latest accoutrements.

At the same time, the technologies of globalizing capitalism have spurred the internationalization of anti-capitalist protest, of truly globalized labor, feminist, anti-racist, queer, environmental, and human rights organizations. Unfortunately, as the postmodernists have never quite learned – while power may be multi-sited, the United States is still the center of capitalist imperialism, and still has the power, if not to prevent such organizing, certainly, in conjunction with the actions of myriad capitalists, to render it relatively ineffective.

As these shifts have taken place over the decades, feminist scholarship has shifted as well in the ways in which it construed the gender/politics arena. The first, path-breaking work both established female political sentience and agency worldwide, and asserted that the unpolitical, "private" domestic domain of Parsonian theorizing and general scholarly neglect was, on the contrary, as much a hotbed of power politics strategizing as the traditionally considered public arena. In Sylvia Yanagisako's for-mulation (1979), there was a need to provide thicker descriptions of domestic domains worldwide, acknowledging their political centrality. The "sentience and agency" impulse led to the rediscovery of female political actors, as in American historian Gerda Lerner's work (1998) on the antebellum Grimke sisters of South Carolina, who moved to Philadelphia to work for abolition, and then joined the fight for suffrage in the face of their Quaker brethren's discrimination against them as women. Or, outside the West, scholars devoted new attention to, for example, the early twentieth-century Egyptian women's movement activist Huda Shawari, who theatrically threw her veil into the sea, and to her contemporaries throughout the Middle East, Africa, Asia, and Latin America (Jayawardena 1986).

The "rethinking public and private" impulse inspired an entire domestic domain literature and a rewriting of earlier Marxist work on the Woman Question. Theorists reconceptualized "reproduction" to include all the labor of bringing the next adult generation into existence, and attempted to account for the varying reproductive roles of women – and even of men – in varying social locations, particularly those of race and class. Using both historical and contemporary materials, looking at what were then labeled the first, second, and third worlds, feminist scholars considered the political implications of women's varying intersections with this larger vision of economic functioning. (One key text of this period was the anthology *Of Marriage and the Market*; see Young, Wolkowitz, and McCullagh 1981). To paraphrase the language of Heidi Hartmann's notorious article of the period, "The Unhappy Marriage of Marxism and Feminism," at least in the hands of these new feminist analysts, was reconciled into amity and new productivity.

A significant element of this retheorizing, along with the renascent Marxism of the period, was social constructionism. Second-wave feminists coined the opposition between sex, or biological differences, and gender, or all differences between human males and females, based on enculturation. (In so doing, ironically, they appropriated the 1930s writings of Margaret Mead and Ruth Benedict to give a cross-cultural imprimatur to Simone de Beauvoir's postwar dictum that one is not born but becomes a woman. While Benedict died at the end of World War II, Mead lived on into the Carter years, and was explicitly a Freudian anti-feminist from the 1940s until the last few years of her life.) Social construction has been extraordinarily productive both theoretically and pragmatically, and is if possible even more of a key element in the present, given the rebirth of sociobiology and its takeover of United States popular culture. Acknowledging the mutability of human categoriza-tions, which we could also derive from Marx's analysis of class under capitalist development, is an essential stage-setting for progressive intellectual and political projects dealing with class, race, gender, and sexual orientation in this era of conservative triumph.

And yet constructionism poses a political problem in two ways. First, a wide variety of political actors, globally, have found essentialist arguments congenial in attempting to effect change. Whether they are pan-Mayan activists, gay rights workers, feminist environmentalists, or Native American or Australian Aboriginal land-claims disputants, the notion of the eternal, unchanging subject whose traditions have the imprimatur of history can be extremely compelling, especially if, as in the cases of Native Americans and Australians, states themselves assert that only such subjects can bear rights. And of course, as Hobsbawm and Ranger noted in their seminal anthology *The Invention of Tradition* (1983), states and elites are among the key historical inventors of traditions.

Second, the 1980s rise of poststructuralism and postmodernism, while offering salutary insights in discursive analysis, also tended to create a false antinomy between culture and economy – even, in some scholars' work, to declare political economy itself simply another fictional representation and thus not worthy of study. And this set of claims became part of the vitiation of progressive politics in the West from the Reagan era forward. Joan Scott's widely hailed piece, "Gender, A Useful Category of Analysis" (1988), for example, adjures historians to study gender as historical discourse – as political semiotics – entirely eliding any concern for actual male and female historical subjects and the shifting political economies in which they lived and live. More recently, philosophers Nancy Fraser (1997) and Judith Butler (1997) engaged in a very high-profile debate over the relative merits of "recognition vs. redistribution," as if we could possibly divorce, for example, the implementation of civil-rights laws in the United States from their economic effects – in this case, the growth of the Afro-American middle class.

These new postmodern antinomies have tended to fuse with earlier scholarly tendencies to locate specific kinds of stratification-based politics in particular social spaces: class, of course, in workplaces, gender in households, and race or ethnicity and immigrant statuses in neighborhoods. (And the "hybrid" identities so celebrated in postmodern writings seem to be located, appropriately, in no particular social space.) Some second-wave scholars have helped to disrupt these spatial givens through considering, for example, the gender politics in proletarian workplaces, in neighborhood or village organizing, in feminist and anti-feminist organizations in a wide variety of locations around the globe. As well, research on sexuality and reproduction from the 1980s forward has opened up our understandings of the myriad ways in which mutually imbricated constructions of gender, sexuality, and race are part of all nationalist, colonialist, capitalist, and anti-capitalist projects.

More recent work has achieved further complexity and breadth through engaging in sophisticated discursive analysis while retaining an historical political-economic vision, with a variety of topical and methodological entrées. Susan Gal and Gail Kligman's *The Politics of Gender After Socialism* (2000), for example, engages simultaneously with shifting labor and reproductive processes, with the complex gendering of official discourses, and with varying popular framings of "proper" gender in the former Soviet sphere. Roger Lancaster's *The Trouble with Nature* (2003) considers the renaissance of anti-empirical and misogynist sociobiology in contemporary American popular culture in the multiple contexts of post-Fordist neoliberal economics, partial feminist and queer revolutions, and transmogrified family forms. Gina Pérez's *The Near Northwest Side Story* (in press) simultaneously narrates postwar circular labor migration between Puerto Rico and Chicago, the specifically raced and gendered economic and familial effects, and the heavily freighted and shifting places of *la isla* and the mainland in her female subjects' fertile imaginaries. And Jane Collins' *Threads* (2003) analyzes material shifts in the global garment industry and the changing gendered discourses of work and community among firm managers, female workers, and union activists in the United States and Mexico.

In what follows, I offer my own efforts to limn shifting gender, class, and race politics in one northern location – the United States – through the fulcrum of what Marx labeled the "historical and moral element" that must always be considered in gauging class formation and capitalist development: the gendered construction, across class and race, of the workings of the "proper home." Like the scholars mentioned above, I engage with the political semiotics of gender within the full historical political-economic contexts of its shifts over time. Thus we can and should consider "the political" both in terms of our older understandings of politics and political organizations and in the newer sense of cultural politics – but without succumbing to the etiolated idealism of postmodernism without political economy.

## HOME IN NEW HAVEN, CONNECTICUT

Let me begin with some urban ethnographic snapshots. First, from the summer of 2000, the tag end of the Clinton years: I am in New Haven, Connecticut, in The Hill, one of the three named ghettos of the town, about four blocks from my former home. My black male companion and I park outside the nondescript brick building with the single neon sign, Cavallaro's. I open the door onto a dark barroom. Black faces at the full bar turn towards me, then back to their conversations. Rhythm and blues pumps from the jukebox at the back of the room. My companion and I find spaces at the bar and order drinks. But the bartender is an elderly white woman, in a dress and matching pearl necklace and earrings, who seems to be having trouble understanding "Stolichnaya." On a hunch, I address her formally, "Signora, è Italiana, lei?"

Italian benedictions rain down on me as the signora, overjoyed to find a *paesana*, calls loudly for her husband and son to come meet me. The drinks are free, the great beauties of our mother country, my appearance, and my competence *nella lingua bella* extolled. The husband tells me at length about his recent trip back to the Abruzzi, checking every paragraph or so, "Ha capito, signorina?" Bar life goes on around us as the excitement fades. A hardbitten woman in a baseball cap, in response to TV news of an international Catholic gathering, shouts, "I want to go the fuck to Rome." The recent gospel convocation comes up, to much criticism of the arrangements: "This is Gospel Fest, you don't rope off shit. It's supposed to be free." Then the signora takes off her apron, totters around from behind the bar, bids me a flowery Italian adieu, and announces to the room, "Io vado adesso." Every barstool habitué turns around to call in chorus, "Goodnight, Mom." Baseball cap says minatorily to Giuseppe, the son, now behind the bar, "She's been on her feet all night!"

On a later evening, I wander in and suddenly realize there are only (almost all black) women customers and a female DJ. The place is hopping, and it is clearly Lesbian Night. I engage the patrons in conversation, and a young black firefighter throws her arms around Giuseppe, declaring "Joe and I went to school together, didn't we, Joe? I been comin here 13 years!"

Then: moving back to 1989 – deep in the Reagan–Bush Senior recession – and I am still living in, not just visiting, New Haven. I have developed a friendly relationship with the new black couple next door in my working-class neighborhood a couple of miles away from the Yale University campus, and go over one evening to interview them. Patty Hendry had said upon meeting me, "I'm not knockin my kind you know, but I never lived with a lot of black people around." I walk into an apartment much like mine next door in that it was a floor-through flat that had been created from a 1920s vintage multi-family house. But Patti's apartment, definitely unlike mine, is a miracle of white, cream, oatmeal, and glass surfaces – and she has a toddler son. She accepts my compliments as only her due, and fusses over providing refreshments. Much happened during that interview, but here I want to note two key points. The first is that Patti repeatedly noticed tiny imperfections in her domestic environment – her little son leaving a handprint on the glass tabletop, a napkin falling to the impeccable white rug – and sharply directed her husband to remedy them. The second is that he and Patti, engaging with my life-history questions, got caught up in a fierce disagreement with one another over whether or not poor black people were to blame for their poverty... Patti was furious about crime and drugs in the neighborhood, and said, "And then you have to fault the parents," while her husband focused on the economy: "I'm just saying, there's some kids that don't know no way out... people doing what they have to do to survive... I'm saying there's no jobs out there right now."

In the summer of 2000, having kept in touch, I catch up with Patti again. She has moved off my old block, due west, into a neighborhood that had been all-white in the 1980s. She is still renting, but now an entire house. This environment is even more impressive than her old apartment, and at the end of our interview, Patti gives me a tour of both floors of the house, pausing to explain how she sponge-painted the bathroom and stenciled a bedroom wall, showing off the vintage furniture and crystal and linen she has collected by haunting yard sales. While all this is going on, her two children wander in and are sharply told what they are allowed to eat in the kitchen and that they cannot go out to the front yard to play. Some little children playing outside come up to the screen door, trying to find out who I am. Patti teases them, but complains to me later that they are poorly trained. "You know, you don't talk to adults that way."

Through the years I have known her, Patti repeatedly lays out for me her sense of the city and its suburban surround, which areas are "nice" and which are "drug city," where she is willing to go and where not. She explicitly warns me against the block that Cavallaro's sits on, and also tells me that she won't walk on the small business block a few streets away from her home, where I regularly attend a storefront black working-class aerobics center in an excess of ethnographic zeal.

In the same more recent period, I also visit with two white families living in Patti's new neighborhood. Both are professional-class heterosexual couples with children, both heavily involved in the renaissance of a local Orthodox Jewish congregation, both with progressive politics. And their home environments are similar as well. Just like Patti and her family in the 1980s, both families rent flats in 1920s multi-family houses. But unlike Patti, their apartments are dingy with old paint, crowded with mismatched, beat-up furniture, children's toys and clothes flung all over, no effort at decoration apparent. In each home, the children wander freely and engage the guest, taking over the conversation with their parents' happy approval. And in both homes, the women talk about New Haven in expansive terms. One boasted to me of her broad knowledge, despite her recent residence in the city, of different black and Latino neighborhoods as a result of exploring them in search of the best thrift shops, in her beat-up station wagon with the kids in the back.

Finally, there is the New Haven native, a progressive black lawyer in her late fifties with a Black Panther past, who befriended me in the aerobics class. For this woman, a wide-ranging familiarity with all areas of the city, specific long-term relationships with black neighborhood shopkeepers, and consumption of local minority journalism are all points of personal pride. She lives with her husband, a retired blue-collar worker, and elderly mother in a nice two-story Victorian house furnished in high style, with orientalist touches, in a neighborhood known since the 1980s as the residential center of the city's black middle class – just a few blocks from my old block, in the opposite direction from Cavallaro's. Her sense of the city, as I have noted, is expansive, and she tends to frame local crime issues in terms of improving communication and saving poor children's lives, rather than in terms of avoidance of certain areas or increased home or neighborhood security. One night she took me to the Black Elk's Lodge, located in the ghetto right next to her neighborhood, to listen to live jazz, and afterwards she drove around the area to show me, with great pride, newly constructed townhouses where falling-down public housing had been. "Where would we go?" she asked me rhetorically, talking about the city and its problems, and announced, "New Haven is home."

Home is an extraordinarily resonant term in American life – a point now highlighted further by George Bush's post-September 11 appointment of a "Homeland Defense" office and czar. My own engagement with the gender, class, and race politics of home arose through the accident of setting up my own residence. In 1986, while teaching at Yale University, I rented an apartment in a working-class neighborhood in New Haven and thereby backed into doing fieldwork in the poor, deindustrialized, and richly engaging city. The "home" theme of this piece is abstracted from the array of issues in my study as a whole, which is an historical ethnography of race, class, gender, and representation in the city from the optic of a shifting working-class neighborhood.

The late Pierre Bourdieu (1977, 1984) wrote compellingly about homes and habitus among both village Algerians and the French working and middle classes – about how the very physical organization of housing space enacts a population's apprehensions of social order, and about the ways in which class habitus is reflected in home organization and décor. Historians and social scientists have also contributed greatly to our understanding of shifting local apprehensions of domesticity in the contexts of global colonial, capitalist, and postcolonial transitions. But as we will see, Bourdieu's and other scholars' insights have not really been adequately translated to the contemporary American scene. God is in the details, and we need to engage with details of home in American history. The people with whom I worked in New Haven, like all of us, have inherited this array of representations, and made and make selective use of them in explaining their lives to themselves and others. So we should be clear at the outset about what they are. For that reason, rather than entering immediately into the lives and apprehensions of Patti Hendry and her sister New Haveners, I will go the long way around, through an historical and political-economic review of "home" in the US.

"Home" underscored the nineteenth-century sense of American differences from Europe – in the Jamesian sense that "we" somehow had nice homes without the decadent baggage of the European class system. It explains the deep strength of the notion of the family farm, and lies behind pioneer, manifest destiny mythology – that Americans could and should domesticate what we defined as uninhabited wilderness. And, of course, along with all of Europe and indeed its colonies, American notions of home became deeply gendered as female over the course of the long nineteenth century with the rise of an ideology of separate spheres. Many scholars have articulated for us the development of the paired notions of the outer, urban, business world as both dirty and corrupting and inherently male, and the inner, tranquil, spiritual, "non-economic" domestic realm as entirely female. So we have inherited a tendency to think about home as a female realm somehow outside the world of economy and labor.

In the post-World War II environment of rapid economic expansion, home took on added symbolic baggage. Widespread suburbanization, widely available household technology like improved vacuum cleaners and automatic washing machines, and postwar anti-working woman ideology (American women stayed in the labor force in this era but were newly invisible after their wartime apotheosis as Rosie the Riveter) combined in an image of the safe suburban home presided over by the contented housewife aided by labor-saving devices. This construction became official in the notorious Cold War "kitchen debates" in which Richard Nixon boasted to Khrushchev about the splendor of American women's household lives.

Betty Friedan's *The Feminine Mystique*, first published in 1963, predated the actual second wave of the feminist movement, but she helped put the ball – the critique of the "housewife in splendor" model – in play. 1970s feminists exploded the notion of the economy-less domestic realm, succeeded in shifting popular consciousness to an apprehension of housework and childcare as real labor, and brought women's labor-force participation, which was in any event already rising rapidly, into sharp visibility. "Home" began to be represented as a site of gender struggle as well as a haven from a heartless world.

This early second-wave period, however, was also the era of civil rights and black power, anti-Vietnam War mobilizations, and the general youth revolution symbolized by the silly but notorious trinity of "sex, drugs, and rock n roll." Popular American notions of home shifted to include – at least in some precincts – unmarried couples, hippie, communal, or movement households. And due to civil-rights organizing, Americans very broadly came to understand themselves as a nation of segregated housing. They varied enormously, though, in their understanding of what should be done about that state of affairs.

Most discussion of housing segregation focused on urban neighborhoods, and here yet another element of the era enters, one I in fact cut my scholarly teeth on back in the 1970s. The very term white ethnicity – meaning European Americans – hails from the 1970s, from what came to be called the "white ethnic renaissance," which had a short flurry of media attention and then was crowded off the public stage by other concerns. White ethnics are important for our discussion, though, both because New Haven historically was a largely white and black city – the growing Latino population is of more recent vintage – and because the nationwide construction of "white ethnics" in that era was both heavily gendered and tied into shifting notions of proper and improper homes.

"White ethnics" discovered themselves and were discovered by others in early 1970s American cities in the context of complex cultural and political-economic shifts: continuing economic expansion, the ongoing war in Vietnam, and a linked set of social movements directly related to these two key political-economic realities – civil rights and black power, the anti-war movement, the student and youth movement, and the revived feminist movement. These multiple movements for reform and liberation challenged federal, state, and institutional structures – such as those of colleges and universities – and individuals who perceived themselves to be threatened by particular demands for social change. The Nixon administration (1969–74), in particular, sought to exploit and enhance these social divisions through the use of the polarizing discourse of the silent majority – as opposed to the protesting anti-administration "minority." Between administration rhetoric and media response, an image grew of this stipulated entity: members of the silent majority were white – implicitly white ethnic – largely male, blue-collar workers. They were held to be "patriotic" and to live in "traditional" families – ones in which males ruled, women did not work outside the home for pay, and parents controlled their children.

This media image, of course, did not reflect an aggregate social reality. This was the era, after all, in which married working-class women were entering the labor force at record rates, and in which their additions to family income maintained working-class living standards in the face of declining real incomes. And sexual adventurism and drug use in the late 1960s and early 1970s were the property of working-class no less than middle-class youth. Nevertheless, as a media construct, as a symbol of the hemorrhaging of Democratic voters to the Republican Party, the conservative, white ethnic, blue-collar worker – Archie Bunker – gained salience in this period. This salience was much enhanced by the shifting populations and power relations in American cities.

In the 1960s, poor black Americans became newly visible, and newly defined as a social problem in northern cities. The two great waves of black migration from the South, during the First and Second World Wars, had each resulted in cohorts of permanent northern black urban residents. These men and women had come north (often through employer recruitment) both to take advantage of lucrative war jobs and to flee Jim Crow and the effects of the mechanization of southern agriculture. They had then often been laid off, and largely had become part of a permanent army of reserve labor. Urban renewal projects in the 1950s and 1960s – an employment boondoggle for white ethnic blue-collar workers – destroyed countless urban black neighborhoods, replaced them with office blocks and sports complexes, and shifted and concentrated the poor black population in areas dominated by inhospitable, poorly built, and badly maintained government housing projects; 90 percent of the housing destroyed by urban renewal was never replaced and two-thirds of those displaced were black or Puerto Rican. The Federal Housing Authority deliberately fostered segregated white housing and refused loans to blacks until the passage of the Fair Housing Act in 1968. Big-city governments refused to shift budgetary resources to basic services for these impoverished areas.

Neighborhood deterioration, increased crime, and urban uprisings – combined with intensive political organizing – stimulated the establishment of highly visible federal Great Society programs. At the same time, a small cohort of socially mobile blacks, emboldened by the civil-rights movement, attempted to buy homes in formerly white urban and suburban neighborhoods. The resulting "white flight" greatly enriched the real-estate speculators who fanned its flames and exacerbated inner-city white racism. Black (and Latino) struggles for higher quality public education, neighborhood services, and civil service and union jobs led to increased friction between white, often white ethnic, and minority citizens in northern urban environments. The first scattered fringe of desuburbanizing better-off whites entered into this polarized and often dangerous environment, benefiting, of course, from its resulting low real-estate values.

Thus the white ethnic community construct arose from an extraordinarily complex historical ground, and this complexity was reflected in its multiple expressions and political uses. Notions of the strength and richness of white ethnic cultures and their repression by WASPS mimicked black cultural nationalist (and white scholars') celebrations of black culture's endurance despite white domination.

Both popular journalistic accounts and grass-roots white ethnic discourse focused on the strength and unity of white ethnic families as opposed to those of black Americans – whose popular image had been shaped in the early 1960s as a "tangle of pathology" by the Moynihan Report. In my own first study, many Italian-Americans' racist expressions against blacks focused on inferior black family behavior as both explaining and justifying widespread black poverty. Then followed the argument that, as the undeserving poor, blacks were not entitled to the largesse of Great Society programs and the approval of elite sponsors, which should instead flow to "deserving" white ethnics.

This relative entitlement frame is attached, as I have argued, to a "report card mentality," in which shifting American class divisions are seen as caused by proper and improper ethnic or racial family and economic behavior rather than by the differential incorporation of immigrant and resident populations in American capitalism's evolving class structure. Scholarship, journalism, and grass-roots expressions celebrated white ethnics for their family loyalties and neighborhood ties. In fact, advertising in this period began to exploit "cute" white ethnic imagery: the pizza-baking grandmother, the extended family at the laden dinner-table – in order to invest frozen and canned foods with the cachet of the *Gemeinschaft* – of community in the deepest sense, of knowing how to live in and reproduce proper homes.

This *Gemeinschaft*, this community, was delineated as an urban phenomenon existing alongside and in opposition to urban black populations. In fact, there was the distinct flavor of a "three bears" analogy in much 1970s and 1980s rhetoric on white ethnicity. (And this Eastern Seaboard and industrial Midwest-based trinity neatly wrote non-black Latinos, Asians, and others right off the American stage.) While WASPs were "too cold" – bloodless, modern, and unencumbered – and blacks "too hot" – wild, primitive, and overburdened – white ethnics were "just right." They could and did claim to represent the golden historical mean between the overwhelming ancientness and primitiveness of *Gemeinschaft* and the etiolated modernity of *Gesellschaft*. For a hot minute in the 1970s, American white ethnics commandeered the baby bear's chair.

Central to the new construction of white ethnic community was the Madonna-like (in the older sense) image of the white ethnic woman. Early 1970s popular writers extolled her devotion to home and family, and many of the more conservative Italian-Americans in my late 1970s study echoed this fusion of ethnic chauvinism and anti-feminism. Part of the appeal of this construction was the notion that white ethnic mothers, unlike "selfish" WASP and "lazy" black mothers, could control their children and thus were exempt from blame for the youth protests then current. But in fact, white ethnic women were no less subject to the pressures and opportunities of the shifting American political economy of the 1970s, and many more of the Italian-American women with whom I worked actively altered or rejected the popular image of the self-sacrificing, kitchen-bound ethnic mother. In an era of rising feminist activism, the sudden celebration of a group of women socially labeled as backward, stolid, and possessive wives and mothers functioned very clearly as anti-feminist rhetoric – particularly against women's participation in the workforce. As well, in focusing on women's "duties" to husband and children, it worked against prevalent civil-rights imagery of heroic black movement women whose duties lay in the public sphere. Many feminist scholars celebrated the strength and endurance of "traditional" ethnic women, and used, for example, narratives of past union and strike activities, or consumer protests, in order to suggest a vision of innately progressive, rebellious, ethnic womanhood. This attempt, however, was overwhelmed by dominant conservative media images, images that live on in say, Olive Garden commercials, while their original political usage has withered.

White ethnic community, since the late 1970s, is no longer a hot topic for academic papers and popular cultural accounts. Festivals and meetings of ethnic historical associations and social groups do not receive the public attention they once did. During the Reagan era (1981–88), we saw instead a return in public culture to the *Great Gatsby* romance – the notion that the really proper American homes were those of wealthy WASPs. *Good Housekeeping* began its "New Traditionalist" advertising campaign featuring obviously affluent, non-working, blond women and their well-groomed children on the spacious grounds of their suburban or country estates: "She knows what she values – home and family." Wealthy whites took back the baby bear's chair with a vengeance, and a new romantic halo was constructed over the image – embodied by First Lady Nancy Reagan – of the elegant, dignified, adorned, and (publicly at least) devoted wife and mother, the curator of the proper WASP bourgeois home and children. Through the Bush and Clinton and now Bush Junior administrations, these images have waxed and waned and ultimately have retreated to the symbolic backstage of American life, but, together with notions of white ethnic community, remain "on hold" for activation in particular social settings for particular ends. The front stage was soon populated by a new construct, symbolically heavily freighted, involving race, class, gender, and notions of home – that of the "minority underclass." Let me lay out its evolution.

The mid-1970s energy crisis, so profitable to the big oil companies, was the first of a series of shocks to the American economy that helped to usher in the new public ideology that we had entered an "era of limits." During the Carter Administration

(1977–80), rapidly escalating inflation, particularly in the rising real-estate market, set the symbolic stage for the dismantling of Great Society programs, newly seen as "too expensive." Welfare cutbacks under Carter became a wholesale shrinkage of the federal social welfare budget under Reagan, and then the abandonment of Aid to Families with Dependent Children altogether under Clinton. The concomitant recession drove unemployment figures into double digits. Numbers of individuals and families made homeless by unemployment, real-estate speculation, and the federal abandonment of low-cost housing programs grew rapidly.

With the economic recovery of the middle and late 1980s, unemployment shrank to early 1970s levels, then rose again with the Bush recession, fell with the Clinton economic renaissance, and are now rising again in the post 9/11 recession. Unemployment always shrinks less for minority Americans, though (thus the Afro-American aphorism, "When America catches a cold, blacks get pneumonia"), and of those successively reemployed, many worked part-time or at jobs with lower status and pay. As a combination of these shifts and regressive tax legislation, over the Reagan and Bush years the numbers of both the very poor and the very rich rose; the shifts of the Clinton years did not alter those tendencies, and they have become even more exacerbated during the second Bush administration. The United States now has the highest levels of poverty and the smallest middle class, proportionately, in the industrialized world. Despite much local and national organizing, popular political discourse shifted significantly rightward from the 1970s into the new millennium. Civil rights, women's, gay, and labor groups were labeled "special interests." But most crucially, public discourse about the poor, particularly poor blacks and Latinos, turned once again nearly hegemonically to automatic deprecation and "blame the victim" rhetoric.

The new underclass ideology functioned specifically, as had older cultures of poverty formulation, to focus attention away from the political-economic production of poverty to the "pathological" behavior of the poor, whose characteristics were presumed (in the hard version) to cause or (in the soft version) merely to reproduce poverty. For Afro-American Harvard sociologist William Julius Wilson, for example, whose 1987 work *The Truly Disadvantaged* rationalized underclass ideology for scholars and policy-makers, advanced capitalism is assumed, and assumed to be benignant. Writing in Reagan's second term, Wilson used passive-verb political economy: blacks "get concentrated" in inner cities, jobs just happen to leave. He scorned "racism" as an explanation for any social change – interpreting it narrowly as malign dyadic encounters in which individual whites do dirt to individual blacks. To put it bluntly, Wilson effectively said, "It's nobody's fault, but poor blacks got screwed and now they're acting ugly." Wilson and other underclass ideologues adduced rising numbers of unmarried mothers, uninvolved biological fathers, welfare abuse, poverty, drugs, and crime to prove the existence of a new pathology in the black and brown poor.

Countering elements of underclass mythology, scholars noted that black adolescent child-bearing rates began falling *in the 1960s*. It was not birthrates but marriage rates that had altered. Further, most poor Americans are white; Afro-Americans were never the majority recipients of welfare, and 40 percent of welfare mothers worked for pay as well. Despite media portrayals, most welfare recipients had few not many children – the average was two – and most cycled off the dole whenever they could line up job, childcare, and health insurance. (Further, it was welfare for the often financially stable elderly – Social Security – not for poor mothers –Aid to Families with Dependent Children – that took up the bulk of the federal social-welfare budget.) Black and white pregnant women consume illegal substances that may be injurious to their fetuses at the same rates – but doctors report black women to law enforcement authorities ten times more often. The exception to the above rule is cigarettes, which of course are legal. A government study indicates that black mothers smoke much *less* than white mothers.

Federal government studies indicate that black adolescents actually consume illegal drugs at *lower* rates than whites. They have admitted that blacks now graduate from high school at close to the same rates as whites, but that "returns to education" (job remuneration and status), at all educational levels, are significantly lower for both male racial minorities and all women than for white men. Employers openly admit to interviewers that they discriminate against minorities in hiring, and federal studies indicate that minorities with the same resources and credit records as whites are denied home mortgages at twice the rate. Minorities are more frequently harassed by police, arrested for crimes when whites are not, convicted more frequently, and given heavier prison sentences. Finally, on the family values front, federal data indicate that the *higher* a man's income, the *less likely* he is to make his court-ordered child-support payments. In sum, underclass ideology, which has faded since Clinton eviscerated welfare and the go-go economy of the 1990s took off, both entirely misrepresents empirical reality, and is waiting backstage much like white ethnic community ideology, should the need arise to redemonize the minority poor.

New Haven's historical political-economic shifts fits all these national urban patterns only too well as a medium-sized deindustrialized southern New England city, with all the impedimenta of abandoned factories, recurrent municipal financial crises, and white flight with which we are so familiar in other deindustrialized towns and cities. The majority of the population is now black and Latino – during most of the twentieth century, though, New Haven had a white ethnic majority, with Italians, Irish, Slavs, and Jews of all nationalities predominating.

In the 1980s, in part because of the depredations of urban renewal that I have described for the country as a whole, but more importantly in tune with the starvation of American cities by successive Reagan and Bush administration policies, New Haven was repeatedly figured in its own local media, and in the national media, particularly in the *New York Times* and a widely read *New Yorker* series, as an emblem of urban dirt, disorder, and danger writ small, a vest-pocket New York, a site of desperate black and brown youth caught up in crack wars – and thus a nicely digestible seemingly empirical rationale for the blame-the-victim pieties of the underclass ideology hegemonic in that era. In *Exotics at Home* (1998), I describe this process from the optic of my working-class neighborhood under the onslaught of wide-scale immiseration, a neighborhood that shifted from nearly all-white to nearly all-black over the five years of my residence.

Spatially speaking, New Haven has an eighteenth-century village green that now defines downtown, with Yale buildings, federal and municipal offices, an urban renewal era mall and other shopping areas, and a medical complex radiating out in different directions from its orienting grid. What we might call the Yale Zone – and Yale is now, after decades of deindustrialization, the city's largest employer – encompasses some neighborhoods north of campus that had been mixed WASP and white ethnic and now are heavily occupied by faculty and graduate students, and some much shabbier areas east of campus, mixed business and residential, where poorer or more cosmopolitan-minded graduate students live. An Italian literature professor recently told me she rented in this latter area when she was a graduate student, calling it the Left Bank, and preferring its racial mix and proximity to black areas to the much whiter complexion of the northern neighborhoods. Since the 1980s, Yale has pushed back the Left Bank, and the ghetto it abuts, through buying up and rehabilitating property, even buying and closing off a public street. This expansion of a *cordon sanitaire*, pushing poor people and their activities away, is not unique to Yale, but is now a common practice on the part of universities and hospitals in the United States, really a part of larger growth politics and gentrifying processes.

Due west of the Left Bank, my neighborhood stretches several miles, with two of the three named city ghettos on its north and south flanks. In terms of what the technocrats call housing stock, New Haven is unlike many large cities in that there are fewer apartment houses and more large multi-family homes that, in poorer areas, have been cut up into individual apartments. The block I lived on was made up of such houses, actually in the process of final cutting-up and renting out during my five years' residence. Farther east, across a large park, was a somewhat more affluent series of neighborhoods that were, in the 1980s, very white. But unnoticed by New Haveners, during the economically expansionist 1990s, the park boundary was erased as both areas became racially integrated. Most astonishing in the last decade, and also unnoticed even by city politicians, the east–west arterial road, which had been lined by heavily Jewish-owned small businesses, including the Hadassah thrift store in which I practically lived in the latter half of the 1980s, became dominated by black ones, including innumerable hair and nail salons, various soul food and Caribbean diners, a small music store, and the storefront aerobics center I have mentioned. In 2002, for example, there was a political fuss over the sale of a small business in the Dixwell area – which is overwhelmingly black – to an Asian couple. A local black alderman, in justifying his protest, astoundingly asked in a public forum whether Jewish shopkeepers on Whalley Avenue would welcome black incomers.

In following urban lives from the mid-1980s to the present, I was highly aware of overarching political-economic shifts – the Reagan/Bush recession, the Clinton recovery – and associated local demographic, economic, and political changes. Over the 1990s, for example, unemployment fell precipitously, the crack wars dried up, and the prostitutes who had come to perambulate my neighborhood nightly at the end of the 1980s either moved indoors or turned to other means of livelihood. But the New Haveners with whom I worked were simply living out their daily lives, and often did not follow these shifts. Thus, not only earlier ethnic and racial residential and business patterns, but also particular images of urban poverty, crime, and danger that were inscribed in New Haveners' minds in the 1980s remained part of their urban imaginary into the new millennium, despite the evidence of their own daily experiences.

Now we are ready to consider the disjunctive elements of "home" in contemporary American public culture, a disconnection which living in working-class New Haven forced to my attention. That is, since the 1970s, we have seen the development of two major public arenas in which "home" is discussed, which we might label the gentry arena and the underclass arena. On the one hand, with the rising cost of real estate, the glorification of the notion of well-off WASP homes (think Ralph Lauren advertisements and Martha Stewart), and the reestablishment of shelter magazines, "home" meaning beautifully appointed living spaces for better-off whites, is a major national industry. As American newspapers' "women's pages" – in part under feminist pressure – were transmogrified into style and living sections, we read more and more each year about sponge-painted walls, great rooms, lofts, ethnic/country/European kitchens, and the installation of vintage or vintage-like bookcases, hardware, and fixtures. Well-off white couples – and sometimes gay couples or single women – pose happily in their "after" living spaces all over mass and middlebrow media.

On the other hand, newspaper front pages periodically run frightening stories, complete with stark black-and-white photos, of ghetto apartments discovered to be overrun with drugs, crime, rats and roaches, and thus from which social services have just yanked children. Front page versus style section, crime and neglect stories versus fluffy gentrifying ones, narratives of the failure of poor black mothers versus the obsessions and triumphs of well-off white ones: this is the new race- and class-divided representation of home in the US. Occasionally, particularly in black and Latino media, we see black and Latino actors, music stars, or athletes in their carefully appointed homes – and the *Village Voice* has a recurrent column in which New Yorkers across race and class are interviewed and comment on their tiny rented or owned apartments – but the very rarity of these representations underscores the underclass norm. And the extraordinary misrepresentation of these representations really comes home to us, as it were, when we reflect that that the vast bulk of the black American population is neither impoverished nor well-off but solidly working-class. In that sense, Patti Hendry and her family are black America.

It is now clear that I developed this analysis of shifts in race, gender, and representation because my New Haven fieldwork virtually rubbed my nose in it. I could not help but be struck with extraordinarily clean and well-appointed living spaces into which I was welcomed by my black and Puerto Rican neighbors, so utterly at odds with what I was reading in the *New York Times* and the *New Haven Register*. And I was thoroughly amused to go into well-off white home after New Haven home that could only be described as Martha Stewart's worst nightmare. We can now also see how Patti Hendry's seemingly anti-black statements and class concerns are defensive, an attempt to define herself and her family outside the dominant underclass characterizations, outside the racial report card, while, sadly, their empirical falsehoods seem commonsensical to her, as they do to most Americans since the 1980s. The black lawyer, on the other hand, has both long-term political and religious reasons for explicitly resisting underclass ideology. And, of course, she is aware of her class status, not to mention her appropriately older-model Mercedes, and does not fear being identified with the black poor she defines herself as in solidarity with and attempting to help.

Afro-American women have inherited not only all the ideological baggage I have just laid out but also the long historically racist white tendency to define them as inherently dirty and degraded, a tendency also extended to other racial minorities and, in the past, to white ethnics. One of the autobiographical sources of my analysis is my strong memory of my Italian-American aunts' obsession with cleanliness and gentility. Their 1950s doilies and Patti Hendry's 1990s sponge-painted walls have the same roots in American women's and racial or ethnic history. And my professional-class white New Haven friends literally could "afford," if they wished, to have disheveled homes and unruly children. There is, of course, tremendous variety in the ways in which American women of all race or ethnic identities and across classes put together interiors, but no one was going to think these Jewish families' house-holds resembled TV video footage of abuse and neglect cases, nor did those wives and mothers worry, as their grandmothers may have done, and my grandmother did, that WASPs would think them dirty, ungenteel sluts.

What can we say, then, about the larger issues of gender, class, and race, and varying home and urban imaginaries on the contemporary American scene? First, individuals in cities extend their notions of "home" outward into other venues, as we saw from the behavior and statements of the patrons at Cavallaro's in my vignette at the beginning of this chapter. But sites of urban pleasure and danger are not at all unambiguous, not widely agreed upon, as we also saw. Cavallaro's is a home away from home for large numbers of working-class New Haven black women, straight and gay – literally a site where family is recognized – but for Patti Hendry it is just a building on a dangerous, dirty street. And again, the stretch of the block with the aerobics center strikes her as low-class, but that is not the opinion of the black lawyer who enjoyed the sweat sessions and the lively company there with me. As well as pure issues of habitus, we have here questions of wildly differing notions of gentility. This latter point is underlined by other ethnographic vignettes: hilarious episodes of working-class black women at other bars skillfully swearing like proverbial fishwives and in the next breath extolling their hardwood floors and crystal ornaments at home. It is buttressed as well by the life-history narratives from the elderly black woman, now dead, who lived across the street from me, who focused away from her cramped, overstuffed apartment and tended to stress instead her friendships with long dead white neighbors, her New England ancestry, and her grown son's executive position in the banking industry.

A further important point here is that neither Patti Hendry's home nor the homes of the aerobics center patrons nor my elderly neighbor, nor the retirement-age librarian with whom I visit – the fulcrum point of black womanhood in the US, statistically speaking – are in any way represented in our contemporary public sphere. Nor, it is important to add, is the easy interracial mingling and open acceptance of homosexuality in the glorious working-class bar part of our public culture where, at best, we see liquor commercials featuring upscale but definitely heterosexual inter-racial friends.

Not only does American public culture misrepresent "home" along gender, race, and class lines, but it cuts off pleasure from danger. Harvard literary critic Marjorie Garber can comfortably write a book like the widely reviewed *Sex and Real Estate* (2000), which blithely assumes an entirely upper-middle and upper-class US in which our only analytic concern should be how the libido enters into home-buying and decorating. And it does, of course, but even for those who cannot afford to buy a house, or even a condo. At the same time, "home" is danger both in the sense of concerns about crime – one need only listen to the narrative of the Puertorriqueña who now lives just below my old New Haven apartment, and who will not walk outside without her husband present – and in the sense of the ways in which people's residences are part of the emotional violence of the evolving American class system.

Finally, all of these points illustrate the complexities of the impoverishment of American civil society in the era of neoliberal capitalism. We can see New Haveners struggling to maintain public spaces, to forge community, within the interstices of the capitalist market. And we see them struggling to invest "home" with meanings no longer expressible in the public sphere, and the particularly privatized class anxieties articulated by Afro-American working-class women in the highly marketized and misrepresentative atmosphere of the neoliberal present.

How New Haveners variously conceive home, then, is William Blake's world in a grain of sand – it reflects wider national and international historical and contemporary realities. And the class, race, and gender inflections of those realities are both occluded by and parallel the current international crisis over homelands here and in Central Asia and the Middle East, a crisis that may soon include the entire globe. Virginia Woolf is well known for having asserted that her country was the whole world. Our homes, and our understandings of them, in ways that American public culture does and does not allow us to see, are fundamentally political. They both index and manifest gender, class, race, power, and the world of nations.

## NOTE

American historical and New Haven material and citations may be found in my *Exotics at Home* (1998), and a history of feminist thought in *Exotics at Home* and in *The Gender/Sexuality Reader* I co-edited with Roger Lancaster (1997).

## REFERENCES

Bourdieu, Pierre (1977) *Outline of a Theory of Practice*, trans. Richard Nice. Cambridge: Cambridge University Press.

Bourdieu, Pierre (1984) *Distinction: A Social Critique of the Judgment of Taste*, trans. Richard Nice. Cambridge, MA: Harvard University Press.

Butler, Judith (1997) Merely Cultural. *Social Text* 15:265–277.

Collins, Jane (2003) *Threads: Gender, Labor and Power in the Global Apparel Industry.* Chicago: University of Chicago Press.

di Leonardo, Micaela (1998) *Exotics at Home: Anthropology, Others, American Modernity.* Chicago: University of Chicago Press.

Fraser, Nancy (1997) Heterosexism, Misrecognition, and Capitalism: a Response to Judith Butler. *Social Text* 15:279–289.

Friedan, Betty (1963) *The Feminine Mystique.* New York: W. W. Norton.

Gal, Susan, and Gail Kligman (2000) *The Politics of Gender After Socialism: A Comparative Historical Essay.* Princeton, NJ: Princeton University Press.

Garber, Marjorie (2000) *Sex and Real Estate: Why We Love Houses.* New York: Pantheon.

Hobsbawm, Eric, and Terence Ranger, eds. (1983) *The Invention of Tradition.* Cambridge: Cambridge University Press.

Jayawardena, Kumari (1986) *Feminism and Nationalism in the Third World.* London: Zed Books.

Lancaster, Roger (2003) *The Trouble with Nature: Sex and Science in Popular Culture*. Berkeley: University of California Press.

Lancaster, Roger, and Micaela di Leonardo, eds. (1997) *The Gender/Sexuality Reader: Culture, History, Political Economy.* New York: Routledge.

Lerner, Gerda (1998) *The Grimke Sisters from South Carolina: Pioneers for Women's Rights and Abolition*. New York: Oxford University Press.

Pérez, Gina (in press) *A Near Northwest Side Story: Puerto Rican Families and the Politics of Belonging*. Berkeley: University of California Press.

Scott, Joan (1988) *Gender and the Politics of History.* New York: Columbia University Press.

Wilson, William Julius (1987) *The Truly Disadvantaged: The Inner City, the Underclass, and Public Policy.* Chicago: University of Chicago Press.

Yanagisako, Sylvia (1979) Family and Household: The Analysis of Domestic Groups. *Annual Review of Anthropology* 8:161–205.

Young, Kate, Carol Wolkowitz, and Roslyn McCullagh, eds. (1981) *Of Marriage and the Market: Women's Subordination in International Perspective*. London: CSE Books.


## SUGGESTED FURTHER READING

Basu, Amrita, Inderpal Grewal, and Caren Kaplan, eds. (2001) Globalization and Gender. Theme issue, *Signs* 26 no. 4.

Bookman, Ann, and Sandra Morgen, eds. (1988) *Women and the Politics of Empowerment*. Philadelphia: Temple University Press.

Coontz, Stephanie (1992) *The Way We Never Were: American Families and the Nostalgia Trap*. New York: Basic Books.

Cott, Nancy F. (1987) *The Grounding of Modern Feminism*. New Haven: Yale University Press.

di Leonardo, Micaela, ed. (1991) *Gender at the Crossroads of Knowledge: Feminist Anthropology in the Postmodern Era*. Berkeley: University of California Press.

Enloe, Cynthia (1990) *Bananas, Beaches, and Bases: Making Feminist Sense of International Politics*. Berkeley: University of California Press.

Ginsburg, Faye D., and Rayna Rapp, eds. (1995) *Conceiving the New World Order: The Global Politics of Reproduction*. Berkeley: University of California Press.

Laslett, Barbara, Johanna Brenner, and Yesim Arat, eds. (1995) *Rethinking the Political: Gender, Resistance, and the State*. Chicago: University of Chicago Press.

Mohanty, Chandra T., Ann Russo, and Lourdes Torres, eds. (1991) *Third World Women and the Politics of Feminism*. Bloomington: Indiana University Press.

Ong, Aihwa (1999) *Flexible Citizenship: The Cultural Logics of Transnationality.* Durham, NC: Duke University Press.

Sassen, Saskia (1998) *Globalization and Its Discontents*. New York: New Press.

Sen, Gita, and Caren Grown (1987) *Development, Crises, and Alternative Visions: Third World Women's Perspectives*. New York: Monthly Review Press.

Yuval-Davis, Nira (1997) *Gender and Nation*. London: Sage.

# CHAPTER 10  Genetic Citizenship

## Deborah Heath, Rayna Rapp, and Karen-Sue Taussig

Since the inception of the Human Genome Project both biomedical practice and popular perceptions have been increasingly "geneticized" (Lippman 1991): a rapidly expansive array of human differences, including health differences, are coming to be understood as genetically influenced or controlled. This widely distributed shift in perspective has traveled across and knitted together complex networks of association linking activists, scientists, politicians, and corporate interests in the collective transformation of the public sphere. In this chapter we outline these incipient developments, and draw out their implications for understanding the parameters of what we refer to as "genetic citizenship."

We argue that the biotechnical reconfigurations of both genetic science and the public sphere have created a significant locus for an emergent "ethics of care" (cf. Morris 2001). We further argue that these practices challenge conventional notions of a divide between lay people and experts. With extensive new arenas of everyday life now open to both personalized eugenics and official regulation, these emergent networks have also given rise to new forms of democratic participation, blurring the boundary between state and society, and between private and public interests. This transitional technosocial terrain is constituted under the shadow of global markets in pharmaceuticals and health care, and considerable public and private interests in containing health-care expenses. It surely has the potential to call forth eugenic practices at the individual level. Yet it is at the same time a site of new forms of power, knowledge, and embodied discipline, along with novel rights and responsibilities.

## MAPPING GENETIC CITIZENSHIP

In order to situate the discussion that follows, we first offer some signposts, pointing to several overlapping modes of social analysis that help to shape our appellation "genetic citizenship." We address here selected works in social theory that provide useful tools in understanding this phenomenon. The literature we have found most helpful has been drawn from science studies, citizenship studies, feminist studies and queer theory, and the "new social movements." Within anthropology, we note the productive convergence of many of these perspectives at the intersection of medical anthropology and the anthropology of science and technology. Collectively, these bodies of scholarship alert us to the terrains of technosocial engagement where emergent forms of public discourse take shape.

The rich and varied science studies literature informs both our present analysis and the work in the anthropology of science that preceded our collaborative venture. Here we briefly draw attention to the overlap and contrasts between two branches of science studies, the first, feminist science studies (cf. Haraway 1994), the second, actor-network theory (ANT) and its variants (cf. Law 1992). Both schools of thought share the following key concepts. The first is the conviction, albeit from decidedly different perspectives, that technoscience embodies the relationship between knowledge and power. Latour (1987), in the classic actor-network theory textbook *Science in Action*, asserts that "Science is politics by other means." Feminist scholars of science studies, including feminist actor-network theorists, have paid close attention to the gendering of science, underscoring the "invisible work" of women and others that is critical to technoscientific networks of association and their claims on progress. (The term *technoscience* here signals the inextricable interdependence between, and joint constitution of, technology and science.)

This leads to a second shared perspective, a focus on the interdependence of or the blurring of the boundaries between technoscience and the rest of society. So, while acknowledging that power relations infuse scientific method, objects of study, and research findings, ANT and feminist science-studies scholars stress that these relations of power are intrinsically grounded in daily practices. Actor-network theory delivers a mandate to study technoscientific networks wherever they lead, for example, beyond the laboratory.

The third concept is an emphasis on the centrality of social-technical "networks of association" or "cyborg" relations between humans and nonhumans. Both actor-network theory and feminist science studies highlight the ways in which knowledge production rests on the relations between humans and their tools, or nonhuman interlocutors. When we follow science studies' dictum to "follow the scientists," we will necessarily encounter an array of both mundane and cutting-edge tools, such as faxes and photographs, as well as engineered mice and bioinformatics databases, all of which form part of the international flow of technoscientific knowledge and power.

The mandate to study technoscientific networks wherever they lead, which dovetails with recent anthropology's methodological move toward multi-site research, also evokes Foucault's emphasis on the "microphysics of power." Our study of genetic discourse and practice is informed by the notion that power is widely dispersed through all levels of society, and that biological knowledge in its many manifestations is both productive, and productive of resistance (Foucault 1979a, b). Many scholars in the social sciences and the humanities have been influenced by Foucault's suggestion that modernity rests on a shift from the absolutist power over life and death by monarchical structure, to the management of life and death as an aspect of dispersed governmental relations: the subjects of the governmental state increasingly have obligations to live (and to die) in relation to the interests of the population being governed.

The discipline and health of the body, including "technologies of the self," both objectify and subjectify modern peoples. Thus, practices of hygiene, fertility enhancement or limitation, reproducing or not reproducing, and regimens of health are aspects of what Foucault calls "biopower," which signals the association between whole populations and the "anatomo-politics" located in the embodied practices of individuals. With the geneticization of both biomedical practice and popular consciousness, we note the emergence of a genetic "micro-anatomo-politics" (Flower and Heath 1993) with identities marked and subjectivities inscribed at the molecular level. As our ethnographic examples in this chapter indicate, the dispersed power relations that mark processes of genetic governmentality introduce potential for new forms of knowledge and power to emerge at the interstices between science and society.

These conceptual tools have helped us to track the flow and interplay of genetic knowledge across multi-sited fields linking scientists, lay health activists, clinicians, and politicians to one another and to a diverse array of nonhuman actors, from the genes and molecules implicated in particular diseases and the technologies used to study them, to the visual images that circulate within and between variously defined experts and amateurs.

## RECONFIGURING ACTIVISM AND GENETICIZING CITIZENSHIP CLAIMS

In the late 1970s, a group of parents brought their children into the Senate Office Building on Capitol Hill. Their daughters and sons suffered from the wounded, blistered skin caused by a debilitating genetic condition called epidermolysis bullosa or EB. Presenting their infants' chronically blistered bodies to legislators like Oregon Senator Mark Hatfield, these parents had a singular objective: to secure federal funding for basic research on this devastating disease. Senator Hatfield, chair of the Senate Appropriations Committee, would become an ardent ally, who for years to come successfully secured funding for biomedical research by attaching line-item riders to other Senate bills. In 2000, when Deborah Heath interviewed him, Senator Hatfield began by saying that he wanted to "lobby" his interviewer to support efforts to find more resources to treat "orphan" genetic disorders. He then went on to describe in eloquent detail how his encounters with health activists 30 years earlier had galvanized his own lifelong support for medical research funding. This convergence between the needs of those families and the Senator's commitments – activism at the intersection between legislative politics and embodied experience with genetic difference – represents one aspect of what we are calling genetic citizenship.

Deborah had originally heard the narrative about the families' pilgrimage to Washington from research biologists in response to her queries about engagements between scientists and people living with genetic conditions. Deborah heard this iconic account from different researchers on several different occasions. For her laboratory interlocutors, this had become part of the scientists' perspective on how their own identities as genetic citizens came into being, an origin story about how scientific work takes shape, in part, where activism and the state intersect with laboratory life. Genetics matters on a daily basis to research scientists and health activists, both as they confront and try to affect public resource allocation and as they engage the complexities of their personal and professional relations with one another.

The parents who made their way to the nation's capital formed the core of a lay activist group known as DEBRA (the Dystrophic Epidermolysis Bullosa Research Association). Like so many other genetic support groups, DEBRA began in family desperation: Arlene Pessar, a Registered Nurse with an affected child living in New York City, set up the first mailing lists, contacted sympathetic researchers and clinicians, and brought the EB families to Washington. In 1998, when Rayna Rapp interviewed Miriam Feder, outgoing head of DEBRA, she was told that "parents used their bloody, blistering babies like a battering ram" to capture Congressional attention: a kinship of affliction figured large in this origin story of an extraordinary coalition for research and treatment, with babies' bodies breaching the boundaries between home, state, and civil society. Arlene Pessar subsequently added that Congressmen had "never seen anything like it, all these cute bandaged kids climbing all over their office furniture, crying for attention. It really made a big impact." Members of DEBRA were subsequently instrumental in creating a registry of EB patients' tissue samples, which have been crucial to laboratory research on the disease. In forging alliances with legislators like Senator Hatfield, and with biomedical researchers, members of DEBRA and other genetic advocacy groups are making citizenship claims on behalf of their genetically vulnerable offspring. We argue that the networks of association arising from these alliances are transforming the public sphere as a site for an emerging "ethics of care."

Peter Marinkovich is a dermatologist, a researcher at Stanford University working on a major project on EB (a program funded by the National Institutes of Health), which involves him in clinical work with patients as well as basic research. The website for the Stanford University Dermatology Department provides clinicians and others with a wealth of information about the diagnosis and treatment of the various forms of EB. Dr. Marinkovich has also used the internet as a forum for his commitment to collaborative patient advocacy. He established an interactive EB website that he moderated with Kelly Drewry, a dynamic college-age woman with one of the more severe forms of EB. Sadly, the electronically mediated networks that facilitate our fieldwork also brought us news of Kelly's death in 2001, through an EB listserv called EBmommas.

Formed in 1997, EBmommas was a family-driven electronic self-help group to which mothers and others posted queries and suggestions on surviving daily life with a fragile child: everything from tips on the endless bandaging problems; recipes that pique the appetites of kids for whom swallowing may be an ordeal; intimate conversations about the marital tensions that accompany life with a chronically ill daughter or son. Here, as in so many other cases, the internet has provided novel possibilities for translocal engagements and intimacies, and for the sharing of both biomedical knowledge and life experience among lay advocates, scientists, clinicians, and their ethnographic interlocutors.

## Cyborg Politics, Embodiment, and the New Public Sphere

We note the ongoing transformations of twenty-first-century spheres of genetic discourse – some public, some less broadly so – that are enabled and mediated by information and communication technologies (ICTs), from genetic databases to online forums. These cultural-technical milieus have transformed an older identity politics, creating venues for participatory knowledge-making in which the distinction between the subjects and objects of scientific inquiry are regularly called into question. We must also note, of course, the potential for a widening of the "digital divide" in which expansion of technoscientific literacy among many increases the exclusion and isolation of those without access in both rich and poor countries.

The web and other social-technical organs of the cyborg body politic instantiate the complexities and contradictions of twenty-first-century citizenship. We maintain that these human/nonhuman interfaces constitute an electronically mediated variant on what Habermas (1989) called the public sphere. This arena is constitutive of the multivocal, densely imbricated relations where claims to citizenship blur the boundaries of inclusion and exclusion, whether between lay and expert, or, in the cases that we study, between the "normal" and "pathological." Indeed, it is precisely the breaching of divides between the genetically disordered and their scientific, medical, and political allies that beckons us to develop the idea of "genetic citizenship."

Classical studies of citizenship have focused on the individual autonomous subject as the rights-bearer within a given nation-state. Yet, as much feminist critique has pointed out, the universal claims of citizenship articulated in classical political theory too often presume a male elite subject on which to construct their universalist arguments. By contrast, contemporary citizenship studies, influenced by feminist critique, point toward contested relations and shifting "postmodern" subjectivities. They are particularly attentive to those whose domains may be global, transitional, or transnational rather than fixed (Ong 1999). The requisite attention of citizenship claims to rights and obligations is conjoined in this literature with an emphasis on recognition and respect, all refracted through a pluralistic lens. Productively reworked by feminist scholars (Fraser 1997) and queer theorists (Bell and Binnie 2000), citizenship seen from these perspectives denotes a multivocal politics of bodies and identities – and their attendant struggles – rather than claims to unity or universalism that efface difference.

Embodiment, difference, and citizenship claims are, of course, long-standing foci of feminist activism, which intersects and energizes many projects in the realm of both health and disability mobilization. More recently, some feminists have also offered political critiques that highlight the implicit masculinism of the normative "independent contractarian citizen." Pointing to the dependency that characterizes long stretches of the human life cycle, feminist critics have analyzed the exclusion of those associated with dependency, whether as care-givers or receivers of care (Kittay 1999).

These contributions by feminist and queer theorists have been fruitfully augmented by work closer to our own realm of inquiry from two directions. Investigators of the AIDS pandemic have highlighted the importance of struggles to gain insider status among scientists, clinicians, and policy-makers. And disability studies analysts have stressed the importance of coalition politics that enable people directly affected by medical, legal, and educational policy to make claims on decisive power. Collectively, these discussions of health/body activism highlight the importance of quite radical claims on civil rights for those whose stigmatized standing is often subject to daily discrimination and prejudice: "Nothing About Us Without Us," as the Disability Rights movement has proclaimed (Charlton 1998).

This insistence on the intimate space of embodied difference as a terrain of public discourse has, of course, been central to theories of sexuality, especially queer theory. Ken Plummer's (2001) notion of "intimate citizenship" usefully points to the significance of bodily and sexual identities as they shape demands for rights and public recognition, which not only explicitly affect sexual minority constituencies, but also potentially affect us all. His work is particularly sensitive to the technosocial mediation of intimate experiences now routinely made public via electronic means. The public mediation of intimate difference is of key concern to us in our investigation of contemporary geneticization. Likewise, many forms of women's activism have transformed the public arenas within which citizenship is recrafted (Yuval-Davis and Werbner 1999).

Building on these diverse literatures, we want to illuminate the emerging arenas of public discourse that link differently embodied subjects to one another. We contend that it is "genetic citizenship" that connects discussions of rights, recognitions, and responsibilities to intimate, fundamental concerns about heritable identities, differential embodiment, and an *ethics of care*. Recent discussions frequently link the notion of an ethics of care to Michel Foucault's notion of "technologies of the self," or of the "care of the self," and to postmodern theories of subjectivity (Foucault 1986). But in the Anglophone literature the concept also has its origins in feminist moral philosophy, from Carol Gilligan's work on moral development in the 1980s to more recent scholarship (cf. Morris 2001). We want to argue for the value and complementarity of both approaches.

## BIOPOWER, ADVOCACY, AND THE PURSUIT OF AN ETHICS OF CARE

In the early twenty-first-century United States, the state's resources and regulatory power, and its role in caring for the health and welfare of its citizens, are volatile issues. And these are unevenly distributed. In the US, beyond the realm of laws and regulations, health care is marked by the influence of a market-driven economy, vested in blue-chip pharmaceutical giants, expanding health maintenance organizations (HMOs), and roller-coaster entrepreneurial biotechnology companies. In the midst of widespread dissatisfaction with the growing corporatization of medical care and rising costs – coupled with an inadequate insurance safety net – health and health care have become sites of political struggle and desire. Indeed, some of the most potent and vociferous social movements of the last two decades involve health-care demands: the women's health and the AIDS activism movements have both combined trenchant critiques of bureaucratic paternalism with demands for concrete transformations in the ways pharmaceuticals are tested, and medical services distributed and delivered.

Yet the claims of these movements have been more radical than this list of activities implies, for they have also demanded the recognition of their desires – for respect, for experiential authority, for inclusion in the research and design of medicines and medical policies. Recognition demands have not conventionally been associated with medicine, yet they are increasingly in play as various constituencies use their "patienthood" as sites to describe health diversity and the needs it generates. This is surely the case across the wide array of genetic advocacy groups discussed below.

Nor are they alone. Increasingly, large and potent health-based social movements, like that associated with breast cancer, have adopted and extended strategies whose goal is to transform therapeutic and bureaucratic processes in light of their lived experiences. And the language and technologies of public health have been engaged by many social movements, running the gamut from extreme left to right, that focus on dilemmas and desires of embodiment. There is often a productive tension between the use of the statistics and technologies of public health and the demand for demedicalization of their political concerns, which has been deployed by activists working for reproductive rights, gay, lesbian, bisexual and queer rights, and some aspects of anti-violence and human-rights movements.

Under contemporary US conditions, a demand for "respectful health care as a right" has a utopian and highly political edge. As such, it is loosely congruent with what are often grouped under the rubric of the analysis of "new social movements" – a label developed in the 1980s to describe collective demands surrounding issues of the quality of life, the colonization of private life by market and state, and identity politics constituted around cultural resources and rights to specificity and difference (Laclau and Mouffe 1985). New social movements theory has addressed the limits of conventional class-based analysis, insisting on the primacy of multiple and new social subjects produced by various political crises of modernity. Health activism can be usefully viewed through this optic, especially when claims for recognition and re-sources proceed through identification with highly specific forms of embodied differ-ence, for example, breast cancer or genetic disorder activism. Likewise, citizenship claims have creatively been made on behalf of disability rights: while modern medi-cine is in large measure responsible for developing technologies and protocols that have helped to keep many people with disabling conditions alive and well, it has also produced a powerful set of discourses and practices that entrap disability as if it were an exclusively medical category of limitation. Disability rights activists are highly diverse in their embodied experiences and needs (e.g., a spinal cord injury produces quite different challenges to daily life than does deafness or mental retardation). But disability activists are united in an insistence that it is social prejudice rather than physical impairment that constrains their ability to lead fully actualized lives. While health activists often make demands for increased access to medical resources, disabil-ity activism is frequently characterized by an opposite strategy: escape from medical definitions to an insistence on political and civic entitlements has produced a distinct and potent agenda.

Alongside the challenges they have posed to biomedical practice, all of the activist constituencies we have indexed have also benefited from and contributed to the use of technoscientific resources as icons and tools of their political projects. Indeed, we are arguing that understanding the dangers and benefits of genetic citizenship re-quires attention to an emergent public sphere which can only be accessed and understood through the lens of technosocial relations. "Intimate citizenship" is largely produced through technosocial networks that constitute the public sphere in the Information Age. For example, both self-help forums on the internet and television talk shows perform multiple functions. They are alternately technologies of the spectacle that may serve as both a modern-day confessional, and a means to achieve technologically mediated intimacy, normalizing the pathological body among geographically dispersed, socially differentiated individuals.

At the same time, some social critics have called attention to the collapse of public citizenship into a potentially more narcissistic "public intimacy" in which the confessional mode – on talk shows, and other highly mediated public displays of sexuality, victimization, and dysfunction – substitutes individual stories of empathy and struggle for more social ground. Yet in normalizing pathological states, and providing genres for the performance of intimate struggles as an aspect of public life, genetic modalities also have the potential to reinvigorate and complicate not just personal but also political life. At these multiple sites of embodied difference and discourse, the possibilities for genetic citizenship begin to be articulated.

Our focus on "genetic citizenship" highlights the intersection between individual rights and responsibilities and the public conditions of their enablement. In that complex nexus where issues like "genetic discrimination" by health insurers, or regulatory guidelines for the Americans with Disabilities Act of 1990 are played out, the cast of interested constituencies is large and growing. It includes associations formed around rare single-gene connective-tissue disorders. Increasingly, however, it also includes those organized around common chronic diseases like arthritis and diabetes, which are now understood to have a multi-genetic substrate. This geneticizing world-view is both a condition and a consequence of material advances in the life sciences. Health activists, biomedical researchers, the public funding apparatus, and the recent and dramatic influx of transnational capital into biotechnology are all implicated in widespread geneticization, as people learn to "think genetically," to see themselves in terms of genetic attributes and limits – or as investment possibilities.

As people come to identify with and make claims based on individual or family genetic conditions or risks, prior coalitions may be refigured. Prioritizing genetic identities may lead individuals to assert claims based on their specific, usually rare, conditions rather than for health care more broadly. At the same time, lay organizations like the Genetic Alliance, which we discuss below, seek to bring together diverse genetic constituencies oriented around genetic identities. Of course, in some senses, "everyone" can be described in terms of genetic susceptibility; indeed, we might argue that people with known, albeit rare, genetic conditions serve as what Faye Ginsburg and Rayna Rapp refer to as the "canary in the gemeinschaft" for the forms which more widespread genetic understanding and interventions will take. While there is ample reason to worry about the eugenic legacies into which such "genetic thinking" easily fits, we want to complicate the story.

## GENETIC CITIZENSHIP AND ITS TECHNOSOCIAL ALLIANCES

Our fieldwork illustrates the technosocial networks of association that have arisen as the Human Genome Project has brought molecular biology and medical genetics into public view. The interpolation of US citizens into genetic perspectives through their workplaces, civic lives, and family responsibilities, as well as through their individual health status now and in the increasingly screenable future, produces not only sites for eugenic discrimination, but also locations in which new forms of subjectification and collective activism come into being. Genetic citizenship may sometimes facilitate democratic possibilities, as well as constraining them. At this juncture, cross-cutting alliances and shifting subjectivities among bench scientists,

Washington lobbyists, and lay genetic advocates move beyond the singular solidarities of conventional identity politics. Emerging from these coalitions, genetic citizenship both marks and potentially transcends the medicalized identities of those living with rare and debilitating heritable conditions like epidermolysis bullosa (EB). It also reveals how the workings of contemporary science in society reconfigure traditional boundaries between state, home, and civil society.

One of our aims is to locate new, or newly configured, sites for citizenship and claims on democracy that emerge from the sometimes uneasy coalitions of the present era. As chroniclers of the AIDS epidemic have taught us, health advocates with chronic, life-threatening diseases have had to face the challenges of crafting complex political-economic relations with the state and market in the quest for medical treatment, social services, and appropriate biomedical research. In this process, they have articulated demands for insider status in scientific controversies and claimed credit for contributing to scientific advances. In their coalitional work, a generative mix of public and private resources has been assembled in the service of new citizenship claims.

And state interventions take many forms. Some recent work on EB has been supported by a surprising source: the US Department of Defense. Although EB is a rare heritable skin disorder, its wounds model those of both conventional and chemical warfare. The Army was therefore eager to award a recent grant of 1 million dollars for basic research on EB. Likewise, this "orphan disease" attracted funding from the pharmaceutical firm Novartis for an innovative interdisciplinary scientific conference that brought oncological and dermatological geneticists into conversation. This pharmaceutical giant was motivated by the potentially huge numbers of consumers for wound-healing technologies, extending far beyond EB to the enormous market niches represented by burn victims and those with diabetes, as well as the victims of war. Thus a small and desperate genetic disease constituency may, through its researchers, find itself in negotiation with the military and the market.

At present, a growing number of research labs and biotech companies are contending with one another to develop engineered tissues, both natural and synthetic, targeted at wound healing. Organogenesis markets an engineered tissue called Apligraf™ that has been used in clinical trials with EB patients. Another biotech company, Ortec, has a patented composite skin product, OrCel™, that has just received limited FDA approval as a humanitarian device: it is being tested on a small number of EB patients who must undergo repeated hand and foot surgery to "de-glove" the scarring of digits that accompanies their disease. The clinical trials run by companies like Ortec and Organogenesis, focused on providing experimental "compassionate care" for patients with orphan diseases like EB, undergird the promise of targeting much larger medical and military markets when and if the product proves successful. At a European conference for connective tissue biologists in 2002, Deborah Heath heard presentations on various models of engineered tissue from several European and US laboratories, many with promise for those living with connective tissue disorders like EB. Still, researchers report that there is currently limited proof of how efficacious this treatment is. Some researchers note that despite the allure of cutting-edge wound-healing technologies, and the ample funding available for such research and development, conventional interventions with animal-skin grafts appear to be just as effective.

This volatile interface of scientific, economic, and medical desires, in which genetic activists encounter the powerful convergence of governance, finance, and technoscience, has recently been recognized within the National Institutes of Health. The establishment of the Office of Outreach to Genetic Support Groups, which collaborates with lay health organizations and consumer groups interested in genetics and genomic research, builds upon the work that NORD – the National Organization of Rare Diseases – accomplished. NORD built a coalition of activists intimately involved with "orphan" diseases, who successfully lobbied to have tax regulations and subsidies entered into the Congressional budget that enable pharmaceutical companies to continue to produce unprofitable medicines on which the lives of relatively small numbers of patients depend. NORD's coalition of biomedical researchers and their Congressional supporters was spearheaded by family and patient activists: like other "orphan" diseases, including the "genetic orphans" from whom we have learned, many activists have told us that "Extreme and rare diseases yield extremely valuable information about how systems of the body work." And, we might add, also about how successful Washington lobbyists and compromise political coalitions work as well. Dramatic stories like DEBRA's bloody-baby march on Congress, or NORD's subsidy and tax regulation successes, are not hard to find in a country where a line-item budget annually determines NIH funding anew, and public support for funds that will go to any particular program must be shepherded through the budget-making process by sympathetic legislators. Indeed, lobbying Congress ("advocacy awareness" in the language of the tax-exempt nonprofit groups who regularly visit Capitol Hill) is virtually built into relationships between US scientists, clinicians, and what we might call their genetic constituencies. For example, at NIAMS (the National Institute of Arthritis and Musculo-skeletal Diseases), researchers brief interested constituencies such as the Coalition of Patient Advocates with Skin Diseases and the Coalition for Heritable Connective Tissue Disorders before these groups make their annual appeal to legislators. Successful health-advocacy groups may well have begun as "mom and pop" operations around the kitchen table of a family with a sick child, but if they are to succeed, they eventually "go national" and "go professional" as well. This "corporatization" of grass-roots voluntary associations represents not merely assimilation into early twenty-first-century capitalist culture, but also a strategic intervention, a move to gain access to resources.

Much of this national, professional, and corporate coalitional presence is "business as usual": a nonprofit group organized around small numbers of interested and desperate participants must, by definition, find allies and create coalitions if its modest cause is not to be eaten up by larger and more publicly visible ones. Nonetheless, we suggest that out of that professionalizing, nationalizing movement to wrest publicity and allocations from Washington, unanticipated claims on democracy may also occur.

"Genetic citizenship" looks somewhat different when viewed from the perspective of systems of health care and scientific funding outside the US. For example, DEBRA was largely modeled on DebRA UK, a British genetic activist group that was formed a few years earlier. In the United Kingdom, where citizen groups do not lobby Parliament because its budget is not amenable to their influence, the organization has succeeded in attaching DebRA's cause to a series of corporate charities and lotteries; the late Princess Diana was their most celebrated sponsor. In the UK, the GIG (Genetic Interest Group), a coalition not unlike the US Genetic Alliance has recently grown in influence, allying itself not only with the Medical Research Council (the UK's equivalent to the NIH) and the Wellcome Trust (which contributed the lion's share of funding toward UK Human Genome mapping), but also with the Genetic Group of the European Union. Like France and other EU nations in which rare disease constituencies tend to be organized from the top down by governmental health bureaucracies, rather than from the bottom up, as has historically been the case in the USA, the GIG and its peer organizations find themselves increasingly involved in setting health and research policy as the EU recirculates some of the NORD strategies borrowed from the NIH. Thus many of the issues to which our label of genetic citizenship applies have specific global aspects, at least in some of the rich countries of the North.

In the US, parental efforts to advance research on EB have focused on public funding: early on, they convinced the NIH to hold a scientific conference and to fund the creation of a registry of patient tissue samples. A registry is both an invaluable tool for scientific researchers, collecting the material they need to construct research data, and an actor network around which the recruitment of interested new scientists looking for "hot" topics and new sources of funding may coalesce. The EB registry became a model for how activists and the NIH have catalyzed researchers to work on other rare but scientifically significant diseases, because it demonstrated the value of centralized access to the material means of scientific knowledge production. Later generations of genetic citizens have adapted this model to fit the specificities of their own situations and objectives.

The Familial Dysautonomia Foundation, for example, raised enough money through affected families and their supporters to fund projects at a major Boston academic laboratory in search of "their" gene (called the FD gene). This dysfunction of the autonomic nervous system (ANS) affects most bodily systems, yet the ANS itself remains poorly understood. Thus researchers were eager to win Foundation funding, hoping that work on this rare condition would clarify other aspects of the ANS. While the Boston researchers quickly found a linkage (in the region of the gene), it took over nine years to find the gene itself, because it turned out to be a splicing defect in the RNA rather than in the DNA, and such entities remain relatively little studied. At the last minute, and under the influence of both the huge bioinformatic public database generated by the Human Genome Project and the biotech corporation Celera's race to outstrip the NIH in declaring the first "map" of the entire genome, an upstart New York lab also found the FD gene. Recognizing the importance of this scientific competition, the FD Foundation is now funding both labs in the quest for animal models and gene therapies. It is also attempting to pioneer non-exclusive patent rights so that both labs and all affected families may benefit from new discoveries.

The case of the Genetic Alliance, which changed its name from the Alliance of Genetic Support Groups in 2000, powerfully illustrates this rapid flexibility of genetic citizens. Founded in 1986, the Alliance brought together a super-coalition of more than 200 genetic lay organizations to provide support to affected individuals and their families. Since its inception it has mushroomed into an organization that coordinates a wide range of activities including, but not limited to, peer support, lobbying, and innovative physician education. The Alliance's own statement on the motivation to change its name demonstrates the unexpected trajectories taken and social formations emerging today through science and culture in action. They explain their name change as follows (http://www.geneticalliance.org):

> A central realization that emerged during strategic planning discussions was that our founding name, "Alliance of Genetic Support Groups," was no longer an accurate representation of who we have become over the past 14 years. In 2000, this organization is much more diverse than a coalition of support groups. We have become a coalition of consumers, professionals, public agencies, biotechnology companies, genetic diagnostic clinics, public health departments, and children's hospitals, to name a few. In recent years, newer consumer groups have expressed ambivalence about joining the Alliance because they saw themselves as foundations, research organizations, advocates or tissue registries with a wide range of services including, but not limited to, peer support.
>
> > SO . . . Because our membership includes all the stakeholders,
> > Because we are a strong Consumer Voice
> > Because our name needs to say Who and What we are . . .
> > We decided to change our name to the Genetic Alliance . . .

As Sharon Terry, Alliance board president and mother of two children with a rare genetic condition, has said, "we're not a bunch of parents crying into our coffee cups." In addition to coordinating activities among genetic lay advocacy groups, today the Alliance engages in a myriad of diverse activities, including the participation of members in basic research and taking places on national advisory boards that aim to reform the process of informed consent. The Alliance works to evaluate and monitor internet resources on genetic disease (a huge and technologically sophisticated task). Its recent efforts include participation in incipient research at the Massachusetts Institute of Technology and the NIH in constructing the Haplotype Map, or "Hap Map" (http://www-genome.wi.mit.edu/media/press/pr_hapmap.html), an innovative project which hopes to simplify the study of complex genetic disorders and differences by mapping the way that blocks of DNA called single nucleotide polymorphisms (SNPs), are inherited together in large, neat units.

Each new generation of genetic citizens benefits from and builds upon the strategic interventions of their predecessors. The work of early health advocates like the EB families, from their march on Washington to the creation of the DEBRA tissue registry, has formed a model that is both emulated and transcended by today's genetic activists. For example, when Pat and Sharon Terry confronted the 1994 diagnosis of their children with pseudoxanthoma elasticum (PXE), another rare genetic connective-tissue condition, they quickly became activists, building far-reaching networks of human and nonhuman allies. They established a lay advocacy organization, PXE International, with the express purpose of facilitating research that would lead to a treatment for their children's condition, building a coalition among members of PXE families, their molecules, and their family and medical histories as a way of drawing researchers into the coalition as well. In spring 2000, Sharon Terry described their work to Karen-Sue Taussig, explaining that in contrast to the NIH-sponsored EB tissue registry, the Terrys insured that PXE International maintained direct control over affected family pedigrees and tissue samples. The organization links individuals in PXE families, the blood, tissue, and family and medical histories that have something to tell about the condition, and researchers who seek to develop genetic knowledge. At the same time, by controlling researchers' access to particular parts of the coalition, the Terrys seek to maintain some control over the process of knowledge production itself. They also volunteered in the laboratory of a Boston researcher from 6 p.m. to 2 a.m. five days a week, determined to move the search for the PXE gene into high gear and gaining the knowledge necessary to insure their status as obligatory passage points (Latour 1987) for anyone interested in PXE. In June 2000 Sharon Terry was a co-author on two of the three scientific journal articles announcing the discovery of a gene for PXE. PXE International and the University of Hawaii have agreed to file their application for the PXE gene as co-inventors. The group is committed to ensuring both open access to the gene for all researchers, and preventing royalty fees that might increase the costs to any individual seeking testing for PXE.

Pat and Sharon Terry regularly consult with other lay genetic health organizations in North America, Europe, and Africa, describing "the PXE model" so that others can adopt the strategies they have employed. In the summer of 2002 Pat Terry was invited to describe "the PXE model" at a meeting of First Peoples in Vancouver, British Columbia, so that they too could consider employing such a model in developing relationships with the researchers who so desire their blood. Elsewhere in the global networks where technoscience and genetic citizenship are intertwined, also during the summer of 2002, Deborah Heath interviewed members of an Italian research lab who described a recent visit by Sharon Terry and her two children. In contrast to the EB activists' legislative intervention 30 years ago on behalf of funding for scientific experts, the Terry family's strategies place them*selves* at the center of ongoing technoscientific practice.

Today the Genetic Alliance considers PXE International a model for lay advocacy organizations seeking treatments for rare genetic conditions. The value of lay advocacy group participation, from the perspective of the Alliance, comes from their interest in the condition "from the bench to the bedside" rather than in what happens to be scientifically "sexy" at the present moment for researchers. Nonetheless, to be this proactive is to confront the culture and politics of both technoscience and the "new economy" in increasingly complex, contradictory ways. Democratic impulses often intersect with economic or political forces far removed from a perhaps idealized ethos of grass-roots politics. We note, for instance that the biotech firm Incyte (and several others) are now major funders of the Alliance. Increasingly, the tension between encouraging an expansion of scientific research and the issue of patenting and regulating the distribution of potential royalties confronts every genetic voluntary health group that has collaborated in and funded genetic research.

## GENETICS IN ACTION

We began this paper by pointing to the ways in which scientific work in the United States today partly takes shape where consumer activism and the state intersect with laboratory life. We have also found cases in which activism has become a significant part of scientists' and clinicians' daily work. For example, in Vermont Alan Guttmacher, a medical geneticist now at the NIH Human Genome Research Institute, put together a coalition of interested organizations, including the University of Vermont, a library-based book discussion program, and a parent-run lay advocacy organization, which successfully sought funding for a project called the Vermont Community Genetics and Ethics Project (CGEP). Among its aims, this project tries to engage all Vermont citizens in a conversation about the implications of emerging genetic knowledge and to provide the state with the local resources to deal effectively with issues raised by this new knowledge. In Oregon, Geneforum has been using the internet and other modalities to bring citizens' values to bear on the state's genetic privacy law discussions; in Michigan, a collaboration between the University of Michigan, Michigan State University, and Howard University in Washington, focuses on genetics and citizens' involvement, especially among communities of color which have historically suffered abuses in medical research settings.

Side by side with these public projects on genetic citizenship, other new arenas for public moral discourse may be emerging: For example, Fritz Bach, a leading xeno-transplantation (animal organs for human transplant) expert, called for a moratorium on his and similar work in 2000. Reflecting on the potential consequences of his work to reconcile pig and human receptors to enable animal organ transplants, Bach is concerned that the unique medical, social, and ethical problems associated with xenotransplantation be addressed before physicians begin using this potential new technology. Moreover, he is deeply committed to engaging a wide-ranging audience in a public discussion of how to resolve these issues: populist and anticipatory bioethics. Bach and other proactive scientist-physician activists work in ways that reconfigure traditional boundaries between science and civil society as they engage ordinary citizens in conversations about the meaning, value, and direction of scientific work and its potential applications in medical practices and wider worlds.

We want to stress that this conversation is taking place in many venues. In Denmark, for example, the government adopted a community consultation model through which genetic policy is actively presented and debated in towns and cities across the nation before laws and regulations are enacted. This policy was much admired by some advocates at the NIH, who tried to adopt it for US usage. New requests for proposals (RFPs, that is, new funding opportunities) now require that some form of community consultation be built into all future human genetics research. And, as mentioned above, the NIH's orphan drug support program served as the model for recent EU legislation establishing consultative patient groups that will help to formulate research and ethics policy.

Here, genetic citizenship indexes both the political economy of state funding and regulation and the unruly aspirations of scientists, health advocates, health-care service providers, and families, sometimes struggling against the market, sometimes seeking, whether ardently or ambivalently, to join it in an effort to imagine other possible futures. We might want to argue, along with Foucault, that in all these examples we see a "genetic panopticon" in active formation. Yet these multivocal strategies to construct a genetic "ethics of care" are widely dispersed, and they engage many new forms of genetic citizenship. As health activists, scientists, politicians, physicians, tissue banks, bioinformatics databases, websites, confessional talk shows, and bioengineered medical devices are brought together to forge innovative "technologies of the self," we also underline that these forms of agency are necessarily part of governmentality as well. The ethnographic instances on which this essay depends all concern extremely rare single-gene disorders. Yet to the extent that the widespread and chronic diseases of "advanced civilization" are increasingly understood to have a genetic basis, we all have "screenable futures." If "Genes R Us," then the potent and protean coalitions on which our work is based now serve as a vanguard of genetic citizenship for us all.

## NOTE

We gratefully acknowledge the support of NIH/ELSI grant 1 RO1 HGO1582 on which the research that supports this essay was carried out.

## REFERENCES

Bell, David, and Jon Binnie (2000) *The Sexual Citizen: Queer Politics and Beyond*. Malden, MA: Blackwell.

Charlton, James (1998) *Nothing About Us Without Us: Disability, Oppression and Empowerment*. Berkeley: University of California Press.

Flower, Michael, and Deborah Heath (1993) Micro-Anatomo Politics: Mapping the Human Genome Project. In *Biopolitics: The Anthropology of the New Genetics and Immunology*. Theme issue, *Culture, Medicine and Psychiatry* 17:27–41.

Foucault, Michel (1979a) *Discipline and Punish: The Birth of the Prison*, trans. Alan Sheridan. New York: Vintage Books.

Foucault, Michel (1979b) Governmentality. *Ideology and Consciousness* 6:5–21.

Foucault, Michel (1986) *History of Sexuality*. Volume 1: *Technologies of the Self*, trans. Robert Hurley. New York: Vintage.

Fraser, Nancy (1997) *Justice Interruptus: Critical Reflections on the "Postsocialist" Condition*. London: Routledge.

Habermas, Jürgen (1989) *The Structural Transformation of the Public Sphere: An Inquiry into a Category of Bourgeois Society*, trans. Thomas Burger and Frederick Lawrence. Cambridge: MIT Press.

Haraway, Donna (1994) A Game of Cat's Cradle: Science Studies, Feminist Theory, Cultural Studies. *Configurations* 1:59–71.

Kittay, Eva Feder (1999) *Love's Labors*. New York: Routledge.

Laclau, Ernesto, and Chantal Mouffe (1985) *Hegemony and Socialist Strategy: Towards a Radical Democratic Politics*. London: Verso.

Latour, Bruno (1987) *Science in Action*. Cambridge, MA: Harvard University Press.

Law, John (1992) Notes on the Theory of the Actor-Network: Ordering, Strategy, and Heterogeneity. *Systems Practice* 5:379–393.

Lippman, Abby (1991) Prenatal Genetic Testing and Screening: Constructing Needs and Reinforcing Inequities. *American Journal of Law and Medicine* 17:15–50.

Morris, Jenny (2001) Impairment and Disability: Constructing an Ethics of Care that Promotes Human Rights. In *Feminism and Disability I*. Theme issue, *Hypatia* 16:1–16.

Ong, Aihwa (1999) *Flexible Citizenship: The Cultural Logics of Transnationality*. Durham, NC: Duke University Press.

Plummer, Ken (2001) The Square of Intimate Citizenship: Some Preliminary Proposals. *Citizenship Studies* 5:237–253.

Yuval-Davis, Nira, and Pnina Werbner, eds. (1999) *Women, Citizenship, and Difference*. London and New York: Zed.

## SUGGESTED FURTHER READING

Bauman, Zygmunt (1993) *Post-modern Ethics*. Oxford: Blackwell.

Berg, Marc, and Monica Casper, eds. (1995) Constructivist Perspectives on Medical Work. Theme issue, *Science, Technology, and Human Values* 20.

Epstein, Steven (1996) *Impure Science: AIDS, Activism, and the Politics of Knowledge*. Berkeley: University of California Press.

Franklin, Sarah (1995) Science as Culture, Cultures of Science. *Annual Review of Anthropology* 24:163–184.

Gray, Chris (2002) *Cyborg Citizen*. New York: Routledge.

Heath, Deborah (1998) Bodies, Antibodies, and Modest Interventions: Works of Art in the Age of Cyborgian Reproduction. In *Cyborgs and Citadels: Anthropological Interventions in the Borderlands of Technoscience*, ed. Gary Downey and Joseph Dumit, pp. 67–82. Santa Fe, NM: School of American Research.

Heath, Deborah, Barbara Ley, Erin Koch, and Michael Montoya (1999) Nodes and Queries: Linking Locations in Networked Fields of Inquiry. In *Virtual Methodologies*. Theme issue, *American Behavioral Scientist* 43:450–463.

Hess, David, and Linda Layne, eds. (1992) *The Anthropology of Science and Technology*. Theme issue, *Knowledge and Society* 9.

Koenig, Barbara, and Monica Casper, eds. (1996) *Biomedical Technologies: Reconfiguring Nature and Culture*. Theme issue, *Medical Anthropology Quarterly* 10.

Law, John (1999) After ANT: Topology, Naming and Complexity. Electronic document, http://www.comp.lancs.ac.uk/sociology/stslaw2.html.

Layne, Linda, ed. (1998) *Anthropological Approaches in Science and Technology Studies*. Theme issue, *Science, Technology and Human Values* 23.

Martin, Emily (1998) Anthropology and the Cultural Study of Science. In *Anthropological Approaches in Science and Technology Studies*. Theme issue, *Science, Technology and Human Values* 23:24–44.

Rapp, Rayna (2000) *Testing Women, Testing the Fetus: The Social Impact of Amniocentesis in America*. New York: Routledge.

Taussig, Karen-Sue (in press) Molecules, Medicine and Bodies: Building Social Relationships for a Molecular Revolution in Medicine. In *Complexities: Anthropological Challenges to Reductive Accounts of Bio-Social Life*, ed. S. McKinnon and S. Silverman. Chicago: University of Chicago Press.

Traweek, Sharon (1993) An Introduction to Cultural and Social Studies of Sciences and Technologies. In *Biopolitics: The Anthropology of the New Genetics and Immunology*. Theme issue, *Culture, Medicine and Psychiatry* 17:27–41.

# 11 The Global City

## CHAPTER

## *Saskia Sassen*

Globalization and digitization have brought with them an incipient unbundling of the exclusive authority over territory and people we have long associated with the nation-state. The most strategic example of this unbundling is probably the global city, which has emerged as a partly denationalized platform for global capital and for the most diverse mix of people from all over the world. This process brings with it operational and conceptual openings for the participation of non-state actors in trans-boundary domains once exclusive to the national state. Among such actors are non-governmental organizations, first-nation peoples, and anti-globalization activists. But they also include immigrants and refugees who become subjects of adjudication in human-rights decisions and thereby become a type of international legal persona. And they include multinational corporations and global markets which can engage in direct transactions with each other, bypassing many of the strictures of the inter-state system that until recently was the necessary context for their cross-border activities. These diverse non-state actors can gain international visibility as individuals and as organizations, and come out of the invisibility of aggregate membership in a nation-state until recently exclusively represented by the sovereign in the international domain.

The large city of today emerges as a strategic site for these new types of operations. It is one of the nexuses where the formation of new claims materializes and assumes concrete forms (Isin 2000). The loss of power at the national level produces the possibility for new forms of power and politics at the subnational level (Brenner 1998). The national as container of social process and power is cracked (Taylor 2000). This cracked casing opens up possibilities for a geography of politics that links sub-national spaces. One question this engenders is how and whether we are seeing the formation of new types of informal transnational politics enacted by the variety of non-state actors concentrated in these cities. These politics may include not only organizations but also individuals, notably immigrants, who may not have politics as their main objective but are de facto creating transnational networks for a growing range of engagements, and a variety of activists often enabled by the new network technologies, particularly the public-access internet (Castells 1996). Beyond being a strategic site, the city would then also emerge as a type of postmodern frontier zone where a variety of often non-formal political subjects engage in types of politics for which the rules of engagement have not quite been shaped or fully formalized.

The first section of this chapter briefly discusses how a focus on cities allows us to see this variety of processes as part of globalization in a way that the typical focus on macrolevel cross-border processes does not. The second section deepens this analysis by focusing on what are often barely visible or recognizable localizations of the global. The third section examines the political implications of these conditions.

## RECOVERING PLACE IN THE ANALYSIS OF GLOBALIZATION

Including cities in the analysis of economic globalization carries analytic consequences. Economic globalization has mostly been conceptualized in terms of the duality national and global, where the latter gains at the expense of the former. Second, economic globalization has largely been conceptualized in terms of the internationalization of capital, and then only the upper circuits of capital. Introducing cities into this analysis allows us to reconceptualize processes of economic globalization as concrete economic complexes partly situated in specific places (Sassen 2001). This contrasts with the mainstream account of globalization, where place is typically seen as neutralized by the capacity for global communications and control. Third, a focus on cities decomposes the nation-state into a variety of sub-national components, some profoundly articulated with the global economy and others not. It signals the declining significance of the national economy as a unitary category in the global economy. And even if to a large extent this was a unitary category constructed in political discourse and policy, it has become even less of a fact in the last 15 years. Fourth, examining globalization from the perspective of cities makes legible the fact of multiple forms of globalization, beyond the many forms of economic globalization.

Recovering place in analyses of the global economy, particularly place as constituted in major cities, brings a focus on the concrete, localized processes through which much of globalization exists. Much of the multiculturalism in large cities is as constitutive of globalization as is international finance, though in ways that differ sharply from the latter. A focus on these cities allows us to see the multiple economies and work cultures, beyond the corporate culture, in which the global information economy is embedded (Low 1999). Finally, focusing on cities allows us to specify a geography of strategic places bound to each other largely by the dynamics of economic globalization and cross-border migrations. I refer to this as a new geography of centrality, at the heart of which is the new worldwide grid of global cities. This is a geography that cuts across national borders and the old North–South divide. But it does so along bounded channels: it is a set of specific and partial rather than all-encompassing dynamics.

The centrality of place in a context of global processes makes possible a transnational economic and political opening for the formation of new claims and hence for the constitution of entitlements, notably rights to places. At the limit, this could be an opening for new forms of "citizenship." The city has indeed emerged as a site for new claims – by global capital which uses the city as an "organizational commodity," but also by disadvantaged sectors of the urban population, frequently as internationalized a presence in large cities as capital. The denationalizing of urban space and the formation of new claims by transnational actors raise the question, "Whose city is it?"

This is a type of political opening that contains unifying capacities across national boundaries and sharpening conflicts within such boundaries. Global capital and the new immigrant workforce are two major instances of transnationalized actors that have unifying properties internally and find themselves in contestation with each other inside global cities. Global cities are the sites for the over-valorization of corporate capital and the devalorization of disadvantaged workers; but they are also the sites for new types of politics that allow the latter to emerge as political subjects.

This dynamic is not present in all cities. It is particular types of cities that bring together key global economic actors and key disadvantaged actors; they are global cities and cities with global city functions. There are about 40 of these in the world today, parts of multiple cross-border networks typically marked by considerable hierarchy. In the next section I examine some of the key elements in the development of scholarship on global cities.

## THE GLOBAL CITY: INTRODUCING A CONCEPT

Each phase in the long history of the world economy raises specific questions about the particular conditions that make it possible. One of the key properties of the current phase is the ascendance of information technologies and the associated increase in the mobility and liquidity of capital. There have long been cross-border economic processes – flows of capital, labor, goods, raw materials, tourists. But to a large extent these took place within the inter-state system, where the key articulators were national states. The international economic system was ensconced largely in this inter-state system. This has changed rather dramatically over the last decade as a result of privatization, deregulation, the opening up of national economies to foreign firms, and the growing participation of national economic actors in global markets.

It is in this context that we see a rescaling of the strategic territories that articulate the new system. With the partial unbundling or at least weakening of the national as a spatial unit due to privatization and deregulation, and the associated strengthening of globalization, come conditions for the ascendance of other spatial units or scales. Among these are the sub-national, notably cities and regions; cross-border regions encompassing two or more sub-national entities; and supra-national entities, that is, global digitized markets and free-trade blocs. The dynamics and processes that are terrritorialized at these diverse scales may in principle be regional, national, or global.

I locate the emergence of global cities in this context and against this range of instantiations of strategic scales and spatial units (Sassen 2001). In the case of global cities, the dynamics and processes that get territorialized are global. Constructs such as the global city are, in my reading, important elements in a new conceptual architecture for the study of globalization. The activity of naming these elements is part of the conceptual work. There are other, closely linked terms that could conceivably have been used: world cities (Friedmann and Wolff 1982; Hall 1996), "super-villes" (Braudel 1984), and the informational city (Castells 1989). Thus, choosing how to name a configuration has its own substantive rationality.

When I first chose to use the term "global city" I did so knowingly – it was an attempt to name a difference: the specificity of the global as it gets structured in the contemporary period. I did not choose the obvious alternative, world city, because it had precisely the opposite attribute: it referred to a type of city which we have seen over the centuries (Braudel 1984), and most probably also in much earlier periods in Asia or in European colonial centers than in the West. In this regard it could be said that most of today's major global cities are also world cities, but that there may well be some global cities today that are not world cities in the full, rich sense of that term. This is partly an empirical question; further, as the global economy expands and incorporates additional cities into the various networks, it is quite possible that the answer to that particular question will vary. Thus the fact that Miami has developed global-city functions, beginning in the late 1980s, does not make it a world city in that older sense of the term (Abu-Lughod 1999).

Global cities are centers for servicing and financing international trade, investment, and headquarters operations. That is to say, the multiplicity of specialized activities present in global cities are crucial in the valorization, indeed over-valorization of leading sectors of capital today. And in this sense, global cities are strategic production sites for today's leading economic sectors. This function is reflected in the ascendance of service-related activities in the economies of these cities. This is not simply a question of the growth in service jobs but, more important, the growing service intensity in the organization of advanced economies: firms in all industries, from mining to wholesale, buy more accounting, legal, advertising, financial, economic forecasting services today than they did 20 years ago. Whether at the global or regional level, urban centers – central cities, edge cities – are often the best production sites for such specialized services. When it comes to the production of services for the leading globalized sectors, the advantages of locations in cities are particularly strong. The rapid growth and disproportionate concentration of such services in cities signals that the latter have reemerged as significant "production" sites after losing this role in the period when mass manufacturing was the dominant sector of the economy. Under mass manufacturing and Fordism, the strategic spaces of the economy were the large-scale integrated factories and the government through its Fordist or Keynesian functions.

The growth of global markets for finance and specialized services, the need for transnational servicing networks due to sharp increases in international investment, the reduced role of the government in the regulation of international economic activity and the corresponding ascendance of other institutional arenas, notably global markets and corporate headquarters – all these point to the existence of transnational economic processes with multiple locations in more than one country. Global cities, whether major or minor, are the key nodes articulating these new or strengthened cross-border networks. We can see here the formation, at least incipient, of a transnational urban system. These cities are not simply in a relation of competition to each other, they are part of emergent global divisions of labor.

Contrary to a very common perspective, the growing digitization of economic activities has not eliminated the need for major international business and financial centers and all the material resources they concentrate, from state-of-the-art telematics infrastructure to brain talent (Graham and Marvin 1996). Telematics and globalization have emerged as fundamental forces reshaping the organization of economic space. This reshaping ranges from the spatial virtualization of a growing number of economic activities to the reconfiguration of the geography of the built environment for economic activity.

Whether in electronic space or in the geography of the built environment, this reshaping involves organizational and structural changes. But global cities are also the sites for the most diverse mixes and growing concentrations of people from all over the world, whose daily life practices reinscribe the urban context with many partly reterritorialized and partly reinvented cultures, including political cultures. These are often not easily coded as political in the narrow sense of the term, and are often invisible to those studying globalization from macrolevel perspectives.

## THE LESS VISIBLE LOCALIZATIONS OF THE GLOBAL

Cities make legible multiple localizations of a variety of globalization processes that are typically not coded as such in mainstream accounts. The global city is a strategic site for these occurrences of globalization in a double sense. Cities make some of these dynamics more visible than other types of spaces, such as suburbs and rural areas. Second, urban space enables the formation of many of these dynamics, and in this regard it is productive space.

Many of these less legible localizations of globalization are embedded in the demographic transition evident in such cities, where a majority of resident workers today are immigrants and women, often women of color, and internal minorities. Global cities are seeing an expansion of low-wage jobs that do not fit the master images about globalization yet are part of it. The embeddedness of these low-paying jobs in the demographic transition evident in all these cities, and the consequent invisibility of these forms of employment, contribute to the devalorization of these types of workers and work cultures and to the "legitimacy" of that devalorization.

This can be read as a rupture of the traditional dynamic whereby membership in leading economic sectors contributes conditions toward the formation of a labor aristocracy – a process long evident in Western industrialized economies. "Women and immigrants" come to replace the Fordist or family wage category of "women and children." One of the localizations of globalization is the process of economic restructuring in global cities. The associated socio-economic polarization has generated a large growth in the demand for low-wage workers and for jobs that offer few possibilities of advancement. This, amid an explosion in the wealth and power concentrated in these cities – that is to say, in conditions where there is also a visible expansion in high-income jobs and high-priced urban space. "Women and immigrants" emerge as the labor supply that facilitates the imposition of low wages and powerlessness under conditions of high demand for those workers and the location of those jobs in high-growth sectors. It breaks the historic nexus that would have led to empowering workers and legitimates this break culturally.

Another localization which is rarely associated with globalization – informalization – reintroduces the community and the household as an important economic space in global cities. I see informalization in this setting as the low-cost (and often feminized) equivalent of deregulation at the top of the system. As with deregulation (for example, financial deregulation), informalization introduces flexibility, reduces the "burdens" of regulation, and lowers costs, in this case especially the costs of labor. Informalization in major cities of highly developed countries – whether New York, London, Paris, or Berlin – can be seen as a downgrading of a variety of activities for which there is an effective demand in these cities – but also a devaluing and enormous competition, given low entry costs and few alternative forms of employment. Going informal is one way of producing and distributing goods and services at a lower cost and with greater flexibility. This further devalues these types of activities. Immigrants and women are important actors in the new informal economies of these cities, and they absorb the costs of informalizing these activities.

The reconfiguration of economic spaces associated with globalization in major cities has had differential impacts on women and men, on male-typed and female-typed work cultures, on male- and female-centered forms of power and empowerment. The restructuring of the labor market brings with it a shift of labor-market functions to the household or community. Women and households emerge as sites that should be part of the theorization of the particular forms that these elements in labor-market dynamics assume today.

These transformations contain possibilities, even if they are limited, for women's autonomy and empowerment. For instance, we might ask whether the growth of informalization in advanced urban economies reconfigures some types of economic relations between men and women. With informalization, the neighborhood and the household reemerge as sites for economic activity. This condition has its own dynamic possibilities for women. Economic downgrading through informalization creates "opportunities" for low-income women entrepreneurs and workers, and therefore reconfigures some of the work and household hierarchies in which women find themselves. This becomes particularly clear in the case of immigrant women who come from countries with rather traditional male-centered cultures.

There is a large literature showing that immigrant women's regular wage work and improved access to other public realms has an impact on their gender relations. Women gain greater personal autonomy and independence while men lose ground. Women gain more control over budgeting and other domestic decisions, and greater leverage in requesting help from men in domestic chores. Also, their access to public services and other public resources gives them a chance to become incorporated into the mainstream society – they are often the ones in the household who mediate in this process. It is likely that some women benefit more than others from these circumstances; we need more research to establish the impact of class, education, and income on these gendered outcomes. Besides the relatively greater empowerment of women in the household associated with waged employment, there is a second important outcome: their greater participation in the public sphere and their possible emergence as public actors. There are two arenas where immigrant women are active: institutions for public and private assistance, and the immigrant or ethnic community. The incorporation of women in the migration process strengthens the likelihood that they will be able to establish stable residence, and contributes to greater immigrant participation in their communities and vis-à-vis the state. For instance, it has been found that immigrant women come to assume more active public and social roles, which further reinforce their status in the household and the settlement process. Women are more active in community building and community activism, and they are positioned differently from men regarding the broader economy and the state. They are the ones that are likely to have to handle the legal vulnerability of their families in the process of seeking public and social services for these families.

This greater participation by women suggests the possibility that they may emerge as more forceful and visible actors and make their role in the labor market more visible as well. There is, to some extent, a joining of two different dynamics in the condition of women in global cities. On the one hand, they are constituted as an invisible and disempowered class of workers in the service of the strategic sectors forming the global economy. This invisibility keeps them from emerging as whatever would be the contemporary equivalent of the "labor aristocracy" of earlier forms of economic organization, when a low-wage worker's position in leading sectors had the effect of empowering that worker, that is, the possibility of joining a union. On the other hand, the access to (albeit low) wages and salaries, the growing feminization of the job supply, and the growing feminization of business opportunities brought about with informalization do alter the gender hierarchies in which women find themselves.

## A SPACE OF POWER AND EMPOWERMENT

What makes the localization of the processes described above strategic – even though these processes involve powerless and often invisible workers – and potentially constitutive of a new kind of transnational politics is that these same cities are also the strategic sites for the valorization of new forms of global corporate capital. The partial loss of power at the national level produces the possibility for new forms of power and politics at the sub-national level, especially in global cities. Global corporate capital emerges as one of the actors that can now engage in cross-border politics, partly bypassing the domain of the interstate system.

But the global city is also becoming a space of empowerment for the disadvantaged. Generally, the space of the city is a far more concrete space for politics than that of the nation. It becomes a place where informal political actors can be part of the political scene in a way that is much more difficult at the national level. Nationally, politics needs to run through existing formal systems: whether the electoral political system or the judiciary (taking state agencies to court). Informal political actors are rendered invisible in the space of national politics. The space of the city, on the other hand, accommodates a broad range of political activities – squatting, demonstrations against police brutality, fighting for the rights of immigrants and the homeless, the politics of culture and identity, gay and lesbian and queer politics. Much of this becomes visible on the street. Much of urban politics is concrete, enacted by people rather than dependent on massive media technologies. Street-level politics makes possible the formation of new types of political subjects that do not have to go through the formal political system.

There is something to be captured here – a distinction between powerlessness and a condition of being an actor even though lacking power. I use the term "presence" to name this condition. In the context of a strategic space such as the global city, the types of disadvantaged people described here are not simply marginal; they acquire presence in a broader political process that escapes the boundaries of the formal polity. The fact of such "presence" signals the possibility of a politics. What this politics will be will depend on the specific projects and practices of various communities. Insofar as the sense of membership of these communities is not subsumed under the national, it may well signal the possibility of a transnational politics centered in concrete localities.

These dynamics are facilitated, and at times brought about, by the new types of connectivity. Most important is the internet, which has enabled a new type of cross-border politics that can bypass inter-state politics, even though these political activities can also thrive without it (Keck and Sikkink 1998). That even small, resource-poor organizations and individuals can become participants signals the possibility of a sharp growth in cross-border politics by actors other than states.

The particular feature that interests me here is that, through the internet, localized initiatives can become part of cross-border networks. This produces a specific kind of activism, one centered in multiple localities yet intensely connected digitally. Activists can develop networks for circulating not only information (about environmental, housing, political issues, etc.) but also political work and strategies. There are many examples of such a new type of cross-border political work. For instance, SPARC (Society for the Promotion of Area Resource Centers), started by and centered on women, began as an effort to organize slum-dwellers in Bombay to get housing. It now has a network of such groups throughout Asia, and some cities in Latin America and Africa. This is one of the key forms of critical politics that the internet can make possible: a politics of the local with a big difference – these are localities that are connected with each other across a region, a country, or the world. Because the network is global does not mean that it all has to happen at the global level. Further, it is a form of political and institution-building work particularly centered in cities and networks of cities, and in informal political actors. We see here the potential transformation of a whole range of "local" conditions or institutional domains – such as the household, the community, the neighborhood, the local school and health-care entities, where individuals "confined" to domestic or local roles remain the key actors – into sites on global networks. From being lived or experienced as nonpolitical or domestic, these places are transformed into "microenvironments with global span."

What I mean by this construct is that technical connectivity will create a variety of links with other similar local entities in other neighborhoods in the same city, in other cities, in neighborhoods and cities in other countries. A partly deterritorialized community of practice can emerge that creates multiple lateral, horizontal communications, collaborations, solidarities, and supports, which arise out of their specific localized struggles or concerns. People can experience themselves as part of global non-state networks in their daily localized political work. They enact some features of "global civil society" in the micro-spaces of daily life rather than on some putative global stage.

One of the most radical forms assumed today by transformations in the linkages that connect people to territory is the loosening of identities from what have been traditional sources of identity, such as the nation or the village. This unmooring in the process of identity formation is, at this time, a condition probably affecting only a minority of people, including the types of groups that concern me here. For these groups it has the capability of engendering new notions of community, of membership, and of entitlement. The mix of focused activism and local or global networks creates conditions for the emergence of at least partly transnational identities. From the perspective of my concerns in this chapter, we might think of the enablement of transnational identities as a condition that can facilitate cross-border relations that at least partly bypass the world of inter-state relations.

## CONCLUSION

Economic globalization and the new network technologies have contributed to produce a spatiality for the urban which pivots on deterritorialized cross-border networks and territorial locations with massive concentrations of resources. This is not a completely new feature. Over the centuries, cities have been at the intersection of processes with supra-urban and even intercontinental scales. What is different today is the intensity, complexity, and global span of these networks, and the extent to which significant portions of economies are now dematerialized and digitized and hence can travel at great speeds through these networks. Also new is the growing use of digital networks by a broad range of often resource-poor organizations to pursue a variety of cross-border initiatives. All of this has raised the number of cities that are part of cross-border networks operating on often vast geographic scales. Under these conditions, much of what we experience and represent as the local turns out to be a micro-environment with global span.

This new geography of centrality constituted by the worldwide grid of global cities, marked by sharp imbrications of digital and non-digital conditions, is perhaps one of the most strategic spaces for the formation of new types of political actors and politics. Global cities concentrate key sectors of global corporate capital and also a vast mix of people and organizations from around the world. This is a cross-border geography characterized by the increasing density and diversity of transactions and actors. It is a space with new economic and political potentialities that is both place-centered because it is embedded in particular and strategic cities; and it is trans-territorial because it connects sites that are not geographically proximate yet intensely connected to each other. It is not only the transmigration of capital that takes place in this cross-border geography, but also that of people, both rich, that is, the new transnational professional workforce, and poor, that is, most migrant workers; and it is a space for the transmigration of cultural forms, for the reterritorialization of "local" subcultures. While these types of developments do not necessarily neutralize attachments to a country or a national cause, they do shift this attachment to include trans-local communities of practice and/or membership, whether they are the new transnational professionals of global finance or activist organizations.

Globalization is a contradictory space; it is characterized by contestation, internal differentiation, continuous border crossings. The global city is emblematic of this condition. Global cities concentrate a disproportionate share of global corporate power and are one of the key sites for its over-valorization. But they also concentrate a disproportionate share of the disadvantaged and are one of the key sites for their devalorization. This joint presence happens in a context where (1) the globalization of the economy has grown sharply and cities have become increasingly strategic for global capital; and (2) marginalized people have found their voice and are making claims on the city as well. This joint presence is further brought into focus by the sharpening of the distance between the two. The center now concentrates immense power, a power that rests on the capability for global control and the capability to produce super-profits. And marginality, notwithstanding little economic and political power, has become an increasingly strong presence through a proliferation of new types of politics and an emergent transnational politics embedded in the new geography of economic globalization. Both actors, increasingly transnational and in contestation, find in the global city the strategic terrain for their operations.

## REFERENCES

Abu-Lughod, Janet L. (1999) *New York, Los Angeles, Chicago: America's Global Cities*. Minneapolis: University of Minnesota Press.

Braudel, Fernand (1984) *The Perspective of the World*, trans. Siân Reynolds. London: Collins.

Brenner, Neil (1998) Global Cities, Global States: Global City Formation and State Territorial Restructuring in Contemporary Europe. *Review of International Political Economy* 5:1–37.

Castells, Manuel (1989) *The Informational City*. Oxford: Blackwell.

Castells, Manuel (1996) *The Networked Society*. Oxford: Blackwell.

Friedmann, John and Wolff Goetz (1982) World City Formation: An Agenda for Research and Action. *International Journal of Urban and Regional Research* 6:309–344.

Graham, Stephen, and Simon Marvin (1996) *Telecommunications and the City: Electronic Spaces, Urban Places*. London: Routledge.

Hall, Peter (1996) *The World Cities*. New York: McGraw Hill.

Isin, Ergin, ed. (2000) *Democracy, Citizenship, and the Global City*. London and New York: Routledge.

Keck, Margaret E., and Kathryn Sikkink (1998) *Activists Beyond Borders: Advocacy Networks in International Politics*. Ithaca, NY: Cornell University Press.

Low, Setha M. (1999) Theorizing the City. In *Theorizing the City*, ed. Setha Low, pp. 1–33. New Brunswick, NJ: Rutgers University Press.

Sassen, Saskia (2001) *The Global City*. 2nd edn. Princeton, NJ: Princeton University Press.

Taylor, Peter J. (2000) World Cities and Territorial States Under Conditions of Contemporary Globalization. *Political Geography* 19:5–32.

## SUGGESTED FURTHER READING

Body-Gendrot, Sophie (1999) *Controlling Cities*. Oxford: Blackwell.

Cohen, Michael A., Blair A. Ruble, Joseph S. Tulchin, and Allison M. Garland, eds. (1996) *Preparing for the Urban Future: Global Pressures and Local Forces*. Washington, DC: Woodrow Wilson Center Press (distributed by the Johns Hopkins University Press).

Cordero-Guzman, Hector R., Robert C. Smith, and Ramon Grosfoguel, eds. (2001) *Migration, Transnationalization, and Race in a Changing New York*. Philadelphia: Temple University Press.

Fincher, Ruth, and Jane M. Jacobs, eds. (1998) *Cities of Difference*. New York: Guilford Press.

Hamilton, Nora, and Norma Stolz Chinchilla (2001) *Seeking Community in a Global City: Guatemalans and Salvadorans in Los Angeles*. Philadelphia: Temple University Press.

Harris, Nigel, and Ida Fabricius, eds. (1996) *Cities and Structural Adjustment*. London: University College London.

Holston, James, ed. (1996) *Cities and Citizenship*. Theme issue, *Public Culture* 8.

Magnusson, Warren (1994) *The Search for Political Space*. Toronto: University of Toronto Press.

Torres, Maria de los Angeles (1998) Transnational Political and Cultural Identities: Crossing Theoretical Borders. In *Borderless Borders*, ed. Frank Bonilla, Edwin Melendez, Rebecca Morales, and Maria de los Angeles, pp. 169–182. Philadelphia: Temple University Press.

Valle, Victor M., and Rodolfo D. Torres (2000) *Latino Metropolis*. Minneapolis: University of Minnesota Press.

## CHAPTER 12

# Globalization

## Jonathan Friedman

The study of class became a very unpopular subject in the 1980s and 1990s in many quarters of anthropology and other social sciences. This was an era in which culture became a dominant mode of understanding the world, even though in principle there is absolutely nothing contradictory about considering the two together. For many, class has been associated with other vulgarities such as exploitation and a whole array of *material* things, which are not considered sufficiently sophisticated for the culturally oriented social scientist. Some of the critique of class analysis is well taken. There was in many approaches a tendency to reduce the basic structures of social life to relations of exploitation, to "relations of production" as they were called in some Marxist discourses. The notion that there were general cultural features of modern capitalist society, for example, that were not class-based, was sometimes rejected by Marxists. In this perspective, culture was seen as a reflection of class position and as such had to be entirely dependent upon such a position. Commercial mentalities, cultural distinctions related to lifestyle, including housing, interior decorating, clothing, and Bourdieu's "taste" were understood as direct products of social position (that is, including sub-class differentiation). It should be noted that the critique of such models was forthcoming even from those who were very much focused on the issue of class.

The shift away from issues of class is not simply a question of taste, but rather is related to a larger reconfiguration of identity and power in Western societies. An excellent example of this shift can be found in much of the sociological work on the advent of information society, globalization, new social movements, etc. The shift is one of the cornerstones of the writings of Alain Touraine (1992). The argument, oversimplified, is that capitalist modernity was based on a class polarization of society that pitted capital against labor in a political struggle for relative advantage. Since the 1980s that modernity, or at least the opposition on which it was founded, has disintegrated. The power of labor has decreased, the working class has fragmented, the middle classes have grown, and as a result working-class movements are being replaced by more local or alternatively more generalized issues such as the environment, feminism, etc. – movements all based on cultural identity rather than class.

Within anthropology there has been a parallel shift of interests since the late seventies toward issues of culture and identity. This is clear enough in the United States, but similar tendencies have also been evident in Europe. The use of the term culture, for example, which was quite uncommon in Europe until the 1980s, became increasingly popular thereafter. This recent shift of interest toward things cultural is part of a more general movement characterized by the decline of some of modernism's primary vehicles (Marxism, developmentalism, rationalism), and by an intensifying critique of science and of universalism that are typical of an emergent "postmodernism."

Much of the discourse produced by cultural studies and anthropology alike in the past couple of decades has been based on this original turn away from class and toward culture. An especially striking reflection of this shift is the following; one well-known anthropologist of globalization, echoing Frantz Fanon (in a perverted fashion), is said to have remarked, "When I hear the word *class* I go for my gun." It is clearly the case that class is not an adequate term when analyzing many of the social forms that are the concerns of anthropologists. Generalizing this insight to all aspects of the modern global system, however, poses serious problems to understanding the reality of the world in which we live.

The purpose of this chapter is to shed light on that reality by suggesting a set of relevant links among phenomena that are quite salient today but that are not often connected. Doing so requires a rethinking of what has been referred to, often without serious analysis, as "globalization." In my view, it is impossible to dissociate questions of the structure of state societies from those of cultural identity and from the larger context within which states are constituted and reproduced. This is not to argue that there is a higher order of determination, the global, above all the rest. On the contrary, it is to argue that the global simply reflects the emergent properties of the articulation of numerous local processes. There may well be hierarchies of control, but these are part of the nature of formal organizations themselves. UNESCO and the IMF should not be confused with global social processes. They may well have as their domains the regulation of international and inter-state relations, but they are largely responses to rather than determinants of those relations. In terms of their social impact, they are small, relatively self-contained worlds of their own, even where they span large geographical distances.

This essay thus seeks to contribute to an understanding of class formation in what has come to be known as the "era of globalization." This requires a reassessment of the term "globalization" itself, so I shall begin with some terminological discussion.

Globalization has become a pop term not only in the media and in business economics, but also increasingly in postcolonial studies and anthropology. I shall not go into detail here, but shall instead briefly summarize the major tendencies and underlying assumptions of this discourse. There is, of course, a literature on globalization-related issues that has emerged in works informed by political economy, in economic geography, critical economics, and sociology. Much of this work is quantitative and is argued in factual terms. It documents a number of changing realities: the rapid increase since the 1970s of capital export in the form of foreign direct investment, the asymmetric distribution of these flows toward East Asia and to a lesser degree to countries like India and Brazil, the increasing salience of multinational companies (sometimes called transnational, to stress what is in fact a false notion of deterritorialization), the enormous increase in financial and speculative transactions in relation to production, and the development of new speculative markets (such as derivatives) – the value of which is greater than the entire world economy measured in terms of goods and service transactions. Very often this development has been interpreted in technological terms, as the product of the computer and internet developments, which have speeded up transaction time and have totally transformed productive activity.

This account is of course anything but new, and it is interesting for an anthropologist who has been through the long critique of technological determinist evolutionism to encounter it yet again. The argument should be taken seriously, but even among otherwise empirically based researchers, the technological connection is simply assumed. In the second edition of his *Network Society*, for example, Castells is at pains to explain away the findings of economist Robert Gordon, one of the US's major specialists on the economics of productivity. Gordon has painstakingly shown that, contrary to the assertions of advocates of the "new economy," the productivity decline that began in the 1970s has *not* changed significantly since the advent of the "new economy." The answer from globalization theorists appears to be, "Wait! Things will change." Well, we are still waiting.

I am not, it should be noted, arguing against the reality of globalization, but about its world historical status. And while it is clear that the last several decades have been witness to novel developments, it is important to be able to challenge what appears as self-evident. In fact, it is the self-evidence that should make us wary. While the globalization literature is certainly important and exciting, especially when it deals with empirical realities, as in much of the work in economic geography and sociology, it is sometimes informed by ideologically based desires. The globalization literature that has found its way into anthropology, I will argue, is far more a concentration of such desires than an empirical and rationally critical endeavor.

## MODELS OF GLOBAL SYSTEMS

The distinction between globalization and global systemic perspectives in anthropology is worth reviewing here, since the two approaches are quite different. Globalization has been proposed as a new stage of world history, an assertion that is based on an experience or a fantasy of things on the move. In anthropological terms this takes the form of a struggle against localism, and of a celebration of movement itself – of what might be called a displacement from roots to routes. In the interests of space, I shall only indicate some of the most general characteristics of the argument. These are reducible to three: (1) the necessary movement from smaller to larger units and from simpler to more complex organizations; (2) following from the latter, the notion that globalization is about the global era that we are now entering, an era fraught with conflicts perhaps, but one which promises a new diasporic way of life that may well supersede the nation-state (Appadurai 1993); in the globalization perspective, the nation-state is understood as the source of most of the evils of modernity, especially essentialism and its twin offspring, nationalism and racism; (3) a new world conceived of as one of border crossing, hybridity, and experimental identification, but also (for some) of hypercapitalism, network society, and increasing exploitation, at least at the beginning. Hypercapitalism is sometimes referred to as millennial capitalism (Comaroff and Comaroff 2000)

Much of the discourse produced in the cultural globalization literature is saturated with a terminology of a trans-x and post-x sort. It is about transcendence of existing borders. A feeling of wanting to escape from all forms of fixed or grounded identities and a profound desire to belong to something higher and more expansive are common characteristics of this discourse. This desire to transcend the self is expressed in a most foundational form in certain versions of post-feminism (Butler 1993). The cultural globalization literature (Malkki 1992; Kelly 1995) finds cosmopolitans in the most dubious of places, and is wont to trash redneck indigenes as enemies of the world society to come.

What is the problem, one might ask? Why is it necessary to take sides in these issues? I suggest that this tendency is the product of a cosmopolitan agenda, one based on a moral classification that divides the world into dangerous classes and locals, on the one hand, and liberal and progressive world citizens, on the other. This popular and proliferating discourse is not, I suggest, an internal theoretical development within any particular social science. On the contrary it is the spontaneous self-understanding of those who occupy a certain position within the contemporary world-system in transformation. The true sources for the conceptualizations of globalization that have emerged from sophisticated academic circles, I would argue, can be found in the mundane activities of those who help manage the contemporary global order. Especially important in this regard is the way people communicate on the internet in certain multinational consultancies, in many of the media, and among top officials in diplomatic, international political and economic arenas, and the way the managerial New Age conceives of the New World. In sum, my assessment of globalization is that it is the expression of a positional identity within the global system rather than a description or theoretical perspective on the contemporary world.

The global systemic perspective is vastly different, not least with respect to the notion of globalization itself. The latter is seen not as a new world-historical stage, but as a phase phenomenon in the cyclical development of hegemonic expansion and contraction. Globalization in this perspective is the expression of hegemonic decline in which a decentralization of capital accumulation results in a shift in investment from old to new centers or potential hegemons (Braudel 1984), and in the process upsets existing sociopolitical and cultural arrangements. On the basis of detailed historical research, Arrighi (1997:2) argues that massive financial expansions of this kind have accompanied all the major hegemonic declines in the history of the European world-system:

> These periods of intensifying competition, financial expansion and structural instability are nothing but the "autumn" of a major capitalist development. It is the time when the leader of the preceding expansion of world trade reaps the fruits of its leadership by virtue of its commanding position over world-scale processes of capital accumulation. But it is also the time when that same leader is gradually displaced at the commanding heights of world capitalism by an emerging new leadership.

This kind of approach has been fully developed in the work of Arrighi, but is also present in much of the world-systems literature. As early as the 1970s my own work led me to suggest that civilizations were all examples of such expansion and contraction processes, and that modern "world" systems were simply a continuation of much older processes. The similarities in this process can be expressed graphically as a set of cycles that tend toward a limit. The individual cycles express shifting hegemony within a larger systemic arena while the larger cycle expresses the ultimate limits of expansion of the system as a whole.

From a global systemic perspective, globalization corresponds to periods of crisis and hegemonic transition. As a phenomenon of transition, globalization has been well documented for the major shifts in hegemony in the Western-dominated world-system. The hegemonic shift from Italy to the Iberian peninsula and then from there to the Netherlands and then Britain, for example, was accompanied by major changes in investment flows from old to new potential hegemons. The most recent shift of this kind came at the end of the nineteenth century. The major themes of this period are similar enough to the present to warrant comment. There was massive globalization of capital, on a scale easily comparable to the present. Foreign direct investment, which had been a minor phenomenon relative to portfolio investment (investment in stocks and bonds) reached 9 percent of world output in 1913, a proportion that was not surpassed until the early 1990s (Bairoch and Kozul-Wright 1996:10). Openness to foreign trade was not markedly different in 1993 than it was in 1913. There were massive British investments in the United States, and Germany was rapidly becoming an industrial giant. Britain was no longer the world's workshop. Its share of world manufacturing declined from close to 50 percent to 14 percent by 1913 as the United States increased its relative industrial dominance. The decline of hegemonic Britain at the end of the nineteenth century occurred in a situation of increasing competition, crises of overproduction, and recurrent depressions. There was also mass migration in this era, which occurred together with expanding trade.

Many of the current debates concerning immigration and "multiculturalism" were already prevalent in this period. This was also an age of technological revolution. Stock markets were connected by cable, and investment could flow between continents at revolutionary new speeds. There was also an enormous celebration of new technologies – electric lighting, telephones, automobiles, and even airplanes and X-rays. This was also a period that witnessed the rise of contradictory ideologies of the same kind that are prevalent today. At one extreme there was the Futurist religion of technology; at the other, cults of tradition, *gemeinschaft*, and the local. In terms of the relative merits of globalization versus global-systems perspectives, however, more important is the fact that this phase of globalization came to an end (by the 1920s), and that it was followed by a long period of de-globalization that lasted until the 1950s (and that involved a major world war). It was only in the 1950s that globalization began again. It has continued to intensify from the 1970s until the present.

This does not imply, of course, that nothing new happens in world history, but simply that some properties of historical processes have remained the same. Indeed, the similarities between the current end-of-millennium crisis and that of the period from 1870 to 1920 does not vitiate the equally important fact that there are also crucial differences in structure as well. The previous globalized era was characterized by stronger national states and nationalism, and by a much lower ratio of direct foreign to portfolio investment. This was an era of national consolidation in the wake of the final breakdown of the Habsburg and Ottoman empires. While there were equivalents to today's multinationals, they were fewer in number and not nearly as complex. Much of this difference has to do with technological developments that have made the internationalization of productive processes a more profitable possibility.

It is often argued that today's global financial economy is a new phenomenon, but here as well there are clear precedents. The very notion of finance capital, discussed at length in a variety of well-known works from the period, emerged in part in an effort to understand the massive expansion of the financial sector with respect to industrial production. This is a crucial issue, because it is a structural rather than an historical phenomenon. The relation between the accumulation of money capital and the accumulation of productive capital, that is, the capacity to produce industrial products and productive services, is a fundamental contradictory relation in capitalist reproduction. This contradiction is expressed in the shift of capital from productive to non-productive activities, a shift that usually occurs simultaneously with capital export (globalization). The latter process is simply the expression of the uneven distribution of profitability in the world arena. The fact that 50 percent of foreign direct investment in 1997 consisted of mergers and acquisitions is a product of a situation in which such activity is more rational than investment in new production. An important aspect of the cycle of expansion and contraction is the increasing divergence of "fictitious" from real accumulation as production becomes increasingly unprofitable in relation to other activities.

This is, of course, an oversimplification of a complex process, but the tendencies to which it points are important, nonetheless. It implies that in hegemonic declines there is not only a tendency toward the massive export of capital (in the form of globalization), but also to a shift from productive to non-productive forms of investment – to real estate, stock-market speculation, derivative markets. This is a process that increases the commodification of the world as demand increases for accelerating accumulation, and as reality is fragmented into clusters of property rights that can be sold on the market. The creation of private titles is a practice of capitalization that creates wealth out of named categories, irrespective of their relation to real production.

According to this model, it is in periods of globalization that international capitalist classes become most salient. This is not to say that they emerge only in such periods. On the contrary, I argue below that they are permanent features of capitalist civilization. What might be said to be specific to globalizing periods is the rapid elaboration of such elites and of the discourses that they produce or that are produced around them. The reason for this is in part the availability of funds to support globalizing elites, who struggle to generalize their particular perspective on the world. This is a perspective that can be characterized as "cosmopolitan."

## STRUCTURES OF THE LONG RUN

Categories such as globalization, cosmopolitan elites, national elites, middle classes, immigrant minorities, regional minorities, and indigenous populations are not categories that appear in a particular historical era. They are basic structural features of the capitalist state system, and more specifically the nation-state system. Their salience may vary over time, but they exist, at least potentially, throughout the history of the system. It might be argued as well that the nation-state itself is no constant in the history of the modern world, but rather that the conjoining of nation and state is a function of historically contingent relations forged among emergent class actors, including the state-class which in the process is transformed into a "government." While the national character of states is thus anything but a constant, there do appear to be certain tendencies in class formation that truly *are* of the *longue durée*. The tendencies to which I refer do not involve a particular set of fixed class categories. Instead, they refer to a process of distribution of positions, local, regional, and global, within the larger territorial entity. These positions define class relations between various kinds of elites and commoner populations. In the pre-nation-state era, for example, the state elites were at the same time cosmopolitan elites, aristocrats who participated in an inter-state realm in which royalties and aristocracies were joined in marriage and political alliances, in which they sent laborers, craftsmen, architects, and artists from court to court in generous gestures.

These states were not nation-states in any sense. They were aristocratic or royal domains linked by marriage and political alliances as well as by conflict and warfare. Territorial populations were not integrated into the larger territory as a mass of individuals. Instead there were numerous regional and local political structures. Migration was certainly an integral part of the dynamics of such states, and was the product of royal policies and demands for specialized labor. But insofar as ordinary people were subjects rather than citizens, they were essentially pawns in a larger set of strategies. National or ethnic identity was limited primarily to local groups and regions or to diasporic populations. And identification with larger political units was primarily the strategy of aristocrats and of those who could gain by becoming attached to royal courts.

What is important for this discussion is the continuum from the local to the inter-state level, and the potential oppositions that developed among them. However, it should be clearly noted that the very praxis of the absolutist state created a social field of national identity. Long before the French Revolution there were letters of "naturaliza-tion" offered to foreigners who came to live in the country, and as of 1697 they were forced to pay taxes. Immigrant status was inherited for three generations for those arriving after 1600. That is, it was defined in terms of descent from specific national origins. There was also a great deal of migration and aristocratic tourism between countries, especially following the war against the Augsburg coalition (1689–97).

As one contemporary described it, "Since the advent of peace, there was such an influx of foreigners in Paris that one could reckon 15 to 16 thousand in the quarter Saint-Germain alone. A year later there were 36,000 in this same quarter" (*Annales de la Cour de la Ville*, 1697–98, in Dubost and Sahlins 1999:15). And the word "nation" is used to identify individuals throughout the period, in terms such as the following (*Annales de la Cour de la Ville*, 1697–98, in Dubost and Sahlins 1999:378, 379, 380):

Anne Sauvage, *anglaise de nation* (English by nation), described as "not married in France, that she does not conform to Parisian custom and that she is not naturalized."

Jacques Lieurard, a Protestant convert from the north of France wrongly taxed as "son of a foreigner, coming from Holland."

"Imperfect Frenchmen."

It is noteworthy that after 1600 immigrant status is inherited for a period of three generations, so that a notion of a local territorial population is clearly in evidence.

One detects in the writings of the period (Fénelon 1920 [1699]) a clear opposition to the urban, commercial, foreign merchants and the international from a position that can be interpreted as Christian and agrarian.

There is a twofold set of representations generated in this division between the peasant and the urban sectors of the larger territory. Urban groups insist on the royal strategy of the state elites to increase their economic base, demographically and in capital, while the peasantry develops on an increasingly salient notion of a national population, sedentary and exploited by the latter. It might be suggested that this growing opposition is the foundation for the French Revolution, in which "the people" are established as sovereign within the confines of the territorial state, thus creating the nation-state. The famous Abbé de Sieyès, one of the ideologues of the French Revolution, defined the Third Estate as the true basis of sovereignty, rather than the king (Sieyès 1963 [1789]).

It is noteworthy that there is a notion of the larger world in opposition to the local and the parochial, which appears as an historical invariant. It is more clearly expressed in the elite sector than in the popular sector. It accounts for the early appearance of religious doctrines that are clearly global in scope. In the early seventeenth century there are fairly clear expressions of a notion of a single humanity in need of a world order – an expression not entirely foreign to the interpretation of the Catholic Church. In 1614, for example, the Rosicrucians published a pamphlet entitled *Fama*. In that pamphlet it is proposed that all learned men throughout the world should join forces toward the establishment of a synthesis of science. Behind this effort allegedly stood an illuminated brotherhood – the children of light, who had been initiated into the mysteries of the Grand Order. This *Brüderschaft der Theosophen* (Theosophical Brotherhood) was said to have been founded by Christian Rosen-creutz (1378–1484), who had become an initiate during his travels in the Middle East in the fifteenth century. He founded a brotherhood that is supposed to have operated in secret ever since.

It is somewhat less clear to what extent there were indigenizing or nationalizing tendencies in the early history of Europe. It is widely accepted, however, that the nation-state was very much a project of state-oriented elites – with the caveat that the latter produced an opposing project rooted in the exploited classes to capture the state and make it an instrument of their own needs. The various regional and local resistances that proliferated within emerging absolutist states are evidence that there were and are numerous sub-state identities of varying strength that have persisted right up into the present. It is necessary to find the resonant bases for the different collective identifications that characterize our history so as to avoid falling into the trap of envisioning such identities as mere intellectual constructs that people have somehow been seduced into accepting.

## PEOPLE, CLASS, AND NATION

The notion of a "people" belonging to a relatively distinct region is at least a virtual category before the emergence of the nation-state, but a series of political reconfigurations of the state, including the French Revolution, established and institutionalized the nation as a replacement for God, as the foundation of sovereignty. These state reconfigurations include the entire relation of representative government and the tendency toward the elaboration of political democracy. The state is reduced to a government, a set of representatives of those granted the right to vote, even as the broadening of the franchise represents the extension of nationhood itself. The rise of representative government is associated with the establishment and institutionalization of national bourgeois elites in competition with the older aristocratic cosmopolitans, over which they gain a clear advantage in the nineteenth century. From this point on, people, nation, and class become an unstable trio of political contest. This applies even to the socialist movement, in which there is a vital and vicious conflict between internationalizing and nationalizing tendencies (with the latter becoming dominant by the time of World War I). The emergent logic here is that which links a definite population to the control over its conditions of existence. Here class merges with peoplehood or nationhood and fuses itself with statehood, which thereby becomes its political expression.

Nationhood is the product of sets of practices of socialization, but also of linkages between local experiences of community, landscape, and language, and larger symbolic orders of the state realm. The capitalization and commodification of society also produce an individualization in which intermediate sodalities increasingly disappear, leaving as an ideal type only the relation between the individual subject and the state. This process of disintegration may create even stronger identification with the nation as the sole concrete expression of a larger collective unity. While assimilation is a variable, both in time and in space, it tends to be strongest in periods of hegemonic expansion and economic growth.

In the above outline I stress the historical variability of such processes. Thus, in the contemporary period, assimilation has been reversed, so that there is a proliferation of identities – migrant, regional, indigenous, and national – all of which have developed simultaneously. This increase in cultural identification combines with growing class polarization to create a highly fragmented lower class of flexible, partly employed, partly legal, and increasingly desperate, disparaged, and enraged people – a "multitude," a new globalized *lumpenproletriat*.

The word "indigenization" is used to indicate an intensification of localized or rooted identities among the downwardly mobile populations of the system at the same time that cosmopolitanism intensifies at the top. It is here we find culture and politics combining in important ways – in the form of an ethnification that generates conflicts among different populations at the bottom (expressed as racisms and nationalisms), and an emergent opposition to the elites themselves, especially the political elites. Some of the extreme examples of militia groups, whose members often come from very different political persuasions, and who express a localism whose main enemy is the class of cosmopolitans that they define as Washington, the Catholic Church, and the Jews (who are often described as allied in a project of world domination). It is noteworthy that many of these groups are ardent supporters of Al Quaeda. The divisions within this lower class are not only politicized, but represent significant aspects of an emergent dominant ideology that pits a humanist elite against the dangerous classes.

France is one of the most interesting countries in which this phenomenon has been charted. The rising culturalism of the elites has replaced class with culture and in so doing has replaced class with ethnicity. Most significant in this fracture was the cleavage of the left itself. Juillard (1997) designates this split as between the *moral left* and the *sociological left*, the elite and the "people." The political elite was (and is) also itself split on this matter, between a more republican and assimilationist and more multiculturalist and even cosmopolitan position. The *loi Debré* (the law introduced by Jean-Louis Debré, president of the National Assembly), which imposed stricter controls on immigration in 1997, sparked a counter-demonstration, while the newspaper *Libération* published a list, classified by professional category, of the signatories to the petition against the law (Juillard 1997:108). More than two-thirds had at least two years of university education and half had university diplomas equivalent to the MA. Only 4 percent of the signatories were workers. It can be argued that this represents a massive change in political identity, the lower end of the population sinking into nationalism or localism while the upper end is increasingly liberal and cosmopolitan. This interpretation is reinforced by the voting statistics from the late 1990s for the National Front, a political party of the extreme right. Upwards of 30 percent of the party's support came from workers.

Juillard's interpretation of these developments (1997:105) fits the model suggested here. There has been a vertical polarization in France. Elites have consolidated around a cosmopolitan identity – a set of representations of reality that are directly contrary to the interests of those whom the elites once thought they represented (i.e., the national working class). Indeed, elites can be said to have switched constituencies in this period.

The cosmopolitanism of certain elites is apparently a well-established European habitus or even tradition. This is clearly evident in the history of Freemasonry. The latter, after being taken over by aristocrats and then wealthy capitalists in eighteenth-century England and France, clearly expressed a set of values that are equally visible in today's world. Thus the new-age managerialism that is so common in the contemporary world of elites has its more aristocratic forerunners in the Freemasonry of the past. These themes can be outlined as follows:

1   An opposition to organized religion in its Western form.
2   An attraction to Oriental religious philosophy, not least its holism.
3   An interest in primitive and ancient religions.
4   The individual as the center of spirituality and a direct link to the sacred or godhead, understood in pantheistic terms.
5   The superiority of the elect who can attain this relation to the sacred.
6   In political terms, an orientation to the world as a whole, to Mankind.
    A   This implies opposition to the nation-state or any other sub-national units except as sources of spirituality.
    B   The internal differentiation between leaders and followers, or the elect and the rest.

7   A millenarian view of the future, of the New Age that is to come.
8   These beliefs represent the identity and ideology of an international elite class.

These themes incorporate notions of holism and of being chosen by higher powers. The elite is the "chosen few," chosen to lead all of humanity to the promised land. This view implies distance rather than identity with populations that are under its rule and this provides a link to the pluralism that is so prevalent in both older and new versions of multiculturalism (Pijls 1999:99):

> The cosmopolitan bourgeoisie in the 18th century came to adopt a perspective [towards its] own society as if it were a foreign one, a target for "colonial" exploitation. Freemasonry provided a cover for developing the new identity on which the exploitation of members of one's own community is premised. By entering the Masonic lodges, merchants and those otherwise involved in the long-distance money economy such as lawyers and accountants, realized the primordial alienation from the community which is the precondition for market relations, exploitation of wage labor, and abstract citizenship.

Another aspect of this particular global position is its association with finance rather than industrial production, which is local and vulgar. Expressly opposed to manual labor, the British masonry defined themselves as above the earthly workings of the economy. They preferred "to sit above the commercial fray, pulling levers, dangling rewards and applying sanctions" (Hampden-Turner and Trompenaars 1993:321). This important logic thus connects finance with the cosmopolitan, and in turn with a sense of a higher power and even mission. The values of the humanism that emerged in the Enlightenment are very much woven together with this particular version of cosmopolitanism.

## The small worlds of cosmopolitanism

One of the outcomes of the continuity in the cosmopolitan elite as an enduring category of the modern state is the production of social worlds that are more or less bounded socially. Cosmopolitan identity commonly represents itself as world-encompassing, as opposed to the smaller worlds of national and other more localized populations. This is a significant misrepresentation of reality, one that confuses geographical with social closure. It has led to the absurd assertion, for example, that diasporas are instances of cosmopolitan openness. Such a claim flies in the face of practically everything that is known of such transnational groups, whose very survival depends on the maintenance of strict boundaries (which in turn implies high levels of endosocial relations, including endogamy and strict control over children).

In this respect, it is enlightening to investigate the life of transnational elites, which display some of the characteristics of diasporas. An interesting study of what has been called *l'immigration dorée* ("the golden immigration") in France (Wagner 1999) reveals a number of interesting properties of the social life of such cosmopolitans. Focusing on foreign elite communities via their relation to international schools and other associations, Wagner depicts a two-layered elite structure. One layer is newer, and is the product of the recent emergence of a transnational managerial class. The other layer is older, and is made up of more aristocratic cosmopolitan elites. Although she has concentrated on a relatively limited period of time, Wagner's work shows that almost a third of all transnationals in her sample marry other transnationals (though not necessarily of the same nationality). They send their children to a limited number of schools, where education consists in learning to be transnational.

These transnationals, Wagner shows (1999:116), play at representing the world, at being a United Nations devoted to a celebration of cultural difference, and they often have official connections with these international organizations. But they also identify themselves in the idiom of blood, even where it is mixed (Wagner 1999:116).

> "I have expatriate blood in my veins . . . I am American by passport and nationality but my family as well as my wife's family have branches in many countries, which means that we always have one foot in the U.S. and one foot abroad."

> "My father was something of a vagabond. It was in his blood. My brothers are like that too: I have a brother in Austria, one in Finland, a sister in Spain. My father was always on the move and I learned from him."

Indeed, they use the term "expatriate blood" to characterize themselves, thus expressing a combination of roots and routes of the kind announced in much of the postcolonial cultural studies literature. In this way the transnational is concretized in biological terms.

The self-definition of a cosmopolitan ethos, which is common to both aristocratic and managerial groups, is an essential part of the self-understanding of transnationals. "Curiosity, openness and tolerance are terms often employed to designate these qualities" (Wagner 1999:142).

This ethos is that of the world traveler always open to new adventures, to new kinds of experience and different kinds of people. But it should be noted that the actual social arenas of these cosmopolitans are limited to a relatively small number of associations, clubs, and schools. Here, they constantly meet and are able to identify one another by their common interests and tastes, but also by means of differences in national origins and cultures. Within these domains cosmopolitans express a clear opposition between themselves and more ordinary nationals, going so far as to refer to the latter as *terrestrials*. This opposition is based on the usual classification of the local as "other" (Wagner 1999:189, 204).

If a cosmopolitan orientation is a constant structure in the modern territorial and national state, it becomes increasingly salient in periods of globalization. One may even speak of an unstable opposition between the local, the national, and the international in which ideological dominance shifts markedly over time. At the very top of this hierarchy are the families that have been designated the *grandes fortunes*. This group keeps its distance from the others, has its own clubs and associations, and is listed and ranked (by members' places of residence) in journals like *Le petit mondain* (The Little Socialite). Wagner (1999) presents the example of the comte de Chatel. His genealogy is mixed in national terms, and encompasses Italy, England, Belgium, and Argentina. It is anything but mixed, however, in class terms, as the family has intermarried exclusively with other *grandes fortunes* families in these countries. The capital of the Chatels is directly linked to the family's international segmentary structure. M. de Chatel is never an expatriate when he travels. He is always on his own property somewhere in the world. But he is also a professional chameleon, in cultural if not class terms (Wagner 1999:122). As Pinçon and Pinçon-Charlot (1996:120) argue, "Cosmopolitan relations and a multiterritoriality extended to foreign countries are two essential components of 'high society'."

The differentiation between the upper crust and the managerial elite, besides being socially marked in very clear terms, is also reflected in identity. The cosmopolitanism of the *grandes fortunes* partakes of an aristocratic world that tends toward homogeneity. The cosmopolitanism of the managers, on the other hand, springs from a more multinational world in which cultures are compared and ranked. This may be more of a variation than a true difference, however, as in both groups there is a tendency for people to distance themselves from the local and the national and to identify with the international or transnational. In Wagner's (1999:212) words, "The ability to be 'at home' materially, socially and symbolically, in several countries, the appropriation of a cosmopolitan identity which affects all aspects of the person, defines the model of emergent international managerial culture."

## Cosmopolitanization and globalization

I suggest that, during periods of strong globalization, such as we have today, elites have the tendency to cosmopolitanize themselves. This can be understood as a product of the convergence of social and spatial mobility, which situates its adherents *above* the world, where they can encompass the diversity that lies below without being part of it (except in the sense of being able to consume it in the form of products). This distinction creates an opposition to the local as something that is decidedly lower in status and conflates immobility with cultural poverty. It is a mistake, however, to assume that the encompassing self-representation of the cosmopolitan implies a real engagement with the world. Geographical movement, yes, but within a narrow sphere of class in which the relations that they establish are bounded and often highly segregated, in which identity is strong and homogeneous with respect to status and position. The negation of social praxis in the self-identification of cosmopolitans is a logical outcome of the nature of their social position within this system. The generalization of cosmopolitanism to all domains of transnational connection appears in this light to express a kind of struggle for ideological hegemony.

This generalization tends to equate cosmopolitanism with globalization itself and to argue for the evolution from local to global, referred to above. Locals are not merely at the bottom of this process, they are also represented as precursors to the present. They are in this sense primitive, but in a way that conflates Freudian primitivity, libidinous and inhabiting all of us, with a temporal sense of being backward. It is this, ultimately, which makes the local dangerous, as in the expression, "dangerous classes." Primitive culture, of course, is perfectly wonderful, but it needs to be extracted from its lived context and transformed into objects that can be consumed without danger. The museological understanding of culture that has become increasingly popular in recent years expresses this sublimation or even displacement of libidinous otherness into objects of consumption/contemplation and celebration. And it is this transformation that enables diversity to be collected and displayed in the salons of the elites. This is also essential to the identification of such elites with diversity and multiculturalism. The strength of this ideology depends on the balance of forces within which it is produced.

Cosmopolitanism tends to emerge simultaneously with and in dialectical relation to localizing ideologies, with nationalism, and other regional identities. This is happening today, just as it occurred in the previous period of globalization (between 1870 and 1920). It is interesting to compare the two periods in this respect. The British empire contained a core of cosmopolitanism that is quite central to developments later in the century. It was Cecil Rhodes and his Society of the Elect whose strategy was to set the agenda for the continued success of the empire. The founding of the League of Nations, one of the significant international developments of this period, may well have been conceived by this group, as was the Union of South Africa and the Commonwealth (Quigley 1981:29).

Despite its cosmopolitan orientation, when expediency required the group was perfectly capable of forsaking internationalism, and following 1931 it embraced the model of national economic regulation. While this all sounds like the extension of empire, the change in the group's orientation must be understood as part of a broader process of hegemonic decline and increasing competition. The turn of the twentieth century was a period of the fragmentation of empire, not least of a formal empire, the Habsburgs. That empire was understood as traditionalist, religiously orthodox, and rigid, yet its ranks were swelled by a new liberal class of cosmopolitans, many of whom were Jews, and all of whom were protected by the imperial court. Thus the cosmopolitanism of this group, which would today be considered progressive, was at that time associated with the past, with absolutism. Nationalism, on the other hand, was understood as the way of the future.

While the situation was actually more complicated than this, since there were other powerful cosmopolitanisms in Europe, the emerging conflict in the world-system was spurred on by national competition, all of which led to the Great War (World War I). The configuration of the period is brilliantly captured by Gellner (1998:12).

> Hence the deep irony of the situation: an authoritarian [Habsburg] Empire, based on a medieval dynasty and tied to the heavily dogmatic ideology of the Counter-Reformation, in the end, under the stimulus of ethnic, chauvinistic, centrifugal agitation, found its most eager defenders amongst individualist liberals, recruited in considerable part from an erstwhile pariah group and standing *outside* the faith with which the state was once so deeply identified.

This competition between states culminated in a world war, which strengthened some nation-states and created others, but which also established the League of Nations. It was riddled with all of the contradictions referred to above. In the end, however, the cosmopolitan was by and large defeated.

In the current situation there are clearly similar tendencies, but political organization seems to have a stronger tendency to empire formation. Thus it might appear that cosmopolitan tendencies are on the rise. International organizations, such as the United Nations (especially its most powerful ideological apparatus, UNESCO), the World Bank, and numerous other instances. such as the World Economic Forum

(WEF), have all converged on a similar set of representations of the world. And although hegemony shifted to the United States, there is nonetheless the heritage of the Rhodes group to consider, one that is visible in post-World War II clubs with overlapping membership. These include the Bilderberg, the Trilateral Commission, the Mount Pelerin society, and the WEF. Global media such as CNN also partake of this cosmopolitan ideology, which is significant, given the force of the media's repetitive (if virtual) imaging and moral framing in the creation of everyday reality. It is also significant that a large number of intellectual elites, academics, and politicians have been socialized into this world-view. Academic anthropology has been deeply influenced by this trend, partaking of the "postcolonial aura" that celebrates movement in itself – and identities of movement (the transnational, trans-local, transsexual, border-crossing, etc.) – as "the good." Also characteristic of anthropology that has been influenced by postcolonial studies is its tendency to denigrate the dangerous redneck locals, who are associated with nationalism, racism, roots, and that greatest of all evils, *essentialism*. This perspective has even generated a critique of what is characterized as the "general anthropological perspective," well epitomized in expressions such as the following (Meyer and Geschiere 1999:3): "anthropologists' obsession with boundedness is paralleled by the ways in which the people they study try to deal with seemingly open-ended global flows." What a pity that the people we study have got it just as wrong as the rest of us. We are all obviously in need of re-education.

It should be noted that cosmopolitanism is not equivalent to internationalism. This important distinction even attracted the attention of Marcel Mauss (1969 [1920]:629), who argued that they were characterized by "deux sortes d'attitudes morales bien distinctes" ("two quite different moral attitudes"). He chose to define cosmopolitanism as a set of ideas and tendencies oriented to the destruction of the nation-state, while internationalism was merely against nationalism as such but was not opposed to the nation-state. Thus the socialist internationals struggled with these two concepts and eventually chose the international rather than the cosmopolitan. But there is another difference as well. The cosmopolitanism of the turn of the last century was largely modernist in the legacy of Kant. It identified itself with universal values, moral, rational, and scientific. Contemporary cosmopolitanism is the descendant of the aristocratic transnationalism discussed above. It is a self-identified status position, one that is quite the contrary of Kantian universalism, in that it celebrates and encompasses (rather than opposes) difference. This is why the notion of hybridity is a logical consequence of the formation of cosmopolitan identities. Cosmopolitanism today is not rationalist–universalist but rather is a fusion of all cultures, as expressed at the Band Aid concert for Ethiopian famine (held in 1984), at which the famous song "We are the World" (composed by Michael Jackson) was first performed.

## Empire?

The large volume by Hardt and Negri (2000) is an interesting example of the continuing reinforcement of a particular ideology of the global. This can be seen in some of their major thematic statements. There is no question for them that we are entering a post-imperialist world, one revealed by the end of the Vietnam war, the disappearance of the Berlin Wall, and the globalization of the world economy. They understand all of this in *evolutionary* terms, even if they are aware of the existence of previous empires, and understand that such structures are themselves fragile in the long run. The main changes that they signal are:

1   Rhizomatic transformations in the organization of power, as a result of which networks replace state forms.
2   A Foucauldian totalization of power conceived of as everywhere and nowhere, and therefore not in any one hegemonic place (such as the US).
3   The obsolescence of boundaries of all kinds, resulting in an extreme openness, so that there is no longer any "outside."
4   The emergence of the "nomadic" as a dominant figure.
5   The formation of a "multitude" to replace the proletariat.

Hardt and Negri regard the United States as the forerunner in this development. Europe is still based on territorially strong national sovereignty, while the US has transcended all that. In the US model we already have the tendency to empire. Unfortunately the Indians had to go as they could never really be *inside*, but the project remains an open one, the frontier that has always to be confronted and transcended and therefore incorporated. This is little more than a self-representation of American pluralism, and therefore is positive for many, both right and left, who vote for the immigrant nation. For these authors empire is also inevitable. Consistent with current globalizing ideology, Hardt and Negri view the *nomad* as the wave of the future, as revolutionary, whereas the local is relegated to the backward. It is even depicted as having fascist potential.

Here is the strongest argument of the globalists. Not only do they represent the good and progressive, but their very existence is enough to perform the historical task of paving the way for the final revolution of the *multitude*. None of this is documented, and the "end of imperialism" that they announce could just as easily be interpreted as little more than the decline of one particular empire – as heralding the arrival of a new dark age, a new feudalism.

Where Hardt and Negri place themselves in all of this is not clear, but the totalizing style of the presentation is clearly something that has resonated with multiple audiences. The book, in its sixth printing, has been hailed from many quarters. It is widely regarded as an extraordinary text, praised by reviewers in such disparate places as *Foreign Affairs* and the *New York Times*, and lauded by authors close to journals like *Public Culture*. The text has a ring of radical chic, perhaps, claiming to transcend a number of former perspectives. The issue of class is relegated to the past. The latter is fast becoming a "multitude" whose principal characteristic is its lack of a single unifying identity or strategic goal. The resistance to emergent empire is the essence of all multitude activities, *by definition*, since these express projects that are not the dictates of higher powers. The world to come is one that is totalized under empire in the same sense that globalization is assumed to make the world into a single place. For both positions, there is no longer an outside. Hardt and Negri's empire is defined as all-encompassing and boundary-less, and the multitude is characterized as migrant and nomadic. They are nomadic not because they are forced to be so, but because they are the essence of global desire, the desire to be on the move, to deterritorialize.

It is this that makes movement in itself, geographical movement, progressive while immobility is reactionary. The same underlying perspective can be found among other globalizers, who see the future in terms of a diasporic world of transnationals (Arjun Appadurai, John Kelly). The latter are regarded as expressing a higher evolutionary stage and higher status than the potentially redneck homebodies who, unfortunately for these authors, make up more than 98 percent of the world's population. The opposition between cosmopolitans and locals is clearly marked in all its morality in their text, "Nomadism and miscegenation appear as figures of virtue, as the first ethical practices on the terrain of empire ... Today's celebrations of the local can be regressive and fascistic when they oppose circulations and mixture" (Hardt and Negri 2000:362).

There are interesting points of similarity and overlap here between this supposedly radical thinking and cosmopolitan ideology. They can be summarized in the following parallel lists.

| *1968* | *1998* |
| --- | --- |
| The national | The postnational |
| The local | The global |
| Collective | Individual |
| Social(ist) | Liberal |
| Homogeneous | Heterogeneous |
| Monocultural | Multicultural |
| Equality (sameness) | Hierarchy (difference) |

These terms are meant to indicate the transition of self-identified progressive thinking over a period of 30 years. Although these oppositions are somewhat oversimplified, they nonetheless capture the nature of the shift. The post-national is today seen as the royal road to the future of mankind, whereas the national is a horrible leftover from a nationalist past that included essentialist and therefore racist tendencies. The global is also regarded as an expression of this new nomadic desire to transcend the prison of locality. Individualism has crept into the former collectivist (that is, nationalist or socialist) ideology and has managed to associate this with Foucauldian totalistic control. The heterogeneous has become a goal in itself, a generalized cultural pluralism of different identities, religions, and political projects. The multicultural quandary is an expression of the same shift toward heterogeneity. Culture is no longer regarded as part of the structure of existence , but rather is seen as a mere role set, as something that the individual can practice by choice, by elective affinity – like joining the golf club instead of the Wahabists, at least on Monday. In the process of this transition equality is increasingly replaced by hierarchy via an emphasis on difference. This is the key to pluralism as a political form, one in which elite rule is essential. Difference becomes the dominant value while equality is seen as an ugly result of totalitarian rule.

It is significant that a work so clearly marked by the radical politics of its authors can become a Harvard University Press bestseller in the United States, enthusiastically welcomed in the pages of *Foreign Affairs* as by authors connected to *Public Culture*.

This book provides a kind of political framework in two ways. It enables the cosmopolitans to reinforce their progressive identities, eliminating the relevance of class and pointing the way to a structure of global power in which the nomadic is defined as the wave of the future revolution. This is a fine piece of ideological fusion, one that is in many ways crucial for the hegemony of the new elites. Lévi-Strauss discussed, in another context, the way in which what he called diametric dualism, egalitarian in form, could be transformed into concentric dualism, which has the quality of being able to represent hierarchy as equality. This is dualism of center and periphery rather than left and right. In political terms the transition captures a process of hierarchization and centralization that is evident in the recent political evolution in Europe, where a former left/right opposition is currently being replaced by what is referred to as the "Third Way," or perhaps more revealing, the German *Neue Mitte* in which there is a fusion of social democracy and neoliberal politics, one in which social democracy is the shell and neoliberalism the core. But similar tendencies were evident in American "New Democracy" (Jacobs and Shapiro 2000). The hierarchic and encompassing theme is also expressed in the discourses of international organizations such as UNESCO, to say nothing of the already mentioned WEF. *Empire* is an almost uncanny expression of many of these tendencies in globalizing discourse and its ambivalent reference to Foucouldian global governance, without a physical center, but all-encompassing, is an excellent concentration of what seems to be "in the air" among certain globalizers. The popularity of the book among certain elites might well be due to the resonance of its message for those who are already tuned in. The relation between globalization, the reconfiguration of class relations, and the production of hegemonic representations is both a viable and important subject to which anthropology, endowed with a clear sense of structural transformation, should be able to contribute. But this cannot be accomplished by the kind of currently popular globalization approaches that are part of the object for which we need to account.

## REFERENCES

Appadurai, Arjun (1993) Patriotism and its Futures. *Public Culture* 5:415–440.

Arrighi, Giovanni (1997) Globalization, State Sovereignty, and the "Endless" Accumulation of Capital. Paper presented at the Conference on States and Sovereignty in the World Economy, University of California, Irvine, February 21–23.

Bairoch, Paul, and Richard Kozul-Wright (1996) *Globalization Myths: Some Historical Reflections on Integration, Industrialization, and Growth in the World Economy.* Geneva: United Nations Conference on Trade and Development.

Braudel, Fernand (1984) *The Perspective of the World*, trans. Siân Reynolds. New York: Harper and Row.

Butler, Judith (1993) *Bodies that Matter: On the Discursive Limits of "Sex."* New York: Routledge.

Comaroff, Jean, and John L. Comaroff, eds. (2000) *Millennial Capitalism and the Culture of Neoliberalism.* Durham, NC: Duke University Press.

Dubost, Jean-François, and Peter Sahlins (1999) *Et si on faisait payer les étrangers?: Louis XIV, les immigrés et quelques autres.* Paris: Flammarion.

Fénelon, Francois de Salignac de la Mothe (1920 [1699]) *Les Aventures de Télémaque.* Paris: Hachette.

Gellner, Ernest (1998) *Language and Solitude: Wittgenstein, Malinowski, and the Habsburg Dilemma*. New York: Cambridge University Press.

Hampden-Turner, Charles, and Alfons Trompenaars (1993) *The Seven Cultures of Capitalism: Value Systems for Creating Wealth in the United States, Japan, Germany, France, Britain, Sweden, and the Netherlands*. New York: Currency and Doubleday.

Hardt, Michael, and Antonio Negri (2000) *Empire*. Cambridge, MA: Harvard University Press.

Jacobs, Lawrence R., and Robert Y. Shapiro (2000) *Politicians Don't Pander: Political Manipulation and the Loss of Democracy Responsiveness*. Chicago: University of Chicago Press.

Juillard, Jacques (1997) *La Faute des élites*. Paris: Gallimard.

Kelly, John (1995) Diaspora and World War: Blood and Nation in Fiji and Hawaii. *Public Culture* 7:475–497.

Malkki, Liisa (1992) National Geographic: The Rooting of Peoples and the Territorialization of National Identity Among Scholars and Refugees. *Cultural Anthropology* 7:24–44.

Mauss, Marcel (1969 [1920]) *La Nation et l'internationalisme*. In *Oeuvres* 3:626–639.

Meyer, Birgit, and Peter Geschiere, eds. (1999) *Globalization and Identity: Dialectics of Flow and Closure*. Oxford: Blackwell.

Pinçon, Michel, and Monique Pinçon-Charlot (1996) *Grandes fortunes: dynasties familiales et formes de richesse en France*. Paris: Editions Payot et Rivages.

Pijls, K. van der (1999) *Transnational Classes and International Relations*. London: Routledge.

Quigley, Carroll (1981) *The Anglo-American Establishment: From Rhodes to Cliveden*. New York: Books in Focus.

Sieyès, Emmanuel Joseph, comte (1963 [1789]) *What is the Third Estate?* Trans. M. Blondel. London: Pall Mall.

Touraine, Alain (1992) *Critique de la modernité*. Paris: Fayard.

Wagner, A.C. (1999) *Les nouvelles élites de la mondialisation: une immigration dorée en France*. Paris: Presses Universitaires de France.

## CHAPTER 13

# Governing States

## David Nugent

Anthropological approaches to the state have undergone a veritable revolution since the 1970s. Max Weber's once normative model of the state as a centralized entity that taxes, conscripts, and monopolizes legitimate violence within a given territory – and further, his conception of rational bureaucratic states as "cages of reason" that stand above society, employing a vast bureaucracy to implement decisions in a neutral, disinterested manner – has been called into question from multiple quarters. Even as some scholars find that modern states impose a structure of hyper-rationality and order on the societies they administer (Scott 1998) – at times with disastrous consequences – other scholars cast a critical eye on virtually every aspect of the Weberian model. Some question the rational, disinterested nature of states, finding instead either dark, irrational, even libidinal passions at work in the very entrails of state processes (Aretxaga 2000), symbolic structures embedded deeply within the workings of seemingly neutral state bureaucracies (Herzfeld 1992), or a near obsession on the part of states with appropriate forms of affect rather than reason (Stoler 1995).

Other scholars question the unity of the state. In place of coherence and consistency of purpose, they find state activities to be chaotic and incoherent assemblages of sites, processes, and institutions that lack any underlying, coordinating logic (Greenhouse et al. 2002), and that often work at cross-purposes with one another. Still other scholars question the boundary between state and non-state, and point to the ways in which these realms interpenetrate and implicate one another in ways that frustrate all efforts at separation (Mitchell 1991). Some document the existence of illicit and dangerous shadow organizations – in principle the avowed enemies of legitimate authority – that not only occupy a gray zone between state and non-state, but that may also be centrally involved in and necessary to the reproduction of state power (Schneider and Schneider 1999).

Yet other scholars retain Weber's emphasis on violence, but extend it beyond police and prisons to consider the violence of everyday life. Their emphasis is on the material and discursive processes by which arbitrary and interested forms of social life are rendered unremarkable and taken for granted as state activities organize the most fundamental times and spaces of social existence, and define legitimate forms of identity, personhood, and life possibility (Corrigan and Sayer 1985). Many scholars argue that the very *idea* of the state is a mystification, one that masks the ways that relations of inequality – patterned by such constructs as race, class, age, and gender – are naturalized and reproduced (Abrams 1988). Rather than emphasize centralized bureaucracy and coercion, a growing number of scholars now look beyond the limits of the state as conventionally defined – to governmental techniques for the management and regulation of populations that are deeply embedded within and widely dispersed throughout multiple domains of public and private life. These techniques are based on plans that allow for rational management, that identify the key objects of regulation upon which management relies, that depend on the generation of expert knowledge about those objects, and on a body of experts who can monitor the behavior of those objects on the basis of the knowledge thus generated (Foucault 1991).

This "post-Weberian" literature offers crucial new insights into the workings of states. In the pages that follow I critically assess this literature, and the Weberian model to which it responds, by applying its insights to processes of state formation in Amazonas – a small agrarian region (and administrative department) in the northern Peruvian Andes – in the middle decades of the twentieth century. In Amazonas, the range of institutions and processes that would conventionally be understood as "the state" did indeed lack coherence, unity, and neutrality, despite enjoying a monopoly on legitimate force, and despite the fact that the institutional outlines of a Weberian state were clearly present. At the same time, however, an underground political movement called APRA created state-like organizational forms that were characterized by a high degree of order, consistency, and shared purpose. It was APRA, and not the state, that oversaw a fundamental reorganization of the time and space of the everyday, that did much to define legitimate forms of personhood and life possibility, and that even generated a "state effect" (Abrams 1988). In other words, despite the fact that it did not monopolize (or even exercise) force, APRA was far more successful at governing than was the state itself.

The fact that APRA succeeded where the state failed raises a series of interesting questions. Among the most important concerns the *conditions of possibility* of state formation – the political, economic, and sociocultural conditions that variously enable or disable efforts to govern. State activities everywhere seek to order and discipline national populations (that may or may not be coterminous with the spatial boundaries of the polity) in relationship to the extraction of wealth and the accumulation of capital. On the one hand, these ordering activities are based on a classificatory discourse that differentiates the population into subgroups (citizens, subversives, aliens, men, women, races, castes, etc.) and that acts as a grid or template for deciding how resources, privileges, rights, and obligations will be distributed. On the other hand, the ordering activities of states take place in the context of a broader field of inter-state relations (which involve relations between regionally or globally hegemonic polities [like the US] and their client states) and global accumulation practices (which undergo crises, reorganization, expansion, and contraction). This broader field has much to do with how effectively a state is able to establish its classificatory grid *authoritatively* – and also the means with which and the ends toward which it seeks to do so. We now turn to a consideration of the broader field of political and economic forces in which efforts at governance unfolded in mid-twentieth-century

Peru. We then consider the attempts of APRA and the Peruvian state to establish their respective visions of governance as authoritative.

## NATIONAL AND GLOBAL CONTEXT

From the turn of the twentieth century the US replaced Great Britain as the most important foreign presence in Peru. American capital flowed into multiple branches of the economy (petroleum, mining, textile production, railroads, and coastal agriculture), and by 1929 the country owed 100 million dollars to US banks. US economic advisors made extensive recommendations regarding how Peru should organize its national finances, and in adhering to these policies the country committed itself to a path of export-led, world-market-driven development, and away from any form of economic nationalism or efforts at autonomous internal growth.

By the time of the Great Depression (1929) uneven development had accentuated long-standing geographic divisions within the national economy. Peru's coastal desert region – the scene of extensive, large-scale, agro-export activities, and also home to the country's largest population centers – became the most dynamic sector of the economy, while its "feudal-like" sierra remained largely stagnant. This process of differentiation undermined an existing, pre-Depression, political alliance between the aristocratic elite of the highlands and coastal elite groups.

The two elites were themselves divided. In the sierra, the tortuous topography of the Andes mountains tended to make of each region something of a world unto itself, where aristocratic landed families battled each other for regional control. The greater dynamism of the coast generated two factions among its elite: a landholding elite involved in the production and export of primary agricultural goods (sugar and cotton) that employed a large labor force, and a commercial and financial elite, whose activities were situated in Peru's large urban centers. These two factions found it increasingly difficult to coordinate their interests.

Despite their differences, these feuding factions of the elite found it necessary to work together as unequal partners in administering the state apparatus. The dynamism of the coast meant that contests for control over the central government increasingly took place between factions of the coastal elite. Although internally divided, these groups were careful to exclude their highland counterparts from important positions of state power. Only in the local administration of the state apparatus in the remote Andean regions where they exercised influence did the established powers of the coast find it necessary to involve the sierra elite. The power-sharing arrangement that emerged in the process is reflected in the relations between elected and appointed officials.

The president of Peru was an elected figure, and among his formal powers was the appointment of an administrative hierarchy that ruled in the name of the executive throughout the national territory. Immediately below the president in this hierarchy were prefects, each of whom administered one of Peru's 24 departments (local states). The prefects appointed subprefects to oversee each of the provinces of which the departments were composed, and they in turn selected governors to manage affairs in each of the districts that made up a province.

Although the executive was in theory free to name its personnel in an autonomous manner, when actually making appointments the president and his staff always consulted with Congressional deputies and senators. These individuals, generally the leaders of powerful landed families, represented a coalition of forces that had out-maneuvered competing coalitions in electoral contests – deputies (one for each province) having prevailed in provincial elections, and senators (two for each department) in departmental contests. Because these individuals represented important power blocs, the president found it necessary to take their wishes into account when appointing personnel to the administrative units where they exercised the most influence. Senators therefore "advised" the president about departmental administrative appointments (prefect, chief of police, and departmental heads of government ministries), while deputies advised him about appointments to provincial-level posts (subprefect, provincial chief of police, and provincial heads of government ministries). Because senators and deputies in effect decided on these appointments, they were able to use their influence with the president to build up local power blocs, rewarding their followers and punishing their adversaries.

State administration was thus a strained affair involving competing factions of the elite, whose opposed interests, differing agendas, and unequal powers reflected their relative positions within a differentiated national economy. And while these conflicts made it extremely difficult for elite groups to act in a unified manner, their problems were not limited to internal struggles. The same processes that had led to the fragmentation of the elite had also produced an increasingly urbanized national population with an extensive *lumpenproletariat* and a well-organized labor movement. Besides fighting among themselves, the elite faced the additional dilemma of how to maintain control over the state apparatus in the face of serious threats "from below." Their inability to resolve this problem led to successive military takeovers. During the 27-year period discussed in this chapter (1929–56), military governments were in direct control for 18 and for the remaining 9 they kept a careful watch over national affairs, containing radical challenges, maintaining an uneasy peace between competing elite factions, and preserving the international, export orientation of the national economy.

The main challenge to the status quo came from an opposition party – the Popular American Revolutionary Alliance (APRA) – a coalition of middle- and lower-class groups that was able to coalesce across the economic and geographic fault lines that divided the elite. The party advocated the nationalization of land and industry, and sought to establish a broad, participatory democracy in which the rural and urban laboring classes, grouped into cooperatives based on production units, would play key decision-making roles in national life. The efforts of successive civilian and military regimes to contain the "Party of the People," as APRA referred to itself, between 1948 and 1956, and the activities of APRA in response to military persecution, have important implications for understanding the literature on the workings of the state.

## POWER, KNOWLEDGE, AND REPRESENTATION IN A MILITARIZED SOCIETY

On October 13, 1948, contingents of Peru's National Police descended upon the homes of some two dozen residents of the town of Chachapoyas, capital of the department of Amazonas in the northern sierra. The police arrived in groups of three or four, knocked at the door, and politely but firmly requested that the individual they sought accompany them to the prefecture. By the next day 13 people had been arrested and were being held in the town jail. All were high-ranking members of APRA.

At about one the next morning (October 14) the Chief of Police, Major Constantino Comeca Tejada, arrived at the jail. In order to soften the prisoners up before interrogating them, Comeca employed a form of torture known as the *tina*. The prisoners were woken and submerged in a large tank (or *tina*) of ice-cold water, with their hands tied behind their backs, and the water level maintained just at their mouths. A lattice framework made of bamboo was then placed over the top of the tank so that the prisoners could not lift their heads more than a fraction of an inch above water level.

Struggling to breathe, and trying to endure the numbing cold of the mountain water, the Apristas were kept in the tank for several hours. One by one they were removed and taken to an adjoining room where Comeca interrogated them. He began by asking each prisoner to confirm that he was an Aprista. Elderly informants who lived through this ordeal still recall his threats and demands: "If you do not give us what we want we will send you to [the jungle prison colony of] Pomará. We are told that you have the [APRA] archive. You must give [it] to us."

Comeca bullied and threatened each man for about half an hour before returning him to the tank. His objective throughout was the same – to obtain the party archive. As he questioned the APRA leaders they all gave him the same response. There was no archive for them to surrender: it had been impossible to maintain one due to the intense, long-term persecution the party had suffered ever since it had been established (1930). By October 16 the leaders of APRA had endured three days and two nights of torture, but had still not confessed to the police the existence of their archive. That same day the prefect received a telegram from the president's office in Lima, ordering that the prisoners were to be released.

The arrests in Chachapoyas followed on the heels of a failed coup attempt hatched hundreds of miles away at a naval base in the port city of Callao, just outside Lima, on October 3. The instigators were a small group of militant Apristas, who had split from the rest of the party, and an equally small body of junior officers and enlisted men in Peru's armed forces, who had been deeply influenced by APRA. Although the coup was put down easily the senior military command and the president viewed it with great alarm, the former because it revealed the degree to which the party had won the sympathy of military personnel, the latter because it showed APRA to be quite treacherous (in turning against President José Luis Bustamante y Rivero, the very individual who had allowed it to climb out of the shadows). APRA gained its legality in 1945 only because it agreed to a secret electoral pact with the then presidential candidate Bustamante. When the APRA vote helped him win the presidency, Bustamante honored his side of the agreement by declaring APRA legal, and by allowing the party the unprecedented opportunity to compete in Congressional elections (in 1945). In the event, APRA won so many seats that it dominated both houses of Congress – a position from which it was able to push for a series of pro-labor reforms that were very alarming to the agro-export elite and senior military command, who were committed to Peru's international, export approach to development.

Ironically, the attempted coup had been led by radical members of the party and the military, who were disgruntled by what they regarded as the slow pace of change initiated by the APRA-dominated Congress. Nonetheless, the failed coup presented senior military officials with the excuse they needed to crack down on the party. Shortly thereafter they staged a coup of their own, deposed Bustamante, and installed General Manuel Odría as the country's new leader.

General Odría immediately unleashed a nation-wide reign of terror against the party in an attempt to rid public administration and public life of APRA. In addition to expelling and arresting Apristas in both houses of Congress, he appointed military men as prefects in departments where APRA was especially strong. His government also claimed sweeping powers of search and seizure, suspended civil liberties and constitutional guarantees, and again proclaimed APRA a proscribed organization. This resulted in widespread insecurity, the imposition of narrow limits on what was do-able or say-able, and the extension of government surveillance into the most intimate spheres of everyday life.

The military conceived of its struggle with APRA as a war to defeat and ultimately eliminate the party. From the beginning the government recognized that this would require engagements along multiple fronts, including the public domain. Their clear objective was to purge it of all affirmative references to the party. They faced major challenges, however, in doing so. From 1945 to 1948 the party had made the most of its opportunity to organize in the open – publishing its own widely read newspaper, forming an extensive network of community centers and youth groups, launching a broad-based popular literacy campaign (in *Universidades Populares*), and providing legal aid, health services, and social assistance to the poor. All these activities extended the movement beyond APRA's original base in organized labor.

The military government employed several tactics in waging war with APRA over the public domain. Viewing the party's newspaper, community centers, popular universities, and social-service organizations as points from which APRA's insidious ideas radiated outward into the population, government officials ordered that all be closed down. Yet they feared that APRA's influence was not limited to the party's own organizations, but extended in less visible ways into society at large. As a result, the military also subjected to official scrutiny neighborhood organizations, rotating credit associations, unions and mutual aid societies, sports clubs, reading groups, and debating societies.

Moreover, the war was not limited to purging the public domain of party influence. The military was also convinced of the need to subject the state apparatus itself to surveillance to rid it of all party members, and to replace them with individuals loyal to the current regime. To be successful, however, they needed detailed information about the identities of all Apristas. In Amazonas, when interrogation and physical abuse failed to provide the police with party membership lists, government officials took a different approach to producing the intelligence necessary to know, control, and ultimately defeat APRA. They transformed the apparatus of state into a vast mechanism for the production of secret military intelligence. Functionaries at each level of the government hierarchy were ordered to provide their immediate superiors with the names of all Apristas under their jurisdiction. Within short order information began pouring in from all corners of Amazonas – from remote rural districts to provincial towns, to the capital of Chachapoyas. Based on this secret intelligence, the prefect compiled a master list of all Apristas.

As state offices reported back to the prefect an alarming picture began to emerge. It became clear that large numbers of Apristas were to be found in virtually every branch of government – including the judiciary and the national police, who were the spearhead of the war against APRA. The secret intelligence revealed that the boundaries of the state apparatus were deeply compromised. It was equally clear that drastic measures would be needed if the state was to purge itself of party influence. And, despite the gravity of the problem, the prefect's subordinates had provided him with the secret intelligence necessary to act decisively. On the authority of the central government, the prefect did so by "cleansing" the state. Beginning in January of 1949 and continuing for several months thereafter, all Apristas in public service in Amazonas were fired. Many were also arrested, and some were tortured.

The military had been quick in ridding the public domain of all manifestations of APRA. They were equally quick in filling the discursive space they had left vacant. The government was at great pains to establish the conditions under which a particular image of APRA, the military, and Peruvian society would appear to emerge spontaneously in discursive arenas. According to this view, Peruvian society consisted of a loyal public that stood united against APRA, a subversive organization of fanatics, criminals, and extremists. The military, on the other hand, was a noble and selfless organization whose historic mission it was to protect all wholesome social elements from the evils of APRA.

The government took anything but a passive role toward waging this war of representation. They employed discursive weapons to effect a familiar military strategy – bombardment. Government officials arranged for the public sphere to be repeatedly and systematically bombarded with new kinds of truth claims in order to demonstrate that most Peruvians really did reject APRA, that there really was a loyal public, and that the military was duty-bound to serve and protect that public.

The government's control over the means of public discourse – especially Chachapoyas' sole newspaper, the *Families' Friend*, allowed it to deploy a series of discursive weapons against APRA. The first consisted of open letters, signed by virtually all the town's prominent (male) citizens, pledging undying allegiance to General Odría and unconditional opposition to APRA. By publishing these letters in the *Families' Friend*, where they would be widely read, the government attempted to define what was normal – a public that was loyal to the military – and to show that "most people" embraced this normative construction. That a series of such letters appeared in the paper meant that the military's normative representation was continually and repeatedly asserted as authoritative, definitive, and true.

The second discursive weapon deployed against APRA consisted of an oath of loyalty to the Odría regime, which public employees were "asked" to sign. Virtually all government functionaries acceded to this request, since refusal meant losing one's job, arrest, and possible torture. One after another these oaths were published in the *Families' Friend*. The third discursive weapon used against the party was based on an offer of amnesty. The military government announced that subversives who were willing to renounce the party would be granted a clean slate. Knowing that the amnesty program represented their best chance of avoiding jail or blacklisting, many Apristas took advantage of the government's offer, and renunciations began to pour into the prefect's office from all over the department. These too were published in the *Families' Friend*, and in a steady stream, showing that Apristas were defecting from the party in droves – that even Apristas had grave doubts about the party, that they were ready to join the broad social consensus that viewed APRA as a dangerous evil. The open letters and the oaths of loyalty were published to demonstrate the existence of a loyal public that embraced the government's definition of what was normal and right. The renunciations were published to demonstrate that more and more people, even former subversives, were embracing this public.

## POWER, KNOWLEDGE, AND REPRESENTATION IN CRISIS

The military government's offensive against APRA appeared to have swept the enemy from the field. Large numbers of subversives had been arrested, APRA institutions had been dissolved, potentially sympathetic organizations were under police scrutiny, and the party itself appeared to be in deep disarray. So successful did the campaign appear to have been that, within just months of the attempted coup, the military began to speak confidently of the "death" of APRA.

Government officials were to discover, however, that the party was not so easily defeated. The military soon realized that the war was far from over – that what appeared to be decisive victories were little more than skirmishes in what threatened to be a long, protracted struggle of an unfamiliar and disturbing kind. Officials ultimately came to believe that not only had they failed to defeat APRA, but that they had been only partially successful even at *engaging* the enemy. They came to believe, for example, that they had failed to purge either the public domain or the state apparatus of party influence, despite the multiple strategies they had employed in order to do so. Government officials also came to suspect that they had lost the war of representation with APRA, despite (or rather because of) having employed a series of discursive weapons in mounting a bombardment of the public sphere.

The difficulties the military experienced in waging war against APRA were a function of its failure to carry out what many theorists of the state, Weberian and post-Weberian alike, regard as crucial governmental functions: the ability to identify key "objects of regulation" (subversive threats), to draw on a body of experts or authorities (government functionaries) charged with political surveillance to monitor the behavior of these objects, and to produce reliable knowledge about these objects (Apristas) that could be used to effect strategies of control. Officials' failure to carry out these crucial tasks of government wreaked havoc with their efforts to do battle with APRA. Especially debilitating to state projects and plans was the fact that officials had extremely faulty information about who was or was not a party member. It was the inability to *know* APRA that made it so difficult to control – or even engage – the enemy in any systematic manner. On any number of occasions government officials were convinced they had dealt a mortal blow to the party, only to learn subsequently that they had mistaken their quarry, that they had been striking out against the wrong people.

Government officials began to question the reliability of their knowledge about the party, and the effectiveness of the war they had waged on the basis of this knowledge, for a quite simple reason. A great many people who had been denounced as Apristas wrote to the prefect protesting their innocence, and swearing their allegiance to the military regime. These letters made officials question their secret intelligence about APRA for two reasons. First, those writing the letters made the disturbing claim that the individuals who had falsely accused them were the very state functionaries that the prefect had relied on to provide him with accurate, impartial information about APRA. Second, the letters made the equally disturbing assertion that it was no accident that these public employees had given the prefect so much faulty intelligence – that in making accusations, functionaries had been utterly indifferent to the state's desire to learn the truth about APRA, but had been motivated by vengeance, greed, or the desire to obey the orders of an elite patron and, possibly, advance their career prospects.

The prefect should not have been surprised at this discovery (although he was!). Most government employees were local people of humble means, who owed their positions to the patronage of one of the region's powerful elite families. Nonetheless, it was difficult for the prefect to ignore the implications of these findings. Government functionaries throughout the entire state bureaucracy, it appeared, had violated the public trust. It had not been beneath them to make false accusations if doing so would result in an adversary being jailed, removed from his job, or punished in some other way. Nor had it been beneath them to conceal the identity of Apristas if it served their purposes to do so – as it often did. As a result, it appeared, the prefect's entire corpus of intelligence was to be regarded as highly suspect. So too were the results of the war he had waged on the basis of this intelligence.

These revelations produced in government officials what might be thought of as a "crisis of faith" in the intelligence they had compiled about APRA, and in the personnel that had gathered that intelligence. Officials' doubts about their subordinate personnel led them to see the state apparatus as deeply compromised. Their doubts about the reliability of their intelligence led them to suspect that they had failed in the all-important task of delimiting the subversive social element. They suspected that a great many party members continued to operate sub rosa, placing in grave jeopardy the state's entire project of ridding public service and public life of APRA's influence. Indeed, believing that they had failed in their effort to identify Apristas, and that there was no dependable body of experts or authorities on which they could rely to monitor the behavior of the subversives, government officials experienced a crisis about their ability to know, and therefore to control or contain the Party of the People. That is, they experienced a deep and profound crisis of power/knowledge/control.

A second crisis associated with government efforts to defeat APRA focused less on the accuracy of its secret intelligence and more on the reliability of its public representations. As part of its efforts to represent itself as defending a broad social consensus that regarded APRA as a dangerous evil, the military used its control over discourse in order to construct a "loyal public" united in its opposition to the party. This public had been constructed on the basis of public testimonials of loyalty made by both rehabilitated Apristas, and forthright and trustworthy social elements that claimed to be staunch defenders of the ruling regime. After these diverse social groups had sworn before society at large to be a part of the broad, anti-APRA consensus, it became common knowledge that their testimonials indicated little about their true political inclinations – that many had testified in order to conceal rather than reveal their actual beliefs. For example, police intelligence revealed that many Apristas who had sworn to have left the party, and whose testimonials to that effect had been published in the newspaper, could not be counted among the supporters of the government. They had in fact continued their involvement in APRA, but in secret, despite public claims to the contrary. Police intelligence also revealed (and it became common knowledge) that many people who had signed loyalty oaths and open letters of allegiance were not part of the "loyal public" in spite of what they had asserted in their public testimonials. Some of these people were out-and-out Apristas, so committed to the party that they had been willing to perjure themselves before society at large in an effort to continue with their secret, underground lives. Others, while not themselves party members, appeared to be alarmingly sympathetic to APRA because they had privileged information about the illicit activities of Aprista friends, relatives, and spouses, but refused to divulge this information to the police.

Once government officials discovered that many people had used the letters of allegiance, oaths of loyalty, and renunciations in order to conceal their actual political inclinations, what suffered was not simply the credibility of these individuals. In a broader context in which officials had come to doubt that they could state with confidence who did and did not belong to the party, they were forced to look with suspicion upon everyone who had claimed to be a trustworthy supporter of the military government. They came to doubt their ability to distinguish between people who really were loyal to the regime and those who only pretended to be – cynically trading on the image of the model citizen or the penitent Aprista in order to deceive the police. As the boundary began to blur between healthy and subversive social elements, officials were compelled to regard as potentially suspect the very act of representing oneself as loyal, honest, and forthright. They were forced to wonder whether or not public proclamations to this effect did not indicate the opposite of what they claimed.

In other words, government officials came to believe that APRA was alive and well in a deep, subterranean realm lying beneath the surface of things – a realm that their campaign against the party had been unable to touch. Untold numbers of people continued to inhabit that realm, they suspected, and remained loyal to APRA despite the grave risks involved in party membership. Although these individuals represented themselves to society at large as part of the loyal public, officials came to believe that they could not trust the level of appearance – that an unknown number of these very people remained deeply committed to the party and everything it stood for. They ultimately concluded, then, that they had failed to purge society of APRA influence, despite having done away with all overt expressions of solidarity with the party, despite ongoing proclamations of loyalty to the military government, and despite a surface appearance of tranquility and calm.

Government officials responded to these discoveries by extending their surveillance to society as a whole, and in the process showed that they doubted the existence of the very loyal public they claimed to be defending. It became clear that even the state did not believe what the "state stated" (Corrigan and Sayer 1985). As state and general populace held each other in mutually intersecting gazes of awareness concerning this fact, the state experienced a deep and profound crisis of representation.

## FIXING ELUSIVE BOUNDARIES: THE "STATE EFFECT" FROM ABOVE

Government officials reacted to these twin crises – of power/knowledge/control, and of representation – in a highly defensive, almost paranoid manner, and not only by lashing out against the public. They also came to view the state as being at major risk from subversive social elements, and as a result became intensely preoccupied with two problems: first, identifying all Apristas who remained in state employ, and second, patrolling the boundary between state and society. As long as this boundary remained unguarded, officials concluded, it would be possible for Apristas to cross over into the state domain, where they could do great harm.

To address these threats the prefect instructed the heads of all government offices to place their subordinates under careful scrutiny – to be on the lookout for any telltale signs of suspicious inclinations or activities. He also charged them with policing the (imaginary) frontier between state and society, in order to insure that the state enjoyed as much "autonomy" from the party as possible. The prefect told them that they were to take a less trusting attitude toward the general populace than they had in the past. In particular, they were to scrutinize with great care anyone who approached them about employment. In this way they could help insure that the state apparatus remained free of APRA influence.

These strategies to protect the state from the party were fundamentally flawed. Although the prefect instructed the heads of government offices to be ever vigilant for signs of suspect behavior among their workers, he failed to tell them how to recognize such behavior. And, although he charged his subordinates with the task of patrolling the boundary between state and society, he provided them with no guidance as to how they were to distinguish Apristas from non-Apristas. Since the inability to know who was or was not a member of the party had been the source of the prefect's problem to begin with, his effort to pass the problem down to his subalterns could not solve his dilemma.

The effectiveness of these strategies was undermined by a contradiction lying within rather than beyond the (hypothetical) limits of the state. The prefect could not really be sure which of his functionaries were sufficiently concerned with the "APRA problem" to follow his instructions. Furthermore, because the prefect could not state with confidence who was or was not an Aprista, he could not be sure that some of the very government functionaries he had charged with policing the state/society divide were not themselves members of the party. This meant that he could not be sure that the fortifications he was seeking to construct between the state and APRA were not continually being breached, due to the indifference or even compliance of the very officials who had been charged with defending his imagined, besieged state.

Government officials resorted to an even more desperate measure in an attempt to make state activities truly autonomous from everyday social processes. They sought to delineate a sphere of communication that would be unequivocally privileged by being restricted to "trustworthy" members of the current regime (that is, the prefect, subprefects, governors, and the departmental and provincial chiefs of police). This would allow them to operate without the risk that APRA would be aware of their activities. Officials sought to establish this domain of privileged exchange by communicating about "sensitive" political matters (especially about those related to APRA) in coded messages.

The fact that an elite inner circle of government officials felt compelled to communicate in coded form about matters of pressing urgency indicates just how much at risk these officials felt the state to be from APRA. It also reflects their suspicion that party members were close to information that should have remained beyond their grasp.

Officials' decision to restrict the use of code to a select few represents their suspicion that the broader arena of government activity and communication, within which their inner circle was embedded, had been infiltrated and contaminated by the party. It also reflects their decision to surrender to APRA the outer domain of the state, and to reinscribe state boundaries further inward – to create a state within a state.

This attempt to redefine the limits of the state (Mitchell 1991) was deeply flawed. High-ranking government officials were still faced with the same problems that had plagued them to begin with. On the one hand, they had no idea who in their inner circle of confidents was sufficiently concerned about APRA to use the coded communication to rid public service of the party's influence rather than use it to pursue alternative agendas. On the other hand, since they had come to believe that they did not know who was or was not an Aprista, they could not be sure that some of the individuals entrusted to communicate in coded form were not themselves sympathetic to the party.

## CONTEXTUALIZING STATE CRISIS: SUBALTERN GOVERNMENTALITY

These twin crises – of power/knowledge/control, and of representation – are indicative of a series of key failures on the part of the military government. Most glaringly, they reflect the military state's failure to "state" – its failure to render natural or taken for granted the premises of military rule (cf. Corrigan and Sayer 1985). Indeed, rather than succeed in normalizing its vision of the national order of things, the application of state power by the military tended to highlight the arbitrary and interested nature of its rule, producing resistance rather than acquiescence, compliance, or indifference. The state also failed to carry out essential governmental functions (Foucault 1991). It failed to identify key objects of regulation and to monitor and regulate the behavior of these objects as part of its more general strategy of managing the national population. Its inability to do so can be attributed in part to yet another failure: its inability to produce a body of experts who could be counted on to operationalize state logics, to obey state dictates, and to respect state priorities.

As a result of these multiple failures in statecraft, government officials were unable to generate a "state effect" (Abrams 1988). They failed to convince anyone (including themselves) that the state was an entity unto itself, wholly autonomous of the social processes in which it was embedded, and that operated according to its own logic, dictates, and priorities. Indeed, so complete was their failure in this regard that, when they became aware of just how compromised the state was, they employed a series of ever more desperate measures in a futile effort to establish some autonomy.

How are we to account for the military's failure to concentrate governmental functions in the state apparatus? What lessons may we derive from these failures about the conditions of possibility that enable processes of state formation? What alternative forces were involved in seeking to order national society in the context of these failures? In order to answer these questions, we now turn to a consideration of the context in which the military regime's efforts at governance and moral regulation was embedded.

As noted above, because of the way that Peru had become integrated into the political-economic center of gravity defined by the United States, its elite had undergone significant internal differentiation, making united action difficult. In addition, for virtually the entire period, 1929–56, the military elite had to contain the threat represented by APRA – an opposition party united across the geographic and economic fault lines that divided the elite. Despite enjoying widespread popular support, the Party of the People had been forced to carry out its activities in secret, beyond the gaze of the government.

As a persecuted party forced underground by government repression, APRA's strategy for survival was based on the elaboration of a complex, subterranean party structure and a highly disciplined membership. In some respects, this amounted to a "state in the making," which reproduced the national territorial grid. Thus there were, in principle, APRA cells or committees for each district, province, and department in Peru, and a national committee (located in Lima) for the country as a whole. The actual make-up of these cells, however, their manner of operation, and the powers and responsibilities allotted to the members of each, reflected a degree of specialization and differentiation that went far beyond the formal state apparatus. APRA conceived of itself as a subterranean state made up of a series of ministries: of the interior, organization, propaganda, discipline, culture, popular education, higher education, economy, social welfare, unions, labor, cooperatives, municipal government, indigenous and peasant affairs, and youth. As their names suggest, each was responsible for attending to the affairs of particular categories of the population. Furthermore, the prerogatives and responsibilities of each ministry were carefully spelled out. In this regard alone, the APRA state in the making was considerably more specialized and differentiated than was the formal state apparatus.

The subterranean APRA state structure did not simply have the longest list of ministries. While the ministries of the formal state apparatus were entirely above ground and visible, they were for the most part "virtual" in nature. Although the state bureaucracy had expanded greatly in size in the 1920s, most state ministries had very little impact on people's everyday lives. This was especially true for those who lived in departments and provinces remote from the national capital. In 1930, for example, while all of the state's (virtual) ministries had a *representative* in Chachapoyas, most of these individuals had only a tiny office from which to run the affairs of their national ministry. All of the representatives operated on an *extremely* limited budget, which was also often more virtual than real. The men appointed to run these offices usually had few if any skills relevant to the functioning of their ministries and had no trained staff (or no staff at all) to assist them. With limited budgets, no staff, and no skills, they and the ministries (and the state) they represented, had little impact on the society they were appointed to administer. Furthermore, because powerful elite families in the region appointed so many members of the government bureaucracy, the impact of the state apparatus on the regional population reflected a composite of central government concerns and local priorities. Most of these revolved around extorting labor from the rural populace for public works, military service, and the elite's own private enterprises.

APRA's underground state structure, on the other hand, was directly involved in the everyday lives of the population, despite the fact that the party was forced to operate in secret, beyond the gaze of the legally constituted authorities. APRA's greater impact on and deeper involvement with the general population can be understood in part in terms of the way the party organized its cells, and the activities of cell members. These were made up of "secretaries," each of which represented one of the 15 ministries that composed the APRA state. The party attempted to have secretaries for as many of its ministries as possible in every cell or committee, whether it was in a remote rural district or a large urban center. Thus, APRA sought to place a secretary of the interior, the economy, justice, indigenous and peasant affairs, etc., in every district, province, etc. where the party had established itself. This meant that the "bureaucracy" that the party generated was considerably "thicker" than that of the formal state apparatus, whose representatives were sparsely scattered about the national territory.

The party drew on this organizational structure in order to prevent the state and the elite from extorting labor from marginal groups. It did so by engaging in what might be called "subaltern governmentality," formulating a careful plan identifying key objects of regulation (such as government officials). This allowed party experts to generate knowledge about these objects that could be translated into strategies of control. APRA focused its regulatory energies on public employees who formulated state plans to extort labor, assigning specially trained party members the task of becoming their close confidents. By carefully cultivating these contacts, the party learned where and when the government planned to extort labor before it was able to do so. An important part of APRA's day-to-day activities consisted of collecting and processing this "secret intelligence," and when necessary sending party messengers on emergency missions to the rural districts to warn the Apristas under threat. They in turn were able to go into hiding, thus avoiding forced labor and military conscription without provoking a confrontation with government officials. By helping poor people evade corvée labor in a way that put neither them nor the party at risk, and by providing them with legal aid, medical services, literacy training, and occasional financial assistance, APRA became a powerful force in the region. The party became sufficiently influential that it was able to collect regular dues from marginalized groups despite the fact that it exercised no coercive power.

APRA's subaltern governmentality also focused regulatory energies on its own followers in whom it sought to instill new standards of individual behavior, personal affect, and group interaction. In order to help make a reality of these new forms and standards of behavior, party cadres sought to inculcate in the rank and file new forms of discipline – mental, emotional, and physical – the aim of which was to produce what APRA referred to as "cultured" individuals. The party considered someone to be cultured if, on the one hand, they had acquired the knowledge and mastered the skills they needed to stand up for their own rights and to help other people stand up for theirs. Equally important to becoming a cultured individual was the cultivation of the courage and integrity needed to face the dangers involved in challenging injustice.

APRA's regulation of social life did not end here. Monitoring people's progress toward becoming "cultured" required an ongoing assessment of their everyday behavior in all walks of life. Toward that end, the party developed a comprehensive security apparatus that employed extensive means of surveillance. It innovated its own court system, which it used to bring the force of the party down upon those who strayed from prescribed forms of behavior. APRA's court generated extensive records of its activities, as did all party offices. Court officers and party secretaries were scrupulous about maintaining and safeguarding the "archives" that resulted from APRA's activities. These archives were intended to provide a permanent record of

APRA's successes and failures toward meeting its long-term goal – the whole-sale transformation of Peru and of Peruvians. Thus, despite the fact that it was an underground movement viciously persecuted by the government, APRA succeeded in taking on many features normally associated with the state. Not only did the party take on many governmental functions, but it also succeeded in engaging the regional population in a project of moral regulation – in defining forms of behavior and thought that much of the population found compelling and authoritative, and in enforcing compliance with these prescribed forms (Corrigan and Sayer 1985).

To what extent did APRA succeed in this regard, and how does the party's success compare with that of the Peruvian government? As we have seen, the state failed in its mission to "state" authoritatively – to forcibly encourage the forms of social life that it sought to proscribe, and to suppress, marginalize, undermine, or erode APRA's vision. Furthermore, the state failed in this regard even though it exercised a monopoly of physical force. APRA, on the other hand, succeeded in just those activities in which the Peruvian state failed. It managed to state with great authority, such that a large number of people listened. So powerful was APRA's appeal that a great many individuals subjected themselves to party discipline even though APRA wielded no coercive power. At the same time, Apristas considered the state's mechanisms for stating – for generating knowledge, and for attesting to the truth – to be of such little consequence that party members did not hesitate to ridicule these practices when it suited their purposes to do so. As we have seen, by "misusing" state-endorsed institutional practices for attesting to the truth, such as renunciations from the party, oaths of loyalty, and letters of allegiance, APRA helped provoke a crisis of representation for the state.

APRA's success in maintaining the loyalty of its members despite government persecution is further reflected in several other factors. First, non-Apristas who wished to run for Congress in Amazonas between 1929 and 1956 knew that they were very unlikely to win an election without the support of the party. Despite government persecution, APRA had the most effective mechanism for turning out the vote. As a result, most candidates sought to make electoral pacts with APRA. Rare was the candidate who succeeded in taking office without one. This was also true nation-wide. By 1956, for example, when the military returned to their barracks and presidential elections were held, although APRA was not allowed to field its own candidate, the party's influence was sufficiently broad nationally that APRA ended up as the "king-maker." It was the party's endorsement of candidate Manuel Prado that allowed Prado to assume the presidency.

What are the implications of this analysis for the literature on the state reviewed briefly at the beginning of this essay? It is clear that Weber's ideal type is problematically applicable to Peru. Although the institutional outlines of a Weberian state are clearly present, the ability of the Peruvian state to wield force, tax, or conscript was undermined to a significant degree by the activities of APRA. The party established underground organizations that offered alternatives to elite and state domination. Indeed, it won the sympathy of many in the state apparatus who were responsible for eradicating the underground opposition movement. It was this ability to alter the normal operation of the state that allowed the party to carry out its clandestine activities without needing to challenge state power directly.

Nor were the rational-bureaucratic institutions of Weberian statehood an "iron cage" of reason that stood above society, employing a vast bureaucracy to implement decisions in a neutral, disinterested manner. The Peruvian state was rather a chaotic assemblage of sites, processes, and institutions that lacked any coherent, underlying logic, and that was unable to impose such a logic, even when it became crucially important to do so. It showed virtually no interest in monitoring appropriate forms of reason or affect either before or after the rise of APRA. Prior to the emergence of the party, the state was only minimally involved in techniques for the management and regulation of the population. With the rise of APRA the state attempted to assume governmental and disciplinary functions, but was unable to do so. These conditions failed to produce a "state effect."

It is thus striking just how much this particular state failed to engage the population in a project of moral regulation, or to carry out key governing functions, even though many of the institutions of the Weberian state were clearly present. Equally striking is the degree to which APRA succeeded where the state failed. The Party of the People established a bureaucratic structure that operated according to principles of "justice" and "the common good." Even though this structure was forced to operate underground, Apristas were scrupulous about ensuring that party ministers faithfully followed procedure. Indeed, an important part of APRA's system of surveillance was focused on this very problem. The underground APRA state was neither incoherent or chaotic. On the contrary; it was characterized by an unusually high degree of order and consistency, and those involved in it worked toward a common goal.

As much as was possible under conditions of political persecution, APRA also sought to reorganize the most fundamental times and spaces of social life (another failing of the Peruvian state) by organizing unions, mutual aid societies, rotating credit associations, neighborhood associations, sports clubs, and reading groups. And, although the party was not able to implement all of its reforms, it nonetheless worked out systematic plans for social transformation and was scrupulous in explaining these plans to party members. APRA also put considerable effort into defining legitimate forms of identity, personhood, and life possibility by means of its focus on "cultured" individuals. It also invested much time and energy in training Apristas in the mental, physical, and behavioral disciplines they needed in order to become "cultured." Many of APRA's techniques for managing, regulating, and improving the population focused on this very problem, monitoring the party's successes and failures in moving toward its long-term goal of transforming the general populace. By drawing on its party apparatus to undermine structural inequality and to effect personal transformation, APRA produced its own version of the state effect. Unlike its Peruvian counterpart, however, the state that party activities brought into being in the imagination of party members stood for justice, equality, and hope.

## CONCLUSION

What general lessons may we derive from this discussion? It would be unwise to seek to generalize about "the state" on the basis of what transpired in northern Peru in the middle of the twentieth century. Instead, what is called for is an appreciation of the specific context in which this set of state processes unfolded. It was the particular position of Peru with respect to the political-economic center of gravity defined by the US that created the tensions between a forward-looking coalition of middle- and lower-class groups who embraced Aprista governance and discipline as forces of emancipation, and an entrenched, albeit internally divided, elite who resorted to military force in an effort to maintain class privilege.

As the foregoing political ethnography suggests, "the state" represents not one but a great many different sets of institutional/governmental processes that respond to, articulate, and seek to mediate material and cultural forces that vary in time and space, and that evolve historically in complex ways as a function of their location within changing global fields of power. An adequate understanding of any actually existing state (which was not Weber's objective in formulating his ideal type) requires a careful consideration of the national society that state processes seek to order – a national society that has its own distinctive historical trajectory. Similarly, understanding how any actually existing state is configured requires attention to the broader field of inter-state relations (especially relations between hegemons and their client states) and global accumulation practices (which undergo crisis, reorganization, expansion, and contraction) within which any particular state is embedded.

Research on the state began to move in just this direction in the 1970s, when the most recent crisis of global capitalism (associated with the end of Fordism) propelled sweeping changes in the organization of state power around the globe. Foucault's writings have been particularly important for scholars seeking to understand these changes, especially his distinction between state (in the Weberian sense) and govern-mentality. This is a distinction that has long been obscured due to the peculiar history of the modern state in Western Europe, where extensive, centralized, bureaucratic structures assumed control over so many governmental functions from the late eighteenth century onward. Some scholars (Rose and Miller 1992) have come to recognize the highly contingent nature of the forces that led to the emergence of "governmental" states in Western Europe, just as they and others (Trouillot 2001) have begun to trace the processes by which governmental forces are becoming increasingly disentangled from state structures. The challenge for the future is to continue in this same direction – to discard the long implicit assumption that the "closed" governmental state is normative, and to focus instead on the wide range of forces that have sought to order national societies in relationship to the extraction of wealth and the accumulation of capital. In other words, one might say that a central challenge facing scholars is to deconstruct the generic category of "the state" so as to reconstruct a more adequate understanding of governing processes.

## REFERENCES

Abrams, Philip (1988) Notes on the Difficulty of Studying the State. *Journal of Historical Sociology* 1:58–89.

Aretxaga, Begonia (2000) Playing Terrorist: Ghastly Plots and the Ghostly State. *Journal of Spanish Cultural Studies* 1:43–58.

Corrigan, Philip, and Derek Sayer (1985) *The Great Arch: English State Formation as Cultural Revolution*. Oxford: Blackwell.

Foucault, Michel (1991) Governmentality. In *The Foucault Effect: Studies in Governmentality*, ed. Graham Burchell, Colin Gordon, and Peter Miller, pp. 87–104. Chicago: University of Chicago Press.

Greenhouse, Carol J., Elizabeth Mertz, and Kay B. Warren, eds. (2002) *Ethnography in Unstable Places: Everyday Lives in Contexts of Dramatic Political Change*. Durham, NC: Duke University Press.

Herzfeld, Michael (1992) *The Social Production of Indifference. Exploring the Symbolic Roots of Western Bureaucracy.* Chicago: University of Chicago Press.

Mitchell, Timothy (1991) The Limits of the State: Beyond Statist Approaches and their Critics. *American Political Science Review* 85:77–96.

Nugent, David (1997) *Modernity at the Edge of Empire: State, Individual, and Nation in the Northern Peruvian Andes, 1885–1935.* Stanford, CA: Stanford University Press.

Rose, Nikolas, and Peter Miller (1992) Political Power beyond the State: Problematics of Government. *British Journal of Sociology* 43:173–205.

Schneider, Jane C., and Peter T. Schneider (1999) Is Transparency Possible? The Political-Economic and Epistemological Implications of Cold War Conspiracies and Subterfuge in Italy. In *States and Illegal Practices*, ed. Josiah Heyman, pp. 169–198. London: Berg.

Scott, Jame C. (1998) *Seeing Like a State: How Certain Schemes to Improve the Human Condition Have Failed*. New Haven: Yale University Press.

Stoler, Ann Laura (1995) *Race and the Education of Desire: Foucault's History of Sexuality and the Colonial Order of Things.* Durham, NC: Duke University Press.

## SUGGESTED FURTHER READING

Comaroff, John L. (1998) Reflections on the Colonial State, in South Africa and Elsewhere: Factions, Fragments, Facts and Fictions. *Social Identities* 4:321–361.

Gupta, Akhil (1995) Blurred Boundaries: The Discourse of Corruption, the Culture of Politics, and the Imagined State. *American Ethnologist* 22:375–402.

Gramsci, Antonio (1971) Notes on Italian History. In *Selections from the Prison Notebooks*, trans. Quintin Hoare and Geoffrey Nowell Smith. New York: International.

Hansen, Thomas Blom, and Finn Stepputat, eds. (2001) *States of Imagination: Ethnographic Explorations of the Post-Colonial State*. Durham, NC: Duke University Press.

Joseph, Gilbert M., and Daniel Nugent, eds. (1994) *Everyday Forms of State Formation: Revolution and the Negotiation of Rule in Modern Mexico*. Durham, NC: Duke University Press.

Moore, Barrington, Jr. (1966) *Social Origins of Dictatorship and Democracy: Lord and Peasant in the Making of the Modern World*. Boston: Beacon.

Roseberry, William (1994) Hegemony and the Language of Contention. In *Everyday Forms of State Formation: Revolution and the Negotiation of Rule in Modern Mexico*, ed. Gilbert M. Joseph and Daniel Nugent, pp. 355–366. Durham, NC: Duke University Press.

Sahlins, Peter (1989) *Boundaries. The Making of France and Spain in the Pyrenees.* Berkeley: University of California Press.

## CHAPTER 14

# Hegemony

*Gavin Smith*

Hegemony is conventionally used to refer to the balance of forces between states facing off in the international arena. But, as a result of the writings of Antonio Gramsci (1891–1937), hegemony is now more often used in the social sciences and social history to refer to the complex way in which power infuses various components of the social world. Power plays a role in the reproduction and possible transformation of social relations, for example, and in daily and longer-term social practices. The notion of hegemony has played an especially strong part in helping us to understand how power works to form the social person, shaping the way in which people variously experience the world they live in.

Over the past 25 years, anthropologists have increasingly used hegemony to better their understanding of the way power works through and beyond the state in different kinds of societies. At just the time when anthropologists were beginning to recognize that the people they studied in the local setting of their fieldwork had long been embedded in the fields of force of larger states, people in cognate disciplines were reworking our understanding of how power works in society. The reexamination of the work of Gramsci (Mouffe 1979), Foucault's work on the specific nature of *modern* power, the work of Raymond Williams and Stuart Hall in shaping a new field called "cultural studies," and Bourdieu's particular framing of the idea of practice in terms of habitus, each of these in its different way rewrote our understanding of the way in which power works to constitute the character of the individual and collective actor: the social subject.

Anthropologists had long worked against other disciplines, such as economics and psychology, to insist that social subjectivity was not a universal, but they tended to understand difference uniquely in terms of culture. Children grew up in certain cultural settings, practices of gender were inscribed in people through their culture, fear of change could be understood in terms of specific cultural beliefs, and so on. Power was certainly a factor, of course, both within a particular cultural setting and in face of "outside" forces from dominant classes, colonial authorities, and/or the state. Once power was understood in more pervasive and formative terms, either there had to be a competition between culture and power over which played a greater role in forming the social subject, or the two would need to be more thoroughly intertwined. Gramsci's notion of hegemony has served this latter purpose. The challenge has been the degree to which anthropologists and other social scientists relying on the term "culture" as a key to understanding politics are able to recognize that older, received ideas of what culture is must change once these more recent understandings of the workings of power are introduced. In recent years some have embraced hegemony with enthusiasm as in some sense giving the idea of "culture" a more realistic and hence more useful meaning. Others have rejected the notion altogether as analytically irrelevant when identity is expressed through consumption in the setting of globalization. Still others have sought to reduce the term to the interplay of discourses.

Here, by starting from the basis upon which Gramsci came to develop the idea, we will unthread the important strands contained in the notion of hegemony. After discussing how some of these ideas have come to be used more recently, we will end by suggesting what the concept can or cannot do to help us analyze and understand the current historical conjuncture. It will be easier to see the relevance of the different elements of Gramsci's epistemology for our current understanding of hegemony if we first provide a concise statement of its features.

Hegemony is about the mastering of history. That is to say, it is about praxis: the use of people's will and agency to drive their own history into the future; and it is about the weight (or lightness) of the past, carried on the shoulders of the present. Fundamental to the concept is a rejection of the idea of the social person as object, passive recipient, or cultural dope. Thus, while it is possible that a person's or a group's ideas about the world might be partial (in both senses: one-sided and incomplete) the notion of false consciousness is not consistent with Gramsci's understanding of hegemony. Regarding the subaltern, the term is invoked to sensitize the analyst to crucial unstable moments when organized collective action can be effective within a field of uneven resources of power. Regarding the powerful, we may speak of hegemonic processes when power is used to organize consent, and when consent is used to facilitate the securing of a political project. Insofar as societies are reproducing historical formations, so hegemonic fields need to be secured for the future, yet carry with them residues of past hegemonic work. Cementing hegemony requires stable institutions, cultural reproductive habits, and the securing of real or imagined territorial mastery. The term is thus intended to capture the unevenness and incompleteness of this work at any given moment in history: the securing of a hegemonic field; and conversely, the destabilizing of that field requires ceaseless work on the part of the forces at play.

## SITUATING GRAMSCI HISTORICALLY AND INTELLECTUALLY

The professionalization of our disciplines today makes it hard for us to imagine the softer lines that distinguished professional from political figures as the social sciences took form, yet anthropology and sociology came into being in the context of easily identifiable social and political currents. The long nineteenth century that began with the French Revolution of 1789 and ended with the Russian in 1917 witnessed the rise and establishment of industrial society, and with it a vast movement of people: a geographical movement in response to the demands of the growing industrial centers and a series of political movements as working people sought some leverage on the motors of history through collective organization.

As the century developed the "societies" to which social thinkers turned their attention appeared increasingly complex and so crosscut by inner conflict that a pressing question became how these kinds of societies could hang together. An element in the equation was the institutional one that drew attention to the proper organization of industrial capitalism on the one hand, and to the modern state on the other. This was the essentially conservative question of social integration. A second was what today we might call "the social movement question." After all, the long century began and ended with revolutions and was much taken up by them throughout, notably in 1830, 1848, and 1870. Moreover, as we have already noted, people were on the move, especially when large urban centers became the major gravitational pull in Europe and the United States. While this represented a threat to "social integration" for some, for others it represented a catalytic possibility. The question became how such a potential force could be harnessed to greatest effect.

Gramsci, a scholarship student in linguistics from Sardinia, abandoned his university career just as this long century was closing, as the Russian Revolution broke out and as World War I drew to an end. The future of Europe was in question and the coherence of Italy as a nation-state was sufficiently unstable that we might, in retrospect, suggest that this was precisely the kind of moment of crisis that calls forth a hegemonic shift. This historical background is worth mentioning, not only because it helps us to situate the kinds of issues and questions that would have been pressing for Gramsci, but also because it bears comparison with our own times, albeit now on a global scale. Worries about integration (now called "national and international security"), a future vastly in question, and a heterodox congeries of "social movements" are common to both.

Gramsci described his own writings as a "body of practical rules for research and detailed observations useful for awakening an interest in effective reality and for stimulating more rigorous and more vigorous political insights" (quoted by Hobsbawm 1999:12). Yet he found himself impatient with the conceptual tools handed down to him by his elders. Like Weber, in terms of the "integration question," he was fascinated by the issue of social power, but Weber's work seemed to place great emphasis on issues of *state* power. Like Lenin, in terms of the "social movement" question, he was concerned with harnessing the collective power of subaltern classes but, as Gramsci saw it, the conditions he faced in Italy were profoundly different from those Lenin had faced in czarist Russia, where crude forms of domination left little room for the space of civil society. In Italy, the situation was almost the reverse: the state was shaking on its newly found legs, while – as Gramsci saw it – there was a long history of a quite effective civil society. Thus, simply to capture the state would be no more than to capture "an outer ditch" behind which lay a vast civil society, yet to be conquered. Past efforts at social transformation in Italy had foundered on this problem; it had to be addressed by first ensuring the thorough advanced preparation of "the troops." Doing so, Gramsci saw, required the development of a new set of concepts appropriate to the social reality of his time and place. What distinguishes Gramsci from Weber is his concern with power within *and beyond* the institutions of the state; and what distinguishes him from Lenin is his emphasis on the need for "prewar" preparations to ensure victory – something he derived from careful analysis of the specificity of Italian history on the one hand and of the current conjuncture on the other.

It is not difficult to see how this makes him an especially attractive figure if we are seeking new political practices beyond either the arena of formal parties or the Machiavellian manipulations of self-appointed revolutionary leaders. Gramsci's thinking on the role of hegemony is a useful tool for gaining insights into the cultural channels through which politics is expressed in the space of "civil society." Yet we need to be careful here – careful about that tricky term "culture" and careful about the revival of a term long relegated to the finer points of political philosophy – "civil society." In Gramsci's writings, crucially, both provide work for intellectuals and both, though in very different ways, need to be understood in terms of what he would call "connectivity." Thus there is no civil society isolated from its dialectical relation with other realms of society. "The state," "civil society," "the economy" – each have their own very particular histories from one social formation to another. Trying to fit them into neat compartments is unhelpful because the history of their interconnectedness will help us uncover the way in which they have dialectically constituted one another. Indeed this issue of "connectivity" is fundamental to Gramsci's political and intellectual project. Moreover, it is especially relevant to students, teachers, and researchers, as well as political activists, since it is an issue that requires us to recategorize the term "intellectual," which in the modern world "has undergone an unprecedented expansion" (Gramsci 2000:307).

"The functions in question are ... *connective*," he noted (2000:306), and it was working on the nature of this connectedness that might make possible a new kind of intellectual, one that could be called "organic." Rather then assigning "domination" neatly to the realm of the state or "political society" and hegemony neatly to that of civil society, Gramsci proposed that the possibility for certain kinds of conduct in the one arose from the offstage rumblings in the other. For example, while "traditional intellectuals" act through the institutions of civil society to generate "the 'spontaneous' consent given by the great masses of the population to the general direction imposed on social life by the dominant fundamental group," the state steps in, providing the coercive power that " 'legally' enforces discipline ... in anticipation of moments of crisis of command and direction when spontaneous consent has failed" (1971:12–13). Minimally, then, we can say that, because hegemony works precisely by being *articulated* between the realm of coercion and punishment represented by the state and a broader realm of "organisms commonly called private," we cannot presume to know that coercion is limited to the state or even "political society," nor that persuasion is limited to a non-economic and extra-state realm called "civil society," without knowing quite a bit about the social formation in question.

Here then is the *connectivity* that we need to bear in mind as we relate hegemony to civil society. But Gramsci was not just a political strategist reflecting on possible arenas for action; he was also "a man almost physically excited by the sheer attraction of ideas" (Hobsbawm 1999:12). And his understanding of reality was at once phenomenological and materialist. This led him to explore the political implications of seeking to understand crucial linkages between people's practical engagement with the daily world that faced them and the historically produced institutional and structural settings within which they worked. Organic intellectuals, therefore, were faced with the difficult task of finding possibilities for political leverage by seeking out what Gramsci referred to as "organic ideology" and distinguishing it from merely "spontaneous" or purely "rational" ideas.

A war of position meant, for Gramsci, the preparation of a "multiplicity of dispersed wills" into a single aim on the basis of "a common conception of the world" *before* a political goal might be secured. In terms of cultural differences, this meant two crosscutting senses of the term "culture" – formal versus popular on the one hand and North versus South on the other: one having to do with the formal propagation of "national" culture by schools, churches, law courts at one level and folklore and practical wisdom at a second, and the other having to do with the distinct cultures of the industrial North and the peasant South.

Exploring the role of intellectuals raised questions about formal "culture," while the southern question directed attention to local cultural practices. Yet the two were bound together. The work to be done required an understanding of both the reciprocal constitution of practical and everyday cultures and more formal expressions of culture. As to the former, Gramsci was less concerned with popular culture as a body of traditions and customs confronting modernity, than with its fragmented, dynamic, and practical activity. While *common sense* has a backward-looking element to it, made up as it is of a fragmented body of precepts picked up as "the afterlife" of traditional philosophy, *practical sense,* though fragmented too and partial, derives less from the past than from forms of attention directed toward daily tasks in the present and future. We have here then the basis of what I call the Janus-face of hegemony – facing backwards and forwards like Walter Benjamin's angel of history (Smith 1999:229–270).

As to more formal culture, in one sense, when Gramsci speaks of traditional intellectuals, he is casting them within a commonly held view of culture and the conventional institutions of cultural production and display – schools, museums, and so on. But in Gramsci's view this kind of culture was also capable of producing personal self-control. Whether this self-control might simply become a subtle form of governance, or whether it might be used as a source of effective resistance and agency, is a question that I will address later. But we can initially note that, in a sense, both kinds of culture, *popular culture* and this *formal culture*, contain elements – practical sense in one case, self-control in the other – that have potential simultaneously for forms of regulation or as the bases for agency.

And intellectuals need to work across this terrain. As "deputies" of a ruling historic bloc they worked in the upper reaches of both political and civil society. But Gramsci referred also to the dialectic between the development of intellectuals and the changing conditions of ordinary people. He extended the idea of "intellectual" well beyond that of the specialized person, using it to refer also to an element within each and every one of us; this is where a crucial opening for making connections occurs. We all have an intellectual sensitivity lying, dozing amid the bedclothes of common and practical sense. And this side of us becomes manifest when we are able not simply to recognize ideologies as "arbitrary, rationalistic, or 'willed'," but also as historically *organic*, "those, that is, that are necessary to a given structure" (1971:376–377). The idea that the market provides a perfect mechanism for distributing goods and services through society would be one example of a highly effective and practical organic ideology.

One role of the professional intellectual is to make these kinds of connections transparent and clear. Gramsci described such a person precisely as an *organic* intellectual – one whose role is preeminently to make connections – both vertically across what he called "the hierarchy of forms" and horizontally, linking up the fragmented situational, personal, and momentary forms of common and practical sense into the coherent whole of a collective will. There are, then, ideologies that are arbitrary, rationalistic (that is, dissociated from practice) and willed (that is, stubborn in their willfulness). As a result they are deprived of historical praxis. And then there is another kind of ideology, *organic ideology*, which, among other things, provides links across variously experienced practical engagements, thereby – however momentarily – producing a collective will, and directing self-control toward autonomous action (agency). As a result, organic ideology becomes a material force.

Especially relevant to us today is the fact that Gramsci, like us, was working in a society that faced an uncertain future: old truisms and well-worn practices were not working. Such moments of instability make us question our old, assumed connections between things. In 1920s Italy the impact of transition on practical sense had a crucial spatial dimension to it because the transition was very unevenly felt across space. On the one hand, transformations leading to the mass-production factory were bringing industrial workers closer together, with obvious political consequences for potential collective action. On the other hand, there was both a disarticulation between these political actors and the southern peasantry and also a problem of spatial dispersal among the peasants themselves, that weakened their political agency. As Roseberry (1994:359–360) puts it, "In addition to *sectoral* differentiation among distinct class fractions, based on different positions and roles within accumulation processes, Gramsci draws our attention to *spatial* differentiation, to the uneven and unequal development of powers in regional spaces."

We might understand any group that interests us then, as probably being caught between overlapping fields of force – workers in the North, peasants in the South. These fields of force need to be understood in terms of both the material conditions that people face in the present, as well as the historical forces that arise out of the past. But there is another feature of instability: it can make philosophers of us all, calling into question the common sense we derive from older, stable forms of knowledge and unsettling the way in which our practical knowledge gets things done for us. As we have seen, the intellectual project once again becomes one of connectivity, but now along slightly different lines.

From what we have so far said, we can see these linkages being made in at least three ways. First, between one fragmented and situated idea and a series of others within a broadly similar group of people, as they begin to become conscious of themselves as indeed "similar" – personal hurt and humiliation becoming understood as the social issue of "abuse," one kind of "abuse" linked to another, until an entire positionality becomes formed. Next, we need to address the kinds of questions Gramsci sought to resolve with respect to the links *across* – in his case, northern workers and southern peasants with very different daily experiences yet shared subalternity. Finally, we need to remember the very particular feature that takes an ideology, as Gramsci sees it, from being random and "rationalistic" to becoming organic – a material force. This is the linking of ideas to effective reality through the proper articulation of practice with the structural conditions of social reproduction that might make that practice historically effective, that is, praxis.

Gramsci's extension of the original notion of hegemony was crucially tied to this notion of praxis: not just any set of social practices, but the driving forward of history by taking the reins of praxis. While the market might empower the individual, well-off bourgeois to achieve her goals, for subaltern people effectivity relies on organic connections: micro-connections among already questioning individuals; connections across social and geographical space; and finally, connections between experience and the principles of social reproduction that characterize the settings of that experience. Hegemony is about how effective will can arise within the context of existing fields of power, thereby reconstituting the possibilities of history. "What hegemony constructs," notes Roseberry (1994:361), "is not a shared ideology but a common material and meaningful framework for living through, talking about, and acting upon social orders characterized by domination."

## HEGEMONY AT THE END OF THE TWENTIETH CENTURY

Key figures like Raymond Williams (1977) and Stuart Hall (1996a, b) have introduced hegemony as a means for understanding the way in which what I have called the offstage rumblings of real threats of power interact with fields of cultural production (both formal and practical in the senses I have so far employed) to form historically specific structures of feeling and social subjectivities. It is important that we understand their contribution in this way because there is a danger that we may employ the idea of hegemony to refer to power relationships expressed uniquely, or even preeminently, through the vehicle of culture.

Jean and John Comaroff have applied an especially careful and effective set of reflections on hegemony to critique this latter position, noting the tendency some writers have to prefix hegemony with the word "cultural." Making a distinction between "agentive" power which is sufficiently acknowledged to be open to discussion and a more obscure non-agentive kind of power "rarely wrought by overt compulsion," and based upon "the unspoken authority of habit" (1991:22), they take "hegemony to refer to that order of signs and practices, relations and distinctions, images and epistemologies – *drawn from* a historically situated cultural field – that come to be taken for granted as the natural and received shape of the world and everything that inhabits it." (1991:23, emphasis added)

Theirs is an understanding of hegemony, then, in terms of the way in which relations of power are secured through – "drawn from" – a prior *cultural* field. The leverage secured through hegemony builds upon the habits of culture rather than the iron demands of a historically specific set of forms for surplus extraction. In the terms I have used above, horizontal connectivities among and between take precedence over connections between experience and the conditions and openings made possible by a historically specific process of social reproduction.

In Sider's work (2003), likewise a historical ethnography, the very particular features that condition social reproduction fertilize the ground in which culture grows. We see how the emergence of collective and fractured senses of subjectivity come to be experienced specifically as culture, through the very particular characterization of the Newfoundland and British imperial social formations and Sider's rich and evocative descriptions of the inter-locational and intra-group micro-processes that arise in the securing of livelihood. Sider argues that merchant capital, unwilling to invest in the social infrastructure of production, relied on sets of relationships that themselves produce what looks like a "distinct culture" among Newfoundlanders and then, as such, serves well to regulate people within it – dividing them and binding them into a perpetual subalternity. Here culture is not understood as the prior pattern on which hegemony operates by being taken for granted, but rather the historical outcome of quite specific ongoing struggles in various sites and at various levels within the context of identifiable forms of domination.

Studies such as these bring us from an older anthropological notion of culture to a newer one in which our understanding of the forms of power specific to a social formation effectively reconstitute the way in which anthropologists can use the notion of culture as the salient means for recognizing differences among people and then interpreting those differences. When difference between people in one part of the world and those in another was understood in terms of "cultures" (in the plural), then "culture" itself became a means of describing and accounting for those differences. Within that frame it became quite straightforward to understand the way a person took on distinctive characteristics simply as the result of growing up to be Trobriand, Mapuche, or Untouchable. The concept of hegemony helps us see that if collectivities become self-conscious in terms of distinct cultures, this is the result of quite specific historical practices – on the part of states, colonial authorities, missionaries, merchants, fisherfolk, and, of course, the cultural analysts themselves.

Yet it would be quite wrong to conclude that hegemony points us toward power relationships expressed uniquely, or even preeminently, through the vehicle of culture. It is far more useful is to ask at what historical conjunctures do particular forms of connection become relevant and thus produce social solidarities. As we have seen, this is not just a spontaneous process; it requires intellectual work. For example, as people moved about in the most shattering and apparently irreversible ways within Europe and across the Atlantic through the nineteenth century, cultural identification with nation or ethnicity vied with other possible emplotments of membership. Many were to be drawn into the world of urban slums and mass-production factories, the resources they could rely upon for livelihood reduced to the sale of their labor power. And once there they were confronted by the visible might of physical capital in the form of factories and built cities. The interaction of such people with organic intellectuals led to an emergent hegemonic project that stressed potential connections and conflicts in terms of class solidarities, which themselves were not spontaneous, natural, or pre-given but required the careful making of connections across diverse experiences as much as the denial of the authenticity of other experiences in the constitution of a selective tradition (Williams 1977; Hobsbawm 1984; Smith 1999:19–49).

In my work I have tried to combine this earlier history of political struggle with Gramsci's subsequent reflections in order to produce a set of methodological tools that work both across history and over a range of scales upon which hegemony might be felt on the one hand and constructed on the other. Like all dialectical conceptualizations then (Bhaskar 1993), hegemony is to be understood less as a stable social configuration within established fields of power than as a process and, as a process, it has both a historical past and potential futures. Once our understanding embraces this *movement* of history, so we begin to see the way in which moments, levels, or sites in the social reality we seek to study are reciprocally constituted.

Thus I have argued (Smith 1999:228–270) that it is useful to understand hegemony by consciously addressing ourselves to two different *currents of time* and to two different *scales of space*. The face of Janus, facing both backwards and forwards, helps us to think about the first of these. On the one hand, we might look at hegemony in terms of the accumulated power struggles that give us the ground on which we stand – literally as the (built) environment, actually as the historical balance of power, and figuratively in terms of selective social memory. This is the face of Janus that provides us with a perspective on the way hegemony shapes our selves and our social setting. The other face of Janus faces forward toward the maneuvers and alliances, the compromises and persuasions that are then made within specific fields of power to build a present and future-oriented hegemonic project. Bits of common sense about the past need to be woven into the fabric of practical issues and urgencies of the present.

Then, alongside these temporal issues, we need also to note the scale at which different fields of hegemony operate. Gramsci, for example, was especially concerned with scale within the bounds of the Italian nation-state. Hence, one scale on which he focused was that of the state. This meant the role of a commanding historic bloc on the one hand and emergent hegemonic connectivities between the peasantry and various elements of the northern working class on the other. But it also meant a concern with how the multiple interests of hitherto fragmented experiences might come together into a collective will. This suggests not just a concern with alliances *across* groups, but with ways of enhancing communication and sympathy *within* groups, producing a second scale that needs attention.

The real challenge comes, then, when we try to put these different scales, time-frames, and practices together. Here we might recall what I have referred to as Gramsci's distinction between formal culture and practical sense in terms of scale. Programs of rule which rely on various formal institutions for the propagation of a broad cultural framework facilitating rule are met in the multiple sites at which people apply practical sense to immediate projects, there to be pragmatically reworked. For example, at a broad scale and from a historically retrospective perspective, we might focus on the way in which hegemony gets to be experienced "to such a depth that the pressures and limits of what can ultimately be seen as a specific economic, political and cultural system seem to most of us the pressures and limits of simple experience and common sense" (Williams 1977:110). But at the more present and smaller scale of interpersonal practical projects it quickly becomes evident that the backward-facing Janus does not simply represent a passive acceptance of "history" but rather requires what is likely to be a shifting between *either* an active collusion in the stakes of history as we assess them at this moment, *or* a critical working *against* the experience given to us through this particular, selective history (Sider and Smith 1997). Thus, when Stuart Hall (1996a:40) remarks that "the same person might position themselves (be inscribed in) vis-à-vis capitalism a) as a consumer, b) as a skilled worker, c) as a gay woman, etc." we need to note that each of these positions invokes different mixes of collusion with the present order and potential critiques of that order. It is not *just* that by prioritizing our skilled-worker identity we trigger a whole chain of meanings discursively connected to work and skill; it is also that we set up the relevant paths of collusion and critique.

I will make a very selective and attenuated attempt to apply this complex set of interwoven processes to shifts in the constitution of economy, society, and social subjectivity. To do this I draw on work I have done in Europe on "regional economies" on the one hand, and on shifts in social-science knowledge production resulting from increasing funding from policy institutions, on the other.

## HEGEMONY IN A NEOLIBERAL WORLD

There is a danger that studies of politics in the contemporary world have shifted too far from a thorough critique of the economy at all its various levels. The result is an understanding of economic relations and practices *exclusively* in terms of market relations, consumption, and speculation or as simply one in an infinite set of discourses (e.g., Laclau 2000). While there is no doubt that studies of discursive regimes and of the effects of patterns of consumption on social subjectivity have helped us immensely in understanding current politics, especially in the wealthier countries of the North, crucial interconnections – beyond discourse, beyond consumption – tend to remain unexplored. A more fruitful exercise would be to try to understand how market discourses, various expressions of the "culture of capitalism" (cultures of consumption, of speculation, of crisis, and the like), practices for the securing of surplus value, different forms for the exercise of power, and the structural features of contemporary capitalism are all interwoven within and between particular sites temporally understood in terms of historical conjunctures. The result of this more holistic exercise would be to reveal the specific dialectical processes by which "economic" practices at a particular historical moment effectively reconstitute what is understood as "culture" or "civil society." The emergence of these reconstituted categories then returns to reconstitute what is understood as "the economy." At the levels of *circulation* and *consumption,* economistic discourses have invoked chains of interconnected meanings that effectively reconstitute the realm of culture. At the level of *production,* dispersed and informalized organizational forms rely on principles of good conduct, neighborliness, and "family values" that in turn rely on a particular understanding of culture and invoke a reformulated arena of "civil society."

While it is true that Gramsci associated the securing of hegemony by a historic bloc in Italy in the 1920s with particular cultural and religious institutions, at that point he was concerned with peasants who were not fully incorporated into market relations, and for whom the church and possibly public education were important channels for the securing of hegemony. But even then hegemony could be secured through other parts of the social fabric, including the economy itself. When talking of industrial workers, therefore, Gramsci identified a very particular compact for securing social order between corporations and the state: "an intensification of exploitation achieved through new forms of management and corporatist strategies, and expansion of state intervention in the economy and society" (Gramsci 2000:223). At one economic level nothing has changed. We still live in a kind of society in which "the reproduction of daily life depends upon the production of commodities produced through a system of circulation of capital that has profit-seeking as its direct and socially accepted goal" (Harvey 2001:312). But the means by which the intensification of exploitation has been achieved and the role state intervention plays have changed, thus recasting the vectors of hegemonic projects.

We can trace the shape of these projects by using what I have called Gramsci's interest in formal culture and the role intellectuals might play therein on the one hand; and on the other hand, the more informal expressions of practical sense in the securing of more immediate and contextually specific projects; these in turn open up different possibilities for intellectuals. In my work I have sought to move backwards and forwards between the broader sweep of hegemony and the work done in the smaller practical world of interpersonal relations to achieve projects in geographically specific sites – a different scale of hegemony. This requires identifying hegemonic programs at a quite broad level, while addressing at a more immediate and local level how these condition the way in which practical projects can be taken up, and over a longer term, how the accumulated effect shapes people's social subjectivities and hence their potential for praxis.

Unlike an earlier kind of economic liberalism, neoliberal formal culture does not assume a natural *Homo oeconomicus* whose freely taken market decisions are encroached on by the state. Rather, one role of the state comes to entail the forming of self-controlled social subjects who conduct themselves in a way appropriate to a social project understood in "economic" terms (Lemke 2001). This, in turn, requires a particular kind of state intervention. An older "welfare" political culture envisaged subjects, deprived of all other resources, selling their labor as a commodity to various kinds of capitalists in return for a wage. Welfare was a decommodifying intervention on the part of the state, both to offset class inequalities and to fill gaps where commodity relations worked inappropriately, such as health and education. The new political culture replaces this rationality with one in which social subjects are essentially no different from enterprises. Workers do possess a kind of capital – human capital – and they or their predecessors have invested in that capital, producing physical strength and skills, of course, but also love, affection, morality, and so on (Burchell 1993). Within such an imagination of the social world, all practices and relationships can be understood in terms of their twofold "economic" benefits – first to the social subject and then, by extension, to the increased productivity of the overall social project in which the person is inscribed. In an older, perhaps more modernist moment, the state was unashamedly engaged in a project shaped by the rationality of progress; this new rationality rejects progress (or history) in favor of intensified socio-economic productivity.

I showed earlier how Gramsci had noted the role of formal culture in contributing to self-control, noting then that this could enhance possibilities for governing people such as workers, or alternatively, possibilities for their own self-willed praxis. We can see now that an especially effective, dominant, hegemonic project need not rely simply on habit and the taken for granted nature of the given world. It can also rely on collusion in terms of a trade-off in which "participation" in the social project promises to empower those recognized as its legitimate members through the intensified productivity of the overall corporate body politic. Such a society replaces the idea of the present as a moment in the historical passage toward "progress," the utopian goal of the future, with the ongoing expansion of units of socio-economic power in a globalized arena. These units could be anything from the body to the family, to the region, to the nation-state, to the supra-state bloc.

We will return to the issue of units of scale and hegemony shortly; for the moment, let us shift levels to institutions of *production*. Here Gramsci spoke of "new forms of management and corporatist strategies" that can be characterized as Taylorism and Fordism. To this day many capitalist institutions of production, services, and finance (factories, offices, and so on) remain sites of authoritarian regimentation where domination, not softened by the velvet glove of democratic representation, outweighs hegemony. In principle, such sites are compartmentalized from the arena of "civil society," where freedom and consumption offset the more disciplined realities of the labor process. One way of understanding this is by adding to the mutual dialectical constitution of political and civil society noted by Gramsci, another set of dialectically constituting fields: the interplay between the domination within the capitalist corporation and a kind of civil society beyond it.

Yet today, Gramsci's "new forms of management and corporatist strategies" have been able to draw on the rationality outlined above to reorganize the labor regimes themselves. In so doing they rework the dialectic between work discipline and civil freedom, breaking down the distinction between corporate regimentation and civil society. My research has been directed toward attempts to establish sub-national regions as social economies into which neoliberal subjects might be induced to invest their human capital as workers, on the one hand, and to invest their financial capital as capitalists on the other. When dispersed capitalist institutions become "flexible" in the form they take, the activities they engage in, and the way in which they use labor, "freedoms" of the so-called civil society combine with the notion of human capital to provide just the hegemonic leverage necessary for the regulation of people's labors. It is precisely because the livelihood settings of these kinds of "informalized" economies are "unregulated" that mastery over hegemonic fields needs to replace the czarist-like, regimented domination of factories. Hegemony thus enters production as a crucial element in the production and extraction of surplus value.

There is a need to maintain dispersed linkages through the continual extension of intimacy. Here sub-national regions become especially suitable for two reasons: first, the spatial limits to regulation through ideologies of intimacy and personal responsibility, and second, the fuzziness, elusiveness, and hence informality that inheres in the very essence of the label "region" itself. On the one hand, the particularisms of family, neighborhood, and community crucial to regulation in flexible and dispersed production regimes limit their spatial extension. On the other hand, the reworking of the relationship between labor and property ownership in terms of human capital relies on quite particular understandings of personal responsibility, which are tied to recontouring the paths of participation in the broader social project. With appropriate interventions by intellectuals, regions simultaneously offer the kind of local scale that allows members to assess returns to investment (of human capital) while at the same time leaving the principles of that participation conveniently vague. For it is evident that these forms of participation linked to productivity stand in a problematic relation to more sharply defined democratic participation. But here, the very fuzziness of the "region" plays its part; regions are not states (much as some might like them to be) and are not, therefore, handicapped by any formal requirements for representative democracy. Yet, since regional economies can be given increasingly recognizable form, for example, through allusions to the distinctive and positive features of the "local culture," so a closer identification of the neoliberal "entrepreneurial worker" with the enrichment of an identifiable social unit – the region – can be achieved. Under such conditions, a region comes to resemble a dispersed kind of firm, and "local culture" becomes part of the region's sales prospectus. "Regional economies," then, are a particular expression of new capitalist forms that effectively reconstitute what is understood to be civil society and culture, responsible social membership (citizenship), individual freedoms (choice), and so on (Smith 1999:133–191; Smith and Narotzky in press; Narotzky and Smith n.d.)

As we have noted, Gramsci imagined hegemonic processes occurring within the scale of the nation-state. For him, hegemony crucially had to be understood within the context of practices of the state on the one hand and projects to capture or direct the state on the other (Roseberry 1994). While we can see now that the role of the state has changed since the time when Gramsci was writing, we can also see that the state's role is far from having been eliminated. Nor has "society" disappeared, neoliberal utterances notwithstanding. Rather, "the social" has become more thoroughly infused with discourses that give value to the productive power that can be achieved – not by a "social economy" as is often proposed, but rather by a thoroughly economistically understood social unit. What becomes crucial, therefore, are the various scales at which hegemonic projects might be undertaken and their stability secured for an extended period of time. This is because neoliberal projects rely on a link being made between the individual's personal investment in "human capital" and the overall expansion of the social economy such that there is a pay-off for collusion.

And here, professional social-science intellectuals have (so far) played an important role of a particular kind. The European Union's increasing interest in guiding capitalist development toward the shaping of regional economies is a project requiring a highly selective reading of history and understanding of "culture." Regional economies, like class formation a century earlier, are only partly the result of the spontaneous patterning of human interaction. They also require the active participation of intellectuals. Thus the task of social-science intellectuals, now increasingly relying on funds from policy-oriented institutions, has become not simply to study "regions" but to invoke them (Lovering 1999). As regions increasingly come to be understood as spatially clustered networks where human capital (labor) is interwoven with financial capital, the issue of membership comes to be defined in terms of positive or negative contributions to the region's "success." Local culture becomes measurable in terms of its positive and negative features. Conduct which exemplifies the positive features of culture enhances membership, while "conduct unbecoming" can be sanctioned with exclusion – exclusion, that is, from participation in the interpersonal networks that regulate and facilitate social relations of production and hence make possible the pursuit of livelihood and ultimately the pursuit of dignified life itself.

## CONCLUSION

Partial and superficial though the above analysis might be, it points us toward a number of useful issues relating to hegemony. While the term can be used with such amplitude as to have little analytic distinction from the commonsense view that complex interweavings of power in modern societies are likely to affect the practices we undertake and the beliefs we hold, were this the end of the question, there would be good reason either to abandon the concept or to relegate it to a very loose and general description. But perhaps the question is too academic in the first place. Were we to ask questions about the practical possibilities for attaining real political goals, it is hard to see how such an enterprise could be understood without some very sharp understanding of hegemony and how it works at various scales and sites in the social world. And, insofar as any political project arises out of a very particular historical formation and in the context of a current conjuncture needing critical assessment, it is hard too to deny that intellectuals play a crucial role.

What we have focused on here might be understood as an assessment of the conditions of the battlefield as social subjects with varying political projects seek to secure potential hegemonic fields. First we are able to see the close interconnection across levels and between sites. Discussion of "regional economies" draws our attention to the possibility of setting different scales for the securing of hegemony. Particular features of capitalist reproduction (described by Harvey above) clearly provide crucial conditions within which quite specific political projects have taken shape. Certain features of this regime can be understood at the broad level of what I have called formal culture, yet we can see too how these are powerfully interwoven with practices at the level of practical experience. Intellectuals, understood as people who work at making crucial yet selective connections, play a vital role in selecting the thread and pattern of this interweaving, invoking different possible chains of interconnected meanings, practices, and material conditions that can catalyze either collusion or critique.

We can see this especially clearly in the case of "progressive" social-science scholarship, which has notably shifted from more or less critical perspectives on capitalism and the state, and skepticism toward scholarship supported by state and capitalist agencies, to "responsible" proposals for the state and capitalism: proposals aimed at remodeling the present for greater resilience and ease of continuity into the future. This is hardly a utopian vision. Intellectuals, as themselves social subjects, are, of course, part of the reality they seek to affect. Their practices are shaped by the changing political economy of their sources of funding and career patterns, just as their accounts of the current political economy represent their attempts to master that social reality.

Perhaps the question should be less whether their accounts of where and how power operates are better than those of others, and more whether they are honest attempts at confronting power, as Eric Wolf put it. At this historical moment, it is only through such an engagement with the political economy of capitalism that we can begin the task of identifying hegemonic possibilities among people whose structural positions provide them with sufficient practical leverage for the emergence of collective structures of effective opposition.

## REFERENCES

Bhaskar, Roy (1993) *Dialectic: The Pulse of Freedom.* Verso: London.
Burchell, Graham (1993) Liberal Government and Techniques of the Self. *Economy and Society* 22:267–282.

Comaroff, Jean, and John Comaroff (1991) *Of Revelation and Revolution: Christianity, Colonialism, and Consciousness in South Africa*. Chicago: University of Chicago Press.

Gramsci, Antonio (1971) *Selections from the Prison Notebooks*, trans. Quentin Hoare and Geoffrey Nowell Smith. New York: International Publishers.

Gramsci, Antonio (2000) *The Gramsci Reader: Selected Writings 1916–1935*, ed. David Forgacs. New York: New York University Press.

Hall, Stuart (1996a [1986]) The Problem of Ideology: Marxism Without Guarantees. In *Stuart Hall: Critical Dialogues in Cultural Studies*, ed. D. Morley and K. H. Chen, pp. 25–46. London: Routledge.

Hall, Stuart (1996b [1986]) Gramsci's Relevance for the Study of Race and Ethnicity. In *Stuart Hall: Critical Dialogues in Cultural Studies*, ed. D. Morley and K. H. Chen, pp. 411–440. London: Routledge.

Harvey, David (2001) *Spaces of Capital: Towards a Critical Geography*. Edinburgh: Edinburgh University Press.

Hobsbawm, Eric J. (1984) *The Worlds of Labour: Further Studies in the History of Labor*. London: Weidenfeld and Nicolson.

Hobsbawm, Eric J. (1999) Introduction. In *The Gramsci Reader*, ed. David Forgacs, pp. 10–13. New York: International Publishers.

Laclau, Ernesto (2000) Identity and Hegemony: The Role of Universality in the Constitution of Political Logics. In *Contingency, Hegemony, Universality: Contemporary Dialogues on the Left*, ed. Judith Butler, Ernesto Laclau, and Slavoj Zizek, pp. 44–89. London: Verso.

Lovering, John (1999) Theory Led by Policy: The Inadequacies of the "New Regionalism" (Illustrated from the Case of Wales). *International Journal of Urban and Regional Research* 23:379–395.

Mouffe, Chantal, ed. (1979) *Gramsci and Marxist Theory*. London: Routledge.

Narotzky, Susana, and Gavin Smith (n.d.) Real Life: Conflicting Histories in a Regional Economy. Files of the Authors, unpublished MS.

Roseberry, William (1994) Hegemony and the Language of Contention. In *Everyday Forms of State Formation: Revolution and the Negotiation of Rule in Modern Mexico*, ed. G. M. Joseph and D. Nugent, pp. 355–366. Durham, NC: Duke University Press.

Sider, Gerald (2003 [1986]) *Between History and Tomorrow: Making and Breaking Everyday Life in Rural Newfoundland*. Peterborough: Broadview Press.

Sider, Gerald, and Gavin Smith (1997) Introduction. In *Between History and Histories: The Making of Silences and Commemorations*, ed. Gerald Sider and Gavin Smith, pp. 3–28. Toronto: University of Toronto Press.

Smith, Gavin (1999) *Confronting the Present: Towards a Politically Engaged Anthropology*. Oxford: Berg.

Smith, Gavin, and Susana Narotzky (in press) Movers and Fixers: Historical Forms of Exploitation and the Marketing of a Regional Economy in Spain. In *Petty Capitalists in the Global Economy*, ed. Alan Smart and Josie Smart. Binghamton: State University of New York Press.

Williams, Raymond (1977) *Marxism and Literature*. Oxford: Blackwell.

*Richard Ashby Wilson*

## HUMAN RIGHTS, CULTURAL RELATIVISM, AND THE COLD WAR

In the middle of the twentieth century, cultural anthropology was largely hostile to the notion of human rights, but by the end of that century, the study of human rights had become a significant strand within political anthropology. This is an account of that realignment of the place of rights in the discipline, from marginality to mainstream.

The key to understanding anthropology's historical opposition to human rights lies in the centrality of the concept of "culture" and the resultant adherence to a moral-ethical position of cultural relativism within the discipline during the Cold War period of 1945–1989. In the United States by the 1940s, cultural anthropology was becoming established in universities as one of the youngest of the social sciences. The founding father of modern cultural anthropology in the US was a German émigré, Franz Boas (1859–1941), who carried out empirical research among Inuit (Eskimos) and North American Indians. Boas reacted against the widely accepted evolutionary theories of the time, advocated by those such as the British anthropologist Edward Tylor, the sociologist Hebert Spencer, and Lewis Henry Morgan, who in turn influenced Karl Marx and Friedrich Engels. Evolutionism broadly asserted that all societies progressed in a unilinear fashion along a scale from the most "simple" to the most "complex," with each stage achieving a higher level of moral and societal improvement. In the context of the European colonialism of the time, this social evolutionism involved an explicit ranking of societies, which reinforced the colonial project and a sense of Western superiority.

Franz Boas sought to explode the myths of the evolutionary writers of the day and adopted a position of moral relativism to do so. He argued that each culture – in the sense of the particular shared symbols, beliefs, and practices held in common by a group of people and passed on through socialization – needed to be understood in its own terms, according to its own unique logic, using fine-grained ethnographic techniques of investigation. This view of culture as the dominant category through which to understand behavior was carried forward by Boas' students such as Ruth Benedict, author of *The Chrysanthemum and the Sword*, a book which tried to understand Japanese personality types through attention to unique Japanese cultural norms and beliefs.

After World War II, the emphasis on cultural specificity and uniqueness in cultural anthropology collided head-on with an international order that was responding to the Nazi holocaust by creating new universal standards and abstract conceptions of humanity. During the Nuremberg trials of 1946, individual responsibility replaced collective state guilt, and a new legal category was created, that of "crimes against humanity," whose violation in any specific place or context constituted a violation against the whole of humanity. The United Nations was created in 1945 and promptly set about writing a list of those 30 rights which all the world's citizens should ideally hold *as individuals*, leading to the UN Declaration of Human Rights in 1948.

The idea of human rights was an old one, going back at least 2,000 years to Cicero and Roman conceptions of "natural rights" which all individuals held by virtue of being human. These ideas had been resuscitated in the Western Enlightenment of the eighteenth century, and in particular during the French and American Revolutions, which threw off the yoke of monarchical rule. Central to the idea of human rights is the view that human nature is knowable and all humans share the same human nature. A humanitarian vision of rights built around an image of the "essential human being" with basic needs and attributes overrides any cultural variations in practice. For the doctrine of human rights, the right to equality before the law regardless of race, religion, or sex, applies whether a culture has traditionally upheld the principle of equality before the law or not.

Within the Kantian tradition, this universalism is underpinned by Reason and the capacity to abstract and generate general propositions using symbols in speech and writing. The ability to reason serves a double function – it is what makes us human and is also the mechanism through which human rights are discovered. Not all humans reason with equal skill, accepts Margaret MacDonald (1984), a modern defender of the neo-Kantian paradigm, but we all have equal rights regardless, since we all belong to the category of "reasoning human being." For MacDonald (1984:32), natural rights are the universal condition for a good society. Human rights protect individual rights and facilitate the realization of human potential, as they are constituted on the Kantian premise that "to treat another human being as a person of intrinsic worth, an end in himself, is just to treat him in accordance with the moral law applicable to all rational beings on account of their having reason."

In the early years after World War II, cultural anthropologists responded to the emergence of universal human rights by rejecting rationalism and abstract humanitarianism and reiterating the inherent worth of cultural variation and local specificity. Melville Herskovits, one of Boas's students, penned the American Anthropological Association's statement on human rights in 1947, which urged the international order to respect cultural difference while promoting an alternative view of the individual and society. Where there was a conflict between rights and culture, say, where a political system denied the participation of a minority population, then the local political culture should be left by the international community to regulate itself. Herskovits stated that each society has "underlying cultural values" which would force states to recognize their transgressions and limit discrimination. Cultures are politically sovereign and morally self-determining communities, and it is not possible to cross cultural boundaries, even for humanitarian reasons.

The AAA statement advanced fundamental tenets of cultural relativism, for instance, in its objection to the assumption of the autonomous and freely acting individual within human-rights discourse. In order to undermine the image of the isolated and rational actor of Western liberalism, Herskovits began with the premise that the "personality of the individual can develop only in terms of the culture of his society." This has implications for human rights insofar as "The individual realizes his personality through his culture, hence respect for individual differences entails respect for cultural differences." In this way, Herskovits articulated a view of the culturally constructed personality type found in the "culture and personality" school that had emerged from a group of Boas's students and included Ruth Benedict and Margaret Mead. By emphasizing how different cultures produce different personalities through socialization and child-rearing practices, then the universal human individual required by human rights starts to disappear into thin air. The AAA statement was thus a communitarian riposte to the growing international emphasis on the universal rights of the individual, regardless of social, historical, and cultural context. In this way, cultural anthropology positioned itself squarely in the tradition of Romantic and communitarian thinkers such as Jean-Jacques Rousseau and Johann Gottfried Herder. These thinkers contradicted French Enlightenment universalism by emphasizing the primitive, the exotic and remote, the uniqueness of each *volk* and its mystical attachment to land and tradition.

## POLITICAL VIOLENCE AND STATE REPRESSION

The views articulated by the AAA held sway in US cultural anthropology for several decades, at least until the 1960s, when cracks began to appear in the cultural relativist edifice. New influences from Marxism and feminism challenged the organicist and culture-bound models of Boas, Herskovits, and Benedict, and instead developed analytical categories such as class and patriarchy, which could be used comparatively and cross-culturally. These new currents within the discipline also called for a different kind of political engagement with the world. Famously, the annual business meeting of the 1966 AAA conference passed a resolution condemning human-rights violations (including torture, genocide, and the use of napalm) in the war in Vietnam, urging all governments to agree on a peaceful settlement.

Although the proponents of the 1966 resolution were motivated more by socialist ideals than anything else, they used the language of human rights in order to denounce US foreign policy in Vietnam, and this allowed them to appeal to mainstream liberals. This increasingly became the pattern – that human-rights talk became the language of denunciation of abuses that united both the left and the liberal center-left and allowed them to make universal statements on suffering across the globe that ruptured the confines of conservative Boasian relativism.

The emergence in anthropology of the language of denunciation of human-rights abuses and US foreign policy was nowhere more evident than in "America's backyard" – Central America. Throughout the twentieth century, the United States had intervened militarily and supported local dictators such as Nicaragua's Anastasio Somoza or Guatemala's Castillo Armas (who was installed by the Central Intelligence Agency during a coup in 1954). These military "strong men" presided over some of the most unequal societies in the world, where racism toward indigenous peoples was endemic, and where a small number of plantation-owning families utterly dominated the political economy of the country. Conditions of extreme deprivation for the majority led to massive levels of conflict in the region. Political violence was particularly acute in Guatemala, a country with a large indigenous majority and, as one might expect, a large number of US anthropologists as well. In the late 1970s and early 1980s, a Marxist guerrilla insurgency managed to win over a section of the Mayan rural poor and was met with one of the most vicious counter-insurgency policies the Americas has ever seen. In Guatemala's 36-year war, the military razed over 600 villages to the ground in its scorched-earth policy, killed up to 200,000 mostly indigenous civilian noncombatants, and made refugees of 1 million people.

In this context, anthropologists ignored cultural relativism and denounced the massive human-rights violations and the role of US governments in supporting the successive military *juntas*. Anthropologists dropped the idea that "underlying cultural values" would come to the rescue and check state repression. Indeed, in the case of racism by *Ladinos* (individuals who claim Hispanic descent) toward Guatemala's Maya majority, "underlying cultural values" seemed to be part of the problem. In anthropologists' denunciations of state violence, their target audience was clear – US public opinion – and so was their aim – to shift the direction of US foreign policy and end covert aid for violent and repressive regimes.

Throughout the 1980s, anthropologists documented the unprecedented wave of violence in publications like *America Watch, Cultural Survival*, and the *New York Times*. Two Latin-American anthropologists played a key initial role in documenting the actual violence and its consequences – Beatriz Manz (1988), author of *Refugees of a Hidden War*, and Ricardo Falla (1992), who meticulously documented the massacres carried out by the Guatemalan army in *Massacres of the Jungle*. A group of US-based anthropologists responded to state terror against Mayan villagers in an edited volume called *Harvest of Violence* (Carmack 1988), in a conscious attempt both to comprehend the utter devastation of the Mayan communities they knew well and to shape US public opinion and alter the direction of US foreign policy.

*Harvest of Violence* concludes by noting that "Anthropologists have not been at the forefront in the study of violence, terror and war," but by the 1990s the anthropology of political violence and human rights began to move center-stage. The style of documentation of abuses also began to change – there were fewer direct narrative accounts from victims, and anthropologists began to ask deeper questions about conflict and violence from more of an analytical distance. Researchers went beyond denunciations of violations aimed at public opinion and attempted to explain the causes, motivations, experiences, and sociocultural consequences of violence.

In Carol Smith's *Guatemalan Indians and the State, 1540 to 1988* (1990), contributors attempted a social history of Guatemala over four centuries. This edited volume asserted that the relationship between Mayan Indians and the state has been the most important determinant of the Guatemalan social, political, and economic order. Using mostly Marxist theories of domination and resistance, it was argued that Indians, far from being passive victims of the political and economic order, have shaped the very nature of the state through their violent and nonviolent resistance. The human-rights violations of the 1980s are contextualized and better understood when placed in this dialectical history of state and community relations. Carol Smith emphasized the structural nature of power and the ways in which the Guatemalan state became increasingly despotic and coercive as it failed to build a lasting infrastructure in rural Mayan communities and thus to create legitimacy and some degree of ideological commitment.

The structural focus of Smith's account was complemented by subsequent studies which emphasized social memory, personal experience, and subjectivity. In Linda Green's article "Fear as a Way of Life" (1994) we get a sense of what a chronic state of fear actually feels like for Guatemalan Mayan women and the anthropologist who interviews them. Green documents not only the observable structures of Guatemalan political economy, but also the invisible experiences of the people of the village of Xe'caj in order to lend her voice "on behalf of those who have witnessed and lived through the macabre." The result is a highly personal and experiential account of a culture of fear and insecurity, and a fine-tuned analysis of the embodiment of suffering among Mayan women. Wilson's 1995 monograph on the Q'eqchi' also focuses on subjectivity and violence, but deals more with collective representations of religious symbols rather than personal experience. Wilson attempts to understand the cultural consequences of the violence for indigenous culture by looking at how the military and the guerrillas struggled over indigenous symbols, such as the mountain spirits. He draws upon Foucault to understand the military's infrastructure of surveillance in Mayan communities and, like Green, discusses the embodiment of violence by referring to the effect of war on indigenous masculinity.

In the first instance, then, anthropologists denounced the human-rights violations carried out by the military in Guatemala, and as time moved on, they tried to explain the causes and consequences of the violence. They produced very different types of accounts, some structural and materialist, and others more personal and experiential, but all generally wrote from a position of opposition to the military and tacit or open support for the opposition. This unanimity was fractured by the publication of David Stoll's *Between Two Armies in the Ixil Triangle of Guatemala* (1993), which advanced an avowedly revisionist account which challenged the widespread assumption held by many anthropologists and all human-rights organizations that Mayan villagers actively supported the Marxist guerrillas.

Instead of being stalwarts of the "revolution," Stoll argues that Ixil Mayas were "rebels against their will," having been caught between the army and the insurgents. Instead, most Ixils practiced an active neutrality, which the guerrillas tried to lever them out of by provoking the army, who then attacked the villagers rather than the armed guerrillas. In this way, argues Stoll, the guerrillas were ultimately responsible for the state terror against villagers, who "were hammered by the army only after being placed on the anvil by the guerrillas." Stoll's iconoclastic argument did not garner a great deal of support within anthropology, and it suffers from weaknesses in its selection of informants (most of whom lived in army-held towns), but its very existence represented a greater maturity in scholarly discussions of political violence in Guatemala. Crucially, it confronted the pro-guerrilla conformity of the left, challenged those who purported to speak for "the masses," and broadened the debate about the causes of the Guatemalan conflict.

The discussion on political violence and state terror we have just seen in Guatemala has been replicated over the last 15 years in a number of other contexts around the world. The end of the Cold War and the collapse of the Soviet empire led to a rise in ethno-nationalism and an intensification of internal and civil wars with massive civilian casualties. There is now a vast literature on political violence within anthropology, and it represents a major focus of research for a significant number of anthropologists around the world. Anthropological research has dealt thoroughly with communal violence in the Indian subcontinent (Das 1990), as well as the rise in ethno-nationalist wars in the Balkans (Cowan 2000). The collapse of the state in parts of Africa has prompted a number of studies, especially in countries with a long history of anthropological research, such as Sierra Leone (Richards 1996; Ferme 2001).

This literature is now rich and varied; some studies are motivated by internationalism and humanitarian ideals, whereas others draw our attention to cultural specificities in experiences of political violence, which are closer to the tradition of cultural anthropology. What all of this literature does is to draw our attention to the interconnectedness of the world and the globalization of networks of terror and conflict. Political violence is never just the product of local circumstances, and is never just caught within the boundaries of one culture. Hegemonic states intervene clandestinely in the political conflicts of other states and provide arms to one side or, in cases like Angola, both sides of the conflict. The guns and weapons used in any conflict are provided by a global arms trade which is greater than the entire gross domestic product of the African continent. The poverty and social exclusion that foments violence is produced in part by the global political economy. The ability of African or Latin-American states to deliver services and build legitimacy is heavily constrained by a number of international factors, including their subordinate position in a mobile and flexible world capitalist economy, the vagaries of development aid, and the structural adjustment policies of the World Bank and the International Monetary Fund.

## GLOBALIZATION AND HUMAN RIGHTS

> The moral imperative must be to stop crimes against humanity wherever they occur.
> (Geoffrey Robertson, international human-rights lawyer)

At the same time that the growing emphasis on political violence began to challenge the certainties of cultural relativism, world events interceded to further erode the position of culture and cultural relativism within the discipline. Since the mid-1990s, there has been a sea change in the terrain of global politics, a shift toward global justice that has shaped how anthropologists approach rights. At this juncture, new global justice institutions with universal jurisdiction have become a tangible reality. From the UN Declaration on Human Rights in 1948 until the early 1990s, international human-rights law had been a marginal, even fanciful, topic with little purchase outside a small community of utopian academic lawyers. In the 1960s, 1970s, and 1980s, the UN issued one convention after another, and these were signed by states that had no intention of ever implementing them. These conventions were diplomatic, paper exercises with no mechanisms of enforcement.

The end of the Cold War and the ethnocidal conflicts in the former Yugoslavia and Rwanda changed all that. For all the failings of the UN Security Council to protect civilians from slaughter in Rwanda and Bosnia, one ground-breaking initiative involved the setting up of two UN war crimes tribunals: one for the former Yugoslavia (ICTY – the International Criminal Tribunal for the Former Yugoslavia) in 1993, and one for Rwanda (ICTR – the International Criminal Tribunal for Rwanda) in 1994. The conviction of Dusko Tadić in 1997 by the ICTY was the first successful prosecution for crimes against humanity by an international tribunal since the Nuremberg trials, some 50 years earlier. At the time of writing, the ICTY trial of Slobodan Milosević for genocide is underway, an historical precedent, since he is the first head of state to be prosecuted for genocide by an international human-rights tribunal.

In the late 1990s, there were a number of other unexpected developments which give more credence to the idea of an international rights regime. Between 1990 and 2000, there were twice as many UN humanitarian missions as there had been in the entire period from 1948 to 1990. In many cases, these were justified on human-rights grounds, as in Kosovo and East Timor in 1999. In October 1998, General Augusto Pinochet was placed under house arrest by Scotland Yard while the Chief Justice and then the British law lords considered a request for his extradition by the Spanish magistrate Balthasar Garzón. Pinochet was eventually released, but not before two important legal precedents had been created: the Spanish *Audiencia Nacional* court asserted that it had universal jurisdiction to try cases of genocide which had occurred to non-nationals outside its territorial boundaries. In Britain, the law lords ruled that a head of state does not enjoy immunity for criminal actions such as torture, which are outside the normal and legitimate functions of a head of state. Finally, in Rome in 1998, 120 countries adopted the statute to set up an International Criminal Court that would be administered by the UN system and would have universal jurisdiction to try crimes against humanity, genocide, war crimes, and aggression.

The above discussion refers to developments in the human-rights regime, but a more diffused rights talk has simultaneously expanded into other areas. Long-standing concerns over gender inequality became reconceptualized as "women's human rights" at international conferences, such as the UN Conference on Women at Beijing in 1995. In the world of economic development, key agencies such as the World Bank and government development ministries became converts to a "rights-based" approach to development. Amartya Sen's *Development as Freedom* has been hugely influential in the policy and academic world, and Sen bases development primarily in ideas of freedom but sees rights as a necessary supplement. Revealingly, the book includes a significant discussion of human rights. Indigenous groups increasingly make land claims and political demands for self-determination with reference to rights charters, such as the International Labor Organization's Convention 169 of 1989. Attempts to prevent discrimination on grounds of sexuality have been enshrined into a national Bill of Rights for the first time in the South African Constitution of 1996. With the expansion of rights beyond the narrow sphere of civil and political rights has come a proliferation in their manifestations, conceptualizations, and implications.

At the same time as these real-world events made human rights more relevant to world affairs than ever before, the literature on globalization gained ground in the social sciences and this had a profound impact on approaches to human rights within anthropology. Globalization theories do appear to take us beyond the confines of a neo-romantic relativism and an unreflexive universalism. A central insight is that globalization is not the same as Westernization or standardization, but involves a proliferation of diversity as well. The globalization of political values does not create uniformity (as universalism might have it) but may generate distinct political and social identities, and diverse legal and moral codes. These are not created out of isolation, as relativists would have it, but out of interaction and relationality. Thus, globalization does not obliterate the local or the particular in the steamrollering fashion of some brands of universalism, but actually presupposes it and engenders it. It is possible to think "locally" only if one has the idea that the global exists, and vice versa.

Globalization theories challenge in turn the isolated fragmentation of relativism by asserting that the world is becoming more integrated instead of being composed of a mosaic of separate and distinct societies or cultures. This occurs through an ever more monopolized communication industry, the deregulation of financial capital, the movement of cultural images and icons across the world, the mass movements of people across huge distances, and finally the application of transnational juridical and political values – from long-distance nationalism to human rights. Human rights may even be considered the global political value *par excellence* as the subject is being taken up by people who may once have viewed it as an alien framework. In my research on human-rights organizations clustered in Braamfontein, Johannesburg, I never encountered African staff who gave even the slightest credence to the view that being black and African precluded them from appealing to international human-rights charters (Wilson 2001). Indeed, the language of the political transition in South Africa, from the Freedom Charter of 1955 to Nelson Mandela's election in 1994, demanded a shift of discourse from the unequal "group rights" of apartheid toward egalitarian concepts of citizenship and human rights based on the individual.

Through what mechanisms does the globalization of political values such as human rights take place? Central to all globalization theories is an assurance of the demise of the nation-state, that we are entering a post-national era caused by the diminution of the state's regulatory capacities. The state is increasingly bypassed as the global comes into direct contact with the local; these levels enter into an unmediated relationship across great distances as both time and space are compressed. Globalization theories do not posit an inherently hierarchical or asymmetrical relationship between the global and the local, as did earlier theories of imperialism, colonialism, or the world system. Instead, globalization theories tend to place emphasis on non-hierarchically organized global structures, which are captured in Hannerz's work on "networks" and in Kearney's on "rhizomic transnational communities." Such nodes and networks are "postmodern" in their lack of boundaries and formal internal structures. In contradistinction to the situation under colonialism, persons, values, information, signs, and commodities flow through them in all directions.

In this new historical juncture in the 1990s, when internal conflicts intensified, when global human-rights institutions claimed an unprecedented authority, and when the globalization literature came to shape anthropology, a number of anthropological works on human rights were published. Anthropologists responded differently from the way they had in 1940s, not with relativism and an emphasis on the importance of culture, nor with the universalist assumptions often found in Marxist and feminist approaches. Instead, they wrote pieces that illustrated a cautious engagement with some of the main ideas of globalization theory and its implications for human rights.

The edited volume *Human Rights, Culture and Context: Anthropological Perspectives* (Wilson 1997) was the first book in which anthropologists directly addressed human-rights talk and institutions themselves. Wilson's introduction asked what happens to local moral or political values within the models of globalization theory of long-distance mediation and communication. Political scientists had focused upon how human rights may extend their reach through international charters or national constitutions, but they had neglected to enquire how human rights are related to and interpreted in different ways in diverse contexts. This interconnectedness is what social scientists should be studying – the complex interactions between overlapping legal and normative codes, where rule-based orders are mutually influencing one another. Within globalization theory, it is still possible to ask micro-social research questions, such as what are the local notions of justice and how do they relate to transnational codes of human rights? Under what conditions are global human rights appropriated, ignored, acquiesced in, embraced, implemented, or resisted? Thus, globalization theories seem to be getting us somewhere, allowing us to problematize historical relationships between transnational and local levels, and at the same time to go beyond the unsatisfactory confines of either an unquestioning universalism or a neo-romantic cultural relativism.

A number of the chapters in *Human Rights, Culture and Context* examined the concrete relationship between global human rights and the specific contexts in which the writers carried out fieldwork. Sally Engle Merry asserted that although human rights was originally a Western legal regime framed in the hegemonic categories of Western law, a close examination of the way it is used in an indigenous rights movement in Hawai'i reveals that this movement operates at three legal levels simultaneously: global human rights law, national law, and local Kanaka Maoli law. This is the process of legal globalization and vernacularization: the deployment and refiguring of Western law in more plural terms, both global and local. Such transnational cultural appropriations are fundamentally creative and represent forms of resistance to global homogenization.

Legal vernacularization is part of a process of the emergence of new national identities, and Merry's study details the appropriation and reinterpretation of international law by the Hawaiian Sovereignty Movement at the People's International Tribunal of Native Hawaiians in 1993. The tribunal was constituted as a criminal trial, with the US government indicted on nine charges, and drew upon the symbolic power of law to recommend the return of Kanaka Maoli land and water rights, and political sovereignty for the Kanaka Maoli people. The tribunal provided a legally plural framework in which to express the claims of an emergent nationalism, in that it drew together claims based upon notions of descent, culture, and tradition, but also used the language of sovereignty, citizenship, and constitutionalism. Merry concludes that law is a site of contestation, where the hegemony of state law may be undermined by the pluralizing of law and the redefining of the legal subject.

In the same volume, Thomas Hylland Eriksen documented multicultural debates and practices in Mauritius in order to explore some of the contradictions between multiculturalist ideas and individual human rights. He argues that the dual origin of nationalism in Enlightenment and Romantic thought created the contradiction between the right to be equal and the right to be different, which has since been exacerbated by the increasing polyethnic character of states. Eriksen asserts that all modern societies are now "multicultural," that "multicultural politics" are universalistic in their operation, and that some versions of multiculturalism are compatible with human rights whereas others are not. Multiculturalism is universalistic in that differences between people are the result of closer relationships which engender comparability and similarity; that is, that the assertion of "cultural uniqueness" implies a shared subscription to a global political discourse.

These points are illustrated in Mauritius by reference to conflicts around discrimination on the basis of religion in private schools, and the application of state and customary law to divorce among Muslims. With regard to the place of customary Muslim family law in divorce, it became apparent that the disparity in perspective between younger female and older male Muslims belied any multiculturalist claim that "cultures" (as bounded and unified) have a single set of discrete "values." Another multiculturalist paradox exists where collectivist notions of cultural identity conflict with the notions of personal autonomy inherent in human rights. In the present climate of movement and hybridity, one must also have the individual right not to have an ethnic identity. Eriksen cites the example of Mauritian socialist politicians, who refused to register their ethnic identity (which entrenches parliamentary representation along ethnic lines) with the result that a white Mauritian of foreign birth was registered as a Hindu on the election rolls. For multiculturalism to coexist with individual human rights, Eriksen asserts that it must include a "dialogic principle" in political communication, as well as being enmeshed in political and economic commonalities and shared meanings.

## HUMAN RIGHTS, NEOCOLONIALISM, AND EMPIRE

Despite its clear advantages over the universalism and relativism debate, the concept of "globalization" has come under attack from a number of quarters. Sociologist Susan Silbey (1997) argues that globalization is not a strong enough term to describe the types of interconnections between local sites and transnational institutions. There is not enough of a sense of the hierarchy of transnational centers which control the flow of finance capital, cultural images, and commodities. Instead, "globalization" posits a kind of benign equivalence between the local and transnational which is very different from the sense of inequality and exploitation inherent in previous epochs of imperialism and colonialism.

For Silbey (1997), international social exchanges are better described as "postmodern colonialism." Transnational forces of economic restructuring and privatization are hegemonic, and in the end do lead to standardization and Westernization. Silbey locates the place of legality in this new world order by drawing attention both to the ubiquity of law and its ideological claims to a transcendent Truth. Legal power is internal to the global market and is therefore a precondition of its functioning, as the "global exchange of persons, capital and culture is managed through legal forms" (1997:209). Law is there to create and police the boundaries between the private and the public, between the economic and the political. Law and rights are ideological in their function, structuring a field of action so as to maintain a set of asymmetrical relationships. In the hands of many social scientists, argues Silbey, globalization is none other than the repackaged and anesthetized version of an old product: free-market capitalism and legal liberalism. Although local practices and expressions of local identities can influence global practices, we cannot lose sight of the fact that nothing like an equal exchange is taking place. The relationship between the local and the global is one of domination and control by transnational centers.

*Empire*, by Hardt and Negri (2000), shares the dystopian vision of Silbey's brand of neo-Marxism and similarly asserts that state sovereignty is being replaced by an asymmetrical global system of domination and regulation. Yet Hardt and Negri's formulation of "empire" draws from the poststructuralism of Foucault and Deleuze and Guattari in order to distinguish itself from earlier theories of imperialism and colonialism. For them, empire is not simply a taking over by one superpower (the United States) of the earlier extensions of state sovereignty by European colonial powers. Instead, a new type of sovereignty is being created, which is decentered, unbounded, and deterritorialized, and which realizes itself through an array of institutions such as the United Nations and transnational non-governmental organizations.

Hardt and Negri place great emphasis on the juridical aspects of this deterritorialization of sovereignty. For them, human rights cannot be emancipatory since they are an integral part of a system of authority which established itself in a context of crisis and emergency, and which justifies international policing operations in the name of peace and humanitarianism. Stated directly, human rights cannot be part of the solution to domination and oppression and war, since they emerge from the global capitalist and universal value system which creates the conditions of war and suffering. Hardt and Negri (2000:18) make this clear when they write, "What stands behind this intervention is not just a permanent state of emergency and exception, but a permanent state of emergency and exception justified by *the appeal to essential values of justice*. In other words, the right of the police is legitimated by universal values" (their emphasis).

Elements of Hardt and Negri's critique of Western liberalism are useful for thinking about the global context of human rights and their place in the new international order since the end of the Cold War. Yet their analytical framework suffers from a number of fatal weaknesses which should preclude its adoption *tout court*. First, there is no single integrated and unified global order that is unhindered by internal contradictions and fissures. National and supranational organisms are not "united under a single logic of rule" (Hardt and Negri:xii). In contrast, we can see a multiplicity of human-rights institutions and processes which are constituted according to different regimes and have diverse and sometimes incompatible trajectories. There are distinct sites of human-rights conceptualization and implementation, from the UN war crimes tribunals for Yugoslavia and Rwanda, to national supreme courts, to the Special Court for Sierra Leone, to the truth commission for East Timor. Reducing them to a single logic is only possible though great abstraction and simplification and at the expense of a thorough and detailed enquiry into their aims, social consequences, and unintended consequences.

Second, *Empire*'s totalizing, holistic, and organicist structuralism utterly denies any agency on the part of local actors and social movements in Asia, Latin America, or

Africa, which are not workerist and revolutionary and instead seek to realize their claims for justice through the human-rights institutions of the international order. Hardt and Negri (2000:14) state that the structural logic of empire "sweeps all actors within the order of the whole," fixing each local strategy within the global hierarch-ization of authority. There seems to be no place in this vision for the pluralistic kinds of strategies which social actors actually adopt in countries characterized by authori-tarian rule. There also seems to be no understanding of how transnational concep-tions of rights and sovereignty might play out differently due to local cultural and political circumstances. For instance, in Africa and Latin America, women's organiza-tions have repeatedly challenged the patriarchal characteristics of domestic legislation by appealing to international human-rights formulations of equality and justice.

Anne Griffiths (2001) documents this well in her consideration of the Unity Dow case in Botswana. Dow, a lawyer, mobilized human-rights language in order to overturn the patriarchal rule in Botswana's Citizenship Act of 1984, which denied citizenship to the children of women who married foreigners but which did not deny the children of Botswanan men who had married non-nationals. She won her case in 1995 and overturned this normative piece of gender discrimination, with the support of national and international feminist groups and by reference to international human-rights charters which upheld the principle of equal treatment for women. As Griffiths (2001:120) concludes, "Power is not confined to, or solely derived from, the formal legal settings in which it operates, but derives more generally from the broader domain of social life." Understanding the complexity of that embedding of rights in social life seems to be one of the main components of anthropological perspectives on human rights, and one of the main components missing from Hardt and Negri's Gothic Left rendering of *Empire*.

## HUMAN RIGHTS, RECONCILIATION, AND THE STATE

> Without the UN and a host of other inter-governmental organizations the nation-state would not be the global form of political ordering that it has become.
>
> (Anthony Giddens 1985:256)

The assumption within globalization theories is that there is an unmediated encoun-ter between transnational processes and specific local contexts. This view is suscep-tible to the criticism that principles of transnational law may be very different, functionally and conceptually, from local social norms. Local and global values and practices may not encounter each other at all, or may do so only via intermediary structuring levels such as the state. The assumptions of globalization theory ask the transnational to do too much and are too general to describe the variety of individual and local responses to international human-rights law. The over-generalizing nature of globalization theories exalts the transnational and its counterpart, civil society, instead of generating empirically based theories of the concrete interactions between a number of stratified and unequal regulatory orders (that is, not solely the "global" and the "local").

Further, the dichotomy between the global and the local is too triumphant about the demise of the nation-state. One thing all globalization scholars agree on is that we are entering a post-national context that represents a radical break with the past. Transnational processes are delinked from nation-states and generate challenges to their regulatory capacities and claims, eroding national sovereignty. State-centered approaches to politics and culture, hopelessly wedded to a previous transitory phase in world-historical terms, are now seen by the advocates of globalization theories as anachronistic and misconstrued. Yet, as Anthony Giddens asserts in the quotation above, supranational institutions such as the League of Nations and its successor, the United Nations, have contributed not to the weakening and demise of state sovereignty, but have instead reinforced and strengthened the power of the state.

In practical terms, the nation-state remains firmly in the picture as a key locus of sovereignty and a dominant and powerful array of institutions of social regulation. Accepting too straightforwardly the claims of gobalist thinkers undermines our ability to comprehend how human rights both constitute and rely upon the power and authority of the state. There is a long and valuable tradition of theorizing state and local relations within legal anthropology, which can help us to understand the new human-rights functions within state institutions. The work of anthropologist Sally Falk Moore (1986) provides a useful point of departure, as she maintains a local and contextual perspective while keeping the state firmly within the scope of her analysis. In Moore's view, local law in Africa is the product of historical competition between local African power-holders and central colonial rulers, each trying to maintain and expand their domains of control and regulation. Law is imposed upon "semi-autonomous social fields" with uneven and indeterminate consequences. We must not overestimate the power of law to exert its will, as the connection between native courts on Kilimanjaro and the British colonial High Court was often "nominal rather than operational" (1986:150). One might apply the same insights to the present relationships between local justice and transnational human rights in order to preserve a space of political agency for Africans.

Moore takes us away from a static view of the articulation of legal systems to examine the historical transformations of regulatory practices, and her work oscillates between small-scale events (individual court cases) and large-scale social processes such as colonialism, imperial rule, and decolonization. Moore accepts that local law was profoundly transformed by colonialism, yet her more interactionist focus upon the Habermasian "life world," and more specifically upon the kinship basis of Chagga society, means that she allows room for local strategizing in pursuit of greater political autonomy. She concludes in one essay (1986:125) that "local law cases reflect the local history of African peoples rather than the history of the Europeans who ruled them."

The application of Moore's legal anthropology to human-rights questions would analyze how adjudicative contexts are transformed over time by the social actions of individuals and collectivities within a wider context of state regulation and discipline. In any locale, there is a variety of institutions and competing value orientations which have emerged via a long process of piecemeal aggregation, rupture, and upheaval, and they continue to be transformed by social action. In order to understand the impact of human rights on conceptions of justice, the question to be answered is how social actors (encompassing both individuals and collectivities) have contested the direction of social change in the area of justice, and what the effects of this are for state formation and the legitimation of new forms of authority. This is a legal anthropology of action, transformation, and interaction between legal orders in the wider context of state hegemonic projects.

In my own work on post-apartheid South Africa (Wilson 2001), this involves looking at how Truth and Reconciliation Commissioners, magistrates, township court officials, Anglican ministers, and others combine human-rights talk, religious notions of redemption and reconciliation, and popular ideas of punishment and revenge in an effort to control the direction of social change, or what the French sociologist Alain Touraine (1995:219, 368) refers to as "historicity." Touraine defines historicity as a set of relations between the social actors who contest the bearing which social change takes. The struggle over historicity in the area of ethics in post-apartheid South Africa presents itself as a struggle over how to deal with the political crimes of the apartheid past, how to construct discontinuities with the past, and in so doing to reconfigure legal authority in the present.

The advantage of Touraine's theoretical framework is that it moves us away from static views of "the global order" toward an examination of the remarkably rapid movement in the production of legal and moral norms. This rapid change in social values is symptomatic of the rise of modernity (Touraine 1995:219):

> Modernity rejects the idea of society. It destroys it and replaces it with that of social change ... The reason why ... I constantly focus my remarks on the idea of *historicity*, is that social life can no longer be described as a social system whose values, norms and forms of organization are established and defended by the State and other agencies of social control, and that it must be understood as action and movement. Social life is therefore a set of social relations between the actors of social change. [Emphasis in original]

Applying this to South Africa, we can see that legal institutions, be they township assemblies, magistrates' courts, or human-rights commissions, are simultaneously subjected to *centralizing* and *pluralizing* forms of social action and knowledge production. Modern states continually attempt to rationalize and institutionalize their legal dominion, and yet encounter resistance from strategizing social actors. These countervailing tendencies emanating from informal justice and popular legal consciousness are a contradiction at the heart of modernity. Weber noted in his analysis of the emergence of legal authority that the character of national law is structured by the competition between central rulers trying to maintain the maximum of power over their subjects and the local power-holders trying to carve out their own domains of arbitrary power over their dependants and limit the central government's claims on them.

At different historical moments, one set of strategies may exercise dominance over another and become hegemonic. In the mid-1980s, as the internal anti-apartheid movement led by the United Democratic Front reached its peak and "popular courts" punitively enforced counter-hegemonic values and political strategies, the dominant tendencies in the area of justice were fragmenting, decentering, and pluralizing.

Since the post-apartheid elections of 1994, the main direction of legal change has been toward greater centralization as state officials attempt to restore the legitimacy of state legal institutions. Government officials and members of the new political elite have sought to integrate certain non-state structures, such as armed units of the liberation movements and the Inkatha Freedom Party, into the criminal justice system, and exclude others, such as township courts. Part of my general thesis about the South African Truth and Reconciliation Commission is that it represented one effort on the part of the new government to formulate a moral leadership and to establish a unified and uncontested administrative authority. This is a common strategy of regimes emerging from authoritarianism, which seek to unify a fragmented legal structure inherited from the *ancien régime*. The notion of "reconciliation" found in human-rights talk is the discursive linchpin in the centralizing project of post-apartheid state governance. Human-rights talk performs a vital hegemonic role in the democratizing countries of Africa and Latin America, one which compels the population away from punitive retribution by characterizing it as illegitimate "mob justice."

The new values of a rights culture are formulated primarily by intellectuals and lawyers representing a new political elite that has sought to superimpose them upon a number of semi-autonomous social fields. These values engender new discursive and institutional sites of struggle and their impact is uneven and emergent, raising questions for research such as: Has the human-rights project of state institutions altered the terms of the debate on post-authoritarian justice, and, if so, how? How can we more precisely conceptualize the specific continuities and discontinuities between local, state, and transnational formulations of justice? In what areas of social life are human-rights ideas and practices resisted, when are they appropriated, and when are they simply ignored?

## NEW DIRECTIONS IN THE ANTHROPOLOGY OF HUMAN RIGHTS

The anthropology of human rights is still an area of political and legal anthropology which is in its infancy. More empirical ethnographic studies and better theorization are needed of human-rights talk and rights institutions and their practices. A number of anthropologists have contributed effectively to the interdisciplinary debate on truth commissions and institutions designed to explore questions of social memory and history-making after authoritarianism and massive human-rights violations (Borneman 1997). Yet there are new areas of global interest that have received less coverage, such as the large-scale, UN-led humanitarian interventions in Sierra Leone and East Timor, and the UN war crimes tribunals for the former Yugoslavia and Rwanda.

Anthropologists interested in human rights also need to respond to the intellectual and political challenges raised by the aftermath of September 11, 2001. The subsequent brutalization and militarization of global politics means that human rights are in a more difficult and demanding position in international affairs than during the era of the "new humanitarianism" of 1991–2001. It seems evident that at one level there has been an attempt at a "securitization of rights," in the sense of a subordination of human rights to a global security regime. Individuals have rights but only so long as they operate within the rules of the game. Once they stray outside the boundaries of acceptable international practice, then they may be deprived of their rights and they may be placed in inhumane conditions that violate international standards of due process and the right to legal representation. The rights of the combatants captured in Afghanistan and placed in Camp X-ray at the US naval base in Guantanamo Bay, Cuba, were clearly violated on a number of accounts, according to a report of the International Committee of the Red Cross. These are individuals who, if guilty of the crimes of which they have still not been formally charged, should engender little or no political sympathy on our part. Regardless of this, their civil liberties must be ensured so that the principles of open societies which are said to motivate the war on terror are not themselves sacrificed in that war. That is, they should be protected as a precondition for any credible claim to be an open and liberal society.

In this context, human rights emerge, as they have done in different historical epochs, as contrary to the aims of international security regimes, and as one way of articulating opposition to empires old or new which seek to curtail civil liberties. As always in this short but rapidly changing history of the relationship between anthropology and human rights, the new global context of human rights requires anthropological theory, ethnographic research, and a renewed political engagement with the world.

## REFERENCES

Borneman, John (1997) *Settling Accounts: Violence, Justice and Accountability in Postsocialist Europe*. Princeton, NJ: Princeton University Press.

Carmack, Robert (1988) *Harvest of Violence*. Norman: University of Oklahoma Press.

Cowan, Jane (2000) *Macedonia: The Politics of Identity and Difference*. London: Pluto Press.

Das, Veena, ed. (1990) *Mirrors of Violence: Communities, Riots and Survivors in South Asia*. Delhi: Oxford University Press.

Falla, Ricardo (1992) *Massacres of the Jungle*. Boulder, CO: Westview Press.

Ferme, Mariane C. (2001) *The Underneath of Things: Violence, History, and the Everyday in Sierra Leone*. Berkeley: University of California Press.

Giddens, Anthony (1985) *The Nation-State and Violence*. Cambridge: Polity Press.

Green, Linda (1994) Fear as a Way of Life. *Cultural Anthropology* 9:227–256.

Griffiths, Anne (2001) Gendering Culture: Towards a Plural Perspective on Kwena Women's Rights. In *Culture and Rights: Anthropological Perspectives*, ed. Jane Cowan, Marie-Bénédicte Dembour, and Richard A. Wilson, pp. 102–126. Cambridge: Cambridge University Press.

Hardt, Michael, and Antonio Negri (2000) *Empire*. Cambridge, MA: Harvard University Press.

MacDonald, Margaret (1984) Natural Rights. In *Theories of Rights*, ed. Jeremy Waldron, pp. 21–40. Oxford: Oxford University Press.

Manz, Beatriz (1988) *Refugees of a Hidden War: The Aftermath of Counterinsurgency in Guatemala*. Albany: State University of New York Press.

Moore, Sally Falk (1986) *Social Facts and Fabrications: "Customary" Law on Kilimanjaro, 1880–1980*. Cambridge: Cambridge University Press.

Richards, Paul (1996) *Fighting for the Rainforest: War, Youth and Resources in Sierra Leone*. London: James Currey.

Robertson, Geoffrey (1999) Crimes Against Humanity. London: Penguin.

Silbey, Susan (1997) "Let Them Eat Cake": Globalization, Postmodern Colonialism and the Possibilities of Justice. *Law and Society Review* 31:207–235.

Smith, Carol A. (1990) *Guatemalan Indians and the State, 1540 to 1988*. Austin: University of Texas Press.

Stoll, David (1993) *Between Two Armies in the Ixil Towns of Guatemala*. New York: Columbia University Press.

Touraine, Alain (1995) *Critique of Modernity,* trans. David Macey. Oxford: Blackwell.

Wilson, Richard Ashby (1995) *Maya Resurgence in Guatemala*. Norman: University of Oklahoma Press.

Wilson, Richard Ashby (2001) *The Politics of Truth and Reconciliation in South Africa: Legitimizing the Post-Apartheid State*. Cambridge: Cambridge University Press.

Wilson, Richard Ashby, ed. (1997) *Human Rights, Culture and Context: Anthropological Perspectives*. London: Pluto Press.

# CHAPTER 16 Identity

## *Arturo Escobar*

It is difficult to appreciate the magnitude of the cultural and political transformation that took place all over the Pacific littoral of Colombia in the 1990s. An entirely new identity emerged and took shape during this decade in this rainforest region inhabited chiefly by black and indigenous groups. This regime was couched in terms of ethnicity and, for the black groups, largely articulated around the concept of *comunidades negras* (black communities). There was nothing in the cultural, social, and political landscape of the Pacific – or even the country as a whole – that made this development necessary. Although the new Constitution of 1991 granted unprecedented collective territorial rights to the black communities of the region, the long-standing forms of self-reference among the black groups of the Pacific had little or nothing to do with what the Constitution referred to as "black communities" or, even more strongly, "black ethnicity." Nonetheless, gatherings of activists, experts, members of non-governmental organizations, local leaders, women's groups – all of them discussing the character and status of the newly discovered "black communities" – became a ubiquitous sight in the Pacific region after 1990, from river hamlets to small towns and cities. A parallel flurry of activity could be seen at many national and regional state planning, environment, and development offices in Bogotá and the main departmental capitals with territories in the Pacific. Within this broad context, black identity became a powerful force among the residents of the coastal region.

How are we to understand this transformation? In the landscape of contemporary social theory, we may consider a number of pertinent concepts. Should we see the emergence of black ethnicity in the Pacific as an instance of the much discussed class of "imagined communities" or "invented traditions"? Should we draw on the burgeoning literature on new ethnicities which, along with fundamentalisms, are often cited as the single most important proof of the forceful return of forms of identification thought long ago to have been left behind by the overpowering march of secular, rational modernity? Or should we appeal to the impressive literature on identity growing out of many fields, from cultural studies and literary, feminist, queer, and critical race theories to social psychology and anthropology? We could also attempt to examine how ethnicity "was put into discourse" by following Foucault, or by appealing to a number of social movement theories. The spectrum of theories that today seeks to account for what is most often stated as "identity" is thus vast, which in itself – as some commentators have pointed out – calls for reflection. Why so much concern with identity in recent times? Who, indeed, needs "identity," as Hall (1996) asks?

Broadly speaking, what has happened in the Pacific can be seen as "relocation of 'blackness' in structures of alterity" and as the inception of a novel order of alterization (Wade 1997:36; Restrepo 2002). What is clear is that the 1990s saw an unprecedented construction of difference through a multiplicity of practices that can be studied ethnographically. These practices involved issues as varied as collective memory, environment, culture, rights, the state, and production. Above all, they concerned the politicization of difference and the construction of a new political subject, "the black communities." If in the 1970s and 1980s anthropologists could still denounce the invisibility of black cultures in expert knowledge and state strategies, in the 1990s this feature was radically reversed. Suddenly there was a tremendous interest in things black, particularly as far as the Pacific was concerned. In broad terms, this was due to the double conjuncture of the political opening fostered by the 1991 Constitution and the irruption of the biological as a global social fact, and it was also related, of course, to the changes brought about by the radical neoliberal policies adopted by the government after 1990. What has to be explained, however, is why this Pacific or black talk took the form it did, particularly in terms of "ethnic identity," "cultural rights," "difference," "biodiversity conservation," and "black communities."

Moreover, more than a decade into the process, it is possible to attempt an assessment of the new regime of identity. Should we see in the sudden appearance of black ethnicity chiefly a reflection of the power of the state – itself responding to the requirements imposed by international capital in the wake of neoliberal models – to create the conditions, even the terms, within which subaltern groups must couch their actions? Or, conversely, should we interpret the emergent black identities a sign of the agency of the subaltern, finally finding a workable formula for collective expression after decades of being silenced? As we shall see, while most analysts gravitate toward one of these positions, the answer to this question is "somewhere in between." This by itself says little. The rest of the story will largely depend on whose voices and perspectives one privileges, one's space of enunciation, and, of course, the framework used to examine the space of encounter between the various actors in the play of identity. Let us then begin our journey through the Pacific (and through theory) with some of these questions in mind.

## The Emergence of Black Ethnicity in the Colombian Pacific in the 1990s

The Colombian Pacific is a rainforest region situated between Panama and Ecuador, and between the Andean mountains and the Pacific littoral. It is inhabited by almost 1 million people, 90 percent of them Afro-Colombians, 50,000 indigenous peoples of several ethnic groups, the most numerous being Emberas and Wounans.

"Forgotten" and relatively isolated for a very long time, in the 1980s it became a new frontier for development, including macro-development projects and new forms of capital accumulation, such as African palm plantations and the industrial cultivation of shrimp. After 1990, with the definitive neoliberal opening of the country to the world economy, and an explicit policy of integration with Pacific basin economies, the region took on new significance. The Colombian Pacific is also one of the richest world regions in terms of biological diversity, and hence of great interest to the conservation establishment. In 1991, a new national constitution granted collective territorial rights to the black communities of the region, and as a result of all these changes, significant black and indigenous movements emerged in relation to the law of territorial and cultural rights (Transitory Article 55, or AT 55, which became Ley (Law) 70 in 1993), and in defense of cultural difference and territory.

As explained above, in this region an entirely new identity regime emerged and took shape between 1990 and 1998 – one couched in terms of ethnicity and articulated around the concept of *comunidades negras*. At the ethnographic level, the investigation of the ethnicization of black identity thus requires a detailed examination of the avatars of the construct of "black communities," particularly the discursive and institutional practices associated with its emergence and dispersion, a project already underway (Restrepo 2002). At a theoretical level, a number of pertinent questions can be raised regarding the transformation, such as: How should the new identities be conceptualized? How are they represented in practice? How is the relationship between identities and their historical context to be investigated? How can one assess the political and cultural effectivity of the new regime? After an initial inroad into approaches to identity on these questions, this chapter moves on to review current debates on identity in the Pacific. Part I begins with a discussion of pre-AT 55 black identities and goes on to examine the various analyses of the ethnicization of identity in the 1990s. Part II studies the particular approach to identity developed by a group of black activists, and ends with a brief assessment of this process from the perspective of the relation between identity, social movements, and the state. First, however, there are some general issues pertaining to identity and its politics.

## Modernity, identity, and the politics of theory

As an explicit problematic of social life, identity is said to be thoroughly modern. Most authors have no qualms in stating that "identity is a modern invention" (Bauman 1996:18). This is chiefly because "identity entered modern mind and practice dressed from the start as an individual task" (p. 19); modernity entrusted the task of self-formation to the individual, even if deeply mediated by a host of experts and trainers. There is also the idea that identity is predicated on a modern logic of difference in which the subordinate term is seen as constitutive of, and necessary for, the dominant (e.g., Grossberg 1996). We will accept this diagnosis here, and bring together the anthropological debates on whether identity, in the form of a definition of self, is a modern Western construct, and the interesting issue of whether there can be forms of belonging without identity. Many anthropologists argue that the modern notion of the self – at least in the quintessential mode of the possessive and discrete individual of liberal theory – does not have a correlate among many non-Western peoples. There are other notions of personhood, but not of "the individual" in the modern sense of the term. Be that as it may, for now it is important to keep in mind that the historical anchoring of identity in modernity is an important referent for the discussion of the Pacific case. We shall ask the question, however, of whether the modern logic of identity is ample enough to describe what is going on with the construction of black ethnicity. If the question of identity has become pressing, can we infer from it that the problems to which it seemingly responds in the Pacific can be fully explained by modern logic?

It is common to refer discussions of identity to the contrasting positions of essentialism and constructivism. According to essentialist theories, identity develops out of an essential and unchanging core. This notion has resulted in primordialist and unitary notions of ethnic, racial, and national identities, in which ontological identity is seen in terms of primordial group ties anchored in a more or less self-contained shared culture. Essentialist notions of identity, while still prominent in the popular imagination and in some scholarly work (often rekindled through debates and repor- tage on "ethnic separatism," "clash of civilizations," balkanization, and so forth), are largely considered inadequate on most counts, if not outright passé. Most scholars and activists today consider that all identities are the product of history. The agree- ment, however, ceases with this statement, because the various radical critiques of essentialism refer to different kinds of subjects (the bourgeois subject; the Cartesian, detached observer; the gendered subject; the agent of subject-centered reason, and so forth, in Marxist, poststructuralist, feminist, and other critical approaches) but also because the various critiques have different political orientations and draw divergent political conclusions.

Poststructuralism has given great attention to conceptualizing identity, and Fou- cault has been the single most influential author in this area. Foucault's theories underline the production of subjects through discourses and practices linked to the exercise of power – practices through which the subject is objectified in various ways, for instance, through mechanisms of discipline and normalization, as much as prac- tices of subjectification that the subject performs on him or herself. For some, however, a theory of identity cannot be complete without an account of the subject's active self-constitution, a point which Foucault left unfinished and which others have continued (e.g., Hall 1996:15). The contributions of Butler and Laclau and Mouffe are perhaps the best-known in this regard. Taking as a point of departure the contradictions of a representational politics within feminism – the fact that within this politics the category of women is produced and constrained by the very structures of power from which it seeks emancipation – Butler (1990) shows the complex and multifaceted character of identity and the limitations of any attempt at constructing a stable subject. The alternative is a constant questioning of representational politics through a critical genealogy of its practices. In the case of feminist politics, this genealogy reveals an underlying heterosexual matrix and an insufficiently scrutinized binary relation between sex and gender – precisely the constructs that ground the regulatory power of patriarchy. The problem is even more complicated, as Butler sees it, since there is no recourse to a utopian notion of a liberated identity outside the matrix of power defined by sex, gender, desire, and the body. Politics thus becomes a constant effort at displacing the naturalized notions that support masculinist and heterosexist hegemony; it becomes a question of making "gender trouble" by continually mobilizing and subverting the very categories that serve as the "foundational illusions of identity" (1990:34).

For Laclau and Mouffe (1985), all identities are "in trouble" in that unfixity has become the rule; all identities are relational and over-determined, leaving a logic of articulation as the only possibility for the political construction of identity. This logic proceeds by the construction of nodal points around which meaning and identities can be partially fixed. For this to happen, the existing relations of subordination (e.g., in cultural, ethnic, or gender terms) must come to be seen as relations of oppression. That is, they must be transformed into sites of antagonism, and this can only happen under certain discursive conditions. Discourses of ethnicity, cultural rights, and biodiversity played this role in the Pacific, making possible the interruption of "subordination as usual" and its articulation as domination; these discourses allowed a novel construction by activists of the situation of the Pacific in terms of external impositions by the state, expert knowledge, and the global economy. Generally speaking, the articulatory model results in novel divisions of the social field on the basis of deeply constructed identities which are partially autonomous, even if their political character is never given in advance but depends on the established discursive articulations.

The seeming fixation on the essentialist/constructivist divide has been increasingly criticized. For Comaroff (1996), constructivism is merely an assertion that all identities are the product of human agency; this assertion might hide an older set of problems. Realist constructivists, for instance, argue that behind identities lie particular sets of interests, thus falling back into an instrumentalist position; cultural constructivists accept that identities are the product of shared signifying practices but tend to treat culture itself as a given; a third perspective, political constructionism, singles out the imposition of ideologies – for example, by the nation-state – as the source of identities; finally, radical historicism follows Marxism in its belief that social identities are the result of the working out of inequalities at the level of consciousness and culture. Contrary to these positions, Comaroff sees identities, first, not as things but as relations that are given content according to their ceaseless historical construction; this means that "ethnic identities are always caught up in equations of power at once material, political, symbolic" (1996:166). Second, identities are constructed through everyday practice, in the encounter between groups. Third, once constructed, "ethnic identities may take on a powerful salience in the experience of those who bear them, often to the extent of appearing to be natural, essential, primordial" (1996:166). Finally, the conditions that give rise to ethnic identity are likely to change, in part as a result of the identity construction process itself, which means that those sustaining it are likely to be quite different. Norval (1996) adds two important factors: the construction of discursive horizons of meaning that go along with how communities interpret their belonging – including the drawing of frontiers through the externalization of an other; and the construction of political imaginaries.

The concern with power and politics can be resolved into theories of identity in other ways. For Grossberg (1996), the discourse of identity as the grounds for struggle, albeit important, is limiting, since its account of its own location within modern forms of power is narrow and, as such, identity politics cannot provide an ample basis for new political communities. Identity's modernist bend, in Grossberg's view, relies on three logics: difference, individuality, and temporality. Even when conceived in terms of fragmentation and hybridity, identity as difference tends to locate the subordinate term as necessary for the dominant, thus ignoring the positivity of the subaltern "as the possessor of other knowledges and traditions" (1996:92). More generally, theories of identity "have failed to open up a space of anti- or even counter-modernity... they are ultimately unable to contest the formations of modern power at their deepest level because they remain within the strategic forms of modern logic" (1996:93). To the logic that transforms identity into relations of difference, he opposes a logic of otherness, productivity, and spatiality. A perspective of otherness enables an examination of identity as difference as itself the product of modern power; and while theories of otherness see both difference and identity as effects of power, they do not reduce the question of the other to being merely constitutive or relational. In other words, in the case of the Pacific, the positivity of black identities cannot be reduced to an articulation of difference dictated by the dominant Euro-Andean order. This would entail denying their otherness as positivity and exteriority.

Theories of identity are also pervaded by modern notions of individuality. Grossberg suggests a useful conception of individuality in terms of three planes: the subject as the source of experience; the agent as the basis for action; and the self as the site of social identity; in short, subjectivity, agency, self and identity. While subjectivity involves attachment to places (even multiple and multiply structured places), agency entails a distribution of acts in space. If places are historical points of belonging and identification, agency is what defines the particular form places may take through the empowerment of particular populations. Agency creates places as strategic possibilities; agency is the empowerment enabled at particular sites or places. The consequences of this conceptualization for rethinking identity – leading to what Grossberg calls "a politics of singularity" and the possibility of belonging without identity – are still to be worked out.

## The ethnicization of black identity in the southern Pacific in the 1990s

To realize the significance of the transformation in the identity regime that took place in the Pacific in the 1990s, it is important to have a glimpse of how identities were previously constructed. Some anthropologists assert the existence of a black cognitive universe that, while constituting a coherent whole with an original logic of its own, is always changing and flexible. Going beyond approaches that emphasized either a proto-identity based on the survival of African traits or, conversely, the inability of black groups to articulate an identity amid the harshness of their marginalization, Losonczy proposes a view of black identities in the Pacific as an "interstitial identity, the result of violent historical discontinuities." Rather than appealing to an ethnic referent, this identity was constructed "in terms of an underlying strategy that systematically reorganized exogenous cultural materials," and which resulted in "a cauldron of identities with open and fluid boundaries" (Losonczy 1999:15, 16). This applies as much to the past as to the present. In the past, this strategy brought together elements of diverse provenance – Catholic, African, indigenous, modern – in ways that called for its own kind of collective memory. This memory was founded on two puzzling absences: about African origins, and about slavery. This is not a total erasure, however, for while explicit memories of these events are nonexistent, they can be gleaned from a series of rituals and symbolic practices, such as mythic narratives and rituals of death and the saints, whose performance, iconography, and musical elements evidence the syncretism of African, indigenous, and Catholic forms (Losonczy 1999; Restrepo 2002).

The same argument has been applied to the most recent past. Speaking of the black society of the northern Chocó area, another anthropologist states that "identity is an artifice made in fine thread (*filigrana*), a tapestry woven from materials from diverse sources, caring not about their provenance nor about the final product" (Villa 2001:207). If throughout most of the twentieth century this strategy entailed the progressive incorporation of a relation to the state and established political parties into local identities, since the late 1980s this logic of recombination has compelled black peasants to discover ethnicity. Villa highlights the role of the progressive church, expert discourses, and some development projects as the source of the threads for the new identity. For Villa, the new identities are part of a process that extends as far back as the colonial society and that finds in the current ethnicization its most recent phase. For Losonczy, similarly, the recent appeal to the idiom of "Afro" (as in the new label of Afro-Colombian) implies a return to the two mythic themes of origins and slavery. For her, however, the reinsertion of identity into this narrative takes place on the grounds of a modern, linear conception of history, and thus runs counter to the previous discontinuous and dispersed regime. It remains to be seen, she concludes, whether this process of bringing black ethnicity into dialogue with modernity (through a sort of "neo-traditionalist memory") will succeed in forging a new figure in the cauldron of identity.

Losonzcy's argument that the ethnicization of identity in the 1990s represents a departure from long-standing logics of identity is shared by other students of this process. Let us return to the previous identity regime to understand this position. A common starting point is the assertion that pre-AT 55 identities were for the most part largely localized, fluid, and diverse. At one level, identities in riverine settlements are strongly place-based, anchored in the river; belonging is most often referred back to the river of habitation. Concepts of territoriality are place-based, and linked to kinship relations, labor practices, and an entire grammar of the environment. Beyond that, some general ways of self-reference do exist, such as *libre* (free person). The origin of this self-referential term is surely to be found in the colonial racial taxonomy, yet it is far from simple. Like the other common category of *renaciente* (a notion of everything being perpetually reborn), *libre* "has a particular meaning in a complex articulation inside a deeply woven set of categories . . . thus the notion of *libre* is not just the local transcription of a racial category of 'black' as simply opposed to 'white' and 'Indian'" (Restrepo 2002:99). In fact, what obtains is a "polyphony of identities that includes multiple notions, such as *cholos* / wild Indians (*indio bravo*) / *indios* / *naturales* / *paisas* / serranos / gringos / *culimochos* / libres / morenos / negros" (2002:101). This fluid and mobile system is further complicated by notions of belonging, occupation, and so forth. One is a worker, a peasant, a *leñetero* (collector of firewood), a fisherman, a *conchera* (shell collector), or a *costeño* (from the coast). These denominations made up the most common subject positions before the emergence of ethnicity.

It is precisely this regime of identity that is seen as having been turned topsy-turvy by the arrival of black ethnicity, even if not all of the previous subject positions disappeared overnight; some have been reconstituted. What is important to empha-size is that the arrival of the 1990s signified a radical rupture with the existing articulations of blackness. To be sure, the overall goal was the relocation of blackness in the new cultural and political imaginary of the nation. In the southern Pacific, the AT 55 inaugurated a series of practices that resulted in a powerful discursive con-struction of ethnic identity in terms of the "black communities." Let us see how.

First of all, the AT 55 called for the creation of institutional mechanisms for the development of the law (which became Ley 70 in July, 1993). These mechanisms (particularly a national-level Special Commission for Black Communities) involved mixed bodies including state officials, experts, and representatives of black commu-nities and organizations. This spurred a tremendous amount of activity. New organ-izations and ways of thinking emerged on the basis of categories that had little previous reference in the Pacific, such as territory, culture, environment, and, very important, the comunidad negra. Here is how Ley 70 defined this term (Ley 70, Article 2, paragraph 5): "Black community is the group of families of Afro-Colom-bian descent who posses their own culture, a shared history, and their own traditions and customs in the context of the town/country division, and who exhibit and preserve a consciousness of their identity that makes them distinct from other ethnic groups."

Numerous observers have commented on how the law, and particularly this defin-ition, which was shaped by anthropologists and other experts in the Special Commis-sion, was based on the only known existing model of alterity, that of indigenous peoples. Be that as it may, the terms introduced by AT 55 and Ley 70 became the nodal points for the articulation of a politics of black ethnicity. There were several conditions that, by the end of the 1980s, prepared the ground for these categories to take root. In the southern Pacific, displacement from the land by *camaroneras* (industrial shrimp farms) and *palmicultoras* (African oil-palm plantations) was fast advancing; international cooperation and development projects, environmental dis-courses such as biodiversity, state decentralization requiring a new type of local subject, and some forms of organizing, particularly by the progressive Catholic Church and peasant unions – all of these factors meant that the concerns expressed in AT 55 found resonance among local groups. For activists, the AT 55 appeared as a great possibility for cultural construction and self-defense. What ensued was a verit-able "pedagogy of alterity" through which experts, progressive church people, state officials, development workers, and, of course, scores of activists, put the novel language into circulation throughout the rivers, hamlets, and towns of the Pacific region. This, however, was not a top-down exercise, but a process of interaction between experts and ethno-territorial organizations, experts and communities, activ-ists and communities, advisers and local groups, etc. These interactions involved a constant negotiation of the terms and of the practices themselves (Restrepo 2002).

These interactions took place through a multiplicity of largely new practices – workshops and meetings in cities and river settlements, map-making and census exercises in communities, the traveling of territories for collective titling, and so forth. It was through these practices that ethnicity was "put into discourse." This putting into discourse of ethnicity relied on a series of operations: it naturalized identity, portraying black groups as environmentalists; it emphasized "traditional" production practices; it represented communities as existing in discrete settlements; and it highlighted specific economic rationalities, traditional forms of authority, and so forth. These operations located black groups in space and time in particular ways; they tended to objectify and regularize notions of territory and culture – away from a fluid and dispersed regime toward a more modern, rational, and normative one. The result was a significant rearticulation of local experience. "To think about the local population in terms of black community, with a territory, traditional production practices, an ethnic identity and a set of specific rights, was an exercise in the construction of difference that only became possible in the [southern] Pacific in the decade of the nineties with the institutional and social positioning of this new regime of representation" (Restrepo 2002:81, 82).

It would be a mistake, however, to see this regime solely as an artifact of the cultural and territorial rights law, or as a result of state manipulation. To be sure, there is a connection between the new identities and the neoliberal state; however, the former can only be seen in part as a result of the latter. As the previous model of a populist and racially homogenous project of nation-building entered into crisis, the state promoted the creation of new identities that it was then unable to control. This was due in part to the impact of transnational factors emphasizing cultural diversity, the environment, and human rights. In other words, it is difficult to defend any simple understanding of the relation between identity, social movements, and the state. Subaltern strategies are neither the creation of hegemonic models nor direct and pure resistance to them. One may find forms of cultural politics that contest the state's institutional discursivity at the local level; as the analyses of everyday practices of state formation and functioning show, local pressures on the part of social movements do have an effect on the state. In places like the Pacific, the ethnicization of identity itself thus needs to be seen as a shared process. This is so because the state hardly functions as a coherent entity, but is rather ridden with internal tensions and conflicts across levels, institutions, and programs. In some cases, local functionaries might seek to capture the fruits of the "eco-ethno boom" to their own advantage, while in other cases they might become allies of local organizations, who also operate as brokers between the state and local communities. Not infrequently, what one finds is that state offices are made up of largely mixed spaces that bring together civil servants, experts, and movement activists – which again make it difficult to decide where the state begins and ends, or whether it can be identified as a discrete entity (Alvarez 2002). Some of this dynamic is missed in recent cultural and ethnographic studies of the state because of what might be described as a lingering state centrism.

Restrepo's (2002) analysis rightly concludes by stating that representations of blackness in terms of ethnicity constitute a field of discursive and hence political contestation; there is no necessary correspondence between a given social location (like blacks) and its representation. Ethnic identities may appear as essential to some, as an imposition on the part of the state to others (e.g., black elites), or as a space for maneuvering to still others. What has made "the black community" thinkable and material is precisely the dense interweaving of expert, state, place-based and activist techniques, with their corresponding mediations. The result has been a significant reconfiguration of modalities of power. This speaks of the profoundly political character of identity, an aspect that social-movement activists know only too well, as we shall see in the next section.

To sum up, the experience of the 1990s exhibits some of the features contemplated in contemporary theories of identity. Identities are historically created by ensembles of discourses and practices. The main discourses of articulation in this case concerned nature (biodiversity) and cultural difference; other important discourses were alternative development and rights. These discourses centered on the notion of "black communities," and operated through a multiplicity of practices bringing together communities, activists, experts, state officials, academics, and non-governmental organizations in various combinations and in a variety of spaces. The ensuing identity regime was the result of a given problematization of difference and can be seen, to this extent, as a modernist process. Modeled after the indigenous experience, black ethnic identities were conceived chiefly as distinct from a dominant Euro-Andean other (whites/*paisas*). As a modernist tool, the construction of black ethnicity may thus be seen as part of a process of negotiating a new mode of insertion into national life. For a time, these identities took on a strong character, even if experienced in different ways by different groups. What was at stake was a rearticulation of belonging – a new discursive horizon of meaning – that enabled the creation of an unprecedented political imaginary in terms of difference, autonomy, and cultural rights. As are all modernist identities, black ethnicity was enmeshed in a representational politics enabled by the very structures of power from which it sought to free itself. The extent to which black activists were able to "trouble" this identity along the way remains to be seen.

Black ethnicity introduced a new economy of power and visibility in the southern Pacific. Yet this is not all; the analysis in the following section will raise some questions about the limits of the interpretations of the ethnicizing process presented in the previous pages. Do the discourses and strategies of the social movements evidence only a conversation with modernity, or do they intuit a counter-modernity in any sense? Can the play of identities be explained solely in terms of the state and the economy, or, conversely, could a different understanding of agency lead to a partially different reading? Do activists craft long-term visions – beyond and perhaps despite modernity – that could make legitimate a different interpretation of their actions? Does the activists' frontal encounter with globalization not lead them to envision a politics of difference that at some level could be seen as defying the logic of capital and the state from another epistemic space, albeit not altogether different? Can a politics of difference be based not only on the exteriorization of an Other but also on a multiplicity of others and, moreover, on a positive construction of place and culture? If this is the case, what other kinds of conversations are activists engaged in besides and beyond "ethnic talk"? Were indigenous and white identities really the main referent points for black ethnic construction, or how, for instance, does nature complicates this picture? Finally, what happens when we shift the framework of interpretation, and how do we reconcile contrasting readings? A closer look at a particular sector of the black movement of the Pacific will suggest tentative answers to some of these questions.

## THE SOCIAL MOVEMENT OF BLACK COMMUNITIES OF THE SOUTHERN PACIFIC

This section analyzes the emergence and transformation of a black movement network organization called the *Proceso de Comunidades Negras* (PCN). As the more visible expression of a larger social movement of black communities of the Pacific, PCN may be seen in terms of the crafting of individual and collective identities through the creation of figured worlds in local contentious struggles. These struggles exist within larger contexts linking communities, the region, and the nation to more extensive networks and to broader socioeconomic, cultural and political histories. What links these levels of identity are discourses of articulation. Rather than approaching the articulatory practices primarily from the side of the state and the economy, however, we shall attempt to see what happens when we look at the politics of articulation from the perspective of the agency and figured worlds enacted by the activists. As in the previous section, we start by introducing a different take on identity as a prelude to the ethnographic presentation and discussion.

## Identity, history, and agency: a contemporary theory

Building on the work of two Russian scholars (the psychologist L. S. Vygotsky and the theorist M. Bakhtin), Holland, Lachicotte, Skinner, and Cain (1998) have developed a dialogic and practice-oriented understanding of identity. Identity, in their view, is a complex form of self-understanding improvised from the cultural resources at hand in a particular historical context. Their focus is on the intersection of person and society, and on how power and culture are negotiated at this intersection to produce particular identities in ways that evince the structured as well as the agential dimensions of the process. In order to conceptualize this process of construction, these authors draw upon Bakhtin's insistence on the ineluctably dialogic nature of human life to arrive at a notion of "codevelopment – the linked development of people, cultural forms, and social positions in particular historical worlds" (Holland et al. 1998:33).

The production of identities entails the construction of cultural worlds; this involves an active engagement with the environment and takes place through recursive improvisations in a sedimented historical background; it also involves various kinds of mediations (e.g., symbolic, linguistic, and other "tools of agency"). In the case of activists, these cultural worlds can be thought of as "figured worlds," defined as locally situated, culturally constructed, and socially organized worlds that make visible people's purposeful agency, that is, their capacity to remake the world in which they live. Although these worlds are subjected to continuous adjustment, they may achieve some durability; indeed, "this context of flux is the ground for identity development" and sets the conditions for "a space of authoring" (Holland et al. 1998:63). Figured worlds of this sort are spaces where cultural politics are enacted, which result in particular personal and collective identities. We can think of activists as having certain competencies for, literally, figuring worlds through a variety of practices, articulations, and cultural artifacts. They do so through forms of "situated learning," in which "identities become important outcomes of participation in communities of practice" (Holland et al. 1998:56, 57). The collectivity called the Process of Black Communities (PCN) can be seen as an example of a cohesive community of practice formed in the process of constructing a relatively stable figured world.

In addition to the dialogic dimension, the second aspect of the authoring perspective is its historical dimension; this is fruitfully conceptualized by these authors through the notion of "history in person" (Holland and Lave 2001). This concept invokes at the same time the structuring effect of historical conditions and the processes by which actors mediate the structuring through the production of cultural forms that take the historical conditions themselves as resources for self-authoring. Holland and her co-workers introduce two notions in this regard. The first is that of "local contentious practice," that is, the actors' situated participation in explicit local conflicts that are generative of identity. The second is that of the "enduring historical struggles," that is, those larger processes that constitute the background within which the former category is located. It is not difficult to see how these two concepts might apply to the Pacific. Local contentious practices around specific territories and their biodiversity, for instance, are clearly linked to broader struggles concerning, say, development, race, environment, the state, rights, or globalization. Here the ethnography should document how "historically institutionalized struggles" linked to long-term conflicts may or may not lead to sustained identities, and how both of these are realized in contentious local practice. In other words, local contentious practice mediates between history in person and enduring struggles, or between historical struggles in person and historically institutionalized struggles. In this non-essentialist view, identities and struggles are always unfinished and in process – persons and institutions are never entirely "made up" previous to, and independently of, their encounter. Whether real or idealized, there are periods when identity becomes habituated and stabilized, so that we are no longer aware of its production since the orchestration of identity has somehow endured, even if for a time.

## History and agency in the practice of the process of black communities

The PCN gathers together some 120 organizations in the southern Pacific and a few other regions of the country. As will be indicated below, these organizations are grouped into regional *palenques*. Some of these organizations are more or less active than others. Most have only a few participants at any given moment. There is an enduring core of activists that includes those on the National Coordinating Committee and some of the main leaders of each palenque. In an informal conversation with two of the leading activists, Libia Grueso and Julia Cogollo (Cali, June 2002), they estimated the number of active PCN members at over a hundred. The smaller core group has remained together and fully active and committed for the better part of the 1990s and until today.

In its initial years (1991–94), and in the context of AT 55, PCN gave preeminence to the social control of the territory and natural resources as a precondition for the survival, recreation, and strengthening of culture. This sustained effort served to lay down the basis, during the 1991–93 period, for the elaboration of Ley 70, and to firm up a series of politico-organizational principles (see below). It also helped PCN activists to recognize the various tendencies found among the array of black organizations involved with Ley 70. At the second *Asamblea Nacional de Comunidades Negras* (National Conference of Black Communities) held in May 1993, delegates revised and approved the text for the law negotiated by the Special Commission. The collective elaboration of the proposal for Ley 70 was a decisive space for the development of the movement. This process was advanced at two levels, one centered on the daily practices of the communities, the other on a political reflection by the activists. The first level – carried out under the rubric of what was referred to as "the logic of the river" – sought a broad participation of local people in the articulation of their rights, aspirations, and dreams. The second level, though having the river settlements as a referent, sought to raise the question of black people as an ethnic group, beyond what could be granted by the law. This level saw the development of a conceptualization of the notions of territory, development, and the social relations of black communities with the rest of Colombian society. This conceptualization took place in a dialogical process with a host of actors, including traditional black politicians and the state. The negotiation with the government entailed a double effort of construction of agreements, between organizations and communities on the one hand, and between these and the government on the other. Given the forceful implementation of the neoliberal opening of the economy and the growing currency of discussions on biodiversity and genetic resources, these negotiations became ever more tense, while the government became more intransigent as its awareness of the capacity of their black interlocutors grew; the black organizing process gained in structure, experience, and coordination. The entire process constituted a veritable social construction of protest that culminated with the approval by Congress of the version of the law (Ley 70) negotiated with the communities (see Grueso, Rosero, and Escobar 1998 for a fuller account).

The Third National Conference was convened in September 1993 in the predominantly black town of Puerto Tejada. With the attendance of more than 300 delegates, the Conference debated the politico-organizational situation of the black communities. Recognizing the diversity of the movement, the Conference (Proceso de Comunidades Negras 1993:27) proposed a self-definition and characterization as

> a sector of the social movement of black communities composed of people and organizations with diverse experiences and goals, but united around a set of principles, criteria, and objectives that set us apart from other sectors of the movement. In the same vein, we represent a proposal to the entire black community of the country, and aspire to construct a unified movement of black communities able to encompass their rights and aspirations.

The objective of the organizing process was stated as "the consolidation of a social movement of black communities for the reconstruction and affirmation of cultural identity... for the achievement of cultural, social, economic, political, and territorial rights and for the defense of natural resources and the environment." A central feature of the Conference was the adoption of a set of politico-organizational principles that encompassed the practice and desires of the black communities. These principles concerned the key issues of identity, territory, autonomy, and development (Proceso de Comunidades Negras 1993:28–29):

> 1. *The reaffirmation of identity* (the right to be black). In the first place, we conceive of being black from the perspective of our cultural logic and lifeworld (*cosmovisión*) in all of its social, economic, and political dimensions. This logic counters the logic of domination that intends to exploit and subject our people. Our cultural vision opposes a model of society that requires uniformity for its continued dominance.

This first principle clearly identified culture and identity as organizing axes of both daily life and political practice.

2. *The right to territory* (as the space for being). As a vital space, territory is a necessary condition for the recreation and development of our cultural vision. We cannot be if we do not have a space for living in accordance with what we think and desire as a form of life. It follows that we see the territory as a habitat and space where black people develop their being in harmony with nature.

3. *Autonomy* (the right to the exercise of being/identity). We understand autonomy in relation to the dominant society, other ethnic groups, and political parties. It arises out of our cultural logic. Thus understood, we are autonomous internally in the political realm, and aspire to social and economic autonomy.

4. *Construction of an autonomous perspective of the future.* We intend to construct an autonomous vision of economic and social development based on our culture and traditional forms of production and social organization. The dominant society has systematically imposed on us a vision of development that responds to their own interests and worldview. We have the right to give others the vision of our world, as we want to construct it.

5. *Declaration of solidarity.* We are part of the struggle for rights of black people throughout the world. From our own particularity, the social movement of black communities shall contribute to the efforts of those who struggle for alternative life projects.

This declaration of principles constituted a major rupture with the political and developmentalist formulations of the left, past black organizations, and traditional political sectors. A final point of interest concerns the organizational strategy of the movement. At a formal level, PCN's organizational structure is simple: (1) Four regional palenques, each of which corresponds to a major region, and which agglutinate the local ethno-territorial organizations; (2) A national coordinating committee; (3) Technical teams at national and, in some cases, regional levels, in charge of economic, development, environmental, and ethno-educational matters. Originally designating the autonomous territories of maroons or freed slaves in colonial times, today's palenques are spaces for discussion, decision-making, and policy orientation in each of the regions with an important black presence. They operate in conjunction with the *Asamblea Nacional de Comunidades Negras, ANCN* (National Conference of Black Communities) and, together, constitute the *Consejo Nacional de Palenques*. Regional palenques are composed of two representatives from each of the region's organizations. The National Coordinating Committee is in charge of coordinating actions, implementing the decisions of the ANCN, and representing the PCN in national and international forums.

It would be a mistake, however, to see this "structure" as a rigid set of norms independent of the day-to-day practices of the activists. There seems to be increasing agreement among social-movement theorists about the need to avoid the dichotomy that has prevailed between structure-oriented explanations and agency, consciousness, or identity-focused ones. Accounting for the dynamics of movements requires models that avoid just such dichotomous thinking. In the newer models, agency and structure are inseparable and mutually constitutive; even when formalized, as in PCN's case, structures are not ready-made, waiting to be filled in by activists. The structure itself is made of movement and enacted in practice. The structure, if anything, is an emergent property resulting from movement over time.

This can be seen in the creation and reproduction over time of the collectivity called PCN. This organization is the product of a varied set of practices developed around local contentious struggles. These practices entail an intense and permanent degree of communication among activists at various levels: horizontally, at the national, regional, and local levels; vertically, across levels. At the national level, there is a high degree of face-to-face and electronic communication among members of the National Coordinating Committee and with some of the main members of the technical teams. This group forms a tight collective which is in permanent contact, with active – not infrequently intense and heated – debates on ongoing issues, decisions, and so forth. For some outside observers, this high level of debate and communications hinders effective action. Be that as it may, it is this practice that has enabled a core group of activists to remain steadfast in their commitment to the collective identity of PCN and what it represents. Communications of this sort are clearly weaker at the local level. While some activists have internalized the organization's principles and political vision, this has been much more difficult at the local level. In some regions, and coupled with growing regional violence, this has led to the dismantling of local organizations and the decimation of the regional palenque.

There is a close connection between culture and identity in the understanding of the activists. As one activist put it, "is not us who will save culture, it is culture who will save us" (quoted in Alvarez 2002:13). This does not mean, however, that activists regard culture as static. On the contrary; they view it as a dynamic and creative process. The collective identity constructed by PCN may be viewed as having a certain doubleness. On the one hand, identity is thought of as rooted in shared cultural practices, a collective self of sorts; this conception of identity involves an imaginative rediscovery of culture that lends coherence to the experience of dispersal and oppression. On the other hand, identity is seen in terms of the differences created by history; this aspect emphasizes becoming rather than being, positioning rather than essence, and cultural discontinuity as well as continuities. For the activists, the defense of certain cultural practices of the river communities is a strategic question, since they are seen as embodying not only resistance to capitalism and modernity but elements for alternative constructions. This defense is not intransigent nor essentializing given that it responds to an interpretation of the challenges faced by the communities and the possibilities presented by a cautious opening toward forms of modernity, such as biodiversity conservation and alternative development. Identity is thus seen in both ways: as anchored in "traditional" practices and forms of knowledge; and as an always changing project of cultural and political construction. The movement builds upon the submerged networks of cultural practices and meanings of the river communities, and opposes, to the static and conventional notion of identity implicit in the 1991 Constitution, a more fluid notion of identity as political construction.

## In, against, and beyond the state? Assessing movements

The 1995–96 period saw the appearance of new organized black sectors with different, and at times conflicting, agendas, seeking to bank on the space created for black people's rights. Over the years, the conflicts and contradictions among all of these groups impinged upon important issues, such as the formulation of the National Development Plan for Black Communities, the negotiation of environmental conflicts, the decision over electoral representation, and so forth; in many of these cases, the bargaining position of communities vis-à-vis the government was weakened.

Notwithstanding, PCN's concrete achievements have by no means been negligible. They include the PCN's central role in the formulation of Ley 70, and in other areas of environmental and cultural policy. PCN also made a major contribution over the years to the creation of community organizations in a number of the rivers in the southern Pacific, to the constitution of community councils, the land-titling process, the funding of specific projects, and to the organization of displaced Afro-Colombians. The group's environmental achievements have been particularly important. By most accounts, the PCN has been the single most visible force engaged in the defense of the southern Pacific rainforest cultures and ecosystems. What makes the PCN so important and unique is a combination of features that include: (1) A courageous and sustained *political strategy* vis-à-vis the state around territorial, cultural, and environmental problems, rights, and issues. (2) The progressive elaboration of a sophisticated *conceptual framework* for problem analysis and alternative policy formulation regarding development, conservation, and sustainability in the Pacific. (3) A persistent engagement with *concrete environmental conflicts* and the search for solutions at local, national, and international levels. From this perspective, PCN can be said to have developed a coherent practice of political ecology.

To sum up, in this section we have attempted to use the framework of "history in person" to interpret the experience of the collectivity called PCN. We have seen how this collectivity arose historically and constituted its identity in practice. This identity was built through dialogical processes of various kinds, some of which involved interpersonal relationships in the interior of the group, others encounters with a host of actors (from state actors and experts to armed actors) in local contentious practice concerning the control of local territories, the defense of cultural and ecological practices, the struggle for the right to difference, and so forth. These local conflicts are related to broader struggles concerning globalization, the destruction of the humid forest, racism, development, and neoliberal capitalism. As a collective identity constructed around a particular figured world – "the black communities," and, indeed, the PCN itself – this collectivity can be seen as constituting a community of practice that, despite ups and downs, has achieved some durability.

The history and agency approach shows the extent to which activists take broader historical conditions (and other conditions arising from local histories *that cannot be reduced fully to the former*) as resources for collective self-authoring. It is certainly the case that by using the tools of modernity, the activists also get further entangled in the worlds from which they seek liberation. In doing so, however, they attempt to redraw the existing hierarchy of power and privilege and to maintain alive the heteroglossic potential of all world-making practices. What this means is that, in the process of struggling with modernist discourses, activists are able to craft spaces that are freer from the authority of the dominant norms and, in so doing, are able to produce differentiated voices – what some have called "alternative modernities," certainly, but also the inklings of alternatives to modernity. In other words, to take the notion of dialogism seriously one has to link the ultimate one-directionality that characterizes most perspectives and that makes the idea of genuine difference or alterity impossible.

## CONCLUSION

One of the most intractable aspects of the situation of the Pacific at present is the problematic of violence and displacement. To the extent that massive poverty and displacement are becoming a ubiquitous consequence of the excesses of neoliberal globalization, the Colombian case (with over 2 million internally displaced people, including a disproportionately high number of Afro-Colombians and indigenous minorities) merits special attention. What are the relations between displacement, capitalism, and modernity? Are development and modernity inherently development-producing processes, and if so, is modernity's own capacity to deal with displacement lagging behind its proclivity to create it? What happens to identities and identity projects under these conditions? These are pressing questions to which there are still few answers. Second, as the modern project presses on in the guise of brutal neoliberal policies, do the conditions not arise for more imaginative forms of protest and alternative world construction? In this regard, the Porto Alegre Global Social Forum dictum, *another world is possible*, is a guiding light. What novel theoretical analyses do we need to illuminate the paths toward these other worlds? Which collective identities might help to bring them about? One of the most patent lessons of today's social movements is the need for new alliances and partnerships between academics and activists. Indeed, today a new breed of intellectual activists and activist intellectuals seem to pose an unprecedented challenge to producers of academic knowledge, one we should be willing to consider.

Finally, the entire problematic of difference needs to be rethought. Identities are relational, to be sure, but this does not mean they are fully explainable in terms of each other. More is certainly at stake, and it is crucial to learn to see and understand this irreducibility with new empirical and theoretical lenses. From Latin America, a new understanding of difference in terms of the long historical suppression of place-based knowledge and the inevitable subaltern exteriority to the modern colonial world-system that this suppression entails is emerging. From this exteriority one may posit a politics of difference – economic, ecological, and cultural difference, as is evident in the black and indigenous struggles of the Pacific – from which other socio-natural worlds, not fully reducible to modern cultural logics, could again be affirmatively possible. I believe it is too soon to declare the possibility of alternatives to modernity – that is, a truly plural multiplicity of cultural worlds – as historically foreclosed, as practically all analysts of globalization and modernity, on all sides of the political spectrum, seem to have concluded. There certainly are risks in wanting to keep alive the promise of an irreducible alterity (including the risk of this wish itself being an effect of modernity), yet the costs of a foregone conclusion on the side of the universalization of modernity everywhere, and for all times, could be even higher in cultural terms. How we give shape to the alternative possibility, in theoretical and political terms, remains an open question.

## NOTE AND ACKNOWLEDGMENTS

This chapter is based on a book in progress on black identity and cultural, environmental, and political mobilization in the Colombian Pacific. Much of importance has been left out, including the relation between personal and collective aspects of identity, the gender dynamics of the movement, and the entire issue of violence and displacement, which became paramount after 1998. I would like to thank the PCN, particularly Libia Grueso and Carlos Rosero, and Eduardo Restrepo for numerous conversations about the issues discussed in this chapter; David Nugent and Joan Vincent for creative editing of a longer version of the chapter; and the John Simon Guggenheim Memorial Foundation and the MacArthur Global Security and Sustainability Program for partial funding for the project's research and writing.

## REFERENCES

Alvarez, Manuela (2002) Altered States: Culture and Politics in the Colombian Pacific. MA thesis, University of Massachusetts, Amherst.

Bauman, Zygmunt (1996) From Pilgrim to Tourist – or a Short History of Identity. In *Questions of Cultural Identity*, ed. Stuart Hall and P. du Gay, pp. 18–36. London: Sage.

Butler, Judith (1990) *Gender Trouble*. New York: Routledge.

Comarofff, John (1996) Ethnicity, Nationalism, and the Politics of Difference. In *The Politics of Difference: Ethnic Premises in a World of Power*, ed. E. Wilmsen and P. McAllister, pp. 163–205. Chicago: University of Chicago Press.

Grossberg, Lawrence (1996) Identity and Cultural Studies – Is That All There Is? In *Questions of Cultural Identity*, ed. Stuart Hall and P. du Gay, pp. 87–107. London: Sage.

Grueso, Libia, Carlos Rosero, and Arturo Escobar (1998) The Process of Black Community Organizing in the Southern Pacific Coast of Colombia. In *Cultures of Politics/Politics of Cultures: Revisioning Latin American Social Movements*, ed. Sonia E. Alvarez, Evelina Dagnino, and Arturo Escobar, pp. 196–219. Boulder, CO: Westview Press.

Hall, Stuart (1996) Introduction: Who Needs "Identity"? In *Questions of Cultural Identity*, ed. Stuart Hall and P. du Gay, pp. 1–17. London: Sage.

Holland, Dorothy, William Lachicotte, Debra Skinner, and Carole Cain (1998) *Identity and Agency in Cultural Worlds*. Cambridge, MA: Harvard University Press.

Holland, Dorothy, and Jean Lave (2001) History in Person: An Introduction. In *History in Person: Enduring Struggles, Contentious Practice, Intimate Identities*, ed. D. Holland and J. Lave, pp. 3–36. Santa Fe, NM: School of American Research.

Laclau, Ernesto, and Chantal Mouffe (1985) *Hegemony and Socialist Strategy*. London: Verso

Losonczy, Anne-Marie (1999) Memorias e identidad: los negro-colombianos del Chocó. In *De montes, ríos y ciudades: Territorios e identidades de la gente negra en Colombia*, ed. J. Camacho and E. Restrepo, pp. 13–23. Bogotá: ICANH/Natura/Ecofondo.

Norval, Aletta (1996) Thinking Identities: Against a Theory of Ethnicity. In *The Politics of Difference: Ethnic Premises in a World of Power*, ed. E. Wilmsen and P. McAllister, pp. 59–70. Chicago: University of Chicago Press.

Proceso de Comunidades Negras (1993) *Tercera Asamblea Nacional Proceedings*. Cali: PCN.

Restrepo, Eduardo (2002) Memories, Identities, and Ethnicity: Making the Black Community in Colombia. MA thesis, University of North Carolina, Chapel Hill.

Villa, William (2001) La sociedad negra del Chocó: Identidad y movimientos sociales. In *Acción colectiva, estado y etnicidad en el Pacífico colombiano*, ed. M. Pardo,. pp. 207–228. Bogotá: ICANH/Colciencias.

Wade, Peter (1997) *Race and Ethnicity in Latin America*. London: Pluto.

## SUGGESTED FURTHER READING

Asher, Kiran (1998) Constructing Afro-Colombia: Ethnicity and Territory in the Pacific Lowlands. Ph.D. dissertation, University of Florida.

Camacho, Juana, and Eduardo Restrepo, eds. (1999) *De montes, ríos y ciudades: Territorios e identidades de la gente negra en Colombia.* Bogotá: ICANH/Natura/Ecofondo.

Edelman, Marc (2001) Social Movements: Changing Paradigms and Forms of Politics. *Annual Review of Anthropology* 30:285–317.

Escobar, Arturo (2003) Displacement, Development and Modernity in the Colombian Pacific. *International Social Science Journal* 17:157–167.

Gros, Christian (2000) *Políticas de la etnicidad: Identidad, estado y modernidad.* Bogotá: ICANH.

Grueso, Libia, and Leyla Arroyo (2002) Women and the Defense of Place in Colombian Black Women Struggles. *Development* 45:60–66.

Hale, Charles (1997) Cultural Politics of Identity in Latin America. *Annual Review of Anthropology* 26:567–590.

Hansen, Thomas Blom, and Finn Stepputat, eds. (2000) *States of Imagination.* Durham, NC: Duke University Press.

Klandermans, Bert, and Suzanne Staggenborg, eds. (2002) *Methods of Social Movement Research.* Minneapolis: University of Minnesota Press.

Melucci, Alberto (1989) *Nomads of the Present.* Philadelphia: Temple University Press.

Mignolo, Walter (2000) *Local Histories and Global Designs.* Princeton, NJ: Princeton University Press.

Mosquera, Claudia, Mauricio Pardo, and Odile Hoffmann (2002) *Afrodescendientes en las Américas: trayectorias identitarias.* Bogotá: UNAL-ICANH-IRD-ILSA.

Pardo, Mauricio, ed. (2001) *Acción colectiva, estado y etnicidad en el Pacífico colombiano.* Bogotá: ICANH/Colciencias.

Scheller, Mimi (2001) The Mechanisms of Mobility and Liquidity: Rethinking the Movement in Social Movements. Department of Sociology, Lancaster University. See http://www.comp. lancs.ac.uk/sociology/soc076ms.html

## CHAPTER 17

# Imagining Nations

## *Akhil Gupta*

Anthropologists like to think of "big" questions by working with people who are not important and famous, though important precisely because they are ordinary. In 1985 I was doing fieldwork in Alipur, a small village in North India. One day I was talking to a man, perhaps not yet 40, who appeared to be perpetually squinting. In the middle of our conversation, he suddenly asked me, "Can I try on your glasses?" People had asked to hold, touch, and scrutinize all the objects that I carried around with me, including a small calculator operated by a solar cell, a camera, and my watch. But this was the first time that someone had asked to try on my eyeglasses. Not knowing how to respond to such a request, I handed them over, warning him to be prepared for the distortions caused by the powerful lenses, the result perhaps of a lifetime of staring at pages of small print. He put them on awkwardly, unused to the crutches that supported them over the ears. He turned his head from side to side, and professed astonishment at what he could see. Giving them back to me, he announced, "That's what I need. I can see so much clearer with them."

Almost a century earlier, on October 4, 1894, to be precise, Friedrich Engels was just putting the finishing touches to his edition of the third volume of *Capital*. Explaining the long delay in the publication of this volume, Engels mentioned the slowing effects of age: "After one is 70, the Meynert fibres of association in the brain operate only with a certain annoying caution" (Marx 1981:92), and he wrote of eye trouble that had forced him to reduce the number of hours he could devote to attending to written material: "I can only rarely take up my pen in artificial light" (Marx 1981:91). As I read this, I wondered about all that is implied by the careless tossing in of that phrase, "artificial light" – light sources that are not yet naturalized enough to make it unnecessary to mention them (there were only 46 electricity generating stations in Britain at that time) or so taken for granted, as they are today, as to make the phrase sound anachronistic, but assumed nevertheless as a normal, daily part of the apparatus of life.

It was this artificial light that occasioned Engels's complaints about his failing eyesight, which in its turn, made me think of that anonymous villager whose poor eyesight will never be a footnote to history. For although the villager would have had some experience of "artificial light," and although he lived in an "electrified" village (the official term for villages that have been provided with electrical connections, perhaps unwittingly conveying the jolt of modernity), and although the sound of radios and later televisions could be heard reverberating in a stereoscopic effect through the narrow by-lanes of the village in the evenings, the artifice of light after dusk was never in question.

In juxtaposing these two stories of failing eyesight, I intend to draw attention to, but not simply reproduce, a pervasive and unavoidable narrative of progress and backwardness, in which the absence of artificial light and the inability to obtain eyeglasses would be central tropes. What interests me here, however, is the emplotment of this narrative of progress in the space of the nation. Thus, the story of the villager becomes a story of the backwardness of India, of the under-development of the nation compared to those other, First-World nations whose level of development a century ago matched or exceeded that of the India of today. But what is the structure of temporality that allows such national allegories to be narrated? How do we understand the time of the nation and the temporalities of nationalism in the "late capitalist" world, without denoting by the term "late capitalism" some teleological understanding of capitalist processes (Gupta 1998)?

In this paper, I reflect on the theme of time and temporality in the literature on nationalism through a postcolonial lens. Although I will draw on a number of different studies on nationalism, the chief focus of my attention will be Benedict Anderson's *Imagined Communities*. Engaging that small and imaginative volume is important, not only because it has transformed the study of nationalism, perhaps more than any other book in the last two decades, but also because of the centrality accorded in it to transformations in time and temporality in the origin and spread of nationalism.

## Rethinking the Temporalities of Nationalism

*Imagined Communities* sets itself the project of explaining why "nation-ness is the most universally legitimate value in the political life of our time" (1983:12) and why nations "command such profound emotional legitimacy" (1983:14). Anderson defines the nation as an imagined political community that is both inherently limited and sovereign (1983:15). In order for nations to emerge historically, a new conception of homogeneous, empty time, the time of the clock and the calendar, had to become dominant against earlier, religious, and messianic notions of time. This new conception of time was central to two eighteenth-century capitalist commodities, the novel and the newspaper. Both forms became possible with the standardization of vernaculars into print languages, which allowed unified fields of exchange and community that were below that of cosmopolitan languages like Latin and above that of vernacular spoken languages.

These ideas of time and print capitalism, so central to Anderson's account of nationalism, have been strenuously debated in the literature on nationalism. For example, Partha Chatterjee argues that "the real space of modern life is a heterotopia" (1999:131) and thinks that Anderson's insistence on empty homogeneous time misrepresents the time in which people live. Claudio Lomnitz (2001) argues in a more historical vein that a mode of imagining empty time became available to elites long before the rise of newspapers and novels in Latin America through state mechanisms such as plans and programs for administration, tariffs, and transportation systems. Similarly, rather than posit this specific connection between a particular arena of capitalist development – print capitalism – and nationalism, Ernest Gellner (1983) has proposed that nationalism was *one* of the many outcomes of the rise of capitalist modernization, a point that fails to account for the specificity of nationalism.

One of Anderson's more intriguing hypotheses is that the national community was formed in no small part by the shared experience of abbreviated itineraries of Creole functionaries in colonial bureaucracies. In these bureaucratic pilgrimages, Creole state functionaries could travel to the colonial capital but not to the metropolitan one. Attention to lower-level state functionaries as they embark on their inevitably frustrating "bureaucratic pilgrimages" (a phrase that evocatively hints at the religious zeal of nationalism) becomes important because it is from their ranks that the first generation of nationalist leaders arises. Once these leaders succeed in creating the first nations, Anderson argues, a model of the independent national state became available for pirating by the second decade of the nineteenth century. Unlike Gellner (1983), Hobsbawm (1990:10), and Kelly and Kaplan (2001), who have emphasized the prior role of the state in the constitution or construction of the nation, Anderson, in his discussion of the historical emergence of the nation, has little to say about the fact that European nations arrived on the scene at least two centuries after the rise of sovereign, territorial states.

Anderson also traces the shift from popular nationalism to the official nationalisms that became dominant in Europe in the middle of the nineteenth century to "the last wave" of nationalisms in former European colonies in Asia and Africa. Third-World nationalisms had their origin in the stunted nature of bureaucratic pilgrimages that limited the educational and administrative journeys of "natives" who began to see themselves as "nationals," people who neither gained admission to the circuits of travel to the metropolitan capital nor to the boardrooms of companies formed by colonial capital. In his influential study, Hobsbawm (1990) offers an alternative to this periodization of nationalisms. Hobsbawm too is concerned chiefly with *changes* in the concept of nationalism, particularly in the nineteenth century. He identifies three stages in the history of nationalism in Europe, the last of which concerns the making of nationalism into a mass movement (1990:12). In a different vein, Kelly and Kaplan (2001:1–29) forcefully argue that it is with decolonization that the world of nation-states as we know it really comes to exist and therefore that Anderson's entire periodization of the different stages of nationalism is incorrect. In a similar vein, Mongia (2002) has pointed out that the last states to actually become *nation*-states were the imperial colonial states of Europe, since before they had completely shed their colonies, they could not be called nation-states but rather multinational empires.

The structure of this chapter is as follows: I begin with the question of whether nationalism inaugurates a new sense of time and then go on to consider whether the novelty of this notion of time lies in the fact that it corresponds to the homogeneous, empty time of the clock and the calendar. Next, I consider how one understands the spread of nationalism, particularly to the Third World. In particular, I will pay attention to the debate between Anderson and Chatterjee on whether modularity or seriality is an adequate explanation for Third-World nationalisms. Then, I consider how paying attention to the temporality of nationalism might force one to think of nationalism as a contested, hegemonic formation that has to be continually renewed, rather than as something that is spread once and for all. In conclusion, I reflect on the changes wrought by late capitalism on some of the temporal premises of nationalism. Thus, each section focuses on closely related but different aspects of the nation's time and the temporality of its nationalism.

## THE NEW, THE NATION

In Anderson's account, the nation was not only premised on new, republican sodalities, establishing horizontal relations among people living in demarcated, inherently limited, territories. It also depended upon, and reinforced, a new consciousness of time. Let us for the moment attend to the larger question of temporality in modernity in order to provide a broader context for the time of nationalism. Nationalism depended upon a modern conception of time in which, to cite Sudipta Kaviraj (1997:326), the plasticity of society and the individual became thinkable. The novel idea that societies could be altered, shaped, planned, and steered in particular directions was matched only by the equally radical belief that individuals could, to some extent, however limited, direct their own destinies. Newness enters this world through a remarkable transformation in the experience of time, a consciousness of time marked by its emphasis on the new. Reading, after structuralism, Marx's oft-quoted phrase that "men make their own history, but they do not make it just as they please" (1963:15), we can too easily forget how revolutionary the first part, about human beings making their own history, must have seemed.

According to Anderson, it is precisely the development of capitalism, particularly that of the now celebrated idea of print capitalism, with its attendant implications for standardizing vernacular languages, that enabled communication and exchange to flourish, but also facilitated new types of exclusion, both of which were necessary for the limited character of the new national solidarities. In addition, the foreshortened nature of bureaucratic pilgrimages cultivated a sense of frustration among Creoles and colonial subjects, while creating new possibilities of association in traveling those circuits. Finally, the coincidence between new national boundaries and old administrative units, particularly in areas where language did not serve to separate one nation-state from another, suggests the possibility that other mechanisms of "state" may also have played an important role in shaping the lived experience of time.

How much of a hold on the modern imagination this call for the new exerted can be gauged from the fact that, in the aftermath of the French Revolution, republican revolutionaries wanted to inaugurate a new calendar starting in the Year One, scrapping the Christian calendar entirely (Anderson 1991:193). But nationalisms in the Third World experienced newness under different, more historical, notions of time. There was thus a fundamental asymmetry between earlier nationalisms and later ones. Already, by the time that nationalism gained ground in Europe in the nineteenth century, history as a discipline had been formally constituted, and the practice of writing the biography of the nation into a horizon-less past was well established (1991:204–205). Having invented this long genealogy, which faded into the mists of time, the problem for subsequent nationalisms was one of reinscribing the newness of the nation, and this is where narratives of national independence were crucial. The nation may always have existed, but its true historical destiny was smothered by despotic monarchs or exploitative colonial powers. (Not all nations fall into this pattern. Dan Segal pointed out to me that Caribbean nation-states are very clear about their moments of origin, and do not seek to invent a horizon-less past.) The newness of the nation was thus instantiated not by a story of geographical origins, but one of republican ruptures.

For those of us born in nations whose independence intersects with the life histories of our parents' generation, it is remarkable how much the affirmative, utopian promise of nationalism, this sense that something new had emerged in the world, has been lost in the scholarship on nationalism. Nationalist affect is now heavily weighted with a negative charge, and quite reasonably so given the disappointments of postcolonial nationalism in the last 50 years. But our view would be seriously askew if we forgot the exhilaratingly positive energies unleashed by nationalism, this allure of new beginnings.

## The Unbearable Emptiness of Time

Dipesh Chakrabarty has persuasively argued that temporality in historicist thinking naturalizes time as a neutral grid in which to record the progress of human history (1997:36–37). Does nationalism presuppose such a grid? Does a historical consciousness of time imply the progression of humankind as moving through a homogeneous and empty time, the time of clocks and of temporal coincidence? The idea of "homogeneous, empty time" comes from Walter Benjamin, who suggests that such a historicist view of time is quite at odds with a historical materialist one. Benjamin does little to hide his contempt for a view of history that, through calendrical coincidence, fills up homogeneous, empty time.

In an innovative and imaginative discussion, Anderson explains why this secular and historical understanding of time is central to the formation of nationalist consciousness by reference to the novel and the newspaper (1991:22–36). Novels represent simultaneity through their plots, which link unconnected characters living in the same clocked, calendrical time, a temporal coincidence apparent only to the omniscient reader (This is another place where Anderson differs from Benjamin, who sharply distinguishes the time of the clock from that of the calendar (1968:261–262). The actors may be unaware of each other's existence, but the connection between their lives is provided by the reality of their society moving through homogeneous, empty time, by the fact, that is, of their actions occurring at the same time. This notion of simultaneity is exemplified by sentences that begin with the word, "Meanwhile" (1991:27–28). Newspapers also enable this imagining of the homogeneous, empty time of the nation by the fact that they are consumed in a mass ceremony of simultaneity. Events reported in a newspaper are linked by little else but their calendrical coincidence, and the very act of reading is one that allows the reader to imagine all those other anonymous people who are also reading the newspaper at the same time, thus forging a sense of imagined community (1991:33–36).

Although the novel and the newspaper are similar in that they are some of the first mass-produced capitalist commodities, Anderson's account of how they generate nationalist consciousness introduces significant differences between them. In the novel, calendrical coincidence is effected through its content, through a plot in which things happen "in the meantime," and where the omniscient narrator or reader links the characters in a temporal space which the characters themselves do not inhabit. By contrast, the newspaper creates nationalist consciousness through a peculiar context, that is, through what, for lack of a better word, we could call the sociological significance of the particular act of reading, of simultaneous consumption. What accounts for this shift from content to context in considering two commodities whose primary goal is to represent, and to represent in a realist mode? (Anderson considers only realist novels in his discussion).

As against an emphasis on homogeneous, empty time, I wonder if it may not be possible to establish a more complicated relation between the temporalities of context, narrative, and reception in novels and newspapers. It would be surprising indeed if objects that are simultaneously commodities and texts had a unitary and overlapping set of temporal assumptions, not least because we might expect textual production and the production of commodities to have their own, relatively autonomous, temporalities. Similarly, in thinking of the temporalities of nationalism and historicism, I wonder if both are equally indebted to a structure of temporality characterized by homogeneity and emptiness (Chakrabarty 1997:36–37). Is there nothing of the messianic and the allochronic in the time of nationalism?

One place to begin thinking about the existence of other times within the space of novels and newspapers is to see how the colonized and the postcolonial are represented in those texts. Discourses about the Other in the colonial and developmentalist era are pervaded by a chronic allochronism, representational practices which position the colonized and the postcolonial as living in another time, one "behind" the West. These discourses of backwardness, of temporal lag, are often naturalized by analogy with the human life cycle. Thus, Third-World nation-states are often represented as being "newly born," "young," "in their infancy," "adolescent," etc., with their attendant implications of "not yet mature," "irresponsible," and so forth (Gupta 1998:40–42). The pervasiveness of these images owes a great deal to their repetition in newspapers. The colonial and postcolonial are represented as occupying another time, a time belonging to the past of the West. The clock under the masthead may tick away steadily – another edition, another day – imposing its own insistent drumbeat of deadlines on journalists, but within the folds of the newspaper, within that methodical, unyielding, empty time of the daily edition are gathered other times as well. To the extent, then, that the imagined community is formed around the breakfast tables of the readers of dailies, nationalism from its moment of conception is composed of different temporalities. Different? Or, would it be more appropriate to say – heterogeneous, split, schizophrenic, ambivalent, tension-ridden, fragmented? (I realize that all these characterizations cannot apply at the same time, but I'd like to argue that a range of such descriptors exists).

Let us leave aside for a moment the complications introduced by the heterogeneous temporalities implicit in the content of newspapers. Focusing now on the context of their production and consumption, is it always the case that the events juxtaposed on a newspaper's pages happen to be there because of calendrical coincidence, that is, because they happened in the same period of time? We know that for events that happen "far away," that is, far from where correspondents are likely to be stationed, it takes days and sometimes months for "news" to reach the reader. Uncommon events in Africa or New Guinea often reach Western readers days, weeks, or sometimes months after they occur, but it is rare indeed, given the structure of global inequalities in the production and dissemination of news reports, for a symmetrical lag in the circulation of major news from the West in Third-World newspapers. Similarly, readers of newspapers who depended on the postal system for delivery also experienced a time lag in reception. (Do we owe newspaper names such as *The Post* or *The Mail* to this phenomenon?) The calendrical coincidence indexed by the daily news thus contains and conceals asynchronous temporalities whose sociological significance may be suppressed by a reading that takes newspapers' self-presentation as today's events too literally (see particularly the excellent essay by Schudson 1986).

Finally, we must consider the status of newspapers as capitalist commodities, as the first mass-produced commodity with built-in obsolescence (Anderson 1991:35). Anderson is quite right to point out that it is this obsolescence of the newspaper that ensures its simultaneous consumption: yesterday's newspaper is worthless as a commodity, although it may acquire some value through the secondary market for recycling. As a commodity, time matters to *The Times* as it matters to few other goods; and it is here that the adage "time is money" is rendered most fully visible in its capitalist garb. However, as capitalist commodities, newspapers are intricately connected with the combined and uneven development of capitalism as a global phenomenon.

My point here is not simply that the temporalities of the novel and the newspaper are much more complex than the simple formula of empty, homogeneous time. If we follow the logic of the argument advanced by Anderson, we arrive at the paradox that the nation has to assert its newness precisely at a time when the historical condition of modernity and the practices of historicism have naturalized empty, homogeneous time as a conceptual grid. If that were all there was to notions of time, it would not be possible to assert new beginnings; any fresh start would have to contend with the fact that it was merely one position on a grid that extended infinitely backward and forward. "Nationalism in the age of Michelet and Renan represented a new form of consciousness – a consciousness that arose when it was no longer possible to experience the nation as new" (Anderson 1991:203). Yet it is precisely new beginnings that nationalism announces. Or it would perhaps be more accurate to say that it is *renewed* beginnings that nationalism emphasizes, not the birth but the *rebirth* of the nation. A historicized understanding of time obligated a different emplotment of nationalist consciousness in Europe, in which the trope of the nation arising from a deep slumber was central (1991:195–196). The nation could awake from its slumber because it was always already there, rather than something that had to be created out of whole cloth. One finds a similar narrative in nationalisms forged in a colonial context. The antiquity of the nation is never in doubt; national liberation is then tied to casting off the yoke of colonialism.

Without positing another mode of temporality, renewal could not be imagined. Furthermore, the imbrications of nationalism in capitalist developments meant that it was infected with the temporality of capitalism, with its fractured and undulating timescape, its cycles of bust and boom, and its rhythms of expansion and consolidation. I will return to this theme in the concluding section of this chapter, after considering the temporal implications of the modularity of nationalism in the next section, and contrasting an understanding of nationalism as a continually renewed process rather than a historical achievement in the following one.

## THE MODULAR NATION

Perhaps no idea about nationalism has proved to be so controversial as that of the modularity of the nation form. Anderson argues that once nations as imagined communities were created in the Americas, they spread rapidly across the Atlantic, and from there to the rest of the world. Models of nationalism became available for copying because "the 'nation' proved an invention on which it was impossible to secure a patent. It became available for pirating by widely different, and sometimes unexpected, hands" (Anderson 1991:67). It is the replicability of the "model" of the independent national state that made it a predominant global institution. Later nations could model themselves on earlier ones, and in fact the later a nation came into being, the wider a range of models it had available for copying. However, once formulated, the models of nationalism also posed constraints, "imposed 'standards' from which too marked deviations were impermissible" (1991:81).

Although Anderson never quite spells out why significant deviations in the model of nationalism were impermissible, and why alternative forms of spatial and political organization did not come into being, and although his discussion of the modular nature of the nation-form is uncannily reminiscent of the cycle by which new products are invented, copied, and standardized in capitalist economies, this remains a powerful and original interpretation of the historical record.

Partha Chatterjee has responded to this formulation: "If nationalisms in the rest of the world have to choose their imagined community from certain 'modular' forms already made available to them by Europe and the Americas, what do they have left to imagine?" (1993:5). Chatterjee questions whether the nation can be seen as a modular form that was simply transported and copied to other places. In such a theory, he complains, "Even our imaginations must remain forever colonized" (1993:5). Chatterjee has brought out the unfortunate political implications of a theory of modularity. However, such a criticism does not depart from the fact that the concept of modularity gets to one of the most striking things about nationalisms in different parts of the world. One would expect them to be different, given the cultural and historical variations among regions; the puzzle is why the national imaginary is so narrowly conceived everywhere, and why nations are so remarkably similar as institutional forms. If the answer is that models of nationalism proved easy to copy, what I wish to ask is what implications this answer has for notions of temporality.

This is a particularly apt question, given that European nationalisms appear to take the form of simulacra. This is one way to think about Anderson's protests that the issue of "derivative discourses" and "imitation" are "bogeys" that are not worth serious consideration (1998:29). Instead, he proposes that nationalism, and politics more generally, have spread in a remarkably uniform way across the world (1998:29).

The spread of such phenomena via modernity and "industrial material civilization" (1998:29) is part of an "unbound series," in which Europe was just one moment, rather than an original that was copied. Andrew Parker emphasizes this aspect of seriality through a Derridean reading of Anderson, in which he argues that "Anderson has rejected in principle the ontologized distinction between origin and derivation on which Chatterjee's criticism depends: for Anderson there can be nothing authentic – West or East – with which to oppose the nation's constitutive secondariness" (1999:43). However suggestive such a reading appears, it is only partially defensible, for the series or the modules do unfold in historical time. In other words, what joins elements in the series together is not a relation of "authentic/copy" but a relation of "before/after": it is not ontological but temporal priority that deserves our attention.

There are at least two broad generalizations that can be made about the temporal assumptions implicit in this theory of modularity of the national form, and they both run counter to the argument that the time of nationalism is a homogeneous, empty time. If one believes that nations that came later pirated or copied earlier models of the nation, then a theory of temporal lag is built in to the time of those nations. Third-World nations, in particular, can never unproblematically occupy the same time as nations in the West. Pick up any speech of the first generation of nationalist leaders in the Third World, and it is immediately clear that this sense of temporal lag fundamentally shapes their view of nationalism. To take an example, let me quote from a letter that Jawaharlal Nehru, India's first Prime Minister, wrote to the leaders of regional state governments in 1954: "We can learn much from the industrially advanced nations of the West. But we have always to bear this fact in mind, that our country is differently situated . . . We are not going to have 100 years in order to make good" (Nehru 1988:72–73). Nehru returns time and again to this idea that India (and he was very much aware that this was a problem faced by all other "underdeveloped" countries as well) had to do in two or three decades what it took the industrial world 100 or 150 years to achieve. What I am suggesting then is that nationalism always has a utopian or messianic time, and that it would be impossible to conceive of nationalist affect, of the love that people might have for the nation, and the hold that the nation might have on them, without this time. In the Third World, the utopian time of the nation is profoundly shaped by a sense of lag and a historical consciousness of lack. Visions of the future are predicated on this sense of belated arrival, of being born into a world of nations competing against each other, but in which the new arrivals are positioned in the starting blocks of a race already underway.

The second broad point I wish to make is that a modular theory of nationalism loses a sense of world-historical time (see Wallerstein 1974:6). By this, I mean that although repetition or reenactment is central to any theory of modularity, not enough attention is given to the changed conditions or contexts that might enable or inhibit the copying of the nation form. For example, the Cold War severely circumscribed the kind of nationalisms that were possible in the Third World, thus removing the possibility of certain types of copying. Another way to make this point about historical context is to ask whether the form in which nations are imagined is fundamentally different for those nations that came into being in the era of competitive capitalism versus those that were born during the heyday of monopoly capitalism or Fordism versus those that have come into existence during our own, neoliberal, late capitalist age. Several authors have noted that nationalism has proved to be an uncomfortable anomaly for Marxist theory, and that Marxists have continued a long tradition started by Marx himself, that the universal struggle between labor and capital would first be conducted on the national stage.

Such a criticism has been made by Anderson (1991:3–4), who does not proffer this as a way to dismiss the importance of capitalism so much as to suggest that nationalism cannot be reduced to, or be deduced from, the nature of capitalism. His theory of nationalism does in fact draw centrally on those kinds of capitalist commodities that are included in the ambit of what he brilliantly terms "print capitalism." However, capitalism's chief role in *Imagined Communities* appears to be in revolutionizing communication technologies and in frustrating natives during colonial rule by keeping them out of corporate boardrooms. Similarly, Partha Chatterjee points out that the nation makes a surreptitious appearance in many places in *Capital*; surreptitious because it is so much assumed as to be completely naturalized. He points out that the whole discussion on money in *Capital* assumes that money takes the form of a national currency, with no explicit reflection on that fact (1993:235). Such criticisms probably reflect on the ubiquity of nationalism in Marx's own life-world.

One way to narrate the articulation of capitalism with nationalism might be to see that technologies of communication and transportation, so necessary for the formation of nationalist consciousness, are constantly revolutionized in the relentless search for higher profits through the reduction of the circulation time of capital. And who understood this better than Marx? Sometime in the middle of the decade of the 1860s, he wrote (in what is now the third volume of *Capital* [1981:164]):

> The main means for cutting circulation time has been improved communications. And the last 50 years have brought a revolution in this respect that is comparable only with the industrial revolution of the second half of the last [the eighteenth] century. On land the Macadamized road has been replaced by the railway, while at sea the slow and irregular sailing ship has been driven into the background by the rapid and regular steamer line; the whole earth has been girded by telegraph cables. It was the Suez Canal that really opened the Far East and Australia to the steamer. The circulation time for a shipment of goods to the Far East, which in 1847 was at least 12 months, has now been more or less reduced to as many weeks. The two major foci of crisis between 1825 and 1857, America and India, have been brought 70 to 90 percent closer to the industrial countries of Europe by this revolution in the means of commerce, and have lost in this way a good deal of their explosive potential. The turnover time of world trade as a whole has been reduced to the same extent, and the efficacy of the capital involved in it has been increased two or three times or more.

If nationalism as a form of imagined community was forged through specific technologies of communication and transportation, how could a massive revolution in those technologies, such as the one described by Marx, have left forms of imagining the nation unaffected? Yet this is precisely the impression conveyed by the notion of modularity; it allows for the speeding up of the mechanisms by which nationalist imaginings are realized, but it cannot account for revolutionary transformations in those modalities, or hence in the character of national sodalities themselves. The broader point that I wish to make here follows from the work of Jameson (1991) and Harvey (1990), arguing that the revolutionary transformations in the nature of capitalism are themselves bound in an uneven and disjunctural fashion to changing perceptions of time. One would therefore expect a corresponding change in the representations of the time of the nation in altered world-historical conditions, and not simply a refashioning and repetition of the structures of temporality of earlier nationalisms.

## NATIONALISM AS EVENT VERSUS NATIONALISM AS PROCESS

Changing conceptions of time resulting from "time-space compression" (Harvey 1990) in late capitalism have implications not only for new nations, but also for existing nationalisms. We have to look beyond the moment when nations are founded – their origins – and cannot just assume that once a nation comes into being, it unproblematically continues to exist. Nations and nationalisms themselves undergo transformations during their existence, and new technologies, changing world situations, and capitalist transformations may fundamentally alter not only the modalities through which nations are imagined and come into being, but also the content of nationalisms and what it means to be a nation.

A Gramscian perspective that treats nationalism not as an achievement but as a fragile, always contested hegemony that was formed within a larger context of global geopolitical, capitalist, and ideological changes would give us a very different picture of the time of the nation than one that focuses on origins alone. Nationalism as an ideology, and the nation as an imagined community, requires constant work of renewal and reaffirmation, and it is this conflict-ridden process that alters the course of nations and nationalisms in unintended directions. Perhaps no one has given us as good an analysis of the transformations in different moments of nationalism as Partha Chatterjee in *Nationalist Thought and the Colonial World* (1986). Chatterjee traces the temporal trajectory of Indian nationalism through three phases, which he terms the moment of departure, the moment of maneuver, and the moment of arrival. The moment of "arrival" is heralded by the consolidation of the passive revolution initiated by Indian nationalism in the form of the postcolonial Indian nation-state. This text is exemplary in that it takes the story of nationalism well beyond the first appearance of the nation on the historical horizon, and shows that the nation was consolidated as the result of intense ideological and material struggles, in which a hegemonic bloc was eventually able to affirm a notion of national community that safeguarded its interests.

By contrast, *Imagined Communities* is preoccupied with the origins (and to a lesser extent, transmission) of nationalism. In the successive movements of nationalism from Creole Pioneers in the Americas to vernacular nationalisms in Europe, followed by official nationalisms in the British empire, and the "last wave" in the Third World, the emphasis is on how nationalism originated in different places in the world. What one gets from this is a sense of nationalism as an achievement and a phenomenon, rather than as an ongoing process. This framework has important consequences for our understanding of the time of the nation. As far as the Third World is concerned, the story of the nation as a traveling, modular form is one that reinstates the temporal lag of the great narratives of modernity centered on Europe and America.

Understanding nationalism as a process, however, allows us to turn this story around: thus, we could narrate the tale of how the official nationalism of imperial powers fundamentally reshaped nationalism in Europe and the Americas; and how Third-World nationalisms that constituted the last wave infused democratic and dissident currents in the nationalisms hegemonic in the First World. The crisis in US nationalism created by the movements against imperialism, racism, sexism, and homophobia that are now indexed by the term "the sixties" would be unthinkable without Third-World national liberation struggles: how could one write the story of the movement led by Martin Luther King without Gandhi or the independence of new nation-states in Africa, or of the anti-war movement without Vietnam and Ho Chi Minh?

If we follow one of many creative ideas in *Imagined Communities* and think about the "biography" of a nation, we could arrive at some understanding of the nation as process. Just as a person changes during the course of her lifetime, so too is a nation changed as a result of growth, different historical situations that are not of its own making, accidents, crises, and its ties to other nations, in fact, to a "family of nations." Anderson points out, however, that a nation's biography differs from that of a person in that the beginnings recede exponentially to a past without an origin, and, unlike a person, the life of a nation has no definite end. In this secular, serial time, an identity has to be forged through the selective remembering of "exemplary suicides, poignant martyrdoms, assassinations, executions, wars, and holocausts" (1991:206). Echoing Benjamin, Anderson points out that nationalist historiography does not recognize the past as it really was, but seizes hold of discrete memories. Benjamin, however, was concerned to rescue the memory that flashes up in a moment of danger, the danger being that tradition and its receivers will become the tool of the ruling classes (1968:255). By contrast, nationalist history aims to make the national tradition a tool of the ruling classes.

If these examples demonstrate anything, it is that representations of time in nationalist ideologies produce a much more complex and fractured temporality than the terms "homogeneous," "empty," "serial," or "secular" would lead us to believe, although it is these temporal features that Anderson emphasizes. He demonstrates that the time of nationalism is one that shamelessly embezzles exemplary moments from the past to produce particular kinds of identities, a Rip Van Winkle time that fitfully awakens after a long period of slumber, rather than the smooth surface of a homogeneous progression over empty time-space. It does not require a leap of faith to propose that other temporalities would be even more visible were we to explicitly consider the dislocations and disjunctions between representations of the time of the nation and the modalities by which national imaginaries are realized. To the extent that nationalism is successful as an ideology, the experience of time for those whom it interpellates is always marked by a heightened intensity, that is, it imbues its subjects with a crisis-like sense of urgency and purpose. This brings me back to nationalism's utopian promise, that which enables vast numbers to make incredible sacrifices for the "future of the nation," which makes it possible to envision "leap-frogging" stages of development, which enables images of "catching up" and being "modern" to be widely shared, and which holds open for Third-World peoples the possibility (or perhaps, more appropriately, the perfumed nightmare) of synchronicity in the temporal rhythms of the world of nation-states.

## Conclusion: Just in (Nationalist) Time or Just in Time Nationalism?

> When philosophy paints its gray on gray, then has a form of life grown old, and with gray on gray it cannot be rejuvenated, but only known; the Owl of Minerva first takes flight with twilight closing in.
>
> (Hegel 1967 [1821]:137)

It has been suggested that, like the owl of Minerva, the study of nationalism takes flight precisely when nationalism as a phenomenon "cannot be rejuvenated, but only known" (Hegel), that is, with twilight closing in on the Age of Nationalism. Proponents of this view often connect the impending demise of nationalism to the coming era of globalization, sometimes glossed as an age of *transnationalism*. Like Mark Twain, nations might justifiably complain that reports of their death are greatly exaggerated. And they would be right, for it is only in a zero-sum world that transnationalism and nationalism can be seen as irredeemably opposed.

Although it is indisputable that globalization is changing the character of nation-states and nationalism, to reduce its effects to an arithmetic of "more globalization-less nationalism" would be to seriously miss its impact. On the one hand, if one thinks of how sovereignty is being compromised by the huge spurt of foreign direct investment, the volatility of capital markets, the growth of global environmental and trade treaties, and the rapid movement of images and ideas, it would appear that national sovereignty is in serious trouble. On the other hand, if one thinks of the ascendance of xenophobia and immigrant-bashing in the West, the rise of deterritorialized nationalisms amongst diasporic populations in different parts of the world, and the quickly multiplying examples of ethnic cleansing, it is also clear that virulent nationalisms are flourishing precisely at this historical moment. To reduce such complex effects and interactions to an arithmetic of more and less, positive and negative, is to assume that globalization and nationalism can be compared and measured on one scale, instead of positing a relation of articulation and disjuncture between them. In my opinion, this has led to a fruitless debate, with each side claiming that they see more evidence of nation-states in decline and a resurgent role for the nation-state respectively.

It turns out that much of the discussion about the implications of globalization for nationalism turns on questions of sovereignty. It is interesting to note how many of the principal phenomena that make sovereignty problematical hinge around the *speed* of global transfers or transactions. If one considers the arguments about what it is that is making it more difficult for nation-states to assert their sovereignty, it is often the speed, or speeding up, of transfers and flows, whether such transactions are finances or images. Why does speed pose problems for national sovereignty?

One way to think about this question is to argue that national sovereignty is constituted not so much by prohibition as it is by regulation (although regulation always has the threat of prohibition built into it). For example, the sovereign space of the nation is regulated by who and what can come into the national space by land, sea, and air: thus the presence of armies, border checkpoints, customs agents, and immigration officials. Sovereignty has a temporal dimension as well, and this involves the regulation of the speed with which these things can enter the national space. The temporal dimension of sovereignty matters because it enables the nation-state to invest the process of spatial crossing with a *durée*, a dimensionality in time that marks it as a regulated domain. The speed of transactions then poses a threat to national sovereignty by erasing that time lag, thereby undermining the regulative operations that mark the exercise of sovereignty. Transactions conducted in "real time," that is, without a time lag, are those that raise these questions of sovereignty most acutely.

The synchronicity introduced by "real-time" procedures in particular, and the time-space compression insinuated by late capitalism more generally, give a distinctive twist to the allochronism of Third-World nationalism. Can Third-World nations continue to be seen as "behind" the West, located in "the past" of the West, when they are participating in just-in-time production in "offshore" factories and export-promotion zones, and "real-time" information flows? Is Third-World nationalism characterized by a schizophrenic temporality?

The key mechanisms that Anderson identifies in his theory of nationalism – print capitalism, bureaucratic and educational pilgrimages, the stabilization of vernacular languages, the operation of state machineries, modularity – are themselves mostly coterminous with the nation's borders, producing what is perhaps a nationalist theory of nationalism. Like the psychic connections between midnight's children (Rushdie 1980), these mechanisms that Anderson identifies as central to the imagining of the nation fail to transmit in real time across the nation's borders. How would the time of the nation be different if one built a theory of nationalism not around these ideas but around immigration, transnational commerce and trade, geopolitics, the global flow of ideas and images, and the worldwide movement of biogenetic resources?

Thinking through these puzzles requires us to return once again to the relation between territory and time. In the critique of allochronism, time and space are bound together by the nation-state, so that Third-World nation-states are seen as "behind" those in the West. The time-space of capitalism is one that cuts unevenly across the space-time of the world of nation-states. Late capitalism connects not just nations but nodes of production and consumption, spaces that do not fill up the map of the nation and times that do not necessarily resonate with the cadences of the nation. The timescape of nationalism in late capitalism is one marked by jagged edges and sheer vertiginous drops rather than the regular drumbeat of homogeneous, empty time. It is to these disjunctures and fissures between the temporality of late capitalism and that of the nation-state that we must attend if we are to reconceptualize the nation-state and nationalism in the present.

## REFERENCES

Anderson, Benedict (1991) *Imagined Communities: Reflections on the Origin and Spread of Nationalism.* 2nd edn. New York: Verso. [First published in 1983.]

Anderson, Benedict (1998) *The Spectre of Comparisons: Nationalism, Southeast Asia and the World.* New York: Verso.

Benjamin, Walter (1968) *Illuminations: Essays and Reflections*, trans. Harry Zohn. New York: Schocken Books.

Chakrabarty, Dipesh (1997) The Time of History and the Times of Gods. In *The Politics of Culture in the Shadow of Capital*, ed. Lisa Lowe and David Lloyd, pp. 35–60. Durham, NC: Duke University Press.

Chatterjee, Partha (1986) *Nationalist Thought and the Colonial World: A Derivative Discourse?* London: Zed Books.

Chatterjee, Partha (1993) *The Nation and Its Fragments: Colonial and Postcolonial Histories.* Princeton, NJ: Princeton University Press.

Chatterjee, Partha (1999) Anderson's Utopia. *Diacritics* 29:128–134.

Gellner, Ernest (1983) *Nations and Nationalism.* Ithaca, NY: Cornell University Press.

Gupta, Akhil (1998) *Postcolonial Developments: Agriculture in the Making of Modern India.* Durham, NC: Duke University Press.

Harvey, David (1990) *The Condition of Postmodernity: An Enquiry Into the Origins of Cultural Change.* Oxford: Blackwell.

Hegel, G. W. F. (1967 [1821]) *Philosophy of Right*, trans. T. M. Knox. London: Oxford University Press.

Hobsbawm, Eric J. (1990) *Nations and Nationalism Since 1780: Programme, Myth, Reality.* 2nd edn. New York: Cambridge University Press.

Jameson, Frederic (1991) *Postmodernism, or, the Cultural Logic of Late Capitalism.* Durham, NC: Duke University Press.

Kaviraj, Sudipta (1997) Religion and Identity in India. *Ethnic and Racial Studies* 20:325–344.

Kelly, John D., and Martha Kaplan (2001) *Represented Communities: Fiji and World Decolonization.* Chicago: University of Chicago Press.

Lomnitz, Claudio (2001) Nationalism as a Practical System: Benedict Anderson's Theory of Nationalism from the Vantage Point of Spanish America. In Claudio Lomnitz, *Deep Mexico, Silent Mexico: An Anthropology of Nationalism.* pp. 3–34. Minneapolis: University of Minnesota Press.

Marx, Karl (1963 [1852]) *The Eighteenth Brumaire of Louis Bonaparte.* New York: International Publishers.

Marx, Karl (1981 [1894]) *Capital, Volume Three*, trans. David Fernbach. New York: Vintage Books.

Mongia, Radhika (2002) Always Nationalize; or, Some Methodological Considerations on Analyses of the Nation and the State. Paper presented at Feminist Interventions: Rethinking South Asia, University of California, Santa Cruz, May 3.

Nehru, Jawaharlal (1988) *Letters to Chief Ministers, 1947–1964. Volume 4. Letters to Chief Ministers, 1954–1957*, ed. G. Parthasarthi. New Delhi: Teen Murti House.

Parker, Andrew (1999) Bogeyman: Benedict Anderson's "Derivative" Discourse. *Diacritics* 29:128–134.

Rushdie, Salman (1980) *Midnight's Children.* New York: Knopf.

Schudson, Michael (1986) Deadlines, Datelines, and History. In *Reading the News*, ed. Robert Karl Manoff and Michael Schudson, pp. 79–108. New York: Pantheon Books.

Wallerstein, Immanuel (1974) *The Modern World-System I: Capitalist Agriculture and the Origins of the European World-Economy in the Sixteenth Century.* New York: Academic Press.

# CHAPTER 18 Infrapolitics

*Steven Gregory*

Paco's Café sits at the bustling intersection of Calle El Conde and Palo Hicado, a broad avenue that forms part of the traffic-choked ring road surrounding Parque Independencia at the edge of the Colonial Zone in Santo Domingo, Dominican Republic. A favorite meeting place for expatriates and seasoned tourists, Paco's largely European and North American patrons pass hours talking among themselves and watching the throngs of people that circulate through El Conde, a modern-style pedestrian promenade lined with fast-food restaurants, clothing stores, and street vendors.

From my table, I could see the military honor guard posted at the Puerta El Conde (Gate of the Count), an imposing redbrick arch and belfry that is the main entrance to the tree-shaded park. It was there that, in 1844, Dominican patriot Ramon Mella raised the new flag of the republic, marking the beginning of the war for independence against Haitian rule. Two young soldiers, dressed in nineteenth-century-style white tunics and baggy blue trousers, stood at rigid attention, rifles shouldered, and indifferent to the traffic mêlée before them. It was late in the afternoon and the pedestrian traffic along El Conde was emptying into Palo Hicado and the park beyond. Shoppers, *colegio* students, and working people, free for the day, fearlessly dodged the traffic maze as they made their connections to public minivans and *guaguas*, or buses, for the journey home.

I was killing time. I had an appointment later in the evening and it was still too hot to do anything productive. A tall, lean Dominican man approached my table and greeted me in Spanish. He was a government-licensed tour guide and was wearing a New York Yankees baseball cap and a plastic ID card clipped to the pocket of his neatly pressed plaid shirt. Earlier, I had watched him trying to interest tourists in a tour of the Colonial City.

*"Ahí,"* I replied, trying to sound Dominican and indifferent. He paused and I could see that he was trying to figure out what I was.

"You're from Puerto Rico?" he continued in Spanish. *"Boriqua!"* He shook my hand with enthusiasm. (A San Juan-based cruise ship had earlier docked in the port and many of the tourists now exploring El Conde were Puerto Rican.) I explained to him that I was North American and that I was working in the Dominican Republic. He frowned.

"But you look Hispanic," he continued in English. I explained that my father was African American and, after puzzling over that for a few moments, he sat down at my table and introduced himself as Alberto.

Alberto, it turned out, had lived in Washington for five years and he spoke English with a southern, African-American accent. "Ain't that some shit," he remarked, twisting his mouth in irony after he described to me how he had been deported by the INS while looking for work in Tacoma. Once back in the Dominican Republic, he told me, a motorcycle accident had left his right leg mangled. No longer fit for manual labor but fluent in English, he had found work as a tour guide.

Two shoeshine boys approached our table, wooden boxes tucked under their tiny arms. "*Limpia!*" cried the older one, beaming and placing his shoeshine box at my feet. "*Boriqua!*" shouted the other, gleefully mistaking me for a Puerto Rican.

Alberto made eye contact with the older boy and shook his head in disapproval. The boy hesitated, frowned, and then began to unpack an odd assortment of plastic bottles filled with white and caramel-colored liquids. "*Limpia!*" chimed the other.

"*Niño, el señor no quiere,*" Alberto said firmly. His face relaxed into a smile. The children pouted but stood their ground. Alberto looked to me with an expression of pride and amusement, and then gave each boy a worn, bronze *peso*.

"You see, I'm not hard on them," he said, watching the children race down El Conde. "Their parents need the money. But they must have respect."

Alberto was still trying to place me, to figure out how I fit into the social landscape of the global economy. He asked me if I worked in the *Zona Franca*, at one of the export-processing factories. I told him that I was a college professor and that I was doing a study on the impact of tourism in the Dominican Republic.

He thought for a moment and then lit a cigarette. Tourism was not helping the country, he said, because the Dominican government's policies prevented poor people from benefiting from the tourist industry. "The rich people in this country want to keep it all for themselves," he continued, clasping his hands and squeezing tightly. "They don't care about the people." He pointed his cigarette at the crowd waiting for *guaguas* along Avenida Hicado.

"Today I have no work. You see me, I am here all day hanging out, not doin' shit." The thought angered him and his gestures and facial expressions seemed to me more black and more American. Alberto explained that he charged only 750 pesos (50 US dollars) to take a group of tourists on an all-day tour of the colonial city. But with the rise of the all-inclusive resort hotels, these excursions were now arranged directly by the resorts with foreign-owned tour operators who charged as much as 50 dollars a head. "It's crazy man! They want it all for themselves and the people have nothing to live."

A bald and sunburned man, looking somewhat disoriented, sat at a nearby table and ordered a beer. Alberto caught his eye and smiled. "*Deutschlander?*"

"No" replied the man in English. "I am from Norway." The Norwegian pulled a guidebook from his backpack and set himself to work.

Alberto lost interest and returned to our conversation. "The government we have now, they make projects and spend money, but it's not for the people. It's for the rich

– *only* for the rich." He gazed at the large banner ads for Burger King and Nokia that were suspended between the kiosks along El Conde. "You see this shit? This is all just paper." He pointed to the four-foot-wide Whopper with Cheese. "It does nothing for the country. It's only a mirror. And the devil is on the other side."

Alberto's metaphor stunned me. After all, how better to put into language the seductive lure of the commodity than as a Narcissus-like engagement with a mirror? And how better to represent the ravenous will to profit of global capital than as a devil behind the mirror, placed as if to ensure that the relationship between the subject and object of consumption would be both immediate and mute – a surface not of reflection, as Jean Baudrillard put it, but of absorption (1990:67). This essay proceeds from Alberto's sharp metaphor to examine how political and economic forces associated with "globalization" and neoliberal economic reforms are affecting and, indeed, restructuring the lives and livelihoods of people in one region of the Dominican Republic.

## GLOBALIZATION, THE STATE, AND ECONOMIC RESTRUCTURING

Globalization has been the subject of much discussion and debate in recent decades, and there is considerable disagreement among theorists as to its defining characteristics, its impact on the contemporary world, as well as its "newness" within the development of the modern world system. Ironically, perhaps, many of these discussions have been far *too* global, pronouncing widespread and, in some cases, epochal transformations in systems of national and transnational political governance (Castells 1997), the structuring of identities and social movements (Appadurai 1996), and in the logic of capital accumulation (Harvey 1989). Rarely, however, have these arguments been submitted to the critical scrutiny of context.

Developments associated with globalization – technological innovation, the internationalization of production and finance, migration, global media, and so on – are often treated as a package of traits that are everywhere inciting a similar logic and process of transformation, hence the very concept of globalization. This tendency has led many researchers to neglect important differences in the ways in which global processes are brought to bear, for example, in developed as opposed to non-developed nations, and to discount differences in how these global flows are materialized within the specific historical and political contexts of nation-states. In some cases, the "systemic" nature of the new world order is asserted in order to discount the analytic significance of these differences in favor of global generalities. For example, Arjun Appadurai, referring to the contemporary "crisis" of nation-states, writes: "Nation-states, for all their important differences (and only a fool would conflate Sri Lanka with Great Britain), make sense only as parts of a system. This system (even when seen as a system of differences) appears poorly equipped to deal with the interlinked diasporas of people and images that mark the here and now" (1996:19; cf. Castells 1997:243–244).

To be sure, scholars have recognized, at least in the abstract, key differences in the ways in which global processes are mediated by less than global contexts, but far more attention has been directed to defining what globalization *is* – thus asserting its newness – than to examining what it *does* in any given context. Few researchers, for example, have examined how the disparate processes tied to globalization have been politically secured and responded to within ethnographic contexts configured by the histories, cultures, and politics of particular nation-states. More to the point, few scholars have examined the political debates and struggles that have accompanied the spatialization of global flows of capital, information, and people within concrete historical and political settings.

A central debate in the rapidly growing literature on globalization concerns the latter's impact on the system of nation-states, the so-called "Westphalian system." Some writers have stressed the diminished capacity of contemporary nation-states to govern their economies and exercise territorial sovereignty due to the internationalization of finance, production, and trade, and as a result of nation-states' participation in regional and international trade organizations and agreements, such as the World Trade Organization and the North American Free Trade Agreement. These developments are said to have resulted in the emergence of institutions of transnational governance, such as the European Union.

Other scholars have stressed the decreased ability of territorially defined nation-states to shape and muster the social identities, interests, and loyalties of their subjects, particularly through appeals to national belonging and citizenship. Manuel Castells (1997), for example, has argued that the globalization of finance and production has undermined the political and economic foundation of the welfare state, since technological advances now enable corporations to shop around the world for labor sources with the lowest and most competitive labor costs related to social benefits. This weakening of welfare statism, he argued, has eroded a key source of legitimacy for nation-states vis-à-vis their subjects – namely, the provision of social benefits – and has undermined an important apparatus of social regulation and control.

In contrast to approaches that, to varying degrees, emphasize the diminished capacity of nation-states to govern their economies and the allegiance of their subjects, there are those that suggest that the novelty of present-day globalization has been exaggerated. Authors writing from this alternative perspective point out that nation-states – or, at least, some of them – now, as in the past, have been active participants in global capitalist development rather than passive spectators. Paul Hirst and Grahame Thompson, taking issue with "extreme globalizers," argue that the contemporary global economy is not unprecedented, but represents one of a number of highly integrated "states" in which the international economy has existed since the expansion of modern industrial technology in the 1860s. Moreover, they point out that the contemporary world economy is far from being truly global. "Rather," they note, "trade, investment, and financial flows are concentrated in the Triad of Europe, Japan, and North America and this dominance seems set to continue" (1999:2).

More recently, Justin Rosenberg (2000) has argued that the model of national sovereignty that emerged from the Peace of Westphalia in 1648 (taken by some to be the ur-moment when territorial sovereignty emerged as the organizing principal for European states) has existed more in principle than in practice. For example, Rosenberg points out that much of the power and influence exercised by British imperialism – as well as US expansionism – was through informal and non-territorial practices of empire which, as he put it, "did not show up on any map" (2000:31). Conversely, as Masao Miyoshi has pointed out, for many if not most postcolonial states, the ideal of territorial sovereignty has been less a real possibility than "a utopian dream often turned into a bloody nightmare" (1996:81). Consequently, to view the current world-system as a radical departure from the Westphalian ideal of territorial sovereignty requires the disregard of the messy political economies of imperialism, past and present, and the elision of sizable disparities in sovereign power among contemporary nation-states.

In fact, arguments for the pervasive "newness" of globalization have often idealized the sovereign prerogatives enjoyed by pre-globalized nation-states in order to make the complexities of the contemporary world-system appear to be a radical rupture with the past. Manuel Castells, for example, while conceding that nation-states have not yet faded away, goes on to add:

> However, in the 1990s, nation-states have been transformed from *sovereign subjects* into strategic actors, playing their interests, and the interests they are supposed to represent, in a global system of interaction, in a condition of systemically shared sovereignty. They marshal considerable influence, *but they barely hold power by themselves, in isolation from supranational macro-forces and subnational micro-processes.* (1997:307, emphasis added)

Clearly, few if any nation-states have ever existed as "sovereign subjects," isolated from forces at work both within and beyond their borders. But as Rosenberg points out (2000:40), this reification of the Westphalian model as a "system" of territorially based sovereignty, serves not only to obscure the specific contexts within which transnational processes operate, but also to exaggerate the territorial boundedness of state power.

In this chapter, I emphasize the importance of situating the analysis of the disparate changes associated with globalization within an ethnographic context – an approach that underscores their *embeddedness* "in differently configured regimes of power" (Ong 1999:4). To stress the ethnographic context here is not to appeal to the "local" as a privileged site of epistemological clarity that is opposed to a "global" register of social experience or theory. Clearly, the global only exists insofar as it is instantiated within particular, though spatially dispersed, locations such as the Dominican Republic. Instead, I argue that an ethnographic perspective is key to understanding the contested *politics* of globalization; that is, the concrete power relations, strategies, and practices through which processes of globalization are politically enabled, inflected, and, to be sure, contested.

In contrast to some treatments of the topic, I underscore the significance of the state, not as a "sovereign subject" or a monolithic agent, but rather as a complex "political field," as Nicos Poulantzas (1978) put it, upon which the conditions of possibility for globalization are secured through the structuring and disciplining of labor markets and, more broadly, through the constitution and governance of subjects. This approach stretches beyond narrow, economic treatments of capitalist production – focused on the circulation of capital, commodities, and people – to examine the production of subjects and social relations. This approach refocuses attention on the social, cultural, and political constitution of the wage-labor relation toward understanding, as Karl Marx put it, "not only how capital *produces*, but how capital itself is *produced*." From this perspective, globalization is not reduced to disembodied and deterritorialized "flows" of capital, commodities, and information that exist external to, or in spite of, the nation-state, but rather as a more complex process – indeed, a *mode* of production – through which capital continually constitutes, negotiates, and enforces its relationship to "free labor" on the historically shaped political field of the nation-state. Attending to the nation-state and its relationship to "the total cycle of the expanded reproduction of capital" is also key to conceptualizing the variability and unevenness with which global processes are restructuring societies within what remains a hierarchy of nation-states (Poulantzas 1978:51).

Second, I explore how people whose lives and livelihoods are being shaped by global economic processes interpret, negotiate, and contest these developments through organized protests as well as through what James Scott (1990:183) has termed "infrapolitics," practices of resistance and critical consciousness that seldom receive the notice of broad publics, academic or otherwise. I shall demonstrate how, in response to these global economic developments, the Dominican working poor are exercising subjectivities, sensibilities, and modalities of agency that elude, disrupt, and sometimes challenge the structures and disciplinary logics of the evolving global division of labor.

Specifically, I direct attention to discourses and practices relating to citizenship (broadly conceived as an unstable and contextually constructed set of relations to the nation-state) as a power-laden political field upon which global economic processes are mediated, secured, and contested. On the one hand, I underscore the state's role in the everyday governance of labor and, more generally, of populations through the disciplinary logic and apparatus of citizenship; that is, the institutional and discursive practices through which citizenship, as an identity tied to rights, obligations, and social goods, is constructed. I contend that this capacity of the nation-state, often elided or discounted in accounts of the demise of state sovereignty and national citizenship, is critical to the structuring and regulation of labor markets under conditions of globalization. Put simply, global capital needs the political apparatus of the nation-state and its ideologies of "belonging" to reproduce itself. On the other hand, I examine how people with weak and compromised claims to citizenship evade, resist, and challenge these structures of labor discipline, in part through informal economic activities that elude regulation by the state.

I begin by discussing my research location, Boca Chica, a municipality in the National District of Santo Domingo and located on the southeastern coast of the country. I examine how state-sponsored, neoliberal economic reforms, and other developments associated with globalization, have restructured the social, political, and economic landscape upon which people pursue their livelihoods. I stress the importance analytically of disentangling the disparate changes that have been associated with globalization – the expansion of tourism, "information age" technologies and media, and export-processing zones, for example – in order to both consider and highlight their specific, variable, and far from congruent consequences for the social division of labor and on the survival strategies practiced by Dominican and Haitian workers.

Next, I examine the ways in which people actively interpret, negotiate, and contest these developments through informal economic activities, organized protests, and everyday practices of resistance that illuminate the "microphysics of power" that are implicated in the structuring of the global political economy (Foucault 1979). I argue that an analysis of these quotidian practices of governmentality and resistance provide key insights into emerging forms of critical consciousness, identity, and agency that are incited by global political and economic changes. To this end, I examine a political debate and struggle in Boca Chica over the construction of a large port facility and free trade zone – a struggle that illuminates the politics underpinning globalization and, more to the point, how global flows of capital are configured upon the political field of the state.

## CITIZENSHIP AND LABOR

Boca Chica is a municipality of the National District of Santo Domingo and embraces three nearby areas of settlement: La Caleta, Andrés, and Boca Chica proper. Located about 30 kilometers from the capital city, the municipality has an estimated population of about 135,000. My ethnographic work centered on the adjoining towns of Andrés and Boca Chica, two communities that have been radically transformed in recent decades by an array of state-sponsored, neoliberal economic reforms promoted by the International Monetary Fund (IMF), the World Bank, and other international agencies.

A community of fishermen at the turn of the twentieth century, Andrés developed as a sugar town, or *batey*, after a US corporation built the Boca Chica sugar mill, or *ingenio*, there in 1916 at the outset of the United States military occupation of the Dominican Republic. During the course of the century, the availability of work at the *ingenio* and in the nearby cane fields attracted a diverse labor force, including Haitian cane-cutters and *cocolos*, migrant workers from the West Indies. Boca Chica, located about two kilometers from Andrés, developed during the early decades of the century as a beach resort, frequented by well-to-do *capitaleños* from Santo Domingo, some of whom built vacation homes along its shore. In 1952, the regime of Rafael Trujillo constructed the Hotel Hamaca, the first of Boca Chica's luxury hotels, as part of an unsuccessful campaign to stimulate tourism and take advantage of the collapse of the Cuban tourism industry after the 1959 revolution.

In the 1970s, spurred by the aggressive promotion of tourism as an economic panacea by the World Bank, the World Trade Organization, and the United Nations, the Dominican government created INFRATUR, a state agency charged with developing infrastructure for the tourist industry, in part through offering tax abatements and other incentives to foreign investors. Boca Chica, designated as a *Polo Turistico*, or tourist pole, by the Secretary of Tourism in 1973, grew rapidly during the 1980s and '90s, witnessed by the expansion of Hotel Hamaca, the construction of two new resort hotels, and the establishment of dozens of small and mid-sized hotels, restaurants, gift shops, and other businesses catering to the arrival of growing numbers of foreign tourists.

The expansion of international tourism in Boca Chica drew migrants from other areas of the country – notably from Santo Domingo and San Pedro Macorís – as well as from Haiti, who, in search of work, settled in Andrés, La Caleta, and expanding squatter settlements north of Boca Chica's tourist zone and town center. The expanding tourist economy, however, provided relatively few jobs for the local population. In 1996, the *Asociación para el desarrollo de Boca Chica* [Boca Chica

Development Association] estimated that hotels and restaurants in Boca Chica employed only 1,662 local residents out of an estimated population of 42,869. With the exception of low-paying work in hotel services – such as housekeeping, security, and laundries – few residents of Andrés-Boca Chica held the educational and other credentials needed to work in the hotels.

An additional source of employment for some residents of the municipality was the export-processing factories located in free trade zones (FTZs) or *Zona Francas*, on the outskirts of the capital and in the nearby city of San Pedro de Macorís. These labor-intensive factory jobs, notorious for their low wages, severe working condi- tions, and forced overtime, were difficult for most to secure and, generally speaking, were frowned upon by residents as being highly exploitative. Most of these jobs did not provide a living wage, and a great many drew on the labor power of poor and working-class women – a group extensively exploited by globalization processes (Safa 1995).

Many more residents eked out a living in the informal economy – that is, in economic activities that are outside of formal, wage-labor relations and are unregu- lated by the state – providing goods and services to both tourists and Dominican visitors to the area. A number of residents worked as beach vendors, selling goods ranging from clothing, crafts, and cigars, to shellfish, fruit, and other foods. Many women from Andrés and its environs worked on the beaches as masseuses, manicur- ists or pedicurists, and hair braiders, catering largely though not exclusively to foreign tourists. Many young men worked as *motoconchos*, or motorcycle taxi operators, that provide inexpensive transportation to residents and tourists. Most men with whom I spoke viewed working as a *motoconcho* as an alternative, albeit a dangerous one, to strenuous, sporadic, and low-paying work as day laborers in the construction indus- try, one of the few sources of employment available to local men.

Although state authorities issued a limited number of licenses for some of these economic activities – beach vendors and manicurists, for example – few workers could afford the stiff licensing fees charged by the authorities to work legally in the tourist zone. Consequently, most who earned livings on the margins of the tourist industry did so illicitly and were subject to arbitrary arrest and stiff fines by the National Police and POLITUR, special tourism police who operate under the aegis of the Secretary of Tourism. For example, though there had been several attempts to regulate the *motoconchos*, by assigning them special ID cards and distinctive vests issued by the police, these efforts were resisted by the *motoconchos* – fearing licensing fees and the placing of restrictions on their areas of operation – and laxly enforced by local authorities. Consequently, *motoconchos*, who number in the hundreds in Andrés-Boca Chica, were routinely stopped by police, sometimes in area-wide sweeps, and fined for lacking proper licenses and documents, resulting sometimes in the seizure of their rented motorcycles.

Another area of informal economic activity in Andrés-Boca Chica was sex work, directed at the largely European and North American tourists who visit the area. During the 1990s, Boca Chica became a notorious destination for male "sex tour- ists," due in part to the proliferation of internet-based sites dedicated to "single male travel." Many of the small and mid-sized hotels, restaurants, currency exchanges, bars, and discotheques owed their livelihood to this sex-oriented and predominantly male tourism. The prospect of making money *"trabajando con turistas"* attracted many young women and men from the capital and elsewhere, as well as from Haiti, to work in Boca Chica's bars and discothèques as hostesses, bartenders, and/or sex workers. Many women who worked with tourists were single mothers, who regarded sex work as the only option available to them to support their families. Prostitution was tolerated by the authorities, but people who pursued it, like others in the informal economy, were routinely arrested and fined by the police, often for lacking proper identification.

Many people were forced to pursue informal economic activities because they lacked birth certificates, without which they could not obtain a state-issued ID card when they reached the age of 18. These ID cards, or *cédulas*, are needed to vote, secure employment in the formal sector, open a bank account, and obtain licenses and other identity papers. According to some estimates, at least 12 percent of the adult population of Andrés (excluding Haitian migrants) lacked birth certificates and other identity papers, and from the perspective of the state did not exist.

In the case of Dominicans of Haitian descent the situation was far worse, since Dominican authorities generally did not issue birth certificates to children born of Haitian parents. As a result, many Dominicans of Haitian descent living in Andrés-Boca Chica were barred from the public school system, the formal job sector, and also from voting. In Andrés-Boca Chica and elsewhere in the Dominican Republic, Haitians are an important source of cheap labor for the sugar and construction industries, in particular. However, in Boca Chica, many Haitians found work in tourist-related businesses because many were bi- or tri-lingual (French, Spanish, and English), and thus could communicate with foreign tourists.

The citizenship status of many people in Andrés-Boca Chica has also been compromised as a result of their interactions with the police and the criminal justice system. Most employers, particularly in the tourism industries and FTZs, require job applicants to present a Good Conduct Certificate along with a state ID card. Issued for a fee by the National Police, the Good Conduct Certificate certifies that the applicant does not have a criminal record. This document is also required when applying for licenses (for example, to work as tour guides or vendors) and by foreign embassies and consulates when applying for visas. Those who have been arrested by the police – not infrequently for lacking identity papers or for working in the informal economy – have great difficulty in obtaining this important document.

Citizenship – here understood as "a continuing series of transactions between persons and agents of a given state in which each has enforceable rights and obligations" – constitutes a critical and contested field of power relations and practices across which struggles are conducted between representatives of state power and the heterogeneous populations under its control over access to employment, political participation, and other rights and social goods (Tilly 1995:8). This ongoing series of transactions, implicated in the making, disciplining, and unraveling of citizens, can be viewed as a nodal cluster of the practices of governmentality. To paraphrase Foucault, these practices are directed at "conducting the conduct" of the people, enabling and disabling their movements through space, labor markets, and other social benefits, and constituting them as subjects marked by class, racial, and other distinctions, who enjoy asymmetrical access to the nation, its political economy, and the space of the licit.

Indeed, it is through these contested practices of citizenship – and their enabling discourses, regulations, and documents – that differences tied to race, class, gender, and national origin are embodied and articulated into a complex system of exclusions that is the social foundation of the division of labor. Social status may be understood as a defining characteristic of citizenship. Far from being merely given as a legal identity, however, social status is situationally forged through everyday, power-laden interactions that transpose socially constructed distinctions – such as race, class, ethnicity, and gender – into formal exclusions from social rights and goods. In this way, the state plays a critical, though not a monolithic, role in articulating and regulating these systems of exclusions through practices of citizenship, making these latter available, so to speak, to capital as a hierarchically structured division of labor.

In Andrés-Boca Chica, this politics of citizenship is centered squarely on the tourist economy, where these identity-based exclusions served to insulate the profits, most notably of the all-inclusive resort hotels. Since these profits depend, in large part, on tourists spending their money within the resort complexes, the hotel industry in Boca Chica has exerted considerable pressure on public authorities to police informal economic activities that compete with goods and services provided by the hotels. Acting through the Asociación Pro-Desarrollo Turistico de Boca Chica [Tourism Development Association of Boca Chica], a group dominated by representatives of the area's three major resorts, the industry has pressured police to crack down on unlicensed vendors, manicurists, *motoconchos*, as well as sex workers who provide relatively cheap, informal goods and services to tourists. These campaigns to *limpiar la calle*, or clean up the streets, typically construct informal economic activities as "criminal," as threatening tourists and the "atmosphere" for tourism. As discussed above, the technology through which state authorities sought to achieve this cleansing was that of citizenship. Consequently, people with the weakest claims to citizenship tended to be both criminalized and marginalized – spatially as much as economically – within the hierarchically structured tourist economy.

## GLOBALIZATION COMES TO BOCA CHICA

In 2000 and 2001, both communities – and the nation as a whole – were being affected by neoliberal economic reforms implemented by the government of President Leonel Fernandez (1996–2000), and advocated by the World Bank, the IMF, and other international agencies. These policies, which centered on the privatization of publicly owned industries on the one hand, and the expansion of the tourism and export-processing sectors on the other, were continued by the government of President Rafael Hipólito Mejía, elected in 2000.

For example, in 2000, Ingenio Boca Chica and other state-owned sugar refineries were turned over to private, multinational corporations, in keeping with a government plan to privatize their management. When Zucarmex, a Mexican multinational, failed to comply with its contract to renovate Ingenio Boca Chica, the mill was shut down, resulting in the dismissal of 3,000 sugar workers in Andrés. The closing of the mill contributed to an already high unemployment rate, estimated at 45 percent in 1998. Many former mill employees and their families were forced to search for work as laborers in the low-wage construction industry, or in the informal economy tied to Boca Chica's tourism industry.

During this same period, the state-owned power industry was also privatized, and both power generation and distribution facilities were sold to foreign power companies, such as the US-based AES and Smith Enron corporations. Consequently, area residents who had not paid for electricity in the past, were now required to pay as much as 500 pesos per month for power – or roughly 20 percent of the minimum private-sector wage. Sections of Andrés and Boca Chica, and elsewhere, that did not pay their electricity bills were punished with *apagones,* or deliberate power outages lasting up to 20 hours. These punitive blackouts provoked widespread social protests and rioting in the capital and elsewhere in 2001, and a vociferous public debate regarding the privatization policies.

This process of privatization, and the protests against it, set the stage for the community's response to the next intervention of global capital in the region. In February 2001, a multinational consortium announced the completion of planning for a large port facility at Punta Caucedo, perched on the Bay of Andrés and just to the west of Andrés-Boca Chica. Officially known as the Zona Franca Multimodal Caucedo [Caucedo Multi-Modal Free Trade Zone], the plan called for the construction of a state-of-the-art, deep-water container port linked to an FTZ industrial park. The *megapuerto* project, as it came to be known, was the result of a 250 million-dollar joint venture between CSX World Terminals, a US corporation involved in the development and operation of international ports, and the Caucedo Development Corporation, a partnership of three Dominican businessmen. The project was financed by a consortium of international investors led by the Scotiabank Group. Permission to operate the port and free trade zone had been granted by decree in 1998 by the then President Leonel Fernandez.

On February 2, 2001, a public hearing was held before the National District's Ayuntamiento [municipal government] in Santo Domingo, at which members of the Tourism Development Association of Boca Chica expressed opposition to the project. Led by Henry Pimentel, a former government tourism official, the association represented merchants, restaurant owners, and other sectors of the tourist industry. Its main function was to lobby government agencies to improve conditions for tourism – by policing the beaches, improving garbage collecting, and cracking down on crime and prostitution.

On March 1, the association called an emergency meeting to debate the impact of the container port on tourism in Boca Chica. Its "experts" asserted that industrial development was incompatible with tourism and that the container port would destroy the coral reef sheltering Boca Chica's popular beach. In addition, they warned, heavy ship traffic through the port would produce oil spills that would harm marine life. Pimentel gave the example of Puerto Plata, where tourism had suffered following the 1994 World Bank-financed construction of a power plant by Smith Enron Corporation.

The association also mounted another argument to oppose the container port: because Boca Chica was the beach most accessible to the capital's residents, tourism had an indispensable "cultural value." Therefore the container port not only posed a threat to the marine environment, but also to popular culture and the national heritage. This appeal to the nation and its cultural traditions was intended to offset charges made by critics of the association that the group was narrowly concerned with the profits of the resort hotels (and the well-being of their foreign guests), and was indifferent to the needs and struggles of the people of Andrés-Boca Chica. In short, the association was attempting to project the interests of the globally oriented tourist industry as those of nation and locality – the cultural patrimony of the nation.

The association's critiques of the container port did not end here. Spokespeople also claimed that the project would violate provisions of Dominican law, and those articles of the Dominican Constitution that protect investments and jobs that had been created as a result of the area's development as a tourist pole. The environmental hazards posed by the container port, the association claimed, would also violate the General Law on Environment and Natural Resources passed in 2000.

Spokespeople for the association appealed to business owners in the audience whose livelihoods would be affected, if not destroyed, by the container port, which was characterized as a "caramel candy" that was tempting people to disregard economic realities in the name of progress and modernization. One spokesman described the free trade zones as an advantage that had been conferred by the United States on countries in Latin America and the Caribbean during the Cold War, with the aims of undermining Cuba's influence in the region and reducing the flow of illegal immigrants to the United States. The FTZs, he explained, were part of a "tributary system" that made it possible for goods to be imported and processed in the Dominican Republic, before being reexported to the US without the payment of taxes or duties. With the expansion of global markets, however, such free-trade regulations now hindered if not disallowed preferential arrangements with nations such as the Dominican Republic. NAFTA, the spokesman continued, was but one example of the "economic logic" of free trade that was having a negative impact on export-processing in the Dominican Republic. Since the future of the FTZs was uncertain, Boca Chica's tourist economy had to be preserved.

The arguments mounted by the association against the container port underscore the complex and fluid relationship between global capital, the state, and discourses of national interests, as they are materialized in practice and within concrete settings. Few in the community believed that the association and the hotel representatives, who dominated its leadership, were concerned about the tens of thousands of local residents who used the area's beaches. Nor did community members believe that the association cared about the residents who eked out a living on the illicit fringes of the tourist industry. The association did, however, succeed in constructing an argument that counterposed US-dominated, free-trade interests against an ecologically conscious hotel industry that was defending the nation's cultural heritage through appeals to the legal apparatus of the state. In fact, the meeting did succeed, albeit temporarily, in defining the terms of the ensuing debate, constructing the container port as an environmental threat to the Dominican way of life.

Here I stress the far from transparent character of the relationships between global flows of capital, the political economy of the nation-state, and contested discourses concerning the nature and trajectory of the global economy. The complex, if not convoluted, arguments mobilized by the association highlight the contextually disputed status of globalization, and the fact that the constitution of the global, in relation to national interests and identities, is as much an *argument* for particular economic policies, as it is a set of intractable, structural relationships between "global" capital and "local" economies. In this regard, the specific political topography of the nation-state conditions not only how global processes are concretized in time and space, but also how "globalization" itself is ideologically articulated, exercised, and received.

Word of mounting opposition to the container port spread throughout Andrés-Boca Chica, in part through programming on *Turivisión*, a low-budget, community-based television station housed at the offices of Boca Chica's cable television provider. Despite its name, *Turivisión* produced a variety of public-interest programs, ranging from *cinéma vérité* reports of local events to talk shows hosted by community leaders. Only days before the association's emergency meeting on March 1, two of the three Dominican partners in the joint container port venture, Manuel Tavares and Jaak Rannik, had appeared on a news and "call in" talk show to discuss the container port and address concerns about its environmental impact. Tavares and Rannik had both stressed the long and rigorous review process through which the project had come. Both assured viewers that environmental risks would be carefully studied, and that the latest technologies would be used in building the port to ensure that the environment is safeguarded.

Opinions among the general populace varied over the matter, complicated by the competing and contradictory claims that were being made by the two sides of the debate. Many who worked in tourism were ambivalent about the project. They were concerned that their livelihoods, though modest and unstable, would be threatened, yet they also believed that the container port would bring general prosperity to the area. The dockworkers at Andrés's existing port were skeptical of the promises being made by the project's sponsors. "They say that there will be work for us," observed Juan Mendez, a retired dockworker, "but I think that this is a lie. Because I have heard that this project, the container port, will be completely automated. They won't need workers, only machines. This is what I have heard."

Some business owners were even more critical. Association member Gabriel Zapata, who owned a medium-sized hotel, told me that the container port was already a "done deal" and that it did not matter what the community thought. Moreover, he added, the project was beyond even the Dominican government's powers of oversight, and no more than a consequence of the nation's debt to the United States. "Before," Zapata continued, "when they wanted to get their money, they sent in the army and took over the customs house. Now, they don't have to do that. They just come in and say, 'Look, we want to buy this piece of land and make this project with it – make a factory, or make a multi-modal, or whatever. That's how they do it now!'"

The diverse interpretations of and responses to the container port underscore the multifarious composition of global capital and the peculiar, context-specific manner in which these global flows, material and discursive, congeal as they are instantiated and inflected on the political field of the state. For example, the association's portrayal of the FTZ system as a relic of Cold War politics, as a tool to stem migration, and as a "tributary" arrangement designed to benefit US corporations, appealed to a historical understanding of the asymmetrical relationship between the US and the Dominican Republic – a view that found support in the protests against privatization that were erupting throughout the nation. Similarly, Zapata's comparison of the project to the seizure of the customs house – which occurred prior to the 1914 US occupation of the country – historicized the container port, providing it with the face and agency of a territorially aggressive nation-state (the US), rather than the shapeless aura of free markets and the global economy.

In short, however diminished the capacity of the nation-state to govern its economy – always an empirical question – the state remains an important, indeed, a key political field, structuring the specific manner in which global flows of capital, people, media, and so forth are materialized in space, whether as multinational projects such as the container port, or as discourses about the nature and future of the world economy and its historically forged relationship to localities.

Precisely these issues lay at the center of the dispute over the container port: What was the container port? Who were its sponsors? Whose interests would really be served by its construction? The answers to these questions were by no means imposed from above by the global economy, but were rather forged through struggles, as Edmund Leach succinctly put it, "on the ground." The hotel industry framed the container port as a US-sponsored project that would not only provide dubious economic benefits but would also violate Dominican law by undermining the nation's natural and cultural patrimony. They sought to mobilize popular opposition to the project by presenting their quite global interests as congruent with those of the nation-state and the local community, and in opposition to foreign, US-dominated capital.

The multinational sponsors of the container port challenged this portrayal, stressing the economic prosperity that the project would bring, not only to its backers but also to disadvantaged groups. Given the long history of conflict between the hotel industry, backed by the police and other authorities, and the region's poor, pressed to survive on the illicit margins of tourism, this argument appeared plausible.

On March 2, the sponsors of the container port held a public meeting at the Hamaca Hotel to present their plan to the community. The lobby outside the spacious meeting room was packed with people – clusters of local officials in business suits, merchants talking on cell phones, and families with children dressed in their Sunday best. Buses had been chartered – one driver told me by officials of local unions – to ferry working-class residents from Andrés to the hotel to attend the meeting. At the entrance to the salon, a table had been set up to distribute information about the project: a small brochure provided an overview of the Zona Franca Multimodal Caucedo and a large booklet in English described Port Everglades, a port facility on the southeastern coast of Florida, that was said to be similar to the one being proposed.

Inside the salon, about 800 people were seated before the dais at the front of the room. The first couple of rows had been reserved for government officials and corporate executives representing CSX World Terminals and Mouchel Consulting, a British firm that would be involved in developing the terminal. Smartly dressed hotel employees scurried about, checking microphone connections and tending stainless-steel chafing dishes and trays that were being readied in the salon's rear. To the right of the dais, an artist's rendering of the container port was projected onto a large screen. To its left, a wooden, soundproof booth housed two simultaneous translators for the majority who would need a translation of the English-language presentations.

A CSX employee approached the podium and welcomed the audience to the "informational" meeting before introducing the dozen or so CSX and Mouchel executives sitting in the first row. The representative then explained that headsets were available in the lobby for those who would need translation of the English-language presentations. A grumble rose from the audience. Only a few left their seats to retrieve the headsets. "This is the Dominican Republic," the woman sitting next to me muttered. "Why are they speaking to us in English?" Others around her agreed. The CSX representative introduced Manuel Tavares, one of the Dominican partners and president of Tavares Industrial, a group of construction and real-estate firms involved in FTZ development.

Tavares, a tall, stately, and deep-voiced man, welcomed the audience and explained that the meeting was part of a long process of public review that was being followed in accord with guidelines established by the General Law of Environment and Natural Resources. He then paused, looking up from his notes. "Having heard the introduction," he began, "it occurred to me that one small issue was overlooked which requires mention. And that is the *local* partners, because only CSX World Terminals was mentioned in the introduction. But it is also important to know who the *Dominicans* are who are moving this project." The CSX and Mouchel executives nodded their heads in agreement.

The slight was telling, and the audience would remain alert to how issues of sponsorship and control of the container port were presented through both the content of the presentations and the meeting's format. Indeed, the charge that the megaport was a US-dominated project, serving United States rather than Dominican interests, had been firmly made by the hotel industry representatives only the day before. Consequently, the issue of how "global," rather than Dominican, the interests controlling the container port appeared would remain a flashpoint, strongly influencing how residents interpreted and evaluated the competing claims made about the project's impact.

Tavares described the port as "a logistics center for the regional transportation and distribution of goods" and maintained that, since the port would handle containers rather than loose cargo, it would operate cleanly. Aided by bulleted discussion points projected onto the screen, he explained that the megaport's proximity to the capital's international airport would – with community support – create a "synergy" that could make the Dominican Republic "the Taiwan of the Caribbean." Tavares then explained the relationship of the Dominican interests to the multinational ones. "Our international partner, CSX World Terminals, contributes various things to this project. On the one hand, they contribute the technology, '*el* know how,' and experience with developing this type of facility. We believe, with much conviction, that realistically, we could not have put together a project of this magnitude if we did not have assistance from a company with the experience and prestige of CSX World Terminals." He added that only a company with CSX's "global reach" could have secured the international financing needed for the project.

Tavares then introduced Jim Rogers, a director at Mouchel, the firm that would conduct the project's environmental impact study (EIS). Rogers spoke at length about the scope of the study, discussing in mind-numbing detail its components. Many in the audience became restless and gathered in groups at the rear of the salon, ignoring the English-language presentation. After an hour or so, Rogers completed his presentation, summarizing the process by which the EIS would be reviewed by the government. There was a flurry of applause, but few in the audience had been listening to the translation over the headsets. Next to speak was Pedro Garcia, a Dominican sociologist who would conduct the social and economic component of the EIS.

As Garcia approached the podium, a man in the audience called out, "*Habla en ingles, usted tambien!*" [Speak in English, you too!]. The audience erupted in laughter. "*Aye mi madre!*" the woman next to me cried out in exasperation, as she removed her headset. Many headsets, it appeared, had not been working properly. Moreover, few in the audience had received them. A CSX employee apologized for the technical problems and encouraged the audience to use headsets for the remaining presentations in English. Hotel employees circulated through the audience distributing the headsets. Irritated, a man shouted out, "*After* the gringo has already spoken?" The CSX executives looked on with concern. Clearly, the use of English was regarded by the audience as an indication that US interests dominated the megaport's multinational partnership.

After the presentations, Tavares provided a summary, stressing once again the scientific rigor of the study that would be done and the economic benefits that the port would bring. He then opened the floor to discussion. Not surprisingly, the opening questions addressed the megaport's impact on tourism and Boca Chica's coral reef.

Juana Sanchez, a councilwoman for the Partido Liberación Dominicana (PLD), relayed concerns that the megaport would damage the tourist industry. She argued that the EIS must address the area's need for "sustainable development," which would ensure the livelihoods of future generations. Next, Jose Antonio Perez, representing the dockworkers of Andrés, stood to speak. He was surrounded by a group of about 40 dockworkers and their families in the rear of the salon. Perez asked what impact the construction of the megaport would have on the existing port in Andrés. "And what will become of the dockworkers of Andrés? Will they also benefit, the dockworkers who have worked in Andrés since the 1940s?"

Tavares placed both hands on the podium and solemnly replied: "I have to say *caballero* that clearly... clearly the dockworkers of Andrés will be taken into account. Who *better* to work the ships than you who have worked here for so many years." Led by the dockworkers, the audience erupted in applause.

One of the last to speak was Gonzalez Troncoso, president of a local environmental group. "What I see here," he began, surveying the audience, "is a conflict of interests between the hotel owners and this corporation, a conflict over which the residents of Andrés and Boca Chica, to use the common expression, 'will lose no sleep.'" The audience laughed, applauded, and then quieted for him to continue. CSX and Mouchel executives pressed their headsets to their ears for the translation from Spanish.

> This project looks excellent... on paper. What we are waiting for now is the *implementation* of the project. Because, just like Falconbridge [a Canadian-owned Ferronickel mine] in Bonao... There they designed a marvelous project. And then we learned that the people of Bonao had taken to the streets, struggling and protesting against the environmental pollution. You spoke to us of Hong Kong, and you spoke to us of Florida... In those places, there are strong institutions, where no one has the ability to violate the law. But here, the multinationals come and do whatever they want. And if you violate this plan, which looks so good on paper, Andrés-Boca Chica and other communities will take to the streets, protesting and demanding the termination of this project.

Once again the audience erupted in applause as Troncoso's voice reached a crescendo. Tavares raised his hands and nodded his head in a gesture of understanding.

"*Caballero...caballero,* and everyone," he began, his deep voice rising above the din.

> You are completely right. You are completely right. And fortunately, our country is making progress. Years ago, there was no...There was a dictatorship. And afterwards, we began a process of democratization that some say is still not complete. But fortunately, we have been making progress. Today, there is still much to do. But we have better justice today than ten years ago. And we will have still better. And if *we* violate our commitment and the law in constructing, and maintaining, and in operating this port, in accord with national and international norms...the project will be removed and taken away.

There was a pause before polite applause as the audience wrestled with the image of the 250 million-dollar Zona Franca Multimodal Caucedo being "removed and taken away." But Tavares's assurances appeared to have tempered key concerns about the project. Four hours into the night, the meeting ended and the audience regrouped around the tables at the rear of the salon, where fruit punch and hors d'oeuvres were being served.

Tavares had succeeded in giving a Dominican voice and face to the project, skillfully parrying questions and comments, while CSX personnel remained conspicuously silent. His manner was authoritative and respectful, suggested by his use of the term "*caballero*" to address male speakers. More significantly, Tavares presented the transnational sponsorship and financing of the project as a guarantee that the EIS and, more generally, the port's operation would be conducted in accord with strict guidelines, rather than under the auspices of an implicitly corrupt and ineffectual state.

To be sure, many in the audience remained skeptical about the project's implementation, but the promises made by these most recent representatives of global capital had been received on a political stage which, peculiar to this context, strongly influenced how the project and its sponsors would be appraised by the audience and the wider community. In the recent past, the development of tourism in Boca Chica had produced a hierarchical, if not a dual economy, in which the high-end formal tourist sector was differentiated, in discourse and in practice, from the illicit and heavily policed informal economy. This order of things had fueled class antagonisms and resentment that undermined the appeal of the hotel owners to the nation's patrimony, let alone the economic interests of the local community; that is, class antagonisms, fueled by this context-specific ordering of the division of labor, shaped how global flows of capital, commodities, and information were structured within the space of the nation-state.

On March 14, an editorial appeared in the newspaper *El Nacional,* criticizing the megaport and based on the environmental arguments that had been made by the hotel industry. Later that day, the editorial was discussed on a community-based talk show broadcast on *Turivisión* and hosted by Hector Peña and Jose Beato, both avid supporters of the megaport. Beato accused the editorial's author of "yellow journalism," and argued that it was an attempt by "a certain interest group" in the community to sabotage the project by spreading false and misleading information about its environmental risks.

"Simply speaking," Peña followed, "there is hegemony in this community. We have to ask [the hotel owners ] for permission to do any kind of project. And we ask,

'Why should we request permission from them, from pirates, to secure the rights of all the people of Andrés, of Boca Chica, and of La Caleta?' For every project that comes into our community, we must ask the permission of *los señores hoteleros.*" Peña dragged out the polite term of address in biting sarcasm. Then, referring directly to Henry Pimentel, president of the association, he added, "Why doesn't he worry himself about the prostitution that is there [in the tourist zone], where children are in the streets until two o'clock in the morning? *Señores,*" he concluded, staring deadpan into the camera lens, "let *us* worry about the development of this community!"

Peña's comments expressed and lent support to beliefs and sentiments that were gaining ground in the community, which cast the hotel owners as elitist "hypocrites," narrowly concerned about the *natural* environment but indifferent to the condition of the poor – the "human environment," as Peña would later put it. To counter the hotel owners's focus on threats to the coral reef, supporters of the megaport pointed to poverty, crime, and prostitution, describing these latter as forms of "contamination" that were the effects, not only of unemployment, but of tourism as well. In this view, international tourism was a corrupting influence that was undermining public morality, Dominican cultural values, as well as the rights and obligations of national citizenship. This argument, which would be exercised often during the course of the debate, resonated with the resentment felt by many toward the international tourist industry and, in particular, the system of all-inclusive resort hotels.

On the one hand, the all-inclusive model locked local vendors and merchants out of the lucrative, "high-end" sector of the tourist industry. Many charged, for example, that the resort hotels dissuaded their guests from leaving hotel grounds by warning that they would be ripped off by local vendors or, even worse, by criminals. Moreover, security policies practiced by the resort hotels excluded non-guests from hotel grounds, as well as from sections of the beach under their de facto control, leading to the complaint that the major hotels were plotting to "privatize" the public beach. Consequently, considerable animosity was felt toward the hotel industry, not only by vendors, merchants, and others working at the low end of tourist economy, but also by Dominican visitors to the beach, who were typically treated as "second-class guests."

On the other hand, the prominence of sex tourists among male visitors to Boca Chica fueled the widely held opinion that foreigners, both tourists and the expatriate owners of local bars, discothèques, and hotels, were undermining the community's morality or, more to the point, the morality of its youth. For example, at the height of the debate over the megaport *El Nacional* published an exposé on prostitution in Boca Chica, which charged that "foreigners" were recruiting young women throughout the Dominican Republic to work as prostitutes in Boca Chica. The exposé provoked quick responses from government officials, as well as a flurry of local investigative reports and commentaries broadcast on *Turivisión*, Boca Chica's television station.

Soon after, an editorial published in *Listin Diario* (2002), entitled "Mega-Ports are Necessary," made this link between tourism, foreigners, and moral corruption even more forcefully. "One preoccupation of the hotel owners," the author began,

> is that the port will produce an "environmental disaster" which will affect the beach at Boca Chica. We believe that every possibility, in this sense, is avoidable and that the

authorities must remain vigilant so that this never occurs. But we also believe that this same level of concern must be shown to ensure that Boca Chica does not remain what it is today: a cavern in which unscrupulous foreigners promote all kinds of sexual aberrations, minors included, and without limits.

Mass support for the megaport, bolstered by these appeals to moral and economic interests, grew rapidly as the terms of the debate crystallized and became common knowledge. A key venue for publicizing the debate was *Turivisión*, whose program hosts devoted considerable air time to discussing the project and to reporting on meetings about it. The campaign provides an interesting case of cable television, the *sine qua non* of the global "mediascape," being put to eminently local use. By mid-April, the public buses in Andrés-Boca Chica carried bumper stickers with the entreaty, *Apoye el Megapuerto!* [Support the Megaport!], and graffiti began appearing in Andrés-Boca Chica, bearing such slogans as *Megapuerto Si, Hoteleros No!*

On February 21, 2002, President Hipólito Mejía, accompanied by officers of CSX World Terminals and the Caucedo Development Corporation, broke ground for the megaport at Punta Caucedo. In a press release recording the event, Arno Dimmling, vice-president of CSX World Terminals, announced: "The new facility, and its associated systems and processes, will allow the Dominican Republic to become one of the most modern and efficient marine terminals in the world today, enhancing the country's ability to compete in the ever-increasing aggressive world market."

## CONCLUSION

The struggle over the Zona Franca Multi-Modal Caucedo highlights the critical role that the nation-state, as a contested political field, plays in configuring global flows of capital, labor, and technology, as well as discourses about the "global economy" in time and in space. The tendency of some theorists to discount the significance of contemporary states by emphasizing the unfettered, transnational character of capital, institutions, information, and so on, obscures the context-specific manner in which these transnational processes are politically secured and materialized in space. Equally important, this tendency also elides the fact that capitalism is, above all, a system for organizing and disciplining labor to produce surplus value; labor which, as we have seen, must be governed, cajoled, disciplined, and, indeed, punished at particular times and in particular places. Time-space compression notwithstanding, capital still must act in time and space, and at times and places not always of its own choosing.

The case of the container port also underscores the complex and, at times, antagonistic composition of global capital, as well as the context-specific barriers, resistances, and, to be sure, opportunities that it encounters within historically formed cultural and political landscapes, such as that of Andrés-Boca Chica. In their struggle against the container port, the hotel industry was compelled, despite the national and international legitimacy enjoyed by the tourism industry, to appeal to the people, and in the name of the cultural and natural patrimony of the nation. To that end, they argued not only that industrial development was incompatible with tourism, but also that the FTZs and the free-trade ideology on which they were based served the interests of US-dominated, multinational capital, rather than those of the Dominican Republic and its citizens.

Nevertheless, their appeals fell on deaf ears in an area that had received few benefits from tourism, and in which the vast majority of workers were forced to eke out a living on the margins of the tourist economy, often beyond the pale of legality and the safeguards of citizenship. In the end class antagonisms, fueled by the hierarchical organization of the tourist economy and by a symbolic economy that counterpoised "valued guests" against poor people to be avoided, exploited, and consumed, galvanized public support for the container port. It is not by chance that the accusation, however overstated, that "foreigners" were sexually abusing the children of Boca Chica, emerged as the most forceful rallying cry against the position of the hotel owners and for the promises of the container port. Against the hotel owners' construction of national interests and traditions, the project's supporters advanced an alternative – one that situated the nation's interests squarely in the economic needs of the poor and against the elitist, socioeconomic landscape of the tourist industry.

To be sure, many residents remained skeptical of the promises made by the megaport's sponsors and were of diverse opinions concerning its impact on the economy and environment. Despite Tavares's efforts to disassociate the project from the abuses of other multinational corporations and other "mega-projects," few could fail to make the connection. Indeed, throughout the review period, communities across the nation were protesting – the authorities claimed they were "rioting" – against the power blackouts, police repression, and a variety of abuses that had been committed by multinational corporations, such as Falconbridge and Smith Enron. Moreover, many people in Andrés-Boca Chica remained bitter over the abandonment of the sugar refinery by its elusive, private-sector managers. Nevertheless, within this *specific* context and at this *particular* time, support of the megaport against the "hegemony" of the hotel interests appeared to be the best course of action for the majority of residents.

It would be wrong, however, to view this community as having been simply duped, once again, by global capital and its promises of free-market prosperity; or, for that matter, as lacking the political resources and "*el* know how" to oppose globalization "globally." The container port controversy provoked a critical public debate, not only about multinational corporations and the interests they served, but also about globalization itself, forcing the project's sponsors – and its detractors – to make explicit and public not only their promises of economic prosperity, but also their claims and assumptions regarding the functioning of the global economy. More generally, people resisted these and other neoliberal reforms through their everyday economic activities and social relations. Precariously positioned on the margins of the formal economy, working people in Andrés-Boca Chica evaded and, indeed, violated the evolving division of labor and its disciplinary technologies, pursuing livelihoods that transgressed the stratified architecture of the formal economy. Although it would be wrong-headed to exaggerate the significance of this infrapolitics, these everyday struggles for livelihood informed and fueled collectively held notions about economic justice and citizenship which, mediated by the nation-state, were not reducible to its conceits.

## REFERENCES

Appadurai, Arjun (1996) *Modernity At Large*. Minneapolis: University of Minnesota Press.

Baudrillard, Jean (1990) *Seduction*, trans. Brian Singer. New York: St. Martin's Press.

Castells, Manuel (1997) *The Power of Identity*. Malden, MA: Blackwell.

Foucault, Michel (1979) *Discipline and Punish: The Birth of the Prison*, trans. Alan Sheridan. New York: Vintage Books.

Harvey, David (1989) *The Condition of Postmodernity: An Enquiry into the Origins of Cultural Change*. Oxford: Blackwell.

Hirst, Paul, and Grahame Thompson (1999) *Globalization in Question*. Malden, MA: Polity.

*Listin Diario* [newspaper] (2002) Mega-Ports are Necessary [editorial]. April 5:11.

Miyoshi, Masao (1996) Borderless World? From Colonialism to Transnationalism and the Decline of the Nation-State. In *Global/Local*, ed. Rob Wilson and Wimal Dissanayake, pp. 78–106. Durham, NC: Duke University Press.

Ong, Aiwa (1999) *Flexible Citizenship: The Cultural Logics of Transnationality*. Durham, NC: Duke University Press.

Poulantzas, Nicos (1978) *State, Power and Socialism*. London: Verso.

Rosenberg, Justin (2000) *The Follies of Globalisation Theory*. London: Verso.

Safa, Helen (1995) *The Myth of the Male Breadwinner*. Boulder, CO: Westview.

Scott, James (1990) *Domination and the Arts of Resistance*. New Haven: Yale University Press.

Tilly, Charles (1995) Citizenship, Identity and Social History. *International Review of Social History* 40:1–17.

# CHAPTER 19   "Mafias"

## Jane C. Schneider and Peter T. Schneider

The word "mafia," although historically associated with Sicilian organized crime, is widely used to label similar, and not so similar, phenomena throughout the world. Indeed, the term has been applied to all manner of violent criminal organizations (and some clique-like formations that are neither violent nor criminal). Since the fall of the Soviet Union, references to mafia have appeared with special frequency in Russia and Eastern Europe, and in the context of transnational trafficking in proscribed commodities.

Early attempts to analyze and account for these apparently rampant mafia formations made use of a market model of supply and demand which paid scant attention to the political and cultural aspects of the various generative situations, or to differences among the crime groups that were generated. Emphasis fell on the unraveling power of states to administer and enforce a legal order, as old regimes collapsed and markets were created or deregulated. Overall, the state's loss of prerogatives in relation to private enterprise, and the emergence of the "information society," were put forward as general conditions, with the nascent mafias seen as everywhere quite similar and easily articulated into global criminal networks.

The work of sociologist Diego Gambetta exemplifies this approach. Conjuring up a market metaphor, Gambetta defines the Sicilian mafia (which he considers a prototype for mafias in general) as "a specific economic enterprise, an industry which produces, promotes, and sells private protection" (1993:1). The legislative creation of private property in early nineteenth-century Sicily, which required institutional arrangements and a regulatory apparatus that the (then Bourbon) state was incapable of introducing, foreshadowed its appearance. The new Italian state, encompassing Sicily in 1860, was only marginally more prepared to quell widespread insecurity and intense conflict over the management and disposition of resources, whether in agriculture, urban markets, or local governance. Such were the structural conditions that made protection by force and intimidation a welcome, hence marketable, service in Sicily, enabling other forms of economic exchange to develop. The advantages of turning to mafiosi as "sellers of protection" were their capacity to control and handle information discreetly, to administer violence and intimidation, and to cultivate a reputation for power and influence.

In Gambetta's model, the Sicilian market for "illegal" protection was vast because protection was not forthcoming from more conventional sources, such as private and public insurance companies, the judiciary, and the police. Similarly, in post-Soviet Russia and Eastern Europe, entrepreneurs quickly surfaced to offer protection as resources were privatized in the absence of a legal apparatus for securing property and enforcing contracts. Much like Sicilian organized crime, the Russian variant, in Gambetta's view, is "a response to a certain institutional demand by the nascent market economy, namely, the need to protect property rights, a need not satisfied by public protection and enforcement agencies" (Volkov 2002:18). Manuel Castells' authoritative essay on the global criminal economy in the third volume of *The Information Age: Economy, Society and Culture,* pursues a similar interpretation. According to Castells (1998:118), "The dramatic errors made by Gorbachev first, in disorganizing the Soviet system without replacing it, and the Russian democrats later, in pushing for an accelerated transition to the market economy without social and institutional control, created the conditions for the takeover (by criminals) of one of the largest and naturally wealthiest countries in the world. It is this wild appropriation of wealth, enacted or tolerated by the powers that be, that explains the overwhelming presence of crime."

Castells (1998:166–167) also theorizes trafficking. With its technologically enhanced communications grid and electronic flows of money, the "information age" has generated a new phenomenon:

> The Sicilian *Cosa Nostra* (and its associates, *La Camorra, Ndrangheta* [sic], and *Sacra Corona Unita*), the US Mafia, the Colombian cartels, the Mexican cartels, the Nigerian criminal networks, the Japanese Yakuza, the Chinese Triads, the constellation of Russian *Mafiyas*, the Turkish heroin traffickers, the Jamaican Posses, and a myriad of regional and local criminal groupings in all countries, have come together in a global diversified network, that permeates boundaries and links up ventures of all sorts.

Indeed, what has made the Russian mafia ruinous in the eyes of Castells is the engagement, in Russia, of what he calls "global organized crime," led by the Sicilian Mafia and the Colombian cartels. These criminal networks "seized the chance of Russian chaos to launder considerable sums of money, as well as mixing 'dirty money' with counterfeited dollars by the billions" (1998:187). As a consequence, "wild Russian capitalism is deeply entrenched in global crime and in global financial networks" (1998:189).

Subsequent analyses, informed by research on the ground, accept this picture only in part. Vadim Volkov, for example, has established that among the "violent entrepreneurs" who rose to the fore in the making of Russian capitalism following the post-1987 economic liberalization were a disproportionate number of trained athletes and body-builders, above all boxers and wrestlers, with something of an esprit de corps – in other words, not simply generic entrepreneurs meeting a market demand. The assumption that they were "merely passive providers of a commodity (protection) the selling of which wholly depends on the level of demand and available choices" (2002:19) underestimates the role of violence or the menace of violence as a "marketing strategy" – as an offer that cannot be refused. In understanding Russian mafia, Volkov would rather emphasize a "whole set of political relations between the owners of the means of violence which produce and change the set of constraints within which economic subjects have to operate" (2002:20). Anthropologists of Russia and Eastern Europe, similarly critical of a market model of mafia formation, have drawn attention to pre-Soviet organized crime traditions, incubated in prisons during the Soviet period, pro-actively reasserting themselves after the "fall" (Humphrey 1999), and to "mafia talk" as a form of labeling with a life of its own, potentially independent of any organized crime reality (see Verdery 1996).

Economist Thomas Naylor criticizes the tendency, illustrated by Castells, to imagine a worldwide "industry" in which all of the major criminal organizations, each bearing an ethnic or national identity but escaping the controls of its home state, are networked into a single "system" that has at its heart the laundering of "hundreds of billions (maybe trillions) of dollars" (Castells 1998:166–167). This vision privileges as new a tendency toward global circulation that is older than Marco Polo, Naylor argues. For its time, the telegraph was more revolutionary – a greater rupture with past patterns of communication – than the breakthroughs in electronic communication today, yet states were immediately able to regulate telegraphic messaging. With a few exceptions, specialized financial investigators, themselves increasingly globally linked, are on top of the most sophisticated techniques for dissociating accumulated funds from their criminal origins, disguising money trails to foil pursuit, and cycling ill-gotten profits back into the criminal world (Naylor 2002:137). Most worldwide hiding and redefining of financial assets is performed by and for legitimate corporate enterprises; most offshore banks are not founded on secrecy (conversely, legitimate banking functions sometimes are); and most of the recycling of illicit funds occurs through the small-scale, face-to-face operations of the sort that evoked the image of the laundry in the first place. Among these is placing ill-gotten money in cash businesses – restaurants, bars, video shops, and the proverbial car washes and laundromats; buying and selling gold, diamonds, antiquities, trading stamps; entrusting cash to innocent-seeming couriers, from priests to members of the diplomatic corps. All the estimates aside, it is impossible to know "how much illegal money is earned or saved or laundered or moved around the world, or how it is distributed among a host of malefactors" (2002:6–8).

## TRAFFICKING AND GLOBALIZATION

Rather than highlighting the deregulation of markets as the decisive framework for trafficking today, it is preferable to understand contemporary globalization in relation to a broader set of processes. First among these is the redirection, worldwide, of public investment away from social services and the transfer of service provisioning to the private sector. Associated with IMF-mandated neoliberal restructuring in the less developed countries – and with neoliberal assaults on the welfare state in the most developed – this process has the effect of marginalizing poor people and subjecting them to severe subsistence insecurity. Inequalities have increased both between and within countries, including within the privileged countries of the "First World." Contemporaneously we find the consolidation of corporate power on a global scale, based on (1) flexible strategies of production (outsourcing, ease of relocation, dispersal to export-processing zones, recruitment of vulnerable immigrant labor); (2) the cultivation of brand names and logos with heavy investment in image creation and advertising; and (3) tie-ins with the staggeringly expansionist new sectors of glitzy name-brand shopping, Disney Worlds, and tourism.

Taken together, these processes spell the increased likelihood of disemployment at one or more points over the life cycle, and the increasing significance of desire as the route to finding moments of warmth and security, excitement and escape from boredom, self-understanding and identity in a continuously shifting world. New and powerful synergisms of supply and demand, desperation and desire are a consequence. In considering these synergisms, it is important to recognize that the regulation of morality has long been an impetus to illegal trafficking. Central to the history of organized crime in the United States, for example, was the widespread interdiction of gambling, above all the gaming practices of immigrant workers, outlawing prostitution, and the prohibition of alcoholic beverages. In each case, moralizing movements produced unrealistic legislation whose contravention was a golden opportunity for violent entrepreneurs. The eventual decriminalization of such "vices," and their heavy taxation by the state, is retrospective evidence for the power of this equation.

Contemporary moral and political movements in various of the world's societies are similarly responsible for more recent pressures on law-makers to criminalize commodities of desire, with a robust evasive commerce being the result. As hearings in the United States Senate underscore, the export of illegal drugs has become an economic niche for entire countries (Colombia; Bolivia until the United States-backed "War on Drugs" intervened; Burma; Afghanistan before 9/11 and perhaps soon again). Drug traffic, these hearings suggest, is "the less celebrated and rarely acknowledged underside of U.S. Mexican economic integration" (Beare and Naylor, quoting a 1996 Senate hearing, 1999:9). Although indexing more open markets, these and other cases illustrate the simultaneous and synergistic presence of, on the one hand, thousands of marginalized peasants and workers who have no alternative livelihood outside of trafficking, given structural adjustment programs and the weakening of state services, and, on the other hand, new rhythms of work and leisure, hyper-employment and disemployment, inter-generational tensions, sexual experimentation, family formation, recreation, and travel, all intertwined with substance use and abuse.

The conditions of neoliberal capitalism have clearly opened a vast space for all manner of entrepreneurs to articulate marginalized, displaced, and otherwise unemployed poor people (wherever they are) with consumers of commodities that, although defined as illegal by states, and even by international conventions, are nevertheless greatly desired (in poor communities, too). This is not, however, to say that the forms of enterprise are universal. Reinvented or newly spawned by the affected communities, they are rooted in these communities, drawing on them for resources at the same time that wider linkages are being forged. Nor do all of the forms qualify as "mafias."

## MAFIAS AND TRAFFICKING

The tendency to attribute contemporary trafficking to market liberalization goes hand in hand with the assumption that various "mafias," understood generically although given regional or national names, are the principal mediators of illegal commerce. In each case, recent or renewed migration and communication, now in the age of email, can be said to have paved the way for transnational networks of kinship and shared nationality, useful for recruiting trusted couriers and managing funds. Each case, too, evokes the use or threat of violence, an asset when it comes to policing illegal operations and contracts. Yet, notwithstanding these affinities, conflating trafficking with mafias gives short shrift to the locally and nationally situated dimensions of mafia formation, and to the multiplicity of traffickers whose roots are not in organized crime. A brief overview of the Sicilian mafia and the yakuza in Japan highlights in particular the political dynamics that contributed to mafia formation before and during the Cold War.

Rather than exhibiting a straightforward coincidence of resource privatization with inadequate state regulation, the formative situations in both cases (and for the Chinese Triads as well) included massive incursions on property and use rights – the kind of huge "takings" that Marxist theory refers to as "primitive accumulation" – substantial enough to set off revolts, revolutions, insurgencies, "social" banditry. Mixed in with the rebels and bandits were persons engaged in predatory crimes, especially armed robbery and kidnapping; mixed in with the criminals were rebels and "Robin Hoods."

Organized thuggery evolved from these situations, with gangs of toughs mediating security for the destabilized populations. Forming themselves into secretive fraternal organizations shored up by ritual practices, and elaborating charter myths in which they claimed not only to restore order but to institute a kind of rough justice, the gangs also exacted a price. Predation at this juncture took on the more parasitic form of extortion and racketeering. Most important, the mediators cultivated the cover of legitimate economic and political elites. For the mafia, the yakuza, and the Triads, the resulting sponsorship became especially pronounced during the Cold War era when the United States, along with allied and proxy governments, tolerated and even encouraged organized crime as a wedge in the fight against communism (Kaplan and Dubro 1986:46–69; Booth 1999; Schneider and Schneider 2003:49–81). In this context, the formations in question became more audacious, especially in relation to the real-estate and construction industries of major towns and cities, winning public contracts, and recruiting and disciplining laborers in these sectors. Control over gambling and gaming, as practiced especially by the working classes, remained a constant.

The classical mafias of course expanded into illegal trafficking. Beginning in the 1960s, Yakuza gangs increasingly trafficked in Korean-produced methamphetamines for Japanese consumers, and in women as well. Indeed, as the Japanese economic bubble inflated, and Japanese businessmen and (disproportionately male) tourists traveled throughout Asia, gang members invested in a parallel expansion of brothels and bars, supplied with sex-workers illegally recruited in Asian countries, including Japan. "The Japanese sex tours encouraged the yakuza to follow the excess of their countrymen across East Asia," say Kaplan and Dubro (1986:200). A parallel traffic in contraband commodities flourished as well (Kaplan and Dubro 1986:197–208). The Sicilian mafia coordinated the international movement of heroin from the late 1970s through the 1980s, taking over from the French Connection while building on prior networks of cigarette smuggling. Clandestine refineries, moving into high gear in 1978, were situated in Palermo and its suburbs, as well as along the western coast and in the mountain town of San Giuseppe Jato. Over the next few years, between four and five tons of pure heroin were refined each year in Sicily, worth 600 million dollars in annual profits and meeting roughly 30 percent of United States demand (Paoli 1997:317–318). Nevertheless, trafficking on this scale was short-lived for Sicilian gangsters and served mainly to help build their power base at home. Specifically, it enabled the most aggressive of the mafia factions to capitalize several new construction firms, broaching their postwar ambition of directing the construction sector of Palermo and the regional economy. According to DIA (*Direzione Italiana Antimafia*) evidence, public works became a privileged locus for reinvesting drug profits, the goal being "complete control and the substantial internal conditioning of the entrepreneurial world" in this sector (DIA, quoted in Paoli 1997:319).

For the Sicilian mafia (as for the Japanese yakuza), anti-mafia prosecutions and reform movements within the "home" regions and locales were already undermining trafficking capacity in the 1980s. Nor was the move into trafficking entirely uncontroversial in the first place. Some US mafiosi, for example, took a moral position in opposition to narcotics, at least initially. At the same time (and with similar moral controversy), other social formations accustomed to using violence with or without state sponsorship have engaged in trafficking as a source of revenue, often to purchase arms. In the 1980s, the Nicaraguan Contras guarded airstrips and served as couriers on behalf of Colombian and US cocaine dealers, receiving in exchange cash, light aircraft, and supplies for their cause. Insurgent groups from the FARC in southern Colombia, to the mujahadeen in pre-Taliban Afghanistan, to the IRA and ETA in Europe also fall into this category, as do the counter-insurgent groups that seek to repress them, and also the secret services and police who collaborate in counter-insurgency. The remnant paramilitaries and secret services of deposed regimes, from Serbia, to the Talaban, and perhaps to Iraq, easily take on a trafficking role. Even Hassidic diamond dealers have found it convenient to raise money for their religious community by helping Colombian dealers unload their cash: a Yeshiva network spanning New York, Miami, Montreal, and Tel Aviv may launder as much 200 million dollars per year (Naylor 2002:157–159).

Since the end of the Cold War, political upheavals have created opportunities for racketeering on every continent. Informal economies, ignored when not harassed by state institutions, depend on more or less extortionist gangs of toughs to police claims, enforce contracts, and settle disputes. It is, nevertheless, an empirical and a local question of what kinds of people (men, really), with what organizational and political resources, become the violent entrepreneurs, and the extent to which they further organize. Whether the resulting mafias and incipient mafias are on a career path toward global trafficking, and how trafficking articulates with their local development, are also variables that need to be sorted out in each case. What follows are some further specifics regarding the Sicilian mafia. Based on our years of anthropological research in Sicily, recently supplemented by the depositions of mafiosi who have turned state's witness, they suggest diagnostic points for comparison.

## RECENT HISTORICAL BACKGROUND

In 1950 a land reform was enacted in Sicily, but by this time mafiosi, historically the racketeering mediators of the latifundist agrarian regime, had something new to offer:

electoral support for regional and national politicians of, primarily, the Christian Democratic Party. Estimates are that, between friends and kin, each mafioso could muster at least 40 to 50 votes, adding up to 75,000 to 100,000 "friendly" votes in the province of Palermo alone. The quid pro quo for these votes was the mafia's relative immunity from prosecution or onerous jail terms, and the *nulla osta* to penetrate several new domains: the administration of the land reform, urban produce markets, and new apartment-building construction and public works, in particular. The failure of the Italian state to prevent the Sicilian mafia from taking over heroin trafficking in the late 1970s is also attributable to that "wicked deal."

Intense conflict over new urban opportunities and drugs led to the insurgence, between 1979 and 1983, of a particularly aggressive group of mafiosi from the interior agricultural town of Corleone, known as the Corleonesi. Feeling excluded from Palermo's postwar real-estate and construction boom, which mafia "families" in the city's environs had pounced on, and apprehensive about being disrespected as junior partners in drug deals, also initially dominated by the Palermo bosses, they launched a series of kidnappings for ransom, committed without the approval of the Palermo groups and against the mafia's own rules. Not only were the targets of these kidnappings rich men; several were construction impresarios who were closely allied to particular Palermo mafiosi.

During their *scalata* or rise to power, which began in the late 1970s, the Corleonesi assassinated many of the Palermo bosses and, more audaciously, 15 police officers, magistrates, and public officials, labeled "excellent cadavers" in the media. They organized the savage bombings that killed two of the most important anti-mafia prosecutors, Giovanni Falcone and Paolo Borsellino, in 1992. Two bomb blasts intended to destroy artistic monuments, one in Rome and the other in Florence, are attributed to them, as are bombings in Milan. Salvatore (Totò) Riina, was the forceful architect of these deeds. (He is nicknamed "the Beast" in Sicily.) Riina's affiliate of long standing, Giovanni Brusca (known as the "Butcher"), from San Giuseppe Jato in the mountains above Palermo, personally detonated the dynamite that massacred Falcone and is notorious as well for strangling the young son of a justice collaborator then dissolving his body in a vat of acid.

## The Mafia as a Violent and Secretive Organization

Underscoring the territorial grounding of classical mafia formations are the central organizational features and cultural practices of the Sicilian mafia. Consider, first, the nucleus of mafia organization, the territorial "family" or *cosca* (evoking the tightly bundled leaves of an artichoke), each one named for the rural town or city neighborhood where it is located. These *cosche* operate like mutual aid societies, enforcing silence vis-à-vis the law while supporting members who are unlucky enough to be arrested and convicted. Prison terms rarely interrupt a mafioso's career, not only because corrupt officials make it possible to conduct business from jail – the Ucciardone (Palermo's massive, nineteenth-century Bourbon prison) is nicknamed the "hotel of the mafia" – but because an incarcerated man has the assurance that his *cosca* will take care of emergency lawyers' fees, subsidies for his wife and children, even a daughter's dowry if it comes to that. According to the depositions of the justice collaborators, ironically labeled *pentiti* or penitents, each *cosca* builds up a fund for this. In addition, when the need to help a prisoner arises, members contribute from their own pockets, aware that to default could jeopardize their security in the future. Mafiosi tell stories of imprisoned affiliates seeking revenge upon their release because they had felt abandoned while in jail.

To some extent, *cosca* organization reflects kinship organization, the status of mafioso being passed from father to son, uncle to nephew. By the same token, mafiosi make much use of the fictive kin tie of godparenthood, naming each other as *compare* or "godfather" to their children. In families where the father, uncles, cousins, older brothers, and godfathers are *cosca* members, it is almost obligatory for up and coming boys to consider a criminal career.

Although the word "family" is frequently applied to the *cosca*, however, it is best understood as metaphorical, an evocation of the presumed solidarity of kinship. Significantly, the son of a mafioso may be recognized from an early age to lack the *fegato* or guts for "criminal reliability." Not only does the mafia pass over inappropriate kin; some *cosche* have rules against admitting too many kinsmen at a time, believing that mafiosi seeking to induct more than one son or brother must be planning a power grab. Fortunately for the mafia, becoming a mafioso is also a career open to talent. From the *pentiti* accounts, it is clear that individual bosses like to choose (even anoint) unrelated newcomers, so much so that young delinquents go out of their way to commit petty crimes in order to impress a would-be sponsor. Antonino Calderone, an early *pentito,* puts it this way: "around every man of honor of a certain rank is always a circle of 20 or 30 kids – nobodies who want to become something . . . there to do small favors, to be put to the test . . . like rock stars looking up to Madonna." Here too, problems can arise, for although recruiting such enthusiasts is crucial to a *cosca*'s viability, it also poses a challenge to discipline and leadership. Care must be taken against "overloading" – "letting in too many youths at a time."

The mafia reinforces a notion of exclusivity and belonging through a symbolically laden initiation rite, in which novices hold the burning image of a saint while their sponsor pricks their finger and, mixing the blood and ashes, gets them to swear an oath of life-long loyalty and silence before outsiders. Exclusively male banquets, hunting parties, and horseplay reinforce a kind of bonding. Mutual goodwill is further induced by an idiosyncratic way of speaking, terms of address, and linguistically playful nicknames, as well as by a charter myth based on an influential novel, *I Beati Paoli,* ("The Blessed Paulists)", published in 1908. This book narrates the adventures of an eighteenth-century secret society of *giustizieri* who, disguised in hoods and masks, met at night in the galleries and tunnels that honeycomb the subsoil of Palermo, pronouncing and executing justice.

As might be imagined, the *cosche* are structured internally along lines of age and privilege, with new recruits, the "soldiers," being expected to take greater risks and accrue lesser rewards. Generally, the senior bosses monopolize the elected leadership positions, but there are famous cases of audacious upstarts proving themselves through exceptional deeds, and taking over. Regarding inter-*cosca* relations, the mafia is, to a large extent, decentralized, yet mafiosi are in constant communication across the various families. More to the point, Palermo and its hinterland is the Sicilian mafia's center of gravity – the locus for the establishment in 1957 of an admittedly fragile overarching "Commission" that continued off and on into the 1990s.

## CONDITIONING AND PROVISIONING

Mafiosi have long established an organic connection to their surroundings through two ongoing processes of association. One is the process of self-consciously *conditioning* elite interlocutors, constructing webs of mutual reciprocity that go beyond any narrow instrumentality. The other, corollary process involves *provisioning* ordinary folk. Because of the vast array of conditioned political connections that mafiosi enjoy, they are often better able than nominal officials of the state to assist ordinary Sicilians – with jobs, access to bureaucratic offices, solutions to other problems. Neither process entails direct blackmail as a *modus operandi*, yet the mafia's reputation for violence surely lurks in the background, ensnaring conditioned elites and provisioned subalterns in a potentially embarrassing, if not frightening, tangle of social relations. At the same time, however, mafiosi invest in making these relations rewarding and normal, even prestigious – such that their interlocutors and clients might think themselves fortunate to be involved.

Mafia *capi* seek to rub shoulders with professionals, politicians, officials, and businessmen in informal settings conducive to mutual enjoyment and casual talk. Such persons are potential allies in the degree that they are "friendly," the point being to condition them to make decisions, or non-decisions, that enable mafiosi to thrive. Typically, a mafioso who must solve a problem involving a key institution asks himself or a close friend, *"cu ci avemu 'dda?"* – slang for "who do we have there?" – meaning, whom can we rely on to lend a hand?

During our first years in Sicily, in the 1960s and 1970s, the web of associations that underpinned conditioned relationships was less hidden than it later became, and our understanding of how it worked comes partly from personal observation. Mafiosi we knew invited local and regional notables – the mayor, the parliamentary deputy, clerics, lawyers, bankers, and owners of land and enterprises – to their major life-cycle celebrations, above all weddings and baptisms. They often also asked such persons to serve in the role of witness to a wedding, or godparent to a child, this being a way to establish a life-long patron–client relation. As a rule, the invitations were not refused. Although they surely elicited varying degrees of apprehension about eventual requests for reciprocity, it was considered flattering and possibly auspicious to be asked. Significantly, large numbers of officials and professionals joined the mourners at mafia funerals.

Besides life-cycle celebrations, a strategic occasion for nurturing relationships was the rustic banquet or *schiticchia* – standard fare at the annual sheep-shearings in the countryside. We participated in several of these at which the parish priest, veterinarian, politicians, and officers of the Carabinieri joined shepherds, mafiosi, and their families in awesome feasts of stewed innards and roasted lamb or goat. Women, it should be noted, were present at these events, cooking and serving the meals. Much as at weddings and baptisms, the wives of mafiosi interacted with the wives of notables, some of whom might already be godparents to their children.

These references to rural properties and rustic banquets should not give the impression that occasions for amicable encounters between the mafia and other elites are only small-town affairs. It is our impression (based on the *pentito* reports) that mafiosi and notables from Palermo made extensive use of secluded country houses to hunt, target shoot, and banquet with "friends and friends of friends" (see Calderone in Arlacchi 1993:116). The estate and villa of Michele Greco, *capo* mafioso of the suburb of Ciaculli, was one such place, replete with a shooting range. The comings and goings of important personages to this property generated constant gossip and a certain mystique. In February, 1985, when Michele and his brother, Salvatore, were fugitives, the police and Carabinieri sealed off and conducted a four-day blitz in and around Ciaculli. Rumors immediately circulated that while searching Greco's house (in vain), they had stumbled upon a torch-lit network of tunnels and galleries accessible through a trap-door in the living room, evoking the *Beati Paoli*. Shortly after this account was published with great fanfare in the newspapers, however, investigators learned that it was largely false – the fantasy of a journalist and the policemen responsible for the search. What existed was merely a basement room fitted with a kitchen for entertaining friends.

If the top bosses and notables of Palermo were welcome guests in country settings, they had at their disposal as well any number of urban locales well suited for privileged encounters. The luxurious *art nouveau* hotel, the Villa Igea, was one marked venue. Its manager and assistant were convicted in 1999 for allowing it to become a retreat for fugitives, a place for the bosses to hold receptions, an employer of "recommended" personnel, and a safe haven for drug traffickers. At one of his hotels, the Zagarella, Nino Salvo, mafioso holder of the tax-collecting franchise for all of Sicily, entertained powerful politicians, among them Salvo Lima, Christian Democratic mayor of Palermo, later a deputy in the European Parliament, and a regular weekend poker companion (Calderone in Arlacchi 1993:175). In 1995 this hotel became a centerpiece in the dramatic trial of former Prime Minister Giulio Andreotti, who was accused of having colluded with the mafia. Introduced into evidence was a photograph taken in June, 1979, showing Andreotti at the Zagarella with Lima, Nino Salvo, and other regional Christian Democrat leaders. The manager of the hotel at the time testified that Salvo had ordered the "best possible" buffet and personally conducted Andreotti on a tour of the finest rooms (Arlacchi 1995:105. In the course of the trial, however, Andreotti denied ever knowing Nino Salvo.)

Thanks to their skill in conditioning – elevating the comfort level of officials and professionals in various sectors and institutions – mafiosi themselves constitute a resource for local populations. They – and sometimes they alone – know where to go to "fix things." Their clients are myriad – people who want jobs, who want to move up on the list of eligibility for public housing, who have a bone to pick with a neighbor, whose children are taking examinations in school and need recommendations. These large and small things are an integral part of the reciprocities that have long sustained poor people in Sicily and continue to do so today. One detects their importance from the very word that is used in approaching employers (*datore di lavoro*, "givers of work"): can they, will they, *assumere* a person? This word, which in English means "to assume," also has a religious connotation in Italian. The Assumption was when God "assumed" – that is took responsibility for – Mary who rose, by His will, into Heaven. In provisioning the supplicant poor of Sicily with mediated access to various institutions, mafiosi pave the way for some of them to be "assumed" in this almost miraculous sense.

Here a quid pro quo exists: the votes of the client and his or her close kin are to be cast as the mafioso dictates. Other reciprocities are open-ended but possible – so much so that most people go out of their way to avoid entanglements. Unfortunately, life is not predictable, however, and things happen. A friend of ours was a young teenager when her father incurred some debts and turned to a mafioso for help. Some time later, he was asked to hide a fugitive in their small apartment. At age 16, our friend found herself giving over her room to this unexplained and uncomfortably inexplicable stranger.

## The Mafia and Deep Politics

As the organized crime groups of southern Italy and Sicily were nurturing their relationship with the Christian Democratic Party after World War II, nuclei of former fascists, secret-service operatives, and military personnel were weaving a different, but eventually overlapping, Cold War structure of power in northern Italy. This web resembled the covert cliques of army officers and secret-service personnel that staged coups d'état in Greece and several Latin American countries during the 1960s and 1970s. Indeed both the CIA and NATO had contingency plans for Italy similar to those deployed in Greece and Chile should a popular front or communist-socialist alliance succeed in forming a government (Ginsborg 1990:258–259, 333–335).

Right-wing counter-revolutionaries actually attempted a coup in 1964, another in 1970, and, although both turbid plans failed to materialize, a possible third in 1974 (Paoli 1996:27). Agostino Cordova, a senior investigating magistrate in Palmi, Calabria, has studied terrorist acts that occurred from 1969 to 1974, as well as the bombing of the Bologna railroad station in 1980 in which 85 people died and 200 were wounded. Although ultra-left terrorist groups were also operating in these years, his 1993 report argues that these particular incidents had "germinated in the 'humus' of Right-wing secret associations" (Paoli 1996:30–31). It is possible, although unproven, that the bombings utilized explosives stolen from secret weapons caches that NATO had "left behind" in Europe in case of a Soviet invasion. NATO's "Project Stay Behind," known as "Gladio" in Italy, had supposedly been dismantled in 1972, but not all of the arms and munitions could be located when the covert training of militias finally came to an end.

Besides the mafia, Italy harbors a rich array of secretive organizations of which Freemasonry is the most important. Recruiting "liberal-minded" elites committed to the right of "free association," Italian masons were estimated to number some 15,000 in the 1980s (Di Bernardo 1987; Mola 1992). They are, they insist, "neither a religion, nor a philosophy, nor a political ideology or socio-economic program; but rather *a meeting place for persons who would otherwise not be able to encounter each other*" (Mola 1992:757; our emphasis).

Apparently, the plotters of the 1970 coup – the so-called Borghese Coup – forged their anti-communist alliance by transforming certain Masonic lodges into meeting places for a more diverse than usual representation of elites, including some skilled in the use of violence. In the language of the Italian press, these branches of transformed Freemasonry were "covert" or "deviated." The model was the infamous Lodge *Propaganda Due*, or P2, founded by a former Tuscan fascist and dual citizen of Italy and Argentina, Licio Gelli, in the mid-1960s. Gelli was prodigious at enrolling in his organization like-minded men of the military, the police, and the secret services, as well as highly placed personages in government, business, and the professions (De Lutiis 1991:284–287). A police raid on his Arezzo villa in March, 1981, uncovered evidence that P2 had developed a so-called "strategy of tension" during the 1970s, aimed at using systematic blackmail, bribes, promises of advancement, and intimidation to displace left-of-center forces from the government (Nicastro 1993:166).

In postwar Sicily as in Italy, professional elites joined Masonic lodges in large numbers. According to the *pentito* Tommaso Buscetta, however, in his day it was "absolutely prohibited for a 'man of honor' to be a member of a masonic order...their aims were totally different and in part incompatible" (quoted in Nicastro 1993:33). Calderone says the same, but from a different angle. Many judges were Masons, he reports, which tempted the mafia to want a relationship, yet the Masons considered mafiosi "too cunning to be inducted." For a mafioso to join, moreover, would have meant to serve two masters – with the potential to betray one or the other (Calderone in Arlacchi 1993:178–179). And yet, sharing a similar logic of secrecy, initiation, and fraternal solidarity, there was an affinity between the two institutions, and some mafiosi did participate in Freemasonry, for example Nino Salvo, Sicily's famed mafioso tax-collector (Nicastro 1993:190). As the Corleonesi gained ascendancy in the 1980s, Riina engaged a Palermitan, Pino Mandalari, as his accountant and business advisor; Mandalari was at once a Mason and collusive with the mafia (Nicastro 1993:188–194).

Calderone reports that in planning for the attempted coup of 1970, the nucleus of plotters approached certain "men of honor" to engage their participation in the installation of new prefects, but the mafia only entertained the idea as a bluff, hoping to "adjust" several trials without actually having to do anything (Calderone in Arlacchi 1993:83–86). Subsequently, in 1977, Stefano Bontade, a formidable player in the expansion of trafficking in narcotics, announced that certain Masons wanted to form a coalition with the mafia's highest-ranking members, two or three from each province. Michele Greco and Bontade himself were chosen from the province of Palermo, Pippo Calderone (Antonino's brother) from Catania (Calderone in Arlacchi 1993:178–179; Nicastro 1993:188). According to a former Grand Master of Italian Masonry, Giuliano Di Bernardo, during the years 1976 to 1980, mafiosi competed to become Masons (Di Bernardo 1987; see also Paoli 1996); it was the drug mafia's way of approaching and infiltrating power. In its 1986 Report, the Parliamentary Anti-mafia Commission claimed there were "2,441 men of honor...distributed among 113 lodges in Sicily" (Ministry of Interior [Italy] 1994); clearly, Masonry "opened roads to a certain level" (Nicastro 1993:187–188).

As the boundary between the mafia and (deviated) Freemasonry became blurred, newspapers reported a growing rift among Sicilian Masons between an older faction, loyal to its traditions, and a new, brazen group that "admitted anyone." Whereas Masonry had once been exclusive, restricted to bankers, professionals, leading businessmen seeking to create a nucleus of power, in the new, "squalid situation," regardless of their place in society, ideologues were joining the super-secret lodges and so were mafiosi and drug traffickers. Calderone traces the initiative for this change to a new secret lodge whose actions were hidden, even from the members of Freemasonry itself (Calderone in Arlacchi 1993:178–179).

At the height of narco-trafficking through Sicily, there was also a growing entanglement between "mafia Masons" and the state-authorized secret services (see De Lutiis

1991; Nicastro 1993; Paoli 1996). Members of Italy's military secret service, SID, later called SISMI, appeared on Gelli's list of P2 associates. According to the journalist Nicastro, by the end of the 1970s, SISMI had developed close ties to P2, having become a "sort of super-SISMI," more secretive and restricted than before. An all-purpose man of affairs (*faccendiere*) and SISMI informer, Francesco Pazienza, close to the Rome-based mafioso of the Corleonese faction, Pippo Calò, participated in this alliance (Di Lutiis 1991; Nicastro 1993:166–171). Perhaps not surprisingly, P2 also held within its orbit a number of shadow financiers adapted for the money-laundering function, most famously Michele Sindona and Roberto Calvi, both close personal friends of Gelli and founding members of the covert lodge.

Sindona purchased the Franklin National Bank in New York in 1973 in order to loot some 45 million dollars from its coffers, driving it into bankruptcy. In the summer of 1979, he attempted to flee US jurisdiction by staging his own bogus kidnapping on New York's streets and his subsequent bogus wounding at the hands of his (Mason) doctor in Palermo. Two *pentiti* of the early 1990s have revealed how several bosses, dependent on Sindona to launder their drug profits, became exasperated by his troubles and wanted his head (Arlacchi 1995:40–47). Eventually convicted on murder charges as well as fraudulent bankruptcy in Italy, Sindona died after drinking a cup of poisoned coffee in a Milan prison in 1986. (Whether his death was a suicide or a homicide is uncertain.)

In the late 1970s, as Sindona's house of cards was collapsing, Calvi, a former ally, became a competitor and enemy. On June 18, 1981, his body was found dangling beneath Blackfriars Bridge in London, weighed down by pieces of concrete, with British authorities unable to determine how he got, or was placed, there. In 1996, Francesco Di Carlo, a former England-based interlocutor of mafia finance, implicated mafioso Pippo Calò as the principal organizer of Calvi's murder, with Sindona and Gelli as possible *mandanti* (sponsors of the crime). Apparently Calvi had tried to kite mafia funds to cover the collapse of his empire's keystone, the Catholic Banco Ambrosiano.

Summing up both the political and the financial entanglements of P2, the Cordova report speculates that "deviated" masonry was "the connective tissue of the organization of power" in Cold War Italy (quoted in Nicastro 1993:186). The journalist Guido Ruotolo uses the word "metastasis" to make a similar point. Reports from the Ministry of the Interior refer to "networks of illicit *lobbying*" (using the English word). All have in mind a capillary formation that extended through virtually the entire national territory – a sort of "transversal super-party" for people of all parties occupying high positions of power. The *pentito*, Leonardo Messina, reminds us that well into the 1980s, narco-mafiosi were plugged in. Inserting themselves into the metastasis, they ended up with adjusted trials and useful financial contacts. "Naturally," he adds, "I am referring to the absolutely secret lodges, for which you would never find membership lists. It is not written anywhere that Riina is affiliated" (quoted in Nicastro 1993:187).

## ANTI-MAFIA

The particulars of one mafia – in this case the mafia that has named the phenomenon – suggest criteria for comparison, among them social organization and cultural practices, modes of conditioning and provisioning, patterns of violence, and depth of political entanglement. We might contrast, for example, how Colombian drug "cartels" take care of local communities. Responsible for a staggering death toll in street battles in the shanty towns of Medellin, and for exposing resident boys and women to risk as couriers, they have also financed churches and projects for community enhancement which benefit these neighborhoods. Meanwhile, conditioning public officials through bribery, intimidation, and outright purchase plays a larger part in the Colombian mafia than was ever characteristic of Sicilian mafiosi (Roldan in press).

Concerned with particulars, we expect all mafias to be grounded, each in its specific context. This makes the image of multiple mafias being networked into a global criminal "industry" or "system" seem greatly exaggerated, even as a trajectory for the future. The networking that occurs is probably better described as a percolating series of fragile coalitions, uniting contingent operators for transient ends. Most important, the particulars, and the significance of place, illuminate a countervailing phenomenon: *anti-mafia*.

Just as the "long 1980s" (the years from the late 1970s to the early 1990s) became a crucible of violence in Sicily, they also framed an intensified police and judicial repression of the mafia, supported by a Palermo-centered anti-mafia social movement. During the years 1986–87, sometimes called the "Palermo Spring" (Palermo *Primavera*), Sicilian prosecutors indicted 475 mafiosi, trying 460 of them in a bunker courthouse specially constructed for this purpose inside the walls of the Ucciardone. Most were convicted and, to the surprise of many, the convictions were upheld through the final stage of appeal in 1992. Following the initial convictions, the prosecutors were undercut by a public-opinion backlash, the purpose of which, they believe, was to delegitimize them. From their perspective, the attacks opened the door to a series of *embrogli* that prefigured the dramatic massacres of Falcone and Borsellino, also in 1992. Yet both the judiciary and the social movement were revitalized in the aftermath of these terrible murders. The social movement, indeed, went on to embrace the mission of educating schoolchildren about legality and engaging them in the recuperation of the built environment, defined as having been damaged by the mafia (see Schneider and Schneider 2003).

The citizens' anti-mafia movement demonstrates the potential for humans to intervene in addressing problems of extraordinary violence and illegality. Between this movement and the concerted police and judicial prosecution of the mafia, the excesses of Sicily's "long 1980s" have given way to a time of relative calm. This is not to ignore the clouds on the horizon. Many Sicilian social scientists and intellectuals are concerned that the current Italian Prime Minister Silvio Berlusconi's campaign against the Italian judiciary and politics of *garantismo* (the single-issue defense of civil liberties) risks undermining the anti-mafia process. Alarmingly, Forza Italia, Berlusconi's political party, does well among Sicilian voters, above all working-class voters, who feel that "too much legality" has cost them jobs. Yet there are reasons to stay hopeful. Sicily has, for the first time, a vibrant and aware civil society; its institutions are less corrupt than they were; and its capital city, Palermo, appears to have adopted a sane and more or less transparent urban plan. As happened in relation to the Ku Klux Klan after the Civil Rights movement in the US South, it is no longer possible to whitewash or valorize the mafia in public discourse. The very terms of the conversation have changed.

Not surprisingly, given the ease of global communication, citizens and law-enforcement authorities mobilizing against other mafias seek to learn from Sicily's experience. Again, however, the particulars matter; not all "anti-mafias" are the same. Beyond the pale of the respectable working class, the residents of the Medellin shanty towns have recently been terrorized by the Colombian state's "war on drugs." In part energized by racial and class discrimination, in part by United States-financed drug enforcement operations, this is an *anti-mafia* of a different, less hopeful sort.

## REFERENCES

Arlacchi, Pino (1993) *Men of Dishonor: Inside the Sicilian Mafia*. New York: William Morrow.

Arlacchi, Pino (1995) *Il processo: Giulio Andreotti sotto accusa a Palermo*. Milano: Rizzoli.

Beare, Margaret E., and Robert T. Taylor (1999) *Major Issues Relating to Organized Crime within the Context of Economic Relationships*. Law Commission of Canada: Nathanson Centre for the Study of Organized Crime and Corruption.

Booth, Martin (1999) *The Dragon Syndicates: The Global Phenomenon of the Triads*. New York: Carroll and Graf.

Castells, Manuel (1998) *The Information Age: Economy, Society and Culture. Volume 1. End of Millennium*. Oxford: Blackwell.

De Lutiis, Giuseppe (1991) *Storia dei servizi segreti in Italia*. Rome: Editori Riuniti.

Di Bernardo, Giuliano (1987) *Filosofia della massoneria: l'immagine massonica dell'uomo*. Venice: Marsilio Editori.

Gambetta, Diego (1993) *The Sicilian Mafia: The Business of Protection*. Cambridge, MA: Harvard University Press.

Ginsborg, Paul (1990) *A History of Contemporary Italy: Society and Politics, 1943–1988*. London: Penguin Books.

Humphrey, Caroline (1999) Russian Protection Rackets and the Appropriation of Law and Order. In *States and Illegal Practices*, ed. J. McC. Heyman, pp. 199–233. Oxford: Berg.

Kaplan, David E., and Alec Dubro (1986) *Yakuza: The Explosive Account of Japan's Criminal Underworld*. Reading, MA: Addison-Wesley.

Ministry of the Interior, [Italy] (1994) *Rapporto annuale sul fenomeno della criminalità organizzata per il 1993*. April.

Mola, Aldo A. (1992) *Storia della massoneria italiana: dalle origini ai nostri giorni*. Milano: Bompiani.

Naylor, Robert T. (2002) *Wages of Crime: Black Markets, Illegal Finance, and the Underworld Economy*. Ithaca, NY: Cornell University Press.

Nicastro, Franco (1993) *Il caso Contrada, le trame di boss, poteri occulti e servizi segreti*. Palermo: Edizioni Arbor.

Paoli, Letizia (1996) The Integration of the Italian Crime Scene. Unpublished MS.

Paoli, Letizia (1997) The Pledge to Secrecy: Culture, Structure and Action of Mafia Associations. Ph.D. dissertation, European University Institute (Florence).

Roldan, Mary (in press) Wounded Medellin: Narcotics Traffic against a Background of Industrial Decline. In *Wounded Cities: Destruction and Reconstruction in an Age of Globalization*, ed. Jane Schneider and Ida Susser. Oxford: Berg.

Schneider, Jane C., and Peter T. Schneider (2003) *Reversible Destiny: Mafia, Antimafia, and the Struggle for Palermo*. Berkeley: University of California Press.

Verdery, Katherine (1996) *What was Socialism, and What Comes Next?* Princeton, NJ: Princeton University Press.

Volkov, Vadim (2002) *Violent Entrepreneurs: The Use of Force in the Making of Russian Capitalism*. Ithaca, NY: Cornell University Press.

# 20 Militarization

## *Catherine Lutz*

Anthropologists have so far found relatively little use for the concept of militarization, focusing instead on but one aspect of the process, which is war. This is unfortunate if not unexpected, given that war is perhaps the most "visible" of human political institutions, a prominence assured by its bloody and embodied spectacularity, its explicit connection to states' pursuit of power, and the ideological heavy hand that emerges to legitimate and even glorify its massive contradiction of life's foundational imperative. Given the original assignment of anthropology to the task of providing just the opening chapters of human political history, and given social evolutionary thinking, the discipline was to focus on so-called primitive warfare, such violence being considered a key index of the savage.

Larger social contexts have directed anthropological attention to non-industrial warfare and away from militarization as well. Anthropology in the US, for example, began working primarily with Native Americans, a predominantly war-refugee population. While the ethnographic method has sometimes militated against the study of modern warfare, by the end of the twentieth century anthropologists had begun examining war and terror in an increasingly militarized world: one where civilians had become the primary victims of war, where weaponry was a key international commodity, and where state terror had grown to unprecedented, epidemic proportions (Sluka 2000). Anthropologists looked at war almost everywhere but in the United States, the country that by then had become a global font of war and militarization. Few post-World War II anthropologists named the US empire that emerged when its German, British, and Japanese rivals had been decimated, but many began to take notice in the atmosphere of the Vietnam intervention. Just a few years later, many of the numerous anthropologists working in what has been considered the US's Central American "backyard" suddenly found themselves on the front lines of the counter-insurgency wars of that era. Not only was war's toll more gruesomely visible (in a few cases targeting anthropologists themselves), but it became easier to see how a putative peace in the US was linked to war overseas, and how the triplets of neoliberalism, impoverishment, and state-sanctioned terror and torture expanded together over time.

There remains a deep conviction among respected military historians, and the public at large which voraciously consumes their work, that the machinery of militarization runs first of all on the oil of aggressive instinct. Anthropologists, political theorists, and other historians have instead asked how political subjectivities are formed, and what social-historical processes accelerate war and militarization. Weberian analysis has seen modernity itself (including bureaucratization and all it entails, as well as notions of progress and the perfectibility of social arrangements) as the necessary condition for mass industrial warfare at the least, and genocide at worst (Bauman 1989). Analysts have asked how both militarization and demilitarization relate to periodic crises of masculinity, to gender more generally (Enloe 2000), and to the process of ethnicization (Malkki 1995).

Scholars have examined how militarization relates or responds to capitalism and its vicissitudes, noting how it appears as a resolution to crises of over-production: the state buys the arms industry's products and then destroys them, or engages in arms races and international arms sales that call for the production of new generations of weapons. Such interests do not prevent massive irrationalities and "blowback" in such state practices, as well as in attempts to manage subordinate arenas of the empire. Historical sociologists have also noted the global pattern of the last two centuries in which hegemonic powers in decline militarize while the hegemon in waiting focuses on technical economic development; for example, Japanese scientists recently developed a new computer 20 times more powerful than existing models, which was designed to model climate change, while development of computers in the US was tailored to the task of modeling the less complex problem of weapons and weapons use. The era of accelerating globalization and flexible accumulation regimes can be related to militarization, as these processes erode the distinction between external and internal violence that the nation-state heretofore had given heightened significance. A growing global arms trade results, as does the outsourcing of violence by the US to accompany and discipline the workforce of the now global assembly line. The rise of neoliberalism and the retraction of the welfare state has also meant growing immiseration, and the social movements or desperation with which people respond are repressed with further militarization.

Inattention to the state in pre-1980s anthropology also meant that warfare was examined as a question of local ecologies, alliance formation, and decision-making. As state processes came into view, anthropologists began to examine two new problems: (a) the erosions in sovereignty that accompany the rise of transnational economic and legal entities like the World Bank, the United Nations, the World Economic Forum, the World Social Forum and the human rights community, and non-governmental organizations; and (b) the related rise of paramilitaries, predatory states, and state terror as an international elite came to be allied (in part through weapons and military training transactions) against the disempowered and to wield more military might internally than across borders.

Theorists of militarization have also related the process to resource shortages, the most important now being oil and water, with the former connected to the epoch-making invention of the car. Militarization has been an implicit part of the relationship between the great migrations of the late part of the twentieth century, often due to war or poverty, and their threats to local capitalist social relations reflected in paroxysms of nativism and nationalism, which can feed in turn into the militarization process.

A number of anthropologists have found or put themselves in the midst of violent whirlwinds that break out in the process of militarization, and they have occasionally traced the vicissitudes of demilitarization. They have shown that war is about social deformation, silencing, and resilience as much as it is about the body's physical destruction. It is important to set alongside these more explicitly war-centered works what might be called "anthropologies of immiseration." They reveal the indistinguishability and interdependence of physical and structural violence. This is in contrast to the notion that violence is a mere tool or accident en route to the pursuit of a state's political interest, or that there are separate "forms" of power, the military, the political, and/or the economic. These works can be used to illustrate the intertwining of the violence of the twentieth century with the widening international and intra-national gap between the rich and poor, and with the surges of old and new forms of racism. I examine here the emergence of this violence, focusing on the historical and anthropological contexts of militarization in, or involving, the United States.

## MILITARIZATION: AN INTRODUCTION

A long process of militarization and empire-building has reshaped almost every element of global social life during the twentieth century. By militarization, I mean "the contradictory and tense social process in which civil society organizes itself for the production of violence" (Geyer 1989:79). This process involves an intensification of the labor and resources allocated to military purposes, including the shaping of other institutions in synchrony with military goals. Militarization is simultaneously a discursive process, involving a shift in general societal beliefs and values in ways necessary to legitimate the use of force, the organization of large standing armies and their leaders, and the higher taxes or tribute used to pay for them. Militarization is intimately connected not only to the obvious – the increasing size of armies and the resurgence of militant nationalisms and militant fundamentalisms – but also to the less visible deformation of human potentials into the hierarchies of race, class, gender, and sexuality, and to the shaping of national histories in ways that glorify and legitimate military action.

While militarization's sources and shapes have emerged within innumerable states, corporations, and localities, the United States is now the largest wellspring for this global process. A nation made by war, the US was birthed not just by the Revolution of 1776, but also by wars against Native Americans and the violence required to capture and enslave many millions of African people. Twentieth-century US militarization accelerated in three major bursts: with the 1939 loosing of fascist forces in a world never recovered from World War I and the US attempt to counter the German empire, again with the establishment of the national security state in 1947, and now with the events of September 11, 2001.

Bitterly watching the US charge headlong onto the slaughter fields of Flanders, and American intellectuals' enthusiastic drumbeat of acquiescence, Randolph Bourne called war "the health of the state" (1964). He meant that the state's power grows in wartime, accumulating legal powers and public wealth to pursue the battle, and that it often maintains that expanded power far into the putative peacetime that follows. Bourne was certainly proven prescient, as the last century's wars enlarged the government and enriched military corporations, shrank legal controls over both entities, and captured an empire of post-conflict markets. And in 1947, with the institution of the National Security Act and a whole host of other antidemocratic practices, the broad latitude of political elites in what is euphemistically called "statecraft" was to be taken for granted.

While many, particularly progressives and libertarians, see and worry about these changes, the entrenched notion that war is the health of the nation has garnered little attention and no irony. It is instead widely accepted that military spending preserves freedom and produces jobs in factories and in the army. The military is said to prepare young people for life, making men out of boys and an educated workforce out of warriors through college benefits. Virtues like discipline and teamwork are seen as nurtured by military trainers and lavishly exported to society at large. That these contentions are problematic becomes evident in the close ethnographic view (outlined below) of communities shaped by military spending.

It is true, however, that the capillaries of militarization have fed and molded social institutions seemingly little connected to battle. In other words, the process of militarization has been not simply a matter of weaponry wielded and bodies buried. It has also created what is taken as knowledge, with just two examples being the fields of physics and psychology, both significantly shaped by military funding and goals. It has redefined proper masculinity and sexuality (Enloe 2000), further marginalizing anyone but the male heterosexual – the only category of person seen as fit for the full citizenship conferred by combat. Militarization emerges from the images of soldiers in recruitment ads that blast across the popular culture landscape through both the 2 billion-dollar annual recruitment budget and Hollywood fare from *The Sands of Iwo Jima* to *Black Hawk Down*. Rearranging US social geography through internal migrations to the South and West for military work, it has accelerated the suburbanization process and the creation of racialized bantustans in the core of older cities (Markusen et al. 1991). It has created the bulk of both the federal deficit and the resistance to social-welfare benefits in a workforce divided into those soldiers and veterans with universal health care, a living wage, and other benefits, and those without them. Finally, it has contributed to the making of race and gender in the US through the biases of military spending toward the whiter and more male segments of the workforce.

This chapter is organized around two central questions. (1) What is the twentieth-century history of militarization, and how is it related to the notion of militarism, to the nation-state, to changing modes of warfare, and to broader social changes? (2) How can we connect global and national histories with specific ethnographically understood places and people involved in the militarization process? I can begin to answer these questions with reference to ethnographic and historical research in a military city, Fayetteville, North Carolina. Its 120,000 people live next to the Army's giant Fort Bragg, and its story tells the history of US cities more generally (Lutz 2001).

## MILITARISM, MILITARIZATION, AND STATES

The term *militarism* has sometimes been used synonymously with the term *militarization*. It is usually much narrower in scope than the latter, however, identifying a society's emphasis on martial values. It also focuses attention on the political realm and suggests that warlike values have an independent ability to drive social change, while *militarization* draws attention to the simultaneously material and discursive nature of military dominance. In addition, North American scholarship has rarely applied the term *militarism* to the United States; it more often projects responsibility onto countries it thereby treats as "others." This makes it hard to identify growing military hegemony in the United States and in other societies where ideological claims suggest the nation is peaceful by nature, and engages in war only when it is sorely provoked. Moreover, there is no universal set of "military values" whose rise indexes a process of militarization, because cultural forms have intersected with and remade society's military institutions. So, for example, faith in technology has supported a high ratio of arms to soldiers in the US military. While some might assume that this is the natural outcome of US affluence or of high-tech weaponry's superior efficacy as a modality of war, neither is necessarily the case, as the Vietnam War and September 11 both demonstrated. Such technological faith comes through the power of military industrial corporations to shape political discourse and decisions in the US through lobbying and campaign contributions, via the revolving door between military and military industrial leadership, and military corporate advertising. The faith is also rooted deeply in advertising campaigns for better living through those sciences that brought advances in transportation, food technology, home appliances, and computers.

Military institutional growth and a glorification of war and its values, however culturally defined, have not always developed in tandem: US military spending remained low in the nineteenth and early twentieth centuries while political culture glorified war and the martial spirit. Oliver Wendell Holmes, Jr. told students at Harvard in 1895 that: "So long as man dwells upon the globe, his destiny is battle . . . War's . . . message is divine" (Karsten 1989:33). William James even argued against war while still assuming a love of battle: "The popular imagination fairly fattens on the thought of wars . . . Militarism is the great preserver of our ideals of hardihood" (Karsten 1989:36). Contemporary American political culture does not tolerate such talk of the merits of violence. Instead, politicians, pundits, and some Fayetteville citizens speak about soldiers as those who are "placed in harm's way," reversing the image of soldiers as warrior-killers and eliding the state's role in their movements. At the same time, substantial resources are allocated to war preparation.

These elisions aside, however, the growth of a behemoth military and of military industrial corporate power have helped make what C. Wright Mills called "a military definition of reality" become the common sense of the nation (see his 1956 classic, *The Power Elite*). That is, it is deeply and widely believed that human beings are by nature aggressive and territorial, that force is the only way to get things done in the world, and that if one weapon creates security, 1,000 weapons create that much more. By this definition, as one soldier told me, "defense is the first need of every organism."

Militarization is a *tense process*, that is, it can create conflict between social sectors, and most importantly between those who might benefit from militarization (for example, corporations interested in expanding international markets for their goods) and those who might not, but who nonetheless may bear some of its costs. This conflict happens on the local level as well. In the 640 US communities with large military bases, realtors and retail owners benefit from the military's presence, unlike lawyers, public-sector workers, and retail workers, who must cope with the shrunken tax base associated with the military bases' federal land. The structural violence a war economy creates is not the simple equation so often painted of subtracting the government's military spending from its social spending. An example of the more complex factors involved is found in Fayetteville, where retail labor is the main category of work created by the post, as Fort Bragg soldiers take their salary dollars there to shop. Not only do retail jobs pay less than any other type of work, but retail workers also face the reserve army of unemployed military spouses whose in-migration to Fayetteville the military funds. Fayetteville wage rates are lower than in any other North Carolina city as a result.

Militarization also sets *contradictory* processes in motion, for example, accentu-ating both localism (as when Fayetteville and other cities compete for huge military contracts or bases) and federalism (as when the fate of dry-cleaning businesses in Fayetteville can hinge on Pentagon regulations on putting starch in uniforms or sudden deployments of large numbers of soldiers). Militarization might seem always to have the latter centralizing tendencies, but there has been in the US especially, a tradition of what has been called the "entrepreneurial city" – competing for interstate highways, county seats, conventions, prisons, and military bases and contracts. This curbs the centralizing tendency of the state, as does citizens' ability to make more claims on a government in exchange for their mobilization for war.

Charles Tilly has argued that most states were birthed by and wedded to war. He in fact names the state a kind of protection racket, raising armies that safeguard the people from violent threats they pretend to see, provoke themselves, or wreak upon their own people. He also, however, leaves open the possibility for legitimate defen-sive armies to emerge in some contexts. "Someone who produces both the danger and, at a price, the shield against it is a racketeer. Someone who provides a needed shield but has little control over the danger's appearance qualifies as a legitimate protector, especially if his price is no higher than his competitors" (1985:170–171). Most of the armies that emerged from the eighteenth century onward claimed to be the primary tool of the state – or, more grandly, the very enablement of a people. These armies could be defined as virtually the sine qua non of both state and nation.

States that formed earlier in the modern period, such as those in Europe and the United States, were better able to externalize their violence, protecting at least the middle and upper classes from the violence their global extraction of resources provoked. States that emerged more recently have often been shaped as clients to those earlier and more powerful ones. For this reason, the more recent states show a much greater disproportion of power between military and civil forces (however much those two categories problematically entail or contain each other). In these client states, the military is favored, as the state strikes bargains more with the foreign patron (who provides military assistance in exchange for commodities, labor pools, and access) than with the people within that state.

Beyond this general relationship between the state and violence, many historians have noted the United States' especially intimate relationship to war. That violence has centered around the idea of race, moreover, and has contributed to the making of races. The early US Army was defined as a kind of constabulary whose purpose was nation-building through "Indian clearance" rather than defense of national borders. The Army also built roads and forts to facilitate colonial settlement, an aim so intrinsic to the military that it was virtually impossible to distinguish soldiering from pioneering. The real and imagined threat of slave insurrection rationalized the raising of local official militias in the nineteenth century as well, and the military fought the Mexican-American and the Spanish-American wars with racial rationales. European colonialism was, of course, rooted in race violence as well, and the World War that ran with a brief interruption from 1914 to 1945 was fueled by contests over colonial holdings and militant expansionism based on racial supremacism (whether European, American, or Japanese). US military power went global as the twentieth century opened, when Filipinos, Puerto Ricans, Guamanians, and Hawaiians were made racial wards of the state.

This long history of race and war is encapsulated in Fayetteville's annual International Folk Festival. It begins with a parade down the city's main street, led by a contingent of the Fayetteville Independent Light Infantry, a militia begun in the slave era and still in existence, though more as a social club than an armed force. The soldiers in archaic costumes are followed by a march of war-refugee nations, from Puerto Ricans and Okinawans to Koreans and Vietnamese, who have made the city their home.

## TWENTIETH-CENTURY MODES OF US WARFARE

To understand how the militarization process has developed historically during the twentieth century, and how social relations have been reshaped in the process, I begin with the notion of an era's dominant "mode of warfare." While many accounts of warfare remain technocentric, that is, focused on the scientifically and technically advanced tool purportedly at its center (such as the machine gun, the atom bomb, or the computer), this phrase draws our attention beyond the central weapon or strategy of a country or era's military organization to the wider array of social features to which any type of war-making leads. The mode of warfare that was associated with industrial capitalism and the nation-state most extensively by the nineteenth century was mass industrial warfare. This required raising large armies, whether standing or relatively episodic. War in this mode also centered on manufacturing labor, with many workers required to produce tens of thousands of relatively simple guns, tanks, and ships, and eventually, airplanes. The advantage of industrial warfare over artisanal warfare was immediately evident in colonial wars in which the European powers captured vast territories. This point can be overemphasized, however; the Belgian Congo represents a case in which a relatively small number of basic tools and techniques – simple guns, chains, and severed hands – did the work of creating a labor force to extract the colony's wealth, while Maori guerrilla warfare in New Zealand was effective for years against the more technically advanced weaponry of the British.

As or more important than the efficacy of a mode of warfare, however, has been the form of life it has encouraged inside the nation waging it. Industrial modes of warfare, for example, pressed governments to extend civil rights and social benefits to gain the loyalty and labor of those larger segments of the population conscripted into the mass army (Tilly 1985). For first of all, mass industrial armies confront the problem of labor, and the symbolic benefits of citizenship have often been exchanged for them. Both World Wars I and II were fought in this mass industrial mode and helped shape the labor geographies and gender/race/class structures of the societies that waged them. They further entrenched patriarchal authority by excluding women from armies (except as sexual aids to soldiers' morale) and from high-paying manufacturing jobs (even if they temporarily involved some women and racial minorities during wartime). These wars also helped absorb excess industrial capacity that increasingly threatened capital accumulation. They did so by producing massive numbers of commodities whose function it was to be destroyed. In round numbers, the US produced 300,000 planes, 77,000 ships, 20 million small arms, 6 million tons of bombs, 120,000 armored vehicles, and 2.5 million trucks in World War II alone. The wars also prevented a crisis within the US economy after the war by requiring retooling of factories for domestic production and by providing new markets, commodities, and desires both overseas and domestically.

The Cold War's beginning has been variously dated from 1917 to 1947, but after World War II, enmity between the US and the Soviet Union became associated with a new mode of warfare. Termed *nuclearism*, it was initiated in 1945 with the bombing of the US western desert and then Hiroshima and Nagasaki. While technocentrism suggests that the new weapon and its massive destructive power were key to the transformation that began that year, what changed, more importantly, was the perception of danger among the people purportedly protected by nuclear weapons, and the new social relations that emerged because of these weapons' manufacture. Nuclearism's economy centered on producing more and more complex forms of the bomb and what are euphemistically called platforms, such as jet fighters, nuclear submarines, and other forms of war machinery. This mode of warfare allows states to have smaller armies since air-delivered nuclear and other weapons replaced ground forces. As weapons became more elaborate and fewer in number, the number of workers needed to produce them (and the unions associated with manufacturing them) declined. Scientific and engineering labor – overwhelmingly white and male both in 1945 and today – became more important than manufacturing labor.

Nuclearism and the military budget undergirding it have not been neutral in their redistributional effects, exacerbating class, gender, and racial disparities in wealth and status. Military industrial jobs migrated to areas of the country with fewer African Americans. When women found work in such industries, they encountered a gender pay gap wider than the one prevailing in the civilian sector. These workers were often non-unionized: indeed, the Pentagon actively advocated relocation of weapons companies to non-union areas, sometimes even billing taxpayers for the move. While North Carolina, for example, has numerous military bases, more Department of Defense tax dollars come out of North Carolina than go back into it, and the inability of localities to tax federal property has further impoverished the several counties from which Fort Bragg land was taken. One of those, Hoke County, with a heavily African American population, has been near the top of the state's 100 counties in its poverty rate, and the jobs it has been able to attract are mainly in its numerous prisons and poultry-processing plants.

This mode of warfare also spawned expanded codes of secrecy to protect the technical knowledge involved in weapons development (as well as to hide the fraud and waste, accidents, and environmental costs entailed): The homosexual in particular was seen as a "weak link" who could be blackmailed to divulge state secrets. Such fantasies envisioned the Soviets undermining US culture from within. This secrecy also fundamentally deformed norms of democratic citizenship already under pressure from consumerist notions of self, and eroded civil liberties. Nuclearism also reshaped forms of masculinity and femininity. The physical bravery and male bonding seen as necessary for earlier forms of warfare were replaced by technical rationality and individual strength. Middle-class womanhood, too, was reframed: the home a woman kept for her family was newly conceived as a bomb-shelter-like haven.

While civilians died in large numbers during the first half of the century under industrial regimes of war (primarily in colonial wars but also in the European theaters of war) the nuclear mode of warfare sharply eroded the practical if not the conceptual distinction between soldiers and civilians, as each was equally targeted by other nuclear powers. This takes Tilly's (1985) point a step further: the power of governments with nuclear weapons is greatly strengthened, as much against its own people as others, forcing the people of nuclear nations into a more lopsided bargain with their states, trusting them with not only their own future, but also that of the human race. Nuclear empowerment also helped both the Soviet Union and the United States administer their populations by suggesting that the nation's survival depended on subsuming internal conflict to the demands of national unity. It is in this sense that the nuclearism-based Cold War has been referred to as "the Imaginary War": war that was more scenario than actual battle, and its cultural force came from managing internal social divisions (for example, controlling the demands of the civil rights movement in the United States) more than from its defense of the nation. So it was in Fayetteville in the 1950s that debates about communism and Jim Crow were wedded. Segregationists argued that the subversive aims of the Soviets would be advanced through "race-mixing" or by race conflict, which communist propaganda would exploit. A local civil-rights leader had to defend the need to integrate schools within the same paradigm: "Our deeds must match our ideals and words concerning the rights of men and their equality before the law, or the two-thirds of the world's population that is not white will turn to the communists for leadership ... America [would then be] doomed to suffer attacks with atom and hydrogen bombs, leaving millions of us lying in unsegregated graves or interned in integrated prison camps" (in Lutz 2001:114–115).

What some nuclear planners discovered, moreover, was that nuclear weapons were unusable, because (as one general observed of war itself) they "ruined a perfectly good army." They were also prone to kill people downwind and to cause accidents whose consequences were as likely to destroy lives at home or in colonial holdings like Micronesia as overseas. The 40 major nuclear accidents of the Cold War era contaminated US and Soviet soil and water at their own hands, not the enemy's (Rogers 2000). This recognition occurred even as other planners fully contemplated first-strike use to disable enemy nuclear capacities, and even though a *single* one of the tens of thousands of extant nuclear weapons in the late 1950s would totally devastate an area of 500 square miles and start fires over an additional 1,500 square miles.

The nuclear mode of warfare also spawned a twin – proxy wars against both nonviolent and violent insurgencies that threatened US and Soviet interests overseas. These movements arose especially in those societies in which class differences were gaping, but the insurgency wars were joined with US and Soviet weapons and military training, particularly where investments or strategic aims were at stake. The arms trade itself became a central feature of international exchange and domestic economic policy, the weaponry originating mainly in the US, the USSR, and Europe. This

military equipment was and continues to be used substantially for domestic repression in the buyer states, as well as to further drain their treasuries. More important,
10 million people lost their lives in the counter-insurgency wars waged on the hot
side of the Cold War (Rogers 2000). But perception is as important as the reality, and
official chronologies now speak of the "blessings" of nuclear weapons, ignoring this
deflected body count, as well as the environmental damage they and their proxy wars
caused. Instead, they focus on the lack of a nuclear exchange between the super-
powers, and call one party the "victor." Despite the dissolution of the Soviet Union,
a nuclear abolitionist movement, and the perception that nuclear weapons are a thing
of the past, the US continued to have 10,500 nuclear weapons in 2000, and to spend
nearly 65 billion dollars on the chimerical idea of a nuclear "missile shield." The
compression of time and space through these and other military means – the focus on
seeing the enemy as tantamount to destroying his "assets" – has led some to call this
another and new mode of warfare, the visual or the postmodern.

During this period, the number of countries with substantial middle classes and
dropping poverty rates increased, but the extent of structural violence intensified in
other states, especially African ones. This was the result of a steady decline in the price
of raw materials, disinvestment in areas both intra- and internationally seen as "basket
cases" or human refuse zones, and the increasing indebtedness of poorer states to
wealthier ones and the banking enterprises within them. These factors meant an
increasing rate of wealth flow from poorer to wealthier states. The promotion of
neoliberalism by the elites of nations rich and poor has meant that whatever legal
protections for local markets had been in place have been dismantled; the people who
suffer as a result look for the source of their immiseration and find local elites rather
than the foreign powers who might have once been so identified.

The post-Cold War period saw the US emerge as human history's first truly global
power. Even before the massive increases of 2002, its military spending was equal to
that of the next 12 most significant national militaries combined. By way of comparison, Great Britain's nineteenth-century empire appears a weakling; the British navy
was rivaled by the two next largest navies together. The reach of the US military that
began to widen in World War II remained breathtaking and unprecedented: there are
currently 672 US overseas military installations, which serve as a far-flung archipelago
of what is euphemistically called "forward basing" rather than imperial outposts
(including all locations, there were 3,660 global US military sites in 1999). "Platforms" such as battleships, nuclear submarines, and jets, as well as spy satellites and
other listening posts, go even further toward creating a grid of operations and
surveillance that comprehensively covers the globe.

The social and environmental costs of US global military operations, however,
include apartheid-like conditions, prostitution, and other retrogressive effects on
women in the surrounding communities, and environmental devastation around
bases at home and abroad. Overseas, these costs have been levied in the name of these
societies, whose people are seen as racialized and feminized helpmates to the explicit
project of US global patronage and policing. What all these military functions share is
the idea of the potential necessity for the violent defense of white and male supremacism, now simply called "civilized values," against those of savagery or barbaric evil.

While many people believe that the Cold War's end shrank the US military substantially, it did not. There was an initial 18 percent drop in military spending, but a

groundswell of aggressive lobbying by defense contractors (whose profits were double those of other corporations in the 1980s), weapons labs, and the Pentagon mended the losses. Budgets had reached the original Cold War levels of 343 billion dollars even before September 11. The military, however, did restructure in the 1990s, just as business had, in tune with the new tenor of a neoliberal age: it downsized and made more of its force part-time (active-duty troops dropping from just over 2 million to about 1.4 million, and reserves increasing), outsourced more of its work (training the militaries of other countries to do proxy work for US interests, while retaining plausible deniability when human-rights abuses occur), and it privatized some of its otherwise public workforce (as when it gave the contract for guarding Fort Bragg's huge ammunition dump to a private security firm). With the demise of the Soviet Union, US military industries became not just the source of the state's coercive power, but of its economic power in a more direct sense. It became the largest global merchant of arms, exporting as much as all other arms-producing countries combined.

New war-making doctrines were developed, their intention or outcome being to protect the military and its industries from decimation. Christened *Operations Other Than War*, they included Evacuation Operations, Support to Domestic Civil Authorities, and Disaster Relief, among many others. Some missions gave the military tasks once seen as civilian jobs, such as famine relief. As it took on social and policing jobs that one soldier from Fayetteville described dismissively to me as "babysitting," it could seem that the army was demilitarizing. Such contradictory effects are also evident in the response to environmental damage found on the military bases that were closed to allow reallocation of funds to military industry purchases. On the one hand, the mess, sometimes of monumental proportions, was cleaned up partly with Environmental Protection Agency funds, which could be considered militarized when allocated to that purpose. On the other hand, military funds might be considered demilitarized when they were used to clean and convert bases to civilian uses.

It was in this flurry of new mission development that "humanitarian war" came to be seen, not as an oxymoron, but as an adjunct to human-rights work and democratic aspirations around the world. It emerged as the newest mode of warfare, and was distinguished from ordinary modern warfare primarily by its ideological force. This is a powerful and paradoxical combination of social evolutionist and human-rights discourse. The reinvigoration of social evolutionism in the United States in the 1980s and 1990s was evident and promoted in books proclaiming a "clash of civilizations" between the Western and advanced, and the barbaric elsewheres, or predicting a "coming anarchy" of clashes between the rich and poor nations, but with a US triumphant because of its superior culture. The humanitarian wars that drew on these various and seemingly antithetical discourses did little to prevent or stop such gross human-rights violations as the genocide in Rwanda, the 1999 massacres in East Timor, and the destruction in Chechnya by the Russians; this is an index of the term's frequent use as a pretext for other national purposes.

Humanitarian warfare has often been twinned (as was nuclearism with counter-insurgency) with what Mary Kaldor identifies as "the New Wars." Paramilitaries fight these wars without clear lines of command; they target civilians with torture, rape, and terror bombings. Their aim is "to sow fear and discord, to instill unbearable memories of what was once home, to desecrate whatever has social meaning" (Kaldor and Vashee 1997:16). The intention of such a war is to prevent dissent or even discussion, as signified by combatants' frequent maiming of eyes, ears, and tongues. These are often civil wars rather than wars between states, and they have involved the use of "small" or inexpensive arms that are thereby made widely available, further raising the death toll of civilians, which reached 90 percent of all war deaths by the end of the century. In some cases, US arms and training are thrown on one side or the other in line with larger strategic interests, and especially in pursuit of corporate access to resources and labor. Some forms of new warfare need no weapons or soldiers at all, such as the deadly use of sanctions in Iraq. Warfare it is, however, with its intention to coerce regime change through bodily suffering.

The US has increasingly relied on executive order for engagement in war, an antidemocratic practice that became ensconced with the national security state in 1947. So did the rise of so-called black budgets in military agencies, which were estimated at 39 billion dollars per year in the late 1980s; these are tax dollars exempt from public knowledge or oversight. Antidemocratic effects also accompanied the turn from a conscripted to an all-volunteer force, which came in 1973 in response to active rebellion within the military against the war. The volunteer army rearranged the exchanges that the state had struck with citizens during the era of conscription: civilians were no longer potential involuntary soldiers or sacrificers of their children, but rather spectators. And the soldiers recruited became increasingly conservative in their politics, something that has changed the political climate in Fayetteville as well as nationally. While tacitly remembering the army's rebellion, however, explicit politically molded memories of the Vietnam era suggest a still unreciprocated bargain with veterans of that war, which continues to shape both political culture and military strategy. These various forms of memory, for example, have lowered tolerance for US battlefield deaths. Together with the long-standing ascendancy of the Air Force and Navy among service branches under the regime of nuclearism in which they specialized, this has meant a sometimes nearly exclusive reliance on aerial bombardment in US-led wars. This is a devastating choice for the people of a host of countries targeted for such attention, but one which ensured fewer political costs for the US, whose populace could be convinced that there was moral virtue (the bombs being labeled *smart*) and little cost to the nation from warfare so waged.

The people of the US emerged from the Cold War 16 trillion dollars poorer, however. If the concept of friendly fire were extended to structural violence, the impoverishment would be much greater. It would include joblessness, the attendant human suffering, and premature deaths and hunger that have resulted from the inequalities the military budget exacerbates. It does this by creating fewer jobs per dollar spent than equivalent social spending, and by derailing the movement for expanded social-welfare benefits, as noted above. In Fayetteville, where the contrast in benefits given to soldiers and civilians is most visible (even as some of the lowest rank enlisted soldiers with families qualify for food stamps), this division plays out rancorously. The upper hand in the debate, however, goes to those who can appeal to the idea of soldiering as an unrecompensable sacrifice for the nation. This argument is made even as the likelihood of death in battle has been minuscule over the last 20 years, when a total of 563 American soldiers died from "enemy" fire, a number far smaller than those people who died in US coal mines over that same period. And with the growing transnationalism of corporate operations and the search for cheap labor overseas, that violence has increasingly been the fist inside the glove of neoliberal trade policies and foreign loans, which together have provided the means and rationale for the flow of resources and wealth from the South to the North, the brown to the white areas of the globe. It remains an entrenched notion among the US population, however – increasingly subject to control of information flows about global realities by media beholden to corporate and state interests – that aid and wealth flows from North to South.

Nonetheless, pressures for demilitarization have exerted themselves throughout global and US national history. In the US, an anti-militarist tradition has been a vigorous force at many points, from the framing of the Constitution through the anti-ROTC movement of the World War I period, to the anti-war novels and films of the 1930s and the 1960s, to the current mass movement to combat the democratic losses and intensified militarization of this most recent period. That tradition has existed within the military as well. Dwight Eisenhower, an important example, declared his unhappiness with the mushrooming military budget of the 1950s, believing it "would leave the nation a militarized husk, hardly worth defending." People around the world have made claims against impunity for repressive government and paramilitary forces from Israel to Colombia to South Africa. The lobbying and educational role of the transnational community of dissident nuclear scientists was one key to the Soviet Union's embarking on a course of denuclearization before its demise. The international human-rights movement helped bring down Eastern European police states, made possible a dramatic rise in international legal mechanisms to control violence, and pressed to define not only physical violence, but also structural violence as a violation of human rights. The Jubilee and nuclear abolitionist movements gained wide support and conventions against the use of landmines, chemical and biological weapons, nuclear-weapons testing, the use of children as soldiers, and state torture have been almost universally accepted. And voluminous and immediate sources of information to counter official lies, as well as being avenues for solidarity and anti-militarization work, have opened up with the internet.

Militarization and demilitarization are connected to particular communities and individual lives. The long home front and its future fate hinge on our reconnecting both sides of the fence that separates the Fort Braggs and the Fayettevilles, and seeing what militarization has wrought globally. The current crisis and the socioeconomic and legal changes that it has already prompted will take their steep toll first in those places like Fayetteville that are most enmeshed in military institutions. An understanding of their past and present predicament can provide transferable insights to other places and help elucidate how they have come to have the textures they do. Ethnographic understanding of militarization's shaping of all the globe's places seems an urgent project for anthropology, as it will allow us to see the seams, fissures, and costs in the otherwise seemingly monolithic and beneficent face of state and corporate and media war-making.

## REFERENCES

Bauman, Zygmunt (1989) *Modernity and the Holocaust.* Ithaca, NY: Cornell University Press.
Bourne, Randolph (1964) *War and the Intellectuals: Essays by Randolph S. Bourne, 1915–1919,* ed. Carl Resek. New York: Harper Torchbooks.

Enloe, Cynthia (2000) *Maneuvers: The International Politics of Militarizing Women's Lives.* Berkeley: University of California Press.

Geyer, Michael (1989) The Militarization of Europe, 1914–1945. In *The Militarization of the Western World*, ed. John Gillis, pp. 65–102. New Brunswick, NJ: Rutgers University Press.

Kaldor, Mary, and Basker Vashee, eds. (1997) *Restructuring the Global Military Sector. Volume 1. New Wars.* London: Pinter.

Karsten, Peter (1989) Militarization and Rationalization in the United States, 1870–1914. In *The Militarization of the Western World*, ed. John Gillis, pp. 30–44. New Brunswick, NJ: Rutgers University Press.

Lutz, Catherine (2001) *Homefront: A Military City and the American Twentieth Century.* Boston: Beacon Press.

Malkki, Liisa H. (1995) *Purity and Exile: Violence, Memory, and National Cosmology among Hutu Refugees in Tanzania.* Chicago: University of Chicago Press.

Markusen, Ann, Peter Hall, Scott Campbell, and Sabina Deitrick (1991) *The Rise of the Gunbelt: The Military Remapping of Industrial America.* New York: Oxford University Press.

Rogers, Paul (2000) *Losing Control: Global Security in the Twenty-first Century.* London: Pluto Press.

Sluka, Jeffrey A., ed. (2000) *Death Squad: The Anthropology of State Terror.* Philadelphia: University of Pennsylvania Press.

Tilly, Charles (1985) War Making and State Making as Organized Crime. In *Bringing the State Back In*, ed. Peter Evans, Dietrich Rueschemeyer, and Theda Skocpol, pp. 67–95. Cambridge: Cambridge University Press.

## SUGGESTED FURTHER READING

Baran, Paul, and Paul Sweezy (1966) *Monopoly Capital: An Essay on the American Economic and Social Order.* New York: Monthly Review Press.

Das, Veena, et al., eds. (2000) *Violence and Subjectivity.* Berkeley: University of California Press.

Evangelista, Matthew (1999) *Unarmed Forces: The Transnational Movement to End the Cold War.* Ithaca, NY: Cornell University Press.

Gill, Lesley (2000) *Teetering on the Rim: Global Restructuring, Daily Life, and the Armed Retreat of the Bolivian State.* New York: Columbia University Press.

Gray, Chris Hables (1997) *Postmodern War: The New Politics of Conflict.* New York: Guilford Press.

Gusterson, Hugh (1996) *Nuclear Rites: A Weapons Laboratory at the End of the Cold War.* Berkeley: University of California Press.

Leslie, Stuart W. (1993) *The Cold War and American Science: The Military-Industrial-Academic Complex at MIT and Stanford.* New York: Columbia University Press.

Lutz, Catherine, and Donald Nonini (1999) The Economies of Violence and the Violence of Economies. In *Anthropological Theory Today*, ed. Henrietta Moore, pp. 73–113. Cambridge: Polity Press.

Mann, Michael (1987) The Roots and Contradictions of Modern Militarism. *New Left Review* 162:35–50.

Virilio, Paul (1989) *War and Cinema: The Logistics of Perception*, trans. P. Camiller. London: Verso.

# CHAPTER 21  Neoliberalism

## John Gledhill

An intellectual genealogy of neoliberalism as an ideology starts from the labors of Friedrich von Hayek and Milton Friedman in the University of Chicago, and traces its progress toward the heart of government through the labors of foundations and think-tanks on both sides of the Atlantic (George 1999). To explain why ideas that would have seemed political suicide in advanced industrial countries for the first 30 years after the World War II became convincing arguments for "reforms" to which "there was no alternative" in Britain under Thatcher and the United States under Reagan, we need to look at changes within advanced capitalism. These are elegantly analyzed by David Harvey, in *The Condition of Postmodernity: An Enquiry into the Origins of Social Change* (1989). In this work, Harvey documents the transition from a Fordist-Keynesian "mode of regulation," characterized by an extensive welfare state and by state intervention to ensure security of employment, to a regime of "flexible accumulation." Although Pinochet's Chile produced a precocious neoliberal "reform" in the South, the generalization of the model was soon guaranteed by the fall of the Soviet empire and the Third World debt crisis. As Peck and Tickell (2001) put it: "What began as a starkly utopian intellectual movement [that] was aggressively politicized by Reagan and Thatcher in the 1980s" was transformed into "a more technocratic form in the self-styled 'Washington Consensus' of the 1990s." By this stage, the relationship between neoliberalism and capitalist globalization takes center stage (Peck and Tickell 2001:1):

> Neoliberalism has provided a kind of operating framework or "ideological software" for competitive globalization, inspiring and imposing far-reaching programs of state restructuring and rescaling across a wide range of national and local contexts. Crucially, its premises also established the ground rules for global lending agencies operating in the crisis-torn economies of Asia, Africa, Latin America, and the former Soviet Union, where new forms of "free-market" dirigisme have been constructed. Indeed, proselytizing the virtues of free trade, flexible labor, and active individualism have become so commonplace in contemporary politics – from Washington to Moscow – that they hardly even warrant comment in many quarters.

Yet, by the mid-1990s, actors tied to the multilateral agencies themselves began to press for significant policy changes that they saw as breaking with neoliberalism. The World Bank responded by sponsoring a "post-Washington Consensus" revision. Although "revisionists" associated with the Bank, such as Poland's former finance minister, Grzegorz W. Kodolko (1998), remained committed to IMF orthodoxy, and to a classical mainstream *liberal* approach, they nonetheless insisted that *neoliberalism* was an ethnocentric theory that failed to take into account crucial institutional differences between the North Atlantic economies and those of regions such as East Asia and Eastern Europe. It was especially flawed, revisionists argued, by its blindness to the role the state could and should play in handling the transitions of post-socialist economies toward a market system.

The World Bank's response to these criticisms was reflected in its influential document, *The State in a Changing World*, which in turn reflected the "liberal" thinking of the Brookings Institution think-tank (Bretton Woods Project 1997:28–29). Brookings analysts argued that both poor and middle-class people in the South (rightly or wrongly) associated stabilization policies and structural reform with rising immiseration and social inequality. This might produce a "populist backlash" that would threaten the continuity of the reform process itself.

The Bank now insisted that the state should take a pro-active role in combating poverty (and gender and racial discrimination), but without returning to interference in the market through price controls, subsidies, and traditional redistributive measures. It also emphasized the need to "strengthen civil society" to build democracy and transparency. The Bank even paid lip service to "the economy as institutionalized process," the concept advanced by Karl Polanyi in his classic work, *The Great Transformation*. There was a certain irony at work here, for Polanyi's classic was published in 1944, and was very much an announcement of the very Fordist-Keynesian consensus to which multilateral agencies had no intention of returning. Instead, the new vision sought to improve poor people's access to services, infrastructure, and education through market-based institutions and a new partnership between the state and non-governmental organizations. Critics of the Bretton Woods Project concluded that since, in practice, "neoliberalism has been less about stripping back the state than about redirecting it" this was "all change but no change" (Bretton Woods Project 1997:2).

In the case of the International Monetary Fund, an absence of significant policy change seemed only too apparent as the Argentine crisis unfolded, with popular mobilization in that country seemingly threatening the survival of the established political parties. As the precarious Duhalde government struggled to convince the IMF to deliver a promised package of aid in March 2002, it was informed that IMF "conditionalities" still included maintaining financial disciplines. In addition, however, the Duhalde government learned that it had to convince the IMF that it could maintain governability in the face of resistance to further austerity measures. Later that month, national leaders gathered in Monterrey, Mexico, for the United Nations Conference on Financing for Development, where they arrived at the "Consensus of Monterrey." Mexico's Foreign Minister summarized the consensus as: "The North agrees to commit more funds to the development of the South on condition that we put our houses in order." Yet spokespersons for the IMF and the World Bank assured delegates to the concurrent *Global Forum for Financing the Right to Sustainable*

*Development with Equity* (organized by NGOs and subsidized by the UN) that the new agreement was not a simple extension of the Washington Consensus. Prakash Loungani, of the IMF's Department of External Relations, insisted that his organization was "trying to change" and establish a new dialogue (*La Jornada* newspaper, March 16, 2002): "It has been said that the Consensus of Monterrey is a continuation of the standard neoliberal model. Everyone can read what they wish into it, but before drawing any conclusions, they should reflect on the fact that we want to help the countries and do not want any top-down imposition of policy but to involve the society in everything that we do."

## FROM NEOLIBERALISM TO NEOLIBERALIZATION

Such a reference to "society" – something Margaret Thatcher, following Hayek, declared not to exist – seems to be moving away from neoliberal premises. Many national governments claim to be building a "Third Way," a modernized social democracy that is not a variant of neoliberalism. Anthony Giddens (2000) argues that Third-Way politics not only advocate continuing provision of public goods, but subject market-based decisions to social and ethical criteria defined by a "healthy" civil society. Yet others deny such a break, arguing that Third-Way politics are simply a "soft neoliberalism" that is one of a series of different transformations within a *deepening* process of *neoliberalization* (Peck and Tickell 2001:4):

> Like globalization, neoliberalism should be understood as a process, not an end-state. By the same token, it is also contradictory, it tends to provoke countertendencies, and it exists in historically and geographically contingent forms. Analysis of this process should therefore focus especially sharply on *change* – on shifts in systems and logics, dominant patterns of restructuring and so forth – rather than on binary and/or static comparisons between a past state and its erstwhile successor. It also follows that analyses of neoliberalism must be sensitive to its contingent nature, hence the non-trivial differences – both theoretically and politically – between the actually existing neoliberalisms of, say, Blair's Britain, Fox's Mexico or Bush's America. While processes of neoliberalization are clearly at work in all these diverse situations, we should not expect this to lead to a simple convergence of outcomes, a neoliberalized end of history and geography.

Despite their stress on diversity, Peck and Tickell also identify a general shift from the "roll-back" neoliberalism of early years – which focused on "the active destruction of Keynesian-welfarist and social-collectivist institutions" – toward a "roll-out" neoliberalism that developed in subsequent years. The latter focused "on the purposeful construction and consolidation of neoliberalized state forms, modes of government and regulatory relations." This has created "a more formidable and robust pattern of proactive statecraft and pervasive metaregulation," although "the diffuse, dispersed, institutional and technocratic form of neoliberalism" also makes it vulnerable to new challenges (Peck and Tickell 2001:6–7).

At first sight, such vulnerability appears the essence of the dialogue between NGOs and agency officials in Monterrey. Yet the NGOs organizing the Forum may have been compromised by their own incorporation into such a structure of metaregulation – as is suggested by the fact that they alienated many of the very "alternative" organizations they sought to involve in the Forum's critical dialogue. Particularly symptomatic was the withdrawal from the Forum of the El Barzón ("The Yoke") debtors' movement, in protest against the 10-dollar registration fee charged per delegate, on the pretext of promoting individual "active citizenship." Contradictions of this kind lead Peck and Tickell to argue that one of the main problems posed by neoliberalism is its diffuse nature as a system of power. Here, they draw on Hardt and Negri (2000:xii–xiii):

> Empire establishes no territorial center of power and does not rely on fixed boundaries or barriers. It is a decentralized and deterritorializing apparatus of rule that progressively incorporates the entire global realm within its open, expanding frontiers. Empire manages hybrid identities, flexible hierarchies and plural exchanges through modulating networks of command. The distinct national colors of the imperialist map of the world have merged and blended in the imperial global rainbow.

Hardt and Negri argue that NGOs are part of the contemporary webs of "empire" as a decentered framework of global governmentality in Foucault's sense, even where their activities have genuinely humanitarian consequences that should not be lightly dismissed. One reason for this is that hegemonic institutions within global power networks have themselves appropriated much of the "progressive" politics launched against the systems of power previously central to "modernist" forms of rule (Hardt and Negri 2000:155–156). While analysts at the heart of US strategic planning, such as Arquilla and Ronfeldt (2000), see transnational NGO networks as a challenge to established systems of global governance no different in form to decentered terrorist networks, the results of NGO interventions on the ground are mixed for a variety of structural reasons.

As professionalized organizations with their own agendas, NGOs may disempower those they seek to aid. Some are directly supportive of the neoliberal focus on "empowerment" through individual self-help. In other cases, NGO intervention produces unintentionally contradictory consequences. Community leaders become detached from their communities as they learn to navigate the circuits of NGO politics and funding. Foreign NGOs pursuing utopias ungrounded in local social and cultural conditions may exacerbate community divisions and inequalities, while the lifestyles of foreign activists may offend local sensibilities and problematize the achievement of changes in gender relations. Local projects must also be adapted to the interests of sponsors in what is, generally, a market framework, while even NGOs that strongly reject neoliberal values may construct the beneficiaries of funds in ways that reflect social and cultural distance. For example, "exotic Indians" preserving a "traditional culture" may seem more worthy of support than "acculturated" people, while "real" flesh and blood Indians may disappoint NGOs precisely because they seem individualistic and self-serving. In contrast to what Ramos (1998) has termed the "hyperreal" Indians that NGO sponsors often construct in their imaginations, real Indians cannot always be trusted to act as guardians of an unspoiled "nature" and often seem uninterested in being objects of "cultural conservation."

The problem this highlights is a need to focus more on the practical, everyday, social effects of the transformations our world has experienced over the past two decades, as well as the way contemporary politics might have become "neoliberalized" at higher organizational levels. I am concerned with the diversity of "actually existing" neoliberalisms, and why and how the diffuse system of power that lends them a certain unity has managed to implant itself with such apparent success in such a wide range of circumstances. In order to understand this problem, it is essential to examine the social and cultural processes that shape the dynamics of both neoliberalism and its counter-movements.

## RECOGNIZING NEOLIBERALIZATION

Neoliberal economic policies in Latin America appear to be the result both of imposition (the price of continuing IMF support in the wake of the debt crisis of the 1980s and subsequent shocks, such as the Mexican crisis of 1994) and changes in the perspectives of political elites. In the case of Chile, special political conditions obtained. Pinochet's objectives were not simply to prevent the future reemergence of the radical left, but to incapacitate the political center as well, and such considerations also applied in other cases, such as Fujimori's Peru.

In Chile, bringing in technocrats from Chicago to design the new economy had a certain resonance with a broader tradition of Latin-American admiration for the capitalist colossus of the North and traditions of positivism found within the elites of many countries. But Latin America's love–hate relationship with the United States had, during the twentieth century, mostly gravitated in the opposite direction – toward economic nationalism and a central role for the state in directing capitalist modernization. In some countries, notably Brazil, landed elites continued to play a significant role in politics even after industrialization. Where they largely disappeared, as in Mexico, urban business groups long preferred protectionism and cozy relationships with a corrupt political regime to the risks of global competition. Yet business interests were not the only, or even the dominant, social and political forces governing the shape of Latin-American political economies before the 1970s. States were run by a variety of actors, few of which directly represented the interests of economic elites. Some of the region's military regimes (such as the Peruvian military under Velasco, and the Guatemalan military in the 1980s) embarked on their own projects of state capitalist development precisely because they were antagonistic to established oligarchies. The Catholic Church, even at its most conservative, also tended to remain antagonistic to neoliberalism, on ideological grounds. Pinochet's technocratic revolution was, therefore, an attempt to restructure the power relations of Chilean society as a whole, a decisively political act that must be understood in its local context.

It is not enough to attribute the general shift to neoliberalism in Latin America as resulting from the imposition of structural adjustment policies on crisis-torn economies. The fact that the countries of the region were in crisis to begin with is very germane to understanding the political context of their initial reception and the political possibility of implementing change. Some of the leaders of the neoliberal turn were required to perform a striking ideological volte-face. Notable in this category were Bolivia's Gonzalo Sánchez de Lozada of the Nationalist Revolutionary Movement (MNR), heir to the authoritarian but decidedly economic nationalist tradition that emerged out of the revolution of 1952, and his successor Jaime Paz

Zamora, leader of the once radical Movement of the Revolutionary Left (MIR). But the appearance of a president drawn directly from Mexico's ruling Party of the Institutional Revolution (PRI) as the model neoliberal reformer for the whole of the South is even more instructive.

Although privatization and cutting state subsidies began under his predecessor, Carlos Salinas de Gortari (1988–94) embarked on a more aggressive course of "roll-back neoliberalism." His election victory in 1988 was heavily disputed, and his last year of office was rocked by a series of crises – the shockwaves of the Zapatista rebellion in Chiapas (under the slogan "for Humanity and against Neoliberalism"), a string of political assassinations, and a mounting sense that unprecedented corruption (linked to the privatization of public enterprises, drug-trafficking, and money-laundering) lay at the heart of government. Yet Salinas still seemed on course for achievement of his ambition to head the World Trade Organization, until a false boom based on speculative capital inflows collapsed almost immediately after he left office. The changes that Salinas sought to engineer ran deep, and the centerpiece of his policy was the North American Free Trade Agreement (NAFTA). Backed by a discourse of "there are no alternatives" (to accepting globalization), Salinas's strategy had a quality of "shock therapy." Subsidies vanished (with few transition measures to cushion the blow) and privatization proceeded apace.

Salinas promised that economic change would promote democratization and transparency in government. In practice, however, his methods for managing economic transition remained profoundly undemocratic. The old corporatist organizations of the PRI were used to manage consent, and the administration's World Bank-inspired social development programs were manipulated politically to divide or co-opt opposition. Although some elements of the old PRI machine displayed resistance to a new order that threatened their tributary powers, at the same time as it generated rapid accumulation of wealth by private-sector groups, their voices remained muted until the regime began to lose credibility. The transition to neoliberalism was favored, at the level of elites, by a series of longer-term transformations. Mexico's big business groups were increasingly operating across national boundaries, and emerging from their previous political quiescence as the vast expansion of public enterprise and state intervention during the 1970s began to impact negatively on their operations. At the same time, leading members of the political class had become key players in their own right within the world of business. Social and business ties at elite levels crosscut party affiliations, while regional elites were no longer isolated from the web of national and transnational elite networks. Capitalizing on the advantages of globalization for the elite of a country with massive reserves of cheap labor and ready access to US markets therefore made sense to a wide range of elite actors, beyond the simple fact that relief from the debt crisis provoked by earlier policies could only be obtained by accepting the new rules of the international game.

Yet the new rules still allowed Mexico to play by its own rules, especially where this mattered for elites. Although the consequences of Salinas's "reform" hardly compared with the "savage capitalism" unleashed in the former Soviet Union, there is one sense in which the Salinas period did replicate the darker aspects of post-Soviet development. The privatization of public assets produced many anomalies: in some cases, investors were allowed to strip assets, plunder failing enterprises, or run them to the benefit of other parts of their operations without regard to the longer term.

A fever of speculative investments in banking led to even greater anomalies, and the Salinas era saw the rise of "new men" closely connected to a political inner circle whose business empires involved activities of dubious legality. When the crash came in 1994 at the beginning of the administration of Ernesto Zedillo, the dominance of political over market mechanisms in the Mexican transition was revealed in its full starkness. The state moved in to protect some of the country's richest families from losses through the controversial FOBAPROA (Fondo Bancario de Protección al Ahorro, Bank Fund for the Protection of Savings) scheme, while leaving smaller businesses to founder.

"Rolling back the state" in some areas thus does not make the use of state power and resources any less necessary for implementing the new regime in other areas. Not only is neoliberalism highly "politicized," but the most important part of the politics may lie backstage. Global "reform" discourses (with their emphasis on the assumed linkages between private enterprise and "good governance") obscure the extent to which capital accumulation processes within market economies may remain embedded in relations that constitute networks of "shadow state" power behind the official institutional façade. The Mexican case also suggests that international regulatory agencies and foreign banks may collaborate (through silence and inaction) in allowing these processes to flourish.

Looking at the Salinas transition from the point of view of ordinary citizens suggests, however, that the account just given does not capture the whole picture. His selective deployment of state clientelism through targeted social-development programs was relatively successful in drawing some popular movements into constructive dialogue with his government and undermining the solidarity of grass-roots opposition. His aggressive approach to tackling the problem of "governability," and to pushing through his modernization plans (which included repression), produced the image of a "strong president." Many families in both urban and rural areas rapidly found themselves losers under the new regime. The neoliberal transition may be understood as a massive process of social retrocession relative to the situation achieved under the "statist" regimes of the 1970s. The government of Vicente Fox, which broke the 70-year monopoly on power of the PRI in 2000, concedes that 40 million Mexicans, three out of five, still live below the poverty line, with 25 million in extreme poverty. Yet the privatization of state enterprises was not necessarily seen as a bad thing by those who worked in them, given the corruption that had characterized state administration, despite local anxieties about lay-offs and the fear that opening doors to foreign capital would enhance the domination of US interests to the disadvantage of Mexican society in general.

The deepest fears in this regard related to the oil industry, whose nationalization is still generally seen as a strategic advantage, despite the fact that few Mexicans harbor the delusion that they are really "owners" of their oil and recognize the way resources were siphoned out of the industry through its union toward the coffers of the PRI. One of Salinas's first acts in seeking to consolidate his authority was to imprison the boss of the oil workers' union (who seemed likely to support his still protesting electoral opponent). This confirmed the scale of resource diversion in the state oil company, since the leader's home region plunged into deep recession once he lost the resources that sustained his patronage. Yet the fact that the case provoked mixed feelings was symptomatic of the way neoliberalism was received in terms of the values orientating Mexican political culture. Imaginaries of the state continued to center on its corruption, but Salinas could be judged worthy of admiration providing his "strong" acts brought tangible benefits to people other than himself. With deep skepticism, many Mexicans were prepared to give the marketeers a chance. In at least some regions, neoliberal rhetoric resonated with local formulations of the virtues of individualism and private property, albeit in tension with new collectivist demands for recognition on the part of indigenous peoples, a counter-current of "identity polit-ics" also linked to globalization, through the proliferation of NGO networks and the growth of postcolonial sensibilities among the more privileged publics of North America and Europe.

There are two possible ways of looking at the apparent resonance between some aspects of neoliberal ideology and grass-roots attitudes. One is to see it as rooted in a local history that created ideologies imbued with a specific kind of individualism. Such ideologies are rooted in local conceptions of social value, but they also reflect people's historical experience of the state in Latin America, coupled with a lively understanding of the pragmatic necessity of seeking solutions to problems via the "levers" of personal relationships of patronage and paying officials their "bite" in routine bureaucratic transactions. These are complicated ideologies, first, because the "legal-rational" alternative is recognized as historically possible (and often located in the United States), and second, because nobody can be successful in life as a true (isolated) "individual."

This kind of individualism is based on a relational model of social personhood, in which respect is due to persons (generally male) who prosper by their own efforts within the webs of family, kin, and patron–client relations. Yet it can also raise the ruthless pursuit of self-interest to a kind of moral value in an unjust world. This latter kind of "individualizing" morality is expressed in the Mexican idea that individuals can be divided into *cabrones* (a "bastard" in an admiring sense) or *pendejos* (literally pubic hairs, with the meaning of fools). The former are ruthless in pursuit of their own interests and adopt the tactics necessary to convince the "other" that it will be less of a hassle to give them what they want, while the latter are naively trusting of the "other's" ultimate goodwill and inevitably get "screwed" (*chingado*) in any social transaction.

A second perspective (not incompatible with the first) would be to emphasize the way changing social conditions (in particular, those resulting from the concentration of population in urban settings), coupled with the implantation of a culture of consumerism, have fostered neoliberalization of everyday life. Such a tendency is deepened by the effects of neoliberal economic policies – in terms of the kinds of solutions available to poor people for coping with the immediate problems of immi-seration – and the failures (and corruption) of the collectivist projects of social progress offered by both populist and leftist regimes. Even when people participate in collective movements, they still have to devise individual day-to-day survival strategies. Harsh circumstances in competition for livelihoods may even divide the family unit, but collective versus individual actions to solve problems are not neces-sarily mutually incompatible *alternatives*. One of the basic contradictions of poor people's struggles is that keeping options open and taking what seems the best bet as opportunities present themselves makes sense for vulnerable families, even if it is a source of friction where other participants see themselves as defending collective projects against egotism, so that solidarity is undermined by internal confrontations around this issue.

Yet to recognize the broader ways in which neoliberalization might have deepened (despite resistance from many sectors of society) we need to ask more searching questions about why it deserves the prefix "neo." Market liberalism and advocacy of free trade are not new. What makes neoliberalism something that a classical liberal such as Adam Smith would have found as disturbing as Pope John Paul II does is its elision of the distinction between a market *economy* and a market *society*, to the point where the latter seems to engulf life itself. One reason why "Third Way" social democracy still seems neoliberal is that citizens who "fail" in their efforts to participate in the market create a *moral* problem that requires remedial action. Although Giddens (2000) recognizes that "social exclusion" reflects structured inequalities, his ultimate goal is to ensure that citizens can fulfill their duty to take advantage of "normal labor market opportunities" and thus to maximize their advantages in market society. Neoliberalism is not simply the response to a crisis of accumulation and a readjustment of the relations between capital and labor following the formation of truly global markets. It is the ideology of the period in which capitalism deepened to embrace the production of social life itself, seeking to commoditize the most intimate of human relations and the production of identity and personhood.

The measurement of social worth in terms of consumption and marketed "lifestyle" symbols penetrates deeply even into the lives of the world's poorest citizens. Indeed, even alternative forms of identity, such as Evangelical Christianity, seem less and less inclined to take an ascetic stance. Other alternative forms of association, such as being the follower of a drug trafficker, also contribute to the propagation of a neoliberal ethic. "Deep neoliberalization" is, however, also promoted by new forms of governmentality embedded in the state and its relationships with its principal interlocutors in "civil society." The "internal market" is now firmly established in the most unlikely of places – for example, throughout the apparatus of government itself, and in a variety of other public institutions (as well as private corporations). The virtues of "competition" as a principle of allocation have produced a multiplication of contracts for the provision of services, and efforts to reduce the period for which contracts remain valid. This line of thinking has been applied with special rigor to the labor market, whose "flexible employees" must be made to realize that their skills date rapidly in the informational society.

This brings us to a paradoxical feature of neoliberalism – its dissemination of what might be called an "audit" culture. In its public-sector manifestations, this audit culture represents a tightening of bureaucratic state intervention, even as the state strives to offload the task of auditing on to supposedly "independent" quasi-governmental bodies. The audit culture's continuous assessment and demands for evidence that goals are being realized has powerful disciplinary effects. For example, measurement of "performance" (or "quality") enables neoliberal governmentality to break down the resistance of workers who once deemed themselves professionals (and who organized to "protect vested interests inimical to the efficient delivery of services at minimum cost"). By increasing insecurity, and by inculcating in people the subjective need to "maximize labor market performance," neoliberal regimes have achieved outstanding increases in the hours regularly worked by white-collar and professional employees. At the same time, these regimes have left professionals with the delusion that they are in a quite different social category than the workers in electronic call-centers who are subjected to a more immediate and oppressive process of surveillance and monitoring. Ultimately, the rationality of neoliberalism has imposed itself on ruler and ruled alike.

Audit culture is also deeply embedded in development agencies and NGOs, leading to a system of project evaluation in which what is really being evaluated is the procedural efficiency of action in terms of the agency's mission rather than its substantive impact on the lives of human beings. This is another form of a *virtualization* most obvious in the creation of virtual markets divorced from the direct production of goods and services in the world of finance. Yet in the last analysis, it is the whole of social existence and personhood that the neoliberal model of market society threatens to desocialize and virtualize.

In a world in which the triumph of the market economy is taken for granted, it seems increasingly difficult to specify "realistic" strategies for those at the bottom of global society that do not entail enhancing their capacity to function in market society. Arguments turn largely on what measures are needed to secure that end. In Fox's Mexico, for example, the emphasis is now placed on giving poorer people access to credit via a "People's Bank," and providing limited forms of assistance to family budgeting. Yet it is absurd to represent "the poor," especially in countries that have never had effective welfare states, as somehow beyond the reach of market society, and therefore in need of being brought into it. What do the plethora of (legal and illegal) activities that have long sustained their precarious livelihoods represent if not efforts to participate in the market, and to behave like the entrepreneurs that neo-liberals recommend they must become? Poor people may be incapacitated when it comes to operating in the "mainstream" economy in terms of their education, but it is not obvious that capitalism has the capacity to offer socially dignifying opportunities to all even if it could deliver improvements in access to education. What is fundamentally wrong with the assumption that it is the moral duty of the citizen to adapt himself or herself to the market is that "the market" is an abstraction that can only deliver to humanity possibilities that are circumscribed by the particular combinations of historically evolving political, social, and cultural forces that Eric Wolf (1999) termed the "structural power" relations that make some outcomes more likely than others.

Some contemporary non-Western elites claim that their societies offer alternatives to Western market society, notably those of China and Malaysia. Ong (1999) has argued persuasively that contemporary East Asian states deploy "modern" forms of disciplinary power in culturally sensitive, adaptive ways so as to be able to play by the rules of global neoliberalism while appearing to "say no to the West." She shows that they have responded to economic globalization by subjecting different sections of their populations to different regimes of valuation and control so as to produce "zones of graduated sovereignty" based on the deployment of different forms of disciplinary power (Ong 1999:217). These evolve in a way that reflects the demands of the global economy, but they are also part of the process of building an "Asian modernity" that plays on what is most meaningful to different kinds of Asian citizens. There are, however, inevitable tensions in such "biopolitical" self-regulation. While, for example, overseas Chinese entrepreneurs can seek to rebuild their social links with the mainland population by investing in clan associations in towns housing their ancestral tombs, there are ongoing clashes between the ideas of ordinary Chinese about civility and responsible behavior, and a new individualistic culture of "family first" in the pursuit of wealth. As a reflection of a broad range of tensions, the Beijing regime resorts to repression in managing the continuing transformation of its society. Its support for the international "policing" project embedded in the West's "war against terror" reflects the way that it legitimates some of its own endeavors.

At the level of the practices of power, the diversity of neoliberal regimes is as striking as the family resemblances between them. In some contexts the privatization of public services has been accompanied by growth of private disposition of the means of violence, manifested in the links between politicians, mafias, and paramilitary forces (Wolf 1999:273). Such scenarios are compatible with transitions to formal electoral democracy and truly heroic efforts within "civil society" to defend human rights and propagate civic virtues. Yet the "shadow powers" mentioned earlier often remain sufficiently entrenched to guarantee continuing violence with impunity. Recourse to both public and private violence may also prove convenient in implementing ambitious transnational schemes to control the last reserves of tropical biodiversity and untapped mineral resources. Even apparently more benign policies, such as those that seek to "market" indigenous peoples and "unspoiled" ecological settings for cultural and ecological tourists, correspond to the deep logic of neoliberalization, the transformation of life itself into a marketable commodity and the imperative for us all to market ourselves.

Yet the failure of neoliberal policies to produce "development with equity" has made it increasingly problematic to express neoliberal ideology in a direct way as an unqualified embrace of the market society model. One of the strengths of US neoliberalism (often dubbed "neo-conservatism") is its ideological grounding through religious forces that supply a layer of transcendent values lacking in more secularized versions of neoliberalism. In general, however, efforts to disguise neoliberalism in this manner have failed to silence critics – as revealed by Carlos Salinas's failure to replace the official ideology of post-revolutionary Mexico with a new doctrine of "social liberalism," and by the negative reception of many "Third Way" doctrines.

Let us therefore turn to the counter-movements. Most analyses to date have focused on the emergence of transnational movements against neoliberalism and globalization that link Northern activists with the South as the positive side of the process of globalization itself. I have argued that excess optimism should be tempered by two considerations. One relates to the limitations of NGOs as organizers of these transnational webs. The other relates to neoliberalization's penetration of society. Even where it now seems in crisis, neoliberalism has set parameters for the history of the twenty-first century that may prove enduring. It is not sufficient to deconstruct the neoliberal ghosts in the machineries of contemporary social, economic, and political life, nor simply to critique neoliberalism's unfilled promises of prosperity, full citizenship, and genuine political democratization. We need to ask what alternatives can be constructed on the basis of the real social and political forces that exist in a world that neoliberalism has comprehensively restructured.

## Rehumanizing Economic Life

As I noted earlier, the NGO forum convened to secure the participation of critical voices in the "dialogue" at Monterrey revealed the limitations of such exercises by alienating local alternative organizations. Its sparsely attended sessions contrasted strikingly with the massive street demonstrations organized in Barcelona to focus the minds of EU governments as they discussed what increase in direct aid to developing countries they should announce before the conference. The Catalan capital echoed to a cacophony of voices representing a vast diversity of organizations and projects, but what was important about this uncoordinated, "decentered" protest was its inclusion of people from different social classes, its expression of deep-rooted social discontents, and its manifestation of a global view that seemed to bring all the different aspirations together. The problem is, however, that this bringing together may not produce a coherent alternative model of how to organize the world that could outlast the euphoria of street protest.

How, for example, do those who (rightly) criticize the environmental devastation produced by neoliberal policies square their concerns with those of peasants in the zones under threat, who are defending modes of livelihood that are seen as damaging to the environment, even as they challenge the right of transnational capital to exploit the resources of their place of residence? How do urban workers or unemployed people struggling on the margins of survival in post-industrial society relate their concerns to those of family farmers fighting to conserve what struggling urban groups regard as a privileged "rural way of life" that increases the cost of farm products or raises taxation? How do the rights of immigrants and minorities fare in a world in which "citizenship" means competing for diminishing public resources? How do the special claims of "indigenous" people balance against the claims of the (generally overwhelmingly more numerous) poor whom history has cast into social anonymity by dispossessing them of identity as well as denying them access to resources?

Is it possible to *think* about ways in which the different demands that cohere in this antagonism to neoliberalism and globalization might be brought together in a model of development that could prove more satisfying to all parties? Efforts toward this end are already apparent, for example, in the debates about sustainable development seen from a social and cultural as well as environmentalist point of view. Social movements with different class compositions and immediate goals have come to see common ground between their struggles in confronting the active opposition of states and capitalist corporations. Yet these convergences remain limited, and very frequently defensive, because of the need to translate utopias into some kind of viable politics. The transnational NGOs and solidarity networks that make local struggles of wider global import (often simply by making it more difficult to wipe the recalcitrant off the map by repression) also participate in the fragmentation and differentiation of movements. At the end of the day, they still have to cope with the fact that local people (inside and outside organized movements) must make their own deals and compromises, based on what alternatives are realistically available to them.

Globalization has indeed opened up new spaces for resistance, by breaking down communicational barriers, unleashing an information revolution that makes global inequalities and human-rights abuses more visible, and by facilitating transnational networking. This is true not only between North and South, but of equal if not greater importance, also applies to relations between different movements in the South itself. Globalization has also promoted the development of postcolonial identity politics that are an asset to those who can use these new tools politically. As I pointed out earlier, however, many of these spaces have been recolonized by the agencies of neoliberal global governmentality. Capitalism's drive to deepen the commodification of social life can only benefit from the proliferation of difference and hybridity, from the consumption of "lifestyle" by the affluent, and from the creation of new market niches even among the world's poorest (in the television and music industries, for example). The virtualized informational economy positively thrives on diversity.

Yet there are still limits to what these new tactics of governmentality can achieve. In 2002, I stood watching the conservative politicians who run the city of Salvador, Brazil, and the surrounding state of Bahia, presiding from their box over the opening parade of the annual carnival. It was given a strong multiculturalist image as "Afro-carnaval," and the intended dignification of the 83 percent of Bahia's population that is black was reinforced by a "pan-African" theme reflected in the opening musical performances and guests from African countries. The politicians did, however, have a difficult moment when the third element in the parade brought more radical black organizations together under the banner of "Drums of Liberty" (*Tambores da Liberdade*). The *Tambores* produced better music, but introduced discordant political elements into the ceremony, beginning with the slogan (borrowed from the US) "Compensation [for slavery] now" emblazoned on every T-shirt. What the politicians could not ignore were placards protesting the fact that the city's airport, whose name previously celebrated national independence, had been renamed in honor of a deceased politician. Nor could they ignore the protesters' demands that the city stop persecuting people who were seeking to make a living by wheeling carts about the streets, selling coffee and cigarettes. When the truck carrying the *Tambores'* trio stopped in front of the politicians' box, the message came out loud and clear that class issues were important and that celebrations of African culture, divorced from measures designed to reduce the poverty and exploitation that most black people suffered, were not going to buy silence, however many subsidies their "cultural" organizations received.

This moment of confrontation past, the *Tambores* moved off toward a working-class district in a slow procession in which all classes and races were welcome to participate. Yet the very nature of the procession already highlighted what had happened to "the world's largest street party" as we moved past the grandstands set up for those who wished to watch a "spectacle" without participating, an impression reinforced on the following night when the official carnival took on its normal form of three separate procession routes. The street was divided into three spaces. One of these was for the spectators in the grandstands. A second was for the paying participant public (local and foreign) that could afford to accompany the *trios* in the middle of the street behind the safety of the rope carried by their employees. There was also a third space, at the immediate margin of the rope, in which young black men danced and jumped aggressively in competition with the rope-bearers. In this situation of exclusion and strongly marked social differentiation, the heavy presence and aggression of military police was not sufficient to prevent fights from breaking out on the margins, while the exchanges between rope-bearers and those on the wrong side seemed to convey the message: "We're all in our places here, but at least we're inside the rope."

Despite its transformation by extremely well-organized government programs to promote a safe and enjoyable tourist experience (and also the politics of multicultural-ism), the official Salvador carnival is not able to cover over the cracks in Brazilian society. Furthermore, this is still not the whole of carnival in Salvador, since there are other parades in working-class districts that have no ropes, no grandstands (though some people prefer to watch from their houses rather than join the crush on the street), no police presence – and little if any violence. This is what made the moment of political protest on the first night possible. There is a *lived* social and cultural basis for organizing that remains resistant to co-optation. No distinct form of life is likely to remain wholly impervious to the individualizing and fragmenting tendencies of neoliberalization. The effects of neoliberalization, however, are also *changing the political implications of* the continuing reproduction of these forms of life.

I will illustrate this with an Argentine example, the Movimiento Mujeres Agrope-cuarias en Lucha (Farm Women in Struggle Movement, MMAL) (Giarracca and Teubal 2001). The MMAL looks, at first sight, like a "backward-looking" effort to preserve the anachronism of the capitalized family farm. Yet in being led by farmers' wives, who developed tactics that did actually stop legal processes of auctioning off land and machinery to repay debts, this spontaneous movement not only surprised the state, but also surprised the more traditional male-dominated organizations representing farmers. Furthermore, the movement showed itself capable of broadening the terms of the struggle on two fronts. First, it posed the issue of family-farm liquidation as a *cultural* question of national importance (what kind of "countryside" do we want and how does this relate to the kind of society we want our children to live in?). Second, the movement took on the problem of debt through a critical analysis of what should constitute "fairness" (in terms of real interest rates). The searching questions posed by the organization, however, concern the structure of bank lending and the fact that only 30 percent of the debt they must repay corresponds to the amount originally loaned. This line of discussion evidently has implications concerning the burden of international debt repayments imposed on developing countries.

Asking such questions rapidly demystifies the notion of neutral "market forces" not embedded in specific power relations and institutional and social conditions with a history. The origins and strength of the MMAL appear to stem from members' descent from European immigrants with a strong sense of cultural tradition and identity. Yet what is notable about contemporary movements such as this one – which are highly "local" in their origins – is that they do not simply advance demands linked to a particular sectional interest. Instead, they present their particular dilemma as part of a broader social problem, and on this basis reach out to allies in quite different social situations. In this regard, the MMAL's most notable outreach effort is with the Brazilian Movimento dos Sem Terra (Movement of the Landless, MST). At first sight, one would think that the MST – a squatters' movement that illegally occupies the property of other people – would be anathema to the Argentine family farmer. Nonetheless, MMAL leaders admire the combativeness of the MST and have sought to build links with other movements struggling for land redistribution rather than simply the defense of existing small-property ownership.

The MST is also not quite what one might expect, since its land-invasion strategy is designed to force the state to legalize private titles. Since the movement's first success in 1987, more than a quarter of a million families have won title to over 15 million hectares. MST political education uses the language and iconography of classical Marxism, and *assentados* (settlers with titles) are expected to work collectively on community projects, but the ultimate goal is to create a land reform based on small individual property-owners. In this sense the distance from MMAL perspectives is less than it might appear. Indeed, the convergence between the two movements does not end here. Like MMAL, the MST promotes rural society and the family farm as a way of life worthy of respect – a "rurality" project that not only critiques urban concentration and cultural bias, but also the role of transnational corporations in the global food system. Yet another paradox is that the MST is working to institutionalize its relations with the state, from which it seeks not simply basic services, but credits for production, extension services, and aid with marketing products. It has even signed exclusive contracts with transnationals to supply commodities such as sugar and milk products. What remains "radical" about the MST, however, is its vision of a completely different Brazil, a vision not necessarily undermined by institutionalization of the means used to consolidate "alternative development" (Mezaros 2000:9).

Yet the appeal of that vision does not eliminate a number of serious internal contradictions that have led to splits within the movement, defections to other organizations, or radically different individual strategies for seeking enhanced social dignity. The MST leadership can behave in deeply undemocratic, authoritarian, and even repressive ways toward its "base." In part this has reflected the growing centrality in MST strategy of the electoral politics of Brazil's left-wing Workers' Party (*Partido dos Trabalhadores*, PT). The PT's candidate, Luiz Inácio "Lula" da Silva, always forthright in his opposition to the "neoliberal model," finally won power on his fourth attempt with an unprecedented 68 percent of the vote in the 2002 general election, on a platform that promised to provide all Brazilians with three square meals a day. Yet he and his party were obliged to tone down their past radicalism very considerably in order to placate the international financial institutions that can now break any national economy overnight. Regional MST leaderships are also prone to conduct backstage negotiations with local politicians that lead to pragmatic, politically useful, outcomes that are not particularly favorable to the interests of their *assentados*. Entrenched political corruption combined with unstable agricultural markets leave MST communities facing problems long familiar to Mexican small farmers from the days when the state supported them with cheap credits and technical assistance. Life as a small farmer is now even harder, and many *assentados* prefer to keep their options open, abandoning the land if an outside paid job comes along or simply failing to pull their weight as full participants, increasing internal conflicts.

In the final analysis, building new social worlds and political cultures is more difficult than defending social worlds under attack, because a new kind of solidarity has to be built among people whose origins may be diverse (and in this case not necessarily even rural). Furthermore the new world has to be constructed within constraints inherited from the past. Land invaders may face social stigma, and may have to renegotiate their identities and right to respect as persons – a particularly difficult challenge within the systems of status differentiation so characteristic of agrarian societies dominated by large landowners. Tenants, sharecroppers, permanent workers, and casual laborers may carve out their own spaces of respect only by further degrading those below them, with their wives as a possible last resort at the bottom of socioeconomic and ethnic hierarchies. Although MST rhetoric projects the image of a coherent and unified national movement, in this as in many other cases, there are considerable differences between regions in what membership of the movement means to people at the grass-roots and in the specific social and economic conditions that shape (or inhibit) its local development.

Yet neoliberalism and globalization have, as the optimists point out, also brought human rights and gender issues into the picture as counter-currents to the negative historical legacies of past systems of domination. For all their contradictions, Southern social movements that can establish transnational links that are not entirely mediated by Northern NGOs are often able to find common ground among a diversity of struggles. In Latin America at least, the neoliberal onslaught has made it possible for organizations of the homeless, jobless, and property-less to make common cause with people who are none of these things. People who were previously middle-class have been hard hit by neoliberalism, and this fact has weakened political parties that have gravitated toward acceptance of neoliberalism's "realism" and inevitability. Fundamental social cleavages do remain important. The El Barzón debtors' movement in Mexico, also an ally of the Argentine MMAL, publicly supported the Zapatista peasant movement in Chiapas against repression. Yet deeper collaboration was impeded by the fact that most of the medium-sized farmers affiliated to El Barzón in the north and center of Mexico continue to view the indigenous peoples of the south as "others," with a different nature and mentality. Nevertheless, there is a trend toward considering what different movements share in terms of common goals, and to use these commonalities as a way to challenge the present model of global development.

On the one hand, movements are converging on the goal of rehumanizing and resocializing the economic process. On the other, they are increasingly engaged in efforts to understand the outlooks and world-views of different kinds of people. This is because there is ultimately no alternative except defeat. Participation in collective movements remains a minority activity, and local struggles focused on specific interest groups have little chance of prospering in isolation. If movements of the kind I have discussed seem unchallenging in their willingness to negotiate with states (and even with capital), this is not an adequate way to assess their potential. In engaging practically with the issue of alternative ways of organizing market-based economic relations, they are more realistic than movements that hope to arrest globalization in its tracks. They are also, however, more likely to impede the project of global governmentality embodied in neoliberalism. They ask the question transnational corporations, neoliberals, and "Third Wayers" have not managed to answer: what is the economy ultimately *for*, and can we not have a real choice about the kind of *life* that we want in a world as rich as this one in which so many remain poor?

**REFERENCES**

Arquilla, John, and David Ronfeldt (2000) Swarming and the Future of Conflict. Electronic document. http://www.rand.org/publications/DB/DB311/DB311.pdf.

Bretton Woods Project (1997) The World Bank and the State: A Recipe for Change? Electronic document. http://www.brettonwoodsproject.org/topic/governance/wbs/pdf.html.

George, Susan (1999) A Short History of Neoliberalism. Paper presented at the Global Policy Forum Conference on Economic Policy in a Globalized World. Electronic document. http://www.globalpolicy.org/globaliz/econ/histneol.htm.

Giarracca, Norma, and Miguel Teubal (2001) The Movimiento Mujeres Agropecuarias en Lucha. *Latin American Perspectives* 121:38–53.

Giddens, Anthony (2000) *The Third Way and Its Critics.* Cambridge: Polity Press.

Hardt, Michael, and Antonio Negri (2000) *Empire.* Cambridge, MA: Harvard University Press.

Kodolko, Grzegorz W. (1998) Economic Neoliberalism Became Almost Irrelevant. Electronic document. http://www.worldbank.org/html/prddr/trans/june1998/kolodko.htm.

Mezaros, George (2000) No Ordinary Revolution: Brazil's Landless Workers' Movement. *Race and Class* 42:1–18.

Ong, Aihwa (1999) *Flexible Citizenship: The Cultural Logics of Transnationality.* Durham, NC, and London: Duke University Press.

Peck, Jamie, and Adam Tickell (2001) Neoliberalizing Space. Electronic document. http://www.tickell.org.uk/papers.htm.

Ramos, Alcida Rita (1998) *Indigenism: Ethnic Politics in Brazil.* Madison: University of Wisconsin Press.

Wolf, Eric R. (1999) *Envisioning Power: Ideologies of Dominance and Crisis.* Berkeley: University of California Press.

## SUGGESTED FURTHER READING

Bourdieu, Pierre (1998) The Essence of Neoliberalism. Electronic document. http://www.analitica.com/bitblioteca/bourdieu/neoliberalism.asp.

Harvey, David (1989) *The Condition of Postmodernity: An Enquiry into the Origins of Cultural Change.* Oxford: Blackwell.

Hertz, Noreena (2001) *The Silent Takeover: Global Capitalism and the Death of Democracy.* New York: Free Press.

Gill, Lesley (1997) Relocating Class: Ex-miners and Neoliberalism in Bolivia. *Critique of Anthropology* 17:293–312.

Gledhill, John (1999) Official Masks and Shadow Powers: Towards an Anthropology of the Dark Side of the State. *Urban Anthropology and Studies of Cultural Systems and World Economic Development* 28:199–251.

Janvry, Alain de, Gustavo Gordillo, Jean-Philippe Plateau, and Elizabeth Sadoulet, eds. (1998) *Access to Land, Rural Poverty and Public Action.* Oxford: Oxford University Press.

Nash, June C. (2001) *Mayan Visions: The Quest for Autonomy in an Age of Globalization.* London: Routledge.

Nazpary, Joma (2001) *Poverty, Chaos and Globalization: Neoliberal Reform and Kazakhstan.* London: Pluto Press.

Polanyi, Karl (1957) *The Great Transformation: The Political and Economic Origins of Our Time.* Boston: Beacon Press.

World Bank (1997) *World Development Report: The State in a Changing World.* Washington, DC, London, and Oxford: Oxford University Press and the World Bank.

# 22 Popular Justice

*Robert Gordon*

Increasing disorder in southern countries is becoming a major concern, not only for the local inhabitants, but across the academic disciplines. It is especially prevalent in so-called failing states assaulted by the economic and political forces of globalization. There is, however, a danger that many different types of violence are being uncritically lumped together under a rather naïve and simplistic catch-all explanation like post-colonialism or globalization. In trying to frame an approach to comprehending these acts of violence, it soon becomes apparent that conventional concepts like "social control" and "law and order" are inadequate. They are everything and nothing at the same time. Rather, what this chapter does is take a deliberate ethnographic stance, a fieldwork-inspired "grass-roots" perspective, to examine what is apparently a populist phenomenon of increasing importance, vigilantism.

By all accounts there appears to be an upsurge in vigilante actions in the former Third World, in particular, sub-Saharan Africa. Vigilantism can be defined as private organized self-help punitive action with a gloss of legalistic ritual, undertaken by people to achieve what they define as justice. Given that most scholars see one of the key characteristics of the state as its monopoly of the means of force and the legal system, this increase in vigilantism raises important questions and issues about contemporary states within the global system. Typically, vigilantism has been ascribed to the perception that the state is ineffective or weak. In effect, vigilantism seeks to mimic the state's judicial system. This raises important questions about how the state is conceptualized by both academics and local people. Its cultural dynamics of moral outrage need to be explored. This chapter argues for an in-depth study of a specific type of violence, vigilantism, at one specific moment of time, so that its characteristics may be more surely related (or not) to a state form, a location within the world economy and its global context.

## VIGILANTES: DOUBLE AGENTS OF LAW AND ORDER

The rhetoric of "law and order" is crucial for the expansion of any state. Given this context, the striking increase in grass-roots judicial self-help activities, sometimes labeled vigilantism and justified in terms of "law and order," raises questions and issues about contemporary states within the global system. Is this because that administrative apparatus is "weak" or losing its legitimacy? Could the increase in vigilante activity be due to the changing contours of the contemporary state in the process of refashioning itself from a "nation-state" that focused on providing such basic services as law and order for its citizens to a "market state," where its priority is to provide market opportunities for its citizens? Or is vigilantism another manifestation of the modern drive toward individualism and "privatization," in this case of the judicial system? Or could it be that at least part of the problem lies in how academics (and ordinary citizens) conceive and study vigilantism, the state, and the role of law?

Vigilantism and activities like it have been surprisingly under-researched. Recent survey articles in the authoritative *Annual Review of Anthropology* ignore it completely. Indeed, except for two recent books, Ray Abrahams's *Vigilant Citizens: Vigilantism and the State* (1998) and Michael Fleisher's *Kuria Cattle Raiders* (2001), it has been largely ignored by anthropologists. Abrahams's study is based on a detailed case study of *sungusungu*, a Nyamwezi vigilante group in Tanzania, where he did fieldwork. He supplements this with a comparison based on the published literature on vigilantes. Fleisher's work is concerned with a similar East African political phenomenon. While it contains much statistical grist, it is surprisingly light on the cultural dimensions. The most interesting recent study is Richard Wilson's *The Politics of Truth and Reconciliation in South Africa* (2001). This includes a valuable chapter, based on fieldwork on a "popular Court" in a small township on the Rand, in order to assess how local legitimacy compares to the national and international rhetoric. The lack of ethnographic studies of vigilante activity is particularly regrettable since it is typically a local phenomenon in which the primary actors are not holders of institutionalized political office or power. Yet, by virtue of this very circumstance, vigilantism is central to the traditional anthropological bailiwick. Indeed, sociologist Alan Hunt (1999) argues that vigilantism derives its moral significance from the very fact that it coordinates dissimilar group projects that lie outside the mainstream of official politics and state institutions.

This chapter examines activities that appear to be increasingly significant outside the official moral realm of the political mainstream. It suggests how anthropologists might critically approach this phenomenon. It concentrates on South Africa in the last 20 years, during which apartheid was finally dismantled. In this period vigilante activity became rampant and, despite the efforts of the government to deal with it through police action and the courts, there was little evidence that the problem was under control. Most donor-funded "think-tanks" believe vigilantism was an important feature of the landscape, both in sprawling squatter settlements outside large cities and in more isolated rural areas. It is seen as part of the country's larger "crime problem" and has spawned numerous private and state research projects. The government has attempted to deal with it in a number of ways – apart from administrative tinkering, increasing penalties for criminal offenses, and reforming police and court systems to make both more accessible to the public, epitomized best by the creation of "Community Police Forums" and "Community Courts" in an effort to combat crime and preempt vigilante-type actions. In striking testimony to the openness of post-apartheid South Africa, the issue has also spawned a rich "gray literature," largely produced by non-goverenmental organizations (NGOs) affiliated to universities, like the Center for the Study of Violence and Reconciliation, the Institute for Security Studies, the Human Sciences Research Council, and even the research arm of various commercial banks. This is available on the World Wide Web.

The focus advocated in this chapter is useful for developing ideas about vigilantism that might be relevant elsewhere in the world. After all, as the tourist brochures put it, South Africa is "A World in One Country." Given the massive discrepancies between the affluent and the poor, South Africa indeed represents in many ways a warped microcosm of global inequalities. It is in no way exceptional, if extreme. As Mahmoud Mamdani has argued in *Citizen and Subject* (1996), apartheid was the generic form of the colonial state in Africa. As a semi-industrialized state where, until recently, authoritarian development was based on patrimonialism exacerbated by racism, South Africa invites comparison with situations in other parts of the world, most notably Latin America.

This is not the place for a controlled comparison of national vigilantisms, as it were. Let me instead observe that most studies of South African vigilantism have focused so closely on verbal evidence (in the form of comments and statements by participants in vigilante actions and by onlookers) that they lack the comparative perspective that problematizes the context and nature of state-making, which an anthropology of politics offers. The South African studies have overlooked crucial points about vigilante activity. First, vigilantism, in essence, mimics the state's formal legal system. Second, vigilante activity is, perhaps above all else, a public performance centering on punishment – usually of a corporeal nature. The vigilante action has an audience: "justice" is seen to be done, quite literally and almost immediately. Finally, vigilante activity is essentially parasitic. It emerges ostensibly in response to state inaction or inability; yet it cannot exist without that state.

Vigilantism entails a subversively undermining paradox. Although it is launched at the local level to uphold law and order, it undermines the legitimacy of state machinery charged with maintaining it at the national level. Centering on these features encourages anthropologists to treat vigilantism as a site for exploring in novel ways the conventional dichotomy between "traditional" and "modern" law, as well as the constitution of the state.

## Vigilantes in their Various Disguises

The *Fontana Dictionary of Modern Thought* (Bullock and Stallingbrass 1974:664) defines vigilantes as "Self-appointed law enforcement groups appearing spontaneously when the established authorities seem unable or unwilling to cope with lawlessness and disorder." The fact that vigilantism occurs in a situation perceived by actors and analysts alike to be lawless and disorderly, and may well be not only nurtured but nourished by this lawlessness, would appear at first sight to be inimical to the interests of the state. It would appear to be a challenge to the state's legitimate monopoly over the use of armed force within its national boundaries. Yet it might be argued that, this being so, all states originate and continue to exist only to the extent that the centralized state machinery practices what might be considered a form of "indirect rule," inasmuch as it delegates the use of armed force, therefore legitimate force, to certain persons among their subjects.

Richard M. Brown (1969), the author of a classic and definitive essay on the history of the vigilante tradition in the US, uses the term to refer to organized *extralegal* movements that take the law into their own hands. They were not *illegal* because it was understood that they arose on the frontier at a time when the state was unable to provide judicial services. In small frontier towns eminent local residents, typically respectable property-owners, organized local vigilance committees whose task it was to punish people believed guilty of basic and obvious crimes. The committees were usually organized in a military fashion. They had constitutions and formal articles or manifestoes requiring speedy formal trials (that is, due process). It is said that attention was paid more to the spirit than the letter of the constitution. These activities, conservative of law and order, as it were, created a parallel or *extralegal* judicial structure. This duplicated the state system, but at a fraction of the financial cost to the local community. Sometimes it also promoted community solidarity, the strong penalties serving as a warning to those who might think of engaging in unacceptable acts (Brown 1969:188–190). What made these movements uniquely American, Brown claimed, was that their ideological justification rested on the doctrines of self-preservation, the right of revolution, and popular sovereignty ("the right of the people").

In this model, the focus is on vigilante committees: regular extralegal organizations that came into existence for a short period of perceived disorder. Their action was usually organized along militaristic lines and, in accordance with law, concluded with a formal (if often abbreviated) trial. Fieldwork-grounded studies of local committees vigilant in the interest of law and order have been carried out in the highlands of Papua New Guinea in the 1970s and 1980s, and more recently in Brazil, Cuba, and Chile.

## Forms of Vigilantism in South Africa

In South Africa the term "vigilantism" has been applied to several political phenomena that might better be kept distinct: (1) political activities of reactionary local groups to hold on to power in the face of radical change; and (2) political activity of the state in mobilizing elements of a local population to suppress others. There is also, I suggest, an intermediary form of judicial activity – alternative dispute settlement, a worldwide movement that entered South Africa in the early 1980s. Before describing these, I apply to South Africa the arguments of Les Johnston, whose essay "What is Vigilantism?" appeared in the *British Journal of Criminology* in 1996.

Perhaps the most valuable elements in Johnston's conceptualization of vigilantism is that he does not assume vigilantism to be necessarily extralegal or entailing punishment. The most important aspect of vigilantism, he claims, is premeditation and planning. It is preeminently a group activity entailing a modicum of organization. There can be no such thing as a lone vigilante, no Lone Ranger or Dirty Harry. This group aspect, whether on an ad hoc or recurrent basis, is an important sociocultural feature of South African vigilantism. A second crucial characteristic, Johnston argues, is that its participants are private citizens whose involvement is voluntary. Thus vigilantism excludes state agents: there is no such thing as off-duty police officers, since they retain discretionary powers even while off duty. Police abuse of power is not to be confused with vigilantism. Crossovers between public and private policing are increasing. In South Africa, for example, the latter currently outnumber the former by a ratio of about four to one. Private commercial security companies practice within the ambit of the law. A third trait Johnston considers crucial is that vigilantism entails autonomous citizenship and takes place without state support or authority. This gives it the characteristics of a social movement. This assumes, however, a definition of citizenship which in the South African context can be problematic (Mamdami 1996). In South Africa it is preeminently denizens (people naturalized into a particular environment) rather than citizens (whose rights and privileges accrue to them by virtue of membership in the state), who partake in such activities.

In sum, Johnston concludes that vigilantism is concerned primarily with personal and communal security and thus morphs between the social definition of crime and social control in a multifaceted way. A necessary condition for vigilantism is a situation in which people feel that they must "do something" and so actively engage in measures to improve the normative quality of life. It must be recognized, however, that others may use the vigilantes' rhetoric of transgression as a cover for a more politically, even criminally, inspired agenda.

There has never been a single accepted adjudicative and enforcement structure in South Africa. While the African "traditional authorities" maintained law and order in the reserves or "homelands," in the urban areas matters were different. Given the government's refusal to recognize that Africans had permanent rights in urban areas, these areas received comparatively little government attention. From the beginning, the process of urban industrialization meant that Africans were obliged to develop their own systems of maintaining law and order. This resulted in numerous coexisting structures, among them largely retributive vigilante-like organizations that arose out of attempts to deal with social and personal fragmentation and alienation in a situation exacerbated by migration, forced removals, insecure employment, constant housing crises, and excessively high rates of youth unemployment. This gave rise to a troubled and ambiguous relationship between these people's courts of no legal standing and the state. A minority of these crypto-vigilante groups was abetted in various ways by the apartheid regime.

This upsurge of vigilantism in both rural homelands and urban areas was almost certainly encouraged by the government's strategic passivity, if not complicity. In the political situation at the time, conventional policing methods were unable to contain the situation of anti-apartheid protest. While apartheid was a particularly odious form of domination, it is one of its ironies that the Republic of South Africa always had one of the lowest ratios of police to population.

South Africa's securocrats were tied into a global network of rather shadowy paramilitary organizations to "combat communism," with nodes at places like the United States' notorious "School of the Americas." They trained in what was known as "low intensity conflict" (LIC) and drew upon French experience in Algeria and Indo-China. Following the principle that 90 percent of all battle was psychological, they adopted a well-tested strategy of clandestinely creating a surrogate irregular armed force to create dissension among an enemy population. The securocrats were well aware of vigilante deployment in other parts of the world and especially in El Salvador, where the South African ambassador was kidnapped and held to ransom by such a force in the early seventies.

In the academic literature, vigilantism has risen to prominence on the backs of the victims, largely in Latin America. The Latin-American version differs substantially from the vintage US model in that its primary purpose is to control civil society at large (Abrahams 1998) and this resonated with the requirements of the South African state. Latin Americanists have depicted vigilantism as informal violence in defense of the status quo – largely conservative forces occupying the high ground in what is usually an authoritarian-style state. For them vigilantism includes a wide range of activities, including paramilitary death squads and *justiceiros*. Kowalewski views these vigilantes as "unconventional counter-movements against a dissident movement [which are] mobilizations of the resources of aggrieved citizens against elites . . . utilized in unconventional ways" (Kowalewski 1996:63). Usually elites resort to such strategies when they are unable to deal with such dissent using conventional (or legal) activities.

Vigilantism becomes prominent in times of increasing dissent. While they are shrouded in populist rhetoric, vigilantes are usually sponsored by elites who use them as a small but flexible private "rapid deployment force" to deal with the protest of common citizens. While scholars agree that vigilante groups are motivated by a desire to deal with crime, it is the social and regime-control roles of vigilantes that these scholars emphasize. Vigilantism emerges in authoritarian states and reinforces their inegalitarian ideologies and practices. Vigilantism is overtly political and death or assassination is the most common result. The most important factor affecting the emergence and proliferation of such groups, these scholars suggest, is the national state and its sometimes clandestine international supporters, the United States or large multinational corporations.

Given their shadowy origins and their intention of undermining civic goals inspired by anti-apartheid, South African vigilantes (sometimes colloquially referred to as *mabangalala*) frequently adopted a vigilante committee model that mimicked the mimics. Applied psychologists and anthropologists instigated a variety of "cultural organizations" in different parts of South Africa and neighboring Namibia, which rapidly became transformed into vigilante committees. Securocrats saw that such local vigilantism might serve the state's strategy of dismantling organizations that opposed it, since both the police and the national defense force were constrained from such activities by legal considerations and negative publicity. By framing part of their repertoire of cultural activities as "restoring law and order," vigilantes could justify support from the police. Since the security forces could neither administer the townships themselves, nor coerce support for the state-sponsored community councils, vigilantes could target the opposition and support the formal township structures that centered largely on allocating and collecting rent on government-built houses. Communities that were cowed and disorganized generated a political vacuum that the vigilante committees could occupy. For the state, vigilantes were inexpensive, and "black on black" violence provided justification for sending the military into the townships to support the police. This served to strengthen white popular ideology that blacks were incapable of keeping the peace themselves. Framed in these terms, South African so-called "hit squads" are similar to what are called "death squads" elsewhere. Both appear to be dedicated to "taking out" criminals on the one hand and popular opponents to the regime on the other. Hit squads and death squads are clandestine groups that engage in extra-judicial violence, usually with some support or acquiescence, either covert or overt, from the government. As with the Ku Klux Klan in the United States, for example, while they thrive on the performance of highly visible public actions, their identity is kept as secret as possible. Their *raison d'être,* as with all such groups, is to counteract a real or symbolic threat to the existing social order.

I would argue that branding this political activity vigilantism so extends the meaning of the term that it comes to lack analytical validity. *The key characteristic of vigilantism is that it arises from lack of action by government officials.* It is action autonomous from the state. Hit squads are engaged in exercises of social and regime control, and do not challenge the sovereignty of state power. Crime control, the focus of classic vigilante action, represents a potential threat to the sovereignty of the state. The violence of hit squads is a reaction by "responsible" but not "autonomous" citizens (Johnston 1996). Thus hit squads might be described as pseudo- or crypto-vigilante activities. Vigilante origins lie in local community concerns, not those of the state, while death squads are often de facto subcontractors of the government. While their rhetoric might overlap, structurally and ritually they are different.

In the mid-eighties (dates are difficult to fix with precision in such shadowy wars) the major political opposition to the white regime, the African National Congress, inspired by a successful grass-roots rent and tax boycott in the townships, was stirred to make the townships ungovernable. Moving into the vacuum or providing an alternative to the formal structure were so-called "people's courts," established as parallel and antagonistic to the formal state machinery. It was part of a strategy to replace the organs of the state and in so doing transform political relations. That the regime viewed these developments as a serious threat is obvious from its brutal suppression of these courts, not that the courts were all that popular. Indeed, schisms rapidly emerged along generational lines. Given the political fervor of the time, the youth claimed a leading role in these courts, and their often cavalier approach to problems of their elders rapidly led to the undermining of the latter's authority, which in turn, on a number of occasions, then organized their own "people's courts" (often with covert state support) to deal with upstart youth.

In South Africa, "popular justice" movements might be considered intermediary between classic community vigilante action and state-acknowledged hit squads. These movements, also known as "informal" or "community justice" movements, have comprised since the early 1980s a worldwide movement toward judicial or legal informalism. They have complex roots that are at once idealist, materialist, political, and professional. Contradictory and complex, they are supplementary to over-crowded and therefore incapacitated state legal systems (as in the case of classic vigilantism). In this case, they may be transformed into institutions very different from what even the most insightful bureaucrats expected them to be.

Popular justice is firmly lodged in the alternative dispute resolution movement (ADR). Nothing could be less like the state's own punitive legal system, particularly in South Africa. The ADR movement rose to popularity in the United States because it was felt that the justice system was being overwhelmed by cases, and it was supposed to provide inexpensive mechanisms for dealing with conflicts that might clog up the court system. Like all significant changes, it developed its own coterie of development experts and has been exported to many former Third-World countries as part of the United States' effort to promote "democratization" and "human rights."

Globally, ADR appears to have had limited success beyond the borders of the United States. It is, by and large, located within aboriginal enclaves in established settler states, where it meets needs that the state cannot satisfy. ADR forums provide a measure of community autonomy in resolving disputes under the aegis of the state. The forums are required to follow a modicum of prescribed rituals and record-keeping. They may, indeed, be just as inflexible as the state, and they are often unable to prevent the intrusion of state power into decision-making. These are not vigilante groups, precisely because it is the government that promotes them. Securocrats may hope that they will counteract perceived vigilante tendencies, but there is always the danger that they may themselves be co-opted and politicized. It is precisely vigilante emphasis on corporal and capital punishment, and their dangerous tendency not to wait until a "crime" has been committed but to act preventatively, that sets off the alarm bells of the state officials, who are increasingly conscious of the publicity impact that such actions might have in the global economy. In particular, tourism would suffer in the face of the universalistic bourgeois human-rights outcry that would ensue. Advocacy of human rights seems able to penetrate even the most obdurate barriers thrown up by totalitarian-style regimes (Wilson 2001).

By the end of 2000, issues of "law and order" had moved to center-stage in South Africa. According to a Human Sciences Research Council public opinion poll taken at that time, 44 percent of respondents felt "safe" and 45 percent "unsafe." This was a vast increase compared with 1994, when almost three-quarters of respondents had felt "safe." Indeed, in 1994 another survey found that only 6 percent of the respondents thought that crime was the "most important problem facing the country." By 1999 this had increased to 65 percent, and by the end of 2002 South African blacks were reportedly growing nostalgic for the apartheid regime. Over 60 percent of all South Africans polled claimed that the country was better run during white-minority rule. This finding was largely attributed to the increase in crime, South Africa having become notorious for the countrywide prevalence of rape, murder, car-hijackings, and robbery. Devising ways of dealing with the increasingly chaotic law and order problem has become a virtual development "cottage industry," with admirable work being done by a number of non-governmental organizations (NGOs). The government has made various attempts to improve outreach by getting local people involved in community police forums (CPFs) and the like. Access to the forums remains limited, while the police attempt to move from a "confession-based" to an "evidence-based" system in order to accommodate local cultural nuances. Meanwhile, the country continues to have one of the highest incarceration rates in the world.

Not surprisingly, there has been an upsurge in vigilante action. The two movements that have garnered the most publicity thus far are People Against Gangsters and Drugs (PAGAD) and *Mapogo a Mathamaga*, a name derived from a Sotho proverb celebrating the fact that a leopard confronted by a tiger turns into a tiger. PAGAD was formed in the Western Cape in 1996, initially as a community group collaborating with the government. By 1998 cooperation with the police had broken down and the US State Department had labeled PAGAD a "terrorist organization," due to its ties to global Islamic fundamentalists, a view shared by many South Africans. Mapogo a Mathagama, on the other hand, continues to thrive, despite internal conflict and much negative publicity resulting from the government's unsuccessful efforts to curtail the organization's illegal strong-arm tactics. Mapogo, like

PAGAD, was established by a community group of businessmen in rural Northern Province near Pietersburg. By September 2001, its leader was chartering a helicopter to attend meetings, while the organization itself claimed over 50,000 members in more than 100 branches in eight provinces.

More pertinently, locally inspired autonomous "people's courts" (*imbizo* or *magotla*) continue to flourish. One such court recently studied by Richard Wilson is in Boipatong, a large African township on the Rand, the hub of South Africa's industrial complex. Wilson's description is particularly valuable because it is based on fieldwork, in contrast to most of the focused interviews and newspaper-commissioned research reports. Fieldwork is integral for *anfuhlung*, that necessary sense of context. Kim Philby, the famous British spy for Russia, made this point well when he claimed that the most important part of his work was to cruise the diplomatic cocktail circuit, because that gave him a sense of the interpersonal milieu essential to interpreting the written documents he had purloined. He had to know who was trying to impress or deflate whom.

In Boipatong a people's court arose out of a concern for the deterioration in law and order. Its moderate success illustrates the complex interplay between local and national interests and actors. Most of the proponents of the court were the older, more established, mostly male community members. Permanent members fall into two distinct groups, the middle-aged and older members who generally belong to the conservative Zion Christian Church (ZCC), one of the most important independent African churches in the country, while the younger members are trained African National Congress (ANC) combatants. Despite this, inter-generational conflict remains endemic in the cases it hears.

Every afternoon between 4.00 p.m. and 5.00 p.m., disputes and complaints, largely concerning petty theft, domestic violence, assault, unpaid debts, and occasionally rape, are brought to the 30 to 40 men of the *imbizo*. The court refuses to deal with murder and "love problems," a gloss for crimes of passion and adultery. The court patriarchs allow extended testimony, examine medical reports when they are applicable, and generally subject parties and witnesses to an inquisitorial style of questioning. They speak of themselves applying "customary law." Justice takes two forms: restorative and retributive. The purpose of the former is to improve existing relationships, largely through compensation. The latter, epitomized by a public beating, is more characteristic. The court is acutely aware of the negative publicity such measures create, especially in the press, because such actions are unconstitutional, and they have met the challenge creatively by first having the accused sign a consent form and then passing sentence collectively, each taking turns in inflicting the beatings. Physical punishment is central to the court's activities. They, and indeed most of the township residents, believe that the "truth" can only emerge under duress. The accused must confess and therefore he must be physically abused to obtain a valid truth or confession. The rights of the accused, they argue, should be suspended in favor of "community" interests. Most people, including females, agree to this *modus operandi* from a lack of an alternative that is inexpensive and accessible. When the accused refuse to consent they are referred to the local police station.

Both police and local civic associations accept the *imbizo*. Initially its founders, showing a keen appreciation of the realities of power, took their proposal not to the local black-run police station, but to the nearest white-run one for approval. One of their aims, according to their written constitution, was to build trust between police and community. That they have succeeded is demonstrated by the fact that cases are referred reciprocally. Community justice adjusts to the cut and thrust of local politics, especially as it negotiates with the state. State jurisdiction has imposed checks on the imposition of certain forms of corporal punishment and, since "human rights" talk has permeated even to the rural local level, this too has had the effect of tempering excessive physical punishment.

Using broad brush-strokes, the situation can be summed up in the following way. While many segments of South African society, including the white middle class, approve of vigilantism, it is found largely in the townships and informal settlements, areas largely characterized by a minimal police presence, minimal services, and rife, unpredictable unemployment. But these townships and informal settlement areas must not be seen as an anarchic void. They are characterized by numerous organizations, some based on kinship, others on common interest or locality. Mainstream churches, independent churches, and sects incorporating elements of both "traditional" and Christian beliefs are ubiquitous. Small rotating credit associations are omnipresent. Entrepreneurs band together. Taxi drivers have a very powerful, indeed militant, association protecting their interests. The strong "unionized" women *shebeen* (illicit liquor establishments) operators pay fines collectively when the police arrest a member for operating an unlicensed drinking establishment. They also pay protection money to survive when, in the absence of official policing, gangs move in and dispense patronage, protection, and justice. And it is the people in these neighborhoods, structurally weak categories of the population, who have recourse to what Victor Turner called *communitas* who support vigilance committees.

These "informal" courts are popular for a number of reasons. Compared with the formal judicial system, renowned for dragging out investigation and court action, judgments are almost instantaneous. They are, moreover, generally held to be conciliatory, accessible, understandable, and inexpensive, yet informality allows for full emotional expression. Sentencing is flexible and generally reflects the public consensus (although there is a suspicion that this can be manipulated). In poor South African neighborhoods, the fact that victims often get their goods back or some form of redress or compensation enhances the attractiveness of these courts. This is rarely the case within the state-run judicial system. Typically, some of the fine levied goes to the victim, but participants in the judgment also receive a token for their work. Rather than being passive, victims and their supporters feel that they are part of the action, and this is not only therapeutic but constructive of community identification. But the most important reason for their popularity is that participants feel they have been "let down" by the formal justice system. The South African justice system lacks credibility. This overwhelming lack of faith, dissatisfaction, and frustration is the one constant upon which all accounts agree.

## THE MAKING OF LAW AND ORDER AT THE LOCAL LEVEL

Both the role of the state as guarantor of "law and order" and the "black-box" model of the state, which assumes it to be some sort of super-organic form of organization floating imperviously above human agency, need to be questioned.

When the man in the street is asked, "What is the state?" he does not enter into abstract discussion but instead points to officials, soldiers, and policemen, claiming that they are the state. He is making the same point that Radcliffe-Brown made when he wrote, "There is no such thing as the power of the State. There are only, in reality, powers of individuals – kings, prime ministers, magistrates, policemen, party bosses, and voters."

In South Africa, as numerous studies have shown, local residents see the police as inadequate, inactive, susceptible to bribes, practicing favoritism, and colluding with criminals or as themselves criminals. This colors their perception of a court system that is dismissed as time-consuming and "soft" on criminals. Thus, in many parts of South Africa, but especially in the townships, the judicial role of the state as under-writer of order and predictability is highly problematic. At the height of apartheid's heyday, most arrests were for offenses such as unlicensed beer-brewing, pass-law infringement, and tax evasion, which were defined as crimes by the state but were not seen as such by the locals. At the same time, local forms of social control, such as public floggings and seizure as a form of debt collection, were considered crimes by the state.

Township rhetoric emphasized that the "Boers" and their dogs – the police – were illicitly occupying the citadels of power. Crime was frequently dismissed as a product of apartheid. "We weep for Mandela" was a commonplace explanation for engaging in theft. The abolition of apartheid and the coming into office of the African National Congress party in 1994 led to rising expectations that were not met.

Bauman (2000) has suggested that, at the same time, challenges to the national state, and increasing demands for the flexibility of labor characteristic of globaliza-tion, led to the conflation of intrinsic insecurity and uncertainty into a single over-whelming concern for personal safety. This is too limited. Given the problematic nature of the state in South Africa, it is necessary to supplement Bauman's analytic framework with Foucault's notion of "governance." This involves not only political and economic subjection and social control via the state and the market, but also the myriad ways in which people organize themselves, attempt to control each other, and imagine what they do in the process. Governance is an acupuncture-like pressure point that influences and impacts other parts of the body politic. In a universe of insecurity generated by state and market volatility, the construction of networks of personal safety places a high premium on cultural creativity. At the macrolevel the state strives for compliance (and hence predictability), not only through legitimacy and coercion, but through legitimacy and co-option as well. It is a complex matter. The brutal and all-encompassing laws of the apartheid regime epitomized evil banal-ity, yet as detailed analyses of court records indicate, many of these laws were either not regularly enforced or unenforceable. A vast number of people controlled by the apartheid state considered it illegitimate. Nevertheless it continued to operate (des-pite its relatively small police force) through a carefully manufactured legitimacy (for the ruling whites) and massive processes of dependency and co-option (for the masses). In the townships and "homelands," for example, officials sought to manipu-late dependency by shutting off services and reallocating them elsewhere. The gov-ernment was an extraordinarily large employer. In the mid-1980s, 35 percent of all whites, 22.5 percent of coloreds, 16.5 percent of Indians, and 19.4 percent of all Africans were employed by the state.

In all efforts at governance, according to Foucault, there is a discrepancy between intention and outcome. At best, people are *bricoleurs* who combine what they stumble across. They rarely anticipate, let alone control, the outcome of their plans, but simply try to make sense of their unintended results. In face-to-face interactions they mostly "muddle through" with a gloss of post hoc and sometimes illusionary predictability facilitated through a number of mechanisms: first, sanctions of approval through manifestations of esteem, public shaming, or respect; second, reciprocity, especially the threat to withdraw from relationships that bind people to that community or group, epitomized by expulsion, exclusion, and ostracism; third, retaliation, or the threat thereof, especially in relationships that are not morally binding; fourth and last, sorcery or the threat thereof (Taylor 1982:80–90) These mechanisms take on a strong cadence of *ceremonialism* as defined by Moore and Myerhoff (1975:13–22, 210–239), as a traditionalizing mechanism with formal properties such as repetition, acting, stylization, evocative presentational style, and a "collective dimension." As Herbert Spencer recognized, long before Foucault, the most basic kind of government is the government of ceremonial observances. It has the largest share in regulating men's lives. Spencerian *government by ceremonial observances* is crucial for understanding the rise and role of vigilante organizations.

## Vigilante Spectacles

Perhaps the most important and most common aspect of vigilantism – so obvious that most writers have overlooked it – is that it needs an audience to be effective. In South Africa, despite these mechanisms for creating order, the social space its denizens inhabit resembles a frontier zone, a vast gray area betwixt and between "civilization" and "savagery," in which ambiguity, unpredictability, and fantasy are key organizing features. While laws successfully shackled the settler imagination, they had less of an impact in the townships. There fantasy, shaped in no small part by television media (up to 20 percent of African households already had access to it in the early eighties), depoliticized the situation, as Heribert Adam has shown in his essay on "Engineering Compliance," by promoting a near obsession with glitz, sex, sport, and crass consumerism. This played a crucial role in social control. And maybe, mass media played a role in inspiring the specific form of social control with which this chapter is concerned – vigilante activity. American gangster movies and B Grade Westerns were popular in the townships in the 1950s and 1960s, but the implications of this still need to be studied systematically.

In the absence of effective state police services in the townships, social order was largely maintained by family and kin groups, a variety of church organizations, traditional healers, and a mix of parastatals and "civics," ubiquitous community organizations concerned with local issues and later linked to the anti-apartheid opposition, the ANC-affiliated United Democratic Front (UDF). Over 30 percent of all Africans belong to a rapidly growing number of independent churches, usually small, largely autonomous congregations belonging to a church which is not affiliated with mainline Christianity and incorporating diverse indigenous elements.

In a discussion of political imagination and popular justice in South Africa, Clifton Crais suggests that vigilante action, with its often authoritarian violence, serves as a powerful constitutive site for conceptualizing both the past and the future. As such, it is often manipulated. Thus Monhle Magolego, the president of Mapogo, is reported to be pleased about widespread reports that his vigilantes have fed criminals to crocodiles. "If they tell terrible stories about Mapogo, I like that. It'll scare the criminals." Any item of information, especially hearsay, is snatched up eagerly, and neither proponents nor opponents of vigilantism have demonstrated much desire to ascertain the validity of rumors that vindicate their own positions. Finding that even unfounded fears work effectively, vigilante groups have even started to market them. Thus Mapogo gives all who pay their fees a T-shirt with the group's logo on it, a sticker to display in a prominent place, and a cell-phone number to call when needed. Clearly a protection racket, these symbolic markers of potential retribution and magical protection fill the coffers of Magolego's organization.

In this maelstrom of uneasy modernity, vigilantism points to the importance of association by both interaction and spectacle, to adopt Herbert Spencer's distinctions. "Interaction" has a strong ritual character about it insofar as it consists of a more or less invariant sequence of formal acts and utterances in an effort to establish conventions, meaning by that term publicly recognized and stipulated rules which, if accepted, entail obligations that invest the sequence with some morality. "Spectacle" refers to a dramatic form of communication that derives its power largely through visual imagery and dramatic action, and that is watched by an audience.

Vigilante activities, as spectacles, must have an audience in order to be effective. The size of the audience may range from a few to upwards of a few thousand. Typically, it includes neighbors, friends, and relatives of the complainant and the defendant, as well as curious onlookers. Certainly, vigilante groups appreciate the importance of ritual and spectacle. This is nowhere more dramatically illustrated than when Mapogo opens a new branch. These occasions are characterized by marches, speeches, special dress uniforms, music, praise songs, and, nowadays, the arrival of the VIPs by BMW or helicopter greeted by an honor guard. In South Africa's Northern Province these performances show an uncanny resemblance to those of the fascist Afrikaner Weerstandsbeweging (Afrikaner Resistance Movement), which had had its stronghold in that part of the country in the latter days of apartheid.

Vigilante courts need a particular mode of spectator and audience reception. Drawing on Baudelaire's essential figure of modernity, the "passionate spectator," Tom Gunning's (1994) notion of a "cinema of attractions" is pertinent to understanding the spectacularity of vigilante action. Vigilante action as "attraction" addresses the viewer or audience directly, soliciting attention and curiosity and collapsing time. Attractions openly acknowledge their own process of display and the onlooker's role as an "outside observer." Held by curiosity and amazement, the gawker is drawn into the drama. One of the consequences of the vigilante spectacle is to draw the onlookers in and to reinforce the engagement of those who already have ties to the defendants or the aggrieved.

The vigilante court performances consist largely of a number of set pieces. These oversimplify and obscure issues as much as they simplify and illuminate. The action focuses on an immediate issue, allowing the larger structures of inequality and dominance to be pushed out of the spotlight and into the dark to such a degree that these overarching structures are strengthened. From this perspective, legitimacy is not so much about getting people to accept what is done as attracting their attention and holding it long enough for them to listen, so that gradually, this "performative" legitimacy can infuse and shape their symbolic systems of action and thereby reduce their perceptions of available choices. These vigilante performances establish a spectral presence, which will continue to haunt and inform the actions of the spectators for the foreseeable future.

In the vigilante court, given the endemic listlessness of public attention and the brevity of public memory, spectacularity, epitomized by the harshness and promptness of the public punishment, is more important than its effectiveness. It is a shortcut to the notorious "feel good factor." As Bauman observes, "Fighting crime, like crime itself, and particularly the crime targeted on bodies and private property, makes an excellent, exciting, eminently watchable show."

At the center of attraction is the prospect and performance of corporal punishment. Flogging appears ubiquitous. It is used to extract confessions, after the suspect has confessed, and even prior to the vigilantes' delivering the suspect to the police for punishment. Vigilantes often call upon parents or guardians in the audience to thrash any of their children found guilty. The public inscription of the body of the culpable signifies the power of the vigilante. Indeed there is an almost exclusive, indeed obsessive concern with the body of the suspect criminal. The body of the guilty is an essential element in the ceremonial of public punishment that invariably takes place in a clearly demarcated place, and sometimes at the scene of the punishment. The condemned or guilty is put on exhibition, sometimes stripped to reinforce humiliation. There is a strong ritual element to both stripping and flogging in a grandiose form of *spiegelstraffen* (mirror punishment) which reflects local theories of what causes wrongdoing. Corporal punishment not only stigmatizes those whose "nature" demands it, but it also creates for the public, the vigilantes, and the victim a visual and symbolic manifestation of domination and duress. Floggings are used to create legitimacy rather than to undergird it. Yet, as a wide array of writers have noted following Foucault, the imposition of horrific punishment is usually a sign of weak authority.

Since an audience is an essential component of vigilante social control, to have their greatest impact courts are held after the working day or on weekends at some readily accessible public space, such as a football ground or community center. The audience attends not simply out of concern for the particular issue but to participate in the discussion, the infliction of punishment, and the "fine." The punishment then symbolizes the collective nature of retribution and, incidentally, absolves individual liability should the complainant decide to sue the group. It also promotes a congenial "feel-good factor." Some members of the audience might simply want to be entertained.

Vigilante actions are a vehicle for the circulation of symbolic statements about the social order, and the audience is as important as the participants, for it is their values and beliefs that determine the meaning of what is said. The vigilantes' legitimacy derives not so much from accepting what is said and done, as from getting people to participate, even passively as onlookers. The fact that "justice is indeed seen to be done" means that as in magical rites, word and deed confirm each other, and the common assumptions of the audience are mobilized in a dramatization of shared values.

Magolego, the Mapogo founder, has justified flogging on a number of occasions: "A doctor does not take the patient to the operating theater to be killed, but to remove the ills from him . . . This is the African way of stopping crime. The criminal must lie on the ground, and we must work on his buttocks and put him right." In an interview with one researcher, he provided the following justification: "I don't want to deny that if a sponge is retaining water and water is needed out of the sponge, we have to squeeze it a little. That is what happens with Mapogo and in most cases [the techniques] are successful . . . I always say that if a patient drinks my medicine, I don't regret it, my medicine is never wasted" (Von Schnitzler et al. 2001). Corporal punishment is often referred to as "African medicine," criminal acts being considered homologous to disease. Viewed as evil, a metaphysical substance lodged in the body can thus be driven out. Historically, there is strong support for flogging not because of its virtues per se but rather to make a virtue of necessity where a lack of resources or high mobility makes restorative or compensatory justice impractical.

Vigilante court performance self-propels fear in an anxiety-ridden society, Bauman claims. According to Gunning, it also reveals the repressed or curtailed utopian, uncanny, or fantastic aspects of modernity that constitute the forgotten future of South Africa's recent past.

While there are important structural differences, for example, vigilante courts presume suspects to be guilty, tend not to follow due process (the ideological centerpiece of Western judicial systems), nor are investigation, prosecution, and conviction kept distinct. A charismatic inquisitorial judge frequently dominates proceedings; both in urban and even in relatively conservative rural areas, vigilante courts mimic the formal justice system in terms of ceremonialism.

Recent studies have shown the centrality of mimicry in understanding the dynamics of colonialism. Many of the concepts and ideas used by anti-colonial movements are the products of imperial culture, and even in opposition these attempts pay homage to their cultural origins. As Homi Bhabha famously put it, "It is almost the same but not quite." There is a profound ambivalence about mimicry, since it contains elements of both disavowal and mockery. By miming forms of authority, mimicry threatens the authorities because it shows that while there is a difference that is almost total, it is yet not complete.

Mimicry takes many forms, from the titles of the court officials to the "service fee" which Mapogo charges, to the special black military-style uniform with gold, black, and brown-fringed epaulets that the president refers to as his gown – "just like a priest has his own gown." Unlike Mapogo, most vigilante courts do not resort to such elaborate regalia, concentrating instead on the court's performance before an audience. Here, gesture and movement are more important than words or costumes. Mimicry is so pervasive that the line between vigilante groups and the gangs they supposedly counteract is a fine one, and, at times, considerably blurred.

Since vigilantism exists because state services are seen to be lacking, vigilantism cannot exist without the state. Ultimately, the state as parameter and resource is critical for the success of vigilante movements. For example, many movements, epitomized by the Boipatong court, originally came into being by cooperating with the police in delivering miscreants to them. PAGAD and Mapogo were originally formed for the same reason, but this soon changed. Mapogo still delivers criminals to the police after beating confessions out of them. This has been curbed to some extent by victims laying charges against the vigilante court. This in turn has led to the innovative Boipatong court now requiring the accused to sign consent forms before they are flogged. Vigilante groups are in a position, by and large, to defy the police through invoking and deploying the formal legal system when it suits them to do so. On other occasions the legal system is ignored and voided.

Ordinary township residents are able to turn this cooperative police–vigilante relationship to their advantage. It has become common practice to lodge a charge with the local police and then use this impending action to shoehorn the dispute into a vigilante court, where hopefully the aggrieved party might obtain compensation rather than the retribution required under the state's criminal-justice system. By and large, the South African state police are ineffectual against vigilante groups. First, vigilante organizations have sufficient financial wherewithal to brief lawyers to represent their members in the state's courts. Indeed, this is touted as one of the prime benefits of joining a vigilante group. Second, the strategy of avoiding a single decision-maker or source of punishment deters potential hostile witnesses. Third, members of the vigilante group intimidate potential witnesses into staying away from hearings, so that the case has to be thrown out.

## CONCLUSION

This foray into vigilantism as social control leads to some tentative conclusions, provocations, and suggestions. A working definition of vigilantism might read: "Vigilantism is privately organized (thus premeditated) self-help action with a gloss of legalistic ritual mimicking the formal state system, undertaken in the public sphere to emphasize what its participants claim is 'justice'." This definition enables me to make a number of observations.

First, perhaps the most important empirical characteristic of vigilantism lies in the public nature of its proceedings and the public spectacle of its punishment. Punishment in vigilante courts is overwhelmingly corporeal and visual. This is in marked contrast to the privatization of punishment increasingly characteristic of modernity. This obliges scholars to rethink the influential theories of Foucault, Weber, Marx, and Elias, which posit an increasing and inevitable drift or march toward privatization as states consolidate. Most famously, Foucault argued that as societies became more disciplined, punishment moved beyond the body to something much more diffuse, such as the life career of the person punished. In contrast, vigilante emphasis on physical punishment is also done in the name of discipline and order. This is not to view such action as a throwback to premodern times, but simply to make the point that it has always been there and continues to the present, albeit sometimes submerged. The politics of scholarly research during the apartheid era often blinded researchers to its ominous presence, dismissing it, sometimes wrongly, sometimes correctly, as part of the machinations of the apartheid regime.

Second, in the realm of public order it is not obedience or disobedience that is important, but rather the occasions which give rise to "remedial work," epitomized in this case by vigilante actions. Such action forms an interconnected web of symbols, discourses, and practices in which the anxieties and outrages that are roused and stirred in moral politics involve the condensation of a number of different discourses, different fears within a single image. Discourses and actions are appropriated from a number of sources, including the national and local levels, and include notions of "traditionalism," witchcraft, sorcery, and masculinity in its embrace of visions of both the past and the future. As such, these actions reveal the anxieties and concerns of the era. Vigilantism must not be seen in isolation, but as part of a shifting complex of projects of governance in which the long-term consequences are not a change of issue but rather in the location of moral regulation within the field of governing others and selves. From this follows the third conclusion, namely that vigilantes are double agents of law and order both symbolically and structurally. Their activities to achieve "law and order" actually undermine it. Vigilante-like actions are self-propelled by fear but generate further anxiety in their slipstream. They create a pattern of symmetrical differentiation and all the conditions for a situation which can lead to what anthropologist Gregory Bateson called *symmetrical schismogenesis*, in which a schism between vigilante and state action is likely to emerge and deepen beyond repair. This raises serious questions about the role of the state, especially in the increasingly volatile Southern countries.

Third, these brief case studies suggest that what makes law effective in maintaining public order is not so much its ability to punish criminals to the maximum allowed by law but because of the judiciary's theatrical ability to conspicuously display authority and law as it evokes terror and mercy.

Finally, the conventional scholarly strategy of treating the state and law as autonomous processes must be questioned. The state is not some black box or sinister octopus, but is better conceptualized as a dispersed residue of varied multi-local sites of power – to use Eric Worby's (1997:75) memorable metaphor, as "tidal pools in which micro-environments of power are iteratively nurtured, but never irrevocably submerged by the sea," and where bubbles of (private) governance periodically surface, eventually forming an expanding archipelago of private governance held together by a form of neo-feudalism.

This perspective of the state challenges the notion so frequently espoused by members of the new legal-bureaucratic elite of Southern countries, who unquestioningly accept the state as a given and see the problem of law and order largely as a matter of developing legitimacy in the judicial institutions. They attribute the rise of vigilante activity to an inefficient judicial system and ignorance of human rights on the part of the local denizens.

This world-view of the new legal-bureaucratic elite is encompassed in a rhetoric of "civil society," and underwritten by international development and funding agencies. It bespeaks an arrogance derived from hearing but not listening to the poor. At the same time, the punitive tendencies of the poor raise profound challenges to the liberal concepts of human rights and pluralism.

## REFERENCES

Abrahams, Ray (1998) *Vigilant Citizens: Vigilantism and the State*. Cambridge: Polity Press.

Adam, Heribert (1988) Engineering Compliance: The Management of Dissent in South Africa. In *Law and Justice in South Africa*, ed. J. Hund, pp. 172–192. Cape Town: CIS.

Bauman, Zygmunt (2000) Social Issues of Law and Order. *British Journal of Criminology* 40:205–221.

Brown, Richard M. (1969) The American Vigilante Tradition. In *The History of Violence in America*, ed. H. D. Graham and T. R. Gurr, pp. 159–217. New York: Bantam.

Bullock Alan, and Peter Stallingbrass, eds. (1974) *Fontana Dictionary of Modern Thought*. London: Fontana.

Crais, Clifton (1998) Of Men, Magic and the Law: Popular Justice and the Political Imagination in South Africa. *Journal of Social History* 32:49–72.

Fleisher, Michael ( 2001) *Kuria Cattle Raiders*. Ann Arbor: University of Michigan Press.

Gunning, Tom (1974) The Whole Town's Gawking: Early Cinema and the Visual Experience of Modernity. *Yale Journal of Criticism* 7:189–202.

Hunt, Alan (1999) *Governing Morals*. New York: Cambridge University Press.

Johnston, Les (1996) What is Vigilantism? *British Journal of Criminology* 36:220–236.

Kowalewski, David (1996) Countermovement Vigilantism and Human Rights. *Crime, Law, and Social Change* 25:63–81.

Mamdami, Mahmood (1996) *Citizen and Subject*. Princeton, NJ: Princeton University Press.

Taylor, Michael (1982) *Community, Anarchy and Liberty*. Cambridge: Cambridge University Press.

Moore, Sally Falk, and Barbara G. Myerhoff, eds. (1975) *Symbol and Politics in Communal Ideology: Cases and Questions*. Ithaca, NY: Cornell University Press, 1975.

Von Schnitzler, Antina, Goodwill Ditlage, Lazarus Kgalema, Traggy Maepa, Thloki Mofokeng, and Piers Pigou (2001) *Guardian or Gangster? Mapogo a Mathamaga: A Case Study*. Violence and Transition 3. Johannesburg: Center for the Study of Violence and Reconciliation.

Wilson, Richard A. (2001) *The Politics of Truth and Reconciliation in South Africa*. New York: Cambridge University Press.

Worby, Eric (1997) Eleven Guilty Men from Goredema: Parallel Justice and the Moralities of Local Administration in Northwestern Zimbabwe. *Anthropologica* 39:71–77.

## SUGGESTED FURTHER READING

Abel, Richard, ed. (1982) *The Politics of Informal Justice*. New York: Academic Press.

Adler, Glenn, and Jonny Steinberg, eds. (2000) *From Comrades to Citizens*. New York: St. Martins.

Harris, Bronwen (2001) *"As for Violent Crime, That's our Daily Bread": Vigilante Violence During South Africa's Period of Transition*. Violence and Transition 1. Johannesburg: Center for the Study of Violence and Reconciliation.

Haysom, Nicholas (1986) *Mabangalala: The Rise of Right-Wing Vigilantes in South Africa*. Johannesburg: Center for Applied Legal Studies.

Huggins, Martha, ed. (1991) *Vigilantism and the State in Modern Latin America*. New York: Praeger.

Matthews, Roger, ed. (1988) *Informal Justice?* London: Sage.

Santos, Bonaventura de Sousa (1995) *Toward a New Common Sense*. New York: Routledge.

Schärf, Wilfried, and Daniel Nina, eds. (2002) *The Other Law: Non-State Ordering in South Africa*. Cape Town: Juta.

Van Onselen, Charles (1982) *Studies in the Social and Economic History of the Witwatersrand 1886–1914: New Ninevah*. Johannesburg: Ravan.

## CHAPTER 23

# Postcolonialism

## *K. Sivaramakrishnan*

Contemplating the fiftieth anniversary of Indian independence, Sunil Khilnani (1998:17) observed that "democracy was established after a profound historical rupture – the experience, at once humiliating and enabling, of colonialism, which made it impossible for Indians to regard their own past as a sufficient resource for facing the future and condemned them, in struggling against the subtle knots of the foreigner's Raj, to struggle also against themselves." This tension between continuity and rupture, mimesis and repudiation, lived hybridity and the quest for authenticity, is a central condition of postcolonialism. It has become the subject of much scholarly inquiry into colonialism and its consequences in India and other countries in Asia and Africa. Disciplinary divides have separated these inquiries into questions concerning institutions (including state formation) and identities (including subject formation). It will be the task of this chapter to demonstrate the fruitful synthesis made possible when both sets of questions jointly animate an anthropological treatment of post-colonialism.

Postcolonial studies have been preoccupied with issues of hybridity, creolization, mestizaje, in-between-ness, diasporas, and liminality. Hybridity evokes both the botanical notion of inter-species grafting and Victorian racist ideas about different races being different species. But in postcolonial theory hybridity is supposed to invoke all the ways in which these two understandings, botanical and racial, are challenged. Colonial hybridity was steeped in the confidence that colonial subjects could be taught to mimic and imitate the authentic colonizer, but there would be no danger of perfect assimilation because of ineradicable differences of race and evolution. But hybridity was also a weapon in the hands of colonized elites fighting for freedom and decolonization. They invoked the ideas of Western societies not only to hold them true to their own beliefs, but also to claim a hybrid identity for the colonized that was a product of foreign and indigenous values (Bhabha 1984). Through notions of mimesis, hybridity, and cosmopolitanism a discourse-oriented postcolonial theory influenced by Said (1978) has attended more to elites, ideation, and representations, at the expense of changes in the economic and political

spheres – especially everyday practices, micro-political economies, and cultural politics. Recently, political anthropologists and some cultural theorists have identified this
bias (see Gupta 1998).

Postcolonialism has been discussed, further, in relationship to the development of
nationalism in the Third World, a process that could only take place through a
contradictory relationship to European social and political thought (Chatterjee
1986). The dilemma of postcolonial nationalism is summed up well by Chakrabarty
(2000:151) when he asks, "How could one reconcile the need for these two different
and contradictory ways of seeing the nation: the critical eye that sought out the
defects in the nation for the purpose of reform and improvement, and the adoring eye
that saw the nation as already beautiful or sublime?" This question is explored in this
chapter, on both national and regional scales, by considering the fashioning of ethnic
identities and the cosmopolitan persona in the context of nature conservation,
wildness, and the regulation of hunting. In particular, it is my argument that both
mimicry and social distancing become key modes of conducting cultural politics in
the context of civilizational processes. As this chapter will show, arguments about
civility and wildness remain central to the divergent discourses and structural forces
that constitute postcolonialism. When related to issues of political modernity, these
arguments also become arguments about variegated forms of citizenship in specifically Asian contexts (Ong 1999). In the Indian case, forms of citizenship emerge at the
intersections of the politics of difference with proliferating institutions of democracy.

What, then, are the ways in which varied nationalisms, regionalisms, and politics of
difference mediate the imagination of the postcolonial world of communities,
nations, and citizens? What role do representations of wildness and nature play in
this process? From the middle of the twentieth century the initiation of state-
sponsored development, the institution of democracy, and the building of conservation agendas were all activities that were figured on the ground of the nation.
Arguments about the place of nature in the Indian nation-space – specifically, how
contending groups imagine, and seek to manage and conserve nature – will serve as
the illustration for this argument. In particular, I shall trace the lineages of a national
conservation imagination, and regionally situated modes of self-recognition, as they
are formed and contested in the context of democratization. As a political anthropology of postcolonialism and nature in India, this chapter works through representations of wildness and the pragmatics of hunting. How these topics illuminate existing
theoretical debates on postcolonial subject formation, and suggest new directions for
a political anthropology of postcolonialism, should become evident below.

## WILDNESS AND THE POLITICS OF DIFFERENCE

In October 1998, the hunter briefly became the hunted when the Indian film star
Salman Khan was chased by Bishnoi villagers for shooting blackbuck in scrub forests
not far from Jodhpur in Rajasthan, western India. The incident gained unprecedented media attention. The press ensured that influential film stars could not hush up
this encounter between villagers and urban hunters. Unexpectedly embarrassed by
the event, the World Wildlife Fund hastily discontinued a calendar they had just
printed with the picture of Salman Khan. Some environmentalists seized upon the

story to celebrate the Bishnoi who, as India's leading environmental magazine put it, "for centuries have militantly conserved their flora and fauna . . . for whom protecting wildlife is an integral part of their sacred tradition and chasing gun-toting thugs, tourists and poachers is a matter of life and death" (Verma 1998:15–16).

This is a narrative that extols the virtues of cultures that embrace wildness in their lived environment. It is also a narrative whose antique genealogy is traced from a precolonial past. The story told here effectively illuminates several key tropes that have become essential to the conceptual architecture of a larger argument on wildlife policy and hunting regulation in India. Some environmentalists have relied upon scattered evidence of villagers respecting wildlife in various part of India to build up an account of wildness that idealizes certain tribal people for their innate wisdom and ability to coexist with wild animals in wilderness areas. Others have celebrated certain farming people for sharing their fields and other domesticated landscapes with itinerant wildlife like migrant birds. This chapter focuses on the play of such tropes: on the powerful work done by political imaginations. It examines the cultural politics at work when the hegemonic ideas of metropolitan environmentalists, conservation bureaucrats, and regional elite groups elicit from the complex realities that constitute any rural environment the simplifying fiction of cultural harmony or wisdom – or for that matter intractable fecklessness or extravagance. As many scholars have noted, essentializing cultural claims are social strategies and the negotiation of stereotypical modes of self-recognition is the stuff of constructing national cultures.

Furthermore, the chapter examines the relationship between these hegemonic constructions of people and nature and the process of forming citizen-subjects worthy of inclusion in the nation. In doing so, I focus on the production and negotiation of social difference in certain forest areas of postcolonial Bengal. Colonial state formation in these areas was partly organized around the definition and expansion of the domain of civility. Corresponding colonial classification of forest tribes by an index of wildness facilitated policies that confined some (like the Paharias) – considered irrevocably wild – to unredeemably wild landscapes. Others (like Santhals) were given land and license to tame the wilderness and so curb their own wanderlust to participate in a wider project that produced settled, industrious, modernizing farmers on the colonial agrarian landscape. The early decades of independence, and the social transformations wrought by Left Front governments in West Bengal since 1977, seemed to continue this trend. But the working of the state, at all levels, was already subject to a new regimen of democratic processes. By the 1980s, especially in the sphere of natural resources and rural environments, the state was experiencing radically new pressures for widening and deepening local democracy. The hallmark of the devolution in government introduced in the last 20 years is the search for "responsible" citizen-subjects. In this new framework for state–society relations, local government requires political enterprise and managerial initiative from villagers, erstwhile primitive tribes, poor uneducated women, and their putative communities of local collective action. In other words, the new citizen-subject is one who can at once bear the rights of democracy and the burdens of conservation.

These recent shifts in defining civility and civic responsibility reward scrutiny. Across the temporal divide marked by decolonization and universal adult political franchise, discourses of wildness, and related practices of hunting regulation, remained important social influences on patterns of mutual recognition among forest-dwellers, conservationists, agency officials, and others caught up in the politics of nature. The colonial regime's policies for forest management, hunting regulation, and disciplining tribal people invented social categories and also filled them by means of criminalization, displacement, or paternalist isolation of specific groups. In regional ethnic conflict and struggles over resources during the postcolonial era, groups variously positioned with respect to this colonial classification have drawn upon the "nature" attributed to them as they jockey for position with respect to each other and the state.

Wildness itself is a concept that needs some unpacking. In the conventional opposition between wildness and civilization the former signifies what comes before, or is placed outside the latter. This notion even pervades primitivist writing that might celebrate wildness. So in evolutionary or modernization frameworks wildness is a shrinking condition. Civility, defined as a progressive and colonizing idea, however, always needs its Other. Civility exists as much by *contrast* with that which is uncivil or wild, as it does by belief in the possible *conquest* of wildness. Juxtaposing civility and wildness becomes a simple summary of more intricate arguments about refinement, sophistication, aesthetic sensibilities, long-range vision, and cultural superiority. These arguments are also salient to issues of authority and voice in the local politics of natural-resource management or wild-habitat conservation. As I will elaborate below, wildness and its antinomies are more usefully considered as crucial media for negotiating social and political power in parts of rural India. This is specially so where identities of caste and tribe, cultivator and hunter, elite and subaltern, were all the subject of contention and coalition.

There are four logical steps to this argument. First, India has a plural democratic political system within a society differentiated in complex ways. Social mobility has increased noticeably in the last five decades and the most potent source of mobility has been the adult franchise. Especially important for the purposes of this essay is the fact that democratic political mobilization has ethnicized caste identities, a situation that has been further complicated by the spread of religious communal politics. In other words, conflict around issues of difference has been magnified as democracy has deepened.

Second, late twentieth-century changes have made autocratic conservation based on forced removal of several million people from parks politically untenable. Elected local government (Panchayati Raj) was constitutionally mandated in 1993, and devolution has emerged as the major strategy for implementing decisions on the environment, promoting governance reform, and encouraging economic enterprise. Two key forms of devolution are decentralization of governance and community-based natural-resource management. This is clearly part of a wider international trend.

Third, the expectation that imagined rural communities will draw on deep cultural traditions of benign intimacy with wildness to facilitate cooperative conservation has foundered on the exacerbation of social difference and increases in malign encounters with wildlife. Fourth, the negotiation of social difference around indices of wildness often seems to participate in new region-specific divisions and coalitions that challenge the existing institutional mechanisms for ordering state–citizen relations.

All this leads me to the central point, that it is essential to examine the structured ways in which social difference is imagined and produced. The term "social difference" in Indian contexts evokes discussions of caste, class, and gender. But for this chapter I am more concerned with an identity politics in which wildness is mapped onto ethnicity and tribal nomenclature.

Postcolonialism, then, is a condition in which such riveting contrasts – like the choice between state regulation and people's conservation – are generated and then reified. Arguably such contrasts arise in prior, historically constituted notions about civility and difference, as everyday aspects of social life, for these notions are at the heart of specific policy interventions and social relations manifest in hunting regulation. I focus on hunting regulation because wildlife conservation is merely the dominant discourse of our times for this more deeply historical theme in interactions between humans and nature. I am also interested in the production of social difference around the idea of wildness. Let me turn, then, to the emergence of colonial regulation of hunting in Bengal. The colonial period is important to construct the history of hunting regulation that influences present wildlife policy, and to consider the way certain tribes were classified by colonial sociology in distinctive ways with respect to wildness, and the impact of this on subsequent identity politics that produce social difference.

## COLONIALISM AND HUNTING

An important facet of the landscape ordering procedures of colonial rule was the systematic redrawing of wildland boundaries. The decimation of carnivores, some herbivorous large mammals, and the eradication of poisonous snakes, a process known as vermin eradication, reached their highest intensity only in the last decades of the nineteenth century. During the nineteenth century, colonial attitudes to indigenous hunting changed from curiosity and admiration to criticism and suppression. Research on India makes it clear that this transformation was achieved by a combination of practical regulatory control over hunting and the development of hunting ideologies grounded in ideas of civility and racial difference. Early British commentators on the Indian hunting scene showed a grudging respect for tribal people, who were credited with the power and skill to avoid large carnivores in the jungles. The overriding importance of pushing back the forest also made it easier to accept, if not admire, those who trapped, fished, hunted, or gathered produce from such lands.

However, much of this activity came to be regarded over the next hundred years as poaching, mindless destruction, or inhumane treatment of wild animals. The spread of British control over general administration in forested areas gradually led to their assumption of the vermin eradication role. So villagers turned to them for protection, particularly when subject to a dire menace like man-eating tigers. Forest protection, vermin eradication, and the creation of a sedentarized peasantry were, however, often contradictory processes. Conservation required the exclusion of most tribal people from forests, curtailed hunting, and caused an increase in vermin. Sedentarization directed communities adept at a mixture of cultivation, gathering, and hunting toward forms of specialization in land use that impaired their hunting. Forest protection also interfered with annual fires and other means by which villagers had controlled vermin in the vicinity of settlements. Complex interrelated activities of agriculture, forest management, and hunting were thus marked off from each other. This approach to resource control increased the burdens of government without securing safe pursuit for, or enhanced returns from, any of these activities.

This brief review underlines some important transitions. Vermin eradication was primarily a program intended to secure agricultural expansion. In its heyday, roughly 1860 to 1890, relations between Indian and British hunting were transformed in several ways. First, if British and Indian hunting had coexisted before 1860, thereafter concerted efforts were made to render the latter completely a servant of the former, or to declare it illegitimate. Second, in the project of vermin eradication, British efforts to secure monopolies over legalized violence converged with the creation of tribal places. In securing these places for their aboriginal pioneers, the colonial government worked to buffer them from predatory carnivores, plains people, and town-dwellers. Third, the establishment of an official monopoly over vermin eradication coincided with the emergence of elaborate codes of conduct relating to sport hunting, and this led to descriptions of native hunting as illegal and cruel, but also occasionally skillful and complementary to elite sport. This meant that the discourse of wildness worked to both criticize and celebrate aspects of native hunting. These representations, by virtue of their impact on livelihoods linked to hunting, had material consequences for the production of social difference among various forest-dependent people in the colonial period. Fourth, hunting regulation was further transformed by a rising conservation discourse that produced a clutch of hunting, shooting, and fishing rules in reserved and protected forests. The legislative mandate was continuously revised over the colonial/postcolonial divide in ways intended to expand the purview of central agencies regulating hunting and wildlife conservation (Sivaramakrishnan 1999).

## SPECTATOR SPORT: NATIONAL MIDDLE-CLASS CULTURE AND WILDLIFE VIEWING, 1950–1990

Aristocrats and other Indian elites lived through the transition to democracy without much dislocation of their attitudes and access to hunting. First, hunting continued to be both a privilege and a pastime for officials, princes, and the landed classes. Until 1969, when princely privileges were abolished, many rulers retained the right of *shikar* (sport hunting). Second, a strong vermin eradication agenda persisted. Authorized killing of black bears to preserve deer, jackal cubs to save game birds, and wild dogs to protect herbivores continued. But by now vermin eradication was not aimed at promoting agriculture. It was strictly part of a selective conservation and hunting preservation policy.

Out of this aristocratic shikari elite and a new urban middle class that had experienced wilderness directly in the USA or Africa, and vicariously through the *National Geographic*, emerged a powerful conservationist coalition that was led by Prime Minister Indira Gandhi herself. It resulted in "Project Tiger," and in a series of other ventures that unequivocally put India's fauna and avian heritage at the center of an ambitious, centrally orchestrated conservation program. The 1972 Wildlife Protection Act provided the legal framework. The 42nd constitutional amendment in 1976 – during the years of the Emergency – placed forests and wildlife on the "concurrent list," thus enabling central legislation that could overrule the actions of state governments. The World Wildlife Fund, the International Union for the Conservation of Nature, and the American Fish and Wildlife Service provided funds and expertise. In short, wildlife conservation was steered onto an authoritarian course by an urban middle-class coalition.

In the period 1980–84 the number of national parks went from 19 to 52, and central law and policy favoring drastic measures for wildlife conservation were greatly strengthened. During the same period, however, the attempt to introduce a similar centralizing forest law failed. Through the 1980s, the forests and wildlife sectors grew apart. Forests were separated into two distinct categories. Some areas were ceded to cooperative projects under growing pressure for inclusive forest management. Other areas were more strongly barricaded than ever before, and were protected against all forms of public intrusion. Wildlife management policy remained unyielding in the face of state, market, and international development or conservation agency pressures for more inclusive, localized approaches. Parks (rather than forests) became objects of an international middle-class form of conspicuous consumption. Rituals of travel to commune with nature, shared experiences of spectacular landscapes and fauna, and the political economy of eco-tourism industries consolidated this class and crystallized its perceptions of wildness in support of authoritarian park management.

By the 1990s, however, a series of research projects and public campaigns had brought the plight of rural people displaced and threatened by wildlife conservation to the center of debates on wildlife policy. Studies carried out by the Indian Institute of Public Administration and the Wildlife Institute of India, as well as the well-publicized *padayatra* (walking tour) of conservationists and rural activists in 1994, which traveled from north to south visiting various protected areas and elicited support from rural residents along the way, contributed to this awareness. But the debate about wildlife conservation remains polarized. In some ways, this polarization appears to have been overdetermined by the accumulation of standardized hunting regulations that have lost touch with the variegated local administrations that had been preserved into the first quarter of the twentieth century. But the consolidation of urban middle-class representations of wilderness and conservation that occurred in the 1960s and 1970s also contributed to this process. In policy terms, the 1990s may have marked a serious departure from the authoritarian wilderness-conservation consensus of the 1970s and 1980s. But the middle-class sensibilities toward wildness that modern naturalists carried around remained less susceptible to change. Recent exponents of these ideas may write in a style that is light, stripped of overt nationalism, but they continue to repeat troublesome polarities.

A period of intense national development, during the years 1950–91, created social space for the emergence of an expansive notion of civility that encompassed, among other things, a substantial elite and middle-class involvement in wilderness conservation. The generation associated with this process, which is linked to organizations like the Bombay Natural History Society, celebrate diversity in the faunal or avian heritage of the country alongside cultural diversity in its human populations without closely examining the relationship between the two. In contrast, young biologists with conservationist zeal are children of the environmental movement that grew in India during the 1970s. This movement has developed many mutually opposed strands, but it has certainly produced responsible citizen-subjects whose vocation is best described as professional conservation. Their civility stems from a scientific appreciation of Indian wilderness and a sophisticate's abhorrence of wild tribes who subsist uncouthly on the sylvan splendor that is their home. These professionals are part of an international conservation vanguard, but they also bear a curious resemblance to the princely elite turned conservationists whom they admire in private. Like the royalty of yore, who sustained their self-image through imperial pretensions, the new international conservationist travels to the world headquarters of global conservation enterprises in Rome, Geneva, Nairobi, London, and Washington for validation and authenticity.

But the very processes through which a strong and multi-sited notion of civility (or cosmopolitan national culture) is constructed also produce the necessary inappropriate "Others" – those people whose actions and representations do not fit so neatly into middle-class narratives involving wild animals, landscapes, and tribal peoples. We consider next the contemporary situation relating to these people, by examining wildness, social difference, and the place of hunting in the dry forest areas of southern West Bengal.

## HUNTING AND SOCIAL DIFFERENCE IN WESTERN MIDNAPORE

Conflicting ideas about wildness, and their changing valence in the politics of social inclusion, have become important for the negotiation of ethnic differences and land claims in dry-land agro-forest regions of India. We can see important shifts, over the last 50 years, in the way regional culture has been formed and reshaped around issues of landscape and memory. One of the key shifts relates to the intertwined ways in which both the land, and the people who lived on it, are imagined as wild. This is not to say that some people imagined others as wild, or certain parts of their landscape as wild, but to argue that we might try to understand how an imaginary of wildness can become a shared basis for historical reconstructions of regional culture. The relationship is not straightforward. Disagreements about the place of wildness in livelihood security have increased even as regional identity politics have rediscovered the empowering qualities of wildness.

My field research in the western uplands of Midnapore was carried out in a cluster of villages populated by three ethnic groups: Mahatos, mostly well-established farmers; Santhals, farmers and pastoralists; and Lodhas, landless laborers who were at the bottom of social, cultural, and economic hierarchies in the region. Historically, these groups have come to coexist in a mosaic of forest and fields. Negotiated transformations of this landscape have shaped the economies of subsistence and the politics of identity that mutually link the different groups. Much of the negotiation has turned on arguments about wildness – its management in nature and its performance in culture. Ethnic group identities – Mahato, Santhal, Lodha – are used here not to deny the existence of social differentiation within these groups on grounds of age, gender, class, and residence, but to maintain our focus, in the regional cultural context, on the construction of ethnic boundaries. Arguments about wildness, its signification in hunting practice, dietary habits, and residential styles, did center on ethnic group identities.

Let me elucidate by describing the following incident. It was a crisp morning in early March and some of us from the Mahato village were out in the low-lying fields that were being ploughed after a light spring shower. A young man began to tell of the appearance of a wild pig in the forests that lay between his village and the neighboring Santhal hamlet. This was a remarkable occurrence, for wild pigs had long vanished from the degraded dry deciduous forest of southern West Bengal. But what made the story more worthy of being told was the commotion that this porcine wanderer had apparently caused in a nearby Santhal village. Boys from there, raised on anecdotes of hunting pig and eager to experience the real thing, had scrambled to dig a pit in the forest and cover it with brush. Knowing of my interest in the changing history of forest cover in the region, the narrator was initially drawn to make inferences about the return of ecological conditions for wild pigs to forage once again in these parts. But soon the discussion turned to the faintly ridiculous prospect of Santhal youth trying to catch the pig.

By referring to a simple-minded and embarrassing wildness associated with Santhals, we quickly transformed the conversation from one about forests and animals to one about people and animality, recreating a process that has several historical legacies. Not least among these was the shift in forest management since the late nineteenth century that had systematically excluded and marginalized wildness. To this end the colonial government, as we have seen earlier in this essay, had concentrated on several things: the most important being a vermin eradication program that worked to eliminate certain carnivores, ungulates, and reptiles, along with livelihoods that coexisted with them in the forests on the fringes of civilization. People living in adjoining farming areas, small towns, and the burgeoning metropolitan middle classes also adopted this colonial opposition between wildness and civilization.

Wildness came to be associated with marginality, social inferiority, political power-lessness, and forest-based livelihoods. One consequence was that, in the colonial period, tribes found themselves pushed into the role of castes in the making. Post-colonial fieldwork allowed me to witness the construction of a regional culture where these processes were being reversed. Wildness had acquired a cachet that sympathetic, paternalist, colonial administrators could not have imagined. If the Mahato lad ultimately restrained the critical reflex activated by the wandering wild pig, and the subsequent exploits of his Santhal neighbors, it was because he would join them in a few weeks for the annual hunt. Mahatos started to join the Santhals and other groups more closely identified with hunting – for subsistence and ritual purposes – since the emergence of Jharkhand (regional autonomy) politics nearly 60 years ago. But they remain ambivalent about recreating regional solidarity through the enactment of wildness in this fashion. This ambivalence reflects the contradictory landscape memories mobilized by farmers, forest-dwellers, land managers, and others who argue about wildness, its provenance, its passing, and its renewed salience to resource control and identity in southern West Bengal.

I am referring to everyday memories that may not bear the burden of transmitting tradition but certainly work to define how people recall their surroundings, the places they call home – familiar landscapes. Ecological nostalgia sits in tension with recollections of brutal oppression. These incompatibilities, and their mutual power over each other, constitute a contested terrain, suggesting ways in which scattered memories may coalesce into more systematic histories. These in turn guide and constrain how the landscape will be imagined.

This insight becomes more analytically powerful when it is extended, by attending to the fractious nature and transformative possibilities of quotidian memory. The cultural construction through which landscapes are made familiar to people in historically shared physical locations involves a precarious consensus. The consensus is produced through the negotiation of ethnic, gender, and class divisions endemic to the place-based community that engages in the cultural politics of constructing a lived landscape that bears designations of wildness and domestication. Any agreement about how landscapes are to be remembered follows fierce negotiations about wildness: its referents, its transformations, and its power. The agreement often masks processes that effect a subtle transposition of wildness from the landscape of fauna and biota to a landscape of citizens: those who inhabit the rural and the urban spheres carved out of a shifting terrain of settlement and land domestication. I will now turn to some of the details about memories of wild landscapes to show how they draw upon and reshape regional culture.

Gently undulating uplands have moderated the transition from forests to fields in western Midnapore. Colonized by gregarious *Shorea* and *Diospyros* trees, or cleared for cultivation, these uplands have historically mediated the boundary between the forested margin and the farmed center in the regional economy. Depending on whom you speak with, dwindling populations of wild animals might be attributed to deforestation, forest fires, or the Santhal annual hunt. Tigers were rare, but one was shot in 1950 in the woods around my field site, and another was sighted the following year in the neighboring Ramgarh forests. Leopards and wolves were present in fair numbers into the 1960s, committing depredations among cattle. Hyenas, jackals, civet cats, and foxes were common in villages bordering the jungles. Wild elephants destroying crops in western Midnapore was common. Wild pigs were found in great numbers, even into the 1940s, and afforded some of the best pig-sticking in Bengal. But by the late 1950s they had become rare.

Santhals are largely held responsible for reducing their numbers. What is often understated is that pigs did interfere with crops, and their elimination mainly benefited entrenched farmers – a category largely dominated by Mahatos after the 1930s. Older Mahato and Santhal villagers spoke of taming the area, in their living memory, between the 1940s and 1960s. In contrast to the alarming reports of deforestation and faunal extinction that the Bengal Forest Committee recorded in 1939, these elders told gripping stories of wild cats and leopards that would boldly enter the village and steal goats in daylight. Fanidol, a pesticide supplied by the government in the 1960s, was used to poison carrion that was left to entice leopards, wolves, jackals, and other wild vermin to their death. The *mandal* (headman) of Belpahar, Narayan Mahato, was particularly eloquent in his accounts of making the village safe for dwelling and cultivation. As the erstwhile chief, who had lost official importance after the abolition of *zamindari*, he may have wished to stress the role played by him and other such village leaders in establishing the village and extending cultivation in the recent past, but far too many villagers from Mahato, Santhal, and Lodha villages told of recent depredations by wild animals to make this implausible.

Within a radius of a mile on any side of the town of Jhargram, the market center and administrative core for the western subdivision of Midnapore, the landscape of mixed forests and fields is dominant: there is no electricity, a scant water supply, no all-weather roads, and very few permanent structures. While the townspeople huddle in their little crowded borough, the rural hinterland becomes a law unto itself, reputed to be dangerous and violent after twilight. This recreates a 200-year-old history in which western Midnapore is associated with banditry, and jungles are regarded as the refuge of criminals. It was almost as if a deal had been struck. From dawn to dusk the townees ply their trades, drawing materials and manpower from the villages; from dusk to dawn, the same channels of communication are controlled by rural bandits, recovering from careless wayfarers a share of the wealth that has been generated. Or at least, so runs the popular account in Jhargram town. After nightfall cars and trucks move in convoys. A tree fallen across the road was cause for great alarm and apprehension among travelers, for it could signal a hold-up. In contrast, villagers moved on foot or on bicycles through the dark, traveling into and through the wooded country with much less trepidation. Living in a village, I was also able to ride a bicycle at all times. When I asked a renowned local boss about this, he said, "you are an outsider, but you are not threatened because everyone knows who you are, and why you are here."

There was some Mahato resentment of Bengali dominance in town and Santhal prosperity in government-sponsored opportunities, but Mahatos remain the domin-ant peasant community. The Mahatos move uneasily between an earlier attempt to claim *kshatriya* (high caste) status and a more recent drive, in the 1980s and 1990s, to be seen as *mulvasis* (original residents) akin to Santhal *adivasis* (indigenes). The latter trend in redefinition of identity is reflected in an alliance between the Mahatos and Santhals – one that is of growing importance in the region, and that is manifest in the Jharkhand movement. In this way, to recall the words of Khilnani that we started with, Mahatos within themselves, and Mahatos in relations with other groups claiming indigeneity in West Bengal forests, are engaged in a struggle of self-defin-ition. Such is the conflict over identity, ethnicity, and territory, that is emerging parallel to the struggle over forests, where the Mahato–Santhal alliance is most easily perceived. Hunting, and the changing character of the fauna in the forest, remains a theme of considerable importance in these politics. The menace of tigers, leopards, and bears has receded only in the last 40 years. In fact, the way that Mahato and Santhal represent the passing of the more dangerous animals presents interesting contrasts. Narayan Mahato, the headman, recounted scary stories of tigers and leopards raiding the village – a mere cluster of ten or so houses in the 1950s – to take animals and children. He added, "geese visited the dighi [pond] in the center of the Rakhagerya jungle from great distances. The sound of hundreds of birds was deafening, and we could not sit the way we are, outside the house, and hope to hear each other."

Clearly this commentary on vermin, deforestation, and diminished bird migrations was cobbled together to present a picture of frontier farmers surrounded by un-desired wildness in their own compounds. To Ashok Murmu, a young Santhal, the loss of avian and floral diversity in the forests was, in contrast, a matter of sad remembrance. His eyes came alive whenever he could drag me off for a walk in the woods, explain the scents and the sounds, and argue about a cultural deprivation experienced in the loss of fauna. Animals elicited neither fear nor hatred in Ashok's memories, at least the way he presented them to me. As he exclaimed, after one of our many animated discussions of hunting, "these days I hunt for *anand* [pleasure] ...there is no game to speak of...even though I am educated I hunt in the appropriate season . . . just like in the Hindu tradition the characters of the Ramayana and Mahabharata liked to hunt." The other term most often used to characterize Lodha or Santhal interest in hunting now, despite the dismal lack of game, was *furthi*, which can only be translated as celerity or energy – a sense of being alive.

Any of my Lodha interlocutors, the poorest community in the region, could point out lianas, creepers, vines, brushwood, grasses, sedges, and describe their uses as we tramped through the jungle. They alone could name all the birds. Clearly their ethnobotanical and faunal lexicon was deeper and wider than that of the other two groups they lived alongside. This is not to suggest that forest knowledge was homogeneous within ethnic groups or tribes. For instance, the *kavirajs* (medicine men) among the Mahatos knew much more plant lore, especially the curative and therapeutic properties of wild plants, than other Mahatos. *Kaviraji*, as an occupation, was more likely to be pursued by poorer Mahato men, as it provided a supplementary livelihood. But this intimate knowledge of everything the forests contained and nurtured was hard to separate from their own subsistence strategies. Only a Lodha house would reveal all manner of traps, snares, fishing and cutting implements, fashioned ingeniously from bamboo, vines, and the mixed jungle woods they knew so well. This knowledge *of* things was more experiential than the knowledge *about* similar things that a Mahato *kaviraj* (traditional healer) may possess.

Not surprisingly, my informants in the Lodha hamlet uniformly agreed that tigers, leopards, wolves, jackals and other such menacing creatures were a distant memory in the forests. Unlike Narayan Mahato and his tales of forests recently tamed, or his celebration of the outdoors as a place recently become safe for recreation; all the older Lodha men I spoke with remembered not the dangers the forests had held, but the loss of meat and sport. Their historical memory was partial to the decline in microfauna, while that of the Mahato headman was suffused with images of threatening macrofauna happily eliminated. It is perhaps easy to partition these memories into those of the farmer and the huntsman, but before I could lapse into such neat typologies, several young men hastened to inform me that Narayan Mahato was "historically unreliable."

The discussion of hunting thus elicited a range of responses. There is still an annual hunting festival (in March) that attracts a lot of people, though all they do now is take a few rabbits and the occasional wild pig. There are contrary tensions at work in the treatment of hunting by the different communities living in western Midnapore. Forests regenerated in the last decade have enriched the population of microfauna but also brought in elephants that are getting pushed out of degraded habitats in neighboring Bihar. These changes are welcomed at one level, since the elephant has religious significance, but the annual damage to crops is increasing. Gathering villagers to deal with the elephant problem creates new points of friction between groups. Lodhas are notably absent from parties assembled for chasing elephants. To explain their non-participation, Shambhu Bhakta, one of my Lodha informants, said, "the presence of elephants in the forests is a good omen, they eat the grain of farmers who prevaricate."

Substantial farmers, especially from among the Mahatos, get agitated by the elephants, and with them I spent many early mornings in *kheddah* – elephant chasing. The tragic irony of this situation is that the irate herd of elephants, pushed back into the inner recesses of the forest, would occasionally retaliate by knocking over a solitary cyclist passing through the woods. More often, Lodha women gathering firewood in the interior became their victims. During my fieldwork, there were a few such instances. In one case, a Lodha woman was trampled to death in the Rakhagerya jungle. In another case, after repeated inroads by a herd into the granaries of certain Santhal villages, and fruitless appeals by the villagers to the forest department for some action, a male adult member of the herd was found dead with several arrows sticking out of it. The matter was hastily closed by a post facto declaration by the forest department, designating the dead elephant a rogue. As these examples suggest, an imagined wildness, recently lost, often worked to bring diverse ethnic groups together in political alliances. But actually returning wilderness threatened those alliances by sharpening the awareness of both cultural and economic divisions be-tween groups. These differences surfaced as Santhals, Mahatos, and Lodhas were compelled, by landscape changes, to renegotiate the place of wildness in their worlds of meaning and subsistence.

## REGIONAL CULTURES OF POSTCOLONIALISM

What has all this meant for regional culture? In western Midnapore a distinctive combination of forest and agriculture-based economy was transformed such that tribal places emerged as wild, yet livable, landscapes. During the postcolonial era the state has identified "tribal development project areas," which map onto earlier tribal regions identified by the British. Along with development in these tribal areas, solidarity movements have also emerged. These political mobilizations, which consti-tute a regional culture, rely on a contested imaginary of wildness of the kind discussed above. Convivial memories of such wildness then become a basis for groups to construct and maintain shared identity. Discord between memories of wildness and the uneven experience of wildness in its reemergent forms can also be viewed as arguments about development. The aggressive mobilization of a collective *adivasi* identity places the regional culture in opposition to the advancement of citizenship in late modern democracy through the practice of development. How forests, as wild landscapes, enter the politics of democracy and development is a larger story that cannot be told in all its complexity here. But I will return, briefly, to the themes with which we began: first, the several levels at which discourses of wildness, civility, and difference can be identified in India as a characteristic of the postcolonial condition; second, the intersection of these levels to constitute somewhat fluid binaries like tribe and caste, rural and urban, local and national, natural park and peopled forests.

The emergence of a regional culture in West Midnapore is anything but unique, but rather is symptomatic of broader processes at work in Indian politics during the last decade. During the 1990s regional political parties proliferated throughout the country, and left a powerful mark on the national political imagination. There were as many as 28 of these parties, for example, represented in the national Parliament of 1996 (Khilnani 1998:57). When due attention is paid to temporal and spatial differentiation in the processes by which several regional modernities are constructed – in this case through the distinction between wildness and civility as markers of social difference – it is possible to detect and describe the arguments within national middle-class culture, regional culture, and across these formations.

Following such an approach I have situated my analysis of wildness, hunting regulation, and social difference in an interrelated set of time–space regionalizations. Briefly stated, these regionalizations, as they pertain to Bengal, are: an agroforestry complex that emerges in colonial southern West Bengal and comes to define the mixed dry-land farming and dry forest-based livelihoods of various social groups; a political-legal formation that was shaped by regimes of exceptional colonial government, special land tenure, and tribal sedentarization and segregation policies; a more recent, post-independence, differentiation of southern West Bengal from its eastern and northern neighbors by patterns of regional under-development generated by the uneven spread of Green Revolution technologies and attendant social change; and a cultural entity that becomes visible in the aftermath of waves of migration and settlement in the jungle areas of southern West Bengal.

Arguments about wildness and processes of hunting regulation were conditioned by these regionalizations in Bengal, but they were also caught up in a different order of identity politics played out at the national level, as urban middle classes articulated their social difference from rural forest-dependent people, especially tribes. Historically generated categories shaped, and were transformed by, new distinctions drawn between wildness and civility. Here processes etched into Indian wilderness landscapes by colonial hunting regulation and attendant discourses of wildness were multiplied, diverted, and occasionally suppressed by the impact of democracy. Finally, a third set of regionalizations, in the realm of environmental policy, has begun to emerge as forest and parks are marked off from each other by different modalities for constructing national or local, or central or devolved, spheres of government.

The issue of social difference as it is organized around the concept of wildness is important because of its centrality to the production of regional culture as a part of these regionalizations in southern West Bengal and India. They describe the dynamic political reality that conservation policy has to encounter. Social difference in the context of hunting provides a concrete and urgent locus for inquiry because when rural livelihoods are reimagined, they often exclude the hunting practices of certain groups who are being disciplined as labor in their area, while they might privilege that of others recruited as civil entrepreneurs or state mercenaries. While hunting becomes important to regional culture as a means to political voice, its selective exclusion also permits rural elites to reproduce historical forms of domination within that regional culture. For instance, in Midnapore, Santhal celebration of hunting as affirming regional culture coexists with their denigration of the Lodha's catching and eating snakes from paddy fields. It would appear that debates about wildness and civility both unify and divide various units of society, and the hunting persona will remain an ambiguous witness to these intense cultural arguments in which ideas of citizenship, community, and nation are forged in a postcolonial world.

## CONCLUSION

The historical processes that have bequeathed to India a myriad of regional political cultures, forged in the context of debates about national culture, civility, and wildness, represent one of the defining features of that country's postcolonial situation. It is this production and proliferation of difference that also represents the essential background in relation to which the preoccupations of postcolonial studies – hybridity, creolization, liminality, and political modernity in postcolonial nations – must be judged. Future research into the condition we refer to as postcolonial must surely examine in greater detail the contested construction of political modernities in postcolonial spaces of identity and state formation. Questions of rights, civility, self-determination, public spheres, and citizenship have to be raised in the context of histories of postcolonial nationalism, development, and globalization. The problem can be situated, at one level, in the general realm of reconciling individual liberty with social equality. To some the reconciliation must rest on a bedrock of rights-based conceptions of civility (Mahajan 1999). Another, more sketchy, position – taken in the name of radical democracy – is that democracy requires both social equality and multicultural recognition. But as Nancy Fraser readily acknowledges, to flesh out this position is to "become immediately embroiled in difficult questions about the relationship between equality and difference" (Fraser 1996:198).

Making the same point in slightly different words, and in the context of East European democratic transitions, Katherine Verdery (1998:293) says, "discussions of citizenship quickly become entangled with the matter of national and cultural identity when, for instance, civic commitments are seen to be precluded by ethnic ones." She also observes that in some East European countries democratization invigorated ethnonational identities. Similar processes have longer trajectories in countries like India, and many other Asian and African "new democracies," where first colonial and then postcolonial politics have produced the very identities and interests necessary to democratic political functioning. Therefore, the affinities and divisions generated by the fashioning of postcolonial polities should remain, both in the realm of imagination and political action, the central focus of continued research in political anthropology.

## REFERENCES

Bhabha, Homi (1984) Of Mimicry and Man: Ambivalence and Colonial Discourse. *October* 28:125–133.

Chakrabarty, Dipesh (2000) *Provincializing Europe: Postcolonial Thought and Historical Difference.* Princeton, NJ: Princeton University Press.

Chatterjee, Partha (1986) *Nationalist Thought and the Colonial World: A Derivative Discourse?* London: Zed.

Fraser, Nancy (1996) Equality, Difference, and Radical Democracy: The United States Feminist Debates Revisited. In *Radical Democracy: Identity, Citizenship, and the State*, ed. David Trend, pp. 197–208. New York: Routledge.

Gupta, Akhil (1998) *Postcolonial Developments: Agriculture in the Making of Modern India.* Durham, NC: Duke University Press.

Khilnani, Sunil (1998) *The Idea of India*. New Delhi: Penguin.

Mahajan, Gurpreet (1999) Civil Society and its Avatars: What Happened to Freedom and Democracy? *Economic and Political Weekly* XXXI:1188–1196.

Ong, Aihwa (1999) Clash of Civilizations or Asian Liberalism? An Anthropology of State and Citizenship. In *Anthropological Theory Today*, ed. Henrietta Moore, pp. 48–72. Cambridge: Polity Press.

Said, Edward (1978) *Orientalism*. London: Routledge and Kegan Paul.

Sivaramakrishnan, K. (1999) *Modern Forests: Statemaking and Environmental Change in Colonial Eastern India*. Stanford, CA: Stanford University Press.

Verdery, Katherine (1998) Transnationalism, Nationalism, Citizenship, and Property: Eastern Europe Since 1989. *American Ethnologist* 25:291–306.

Verma, Jitendra (1998) Reel-Heroes and Real Ones. *Down to Earth* 7:15–16.

## SUGGESTED FURTHER READING

Anagnost, Ann (1997) *National Past-Times: Narrative, Representation and Power in Modern China*. Durham, NC: Duke University Press.

Chatterjee, Partha (1993) *The Nation and its Fragments: Colonial and Postcolonial Histories*. Princeton, NJ: Princeton University Press.

Dirks, Nicholas B. (2002) *Castes of Mind: Colonialism and the Making of Modern India*. Princeton, NJ: Princeton University Press.

Gilroy, Paul (1993) *The Black Atlantic: Modernity and Double Consciousness*. Cambridge, MA: Harvard University Press.

Grove, Richard, Vinita Damodaran, and Satpal Sangwan, eds. (1998) *Nature and the Orient: Essays on the Environmental History of South and Southeast Asia*. Delhi: Oxford University Press.

Guha, Ramachandra (2000) *The Unquiet Woods: Ecological Change and Peasant Resistance in the Himalaya*. Berkeley: University of California Press.

Guha, Sumit (1999) *Environment and Ethnicity in India, 1200–1991*. Cambridge: Cambridge University Press.

Hall, Stuart (1996) When Was the "Postcolonial"? Thinking at the Limit. In *The Postcolonial Question: Common Skies, Divided Horizons*, ed. Iain Chambers and Lidia Curti, pp. 242–260. New York: Routledge.

Merry, Sally (1999) *Colonizing Hawai'i: The Cultural Power of Law*. Princeton, NJ: Princeton University Press.

Neumann, Roderick P. (1998) *Imposing Wilderness: Struggles over Livelihood and Nature Preservation in Africa*. Berkeley: University of California Press.

Peluso, Nancy and Michael Watts, eds. (2001) *Violent Environments*. Ithaca, NY: Cornell University Press.

Prakash, Gyan (1999) *Another Reason: Science and the Imagination of Modern India*. Princeton, NJ: Princeton University Press.

## CHAPTER 24

# Power Topographies

## James Ferguson

## BEYOND "THE STATE" AND "CIVIL SOCIETY" IN THE STUDY OF AFRICAN POLITICS

If there is to be an anthropology of "globalization," it is evident that it will require analytical tools, concepts that will enable critical analysis and open new understandings. As is so often the case, however, in the anthropological study of modernity, the analytical tools closest to hand are themselves part of the social and cultural reality we seek to grasp. There can be no neat separation of analytic categories from "folk" categories when the folk categories in question include such key items of the social-scientific lexicon as "culture," "transnational," "diversity," "flows," "hybridity," "network," and so on. Such a situation calls for a heightened level of reflexive scrutiny of our categories of analysis, if we are to gain critical purchase on the emerging ideologies and world-views of our era, rather than simply (re)producing them.

This is an issue that arises immediately when one looks at the recent literature on "democratization" in Africa. Here, the idea of "civil society" has emerged as a keyword, ubiquitous in both scholarly analyses of "democratization" and the "real-world" practices they seek to describe and explain.

The fad for "civil society" has perhaps been most in evidence among political scientists, who have been understandably eager to leave behind their Cold-War paradigms for livelier topics such as democratization, social movements, and what they call "state/society relations." But anthropologists, too, have been bitten by the bug, finding in "civil society" a new and improved incarnation of their old disciplinary trademark, "the local." Rising numbers of anthropology dissertation students, it seems, are nowadays heading out to "the field" in search not of an intriguing culture or a promising village, but an interesting non-governmental organization. But if such anthropological engagements are to be fruitful, it will be necessary to devote some critical scrutiny to the common-sense mapping of political and social space that the state/civil society opposition takes for granted. Beginning with the category "civil society" itself, I will try to show how the state/civil society opposition forms part of an even more pervasive way of thinking about the analytic "levels" of local, national, and global – a way of thinking that rests on what I call the *vertical topography of power*. I will argue that calling into question this vertical topography of power brings into view the transnational character of both "state" and "civil society," and opens up new ways of thinking about both social movements and states.

I will not attempt a genealogy of the term "civil society," but will only note a few aspects of the changes in its meaning. Its origins are customarily traced to eighteenth-century liberal thought, and especially to Scottish Enlightenment thinkers such as Francis Hutcheson, Adam Ferguson, and later, Adam Smith, in whose thought the term is associated both with the developing conceptualization of society as a self-regulating mechanism, and with concepts of natural law. Better known to many is the Hegelian usage of the term to denote an intermediary domain between the universal ideal of the state and the concrete particularity of the family, a conception famously critiqued by Marx, and imaginatively reworked by Gramsci. Today, the term most often comes up in discussions of democracy, especially to refer to voluntary or so-called non-governmental organizations (NGOs) that seek to influence, or claim space from, the state.

The term "civil society" still had a rather antique cast to it when I first encountered it in graduate seminars on social theory. But since then, it has gotten a new lease on life, chiefly thanks to the dramatic recent political history of Eastern Europe. There, of course, communism had promised to lead to the gradual demise of the state. But instead, the state seemed to have swallowed up everything in its path, leaving behind no social force – neither private businesses, nor church, nor political party – capable of checking its monstrous powers. It was not the state, it seemed, but civil society that had "withered away." In this historically specific context, the old term had a remarkable resonance, and it licensed otherwise unlikely coalitions between actors (from dissident writers to the Catholic Church) who had in common only that they demanded some space, autonomy, and freedom from the totalitarian state.

Coming out of this rather peculiar and particular history, the term "civil society" came for many to be almost interchangeable with the concept of democracy itself – nearly reversing the terms of Marx's famous critique, which had revealed the imaginary freedoms of capitalism's democratic political realm as an illusion, to be contrasted to the real *unfreedom* of "civil society," conceived as the domain of alienation, economic domination, and the slavery of the workplace. But this new conception (of "civil society" as the road to democracy) not only met the political needs of the Eastern European struggle against communist statism, it also found a ready export market – both in the First World (where it was appropriated by conservative Reagan/Thatcher projects for "rolling back the state") and in the Third World (where it seemed to provide leverage both for battling dictatorships and for grounding a post-socialist mass democratic politics). With little regard for historical context or critical genealogy, and in the space of only a few years, "civil society" has thus been universalized. It has been appropriated, for different reasons (if equally uncritically), by both the right and the left. Indeed, it has become one of those things (like development, education, or the environment) that no reasonable person can be against. The only question to be asked of civil society today seems to be: how can we get more of it?

I will argue that the current (often ahistorical and uncritical) use of the concept of "civil society" in the study of African politics obscures more than it reveals, and indeed, that it often serves to help legitimate a profoundly anti-democratic trans-national politics. One of my aims in this essay, then, is to point out the analytic limitations of the state/civil society opposition, and to trace its anti-democratic political and ideological uses.

But I also have a second, and less reactive, aim in exploring the specifically African career of the "civil society" concept. For in the course of criticizing the state versus civil society formula, I hope to arrive at some suggestions about other ways of thinking about contemporary politics in Africa and elsewhere. In particular, I will argue that the "state/civil society" opposition brings along with it a whole topography of power, revealed perhaps most economically in Hegel's famous conception of "civil society" as, in Mamdani's phrase, "sandwiched between the patriarchal family and the universal state" (Mamdani 1996:14). This conception rests on an imaginary space, with the state up high, the family low on the ground, and a range of other institutions in between. In what sense is the state "above" society and the family "below" it? Many different meanings characteristically get blurred together in this vertical image. Is it a matter of scale? Abstraction? Generality? Social hierarchy? Distance from nature? The confusion here is a productive one, in the Foucauldian sense, constructing a common-sense state that simply *is* "up there" somewhere, operating at a "higher level." This common-sense perception has been a crucial part of the way that nation-states have sought (often very successfully) to secure their legitimacy through what Akhil Gupta and I have termed claims of vertical encompassment – claims that naturalize the authority of the state over "the local" by merging three analytically distinct ideas – (1) superior spatial scope; (2) supremacy in a hierarchy of power; and (3) superior generality of interest, knowledge, and moral purpose – into a single figure: the "up there" state that encompasses the local and exists on a "higher level."

Such an image, of course, underlies the familiar public-private split, and the idea (of which Habermas makes much) of a "public sphere" that mediates between state and citizen. By imagining the family as a natural ground or base of society, as feminists have pointed out, it leaves the domestic out of the sphere of politics entirely. But this imagined topography also undergirds most of our images of political struggle, which we readily imagine as coming "from below" (as we say), as "grounded" in rooted and authentic "lives," "experiences," and "communities" (cf. Malkki 1992). The state itself, meanwhile, can be imagined as reaching down into communities, inter-vening, in (as we say) a "top-down" manner, to manipulate or plan "society." Civil society, in this vertical topography, may appear as the middle latitude, the zone of contact between the "up there" state and the "on the ground" people, snug in their communities. Whether this contact zone is conceived as the domain of pressure groups and pluralist politics (as in liberal political theory) or of class struggle in a war of position (as in Gramscian Marxism), this imaginary topography of power has been an enormously consequential one.

What would it mean to rethink this? What if we question the self-evident "vertical-ity" of the relation of state to society, displace the primacy of the nation-state frame of analysis, and rearrange the imaginary space within which civil society can be so automatically "interposed between" higher and lower levels? As we will see, such a move entails rethinking "the state" and looking at transnational apparatuses of governmentality which I will suggest are of special significance in many parts of contemporary Africa, where states are, in significant ways, no longer able to exercise the range of powers we usually associate with a sovereign nation-state, or even (in a few cases) to function at all as states in any conventional sense of the term. But it also, and at the same time, entails rethinking received ideas of "community," "grass-roots," and "the local," laden as they are with nostalgia and the aura of a "grounded" authenticity. Using the politics of structural adjustment in Zambia and the South African civic movement as examples, I will try to show that both the "top" and the "bottom" of the vertical picture today operate within a profoundly transna-tionalized global context that makes the constructed and fictive nature of the vertical topography of power increasingly visible, and opens up new possibilities for both research and political practice. First, however, I wish to continue the interrogation of the contemporary conceptualization of the problem of "state/civil society relations" by showing how much it shares, at the level of the topographic imagination, with the older "nation-building" paradigm which it has largely replaced.

## The Vertical Topography in the Study of African Politics: Two Variants of a Mythic Structure

I will begin by considering two views of African politics that, sometimes in explicit opposition, often in implicit and confused combination, have dominated the intellectual scene in recent decades. The older paradigm sees nation-building as the central political process in postcolonial Africa, with a modernizing state in conflict with primordial ethnic loyalties. The newer view recommends the roll-back of an overgrown and suffocating state, and celebrates the resurgence of "civil society," often putatively linked to a process of "democratization." In deliberately presenting a highly schematic and simplified account of their distinctive features, my purpose is to reveal an underlying set of assumptions that they share.

### "Nation-building"

The key premise of the "nation-building" approach to African politics is the existence of two different levels of political integration, and a necessary and historic movement from one to the other. The first such level, logically and historically prior, is the local or sub-national; this is the level of primordial social and political attachments, left over from the premodern past. Originally referred to by such labels as "tribal organization" or "traditional African society," these supposed "givens" of African political life were thought to include structures of kinship, community, and (in some formulations) ethnicity. Later, Goran Hyden would summarize such local "primordial affiliations" under the singularly unfortunate rubric, "the economy of affection" (Hyden 1983). Indeed, it should be noted that while such "primordialist" approaches to sub-national identities may fairly be described as out of date, they are very far from having vanished from the contemporary scene.

The second level of integration, in the "nation-building" scheme, is, of course, the national. Emergent, new, modern nations were understood to be in the process of construction – stepping out, as it were, for the first time onto the stage of world history. With national structures of authority struggling to establish themselves in the face of "primordial" commitments, "nation-building" appeared both an urgent task and a historically inevitable process. Yet the generally hopeful tone of the work in this tradition is shadowed by the phantom that stalks "nation-building" – the specter of premodern resurgences such as "tribalism," or such manifestations of the lingering "economy of affection" as nepotism, corruption, and other banes of "good government." Failed nation-building, it follows, can only mean a resurgence of primordial affiliations (still the usual journalistic explanation for civil wars in Africa). State success, on the other hand, means the construction of new bases of authority resting on nation-state citizenship. Above the national level, finally, appears the international, understood largely as (1) a source of "aid," a helping hand in nation-building; and (2) a utopian image of the union of nation-states, with the key symbol of the UN as the promise of the universality of the nation form.

"Development," in such a view, is the natural reward for successful national integration, just as nation-building is the characteristic rhetoric of the developmental state. The strong, activist state thus naturally becomes the protagonist in the optimistic narratives of "national development" that flourish within this paradigm. This view of the world is perhaps sufficiently familiar to make it possible to move ahead without further elaboration.

## "State and society"

"State and society" – the self-proclaimed "new paradigm" in the study of African politics – regards the state and its projects with new skepticism, and rediscovers "the local" as the site of "civil society," a vigorous, dynamic field of possibilities too long suffocated by the state. In place of a modernizing national state bravely struggling against premodern ethnic fragmentation, the image now is of a despotic and overbearing state which monopolizes political and economic space, stifling both democracy and economic growth. Instead of the main protagonist of development, the state (now conceived as flabby, bureaucratic, and corrupt) begins to appear as the chief obstacle to it. What are called "governance" reforms are needed to reduce the role of the state, and bring it into "balance" with "civil society" (Harbeson, Rothchild, and Chazan 1994).

The local level, meanwhile, is no longer understood as necessarily backward, ethnic, or rural. New attention is paid to such non-"primordial" manifestations of the local as voluntary associations and "grass-roots" organizations through which Africans meet their own needs, and may even press their interests against the state. There is, in much of this newer research, an unmistakable tone of approval and even celebration – not of the nation-building state, but of a liberated and liberatory civil society. Society, left to its own devices, it seems, might make political and economic progress; the problem now is how to induce the state to get out of the way, and to make it more responsive to "civil society's" demands. Hence the connection, repeatedly asserted in the "governance" literature, between democratization (conceived as making space for "civil society") and development (conceived as getting the state out of the way of a dynamic non-state sector). It is such a link, too, that accounts for the otherwise peculiar idea of a natural affinity between the draconian and decidedly unpopular measures of "structural adjustment" on the one hand, and populist demands for "democratization" on the other (a point I will return to shortly).

The "new" state and society approach is often posed as a simple opposition to the "old" nation-building (or "statist") model. But the two paradigms are not as different as might at first appear. In particular, the state and society paradigm uses the very same division of politics into analytic "levels" as does the "nation-building" one, altering only the valuation of their roles. The "national" level is now called "the state," the "local" level "civil society." But where the older view had a new, dynamic, progressive national level energizing and overcoming an old, stagnant, reactionary local level, the new view reverses these values. Now the national level (the state) is corrupt, patrimonial, stagnant, out of date, and holding back needed change; while the local level (civil society) is understood as neither ethnic nor archaic, but as a dynamic, emerging, bustling assemblage of progressive civic organizations that could bring about democracy and development if only the state would get out of the way.

The international, too, appears in both paradigms, but with largely opposite functions. International agencies, especially financial ones, appear in the state-and-society view less as state benefactors and providers of "aid" than as the policemen of states – regulating their functioning and rolling back their excesses through "structural adjustment." If the nation-building view imagined the international in the form of an idealistic UN, the state and society paradigm pictures a no-nonsense IMF: stern, real-world bankers, speaking what I have elsewhere called the language of economic correctness (cf. Ferguson 1995).

The implications for "development" are clear, and again nearly the reverse of those of the nation-building approach. For the state and society paradigm sees development not as the project of a developmentalist state, but as a societal process that is held back by the stifling hold of the state; "structural adjustment" is needed to liberate market forces to work their development magic. Where the first paradigm saw the development problem as too much society, not enough state, the second sees it as too much state, not enough society.

The two views, it should by now be clear, bear a remarkable resemblance to one another, even as they are manifestly opposed. Indeed, everything happens as if the second model were, as Lévi-Strauss might say, a very simple transformation of the first. Through a structural inversion more familiar, perhaps, to analysts of myth than of politics, we are left with two paradigms that are simultaneously completely opposed to one another and almost identical.

## The Topography of "State and Civil Society"

It is obvious that there exists a range of phenomena in contemporary Africa that are not captured in the old nation-building optic that saw politics as a battle between a modernizing state and primordial ethnic groups – hence the recourse to the idea of "civil society" to encompass a disparate hodge-podge of social groups and institutions that have in common only that they exist in some way outside of or beyond the state. Indeed, while the term "civil society" is often not defined at all in contemporary Africanist literature, most authors seem to intend the classical Hegelian usage that, as I pointed out, imagines a middle zone of "society" interposed between family and state. Others speak more specifically of civil society as a frontier of contact where a politically organized and self-conscious "society" presses against, and sets the bounds of, "the state" (see the essays in Harbeson, Rothchild, and Chazan 1994; for an illuminating critical review of the uses of the "civil society" concept in African studies, see Comaroff and Comaroff 2000).

But while definitions of "civil society" in this literature are usually broad and vague, in practice writers move quite quickly from definitional generalities to a much more specific vision that is restricted almost entirely to small, grass-roots, voluntary organizations, leaving out of the picture some rather important and obvious phenomena. One is never sure. Is the Anglo-American Corporation of South Africa part of this "civil society"? Is John Garang's army in Sudan? Is Oxfam? What about ethnic movements that are not so much opposed to or prior to modern states, but (as so much recent scholarship shows) produced by them? Or Christian mission organizations, arguably more important today in Africa than ever, but strangely relegated to the colonial past in the imagination of much contemporary scholarship? All of these phenomena fit uncomfortably in the "state" versus "civil society" grid, and indeed cannot even be coherently labeled as "local," "national," or "international" phenomena. Instead, each of these examples, like much else of interest in contemporary Africa, both embodies a significant local dynamic and is indisputably a product and expression of powerful forces both national and global.

The state, meanwhile, when apprehended empirically and ethnographically, starts itself to look suspiciously like "civil society." Sometimes, this is literally the case, such as when NGOs are actually run out of government offices as a sort of moonlighting venture ("An NGO?" a Zambian informant of mine once remarked. "That's just a bureaucrat with his own letterhead.") Perhaps more profoundly, as Timothy Mitchell (1991) has argued, the very conception of "state" as a set of reified and disembodied structures is an effect of state practices themselves. Instead, recent work on actually existing state practices (e.g. Gupta 1995) suggests that states may be better viewed not in opposition to something called "society," but as themselves composed of bundles of social practices, every bit as "local" in their social situatedness and materiality as any other.

Such work suggests that to make progress here we will need to break away from the conventional division into "vertical" analytic levels that the old "nation-building" and the new "state and society" paradigms share. In the process, we will manage to break out from the range of questions that such a division imposes (how do states rule, what relations exist – or ought to exist – between state and society, how can civil society obtain room to maneuver from the state, etc.), and open up to view some of the transnational relations that I will suggest are crucial for understanding both ends of the vertical polarity. Let us consider what a focus on transnational contexts has to tell us, first about the putative "top" of the vertical topography ("the state") and then about the supposed "bottom" ("grass-roots" civic organizations).

## "The top"

If, as neoliberal theories of state and society suggest, domination is rooted in state power, then rolling back the power of the state naturally leads to greater freedom, and ultimately to "democratization." But the argument is revealed to be fallacious if one observes that, particularly in Africa, domination has long been exercised by entities other than the state. Zambia, let us remember, was originally colonized (just a little over a hundred years ago) not by any government, but by the British South Africa Company, a private multinational corporation directed by Cecil Rhodes. Equipped with its own army, and acting under the terms of a British "concession," it was this private corporation that conquered and "pacified" the territory, and set up the system of private ownership and race privilege that became the colonial system.

Today, Zambia (like most other African nations) continues to be ruled, in significant part, by transnational organizations that are not in themselves governments, but work together with powerful First-World states within a global system of nation-states that Frederick Cooper has characterized as "internationalized imperialism."

Perhaps most familiarly, international agencies such as the IMF and the World Bank, together with allied banks and First-World governments, today often directly impose policies upon African states. The name for this process in recent years has been "structural adjustment," and it has been made possible by both the general fiscal weakness of African states and the more specific squeeze created by the debt crisis. The new assertiveness of the IMF has been, with some justification, likened to a process of "recolonization," implying a serious erosion of the sovereignty of African states (e.g., Saul 1993). It should be noted that direct impositions of policy by banks and international agencies have involved not only such broad, macroeconomic interventions as setting currency exchange rates, but also fairly detailed requirements for curtailing social spending, restructuring state bureaucracies, and so on. Rather significant and specific aspects of state policy, in other words, are, for many African countries, being directly formulated in places like New York and Washington.

Such "governance" of African economies from afar represents, as critics have not failed to point out, a kind of transfer of sovereignty away from African states and into the hands of the IMF. Yet since it is African governments that remain nominally in charge, it is easy to see that they are the first to receive the blame when "structural adjustment" policies begin to bite. At that point, democratic elections (another "adjustment" being pressed by international "donors") provide a means whereby one government can be replaced by another. But since the successor government will be locked in the same financial vice-grip as its predecessor, actual policies are unlikely to change. (Indeed, the government that tries can be swiftly brought to its knees by the IMF and its associated capital cartel, as the Zambian case illustrates vividly). In this way, policies that are in fact made and imposed by wholly unelected and unaccountable international bankers may be presented as democratically chosen by popular assent. Thus does "democratization" ironically serve to simulate popular legitimacy for policies that are in fact made in a way that is less democratic than ever (cf. Ferguson 1995).


## "The bottom"

Civil society often appears in African studies today as a bustle of grass-roots, democratic local organizations. What this ignores is, of course, as Jane Guyer has put it "the obvious: that civil society is [largely] made up of *international* organizations"

(Guyer 1994:223). For indeed, the local voluntary organizations in Africa, so beloved of "civil society" theorists, very often, upon inspection, turn out to be integrally linked with national and transnational-level entities. One might think, for instance, of the myriad South African "community organizations" that are bankrolled by USAID or European church groups; or of the profusion of "local" Christian development NGOs in Zimbabwe, which may be conceived equally well as the most local, "grass-roots" expressions of civil society, or as parts of the vast international bureaucratic organizations that organize and sustain their deletion. When such organizations begin to take over the most basic functions and powers of the state, it becomes only too clear that "NGOs" are not as "NG" as they might wish us to believe. Indeed, the World Bank baldly refers to what they call BONGOs (Bank-organized NGOs) and now even GONGOs (Government-organized NGOs).

That these voluntary organizations come as much from the putative "above" (international organizations) as from the supposed "below" (local communities) is an extremely significant fact about so-called "civil society" in Africa. For at the same time that international organizations (through structural adjustment) are eroding the power of African states (and usurping their sovereignty), they are busy making end runs around these states and directly sponsoring their own programs or interventions via NGOs in a wide range of areas. The role played by NGOs in helping Western "development" agencies to "get around" uncooperative national governments sheds a good deal of light on the current disdain for the state and the celebration of "civil society" that one finds in both the theoretical and the policy-oriented literature right now.

But challengers to African states today are not only to be found in international organizations. In the wake of what is widely agreed to be a certain collapse or retreat of the nation-state all across the continent, we find a range of forms of power and authority springing up that have not been well described or analyzed to date. These are usually described as "sub-national," and usually conceived either as essentially ethnic (the old primordialist view, which, as I noted above, is far from dead), or alternatively (and more hopefully) as manifestations of a newly resurgent "civil society," long suppressed by a heavy-handed state. Yet can we really assume that the new political forms that challenge the hegemony of African nation-states are necessarily well-conceived as "local," "grass-roots," "civil," or even "sub-national"?

Guerrilla insurrections, for instance, not famous for their "civility," are often not strictly "local" or "sub-national" either – armed and funded, as they often are, from abroad. Consider Savimbi's UNITA army in Angola: long aided by the CIA, originally trained by China, with years of military and logistic support from South Africa, and continuous funding from US right-wing church groups. Is this a "sub-national" organization? A phenomenon of an emerging "civil society"? What about transnational Christian organizations like World Vision International, which (as Erica Bornstein [2001] has recently pointed out) play an enormous role in many parts of contemporary Africa, organizing local affairs and building and operating schools and clinics where states have failed to do so? Are such giant, transnational organizations to be conceptualized as "local"? What of humanitarian organizations such as Oxfam, CARE, or Doctors Without Borders, which perform state-like functions all across Africa?

Such organizations are not states, but are unquestionably state-like in some respects. Yet they are not well described as "sub-national," "national," or even "supra-national." Local and global at the same time, they are transnational – even, in some ways, a-national; they cannot be located within the familiar vertical division of analytic levels presented above. Not coincidentally, these organizations and movements that fall outside of the received scheme of analytic levels are also conspicuously understudied – indeed, they seem to be largely invisible to theoretical scholarship on African politics, tending to be relegated instead to the level of "applied," problem-oriented studies.

In all of these cases, we are dealing with political entities that may be better conceptualized not as "below" the state, but as integral parts of a new, transnational apparatus of governmentality. This new apparatus does not *replace* the older system of nation-states (which is   let us be clear – far from being about to disappear), but overlays it and coexists with it. In this optic, it might make sense to think of the new organizations that have sprung up in recent years, not as challengers pressing up against the state from below but as horizontal contemporaries of the organs of the state – sometimes rivals, sometimes servants, sometimes watchdogs, sometimes parasites, but in every case operating on the same level and in the same global space.

Such a reconceptualization has implications for both research and political practice, insofar as these depend on received ideas of a "down-there" society and an "up-there" state. In particular, I will examine some of these consequences for two sorts of actor with a special stake in the "grass-roots": social movements, on the one hand, and anthropologists on the other.

## "GRASS-ROOTS" POLITICS WITHOUT VERTICALITY?

What does the critical scrutiny of the vertical topography of power mean for progressive social movements that have long depended on certain taken-for-granted ideas of locality, authenticity, and "bottom-up" struggle? An extremely illuminating example comes out of the practice, and self-criticism, of the South African civic movement. Organized, politically powerful, local civic organizations played a huge role in the struggle for democracy in South Africa. With national political organizations banned, township civics built networks, organized boycotts and demonstrations, educated cadres, and made many townships no-go areas for the white regime's troops and policemen. Civics took up key government functions, and sometimes developed remarkably democratic internal institutions. At the height of the anti-apartheid movement, the civics were not just protest groups, but something approaching a genuinely revolutionary force – as the apartheid regime itself recognized.

I will here draw on the recent writings of Mzwanele Mayekiso, a township organizer in the Johannesburg neighborhood of Alexandra, and a true heir of Antonio Gramsci (in an age of many pretenders). Mayekiso sees very clearly the shortcomings of much fashionable celebration of "civil society." Simply lumping together everything outside of the state may have had its utility in the struggle against totalitarian rule in Eastern Europe. But in South Africa, he insists, it is disastrous; it conceals the diametrically opposed political agendas of distinct and antagonistic social classes. For Mayekiso, the socialist, it makes no sense to allow the Chamber of Mines and the

Mineworkers' Union to be simply thrown together as "civil society," in opposition to "the state." Moreover, the unthinking valorization of "civil society" for its own sake contains the risk of "following the agenda of imperialist development agencies and foreign ministries, namely, to shrink the size and scope of third world governments and to force community organizations to take up state responsibilities with inadequate resources" (1996:12). Instead, Mayekiso proposes an eminently Gramscian solution: a determination to work for what he calls "working-class civil society." It is this that must be strengthened, developed, and allowed to preserve its autonomy from the state. Mayekiso cites two reasons for this: (1) to build a base for socialism during a period when a socialist state is not yet a realistic expectation; and (2) to serve as a watchdog over the state while pressing it to meet community needs in the meantime.

It is useful to keep in mind that Mayekiso is writing from the position of an extraordinarily successful political organizer. The South African civics have been a formidable force to be reckoned with, not only in the anti-apartheid struggle, where their organization and political energy proved decisive, but also in their post-independence role. The civics have been successfully transformed from agents of all-out resistance to the apartheid state (aiming – among other things – to make the townships "ungovernable"), to well-organized autonomous structures ready to lend support to some state campaigns while vigorously attacking and protesting others. A national organization of civics, SANCO (South African National Civic Organization), which Mayekiso headed, is today a major player on the national scene, and serves as an independent advocate for worker and township interests – all of which makes it at least a bit more difficult for the ANC government to sell out its mass base.

But the post-independence era has also presented some profound challenges to Mayekiso's Gramscian praxis, which he analyzes with remarkable honesty and clear-sightedness. In particular, Mayekiso has come to recognize that the policies of the new South African government are constrained not only by the balance of forces in South Africa, but also by the forces of transnational capital, which "denude the ability of nation-states to make their own policy" (1996:280). Faced with the threat of a capital boycott, there may be limits on how far even the most progressive South African government can go down the road to socialism. The traditional nationalist approach, based on organizing the masses to put pressure on the government, has no effective response to this situation. Vertical politics seems to have reached its limits.

Such failures of strictly national politics from below lead Mayekiso to a very interesting critical reflection. Recalling the long struggle of the Alexandra Community Organization during the apartheid years, he acknowledges that its success grew not simply from its strong base in the community but from strategic transnational alliances. In fact, the ACO, he reports, received *most* of its funds not from the community, or even from within the country, but from international sources. Dutch solidarity groups, US sister city programs, Canadian NGOs, Swedish official aid, even USAID at one point – all were sources of aid and support for Mayekiso's "local organizing," which (we begin to realize) was not quite so "local" after all. But Mayekiso does not apologize for this. On the contrary, he uses a reflection on the successful experience of the ACO to begin to develop what he calls "a whole new approach, a 'foreign policy' of working-class civil society" (1996:283). After all, he says, "there is a growing recognition that poor and working class citizens of different countries now have more in common with each other than they do with their own elites" (1996:283), while "the ravages of the world economy are denuding the ability of nation-states to make their own policy" (1996:280). In such circumstances, challenges from below within a vertically conceived national space cannot succeed; but "international civic politics is a real alternative to weak nation-states across the globe" (1996:280).

Traditional leftist conceptions of progressive politics in the Third World (to which many anthropologists, including myself, have long subscribed) have almost always rested on one or another version of the vertical topography of power that I have described. "Local" people in "communities" and their "authentic" leaders and representatives who organize "at the grass-roots," in this view, are locked in struggle with a repressive state representing (in some complex combination) both imperial capitalism and the local dominant classes. The familiar themes here are those of resistance from below and repression from above, always accompanied by the danger of co-optation, as the leaders of today's struggle become the elites against whom one must struggle tomorrow.

I do not mean to imply that this conception of the world is entirely wrong or entirely irrelevant. But if, as I have suggested, transnational relations of power are no longer routed so centrally through the state, and if forms of governmentality increasingly exist that bypass states altogether, then political resistance needs to be reconceptualized in a parallel fashion. Many of today's most successful social movements have done just that (as the example of the South African civics in part illustrates). But academic theory, as so often, here lags behind the world it seeks to account for.

To be sure, the world of academic theory is by now ready to see that the nation-state does not work the way conventional models of African politics suggested. And the idea that transnational networks of governmentality have taken a leading role in the de facto governance of Africa is also likely to be assented to on reflection. But are we ready to perform a similar shift in the way we think about political resistance? Are we ready to jettison received ideas of "local communities" and "authentic leadership"? Critical scholars today celebrate both local resistance to corporate globalization as well as forms of grass-roots international solidarity that some have termed "globalization from below." But even as we do so, we seem to hang on stubbornly to the very idea of a "below" – the idea that politically subordinate groups are somehow naturally local, rooted, and encompassed by "higher-level" entities. For what is involved in the very idea and image of "grass-roots" politics, if not precisely the vertical topography of power that I have suggested is the root of our conceptual ills? Can we learn to conceive, theoretically and politically, of a "grass-roots" that would be not local, communal, and authentic, but worldly, well-connected, and opportunistic? Are we ready for social movements that fight not "from below" but "across," using their "foreign policy" to fight struggles not against "the state" but against that hydra-headed transnational apparatus of banks, international agencies, and market institutions through which contemporary capitalist domination functions?

Consider a recent article in the *Los Angeles Times* on the worldly engagements of the Zapatistas of Chiapas, Mexico (Fineman 1996). The Zapatistas, we learn, have become celebrities, and have been discovered by the jet-set. The Hollywood film producer Oliver Stone was photographed receiving the trademark wool mask and pipe from sub-commander Marcos during a recent visit to the guerrillas' headquarters. Danielle Mitterand (widow of the former French president) recently dropped by. And so on. Most shockingly, Marcos himself has apparently appeared in a fashion spread for the Italian clothing firm Benetton. The sub-commander appears in camouflage dress, the glossy photo captioned: "You have to go to war. But what will you wear? Camouflage visual dynamic: light, photogenic . . . ideal for the soldier who goes from war to war and who doesn't have time to change." Benetton even offered to be the official outfitter of the Zapatistas, but here Marcos drew the line. "Compañeros," he told reporters solemnly (through his mask), "we have decided that it is not suitable to wear sweaters in the jungle."

If this strikes one as funny (as it did me), it is useful to think about exactly what the joke is here. For at least part of the humor in the story comes from its suggestion that a group of supposed peasant revolutionaries have, in their inappropriate appetite for Hollywood celebrity and Italian clothing, revealed themselves as something less than genuine ("from fighting to fashion"). After all, what would a "real revolutionary" be doing in a Benetton ad, or lunching with Oliver Stone? But this reaction may be misplaced. As Diane Nelson (1999) has recently argued, First-World progressives need to rethink our ideas of popular struggle, and to prepare ourselves to learn from Third-World transnational "hackers" with a sense of media politics, as well as a sense of humor – and from movements that offer us not a pure and centered subject of resistance, but (like the sub-commander) a quite different figure: masked, ambivalent, impure, and canny. Like the South African civics described by Mayekiso, the Zapatistas present us not with authentic others fighting for a nostalgic past, but with media-savvy, well-connected contemporaries, finding allies horizontally, flexibly, even opportunistically, but effectively. For there is obviously real political acumen in the Zapatista strategy. Celebrity attention and world press coverage may well help to protect Chiapas communities against potential aggression; the cost to the Mexican state of political repression surely rises with the amount of press coverage (and public-relations damage) that it entails. More profoundly, the *image* of destabilization through guerrilla warfare, properly circulated, is perhaps the Zapatistas' most potent political weapon. Capitalism is built on perceptions, and Mexican capitalism is built on an especially precarious set of perceptions – particularly, on the idea that it is an "emerging market" on the path of the "tigers" of East Asia, a carefully nurtured perception that has supported a huge burst of speculative capital investment in the Mexican economy from the US and elsewhere. The real damage to the Mexican economy (and thus to the Mexican ruling class) may not come so much from the Zapatistas' actual raids, as from the effect that the *fear* of such raids has on the Mexican stock market, and on the all-important "confidence" (as they say) of the international bond-holders who have the Mexican economy in their pockets. A guerrilla war conducted in images on the pages of an international fashion magazine, then, may not be so out of place after all. Indeed, it may well be the most tactically effective sort of warfare that the terrain will support.

The globalization of politics is not a one-way street; if relations of rule and systems of exploitation have become transnational, so have forms of resistance – along lines not only of race and class, which I have emphasized here, but also of gender, sexuality, and so on. Gramsci's brilliant topographic imagination may be a guide to this new political world, but only if we are willing to update our maps from time to time. The image of civil society as a zone of trench warfare between working people and the capitalist state served the left well enough at one moment in history, just as the vision of a self-regulating zone of "society" that needed protection from a despotic state served the needs of an emergent bourgeoisie in an earlier era. But invoking such topographies today can only obscure the real political issues, which unfold on a very different ground, where familiar territorializations simply no longer function. Rethinking the taken-for-granted spatial mapping that is invoked not only in such terms as "the state" and "civil society" but also in the opposition of "local" to "global" (and in all those familiar invocations of "grass-roots," "community," etc.), in these times becomes an elementary act of theoretical and political clarification, as well as a way of strategically sharpening – and not, as is sometimes suggested, of undermining – the struggles of subaltern peoples and social movements around the world.

## Toward an Ethnography of Encompassment

Just as a rethinking of the vertical topography of power has special consequences for political practices that depend on unexamined tropes of "above" and "below," it also contains special lessons for forms of scholarship that have traditionally found their distinctive objects in vertically conceived analytic "levels." Working through these conceptual issues, I suggest, might well point in the direction of promising new directions for research. For making verticality problematic not only brings into view the profoundly transnational character of both the state "level" and the local "level," it also brings the very image of the "level" into view as a sort of intensively managed fiction.

To say this is to point toward an ethnographic project that I am only beginning to explore, in collaboration with Akhil Gupta – that of exploring the social and symbolic processes through which state verticality and encompassment are socially established and contested through a host of mundane practices (Ferguson and Gupta 2002). On the one hand, the project we envision would entail the ethnographic exploration of the processes through which (insofar as state legitmation goes smoothly) the "up-there" state gets to be seen as (naturally and common-sensically) "up there." The spatialization of the state has usually been understood through attention to the regulation and surveillance of the boundaries of nations, since the boundary is the primary site where the territoriality of nation-states is made manifest: wars, immigration controls, and customs duties being the most obvious examples. But while this is a rich area of investigation, it is only one mode by which the spatialization of states takes place. The larger issue has to do with the range of everyday technologies by which the state is spatialized, by which verticality and encompassment become features of social life, commonsensical understandings about the state that are widely shared among citizens and scholars. The policing of the border is intimately tied to the policing of Main Street in that they are both rituals that enact the encompassment of the territory of the nation by the state; these acts represent the repressive power of the state as both extensive with the boundaries of the nation and intensively permeating every square inch of that territory; both types of policing often demarcate the racial and cultural boundaries of belonging, and, are often inscribed by bodily violence on the same groups of people. Nor is this simply a matter of repressive state power: state benevolence as well as coercion must make its spatial rounds, as is clear, for instance, in the ritual touring of disaster sites by aid-dispensing US presidents. It is less in the spectacular rituals of the border than in the multiple, mundane domains of bureaucratic practice that states instantiate their spatiality. Rituals of spatial hierarchy and encompassment are more pervasive than most of us imagine them to be; an ethnographic focus allows these everyday practices to be brought more clearly into focus.

At the same time, however, it is part of our argument that new forms of transnational connection increasingly enable "local" actors to challenge the state's well-established claims to encompassment and vertical superiority in unexpected ways, as a host of worldly and well-connected "grass-roots" organizations today demonstrate. If state officials today can still always be counted on to invoke "the national interest" in ways that seek to encompass (and thereby devalue) the local, canny "grass-roots" operators may trump the national ace with appeals to "world opinion" and email links to the international headquarters of such formidably encompassing agents of surveillance as "Africa Watch," "World Vision," or "Amnesty International." Where states could once counter local opposition to, for example, dam projects by invoking a national-level interest that was self-evidently "higher than" (and superior to) the merely "local" interests of those whose land was about to be flooded, today "project-affected people" are more likely to style themselves as "guardians of the planet," protectors of "the lungs of the earth," or participants in a universal struggle for human rights, and to link their "local" struggles directly to transnationally distributed fields of interest and power. Such rhetorical and organizational moves directly challenge state claims of vertical encompassment by drawing upon universalist principles and globally spatialized networks that render the claims of a merely *national* interest and scope narrow and parochial by comparison. The claims of verticality that I have reviewed here (claims of superior spatial scope, supremacy in a hierarchy of power, and superior generality of interest, knowledge, and moral purpose) have historically been monopolized by the state. But today these claims are increasingly being challenged and undermined by a newly transnationalized "local" which fuses the grass-roots and the global in ways that make a hash of the vertical topography of power on which the legitimation of nation-states has so long depended.

What this implies is not simply that it is important to study NGOs and other transnational non-state organization, or even to trace their interrelations and zones of contact with "the state." Rather, the implication would be that it is necessary to treat state and non-state governmentality within a common frame, without making unwarranted assumptions about their spatial reach, vertical height, or relation to "the local." What is called for, in other words, is an approach to the state that would treat its verticality and encompassment not as a fact taken for granted, but as a precarious achievement – and as an ethnographic problem. Such a project would be misconceived as a study of "state–society interactions," for to put matters thus is to assume the very opposition that requires to be interrogated. Rather, what is needed is an ethnography of processes and practices of encompassment, an ethnographic approach that would center the processes through which the exercise of governmentality (by state and non-state actors) is both legitimated and undermined by reference to claims of superior spatial reach and vertical height.

Such a view might open up a much richer set of questions about the meaning of transnationalism for states than have up to now been asked. For in this perspective, it is not a question of whether a globalizing political economy is rendering nation-states weak and irrelevant, as some have suggested, or whether states remain the crucial building-blocks of the global system, as others have countered. For the central effect of the new forms of transnational governmentality is not so much to make states weak (or strong), as to reconfigure the way that states are able to spatialize their authority and stake claims to superior generality and universality. Recognizing this process might open up a new line of approach into the ethnographic study of state power in the contemporary world.

## REFERENCES

Bornstein, Erica (2001) The Good Life: Religious NGOs and the Moral Politics of Economic Development in Zimbabwe. Ph.D. dissertation, University of California at Irvine.

Comaroff, Jean, and John L. Comaroff (2000) *Civil Society and the Political Imagination in Africa: Critical Perspectives.* Chicago: University of Chicago Press.

Ferguson, James (1995) From African Socialism to Scientific Capitalism: Reflections on the Legitimation Crisis in IMF-ruled Africa. In *Debating Development Discourse: Popular and Institutionalist Perspectives,* ed. David Moore and Gerald Schmitz, pp. 129–148. New York: St. Martin's Press.

Ferguson, James, and Akhil Gupta (2002) Spatializing States: Toward an Ethnography of Neoliberal Governmentality. *American Ethnologist* 29:981–1002.

Fineman, Mark (1996) Zapatistas in Transition from Fighting to Fashion. *Los Angeles Times,* April 21:A4.

Gupta, Akhil (1995) Blurred Boundaries: The Discourse of Corruption, the Culture of Politics, and the Imagined State. *American Ethnologist* 22:375–402.

Guyer, Jane, 1994 The Spatial Dimensions of Civil Society in Africa: An Anthropologist Looks at Nigeria. In *Civil Society and the State in Africa,* ed. John W. Harbeson, Donald Rothchild, and Naomi Chazan, pp. 215–230. Boulder, CO: Lynne Rienner.

Harbeson, John W., Donald Rothchild, and Naomi Chazan, eds. (1994) *Civil Society and the State in Africa.* Boulder, CO: Lynne Rienner.

Hyden, Goran (1983) *No Shortcuts to Progress: African Development Management in Perspective.* Berkeley: University of California Press.

Malkki, Liisa, (1992) National Geographic: The Rooting of Peoples and the Territorialization of National Identity among Scholars and Refugees. *Cultural Anthropology* 7:24–44.

Mamdani, Mahmood (1996) *Citizen and Subject: Contemporary Africa and the Legacy of Late Colonialism.* Princeton, NJ: Princeton University Press.

Mayekiso, Mzwanele (1996) *Township Politics: Civic Struggles for a New South Africa.* New York: Monthly Review Press.

Mitchell, Timothy (1991) The Limits of the State: Beyond Statist Approaches and their Critics. *American Political Science Review* 8:77–96.

Nelson, Diane (1999) *A Finger in the Wound: Body Politics in Quintencennial Guatemala.* Berkeley: University of California Press.

Saul, John S. (1993) *Recolonization and Resistance in Southern Africa in the 1990s.* Trenton, NJ: Africa World Press.

## SUGGESTED FURTHER READING

Arato, Andrew, and Jean-Louis Cohen (1994) *Civil Society and Political Theory.* Cambridge, MA: MIT Press.

Bayart, Jean-François (1993) *The State in Africa: The Politics of the Belly.* New York: Addison-Wesley.

Bayart, Jean-François, Stephen Ellis, and Beatrice Hibou (1999) *The Criminalization of the State in Africa.* Bloomington: Indiana University Press.

Chatterjee, Partha (1990) A Response to Taylor's "Modes of Civil Society." *Public Culture* 3:119–132.

Marx, Karl (1978 [1844]) On the Jewish Question. In *The Marx-Engels Reader*, ed. Robert C. Tucker,. New York: W. W. Norton.

Mbembe, Achille (2001) *On the Postcolony.* Berkeley: University of California Press.

Reno, William (1999) *Warlord Politics and African States.* New York: Lynne Rienner.

Taylor, Charles (1990) Modes of Civil Society. *Public Culture* 3:95–118.

## CHAPTER 25

# Race Technologies

## *Thomas Biolsi*

One of the central challenges in understanding race and racism is to grasp simultaneously the utter *social constructedness* of "race" (the fictional nature of race) and the *social fact* of race (the inescapable human consequences of race for the individual in a racist society). As historian Barbara Fields (1990:96) describes the fictitious nature of race, "Anyone who continues to believe in race as a physical attribute of individuals... might as well also believe that Santa Claus, the Easter Bunny, and the tooth fairy are real, and that the earth stands still while the sun moves." But race is a "fiction" in the same way that money is a fiction; race is a *concrete* abstraction, and to be black in the United States, for example, is to live on the receiving end of the fiction of "race" in deeply brutalizing ways. And, as scholars have only recently come to recognize, to be white is to inherit racial privilege in profoundly material ways.

This chapter will start from these two grounding premises and make the case for understanding race, not as a thing, but as a process or activity. As Michel Foucault advised us to do in the study of power, rather than ask what race is, it is fruitful to ask: How is race exercised? By what means? And what happens when an individual asserts her race in relation to another? Just as in the Foucauldian approach to power, this chapter argues that we can learn a great deal if we see race not as some social thing that one holds (such as an identity, a status, an ideology, or a world-view) or that can be observed (such as a structure, or an institution), but as a *technique that one exercises*.

The key to this approach is to understand race-making in terms of the micro-practices used by situated actors in concrete, historical situations. This "technological" approach to race shifts attention to the practices by which "a human being turns him- or herself into a subject" (Foucault 1983:212). A subject is here understood in modern philosophy's sense of an active consciousness aware of itself (or, often, deceived) as a bounded individual in relation to others, with a certain inescapable will, and an array of self-determined interests. One of Foucault's contributions was to show how this subject can be neither pre-given and natural, nor voluntary and sovereign, but can only be actively formed through socially – and historically – available technologies of the self (and the Other). The racial technologies that will be described in this chapter include active techniques of *stating*, *mixing*, *classifying*, and *spacing*. The substantive focus here will be on the technologies that produce black–white race lines on the one hand, and American Indian–white race lines on the other, within the United States. The point is not to give any theoretical emphasis to these particular race lines rather than others. These cases are simply drawn upon for the purpose of illustrating how one might approach race in terms of technologies of the self.

## STATING

Let us begin with Thomas Jefferson's *Notes on the State of Virginia* (1982 [1787]). Jefferson was, of course, the drafter of the Declaration of Independence and one of the key US Enlightenment thinkers. As has been widely recognized by scholars of race, one of the more interesting themes in Jefferson's *Notes* is a comparative treatment of African Americans and Native Americans – as against whites. Jefferson did not have nice things to say about what he called the "physical and moral" characteristics of African Americans (Jefferson 1982 [1787]:138–139):

> They secrete . . . more [than do whites] by the glands of the skin, which gives them a very strong and disagreeable odour . . . They are more ardent after their female: but love seems with them to be more an eager desire, than a tender delicate mixture of sentiment and sensation . . . Their griefs are transient . . . In general, their existence appears to participate more of sensation than reflection. To this must be ascribed their disposition to sleep when abstracted from their diversions, and unemployed in labour . . . Comparing them by their faculties of memory, reason, and imagination, it appears to me, that in memory they are equal to whites; in reason much inferior, as I think one could scarcely be found capable of tracing and comprehending the investigations of Euclid; and that in imagination they are dull, tasteless, and anomalous.

Jefferson insisted that none of this was merely a product of "circumstance," of having been deprived of learning by the condition of slavery. Even though some blacks had received liberal educations and other exposure to civilization, "never . . . could I find a black had uttered a thought above the level of plain narration; never seen even an elementary trait of painting or sculpture." Jefferson concluded, "I advance it therefore . . . that the blacks, whether originally a distinct race, or made distinct by time and circumstances, are inferior to the whites in the endowments both of body and mind" (Jefferson 1982 [1787]:143).

The white negrophobia at work here is as old as it is widely known in the United States, and anyone who has lived for more than a little while in the United States is familiar with its basic outlines: the complete and unalterable otherness – difference – of the negro, as well as his utter "savagery" – if, indeed, he is human at all – and "inferiority." Frantz Fanon summarized this white insistence on the inescapably uncivilized otherness of the black person by starkly enunciating the terms by which the black person is hailed in racist society: " 'Dirty nigger!' Or simply, 'Look, a Negro!' " (Fanon 1967 [1952]:109).

It is important to recognize that negrophobic statements are not, in Foucauldian terms, best understood as expressions of an underlying white racist "ideology," "world-view," "habitus," or "structure." To understand racist narrations as symptoms of a deeper racist "culture" is to miss how an act of racist narrating is better understood as a technology of the self, or as a process of subject-formation. As Robert Young explains, for Foucault, a discursive statement is to be understood as "the *act* of making the statement"; "[t]he statement itself constitutes a specific material event, a performative act or a function, an historical eruption that impinges on and makes an incision into circumstance." A paradigmatic example of a statement is a press statement or a statement to the police (Young 2001:401–402, emphasis added). The emphasis, in other words, is not upon elucidating an abstract collective representation that is supposedly expressed in a statement, but upon the tactical or strategic project of subject-formation that is tied up in the making of the statement, as well as upon the unintended effects of the statement in its subsequent relationships with other statements.

The projects of racial subject-formation at play in the long history of white stating about blacks are intimately linked to modern Euro-American selfhood. At the most global and strategic level, the Enlightenment's "Man" and the "Citizen" of social-contract theory are founded upon the premise of a free, individual actor, which in turn is premised on abstract notions of pure, archetypical Reason and Progress. These archetypes of Western subject-formation necessarily require an imagined Other for delineating the boundary and the content of the rational self. That imagined Other has been both gendered (Woman) and racial. John Locke, as just one example, contrasted the modern state, with its rational citizens bound together by the social contract, against the state of nature inhabited by supposedly pre-rational Africans and American Indians.

This process of self-making implicated in statements about the black Other is also fruitfully understood as the construction of whiteness (or of the white "race"). Key to whiteness is the systematic modernist disciplining of the self, including deferral of gratification, sobriety, civility, respect for constituted authority, orderliness, rational management of time and money, individual autonomy, avoidance of "dependency," and suppression of – or at least highly disciplined control over – various "uncivilized" drives. The particular disciplines, gratifications, and drives in question have, of course, varied through time with the historical development of capitalism. Part of the work of subject-formation here entails the projection onto an imaginary black Other of all that must be exorcised from civilized (or modern) life, and all that threatens to undermine and disrupt it.

The civilized, modern white self is not only rational, but also democratic, humane, and moral. Therein lies an historical and perennial challenge to white subject-formation: how to explain the glaring "anomaly" of how blacks experience their presence in the US, in comparison to whites, how blacks have fared under "modernity." During slavery, that anomaly was the disturbing presence of slaves in a democratic republic founded on the premise that all men (*sic*) are created equal and endowed with the inalienable right of liberty. The exoneration for whites was the claim, as Thomas Jefferson put it, that "blacks are inferior to whites." Jefferson's negative appraisal of blacks makes perfect sense as his self-constituting struggle to make sense of himself, and those like him, as a radical defender of the natural rights of Man, but also as a slave-owner. Jefferson the slave-owner deployed the negrophobic statements in *Notes* as a slave-owner who was also an Enlightenment subject in the making. Race is at least as central a constituent of "modernity" as is gender.

The unsettling anomaly of the inhumane and unjust situation of blacks in the US threatens whiteness just as much in the present, when the putatively natural and open market economy touted by neoliberalism would seem utterly *incapable* of allocating the basic necessities of life to so many Americans. The radical inequality among Americans in the present can only be explained, short of a radically destabilizing critique of the economy, as a result of "race." What is remarkable is how little the thrust of white race-stating about blacks has changed since Jefferson's day. While he spoke of "racial inferiority," contemporary scholars, the media, and the white imagination loquaciously expound on the black "culture of poverty"; the black family as a "tangle of pathology"; the black "underclass" characterized by "skyrocketing" rates of crime and illegitimate births; and all the other negrophobic images that come, seemingly naturally, to (the white) mind: "welfare queens," "gangsters," "drug dealers," and even "genetic inferiority" – "No wonder the blacks are at the bottom!"

But it is critically important to understand that racial narration is not only an *imposition* by the racially powerful upon the racially oppressed. Racially oppressed peoples have developed counter-statements that, while accepting the proposition that "the races" are distinctly and essentially different, challenge the terms of the white statements. Malcolm X *embraced* his blackness, indeed, made it the center of his existence, but in ways that directly challenged the content of white racist statements. Indeed, race could not exist without both whites and blacks agreeing that there is such a racial thing as black and white.

It is also important to understand that *within* "races" there will always be multiple forms of racial practice – inconsistent in terms of meaning, but consistent in terms of the architecture of race. Consider, for example, the differences between the racial projects of Booker T. Washington and W. E. B. Dubois, or Malcolm X and Martin Luther King. Or consider the historical instances of middle-class whites admiring black culture, perhaps, in part, because it is transgressive to do so (this transgression does not, of course, call the architecture of black and white into question, but on the contrary, reinforces it). The phenomenal popularity of hip-hop culture among white young people is just a recent example of a long history of white negrophile practices (no less racist than negrophobia, of course). The point is the formidable diversity and contradiction of race-stating, even while the architecture of race is left unchallenged.

An imagined Indian Other has been used no less than the black Other to secure white personhood and to ward off morally and politically uncomfortable questions that might undermine it. Indian phobia is most visible in historical moments when, and geographical zones where, settlers cleared territory of indigenous peoples. The practical utility of frontier Indian-hating narratives for both mobilizing extermination and denying the settlers' own savagery is obvious. Indian-hating also served, as did the image of the black Other, in the discursive production of the white, American subject. This master narrative did not disappear with the clearing of Indians from "the public domain," but is obvious in many twentieth-century films, and continues to live on in locally popular white stereotypes of "the drunken Indian," the "godlessness, joblessness, and lawlessness" of "reservation culture" (quoted in Biolsi 2001:192), the Indian "welfare queen," and, of course, in school and professional sports-team mascots.

But, recognizing the complexity of statements about race, as we saw in the case of white stating about blacks, there is another kind of stating about Indians. Let us return to Thomas Jefferson. While it was true that to him Indians were, like blacks, a "barbarous people," this was a matter of "circumstances" rather than *race* (1982 [1787]:60–61). Indians "are formed in mind as well as in body, on the same module with the 'Homo sapiens Europaeus'" (1982 [1787]:62). And it is also worth examining what the Supreme Court had to say in 1856 about Indians in *Dred Scott vs. Sandford*, where the Court announced that because negroes were "considered as a subordinate and inferior class of being," they "had no rights which the white man was bound to respect." Indians could, however, "like the subjects of any other foreign government, be naturalized by the authority of Congress, and become citizens of a State and of the United States . . . and if an individual should leave his nation or tribe, and take up his abode among the white population, he would be entitled to all the rights and privileges which would belong to an emigrant from any other foreign people."

Thus, in addition to the ignoble savage, the noble Indian savage has been critical in white American self-constitution. This good Indian is redeemable, or more particularly, able to be civilized and assimilated, since he is basically made of the same stuff as are whites. Since the end of the Indian wars in the last quarter of the nineteenth century, the solution to "the Indian problem" has almost universally been seen as a policy of education for civilization. The height of this civilization project was the period from approximately 1880 into the early 1930s.

Along with the white projects to civilize Indians appeared the contradictorily related – perhaps akin to transgressive Negrophobia – projects of imperialist nostalgia. The noble savage may lack "civilization" – or, in more contemporary terms, "modernity" – but this is precisely what makes her or him desirable – desirable for assimilation and for rescue, but also for salvage ethnography, for display and spectacle in art, museums, and wild west shows, and even for marriage, adoption, and for racial cross-dressing and other forms of admiring racist mimicry. The white–Other binary has not ceased to operate in narratives of the noble savage, but the moral evaluations have reversed poles. For those whites who are critical of or ambivalent about fundamental components of "civilization" or modernity (which means *all* whites), "the Indian" can represent what has been "lost" – spirituality, kinship with nature and with "all" of humanity, genuine community, and so on. Thus we find a long history of the appropriation of supposedly Indian costume, music, and ceremony by antiquarians and anthropologists (for example, Lewis Henry Morgan), fraternal organizations, Boy Scouts and Campfire Girls, almost all summer camp programs, "hobbyists," and New Age spiritualists. Many such consumers of things "Indian" believe that "real" or "authentic Indians" have disappeared or are "fast disappearing," and that "mixed bloods" or "assimilated Indians" – which is to say, *living* Indian people – are inauthentic Indians. It is the "traditional Indian" that is the object of consumption for imperialist nostalgia.

Just as white statements about blacks were put to both abstract strategic (white selfhood) and local practical uses (exclusion and containment), white statements about Indians are not only made in the abstract constitution of white identity. Very material matters are involved. To begin with, there was the problem that the "New World" was not "virgin land" waiting for Euro-American "penetration." Approximately 5 million Native people lived in what would become the lower 48 states in 1500. While much of this population would "disappear" in what many Indian people call a holocaust, how could this land be appropriated by the settlers from the remnant native populations "morally" and "legally"? This was not only a key question in modern, democratic subject-formation, but it was critical to the international diplomatic recognition of the fledgling United States. The revolutionary republic was on the world stage – or, at least the European world stage – and what it *did* would be perhaps even more closely scrutinized than what it said about the natural rights of Man. One tactic for the Americans was to racialize the aboriginal inhabitants into primitives who could claim no – or only much impaired – property rights to North America. This was effected through the European doctrine of discovery, which was enunciated by the Supreme Court in 1832. In *Johnson vs. McIntosh* the Court made it clear that "discovery" of the New World had been made by the worldly Europeans, not the savage natives already resident, and "discovery gave exclusive title to those who made it." Supposedly all hunters, the natives had no real claim to property.

While the racial primitivizing of native peoples for "legal" purposes had its pragmatic uses, there was nevertheless the stubborn historical fact that native people were members of distinct polities that had some degree of strategic and even legal claim (on the basis of natural law theory and the tenets of international law) to their aboriginal territories. Some of these polities had been formally recognized by the British as nations, and were later so recognized by the United States in treaty negotiations. Whether the United States liked it or not, it was in no position strategically or diplomatically during its early years to interfere in the internal affairs of native nations, or to enter their respective territories without their leave. And there lay the practical problem: How was the United States to get access to the lands and resources held – or blocked – by the Indian nations? The answer was: by legally liquidating the tribal nations, by assimilating Indians and absorbing the populations of the erstwhile native nations into the United States. The manner in which this was pursued was through converting Indian nationhood and individual citizenship in such nations into a racial status – and a racial status that was conceived as only *quantitatively* different from white citizenship, and that was only temporary. Indians would sooner or later, one way or another, *become* white. The Indian–white race line needed to be erased, not preserved, and this goal was pursued by a racial regime quite different from that surrounding the black–white race line.

## MIXING

We turn again to Thomas Jefferson. His statements on the racial difference of African Americans and whites, mentioned above, had not been penned merely for the purpose of advancing scientific knowledge on race. Rather, Jefferson was arguing for a clear racial policy. Indeed, his "scientific" statement on race follows his argument to emancipate children born into slavery, followed by their removal somewhere beyond the borders of Virginia. The danger, if ex-slaves remained as freemen in Virginia, was that "mixture" might result in "staining the blood" of whites (1982 [1787]:143). And there was even a more insidious likelihood of this staining than might at first be thought. Since their black skin and African hair and body form made them less "beautiful" than whites, black men came to prefer white women over the females of their own kind, just as the "Oran–ootan [prefers] the black women over those of his own species" (1982 [1787]:139).

Laws against black–white miscegenation and intermarriage appeared very early in US history. In an effort to prevent "abominable mixture and spurious issue," Virginia enacted a law in 1691 which made it a crime for any "English or other white man or woman . . . [to] intermarry with a Negro, mulatto, or Indian man or woman". Virginia singled out miscegenation outside of marriage as a crime distinct from mere fornication in 1662. The linkage of such laws to both racial subject-formation and political economy is widely recognized by scholars: the ambiguity of racially "impure" individuals in a society in which all human beings were fast becoming discretely divided into free and slave on the basis of race. This distinction became even more important to make once slavery coexisted with the US revolutionaries' Enlightenment claim of Man's natural right of freedom. After emancipation, blurring the black–white race line threatened to undermine the very basis of racial segregation under Jim Crow, and later, up through the present, the "colorblind," transparent – but no less material – boundaries of white privilege. Virigina's intermarriage prohibition was on the books until it was overturned by the Supreme Court in 1967.

Of course, plenty of miscegenation, if not intermarriage, has been common in the United States. Whatever Jefferson's erudite expositions of the dangers of "mixing" and "staining," he was not able to keep himself from mixing with his own slave, Sally Hemmings, and thus "staining" his own children. Indeed, since the offspring of white men and black slaves, contrary to the precedent of English common law, took the status of the mother and not the father in the United States, the economizing slave-owner actually had a financial incentive to impregnate his slaves. The real danger to slavery's necessarily discrete binary of free white citizens and enslaved black property did not come from mixed children of white slave-owners and their female slaves, since those children could simply remain with their mothers and be raised as slaves – as, indeed, untold numbers were. The interracial mating to guard against was that between the black man and the white woman, since it was this progeny, raised presumably by the woman in a presumably white (free) family, who would call into question the fiction of a clear race line, indeed, the very idea that black and white were mutually exclusive "races" entitled to radically different statuses of freedom and bondage in slave society. Thus, it should not surprise us that this dangerous possibility was not only outlawed, but culturally tabooed and elaborated into a systematic social anxiety, as well as "combated" through a virtual industry in race-specific rape laws. In Virginia, for example, rape was originally merely "aggravated assault" – a misdemeanor – for either black or white perpetrators, but by 1823, attempted rape of a white woman by a black was punishable by death. While race-specific provisions were removed from rape statutes after the Civil War, unlicensed terror against black men "suspected" of rape or attempted rape of whites was prevalent in the form of lynching. One estimate is close to 3,000 lynchings between 1890 and 1950. But it did not stop at unlicensed terror against black men: "legal lynching" involved the prosecution, conviction, and sentencing with a vengeance of black men charged with raping white women. Between 1930 and 1967, 89 percent of men executed for rape in the United States were black (405 individuals).

Mythical statements about black rapists had their primary role in the justification of unlicensed terror against black people in the wake of emancipation. The imagined "emergency" was critical in shoring up racial and class hierarchy in the South. Just as in European overseas colonies, the mythified white paranoia about the "black peril" helped solidify the loyalty of the white working class and poor on the basis of race and not class. Without the imaginary "necessity" for whites (both men of different classes, and men and women) to stick together, marginalized and disempowered whites might have come to see that they had more in common with black sharecroppers and workers than with the white elite. Race (and perhaps gender) can be used – and commonly is around the world – to trump class.

To examine the situation regarding Native Americans, let us listen again to Jefferson, whose statements on the nature of Indian people had clear implications for national policy. Jefferson once told a group of Native Americans: "You will mix with us by marriage, your blood will run in our veins, and will spread with us over this great island" (quoted in Takaki, 1982 [1979]:59). His policy proposal for dealing with Indians was "to let our settlements and theirs meet and blend together, to intermix, and become one people. Incorporating themselves with us as citizens of the United States, this is what the natural progress of things will of course bring on" (quoted in Sheehan 1973:174).

It is noteworthy that the 1691 Virginia law prohibiting intermarriage between whites and negroes, mulattoes, and Indians was amended in 1705 to remove Indian–white intermarriage from the prohibition. Most anti-miscegenation/intermarriage and racialized rape laws in the United States have not had provisions regarding whites and Indians. In South Dakota, for example, where there has always been a high proportion of Indian people, the legislature itemized a list of prohibited marriages in its anti-miscegenation law, still on the books in 1950: "any person belonging to the African, Korean, Malayan, or Mongolian race with any person of the opposite sex belonging to the Caucasian or white race." What deserves our attention, however, is not just that Indian–white marriages were not proscribed. The Bureau of Indian Affairs (BIA) actually encouraged intermarriage as a means of bringing about the civilization of Indians, and used the reduction of Indian "blood quantum" as both a means and a measure of doing away with Indians. Even though it would be more than a little inaccurate to say that race relations between whites and Indians in South Dakota have been historically harmonious, there were no race-specific rape laws, no rape-phobic violence, and no culturally elaborated concern for the sexual security of white women in the state. In 1934 approximately 149 of the 1,575 married couples (9 percent) on Rosebud Reservation were composed of white men married to Lakota women, and 68 (4 percent) were composed of white women married to Lakota men. This was a long way from Mississippi in 1934.

While black–white sexual and love relations have historically been the stuff of prohibition, transgressive desire, and pornography, Indian–white sexual and love relations have often been, and continue to be, wholesome white family fare. The marital love between John Smith and Pocahontas in Disney's animated *Pocahontas* is only the most recent instance of this. A white man finding an Indian woman alluring, and in fact marrying her, has seldom seemed to raise white eyebrows. An example from my field site on Rosebud Reservation makes the point: In 1972, a young (presumably white) woman from Philadelphia wrote to the editor of the *Todd County Tribune*, a reservation newspaper: "I have been interested in the Indian people for a long time . . . I have written many places in order to find an Indian pen pal . . . I would appreciate it if you could find a guy of about 27 . . . This will make me very happy as I said I think they are beautiful people." The (white) editor responded in print: "Christine Honey, I think they are beautiful people but I have this newspaper to print so really don't have time to hunt up a 27 year old, obviously single male for you. Would one of you young, good-looking men please write to this lady?" (Anonymous 1972). Racial difference does not even appear "spicy" in this publicly imagined romantic encounter; it would be difficult to conjure up a parallel scene involving a white Christine looking for a "good-looking . . . obviously single" black man to correspond with from Mississippi in 1972. Indian partners appear to be in relatively high demand among whites, and many whites feel no guilt in being direct about their race-specific desires regarding Native Americans. For example, a 1999 personal advertisement in *Indian Country Today* (the major national American Indian news-paper, widely read by whites), which is not at all unusual, read: "Attractive SWF [single white female] . . . seeks beautiful, brown-skinned AI/M [American Indian/ male] companion with beautiful dark eyes that melt ones heart and long, black shining hair" (Anonymous 1999). There is no equivalent *innocent* interracial desire expressed in white popular culture for specifically black partners, although, as men-tioned above, transgressive subcultures may articulate such desires.

But there are other forms of mixing Indian and white that deserve our attention. The civilization policy itself was a mixing project in its teleology of assimilation and incorporation into the nation. Among the most important tactics deployed by BIA personnel to do this was the allotment of reservation lands in severalty, enabled by the 1887 General Allotment Act (also known as the Dawes Act). The theory was that individualizing land would not only liquidate reservations and tribes, but would create Indian property-owners and foster appropriately self-interested rational subjects. Of course, the theory went, there would be an extended period during which many, if not most, Indian adults would necessarily be wards of the government, not yet capable of handling private property or money, and not yet prepared for citizenship. During this period, their allotments would be held in trust for them. But within, perhaps, a generation, almost all Indian adults would presumably become *competent* to manage their own affairs, the trust status would be removed from their allotments, and they would graduate into US citizenship with legal rights no different from those of whites.

Race is also made or unmade through other forms of affiliation, love, and family formation – as well as their opposites, personal boundary-formation on the basis of race. One of the most noteworthy characteristics of Indian–white race relations during the twentieth century was the demand among white families – especially childless families – for specifically Indian children. The pretext for supplying this demand was usually, before the passage of the Indian Child Welfare Act in 1978, an allegation of "neglect" on the part of Indian families – which could refer to such things as living in an extended rather than a nuclear family, or simply the presence of poverty and material deprivation. As one US senator put it, "Public and private welfare agencies seem to have operated on the premise that most Indian children would really be better off growing up non-Indian" (quoted in Johnson 1981:437). An attorney involved in Indian child welfare summarizes the consequences of all this, "Before 1978, as many as 25 to 35 percent of the Indian children in certain states were removed from their homes and placed in non-Indian homes by state courts, welfare agencies, and private adoption agencies" (Jones 1995:18). No such figures for adoption by white families exist in the case of African American children.

## CLASSIFYING

In June 1892 one Homer Plessy bought a first-class railway ticket and boarded a "whites only" car in New Orleans. Plessy, who had some minimal amount of "Negro blood," and was thus *colored* under Louisiana law, was in violation of the state's Separate Car Act. When the train conductor, in an arranged confrontation, ordered Plessy to vacate the seat and remove himself to the colored accommodations on the train, Plessy refused and was arrested. Plessy challenged the law, and his case eventually reached the US Supreme Court. *Plessy vs. Ferguson* (1896) is now remembered for having posed the question of whether racial segregation was consistent with the Fourteenth Amendment, which guarantees equal protection for citizens. The Court's notorious answer was that, yes, "separate" was constitutional, as long as it was "equal."

What has been forgotten about the case in popular memory is that Plessy's lawyers had launched a direct attack upon the very idea of distinct black and white races – not just an attack on racial segregation. Here is part of their argument to the Louisiana Supreme Court: "[Plessy] is of mixed Caucasian and African descent in the proportion of seven-eighths Caucasian and one-eighth African blood...the mixture of colored blood is not discernible in [him], and he is entitled to every recognition, right, privilege, and immunity secured to citizens...of the white race by the Constitution and laws of the United States." He was "really a white man...[arbitrarily] classed as a colored man." The attorneys also argued that a non-arbitrary separation of those who are "white" from those who are "colored" is simply not possible in a society in which miscegenation had gone as far as it obviously had at the time. After all, rather than counting as black everyone who has any trace of black blood, "Why not count every one as white in whom is visible any trace of white blood?" – which, of course, would include almost all African Americans. Plessy's lawyers meant to challenge what is commonly known as the "one-drop rule."

The one-drop rule as a race-making technique has the effect of producing discrete, mutually exclusive, "black" and "white" races in the social and legal imaginaries. As Plessy learned, the race line is literally a line – clear, indelible, and permanent. Furthermore, it is, in a classificatory sense, easy to be black; one cannot be a little bit "colored," since any amount of "black blood" makes one black. It is, on the other hand, not easy to be white in classificatory terms. And one cannot hope to move from black to white during the course of one's lifetime, unless one attempts to "pass." The one-drop rule had its origins in racial slavery and made perfectly good sense from the standpoint of slave-owners. As mentioned, one of the central political and moral quagmires facing the racial and class elites in the young United States was the glaring presence of slavery in a republic founded on the principles of freedom and equality. The "solution" to this logical puzzle – puzzling, of course, only to whites and slave-owners – was the proposition that blacks were racially inferior to whites, not fit for freedom, and, in fact, naturally fitted for slavery, however regrettable that may be. Should it surprise us that Thomas Jefferson, the slave-owner *and* drafter of the

Declaration of Independence, impugned the racial character of blacks (even though he fretted over slavery)? It is not difficult to see why it came to be – or, rather, came to be willfully asserted – that it was only "natural" that blacks should be slaves and slaves should be black.

The problem with this "explanation," however, was that those who were enslaved were coming to look, generation after generation, much less "black" than slaves had earlier. Because slave-owners regularly impregnated their own slaves, slaves were becoming increasingly "whiter." In fact, the veritable industry of white slave-owners fathering children by their black slaves was an open secret, and some mixed-race slaves were said to "resemble" their slave-owning fathers – as was Jefferson's slave son. By the mid-nineteenth century, the population of mulatto slaves was increasing at a rate three times that of "pure" black slaves. If slavery and freedom were to be mutually exclusive legal statuses, and if slavery was to be justified by race, something needed to be done, if not practically, then at least conceptually, about miscegenation and racial *hybridity*. In defense of slavery, the one-drop rule became customary by the 1850s.

After emancipation at the end of the Civil War, the one-drop rule became even more entrenched, and eventually codified in law. The prohibition of slavery (Thirteenth Amendment, 1865), the extension of citizenship to all persons born in the United States (Civil Rights Act, 1966; Fourteenth Amendment, 1868), and the guarantee of the rights of citizenship regardless of race (Civil Rights Act, 1966; Fifteenth Amendment, 1870), opened the legal possibility for racial equality in the United States – at least as far as African Americans and whites were concerned. Much was a stake here for the old order – not just in the South, but also in the North. To begin with, there was the matter of control of black labor for agricultural production in the South, and, a little later, for industrial production in the North. Both employers/landowners and workers had interests in keeping African Americans "racially" distinct in a segmented labor force. There was also the question of how working-class whites would perceive and calculate their material interests: would they come to recognize the overriding *similarity* of their situation to that of their black neighbors and co-workers, and their *parallel* exploitation by large landowners and industrialists? In the end – but not without struggle – white supremacy simply served too many powerful interests, and racial segregation was progressively implemented legally throughout the United States through Jim Crow laws.

Just as slavery was based upon an absolute, qualitative distinction between the status of freedom and the status of slavery, segregation was all about discrete and mutually exclusive social space. And just as slavery required an absolute and impermeable *line* between "black" and "white," so Jim Crow required that everyone be clearly raced, and that blackness not be allowed to visibly inhabit white space. A person who was obviously of even *some* negro descent riding in a "whites only" car would threaten the entire (arbitrary) system of racial privilege and exclusion. The one-drop rule also helped to guarantee to whites that they could in no way come to be classified as blacks, and that what was happening to blacks could never happen to them, because the classificatory boundary was crystal clear to everyone. The one-drop rule, in other words, was critical in securing the participation of all whites in white supremacy. Thus the increasingly stark concerns with white racial purity and the dangers of miscegenation, and the hardening and codification of the one-drop rule during the Jim Crow period, which was effectively on the statute books of 16 states by 1910.

As we saw in the case of stating about black and white, it is important to recognize that the one-drop rule as a racial technology was not simply imposed by the state and by whites upon people who were denied the status of being white. In other words, not all mixed-race people wanted to "be" or "pass" as whites or near-whites. During the Jim Crow era, when all "negroes" were defined and treated as just that, lighter-skinned people who might have had reason to think of themselves as "mixed race" found themselves having much more in common with other blacks, as defined under the one-drop rule, than with any whites – even their white relatives. During the Harlem Renaissance of the 1920s, many of these formerly elite mulattoes came to fill the critical roles of organic intellectuals, constructing and articulating a common black culture shared by an emergent and self-consciously *black* people – including all "mixtures" of black and white. Building black peoplehood or nationhood on the basis of resistance to oppression necessarily defined the boundaries of "the people" through the oppressors' delimitation of the races, and the implicit recognition of the one-drop rule is clear in this intellectual work of black nationalism. W. E. B. Du Bois described what must have been his racial epiphany regarding the one-drop rule upon his arrival at Fisk University in 1885: "It was to me an extraordinary experience. I was thrilled to be for the first time among so many people of my own color or rather of *such various and such extraordinary colors,* which I had only glimpsed before, but who it seemed were *bound to me by new and exciting and eternal ties*" (quoted in Zack 1993:104–105, emphasis added). Black had become a race for itself.

Some black nationalists have been even more explicit in their embrace of the one-drop rule for building the black nation. In his 1965 autobiography, Malcolm X recalled his preaching as a minister of the Nation of Islam (X 1999 [1964]:205–206):

> my *beautiful*, black brothers and sisters! And when we say "black," we mean everything not white, brothers and sisters! Because *look* at your skins! We're all black to the white man, but we're a thousand and one different colors. Turn around, *look* at each other! What shade of black African polluted by devil white man are you? You see me – well, in the streets they used to call me Detroit Red. Yes! Yes, that raping, red-headed devil was my *grandfather*! ... If I could drain away *his* blood that pollutes *my* body, and pollutes *my* complexion, I'd do it! Because I hate every drop of the rapist's blood that's in me!

Here is a concrete example of racial subject-formation with a vengeance. The critical point for immediate purposes is that Malcolm X's white blood was, in the self-understanding he struggled to achieve – *part of the oppression of black people.* His white ancestry in no way made Malcolm X less black and, indeed, its presence actually valorized the authenticity of his racial self – a self understood in terms of the object of white racist oppression.

In the case of identifying American Indians, a drop of "Indian blood" has almost never been enough to make one legally Indian; it has historically taken more Indian blood (as well as other qualifications) to make one legally Indian than it has taken black blood to make one black. Indeed, even being "full-blood" Indian may not be sufficient. Looked at from a different standpoint, a mixed-race person can have a significant amount of Indian blood and still be legally white. In 1924, for example, Virginia formally defined white as a person who had " 'no trace whatsoever of any blood other than Caucasian' or no more than one-sixteenth American Indian blood."

Beginning in the mid-nineteenth century, federal and state courts in the United States developed a "two part test" of Indian legal identity that requires the presence of both Indian "blood" and some form of social "recognition" as an Indian. This is commonly known as the "*Rogers-St. Cloud* test," after two federal cases that set the precedent. The 1988 federal case of *St. Cloud vs. United States* is a good illustration of the classificatory scheme. In this case, a defendant claimed that he was not subject to federal jurisdiction for a crime committed on an Indian reservation because he was not Indian (he would have been subject to federal jurisdiction only if he was legally Indian). The defendant was "approximately 15/32 Yankton Sioux and 7/16 Ponca." "As virtually a full-blooded Native American," the court opined, "St. Cloud is ethnically [racially] an Indian. [Furthermore, h]e is socially recognized and lives as a Native American." However, merely having Indian blood, and some recognition as an Indian (including appropriate cultural behavior) was not sufficient in the view of the court because St. Cloud did not have the most important criterion of recognition – official enrollment in a federally recognized tribe. An American Indian can enroll officially in only one federally recognized Indian tribe, and St. Cloud had been enrolled in the Ponca Tribe, which was "terminated" (declared no longer to be in legal existence as a tribe) by Congress in 1962. The court declared that he was a "non-Indian" under the law and ordered his release from federal custody. Thus while St. Could was apparently "a virtual" full-blood, was visibly Indian, lived and participated in a reservation community, and had once been legally Indian and a member of a federally recognized tribe (prior to termination of the Ponca tribe), he had become non-Indian.

Some courts have delved deeply into the behavior of individuals in order to ascertain the degree of their "recognition" as Indians. The Supreme Court of Wyoming, for example, was called upon to decide if the state courts had jurisdiction over a defendant convicted of a felony on the Wind River Reservation. If the defendant was Indian, the state would not have had jurisdiction, and the defendant would have been wrongly convicted. The court determined that not only was the defendant's "one eighth Indian blood" insufficient to make the defendant Indian, but "his life style is not that of an Indian; he lives in a mobile home in a trailer court . . . and he has been employed by drilling companies which work 'all over the east and western United States'." Perhaps the defendant's not living in a reservation housing project (or a *tipi?*), and not staying put on the reservation made his lack of recognition as an Indian a no-brainer for the court.

Since the early twentieth century, the federal government has systematically recorded the degree of blood of American Indians, which has served as both a measure of, and a technique for, the legal liquidation of tribes and Indians. In 1917, for example, the BIA sought a means by which to relieve itself of supervision over "competent Indians" and "white Indians" and to give "even closer attention to the incompetent that they may more speedily achieve competency." The administrative criterion for this division was simple: "all able-bodied adult Indians of less than one-half Indian blood" would have the trust status removed from their allotments and would become US citizens.

Tribal governments have also found the blood quantum useful, not for liquidating tribal membership, but for limiting membership in the face of an overwhelming demand for tribal enrollment, especially in the wake of the recent take-off in tribal gaming. So, for example, the Confederated Tribes of the Grand Ronde Community of Oregon, in a tribal referendum, voted in 1999 to amend their constitution to replace the enrollment requirement of "one-sixteenth . . . or more degree of Indian Blood," which would include "blood" from other tribes, with "one-sixteenth . . . or more degree Grand Ronde Blood," a much more exclusive category.

## SPACING

Racial segregation in the United States was and is all about clearly marking off white space from black space. Jim Crow involved segregation of all aspects of daily life. Segregation of railways – which was challenged by Homer Plessy – had begun well before 1900. Jim Crow laws in the South prohibited black and white workers from fraternizing on the job; separated the races in hospitals and mental institutions; and segregated inmates in prisons. "Separate park laws" also appeared, and circuses, tent shows, sideshows, theaters, picture houses, and amateur sports teams were increasingly required to separate the races. Segregation even went so far as "Jim Crow Bibles for Negro witnesses in Atlanta courts and Jim Crow elevators for Negro passengers in Atlanta buildings" (Woodward 1974 [1955]:102).

Beyond classic Jim Crow segregated social space, residential segregation has also been, and continues to be, one of the inescapable facts of blackness (and whiteness) in the United States. Critically, residential segregation has been strongest in the North, from the early twentieth century, as African Americans moved north in what is commonly called "the Great Migration." The techniques by which residential segregation has been produced have historically included intimidation, terror, and discrimination in housing and home-finance markets. We are all familiar with the geography of race produced by these practices, as well as by public policies such as urban renewal – clearly demarcated *lines* between largely homogeneous black neighborhoods and white neighborhoods. The boundary is stark, clear, and every American knows about it, and keeps it in the back of their mind so as not to be dangerously "out of place." Even in New York's diverse Elmhurst-Corona studied by Roger Sanjek, in which "peoples and languages [run] into each other in a mix never before seen," blacks are segregated in one housing development (Sanjek 1998:223). Black people are kept, and largely remain, in their place.

Geographic separation was at one time the policy of the United States toward American Indians. Beginning with the removal of native peoples from the Southeast to beyond the Mississippi during the expansion of the slave-based cotton economy in the 1830s, the policy was to establish reservations outside of the states, to which Indian tribes would be relocated and largely left to their own devices, and which whites would be prohibited from entering without special permission and federal oversight. The largest such project was Indian Territory, where both eastern and western tribes were concentrated, and which became part of the state of Oklahoma in 1907 (after native plans for a separate Indian state to join the Union were quashed).

By 1880, however, open territory for warehousing Indians had disappeared in the West, and there was an increasing demand by potential homesteaders, land speculators, railroads, banks, the mining industry, and other interests to make Indian lands available for development. Indian policy also needed to be rethought, because it was no longer possible to leave tribes to their own devices. The "Indian problem" could no longer be solved by exporting Indians beyond the borders of the states. Indians would have to be "civilized" and eventually become citizens, and the reservations would eventually have to be fully incorporated. As mentioned above, the 1887 General Allotment Act was a critical component of this policy. While individual allotments were initially held in trust by the government, the assumption was that as an individual became civilized, the trust status would be removed, that little piece of reservation would disappear *qua* reservation, and the "civilized" Indian would graduate into citizenship. One of the goals associated with the policy was also to bring white homesteaders to reservations and former reservations, and to pepper white families among Indian families on the landscape. This was accomplished by "opening" to homesteaders Indian land declared "surplus" after each allottee had received her/his allotment, and by making available for sale to whites allotments from which the trust status had been removed. It was assumed that having white neighbors was good for Indians. As the Pine Ridge Reservation BIA superintendent put it in 1922, "It is without question, advisable, in the matter of bringing the Indians to a reasonable standard of competency, to provide for an intermingling of the races" (quoted in Biolsi 1999:41). The result of this policy was precisely the opposite of the spatial segregation of black and white described above. Reservation lands throughout the United States became "checker-boarded" during the early twentieth century: white-owned homesteads and purchased tracts became interspersed with tribal land and individual Indian-owned allotments under federal trust status. Municipalities and counties organized under state law – largely representing white constituencies – also appeared within reservation boundaries. All of this was assumed to be a "natural" step toward the assimilation of Indians into the nation, and the gradual withering away of the reservations as "the Indian problem" was solved, one individual, and one piece of land, at a time.

In the end, the Indian problem was not thus solved because a fundamental change in policy during the New Deal period froze the withering-away process in midstream. As economic demand for Indian lands and other reservation resources disappeared during the Great Depression, white critics of the Indian assimilation and allotment policy found an opportunity to intervene. A new head of the BIA, brought in by the Roosevelt administration, began implementing what came to be called the Indian New Deal by halting the allotment and sale of trust land to whites, making reservations into *permanent* tribal homelands, and organizing modern tribal governments as federally recognized bodies. The checker-boarding of reservations became permanent, and whites living on reservations have become one of the chief ways that the authority of tribal governments has been undermined in the present. It is the non-Indians living on reservations who have organized subdivisions of state government on the reservations – counties in particular – and who have argued via the rhetoric of "equal rights" – in both the courts and through their delegations in Congress – for state jurisdiction on the reservations, for exemption from tribal jurisdiction over non-Indians, and ultimately for termination of tribal governments. The logic of this racial geography has historically – since approximately 1880 – been penetration, liquidation, and atomization, not exclusion and containment, as in the case of African Americans.

## CONCLUSION

One conclusion that might seem reasonable is that we can identify distinct racial *structures* at work here, one that underlies the black–white race line, the other the Indian–white line. Clearly both the historical staying-power of these two distinct race lines, and the combined systemicity of the diverse technologies making up each regime of race-making, are formidable and linked logically to larger political-economic processes in US history. In each case, the social consequences of the regime are systemic – exclusion and containment of the subordinated in the one case, and penetration, atomization, and liquidation in the other. Furthermore, the practices comprising each "structure" have a mutually dovetailing relationship. To fear ne-groes, especially male negro sexual aggression, has a certain "logical" (and practical) consistency with the "protection" of white women, the racial segregation of social space, concepts of pollution and contamination, anti-mixing laws and customs, and the one-drop rule. With regard to Indians, "loving" and consuming them through intermarriage, saving them through adoption, integrating and assimilating them, and watching anxiously their inevitable "disappearance" and the relentless diminishing of their "Indian blood," also seem to constitute a coherent "system" of racial technolo-gies. As Winthrop Jordan argues convincingly, much of this systemicitiy can be observed in Thomas Jefferson, whose thinking "recapitulated major tenets of the U.S. racial complex" (Jordan 1974:180) – as if the deep structure of American race can be found in any truly representative American.

The Foucauldian frame of analysis pursued here, however, would avoid the notion of stable deep structures of race, and would instead make use of the more complex concept of discourse. In contrast to a structure which, at least at an underlying level, is unified, a discourse is *not* "a logical totality or coherent whole." Rather, discourse is "fragmented, dispersed and incomplete" (Young 2001:404). We saw obvious in-stances of this in the simultaneous existence of negrophobia and negrophilia, as well as the coexistence of the great project to civilize Indian savages and imperialist nostalgia. A dominant discourse, no matter how widely distributed among the insti-tutions and actors of a society – as obviously are the white projects to exclude blacks and to assimilate Indians – is never "totalizing." Racial projects are always local, and there is no monolithic racial standpoint (such as "black," "white," or "Indian") that is not crosscut by other systems of difference – class, gender, sexuality, and region, among the most obvious of these. Whatever Jefferson said about Indians from his desk, many citizens on the frontier had no intention of "mixing their blood" with Indian savages, from whom they were wresting a continent. This all means that the constituent technologies (stating, mixing, classifying, and spacing) of an historically concrete and socially dominant racial discourse can be, and commonly are, *disaggre-gated* from the discursive formation and *redeployed* in unpredictable and antagonistic ways in particular local settings, by specific racial subjects in the making, for determin-ate racial projects. Race technologies are mobile and flexible.

Take, for example, the race-stating technology of *foreignness*, which as is widely recognized, has been used historically to create white racial difference from Asian immigrants and Asian Americans, and was critical in the internment of Japanese Americans during World War II. But foreignness has not only been used to make

"Japs," "Orientals," or "Asians." In 1924, when Congress instituted a quota system to limit the "new immigration" from southern and eastern Europe, the culturally alien nature of these newcomers was linked up to the "scientific" fact that they constituted races ("Alpines" and "Mediterraneans") distinct from the "Nordics" native to western and northern Europe. From the latter, of course, came the Anglo-Saxons who had "founded" and "built" the US. Anti-Asian racism on the West Coast, and racism directed against Jews, Italians, and other non-"Nordics" in the Northeast, unfolded historically in the racial technology of stating their inescapable and dangerous foreignness during the 1920s. Indeed, one congressman who championed racial restrictions on immigration in 1923 followed his remarks on the floor of the House regarding "the Japanese peril" with a self-consciously racist analysis of the dangers of southern and eastern European immigration.

The ability of real historical actors to recombine and redeploy race technologies in mobile and flexible ways implies that apparently *established* and stable "races" are always susceptible to discursive undoing, which is to say, social and material deconstruction. It would not be going too far to say that "the white race" was discursively disaggregated – as was done previously in the face of Irish immigration – at sites in the Northeast (including the halls of Congress) during the 1920s through the technologies of racial foreignness, and that it was reknit (grudgingly, from the standpoint of self-proclaimed Anglo-Saxons and Nordics) only through new racial technologies that turned Jews, Italians, and other southern and eastern European immigrants into white folks.

## REFERENCES

Anonymous (1972) Letter to the Editor. *Todd County Tribune*, December 7.

Anonymous (1999) Personal advertisement. *Indian Country Today*, June 7–14.

Biolsi, Thomas (1999) The Birth of the Reservation: Making the Modern Individual Among the Lakota. *American Ethnologist* 22:28–53.

Biolsi, Thomas (2001) *"Deadliest Enemies": Law and the Making of Race Relations on and off Rosebud Reservation*. Berkeley: University of California Press.

Fanon, Frantz (1967 [1952]) *Black Skins, White Masks*, trans. C. Markmann. New York: Grove Press.

Fields, Barbara (1990) Slavery, Race and Ideology in the United States. *New Left Review* 181:95–118.

Foucault, Michel (1983) The Subject and Power. In *Michel Foucault: Beyond Structuralism and Hermeneutics*, 2nd edn., ed. H. L. Dreyfus and P. Rabinow, pp. 208–226. Chicago: University of Chicago Press.

Jefferson, Thomas (1982 [1787]) *Notes on the State of Virginia*, ed. W. Penden. Chapel Hill: University of North Carolina Press.

Johnson, Barbara Brooks (1981) The Indian Child Welfare Act of 1978: Implications for Practice. *Child Welfare* LX:435–446.

Jones, Billy Joe (1995) The Indian Child Welfare Act: The Need for a Separate Law. *Complete Lawyer* 12:18–23.

Jordan, Winthrop D. (1974) *The White Man's Burden: Historical Origins of Racism in the United States*. New York: Oxford University Press.

Sanjek, Roger (1998) *The Future of Us All: Race and Neighborhood Politics in New York City.* Ithaca, NY: Cornell University Press.

Sheehan, Bernard W. (1973) *Seeds of Extinction: Jeffersonian Philanthropy and the American Indian.* Chapel Hill: University of North Carolina Press.

Takaki, Ronald (1982 [1979]) *Iron Cages: Race and Culture in 19th-Century America.* Seattle: University of Washington Press.

Woodward, Comer Vann (1974 [1955]) *The Strange Career of Jim Crow.* 3rd edn. New York: Oxford University Press.

X, Malcolm, with the assistance of A. Haley (1999 [1964]) *The Autobiography of Malcolm X.* New York: Ballentine Books.

Young, Robert J. C. (2001) *Postcolonialism: An Historical Introduction.* Malden, MA: Blackwell.

Zack, Naomi (1993) *Race and Mixed Race.* Philadelphia: Temple University Press.

## SUGGESTED FURTHER READING

Berkhoffer, Robert F. (1978) *The White Man's Indian: Images of the American Indian from Columbus to the Present.* New York: Vintage.

Brodkin, Karen (1998) *How Jews Became White Folks, and What that Says about Race in America.* New Brunswick, NJ: Rutgers University Press.

Davis, Floyd James (1991) *Who Is Black? One Nation's Definition.* College Park: Pennsylvania State University Press.

Hartigan, John (1999) *Racial Situations: Class Predicaments of Whiteness in Detroit.* Princeton, NJ: Princeton University Press.

McClintock, Anne (1995) *Imperial Leather: Race, Gender and Sexuality in the Colonial Contest.* New York: Routledge.

Omi, Michael, and Howard Winant (1994 [1986]) *Racial Formation in the United States: From the 1960s to the 1990s.* 2nd edn. New York: Routledge.

Roediger, David R. (1991) *The Wages of Whiteness: Race and the Making of the American Working Class.* New York: Verso.

Sanjek, Roger, and Steven Gregory, eds. (1994) *Race.* New Brunswick, NJ: Rutgers University Press.

Smedley, Audrey (1999 [1993]) *Race in North America: Origin and Evolution of a Worldview.* 2nd edn. Boulder, CO: Westview Press.

Stoler, Ann Laura (1995) *Race and the Education of Desire: Foucault's History of Sexuality and the Colonial Order of Things.* Durham, NC, and London: Duke University Press.

Stoler, Ann Laura (2002) *Carnal Knowledge and Imperial Power: Race and the Intimate in Colonial Rule.* Berkeley: University of California Press.

Sturm, Circe (2002) *Blood Politics: Race, Culture, and Identity in the Cherokee Nation of Oklahoma.* Berkeley and Los Angeles: University of California Press.

Susser, Ida, and Thomas Patterson, eds. (2001) *Cultural Diversity in the United States: A Critical Reader.* Malden, MA: Blackwell.

Thomas, Nicholas (1994) *Colonialism's Culture: Anthropology, Travel, and Government.* Princeton, NJ: Princeton University Press.

Wolfe, Patrick (2001) Land, Labor and Difference: Elementary Structures of Race. *American Historical Review* 106:866–905.

CHAPTER **26** Sovereignty

*Caroline Humphrey*

Most theories of sovereignty operate at the level of states and nations. If we accept the common definition of sovereignty as the capacity to determine conduct within the territory of a polity without external legal constraint, then the "polity" in question is normally considered to be the nation-state and the "territory" a geographical space bounded by state frontiers. The dominant "realist" theory of international politics, stemming from Hobbes, posits that the system of sovereign states is inescapably anarchic in character, as each state, recognizing no superior authority or moral code, pursues its own interests (Held 1992:10–39). With regard to the interior constitution of the state, theories from the earliest philosophies of politics onward have focused on the forms taken by the sovereign authority (tyranny, monarchy, elective democracy, etc.) and their legitimacy. This raised in particular the issue of freedom. Isaiah Berlin (1997 [1958]:411), for example, argued that the crucial question was *how much* authority should be placed in any set of hands. Democracy in this respect might prove no more enabling in respect of freedom than medieval tyranny.

Foucault challenged the entire set of issues concerned with the nature of the juridical apparatus that invested sovereign power and the rights that could legitimately place limits on it. His essay "Power, Right, Truth" (1980) aimed to replace the analysis of sovereignty and legitimacy with that of governmentality, by which he referred to the complex of apparatuses, institutions, and regulations that can be exercised as manifold forms of domination within society. Foucault's attention thereby shifted from the forms of power at their central locations to a concern with power at the extremities, "in its ultimate destinations, with those points where it becomes capillary, that is, in its more regional and local forms and institutions" (1997 [1980]:545). His paramount concern was with the point where power surmounts the rules of right that organize and delimit it and extends beyond them. "Biopolitics" was his name for the penetration of circulating webs of power relations into the very constitution of bodies, which become politically peripheral *subjects* as a result of the effects of power.

Yet the issue of sovereignty has reemerged with the work of the philosopher Giorgio Agamben, for he argued that Foucault never managed to deal with the intersection between the juridico-institutional and the biopolitical models of power (1998:6). At the end of Foucault's life a "blind spot" was left, where he was not able to reconcile his research into the *political techniques* of the state with that concerning the *technologies of the self* (the processes of subjectivization binding the individual to his own identity and to external power). These two analyses cannot be separated, Agamben writes. For sovereignty in the end rests on its capacity to threaten or even inflict death, which is historically linked to the Roman-law juridical concept of "life" as the simple fact of living (2002:15). It is in this light, he insists, that we must reconsider our idea of sovereignty, for "the inclusion of bare life in the political realm constitutes the original – if concealed – nucleus of sovereign power" (1998:6).

Agamben's thought-provoking line of thinking may be qualified in the light of anthropological concerns inspired at least partly by Foucault. Agamben begins his book *Homo Sacer* (1998) with the idea of "bare life," that is, the simple fact of living, which, according to Plato and Aristotle, was not to be confused with a qualified life, the "good life" proper to the *polis*. Modern languages do not distinguish these ideas. But Agamben reminds us of them, for he wishes to distinguish "bare life" first from "ways of life," the various customary activities of collectivities, and second – and above all – from something that seems for him to be an ideal, the "form-of-life." By this he refers to a life that can never be separated from its form, a life in which it is never possible to isolate bare life. "Form-of-life" denotes the concept of life in which acts and processes are never simply facts but always also possibilities and abilities, a life pursued through communicability with others, and a political life oriented toward happiness – for humans are the only beings for whom "life is irrevocably and sadly assigned to [achieving] happiness" (2002:14). This ideal of the form-of-life is "unthinkable," he writes, in the presence of sovereignty (2002:19). This is because sovereignty as a properly *political* form rests on its menace, that is, its ability to separate bare life from ways of life and its capacity in the end to snuff out life without regard to its sacral quality.

Agamben's work is about the politicization of bare life. But, unlike Foucault, he does not locate this process – the inclusion of "natural life" in the mechanisms and calculations of state power, that is, the emergence of biopolitics – straightforwardly with the modern era. It is true, he writes, that the modern Western state has integrated to an unprecedented degree the techniques of subjective individualization with procedures of objective totalization (1998:5). But what is the point, he asks, where the voluntary servitude of individuals comes into contact with objective power? This point cannot be identified with a historical moment – the inclusion of bare life into the political was there from the beginning. "The modern state does nothing other than bring to light the secret tie uniting power and bare life, and reaffirms the bond between modern power and the most immemorial *arcana imperii*" (1998:6). Thus Aristotle's opposition between the good life and bare life must be reconsidered: bare life is always implicated in politically qualified life.

Sovereignty conceived in this way and for the contemporary period forces us to confront "the exception," an idea originally propounded by the political philosopher Carl Schmitt (1966 [1932]). For Agamben, "the exception" refers to those paradoxical spaces where bare life is excluded from political life and yet, simultaneously, is included in it. He has in mind here the paradigm of the concentration camp. In the contemporary period, such "irreducible indistinction" (1998:9) is emergent all around us. "At once excluding bare life from and capturing it within the political order, the state of exception actually constituted, in its very separateness, the hidden foundation on which the entire political system rested" (1998:9).

Today, as state structures are compromised by global forces, as biopolitics becomes ever more invasive, as the emergency becomes commonplace, and the exception everywhere becomes the rule, bare life remains marked as subjection, Agamben insists, and it continues to be included in politics solely through an exclusion. Studies making use of his ideas have focused, accordingly, on sites of state-defined exception, such as borderland refugee camps, displaced persons, and detention centers. Yet Agamben also invites us to reconsider politics *as such*, that is, the emergence of sovereignty in *any place*, when he asks: "How is it possible to 'politicize' the 'natural sweetness' of mere living" (1998:11)?

Notwithstanding the importance of the Foucauldian literature on global governmentality, important dimensions to contemporary political processes are not captured by its ideas. I refer to these processes as *localized forms of sovereignty*. Although nested within higher sovereignties, these localized forms of sovereignty nevertheless retain a domain within which control over life and death is operational. Although such domains may be "exclusions" in terms of a central state, they may nevertheless construct the quasi-juridical terms in which exclusions can be made from their own body. Analysis of localized forms of sovereignty therefore enables us to come to a better understanding of the political life as such. Agamben's is a philosophical theory with a general and prescriptive character. Anthropology has to take a less programmatic tack.

In exploring the space opened out by Agamben's questions, an anthropological approach draws attention to the *actualities of relations* within the ways of life that exist under conditions of sovereignty. The deficiencies of Agamben's somewhat pallid notion of ways of life as merely the habitual activities of politically and juridically defined groups (electors, employees, journalists, students, the HIV-positive, the aged, etc.) (2002:17) become apparent. Ways of life need to be conceptualized as "thicker" than this; they have their histories and their modes of governmentality. They do not simply acquiesce to the menace of sovereignty but interpose a solid existence of their own that operates collaterally or against it. Perhaps we can even perceive in them flickering moments of the qualities Agamben attributes to the "form-of-life." Thus, while accepting his arguments that we cannot cast aside sovereignty as the concept of a defunct political theory (as Foucault does) and that we must recognize it – cast in a new light – as integral to the contemporary political landscape, we may also investigate, and indeed in some ways query, the delineation the philosopher proposes for its internal social characteristics.

To demonstrate the importance of this issue, I examine the processes that led to the emergence of a localized form of sovereignty in the Russian city of Ulan-Ude from the 1950s to the 1990s. The character of such local – even mundane – forms cannot be anticipated or understood on the basis of either national assertions of sovereignty or supra-national processes of governmentality – although political processes in Ulan-Ude have certainly partaken of and participated in these broader fields. By describing how issues of sovereignty can occur in ordinary urban life, this chapter shows how anthropology can fill in and help explain certain lacunae left in the wake of the influential political theories introduced in the previous section. When sovereignty is identified within a particular configuration, then sovereignty itself, which has to consist of practices, may be rethought not simply as a set of political capacities but as a formation in society that engages with ways of life that have temporality and their own characteristic aesthetics.

## SOVEREIGNTY AND WAYS OF LIFE: THE MASHRUT SYSTEM IN THE CITY OF ULAN-UDE, RUSSIA

Why should the anthropology of politics be concerned with these issues in Russia now? The upheavals of the post-communist years created conditions for the opening up of a host of previously undreamed-of social spaces in officially unattended locales. Alexei Yurchak (1999:88), following Hakim Bey (1991), conceptualized these as "temporary autonomous zones," unnamed operations that are suspended outside (and yet within) institutional state power. Varying greatly in scale, the great majority of these – communal squats or sites of rave culture in the early 1990s, the barter networks of the mid-1990s, or the financial enclaves of banking culture of the end of the decade – are not "sovereign" in Agamben's sense. But they share certain characteristics with localized sovereign domains. These include non-legality – that is, being unenvisaged and unrecognized by, and hence "invisible" to, state legislation. They also share the quality of being created by "ways of life" that poured in to new interstices within Russian society. Because localized sovereign domains are continuous with these similar zones of autonomy, the former have to be understood as part of wider social transformations in Russia. Thus, while the concept of "bare life" is essential for defining the bottom line of sovereignty, it will not suffice to explain the actual operation of these domains.

### The political context

In order to understand the relationship between national and localized forms of sovereignty in Ulan-Ude, it is first necessary to discuss Russian federalism. The Russian Federation was set up as an amalgam of 88 "subject territories" following the break-up of the USSR and the creation of "successor states" in Central Asia and the Baltic republics at the beginning of the 1990s. These were units that had clearly ranked status in the USSR as *oblasts* (provinces), *krais* (territories), and federal cities – all administered on a non-ethnic basis – and autonomous republics comprised of non-Russian nationalities as well as ten ethnic-based "autonomous districts" and one national *okrug* (the Jewish National County).

In the late 1980s, Mikhail Gorbachev encouraged regional communist elites to declare sovereignty in the autonomous republics, and his successor Boris Yeltsin went on to instruct the new post-Soviet provincial governments to "take as much sovereignty as they could swallow" (Urban 1997:282–283). As a result, the Russian Federation became a seething cauldron of identity politics and claims for rights and status. Few boundaries were changed, but the centralized hierarchical structure was in convulsions. Many provinces declared complete sovereignty, including the right to conduct independent foreign relations and withhold taxes from the center. Some promulgated their own constitutions at odds with that of the Federation, while "lower" units sought to jump up the hierarchical ladder by establishing direct relations with Moscow. The presidents of republics and the governors of provinces were now directly elected by the population.

The 1990s saw a flourishing of competitive difference. Inside the provinces, cities with their independent budgets and directly elected mayors challenged the governors of the provinces in which they were situated. Even obscure districts (*raion*) started to brandish the word *suverenitet* (sovereignty). Yet in many regions, elite holders of official posts, the old communist *nomenklatura*, retained control and have been relatively cautious in flying the sovereignty flag. In others, new leaders appeared, bringing in idiosyncratic political and economic regimes, with innovative "ideologies," rituals, and value systems. The great majority of all these provincial regimes were "authoritarian," being founded on presidential as distinct from parliamentary powers, and political parties were weak and shifting everywhere. But the practical effects of these changes were wildly disparate for reasons other than the purely political. The provinces varied vastly in size and resources: some were perpetually and miserably in debt to Moscow, while others contributed substantially to the federal budget. Regional lobbies (such as local industries, quasi-monopolies in electricity, gas, and oil, ethnic and religious interests, and those of criminal networks) articulated particular interests *outside* formal political institutions,

From the moment of his election in 2000, President Putin tried to reestablish central control over these unruly sovereignties. In seven new super-regions, he appointed plenipotentiaries drawn mostly from former KGB or military personnel to promote "vertical authority," and he punished overt independence (especially in Chechnya). It cannot be said that he has definitively succeeded. There have been abrupt shifts in the central political values of Russia, leading it is not clear where. Many provincial governments have supported popular movements for distinct "Russian values," such as collectivism, egalitarianism, strict controls on capitalism, "anti-Atlanticism" and "Eurasian" spirituality (Humphrey 2002), that seemed to have been halted in their tracks by Putin's decision to align Russia with the Western powers after the attack on New York's twin towers on September 11, 2001. Yet rightist (quasi-fascist) and leftist (essentially socialist restorationist) movements continue to seethe beneath the surface. Along with all this, a range of discourses has emerged in globalized arenas with diverse international links. Patchily across Russia, we find discourses on ethnic rights, ecological concerns, gender equality, law reform, and civil rights. Religious activism flourishes, often with international connections and funding. This includes mystic, shamanistic, magical, and healing movements, and pagan "revivals" as well as the reconstruction of established religions of Orthodox Christianity, Buddhism, Judaism, and Islam.

## The *marshrut* system and political life

The following section does not focus on explicit notions of *suverenitet* propounded by provincial leaders, nor on the ideologies and rituals they have attempted to establish. For these, see Humphrey 2002. It attempts rather to understand practices of sovereignty at the street level in a Siberian city, Ulan-Ude in eastern Russia. In 2001, when field research was carried out there, the notion of *suverenitet* remained inchoate and largely unspoken. This is an ethnography of the emergence of sovereignty before it could ever have been called that by its subjects.

The closed *marshrut* system organizes public transport in the city of Ulan-Ude. It is a mafia-dominated organization of taxi-drivers operating along set routes – hence the name *marshrut* (route, itinerary). The system has constituted itself as a micro-realm separate from the branches of the state, organizing itself along different principles. When it comes into contact with local state agencies, the system either rebuffs them or forces them to act, at least in part, according to *marshrut* logic.

Around 1991 the state-run bus service collapsed and was replaced by what inform-ants described as a "movement" (*dvizhenie*) – the emergence of all sorts of individ-uals as providers of *marshrut* taxi transport. People with their own cars or vans joined first, and others borrowed money to buy micro-buses or even old, large, state-owned buses. They formed themselves into groups to take over the old bus routes, but soon realized that new routes would be more profitable. New teams and new itineraries zigzagged across the city, and orbital routes were added until it appeared that every conceivable track had been exploited. This was strictly individual private enterprise – each driver made his or her profit from the value of the fares they took minus the costs of petrol, car maintenance, etc.

Yet drivers cannot act completely independently. From a purely functional point of view collaboration is necessary. The *marshrut* taxi operation is in competition with opportunistic car drivers, cruising around the streets, who will take people anywhere from door to door but demand far higher, unpredictable fares. *Marshrut* drivers struggle to keep fares down by strict calculation of the costs of set routes and the volume of passengers. They must establish routes and inform the citizenry about them, and they must avoid bunching up on any given route so as not to miss valuable passengers. Ulan-Ude is one of those extraordinarily spread-out towns, in which socialist planning sited factories, offices, shops, and dormitory districts far apart from each other. People have to travel long distances, therefore, and taxi routes often span 15, 25, or even 35 kilometers from the city center.

By around 1994, this had developed into what the taxi-drivers themselves call a "system" (*sistema*) that has its own internal "law" and is entirely run by what (for want of a better term) we may call a mafia. Every driver pays a regular toll or tribute (in Russian this is called *dan'*) to these gangsters, initially at the point of a gun. The mafia widely avoids state taxes. The police categorize its members as "organized criminals" and a special directorate has been set up to combat them. A differentiation between "the state" constructed by official law and the actual operations of state institutions will enable us to understand the curiously suspended situation of the *marshrut sistema*. Being run by mafia groups, it is strictly illegal from the point of view of "the state" insofar as that idea is enshrined in federal and republic law. Yet a great deal of what "the system" actually does is not provided for in law and hence is "invisible" to it. Yet the *marshrut* "system" provides the only means whereby the vast majority of the population travel and in this sense is completely integral to the functioning of the city. The *sistema* also collaborates secretly with compliant officials, that is, with elements of "the state" considered as a set of institutions and practices.

This "privatized" *marshrut* system is an extremely efficient economic arrangement. It is regarded by ordinary people as cheaper, faster, more reliable, and in some ways more pleasant to use than the legal *marshrut* services in other Siberian cities that are run by the municipality.

This mafia-run phenomenon has been described in two ways in the literature. One analyzes it in economic or "rational choice" terms (Varese 1994). The other focuses on the political context of the phenomenon, the idea of the weak or disintegrated state and its inability to carry out certain functions that are then taken over by private groups (for example, Volkov 1999). These are top-down studies, in which the notion of politics employed radiates outward from the state, elections, and the overall domination of the means of violence. There have been very few studies of govern-mentality, a more socially pervasive and contextualized art of politics, which has extended through the late Soviet era into the present (Yurchak 2002). There may be a good reason for this. It is difficult to perceive any consistent or coherent overall governmentality in the myriad of diverse forms of political action now seen in Russia.

A strong impulse toward local autonomy at all levels suggests that issues of sovereignty might be more relevant than governmentality. Although most theories of sovereignty operate at the level of states and nations, aspects of them can be employed profitably in looking at the grass-roots (or more appropriately, the tarmac) operations of politics. Because such theories have left sovereignty as such a "thin" description, anthropology can and should engage with them in order to enrich them. In this respect, *pace* Foucault, there is no contradiction between his idea of govern-mentality and an anthropology of sovereignty that includes those aspects of governmentality that focus on it as a *way of thinking* about, or imagining, the practice of government as well as the actions people take in relations of domination.

The *marshrut* system provides an example of a new, post-Soviet institution that did not exist before 1991. It therefore serves as a thought experiment about the emergence of "the political" in relation to both sovereignty and governmentality. It helps us to think about how particular ways of life are related to "the political" as an emergent form of relations between people. An obvious question arises, however. The people who created the *marshrut* system were not innocents, as it were, but had previous experiences and ideas, not to speak of concurrent political ties, however weak or fluctuating, as subjects of the state. Nevertheless, we can separate sovereignty from previous modes of existence *conceptually* (if not historically or ethnographically) by adopting Agamben's definition. Yet, because it is these earlier and alternative experiences that provided the resources to open out and fill the domain of the *marshrut* system, it is essential that this chapter should discuss them.

## The emergence of "the system"

The information in the following section comes mainly from one middle-aged woman taxi-driver, as well as from conversations with some of her male colleagues, with other inhabitants of Ulan-Ude, and from local newspaper articles.

The woman said that from 1991 to 1994 the new taxi service was both spontaneous and peaceful. Drivers, mostly experienced men, simply got together and followed the old bus routes. But in 1994, when the citizens were forced to face widespread unemployment and delays in the payment of wages, there was a mad rush to join in. People found every possible way to get money to buy a car, van, or microbus and open up a new route. In Ulan-Ude, unlike certain other cities, this happened so suddenly and on such a scale that the Mayorate (the new town council) was unable to take control and "criminal elements" moved in. They simply claimed a given route as "theirs" and demanded that the drivers on that route pay them to use it. They beat up individuals, threatened others, and set up ambushes in remote areas to attack anyone who resisted. The police were unable to cope. The drivers then got together at a mass meeting and decided that "If the 'roof' [*krysha*] exists, then after all it is better for us to have some kind of 'roof'." "Roof" was a term widely used throughout Russia for protection in general and mafia personnel in particular. Drivers then began to pay up regularly. Meanwhile, the controllers of the different routes quarreled, especially when the mafia groups themselves invented new routes to mop up the best passengers. Drivers and mobsters together set up fights all over the city. Finally, in 1995, there was a massive "settling of accounts" (*razborka*) between the various *struktura*s at a central patch of bare ground called the Komsomol Peninsula. Several people were killed. These were, significantly, interstitial people who tried to get round the opposed blocks, to blur the boundaries of "those ranks of inter-connected criminals." After this the "roofs" agreed on how to divide all the routes among themselves and (in the words of our woman taxi-driver) "Everything died down."

Meanwhile, our informant said, she and some other women drivers felt unsafe. "In the case of our route," she said, "we invited five to six young men to join us as co-drivers, aged about 32–35, all very good boys, with drivers' documents, they all graduated from the Technological Institute, they had education, some had been in the KGB." One of them was chosen by our roof to be our brigadier, to register the members of the team and collect and pay up the money. "On all these routes," she continued,

> "there was very strong discipline. I was amazed. No sooner had we opened our new route under the Wrestler [*Bortsy*] roof than every week there was a meeting [*sobranie*]. The agenda and the time were announced beforehand, and then the roof arrived, two or three people in their own cars, and they had a sorting out [*razborka*] to discipline the drivers. It was almost like a Party meeting in the old days, but with even stricter, stronger discipline. Everyone connected with any of the routes owned by a given roof comes to these meetings, perhaps 40 or 50 people. You can't put your feet up or smoke, and you have to pay attention. If you don't come to one meeting you get a first warning [*preduprezhdenie*], if you don't come twice you get a second warning, if you don't come three times you are sacked from the route. 'Infringers' are punished."

At this point, our interviewer asked, "Who are these 'infringers'?" The reply was, "People who get drunk, who don't have the right documents and licenses, whose cars are not kept in order." And the driver added that "illegals" (*levyye*) are not allowed in. "You know how a white rook is thrown out of the nest, an alien bird? It's the same here, an alien [*chuzhoi*] cannot appear on our route." "And how do they get rid of him?" "Simple. They beat him up and put sand in his tank, he wouldn't venture on our route again." In fact, the occupation of *marshrut* taxi-driving is now (2001) saturated. This means that someone joining a route has to pay a huge sum of 10,000 rubles to the brigadier, who pays it to the roof, which then gives permission to start work, but only if some other driver can be dismissed.

The woman driver described how she suddenly came to realize what she was involved in. "My husband Bair," she said,

> "One day he got so angry when the guy came round from the roof to collect the money. Bair spoke out, 'What's this? You are still young, you do nothing, and we work from day to night, we don't owe you any money!' A real row. Two days later, two threatening figures from the roof came round to our apartment and told Bair he was excluded from the route. Then we realized! Driving was our livelihood. We had to get back a route, but to do that we'd have to reestablish the roof and pay them a massive fee. God, it was difficult. We faced ruin and we had to rent out our car for a time to make the money... So today in Ulan-Ude the *marshrut* system is completely regularized. Maybe one roof or another will weaken and another will come in, but it will be according to the same scheme. You have to deal with the roof, and whoever among them wins, the drivers have to pay."

Further inquiries revealed the strength of "the system," its capacity to incorporate branches of public bodies and defy those that attempted to reform it. Suddenly, a new route appeared, No. 55. Normally the drivers would have been attacked, but everyone said not to touch this one, even though it crossed many other routes. It was rumored that this was Aidaev's route – Aidaev being the mayor of Ulan-Ude. Then, amid much hedging, because Aidaev is still the mayor and an extremely powerful figure, our informant revealed her suspicion that the drivers of No. 55 are secretly paying a roof called the Dvortsovskaya Struktura (the Palace Structure, probably referring to the Palace of Sport) and that this roof then pays directly to Aidaev personally.

Next to appear on the scene was the *mayorate* as an institution, this being the public body headed by the mayor but distinct from him as a private person. The *mayorate* set up routes 90, 91, and 97, and in the words of our driver tried to "subordinate" (*podchinit'*) its teams, by forcing them to rent cars at high rates from the town council and also to pay them a large percentage of the fares through a metering system. Aidaev, in his capacity as mayor and attempting to follow the example of the city of Irkutsk, decided to try to extend this differently organized municipal operation over the whole city. He gave an order (*prikaz*) to this effect. In revolt, the private drivers supported by the "roofs" then joined together under a former Soviet trade-union official, each route elected its own representative to the new union, and all went to court to contest the order. Quite probably through illegal pressure, but ostensibly because the drivers had licenses and some of them could be shown to have paid certain nominal taxes, the *mayorate* lost the case and everything went back to the mafia-run system as it was before.

The public powers having been defeated, the 6th Directorate for the Fight Against Organized Crime, a section of the police under the Ministry of Internal Affairs (MVD), decided to join "the system." They carefully studied the strengths and weaknesses of the various roofs to see where they could make an alternative offer of "protection" to the drivers. "In general," our taxi-driver said, "the MVD has complete information about who is in each roof and who controls whom. Everyone knows about everything. In fact, the MVD 6th Directorate already had its own route, Number 130. We all know that that is theirs and that no one should touch it. How do we know? Because in 1997 when there was a period of disorder and drivers were getting beaten up and robbed, we asked for help from the 6th, the 5th,and the 10th Police Directorates, and only the 6th gave any active help, and then only to drivers on route 130! Of course, if you ask those drivers concretely, 'Who is your roof?' they deny the whole thing and say they don't know."

The implication of what our informant said is that the police are trying to take over other routes as well, but she was adamant that neither the police, nor the town council, nor the mayor, would change "the system." "That cannot happen in Ulan-Ude," she said, "because they are all privatized drivers [ *oni vse* individually]. The state is not strong enough to unite them, nor can it afford to supply them all with petrol, spare parts, oil, technical checks, and all the rest of it – colossal money – for them to go onto the wage system."

So, in this micro-world it is the roofs that are in control. Having more or less agreed on a division of the spoils, they unite to rebuff outside interference through their new union. They suck money up through the brigadiers and pay it into their *obshchak* (common pot or treasury). For return favors, they pass some on to the mayor personally, as we have seen, and no doubt also to some other official figures. Yet such links are secret and have to be disguised, as is the participation of the police. This secrecy acts as a screen that separates the domain of the *marshrut* operation from the public activities of the state. In effect, secrecy constitutes a boundary between sovereignties. In this curious situation, the taxi service is *simultaneously* open and part of the daily life of every citizen and at the same time illicit, with its governing bodies hidden. The drivers, with the exception of the brigadiers, do not know the roofs personally, do not know their real names, and do not socialize with them. "We just *see* these people, we have no idea what they do," as our driver put it. "In the first days it was very unpleasant," she continued. "Perhaps it was the Soviet mentality, but to sit in those meetings and listen to that roof laying down the law, well, I know we sat and clenched our teeth. It was somehow insulting when young boys ordered you around and could spit on you." The interviewer then commented that she herself as a passenger hated it when "you are sitting in the taxi and in come two boys, completely young and green, just 18 or 19, and roughly give orders to the driver, and you see him handing over money." The driver thought for a bit and then said, "In the old Communist days, we had someone to complain to. I could go to the *partorg* or the *mestkom* [low-level Party officials]. Nowadays I have no one to go to. These are new times. Anyway, a criminal now is not the same as he was in the past, with blood-stained fingers opened wide. Now the criminals are very proper and even nice people [ *vpolne prilichnyye dazhe simpatichnyye lyudy*]."

Another driver commented that since the various mafia "structures" that dominate in Ulan-Ude are all groups of athletes, you have to understand their situation. "They were given advanced special training in the Soviet system, they are incredibly fit and strong and energetic, way beyond ordinary people. Remember, they were trained to beat the world at the Olympics! Now there are no jobs for them. What else are they to do?" In such statements, the roofs appear almost in heroic guise. They consist in fact of groups who call themselves the Wrestlers, the Boxers, the Karate group, and so on, and these are the images they project even if most of the members these days are not athletes at all. Note, because it will be relevant later, that the Wrestlers (*Bortsy*) run the *marshrut* system and are currently the dominant group in Ulan-Ude.

## THE "SYSTEM" AND THEORIES OF SOVEREIGNTY

How can we analyze this phenomenon? First, it has to be seen as a process, rather than as a timeless structure, a process whereby what the driver called "the system" came into being, evolved (as it were), and probably will mold itself into yet other shapes in the future. Second, this micro-world involves a kind of sovereignty. At the extreme, people were killed in order to set its boundaries. Further, "the system" was able to rebuff the control of the legal state (in the form of municipalization) and, within the practicing state, it could transform both the mayor's and the Police Department's interventions into minor examples of its own methods. Finally, "the system" – while being itself an exception – could decide on what (or whom) it could exclude, an ability that is inseparable from creating and guaranteeing the situation that its internal law requires for its own validity. As Agamben paraphrases Carl Schmitt (1998:16):

> The exception appears in its absolute form when it is a question of creating a situation in which juridical rules can be valid. Every general rule demands a regular, everyday frame of life to which it can be factually applied and which is submitted to its regulations. The rule requires a homogeneous medium. This regularity is not some external matter, but belongs rather to the rule's immanent validity. There is no rule that is applicable to chaos. Order must be established for juridical order to make sense. A regular situation must be created, and sovereign is he who definitely decides if the situation is actually effective.

It was exactly such an "everyday frame of life" that the Bortsy created when they took control of the *marshrut* system. They established team memberships, firmly cut off "illegals" (illegal from their point of view, but no more illegal than they themselves from the point of view of the legal state), and set up the regular disciplinary meetings. In such a "homogeneous medium" their own law could have validity, that is, the tariffs charged, the apparatus of warnings for non-attendance at meetings, the idea of "infringements," and the punishments for them.

Agamben, as we have seen, reworks Schmitt's ideas on sovereignty and law in order to examine their relation to "nonpolitical" everyday life. He insists that the problem of sovereignty is not to be reduced to who within the political order is invested with certain powers, but refers to the "threshold of the political order itself" (1998:11–12). In this light, Agamben's notion that the ban is the originary political act is significant. "The ban" refers here both to exclusion and to the command of the sovereign. The topography of legality defines itself in relation to what is external to it. Yet, as Agamben argues, the person who is banned, like Bair the driver, "is not in fact simply set outside the law, but rather abandoned by it. That is, he is exposed and threatened on the threshold in which life and law, inside and outside, become indistinguishable" (1998:28). In the case of Bair, a decision was taken to write him off, as it were, and yet he was still present as a driver in the city. And he never mentally left the system. As soon as he was excluded, he and his wife could only think about how to get back in again.

Agamben does not draw out the full implications of this idea, including its psychological implications, because his point of originating action is always (only) the sovereign. He writes, "Contrary to the modern habit of representing the political realm in terms of citizens' rights, free will and social contracts, from the point of view of sovereignty only bare life is authentically political. This is why in Hobbes the foundation of sovereign power is to be sought not in the subjects' free renunciation of their natural rights but in the sovereign's presentation of his natural right to do anything to anyone, which now appears in the right to punish" (1998:106). We may accept Agamben's definition of the basis of sovereignty in the "right" to kill, but a definition only goes so far toward understanding a phenomenon that is, in fact, a complexity of interrelations. Prioritizing the "intrinsic right" of the sovereign in this way underestimates the richness and weight of the "ways of life" of the people, which Agamben sees only in terms of bare life, its vulnerability to violence, its liability to be snuffed out in killings or incarcerated in camps.

The payment of tribute by the drivers, for example, is not just a matter of fear. It is conditioned by the struggle to live which Russians call *vyzhit'* (to survive, to hold out). People in Ulan-Ude have to make payments wherever there is scarcity. They have *to buy*, in effect, jobs, have to pay for promotions, to get their children into college, to acquire a trading license, and so on. These payments are not simply economic in character. They are thought within convoluted ethical considerations and ruminations about what one might expect from other people of various kinds. In the case of payments to racketeers, these musings do not exclude even empathy for the men of violence. Thus our woman driver said of one member of her roof, "I was on his side, because, really, he's just a little boy, just 12 or something, not even shaving, and he opens the door and asks you for money." And about the men of her own brigade, who at one point had gone out to block a competing route and beat up its drivers, she said, "Well, our lads, it's their age, 32–35, the very age for fighting." For payments to state officials, she had the following comment to make. "It's not like the roof there. Those are state structures after all. The person who sits there in a state post, he *has a right* to receive money, valuable gifts or services. Because, you know, a state seat is an 'income-giving place' [*doxodnoe mesto*]." In this light, the tribute given to the roof can be seen as part of a wider imaginary of political-economic acts. A person does not pay up as a negotiated strategy, nor out of sheer fright, but as someone who *has adopted a way of life* and submits to the way its necessities are conceived. Giving tribute is a crucial element in governmentality, in what we may call the "technologies of sovereignty," and, at the same time, it cannot be separated from the wider symbolic imaginary of "survival" in urban life.

Thus, as anthropologists, we have to see such objects as "natural rights" in terms of the ideas in which they are held. The people who sign up as drivers, whose bare life, in Agamben's terms, is thereby included in the micro-polity of the Bortsy, are not to be seen as mere eaters and sleepers and family reproducers in the Aristotelian mode. They are not devoid of experience in political life. What would be the ideas whereby Russian and Buryat drivers would subordinate themselves and "leave" to the Bortsy the exercise of their power? And would these notions not in some degree impinge on the actual forms taken by the practice of sovereign power? Indeed, might not other ideas, springing in some sense from the wide totality of everyday life and global imagining, spill over and infuse into the political, so that we could not truly understand the political life without taking account of them?

## PRECURSORS IN THE IMAGINING OF A WAY OF LIFE

These questions are explored by making a brief excursion into a significant precursory context of the *marshrut* system, considered as a sphere of politics. I refer here only in passing to the official Soviet institutions, because they are well known to readers in their broad outlines. What I draw attention to is another rebellious foundational experience that would be part of the "political" life (in a non-official sense) of any contemporary inhabitant of Ulan-Ude. This draws upon the idea, explored by Nugent (2001), that local people's relation to the state and politics in general is imagined in frameworks that have spatial and temporal dimensions. In Ulan-Ude, the former Soviet imaginary of the all-USSR and future-oriented spatio-temporal frame has fractured into a literally provincial and somehow self-oriented outlook. This is fully understandable only in relation to its precursory perspectives, because those are what people today refer to when explaining their new attitudes.

The history that illustrates this point is that of youth-gang conflict on the streets of Ulan-Ude. This is something – a combination of practices and imagination – that almost everyone, women as well as men, must have participated in, if at times only peripherally, since between the late 1950s and the late 1980s the city became saturated with gangs. At first the conflict was between predominantly Russian urban working-class kids and immigrant Buryat youths from the surrounding countryside. The Buryats, the indigenous people of this region of Siberia, seen by the Russians as country hicks, called themselves by defiantly oriental names, such as Chiang-Kai-She, referring to the 1940s anti-communist Chinese leader, or Hung-hu-dze, the local pronunciation of the Chinese term for "Red Beards," bandits (possibly originally Russian) who infested the Russo-Chinese borderlands in the early twentieth century. Street battles were part of the urban scene during the late 1950s, but sometime in the early 1960s a mass battle took place on the bridge that linked the center of town with a district across the River Ude occupied mostly by Buryats. The police intervened and "imposed order," as it were, only for the Chiang-Kai-Shisty to use this as a shelter to strengthen their grip over the entire riverine area. Through the 1960s and 1970s they subdivided into several, often warring, gangs and established outposts in nearby villages. The central city groups did likewise. In this shifting scene, at any one moment the entire city was divided up into delimited gang territories, down to each apartment block. If members from an enemy gang strayed onto alien territory, they would be beaten up. The incident would then count as a provocation for a more general battle.

Each gang had its own name, war cry, distinctive dress-code and hairstyle. Some even had hymns or anthems. The images gloried in heterodoxy. Some gang territories were named after American states such as Louisiana or Nebraska, or after Chinese cities, such as Shanghai. Gang names included "the Anarchists," "the Bourbons," "the Colonialists," "the City Wreckers," and, in the case of a women's gang, "the

Sultanki" ("the Sultanas"). Defying the derogatory stereotype of Buryats as backward nomads, certain gangs chose names like "the Huns" or "the Barguty." Cocking a snook at sexual stereotypes, one central city gang called itself "the Babochki" ("the Butterflies," a reference to their territory around the Opera and Ballet Theater, associated with homosexuals). Gang leadership was shifting, but chiefs called "Boss" or "Papa" were supposed to demonstrate strength and fairness. They often acquired additional authority through having served a prison term (Mitupov 2002). The leadership, which dominated over a three-tiered hierarchy according to age (within the range of about 16 to 25), collected a nominal sum from all gang members. This was supposed to provide support to the families of those who were arrested. To refuse to fight was to incur ignominy or bullying, yet for decades these payments were strictly voluntary.

This whole situation of gang warfare, according to those who remember it, was driven by a desire for sheer domination – glorious victory over the enemy and intimidation of the weak or undecided. In its perpetual violence, its collectivism, lack of structure, the absence of anything definite to fight over, or any ideological reason for conflict, this looks like an example of what Norbert Elias (1978) modeled as the "primal contest," or Carl Schmitt (1996) as the "pure politics" of the friend/enemy. Yet, although the gang world had its own kind of order, it was firmly encased within another order, that of the Soviet state.

It is very significant that the gangs withered with *perestroika* (Gorbachev's campaign to restructure the socialist system) in the late 1980s and morphed into something very different during the 1990s. After the end of communism the "romantic period" of the gangs was over, as one Buryat observer put it (Badmaev 2002:99). Ulan-Ude's gangs created an archetypal "temporary autonomous zone" of the kind mentioned earlier – the flow of life into unrecognized spaces within and between rigid structures. They are evidence that the Soviet state did not have a complete monopoly over violence (*pace* Volkov 1999), but nevertheless the gangs cannot be described as sovereign. The legally defined state and the state in practice were very much closer to one another in Soviet times than they are today. Soviet overarching dominance, if not monopoly, created the situation in which the stakes of gangland violence were – and could be – nothing but glory.

If this state of perpetual conflict was the precursor of the *marshrut* system, the transformation of the gangs after 1991 shows something of the social landscape in which the system now exists. The trade and entrepreneurship allowed in the late 1980s brought real economic gains to be fought over. The gangs ceased to be purely territorial and began to establish bases in schools, colleges, and workplaces. The collection of money dues then became obligatory. Primary-school gang members sometimes stole from their parents in order to accede to the demands of extortionists.

As police supra-domination of the street withered, this newly economically rapacious system flourished. It still exists and is countered by well-organized vigilante groups (one such, called Black Rider, is a militant Buryat movement trained by ex-army officers). The criminal subculture, with its jargon, ways of behavior, and styles and rules of interrelationships, spread into society through these same networks (Badmaev 2002). Remembering that between 1960 and 1990 around 73 million people in Russia served terms in prisons or labor camps (Mitupov 2002) and that Ulan-Ude was located in a region known for such institutions, it is not surprising that the influence of the "zone" (slang for the Gulag) has a strong social foundation. The tribute flowing into the common treasuries (*obshchak*) along a well-established hierarchical chain became by the mid-1990s the internally "legal" (*zakonnyi*) economic basis for the criminal racket. The image of "the enemy" is no longer another street gang but the so-called *barygi*, traders and kiosk-owners who are also trying to wrest a living from the street. It is their territory that the racket is trying to "occupy." And who dominates this racket in the city of Ulan-Ude but our friends the Bortsy (Wrestlers).

This brief chronology indicates how different kinds of domination succeeded one another. The more spontaneous and rebellious form of the early street-gang had its conditions of existence guaranteed by the Soviet state. It could take the "romantic" form of pure conflict (pure "politics") because "the economy" was provided for – everyone was simultaneously either in education or at work. It was imagined in global terms because the USSR itself was imagined that way. By the late 1990s, however, the region of Buryatia had become one of the poorest in Russia, and 40 percent of its adolescents were neither working nor in education (Badmaev 2002, quoting *Trud* 1997, March 6). The almost theatricalized performance of anarchic autonomy melted away and was replaced by a struggle for economic survival.

Gangs, no longer quasi-universal but specialized in racketeering, became serious elements in the political economy of the city. Their fighting quality (*boevitost'*) no longer springs from the strength and aggression of young people who happen to live in given territorial districts but rather is constituted by *the ability to rule* of professional thugs who provide "protection" from above. These professionals, instead of avoiding state agencies as the gangs do, connect with them in various discrete ways. Yet, as suggested earlier, the secrecy of these links constitutes an invisible boundary for the emergence of domains in which prototypes of sovereignty may be recognized. The aesthetics of these rulers has shifted: the toponymy of ironic autonomy has been replaced by names intended to evoke respect.

This is the contemporary context for the *marshrut* system, which now can be seen as a quasi-sovereign protection racket with its own dynamic – even perhaps a relatively benign one – in a differentiated landscape of networks. True, it takes dues by threats of violence, but at least it does not rob children and it does allow taxi-drivers a decent living. The Bortsy have become a sprawling and variegated conglomeration. One driver respondent said, "The Bortsy are not just wrestlers, of course. They link up bank structures, commercial structures. Bortsy is just their general name. Lots of different people are joined up there, those who are very occupied with violence and those who have real money, real power [*vlast'*]. It's a very complex structure."

The implication of this is that the Bortsy exercise their rule in different ways in their various spheres of operation, a point supported by Varese's (2002) study, *The Russian Mafia*, which makes it clear that a highly variegated repertoire of tactics is present. What we see here are different forms of governmentality present in various sites of operation and engaging with different concrete ways of life. Yet, however politely the threats are couched, anthropologists should not lose sight of the fact that these operations are ultimately about sovereignty when the fundamental, realistic threat is that of an ignominious death. Informants among the taxi-drivers spoke of an uncle murdered in his apartment, a young man found with his throat slit in a stairwell, a debtor discovered burnt to death so that his remains would not be identifiable. This is "the life that may be killed but not sacrificed" of which Agamben writes (1998:107). Yet our analysis cannot be restricted to this horror since a sphere of threats precedes it that exists in the world of the living. Here there must be different manners if, as I have argued, sovereignty is always qualified by ways of life.

We therefore need to take account of the values and symbolism that give legitimacy to the Bortsy. A Buryat writer suggests that the dominance of the Wrestlers is quite understandable, since wrestling and archery are the national sports of the Buryats (Badmaev 2002). This is inadequate, because the Bortsy are mostly not Buryats but Russians, and in any case the sportsmen–mafia association occurs all over Russia. More pertinent is the previous cult of sport in the Soviet Union and its link to images of world glory through the medium of the physically honed, powerful male body and the idea of the loyal team. Certainly such images are exploited in the governmentality surrounding the Bortsy. Their dominance is expressed in the image of the heroic Spartachi ("Spartan warriors," a term commonly applied to all sports-based mafia-type groups) in the supposition they foster that they are secretly training hard, and would prevail in any physical encounter. Their symbolic face is at once a heroic exemplar and an utterly practical threat. Yet, the mobsters' practice of using aliases, noms de guerre, code-names, and nicknames (Varese 2002) distances the face from the person behind it. In this context we should remember the taxi-driver's sympathy, even admiration, for the actual members of the roof she encountered ("the 12-year-old who was not even shaving," the "young men of perfect age for fighting"). Such views are carried forward, I suggest, from half-remembered youthful participation in the adventures of the Soviet-era gangs. The mobsters themselves adopt a similar self-identification technique (naming by iconic image) to that of the youth gangs. This points to the complex psychological relationships that exist when people are aware of changing temporalities, masks, and more vulnerable faces. We see a multiple relation between the familiar Soviet images of prowess and fame (now lost for ever), the hard surface the Bortsy project (but cannot always sustain), the struggle of everyone to wrench economic gain from the streets, and the ordinary people's understanding of the pathos of these contradictions.

This leads to a final observation in my attempt to understand the marshrut system. I have argued that there is sovereignty here, but that idea as expounded by Schmitt and Agamben fails to take account of what the ordinary participants bring to the relation. Their everyday life "throws in" its own exigencies and excitements. These burst beyond the confines of the notion of sovereignty and qualify it by responding to a different logic. True, the taxi-driver explained how every member of her team is now "disciplined," which might be understood simply as subjection to sovereign power. But in fact, this is a self-discipline, which does not lie only in menace or in submissiveness, but has other origins too. She explained, "You know how it used to be, you went to work in a factory, every day at the same time, you waited for the whistle, you got up at seven. That was very hard psychologically. Now the marshrut drivers get up even earlier at five, but they don't have that feeling of heaviness because they know they could go at 12 o'clock. But I go out before six because I know that I'll get money right from six o'clock." Certainly the rulers tap the economic impulse ("I'll get money"). But that impulse also interjects its own rationale, which cannot be summed up by the notion of pure subjection.

Let me explain by describing some nuances of the drivers' practices. They have instituted a rigidly upheld order according to which they must set out from the beginning of the route and follow one another in sequence. To start in the middle or overtake another driver is regarded, except when it happens by accident, with harsh disapproval, as this is seen as collecting other drivers' rightful fares. The drivers observe strict mutual surveillance in this matter and beat up drivers who "infringe." We should beware of assuming an overwhelming oppressiveness in this situation because people bring to it an awareness of experiences of even more grim Soviet contexts. The women taxi-driver said:

> "What's good about these days is that a person for the first time can…well, I'm speaking about myself, I always worked in the state structure, I received wages regularly. But they could insult you and what could you do? But the entrepreneurial movement gives me a kind of freedom. I have a car of my own, I can just sit in it and go to work, I earn money for myself, and it seems to me this is a very pleasant feeling, despite the roof, in spite of all the difficulties."

In other words, we cannot understand the life of taxi-drivers unless we see that it does not stand on its own – they are contrasting it with the perspective of an earlier time.

Furthermore, however authority-ridden the *marshrut* system, its actuality can be infused with *joie de vivre*. "Let's say," the woman continued, "we decide to start the route at 7 o'clock. And sometimes it happens that several cars go to the starting point together. And there's such a race for who'll get there first, because the others will have to wait their turn. We have such a great time racing there wildly through the streets. And everyone knows it's no big deal, because shortly after seven there are lots of people going to work and we'll all be making big money." She went on,

> "On almost all routes, people work there a long time and are friends. In our route, for example, we had an opening party [*otkrytie*] when we started, and then we always celebrate our anniversary [*godovshchina*], and we have set up a common fund [*kassa*] for people's birthdays and to help people. If I need an urgent repair and I have no money I can park at the last stop and one of the other drivers will always help me. People borrow money from one another freely in our team, because the guarantee is always your car, or the fact that you have a place on the route. This pleases me, these human interrelations."

Two points can be made about this statement. First, it is impossible not to see here certain long-standing habits of sociality being carried forward into the new micro-world. Opening parties, anniversaries, common funds, etc. were all features of the old Soviet *kollectiv*. To these are added the invigorating bolsters of the newly imagined world of entrepreneurship and "capitalism" in which the Bortsy are participants: valuable private property (the car), entitlement to earn (one's place on the route), and the sense of freedom. Second, more tentatively perhaps, one can see a certain "economy" of vitality here. Negative quashing of life ("the ban," the beatings and threats) may be the ultimate guarantee of sovereignty, but are they not countered in the sphere of daily life by this *joie de vivre*?

## Conclusion

This chapter has suggested that analysis of sovereignty need not be opposed to studies of governmentality, and that both concepts are essential in explaining how the political life emerges and may be constituted. In particular, localized "everyday" spheres of politics, because they are constituted by particular ways of life, offer the most vivid opportunities to question aspects of theories on sovereignty. The *marshrut* operation is a micro-polity that operates on its own terms and maintains its own "law." Because its initial operations created an unforeseen and uncharted space, it was for a period "invisible" to the black letter of the law, which has never quite caught up with it. It is still not absolutely clear, for example, whether tribute paid to the roofs is illegal or not. Meanwhile, as regards the practical agencies of "the state on the street," the *marshrut* operation has either kept them at bay or forced them to participate in the racket system.

I have argued that this is a system of micro-sovereignty. Yet "pure sovereignty" is qualified by the necessity of manifesting itself in life. The Ulan-Ude ethnography shows that micro-sovereignty has its own distinctive ways of instantiating symbolizing authority, which imposes a specific kind of relationality with its subjects. At the same time, in any historical situation those subject to sovereignty will have prior experiences and alternative lives people construct for themselves – previous "states of imagination" in Nugent's (2001) terms. Both the street gangs and the Soviet labor *kollektiv* are such prior worlds. In the case of the street gangs, the sense of belonging, of having enemies, of fiercely observed territoriality, and paying tribute to leaders, as well as a kind of rebellious independence, all pervade the actual practice of the taxi system. It is, perhaps, no accident that the neighboring city of Irkutsk, which never had such pervasive street gangs, also does not have an independent mafia-run transport system.

Yet we are dealing here with a new era. The images that enhance the authority of the roof are not just after-images of Soviet athletes. They also embody the figure of the ruthless capitalist, with all that that implies for people who have been taught from childhood about such people but never experienced them. The subjects in this arena of sovereignty bring to it new, yet historically specific, political ideas – such as that they constitute "a movement," that they are all "privatized," and that a certain freedom is possible within an oppressive system. Agamben may be right in general terms that across the world we are coming to see the increased presence of paralegal measures beyond the state that embrace "biopolitics" and create enclaves alien to democracy (see also Žižek 2002). But it would be a mistake to think that new sovereignties emerging within and beyond nation-states are all alike, simply because they do indeed have the characteristics of sovereignty. Sovereignties are saturated with "ways of life."

## REFERENCES

Agamben, Giorgio (1998 [1995]) *Homo Sacer: Sovereign Power and Bare Life*, trans. Daniel Heller-Roazen. Stanford, CA: Stanford University Press.

Agamben, Giorgio (2002) *Moyens sans fins: Notes sur la politique.* Paris: Editions Payot et Rivages.

Badmaev, André (2002) Neformal'nyye molodezhnyye assotsiatsii v Ulan-Ude. *Vestnik Yevrazii* 1:89–103.

Berlin, Isaiah (1997 [1958]) Two Concepts of Liberty. In *Contemporary Political Philosophy: An Anthology,* ed. Robert E. Goodin and Philip Pettit, pp. 391–417. Oxford: Blackwell.

Bey, Hakim (1991) *T.A.Z.: The Temporary Autonomous Zone, Ontological Anarchy, Poetic Terrorism.* Brooklyn, NY: Autonomedia.

Elias, Norbert (1978) *The Civilizing Process,* trans. Edmund Jephcott. New York Urizen.

Foucault, Michel (1997 [1980]) Power, Right, Truth. In *Contemporary Political Philosophy: An Anthology,* ed. Robert E. Goodin and Philip Pettit, pp. 543–550. Oxford: Blackwell.

Held, David (1992) Democracy: From City-States to a Cosmopolitan Order? *Political Studies* 40:10–39.

Humphrey, Caroline (2002) "Eurasia," Ideology and the Political Imagination in Provincial Russia. In *Postsocialism: Ideals, Ideologies and Practices in Eurasia,* ed. C. M. Hann, pp. 258–276. London: Routledge.

Mitupov, Konstantin (2002) Gurppirovki semidesyatykh: vospominanie-kommentarii k stat'e A. Badmaeva. *Vestnik Yevrazii* 1:104–119.

Nugent, David (2001) Before History and Prior to Politics: Time, Space and Territory in the Modern Peruvian Nation-State. In *States of Imagination: Ethnographic Explorations of the PostColonial State,* ed. Thomas Blom Hansen and Finn Stepputat, pp. 257–283. Durham, NC: Duke University Press.

Schmitt, Carl (1996 [1932]) *The Concept of the Political,* trans. George Schwab. Chicago: University of Chicago Press.

Urban, Michael, with Vyacheslav Igrunov, and Sergei Mitrokhin (1997) *The Rebirth of Politics in Russia.* Cambridge: Cambridge University Press.

Varese, Federico (1994) Is Sicily the Future of Russia? Private Protection and the Rise of the Russian Mafia. *Archives Européennes de Sociologie* 35:224–258.

Varese, Federico (2002) *The Russian Mafia: Private Protection in a New Market Economy.* Oxford: Oxford University Press.

Volkov, Vadim (1999) Violent Entrepreneurship in Post-Communist Russia. *Europe–Asia Studies* 51:741–754.

Yurchak, Alexei (1999) Gagarin and the Rave Kids: Transforming Power, Identity, and Aesthetics in Post-Soviet Nightlife. In *Consuming Russia: Popular Culture, Sex and Society since Gorbachev,* ed. Adele Barker, pp. 76–109. Durham, NC: Duke University Press.

Yurchak, Alexei (2002) Entrepreneurial Governmentality in Post-Socialist Russia. In *The New Entrepreneurs of Europe and Asia,* ed. V. Bonell and Thomas Gold, pp. 127–156. Armonk, NY: M. E. Sharpe.

Žižek, Slavoj (2002) Are We in a War? Do We Have an Enemy? *London Review of Books,* May 23:3–6.

# CHAPTER 27 Transnational Civil Society

## June Nash

Recent decades have witnessed the emergence of novel networks of association in the civil domain that have expanded the parameters of political engagement for poor and marginal groups. These networks consist of extra-governmental associations of people from multiple national backgrounds who dedicate themselves to monitoring and reforming the institutions that exercise power within national domains. This "transnational civil society," as it is sometimes called, differs in important ways from classic civil society, famously discussed by John Locke (in *Two Treatises on Government*). The origins of classic civil society are inseparable from the emergence of mercantile and industrial capitalism, and the efforts of predominantly male, property-owning, bourgeois classes in the countries of Western Europe to consolidate a group of entitlements, a set of social institutions, and a domain of communicative action that were independent of central state power. In addition to having been organized on a national basis, classic civil society was further distinguished by its homogeneity (in racial, class, and gender terms), and also by the historical and political context out of which it emerged.

Contemporary civil society has come into being not in relation to the birth of capitalism in Europe, but in response to a major shift in capitalist accumulation practices on a global scale. Particularly important in this regard is the crisis of Fordism and the rise of flexible accumulation (Harvey 1989). As Gledhill (1998) has shown, the set of economic policies known as "neoliberalism" may be understood as one expression of flexible accumulation. Neoliberalism is characterized by: (1) a commitment to the logic of the market (Adam Smith's "invisible hand"); (2) the abandonment of national systems of redistribution and the down-sizing of government; and (3) maximizing profits in low-wage production sites where investors are promised tax-free entry.

As implemented by the International Monetary Fund (IMF), one of the major architects of neoliberal policy, these practices have had devastating consequences for low-income groups in "Third-World" countries. They include a widening gap between the wealthy and the poor (also a worldwide phenomenon), a decline in social welfare, and the fragmentation of families and communities as capital abandons old production sites in search of more lucrative locales.

People have turned to civil society as a locus for mobilizing social change in nations where neoliberal policies have exacerbated conditions of poverty, where elections and political parties have been corrupted, and where state coercion has brutalized the civilian population. It is especially low-income groups adversely affected by the reorganization of global capitalism (peasants, indigenous and informal sector groups, wage laborers) that have been drawn into this movement. The socially heterogeneous civil society that has resulted has little in common with its eighteenth-century forerunner. Not only is today's civil society distinctive in terms of its hybridity, it is also distinguished from classic civil society in having important transnational dimensions. It brings together groups from many different nation-states, often acting through non-governmental organizations (NGOs), who find common cause in promoting principles of a global nature – such as human rights, the environment, and indigenous autonomy. Finally, many of the groups that form the core of contemporary civil society are inspired by religious principles. The moral basis of an emergent world order is increasingly dependent on a sense of *communitas* nurtured by transnational civil society as it reaches out to a broad, global constituency. Transnational NGOs have opened up an expanded arena for dissent as citizens of modernizing states have lost confidence in national law-making and law-keeping organizations, and have looked to the global networks of association and community provided by human-rights and church-based activities.

Operating beyond the reach of state institutions, sacred and secular NGOs alike seek to address the growing inequities that prevail in countries where governments have abandoned national redistributive systems. These NGOs may serve as alternative models for development, and in some cases help to cultivate environmental consciousness. Although there is some truth in the claims of critics who regard NGOs as a means of dismantling the national welfare state, NGOs can nonetheless ensure an expanded arena for political action and promote a sense of belonging in a global society.

The key word with regard to the potentially transformative nature of NGOs is *alternative*: their ability to provide alternative models of economic development and political organization. By providing a political space to mobilize public opinion at home and abroad, transnational NGOs are keeping alive the basis for opposition to entrenched national power structures whose claims to sovereignty enable their leaders to arrest, torture, and even kill dissidents. In this role, transnational civil society constructs a moral basis for global society.

In this chapter I analyze the role of transnational civil society in monitoring and reforming the institutions that wield national power by focusing on the conflict between the government of Mexico and the Zapatista Army of National Liberation (EZLN) – a rag-tag but disciplined army of young, predominately indigenous women and men in the southern Mexican state of Chiapas, who took up arms against the Mexican government in 1994 in protest against the conditions of poverty and marginality in which so many Mexicans lived. Although the ensuing struggle between the Zapatistas and the state threatened to become exceptionally bloody, transnational civil-society organizations were able to play a crucial mediating role in the conflict, monitoring the behavior of the government, publicizing the activities of the armed forces, bringing world public opinion to bear on the situation, and in some cases engaging in acts of civil disobedience.

## CIVIL SOCIETY, MILITARIZATION, AND TRANSNATIONAL NGOS

Civil society groups representing the interests of indigenous and non-indigenous semi-subsistence farmers began to emerge in Mexico in the early 1970s, when the national government retreated from its historic commitment to small-scale agriculture, and to land-reform policies that had long provided a subsistence base for a growing rural population. In Chiapas, the proliferation of these groups occurred under the encouragement of the Catholic Church, and Bishop Samuel Ruiz García – a noted theologian and committed advocate of liberation theology. Ruiz also helped establish Christian Base Communities throughout Chiapas, adding to the proliferation of civil-society groups in the region that was to become the focal point of the struggle between the EZLN and the state.

By the time the Zapatista rebellion broke out, religious and secular civil-society groups had been diffusing throughout Chiapas, and Mexico as a whole, for two decades. Regional and national confederations of these groups had formed, providing an extensive civil-society network that was capable of advancing collective interests and of opposing entrenched elites. As the struggle between the EZLN and the government unfolded, regional and national groups joined forces with NGOs from abroad to form the transnational civil-society movement that has played a key role in mediating conflict.

On January 1, 1994 – the day that the North American Free Trade Agreement (NAFTA) was to take effect – the Zapatista Army of National Liberation surprised national security forces in the southern state of Chiapas by seizing towns in its eastern and central highlands. The Zapatistas ransacked government buildings in many towns, including San Cristóbal de las Casas – once the colonial seat of government in Chiapas and now a major center of commercial and tourist activity. The EZLN declared itself in rebellion against the government, the army, and the police. They called for the end of the "illegal dictatorship" of Mexican President Carlos Salinas de Gortari, and issued proclamations demanding economic, social, and political justice and cultural autonomy. Having declared war on the Mexican state, they invited international organizations and the Red Cross to monitor the conflict under the provisions of the Geneva Convention. They also appealed to all Mexicans to join them in their struggle for justice and equality. The Mexican government was quick to respond, moving large numbers of troops and military equipment into the region. After several fierce battles with the Zapatistas, federal troops, supported by air strikes, forced the rebels to abandon the highland towns they had occupied, and to retreat into the inaccessible Lacandón rainforest of eastern Chiapas.

Since the uprising Chiapas, and Mexico as a whole, has become the staging ground for "low-intensity warfare," a mode of organizing conflict that minimizes body counts while maximizing divisive tactics within the civilian population. Although the militarization of civil society that accompanies low-intensity warfare (Klare 1988) had pervaded much of Central America during the interventionist, Reagan–Bush years (1980 to 1990), prior to its struggle against the EZLN Mexico had kept its distance from US anti-communist, counter-insurgency practices. So much so was this the case that Mexico allowed the Guatemalan National Revolutionary Unity, a coalition of four leftist guerrilla groups, to base its political directorate in Mexico City. Mexico has also offered refuge to nearly l00,000 Guatemalan Indians, regarded by the Guatemalan military as guerrilla sympathizers.

When the Zapatista uprising occurred, the Mexican government also began to employ low-intensity warfare. The first stage in an escalating process by which the government militarized civil society took place in the immediate aftermath of the uprising, when President Salinas ordered an estimated 40,000 federal troops to take up checkpoints on the perimeter of the zone of conflict in Chiapas. In an effort to maintain a good public image, however, Salinas also tried to maintain the ceasefire agreement that his government had signed with the Zapatistas. In February of the following year (1995), as support for the Zapatistas grew, Mexico's new President Zedillo decided to take action. He responded to what he perceived as a growing challenge to government control by ordering an invasion of rebel settlements in the Lacandón rainforest itself. By the time additional troops arrived in the region there were approximately 60,000 soldiers stationed at checkpoints within the conflict zone.

At this point the militarization of civil society began in earnest. The army attempted to validate its presence in the zone of conflict by taking on a pseudo-developmental role in which soldiers took over civilian positions as the major policing force, and also as development agents responsible for the construction of roads and other elements of infrastructure. By vastly increasing the number of military personnel in the region, and by placing soldiers in key positions involving policing, political decision-making, and infrastructural development, the military sought to accomplish two goals. On the one hand, the army sought to habituate people to the ubiquitous presence of the soldiers, and in this way to overcome the resistance of the general population. On the other hand, the military also sought to undermine people's ability to manage their own lives – to make them dependent on the military.

These two elements of strategy were combined with a third – a concerted effort by the military to escalate violence in the region, by arming pro-government paramilitary groups. In order to make these latter efforts as effective as possible, Mexico did an about-face with respect to its neighbors in Guatemala. Mexican military and government officials began consulting with their Guatemalan counterparts about how to control the Zapatista uprising. The Guatemalan military were considered experts on such matters because they had already fought a decades-long counter-insurgency war of their own.

The Mexican government used the threat (and reality) of force first to fragment civil society, and then to reconstruct it in a militarized form so as to undermine support for the Zapatistas and build support for federal troops. Thus it was, for example, that the Asociación Rural de Interés Colectivo (ARIC), an organization consisting of peasants from many rural areas that had provided important non-military aid to the EZLN, found itself threatened by the government. If they refused to accept a barracks in their midst, villagers were told, the army would burn their settlements to the ground. In addition to threatening (and employing) the use of force, the government also funneled arms and resources to its own support groups, even as it disavowed any knowledge of or responsibility for their actions. These paramilitary groups went on to carry out unusually brutal acts of violence against opponents of the government, and on a massive scale.

The government's decision to adopt a policy of low-intensity warfare, and to arm paramilitary groups, escalated levels of violence in everyday life, and did much to fragment the civil-society organizations that had formed in previous years. At the same tine, however, because the government sought to restore its waning legitimacy, it pursued a program of domesticating the military, and attempted to make it a normal part of everyday life in the colonized settlements and highland villages. Soldiers distributed sweets to children, and tried to pass out gifts of food and medicine to women (many of whom refused the handouts). Military personnel performed haircuts and provided dental services to people without medical clinics. Armed aggression against the local population continued, but it was increasingly carried out by paramilitary groups, who worked in close conjunction with (and who obtained their arms from) the military.

The ability of transnational civil society to open a political space within which acts of civil disobedience and the pressure of public opinion can be employed to oppose entrenched, national, power structures is revealed with great clarity by examining the tense months following the government's invasion of Zapatista territory in the Lacandón rainforest on February 9, 1995. Groups of concerned citizens from the Midwest and West of the United States arrived in San Cristóbal, where they were met by representatives of two prominent transnational NGOs – Global Exchange and International Services for Peace, which coordinated work with regional and national civil-society groups seeking a peaceful solution to the conflict. By the time they arrived, the military had already established a powerful presence in the zone of conflict. Patrols of soldiers routinely harassed visitors throughout the zone, detaining peasants as though they were foreigners, and even made their presence felt to tourists in the nearby Maya ruins. Helicopters and military observation planes, equipped with sensitive surveillance technology provided to Mexican anti-drug units by the US, flew missions over the villages of the conflict area.

In this context, a transnational NGO called Pastors for Peace decided to follow the troops into action. I was with this group when it was turned away by army personnel on February 11, 1995. The group of ministers, secretaries, and other professionals persisted, however, and later that day gained access to the conflict area. Pastors for Peace then became a conduit that passed essential information about the conflict to the assembled press and television crews that arrived in San Cristóbal from all over the world. Pastors for Peace was not the only NGO that was turned away by federal troops. National NGOs, representatives of the Mexican press, and even the Red Cross were also refused entry into the conflict zone during the first days of the February invasion.

A series of peace talks between the Zapatistas and the government were held from April to September, 1995, at several different locations in the conflict zone. During the first of these talks, held on April 12 in the peasant town of San Andrés, civil society groups organized press conferences that were attended by hundreds of press representatives from all over Europe (but by many fewer from the less sympathetic US press). Stationing themselves in concentric circles around the Zapatista spokespeople and government representatives, cordons of supporters made up of peasant and indigenous civil-society groups (many organized by gender) formed "peace lines" that prevented interlopers from disrupting the negotiations. Acting as bodyguards, they surrounded the Red Cross that took the innermost ring, with international observers and non-indigenous Mexicans in the outer ring. International and national peace NGOs played an essential role in the protests by organizing and registering thousands of witnesses, participants, and observers – development workers, students, teachers, merchants, housewives, who had traveled long distances to support the Zapatistas and discourage an attack by the armed forces. There were no outbreaks of violence despite the frustration of people who had walked for hours to be part of the historic occasion, and despite the menacing presence of thousands of federal troops surrounding the town.

In the course of these mobilizations, indigenous people learned that there was widespread support for their cause. The national and international press projected a new, less primitivizing image of indigenous people than did the provincial media (Nash 1997). Having seen the deep commitment and the serious intent of indigenous participants, it was difficult for international observers to persist in representing them as marginalized "tribal" or "peasant" populations.

The active intervention of civil-society organizations protesting the militarization of the conflict in the Mexico City plaza, along with the presence of NGOs in peace camps distributed throughout the conflict zone in Chiapas, may have made the difference between the Mexican army's low-intensity warfare and the Guatemalan war of extermination in the 1980s – as a result of which approximately 200,000 people lost their lives, and another million were displaced. Religious and secular NGOs working with Mexican civil-society groups ultimately succeeded in bringing the government to the negotiating table. After a series of meetings with the EZLN, in February of 1996 the government signed the San Andrés Accord, agreeing to auton-omy for indigenous people in the selection of their representatives in areas where they constituted a majority, along with direct representation through them in the federal congress. This accord was heralded by large sectors of Mexican society as reflecting a changed relationship between the state and indigenous people.

## INDIGENOUS CIVIL-SOCIETY GROUPS

Regional, national, and international organizations have played a major role in mediating the conflict between the EZLN and the government. The contribution of these groups, however, rests on a foundation provided by the organizations of indigenous and non-indigenous semi-subsistence farmers that began to emerge in Chiapas in the 1970s, with the encouragement of the Catholic Church. Indigenous groups have been especially important to the growth of the civil-society movement, and have been singled out as targets of military and paramilitary repression. We next examine the key role played by organizations of indigenous men and women as the conflict between the Zapatistas and the state unfolded.

### Men's groups

As civil society became increasingly militarized during the 1990s, violent conflicts took place in the borderlands of several highland indigenous municipalities in Chi-apas, in the Lacandón rainforest, and on Chiapas's northern frontier. The mode of organization of civil-society groups in these borderland regions differed from that of the nationally and regionally based organizations discussed above. In the border zone indigenous action groups tended to work toward collective goals in a highly autonomous, egalitarian manner. They employed distinctively Mayan naming practices in order to emphasize the collective, consensual nature of their activities. In Maya folk belief, bees and ants are auxiliaries to Mayan heroes and gods, in part because they embody the much-admired qualities of cooperation and collective action. Accordingly, action groups in this frontier region commonly called themselves "La Hormiga" (the Ant), and "Abejas," (the Bees) – as the following notice from "the Bees" indicates (SIPAZ 1998:16):

> We came together in 1992 because we are a multitude and we want to build our house like a honeycomb where we all work collectively and we will all enjoy the same thing, producing honey for everyone. So we are like the bees in one hive. We don't allow divisions, and we all march together with our queen, which is the reign of God, although we knew from the beginning that the work would be slow but sure.

The use of such symbolism was widespread. Referring to themselves as the "Bees Civil Society" (Sociedad Civil Las Abejas), a group of 25 Christian Base Communities in the municipality of Chenalhó came together to object to the attempts of government officials and paramilitaries to force them to take up arms against the EZLN. These communities consider themselves to be civilian support bases for the Zapatista Army of National Liberation (EZLN), but they make it very clear that they seek to exert their strength through peaceful means, through fasting and prayer, and not by force of arms. As one member stated to anthropologist Christine Eber (in press):

> It's that God is all powerful. He gave one group [the EZLN] arms. He gave another group [the Bees] the peaceful path. When the shooting starts the other group comes by the peaceful way to urge a solution. However, if we only use the peaceful way, the oppressors don't understand. That's when the first group comes with arms to organize so that the government listens. It's that the government needs a slap in the face to make it listen.

## Women's groups

Indigenous women have become deeply involved in the civil-society movement, in many cases forming their own groups, and in the process they have asserted their gender-specific rights alongside those claimed by other organizations. The proliferation of indigenous organizations in general has allowed women from many different villages to associate with one another – promoting solidarity among them. Indeed, changes for women have been even more dramatic than those experienced by men. A statement formulated by a group of women in December, 1995, at the fourth assembly of the National Association of Indigenes Plan de Ayala (ANIPA), an organization inspired by Zapata's program for smallholders in the 1910–17 revolution, reflects the women's recognition of the specificity of their oppression, and their willingness to speak out against it (Gutiérrez and Paloma 1999:83):

Autonomy for us women implies the right to be autonomous . . . to train ourselves, to seek spaces and mechanisms in order to be heard in the communal assemblies and to have posts. It also implies facing the fear that we have in order to dare to take decisions and to participate, to seek economic independence, to have independence in the family, to continue informing ourselves because understanding gives us autonomy. To be able to participate in this type of reunion enables us to diffuse the experiences of women and animate others to participate.

Women show a clear awareness of their responsibility to cultivate the practice of autonomy in society as well as in the home and family, since it is there that children are enculturated in the patterns that define future behavior. Those women who live in fear of abuse, who accept subordination in the home, diffuse sentiments that reproduce subordination and marginalization.

Women's growing sense of empowerment, and their willingness to confront injustice, is reflected in the fact that, with the militarization of the Maya conflict, and with the invasion of Zapatista territory by federal troops in February of 1995, women became the most vocal opponents of the war. A "March for Peace" that they organized on March 8 of that year exemplified their solidarity and collective strength. They distributed leaflets bearing their denunciation of the military in their communities. Looking more like a religious procession than a political movement, women from throughout the diocese of Chiapas marched through the town of San Cristóbal de Las Casas, carrying flowers and candles, their babies on their backs, while their leaders wafted incense to mark their way. Employing loudspeakers, they made speeches in San Cristóbal's central park, in which they protested not only the invasion of their communities and the deployment of troops in the rainforest, but also their general oppression as women (Gutierrez and Paloma 1999:84):

We are educated to serve in house and communit[y]. Families give preference to boys while girls leave school to work in the house. The government does not give credit or land to women. We do not work for wages, and we [are not paid] for cultivation. When we ask for legal aid, officials ask for a marriage license, and if we are not married, they say they will not write a warrant. Women cannot be officials in their communities, and do not have the right to a voice, and our word is [worth nothing] in court. With the bad treatment we receive, we see rage and suffering as something normal. We seek democratic and harmonious relations with equality and without discrimination and the sharing of household responsibilities.

As a result of the discrimination they have experienced within male-dominated organizations, women have formed separate groups within these organizations, where they have established their own agendas for change. Spokeswomen explain why they have followed this course (Gutierrez and Paloma 1999:86):

So we are convinced that the relations of our lives are also determined by the relations that we establish with men (those of our ethnicity and those who are not indigenes), and that these relations . . . have oppressive consequences for us and ought to be transformed. Therefore, the spaces that we value and that we seek to construct are the organizations of women, where we construct our own identity that marks and defines the gender condition and permits the flow and interaction with both male and female "others" and allows us to establish a dialogue of reentry with our own pueblo, with our customs, and to make alliances and actions with women in general to demand a recognition as indigenous women.

Indigenous women can state with pride that they have maintained, reproduced, and enriched the great cultural richness of their people. They have also vowed to prevent outsiders from exploiting the richness that women have done so much to preserve – to keep outsiders from using indigenous culture in ways that are foreign to indigenous views of life. Because of their responsibilities in the family and community, changes of the sort that women are experiencing and advocating can radically change expectations regarding what behaviors are acceptable, not only in the intimate spheres of the home, but increasingly in the mainstream of political protest and action.

The participation of women in civil society has transformed the actions and ideology guiding political life in the state. Yet at the same time, women's growing assertiveness and autonomy has threatened some sectors, particularly the young men of their communities, who sense their loss of control over women's labor and bodies at the same time that they are losing a sense of their own future in a declining agrarian economy. As the repositories of indigenous culture in communities that have long relied on women's exclusion from political and social life, women's demands for full participation in the emergent civil society they are helping to forge exemplify the struggles of the indigenous movement as a whole. In short, women's assertion of autonomy is crucial for the attainment of indigenous autonomy.

## CONVERGENCE OF HUMAN-RIGHTS NGOS AND CIVIL SOCIETY

Indigenous people are increasingly appealing to human-rights accords, thereby gaining support from international agencies (Kearney 1995). As "Fourth-World" enclaves, they are just now seeking the rights of man proclaimed in the French and American revolutions. Revolutionary groups in their midst add to those the collective rights to social and cultural programs that were central to the Russian revolution in 1917. Because these populations often live in the last remaining rainforests or in sites rich in unexploited natural resources, their rights to retain their habitations are threatened by lumber and oil predators. They are therefore likely to cast their demands in terms of global rights to peace, development, a healthy balanced ecology, and the right to share the common heritage of mankind. This is in accord with the Vienna declarations on human rights of 1993, which challenged the concept of rights phrased in terms of individuals. The new declaration replaces the civil and political rights as phrased by Western powers in terms of freedom of speech, assembly, and religion with communalistic aspirations.

Since the implementation of United Nations covenants on human rights and cultural autonomy has depended on the very nation-states that were often the major perpetrators of violations, they have rarely been implemented. Yet they provide a basis for outlawing "rogue" states in developing global arenas, especially by means of trade agreements, embargoes, weapons inspections, and other spaces where nations agree to disagree. This is precisely the arena in which transnational civil society is expanding as it counters the violence of nation-states delegitimized and down-sized in the context of neoliberalism. The new thrust in human-rights conventions, in declaring the rights of people to peace, seeks to transform the very basis of sovereignty. These conventions challenge the use of armed force against civilian populations, arbitrary arrests, torture, covert operations, and the denial of their own civil laws that has been taken for granted in the exercise of brute force to maintain elites in power.

It is ironic that, although recognition of the economic, social, and cultural rights of all members of the human family was posed as the foundation for international peace in the Universal Declaration of Human Rights, attempts to add to this list the "Right of Peoples to Peace" as constituting a fundamental obligation of each state have never been formalized (Forsythe 1992:4). Given the proclivity of nations to turn to militarism in the current historical conjuncture, the right to peace should move into top priority for transnational civil society – even if it never appears on the United Nations agenda. The potential of transnational civil society to effect social change is evident in their promotion of these international human-rights covenants and in the subsequent attempts of activists to ensure compliance in countries where these agreements have been ratified. The transnational human-rights networks established by transnational NGOs have also been instrumental in alerting members and a wider public to mobilizations organized in defense of their appeals.

## CONCLUSION

Indigenous people who have maintained a collective identity even within repressive states are becoming leaders in the spaces opened up by national and transnational civil society. The society of semi-autonomous multicultural entities that they are seeking to construct within a national federation of ethnic groups is based on resistance to 500 years of domination. It represents a kind of pluricultural and multi-centered society that is more adapted to the emerging global ecumene than are nation-states. Giddens (1990) argues that the quintessential feature of modernity is the disembedding of social relations from local contexts of interaction and their restructuring across indefinite spans of time–space. The corollary of this is the challenge to a system of morality that relies on community as the unique framework of actors related to specific sanctioning powers. The morality once enshrined in national institutions of the church and state must be replaced by a broader field in today's multicultural environment, where distinct religious and political allegiances prevail. Transnational NGOs that ascribe to human rights are restructuring a new, more flexible response that builds on the premises of heterogeneous religious and secular moral orders in their alliances with local civil society. As yet, NGOs lack the military sanctioning power of the nations they confront, but they are moving toward trade sanctions and banking credit as a means of achieving commitment to human-rights covenants. This is the challenge for the coming millennium.

## REFERENCES

Eber, Christine, (in press) *Buscando una nueva vida* (Searching for a New Life): Liberation Through Autonomy in San Pedro Chenalhó, 1970–1998. *Latin American Perspectives.*

Forsythe, David P. (1992) *Human Rights and Peace: International and National Dimensions.* Lincoln: University of Nebraska Press.

Giddens, Anthony (1990) *The Consequences of Modernity.* Stanford, CA: Stanford University Press.

Gledhill, John (1998) The Mexican Contribution to Restructuring U.S. Capitalism: NAFTA as an Instrument of Flexible Accumulation. *Critique of Anthropology* 18:279–296.

Gutiérrez, Margarita, and Nelly Paloma (1999) Autonomía con mirada de mujer. In *Mexico: Experiencias de autonomía indígena*, ed. Aracely Burguete Cal y Mayor, pp. 54–86. Copenhagen: Documento IWGIA No. 28.

Harvey, David (1989) *The Condition of Postmodernity: An Enquiry into the Origins of Social Change..* Oxford: Blackwell.

Kearney, Michael (1995) The Local and the Global: The Anthropology of Globalization and Transnationalism. *Annual Review of Anthropology* 24:547–565.

Klare, Michael T. (1988) The Interventionist Impulse: U.S. Military Doctrine for Low-Intensity Warfare. In *Low Intensity Warfare*, ed. Michael T. Klare and Peter Kornbluh, pp. 49–79. New York: Pantheon.

Nash, June (1997) The Fiesta of the Word: The Zapatista Uprising and Radical Democracy in Mexico. *American Anthropologist* 99:261–274.

SIPAZ (1998) Report on Las Abejas, volume 3, number 2, April.

## SUGGESTED FURTHER READING

Bonfil Batalla, Guillermo (1996 [1989]) *México profundo: Reclaiming a Civilization*, trans. Philip A. Dennis. Austin: University of Texas Press.

Centro de Derechos Humanos Fray Bartolome de Las Casas (1998) *Camino a la masacre. Informe especial sobre Chenalhó.* San Cristóbal de Las Casas: Centro de Derechos Humanos Fray Bartolome de Las Casas. Comunicación Popular Alternativa, Grupo de Trabajo.

Kovic, Christine (1997) Walking with One Heart: Human Relations and the Catholic Church Among the Maya of Highland Chiapas. Ph.D. dissertation, City University of New York.

Leyva Solano, Xochtitl (1995) Del común al leviatán: Síntesis de un proceso sociopolítico en el medio rural Mexicano. *América Indígena* 1–2:201–234.

Rojas, Rosa (1995) *Y las mujeres qué? Collección del Hecho al Hecho, tomo II.* Editorial La Correa Feminista, Centro de Investigación y Capacitación de la Mujer.

Warren, Kay (1993) Interpreting la Violencia in Guatemala: Shapes of Mayan Silence and Resistance. In *The Violence Within: Cultural and Political Opposition in Divided Nations*, ed. Kay Warren, pp. 25–86. Boulder, CO: Westview.

# CHAPTER 28 Transnationality

## *Nina Glick Schiller*

In 1986 we were three women, living on the margins of Manhattan and the academic world; at the time none of us had a faculty position and we lived in the Bronx, one of the outer boroughs of New York City. We always felt that it was this marginality, a mutually constituted positioning of gender, employment status, and geography, that helped us rethink outside of the dominant migration paradigms and begin to talk about transnationalism. But there were other reasons as well. We began our discussions at a moment when corporate capitalists were globally restructuring the processes of production and consumption. The processes of global interconnection and the study of transnational connection, restrained to some extent by World Wars I and II and the Cold War, were once again intensifying. Linda Basch and I, as Caribbeanists, were particularly well situated to think about the transnational connections. Globe-spanning connections, cultural syncretism, and cultural flows were in fact the substance of Caribbean history and society. Working with three Caribbean scholars, Rosina and Winston Wiltshire and Joyce Toney, Linda Basch had already begun to speak of transnational migration in a Caribbean context by the time the three of us sat together to discuss our work. Cristina was herself a transmigrant, her life stretched between the United States and Italy.

It soon became apparent that all three of us were observing immigrants who were living their lives simultaneously across national borders, incorporated into two or more nation-states. We understood that the academic discussions of assimilation and multiculturalism had no conceptual space to encompass migrants living in more than one society. Equally inadequate was the widely disseminated imagery of the US as a melting pot or a salad bowl, with new immigrants adding to the flavor of the homemade dish. A new paradigm for migration studies was needed, one that allowed researchers to explore simultaneous embeddedness. After some debate, we named the paradigm "transnationalism" and the persons who lived their lives across borders "transmigrants," and we did what academics do in such circumstances. We called a conference and managed to convince our friends, some more skeptical than others, to try out the new paradigm (Glick Schiller, Basch, and Szanton Blanc 1992).

In due time Linda, Cristina, and I learned, of course, that the term transnationalism was used by Ralph Bourne in an article in the *Atlantic* as early as 1916. Not only that. While we were hard at work at defining the terms of our new "discovery," on the west coast of the US anthropologists Michael Kearney and Roger Rouse were also beginning to speak about migrants who lived their lives across borders and had also called for a new scholarship of migration. Just a few years later, and independently of the work in US anthropology, Canadian sociologist Luin Goldring and US sociologist Peggy Levitt initiated ethnographic transnational studies in their discipline, while in France Mirajna Morokvaisc began to speak about transnational migration. The study of transnational migration was an idea whose time had come.

By the beginning of the twenty-first century transnational migration had become one component of a thriving field of transnational and global studies. This new field has the potential to make visible historical and political processes that have previously been obscured, and to contribute to social justice by participating in social movements sometimes collectively called "globalization from below." It may, on the other hand, create its own forms of obfuscation. I begin this paper by examining the barriers that initially blocked the emergence of transnational studies, and the ways in which the new paradigm facilitates the analysis of structures of power that legitimate social inequalities. The paper concludes by returning to this theme, cautioning that as transnational studies emerge as a new hegemonic concept, it may obstruct some types of analysis, including the analysis of imperialism.

In order to proceed, it is important to distinguish between the terms "global" and "transnational." When I speak about transnationalism or transnational processes I wish to emphasize the ongoing interconnection or flow of people, ideas, objects, and capital across the borders of nation-states, in contexts in which the state shapes but does not contain such linkages and movements. The exercise of political power by governments is within the scope of transnational studies. So too are specific national forms of "governmentality" that shape daily experience, the "everyday forms of state formation," cultural subtexts, and identity markers that constitute nation-state building (Joseph and Nugent 1994).

In contrast, the term "global" is best deployed for the world-system's phenomena that affect the planet, regardless of borders and local differences. Capitalism, for example, is now a global system of economic relations that has extended across the entire planet and has become the context and medium of human relationships, although with differential effects. The term "globalization" is a useful way to speak about periods of intensified integration of the world through capitalist systems of production, distribution, and communication.

## BARRIERS TO THE TRANSNATIONAL PARADIGM

Transnational studies reminds us that nation-states, as products of modernism, arose from and contributed to the global development of capitalism. Nation-states are always constructed within a range of activities that strive to control and regulate territory, discipline subjects, and socialize citizens, but these processes and activities are not necessarily located within a single national territory. Transnational studies draws attention to this fact, and in the process challenges: (1) a bounded and ahistorical concept of culture and society; (2) methodological nationalism, and; (3) migration studies that were mired in assimilationist or multicultural paradigms.

## Unbounding concepts of culture and society

The sanctity of borders and boundaries is recent both in human history and anthropological theory. Until World War II scholars used concepts of culture and society that were not confined to the borders of nation-states. They understood that migration has been the norm through human history, including the history of the modern state, and that ideas as well as objects could travel long distances and not be associated with a specific territory. Today, the British diffusionist school of anthropology, which read the entire history of cultures as one of migration, is often used as an illustration of theory gone awry, as well as an example of the manner in which European scholars tried every possible means of dismissing indigenous creativity all around the world. But diffusionists were aware that cultural flows and social relationships are not limited by political boundaries; there are long-standing connections between disparate regions and localities. These insights informed the founders of US anthropology. Transnational studies have now begun to recover and reinterpret the strengths of cultural diffusionist perspectives.

To do so, it has been important to set aside the organic, territorially embedded view of culture popularized by British functionalist and structural-functionalist anthropology. This scholarship failed to examine social and economic relationships that shaped the history and political economy of a particular locality. It overlooked the influence of colonialism and capitalism on the subject peoples. Beginning in the 1940s, US anthropologists adopted a similar mindset by studying "communities" as if they were discrete units subject only to local historical developments and divorced from larger social, political, and economic processes. The popularization of Clifford Geertz's influential work on culture as localized text continued this bounded approach to culture in anthropology, long after the demise of community studies and forms of functionalism. For Geertzian-influenced anthropology, culture is a discrete, stable, and historically specific local system of meanings.

Even when anthropology began to examine transnational processes, the legacy of this bounded theory of culture continued to impede historical analysis. Those anthropologists who work within the Geertzian tradition of cultures as discrete webs of signification spoke as if transnational processes were novel and transgressive, occurring in response to dramatic changes in communication technology and global capitalism. They framed the outcome of transnational processes as hybridity, which implicitly defined a previous stage of cultural production unblemished by diffusion. In the new "post-national moment" the borders and structures of nation-states would become increasingly meaningless.

Scholars who developed a transnational paradigm for the study of migration began with a very different approach to culture. Many of us deployed a broader and older Tylerian concept of culture that encompasses social relations, social structure, and trans-generationally transmitted patterns of action, belief, and language. We also utilized a body of theory, methodology, and data that was not place-bound. Especially important were the ethnographies of Southern Africa and the Copper Belt dating from the period between World Wars I and II, and the methodological approaches to complex societies and colonial relationships developed by Max Gluckman and the Manchester School.

The Manchester School researchers gave us a conceptual and methodological toolkit appropriate for the study of transnational processes. Because many of their studies were of the ongoing home ties of urban labor migrants, their observations of social relations extended across time and space. The development of ethnographies "as long stories of quarrels," as Adam Kuper put it in *Anthropologists and Anthropology: The British School 1922–1972*, provided anthropologists with strategies for studying the embodiment of dominant values and their contestation and reshaping within the processes of everyday life. Manchester School anthropologists approached the study of networks and social situations as a study of dynamic processes. They were adept at "taking a series of specific incidents affecting the same person or groups, through a period of time, and showing how these incidents, these cases, are related to the development and changes of social relations among these personae and groups" (Gluckman 1967:xv)

In fact, these scholars were taking important steps in documenting the effects of globalization, although they described it as an industrial urban social system or in terms of colonialism. Using these methods, scholars of the Manchester School were able to show that rather than becoming acculturated and "detribalized" within urban industrial settings, African workers kept their home ties. In fact, their remittances home often helped maintain the rural "traditional" society. They placed the continuation of rural life and the persistence of home ties in the context of colonial and industrial structures of unequal power drawn along lines of race.

Other anthropological studies of migration, while less engaged in relations of power, also pointed to the significance of the rural–urban connections of urban migrants, and also provided an intellectual and ethnographic foundation for transnational studies. Research in West Africa noted the continuation of hometown ties in voluntary associations. Anthropologists working in Latin American cities challenged the view that migration always swiftly led to acculturation by writing about "peasants in the city."

## Methodological barriers to envisioning transnational processes

Methodological nationalism has been a potent barrier to the study of transnational processes. Methodological nationalism is an intellectual orientation that assumes national borders to be the natural unit of study, equates society with the nation-state, and conflates national interests with the purposes of social science (Wimmer and Glick Schiller 2002). If we shed the assumptions of methodological nationalism, it is clear that nation-state building was from the beginning a trans-border process. The political economy and the ideology of the modern state and of national populations developed across the borders of states rather than within territorially fixed spaces. From the earliest development of the nation-state, in the Americas and Western Europe, political boundaries have never confined or delimited its economic, social, cultural, or political activities. But you have to think outside of the box of dominant national discourses to see the trans-border foundations of nation-states.

Modern states were formed within imperial projects through which distant lands were colonized or dominated. At first, persons in disparate territories saw themselves as creating home through "civilizing" barbaric landscapes and habitats. Benedict Anderson (1994) reminds us of this fact when he describes the experiences of a white woman kidnapped by Native Americans within the territory of the British 13 colonies. When this woman encountered the cultivated fields of the colonists, while being moved by her captors from one location to another, she saw those fields as part of England, differentiating herself and the cultivated spaces from the native people through her Englishness. England was a cross-border, transatlantic location for this eighteenth-century woman. In a related process, middle-class women in Birmingham, England, in the mid-nineteenth century came to see themselves as English in relationship to the building of a globe-encompassing British empire.

Scholars of colonialism and postcolonialism have demonstrated that concepts of the territorially based nation-state emerged within the context of empires. Partha Chatterjee's now classic work, *Nationalist Thought and the Colonial World*, deconstructs the claim that Third-World nationalist ideology is a derivative discourse, and places the Indian nation-state building project within worldwide debates about the meaning of modernity.

The legitimation of modern states through Enlightenment ideologies of popular sovereignty and republicanism developed within colonial regimes in which independent states were differentiated from colonies. In point of fact, the ideologies that first delineated concepts of sovereign peoples and equated nation, history, territory, and culture – the foundational concepts of modern nation-states – were produced in trans-border debates about the rights of man and the nature of peoplehood. The American, Haitian, and French intellectuals who popularized these ideas in the first states founded on these ideologies participated in political dialogues that were not confined to national territories. However, if you accept the prevailing paradigm that divides a state's affairs into internal, national matters and international affairs that have to do with state-to-state relations, the history of trans-border and transnational nation-state building becomes invisible.

The writing of national histories compounds this invisibility by confining the national narrative within the territorial boundaries of the state. This restricted view of national history became increasingly marked after World War I and continued until the end of the Cold War. While alternative histories developed during this period, including Immanuel Wallerstein's world-systems perspective, and Eric Wolf's historically informed anthropology, most historical writing about states viewed them as discrete entities. Relationships to other states were placed within a rubric of "international relations," and transnational processes (including the flow of ideas, people, goods, and capital) are minimized in these accounts. As Andreas Wimmer and I (2002:305) have argued, scholars were "deeply influenced by the methodological nationalist assumption that it is a particular nation that would provide the constant unit of observation through all historical transformations, the 'thing' whose change history was supposed to describe." As a result, although transnational processes are as old as modern nation-states, transnational and global studies only emerged at the end of the twentieth century, during a high point of globalization.

In the 1970s and early 1980s, large corporations and financial institutions, aided and abetted by national and local governments, began a massive restructuring of capitalism around the globe. During the same period anthropologists noted aspects of this transformation, studying the global assembly line, rural–urban migration, the international division of and feminization of labor, and the continuing and deepening dependency of peripheral states. However, neither anthropologists nor other social scientists developed a term or a theory to address the totality of the changes that link economic restructuring to global cultural processes. Even when they looked globally, researchers identified nationally and could not develop paradigms that took them beyond the interests of their own state. Divisions between the social sciences and the growing fragmentation of individual disciplines into separate fields of study, such as media, gender, migration, politics, economics, and identity, further impeded social scientists' ability to look beyond dominant paradigms.

## The specific case of migration studies and immigrant identities: assimilation, multiculturalism, and the return to assimilation.

A combination of methodological nationalism and bounded views of society and culture produced a particular kind of shortsightedness among scholars that excluded theory or methods to study transnational processes. Migration studies are a case in point. Scholars in both the United States and Europe looked at migration processes only through the political agendas of their own state and its particular migration policies. In the United States, until the 1960s and the turn to a more multiculturalist imagining of the national landscape, political leaders, historians, and social scientists expected immigrants to assimilate. The paradigm of assimilation was broadly disseminated beyond the borders of the US and had an impact on Latin American research on migration settlement. That is to say, there was a general expectation that migrants would and should abandon their own culture and identity and merge into or help forge the mainstream culture. This process was generally expected to take several generations and there might be ethnic communities formed along the way, but assimilation was the ultimate outcome and political goal.

Looking back now at earlier scholarship, especially studies produced before World War II, it is interesting to note that many scholars actually documented the transnational ties of European and Asian immigrants, their patterns of sending home remittances, their continuing family ties, and their political engagement with homeland politics. Writing in 1949, the sociologist Schermerhorn used the term "home country nationalism" in his classic work, *These Our People: Minorities in American Culture*, to refer to the transnational political activities of immigrants. In 1954, Nathan Glazer (1954:161) reported:

> in America, great numbers of German immigrants came only with the intention of fostering the development of the German nation-state in Europe ... the Irish, the second most important element in the earlier immigration, were also a nation before they were a state and, like the Germans, many came here with the intention of assisting the creation of an Irish state in Europe. On one occasion they did not hesitate to organize armies in America to attack Canada.

Many of these earlier researchers also understood that many immigrants left home with only very local or regional identities and dialects, and actually learned to identify with their ancestral land only after they had settled in the United States. However, the home-country nationalism and the transnational ties of immigrants were portrayed as short-lived because migration theory took assimilation to be an inevitable process.

In the postwar years in the US, even an acknowledgment of the home ties of migrants tended to disappear with the popularization of Oscar Handlin's highly influential work, *The Uprooted*, and his concept of immigrants as "uprooted," that is, without transnational ties. This approach prevailed, even though Handlin himself was aware of transnational connections and return migration.

The multiculturalist turn, first in the United States in the 1960s as cultural pluralism, and then in various forms of multiculturalism in Canada, Australia, the United Kingdom, and the United States, acknowledged that generations after a migration, cultural differences and identities remained among some sectors of the immigrant population. However, this acknowledgment did not lead to a theory of transnational connection in migration studies. Instead, methodological nationalism prevailed and cultural diversity became an alternative narrative for celebrating na-tional unity. Most recently, a significant group of sociologists in the United States has resurrected the term "assimilation," critiquing multicultural theory with evidence that most immigrants become well incorporated into US daily life. French public policy-makers, after only a brief flirtation with multiculturalism, have continued with the project of shaping a single national culture. French social scientists, while they may document circulatory migration and the cross-border trading patterns of migra-tion, have tended not to theorize transnational connections. Only in Germany, which until very recently contended it was not an immigration country and made the acquisition of citizenship difficult and lengthy, are the homeland ties of migrants visible in the social-science literature. However, with some significant exceptions, such ties are seen as barriers which impede the integration of foreigners into the German social fabric.

The dominant paradigms have not only obscured the continuing transnational connections of immigrants, but have also made it impossible to see that many migrants simultaneously become incorporated into a new land while keeping some kind of transnational connection. The failure until recently to attempt to theorize or operationalize the concept of simultaneous incorporation is an outcome of methodo-logical nationalism. It reflects the inability to observe and think beyond the borders of the nation-state.

## THE EMERGENCE OF TRANSNATIONAL STUDIES

We can use the enthusiastic reception of David Harvey's *The Conditions of Postmod-ernity: An Enquiry into the Conditions of Cultural Change*, published in 1989, as an indicator of the moment in which the paradigm changed and transnational processes once again became visible. Harvey, a geographer by training, stepped beyond discip-linary boundaries to link changing structures of capital accumulation, which he called flexible accumulation, with cultural transformations, including the development of new analytical paradigms such as postmodernism. Beginning in the 1980s and with increasing momentum and confidence throughout the 1990s, a transnational perspective developed in anthropology.

## Divisions and interconnections

As the interest in global connections and transnational processes flourished, scholarship went in several different directions, which have emerged as distinct areas of transnational studies: trans-cultural studies; diasporic studies; migration; and globalization. Trans-cultural studies focuses on "global cultural flows." With the growth of global communications, media, consumerism, and public cultures, these flows have rapidly and readily transcended borders. Anthropologists have been careful to insist that global flows should always be reinterpreted locally with a consequent creolization, hybridification, and indigenization rather than the homogenization of culture. However, many studies of global flows ignored "power relations, [and] the continued hegemony of the center over the margins. Everyone became equally 'different,' despite specific histories of oppressing and being oppressed" (Lavie and Swendenburg 1995:3).

Meanwhile, a field of diaspora studies began to emerge, spurred by developments in literature and cultural studies. Scholars in this field were concerned more with identity than place. They examined narratives of identity that are legitimated by myths of common origin and dispersal. Because their focus of interest was on populations who maintain trans-border connections on the basis of a shared sense of history, culture, and descent, the first wave of diaspora studies focused more on cultural representation than on political practice or the state. The state entered the debate as a giver of passports or a source of narratives of transnational culture more than as a homeland with its own politics enacted within a transnational sphere of practice.

In this same period, researchers also began to study migration as a transnational process in which migrants maintain and construct social, political, and economic relationships across borders. The term "transnational community" became widespread, especially in the work of sociologists. Alejandro Portes (1997:812) refers to transnational communities as "dense networks across political borders created by immigrants in their quest for economic advancement and social recognition." Other researchers used the term "transnational community" to refer to a specific locality in which a communal system of leadership and collective action extends across international borders. Anthropologists, building on the critique of community studies and the concepts of social "network" and "field" developed by Manchester School scholars, preferred the term "transnational circuit" or "transnational social field" (Glick Schiller, Basch, and Blanc Szanton 1992; Rouse 1991). I have defined "social field" as an unbounded terrain of multiple interlocking egocentric networks. "Network" is best applied to chains of social relationships that are egocentric and are mapped as stretching out from a single individual. "Social field" is a more encompassing term than "network," taking us to a societal level of analysis.

Meanwhile a field of globalization studies emerged. At first, globalization studies was primarily the domain of geographers and focused on the reconstitution of space and time within global cities. New flexible ways of transferring capital had moved it beyond the boundaries and controls of states so that global cities flourished, while their peripheries were stripped of services and infrastructure. As did the scholars in transnational studies, those who studied globalization emphasized the novelty of the current moment. Many researchers tended to see communications technology – computers, telephones, televisions, communication satellites, and other electronic innovations – as the motor of change. Suddenly we could all visually experience the same war, the same concert, or the same commercial and share the information age. The power of the new technology, combined with the insistence of postmodern theorists that the past was stable and the present fluid, led to a form of technological determinism. The impact of past technological leaps including the steamship and the telegraph, was dismissed or forgotten. In *Nations Unbound*, (Basch, Glick Schiller, and Szanton Blanc 1994:24) Linda, Cristina, and I critiqued this trend, arguing that "the presence of technological innovation...[does not explain] why immigrants invest so much time, energy, and resources in maintaining home ties...Rather it is the current moment of capitalism as a global mode of production that has necessitated the maintenance of family ties and political allegiances among persons spread across the globe."

Whether or not the new technology was seen as key, there was a tendency among the first wave of studies to see transnational processes as a phenomenon linked solely to the current moment of capitalism. The fact that the current period is marked by *both* a paradigm change and a restructuring of processes of capital accumulation was not made clear, and the two related but different phenomena were conflated. There was a widespread acceptance of the previous hegemonic anthropological paradigm as an actual description of social relations, as if people actually lived within fixed, bounded units of tribe, ethnic group, and state. The past contained homogeneous cultures while now we lived in a world of hybridity and complexity. Scholars continued the myth that the subject of anthropological scrutiny had been small isolated societies and only now had the world become our terrain.

A more historical turn, however, led by those in globalization studies, soon made it clear that while there are different ways to define and date globalization, people around the world have been affected by the same economic and cultural processes at least since the expansion of Europe. If we define globalization as the myriad of cultural, social, political, and economic processes that integrate the world into a single system of relationships and value, then it is clear that the period between about 1870 and World War I marked an intensive period of globalization. Contemporary globalization differs from previous processes of connection significantly in the ways in which capital is accumulated, the degree of the commoditization of everyday life around the world, and the rapidity of the movement of information and capital.

Currently scholars in all fields of transnational studies have turned their attention to a reexamination of state processes, noting that the current phase of globalization has been marked by the "hyper-presence" and "hyper-absence" of the state (Suárez-Orozco and Thomas in press). On the one hand, the state is absent to the extent that its regulatory mechanisms have been relaxed or abolished in the domain of financial markets, production, and the generation of information and communication. On the other hand, while during the previous stage of globalization passports were by and large abandoned, allowing for the free flow of labor, today in fortress Europe, the US, and among nations in Asia and Africa, borders are under surveillance, access to visas and work permits is restricted, sharp lines are drawn between citizens and denizens, and deportations are frequent. States maintain the role of identity containers, formulating categories of national identity through differentiating foreigners from those who can claim the right to belong. These identity processes become the lens through which globally disseminated media, music, and commodities are experienced and consumed. However, tensions exist between the intensity of global connection and the production of differences of wealth, gender, race, religion, and nationality.

## Differentiating among transnational social fields, cultural practices, actors, and migrants

As transnational studies has developed there continues to be confusion about the subject of study. The division between the study of migration and the study of cultural flows has contributed to this confusion. By distinguishing between transnational social fields and transnational processes of communication, we will be in a better position to advance research and theory. Transnational cultural processes may include but do not depend on direct people-to-people relationships and interaction. In reading a book, newspaper, or magazine, listening to a radio, watching a film or television, or surfing the internet one can obtain ideas, images, and information that cross borders. From the period in which political borders marked differentiated nation-states, people have lived beyond them through such means of communication. Sometimes the effect has been profound, contributing to various forms of transnational solidarities. The contemporary dissemination of the Bible and the Koran, and the growth of cross-border religious movements, is one such example. However, as this example makes obvious, while transnational cultural processes are increasingly communications that occur without direct relationships with other human beings, often people experience both kinds of cross-border connections. For example, since the fifteenth century Christian missionaries have been transnational actors who accompanied the dissemination of the written text, and who lived in transnational social fields which came to include the people they converted.

Transnational social fields include individuals who have never themselves crossed borders but who are linked through social relations to people in distant and perhaps disparate locations. The concept of transnational social field directs attention to the simultaneity of transmigrant connections to two or more states. It allows ethnographers to operationalize and investigate the ways in which transmigrants become part of the fabric of daily life in their home state or other states and participate in their forms of nation-state formation, while simultaneously becoming part of the workforce, contributing to neighborhood activities, serving as members of local and neighborhood organizations, and entering into politics in their new locality. Transnational social fields are not metaphoric references to altered experiences of space but rather are composed of observable social relationships and transactions. Multiple actors, with very different kinds of power and locations of power, interact across borders to create and sustain this field of relationships. As networks of interpersonal connections that stretch across borders, transnational social fields are people-to-people relationships through which information, resources, goods, services, and ideas are exchanged. Social fields form a network of networks that allows us to map the indirect connections between disparate individuals who do not know each other or even know of each other, but yet are shaped by and shape each other.

In order to study transnational networks, the social fields they constitute, and broader cultural processes that link disparate individuals, we must disentangle actual migrants from persons who rarely or ever travel and yet actually live within transnational social fields that connect them regularly to persons located within the borders of other states. While making this distinction, we miss much of the significance of transnational connections if we confine our study to persons who frequently cross borders, as some researchers have suggested. Today, as in the past, the vast majority of the world's people never move from their home locality, and large numbers of those who have migrated cannot or do not return to the place from which they originated. Nonetheless, through interpersonal relations and various forms of communication large numbers of people in both categories live connected to others across borders. To build transnational theory we must reexamine the growth of ideas and identities, the development of cultural patterns, and the forms of political action, both past and present, by means of which people maintain connections within transnational social fields.

Stepping outside assumptions about history shaped by methodological nationalism, we can see that the national identities of the United States, and states in Europe, the Middle East, and Asia, were forged within the context of debates and intellectual exchanges that spanned borders, many of which took place within social relations that composed transnational social fields. Leaders striving to build Japanese, Chinese, Korean, and Philippine national identities used concepts of race, blood, and nation that were globally disseminated by European colonialism. Meanwhile, poor and disempowered migrants, as well as migrant political leaders and intellectuals, played an important and as yet untheorized role in nation-state building in emigrant-sending countries such as Italy, Poland, Greece, Ireland, Hungary, Turkey, China, and Mexico.

## Distinguishing between identity and social practice

As we develop transnational theory, it is also essential that we distinguish between *transnational ways of belonging* and *transnational ways of being*. *Transnational ways of being* include various quotidian acts through which people live their lives across borders. Here we watch people who, as members of a transnational social field, may not themselves frequently or ever cross borders but who interact across borders. They are transmigrants in terms of their life ways. They raise children, sustain families, and act out family tensions and rivalries within transnational networks. They juggle, build, and break social relationships with sexual partners, spouses, friends, business connections, and acquaintances who live elsewhere. They engage in trade, investment, and the transfer of goods and information across borders. Their actions are shaped by gossip, rumor, and cultural production which are generated within their cross-border social relations. The fact that these ways of being take place in transnational social fields tells us nothing about how these activities will be represented, understood, and translated into an identity politics, that is, into a transnational way of belonging.

When we study *transnational ways of belonging*, we enter the realm of cultural representation, ideology, and identity through which people reach out to distant lands or persons through memory, nostalgia, and imagination. They may do this, whether or not they live within transnational social fields. Transnational belonging, while not rooted in social networks, is more than an assertion of origins, optional ethnicity, multiculturalism, or "roots," which are all forms of identity which place a person as a member of a single nation-state. Ways of belonging denote processes rather than fixed categories. Persons who adopt certain forms of cultural representation may find themselves as new participants in transnational social fields. Take, for example, a New Hampshire politician who speaks no Spanish and has never visited Latin America but whose father came from Mexico. When this man, identified by his Spanish name, became known as a representative of the "Hispanic community," he was acting on a US-based ethnicity. However, as he asserted his Mexican roots, on some level he began to define his identity, not only as a member of a Mexican-American ethnic group but also as someone connected to Mexico, although he had never been there. If, as a result of such an identity claim, he finds himself working with representatives of the Mexican government to facilitate their connection to the Mexican migrant population in New Hampshire, he will have become a participant in a transnational social field.

On the other hand, persons who live in transnational social fields may adopt, at various times, different forms of cultural representation. Transnational belonging is an emotional connection to persons who are elsewhere – a specific locality such as a village, a region, a specific religious formation, a social movement – or are geographically dispersed but bound together within a notion of shared history and destiny. It is these myriad types of transnational belonging that some scholars wish to term transnational communities, but more specific terms of reference seem warranted. Tölölayan (2001) employs the term "exilic nationalism" to focus attention on the nation-state building processes through which dispersed elites organize to establish or reestablish a political regime within a territorial homeland. He uses the term "diasporic transnationalism" for the ideology and practices of belonging deployed by dispersed populations as part of a distant homeland after the establishment of a nation-state. I have suggested the term "long-distance nationalism" for a set of identity claims and practices that link together persons who claim descent from an ancestral land (Glick Schiller 1999; Glick Schiller and Fouron 2002). These persons see themselves as acting together to constitute, strengthen, overthrow, or liberate a homeland.

In a path-breaking study of transnational Turkish media in Germany, Caglar (2002) demonstrated the complexities that underlie ideologies of belonging and transnational cultural politics. Setting aside simplistic notions of cultural hybridity or cosmopolitanism, she provided an ethnography of Turkish and Kurdish media in Berlin to illustrate the practice of cultural politics that were neither fully within nor totally independent of the agendas of multiple states. Such ethnography necessarily combines the study of transnational social fields with the production and reception of transnational cultural flows. The result is a series of interlinked transnational political projects that bridge the domains of religion, homeland identifications, and the identity politics of disparate European locations.

## Types of transnational actors

The growing interest in the state in transnational studies is a gratifying development for those of us who from the beginning have advocated this perspective. This new scholarship provides the foundations for the exploration of everyday forms of transnational nation-state formation as they are experienced within the transnational cultural practices of home, community, school, and religious congregations. The standard textbook version of the nation-state envisions a polity in which the people within a territory share a history, culture, and government, and envision themselves as a nation. Today, both political leaders and disparate others are reviving and updating earlier notions of the state in which membership in the polity extended across state borders to include persons living or even born elsewhere. The people whom the government of a state claims and/or the people who claim the government may live outside its national territory.

Emigrant-sending countries, including Mexico, Colombia, the Dominican Republic, the Philippines, Eritrea, India, Croatia, Ecuador, Brazil, Portugal, and Haiti, have recently created or revived laws and policies that reach out to their diasporas, seeing them as a source of remittances, development capital, and funding for campaigns to maintain national independence or expand the borders of the state. The "Croatian diaspora" was allocated 12 of the 92 seats in Parliament (Skrbiš 1999:184). The Colombian Constitution now provides for the representation of populations abroad, while Portugal, Mexico, and Haiti have ministries or councils for their "communities abroad." The Eritrean rebels organized a referendum for independence which included the diaspora, and since independence have collected a voluntary tax of 2 percent from those living abroad (Ali-Ali, Black, and Koser 2001). Increasingly, emigrant-sending states see their populations settled in the United States as political lobbies that can defend the homeland. States as different as Ireland, Mexico, France, and China recognize various forms of dual nationality. States in all regions of the world now recognize dual nationality so that emigrants can carry two passports or dual citizenship, which extends voting to emigrants who have become citizens of other countries. Nonetheless, both emigrants and sending states often portray the connections of emigrants and their children to the homeland as blood ties, rather than a formal legal status, revitalizing notions of biological belonging. Such notions, which are the basis of racial categorization and hierarchies of essential difference that were popularized at the beginning of the twentieth century, are with us again.

In general, it is the political leaders of present or past emigrant-sending states that have recently worked to reconstitute their nations as transnational nation-states and to encourage long-distance nationalism among their emigrants, but there are significant differences in the degree to which and the ways in which migrants have responded to these state projects. In addition, political leaders of states that have had their borders reshaped by war are claiming populations beyond their borders. For example, the logic of blood ties that stretch across borders has been articulated by the Hungarian state, which has extended rights to "ethnic Hungarians" settled in neighboring states (Stewart 2002). The same kinds of symbols of blood ties and common history used by an emigrant-sending state such as Haiti to maintain the loyalty of remittance-sending emigrants and their descendants can be used for expansionist aims by states that wish to claim territories now held by neighboring governments. Because nationalist symbols are polyvocal, carrying multiple simultaneous contradictory messages, they can be used transnationally for disparate political agendas.

It is important to note that at the present historical conjuncture disparate situations seem to stimulate long-distance nationalism. We are seeing the flourishing of a politics in which ancestral identities are made central by diverse sets of actors, including emigrants, political refugees, homeland governments, and intellectuals. One can identify very different sets of actors with different or opposing sets of interests, who currently deploy a variant of long-distance nationalism.

Politicized transmigrants and homeland political leaders and officials are only two variants in a long list of types of transnational actors, if we define that term as persons who maintain ongoing connections across borders. Disparate sets of actors, who on a daily basis may engage in transnational relations and connections without engaging in culture representation or political activities, may in certain moments be drawn into transnational political activities to influence public policies. The list includes migrants and refugees and their descendants who maintain familial, economic, religious, or social forms of home ties, members of transnational organizations ranging from non-governmental development organizations to various types of religious missionaries and activities, and the employees of businesses, corporations, and organizations who maintain transnational connections. A significant category of transnational actors are those who maintain illegal and hugely profitable businesses in trafficking drugs, sex workers, and arms. Their control of considerable amounts of capital makes these transnational businesses potent, although often unmarked, participants in political affairs.

## TRANSNATIONAL THEORY: THE CURRENT STATE OF THE ART

The exhilaration of new insights that comes from setting aside old paradigms continues to mark transnational studies. Here I focus on the second wave of scholarship that brings together the study of transnational migration and transnational cultural processes. I note three important and interrelated developments, each of which is being enriched by ethnographic interventions: (1) the critique of the concept of transnational community and the growing interest in the study of transnational social fields and their shaping by transnational cultural processes; (2) the increased efforts to study forms of simultaneous incorporation of migrants and their descendants; and (3) the study of cross-border social citizenship.

One cannot assume community or even shared identity when people participate together in a transnational network. Networks that stretch across borders may include actors with different class, gender, and power positions and conflicting politics. Many of the rich array of studies sponsored by the Oxford University Transnational Communities Project between 2000 and 2002 called into question the utility of the term. These studies distinguished between patterns of connections on the ground and the conditions under which ideologies of connection and community emerge, clarifying the distinction between *ways of being* and *ways of belonging*. They demonstrated that any social or cultural capital shared within kin networks or broader ethnic networks cannot be assumed to constitute a community of interest able to generate access to economic capital. As the recent comparative research of Edmund Gomez and Gregor Benton demonstrates, transnational family networks may provide resources to migrate and settle, but business networks are often built on cross-ethnic rather than inter-ethnic bases. The degree to which commonalities of identity exist and can be used to generate material support must be investigated. Ethnic or national identifiers such as "Chinese" are not descriptors of persons who necessarily share either a community of interest or connection.

Increasingly, researchers have put aside the rubric of transnational community and have explored the construction, maintenance, and meaning of transnational kinship. Studies of transnational kinship document that familial networks that stretch across borders are marked by gendered differences in power and internal rankings of status and class. There is the potential for kin networks to be used for exploitation, a process of transnational class differentiation in which the more prosperous extract labor from persons defined as kin. Even kin networks maintained between people who send remittances and those who live on them can be fraught with tension. Persons who live in the homeland live not only in a transnational field of social relations but within a domain of media and advertising. These portray life in the centers of capitalist power as one of luxury and opportunity for all. Increasingly, studies of transnational migrant connections must examine the way in which they are shaped by the flow of ideas and goods that fashion dreams, desires, and discontents for both migrants and those who are "left behind."

As it deconstructs transnational community and highlights contradictions and disparities within transnational social fields, the new research leads us to study and theorize the transnational intersections between specific kin, local, and national institutions. For example, we are now at the point when we can conceptualize and theorize the intersections of family networks that stretch between a village in the Dominican Republic and the United States, village-based institutions that extend between the US and the Dominican Republic, and the efforts of the Dominican government and various political parties to develop transnational constituencies (Grahm 2002). We can document the processes through which *ways of being* and *ways of belonging* become fused and the new tensions and contradictions that arise from such fusion.

Until recently, the excitement generated by the new paradigm of transnational studies, combined with the continuing blinders of methodological nationalism, led many researchers to neglect the study of the simultaneous incorporation of immigrants into multiple states, despite the fact that it is in some ways the most obvious and observable of social processes. People can readily be observed participating in different sets of activities as well as identities, some local, some national, and some transnational. And yet, *simultaneity* is just now beginning to be systematically studied and theorized. It contradicts established notions of society and the nation-state and seems threatening to the need of governments to ensure the loyalty of their citizens. Researchers are beginning to document that it is migrants who have become citizens and have stable bases in the US or Europe who participate most frequently in transnational politics that connect them to a homeland. By maintaining transnational networks and identifying with their homeland, migrants are able to maintain their personal self-esteem despite experiencing a loss of social standing as they incorporate in a new land.

Often the same actors engage in homeland, new land, and international politics. Kurdish and Turkish migrants settled in Germany, the Netherlands, Denmark, and the UK become active participants in the political structures of sending states, receiving states, and transnational federations of migrants (Østergaard-Nielsen 2002). In many cases the same political organizations may have dual agendas, addressing political issues in their host country, while they engage simultaneously in homeland politics. Activists create forms of struggle, religious and cultural identities, ideas about rights, and expectations about the state that transgress the established notions in both states and become a potent force for change. For example, Kurdish immigrants who seek cultural and religious recognition in Europe also send messages to Turkey, Syria, and Iraq, where their rights and cultural distinctiveness have been suppressed.

Research on simultaneity challenges strongly held ideas about immigrant incorporation. It sets aside the argument, which has become common sense in Europe, that differing "political opportunity structures of particular countries" shape the degree to which migrants become integrated into the political life of the receiving society or maintain transnational connections. The concept of *simultaneity* also challenges established notions of society, opening up new ways of understanding the structuring of social relationships, including trans-border citizenship.

In the initial development of transnational studies, migrants were sometimes portrayed as forging a new type of citizen, freed from the constraints of individual regimes. The second wave of transnational studies continues the discussion of citizenship, but this time within an analysis of the continuing viability of states whose legal systems limit movements across borders and extend or restrict legal rights. *Trans-border citizens* are people who live their lives across the borders of two or more nation-states, participating in the daily life and political practices and debates of these various states. As with all other citizens, they claim rights and privileges from governments, but trans-border citizens claim a relationship to more than one government. The fact that within the past decade an impressive number of states have adopted some form of dual citizenship or dual nationality is an important foundation of the development of cross-border citizenship. But an understanding of the development of trans-border citizenship takes us beyond legal citizenship into the subject of governmentality and social citizenship, while not abandoning an appreciation of the role of the state to restrict or eliminate rights.

In many states, migrants who have legal residence but not citizenship are given access to a range of rights, including access to state services, and many even participate in some form of local elections. Such persons are *social citizens* who comprise a population which is not accorded the same political role in the state as citizens, but which experiences the governmentality of the state in its positive form. Persons who are accorded rights from the state in which they reside often respond by acting as if they belong to the state that has accorded them rights. They organize to protect those rights, counter discrimination, or to make further claims to rights, services, and opportunities from the state. A considerable number of social citizens become simultaneously incorporated in more than one state, making such claims in several locations simultaneously.

Because trans-border citizens participate in the political processes and political cultures of more than one state, they may draw on concepts of the state and the ideas of civil and political rights of more than one polity. In so doing, they contribute to the development of the political processes and ideologies of more than one state and the lives of people within them. In the Haitian case, for example, many poor people became a politically engaged trans-border citizenry, with political repercussions in both the United States and Haiti. The Haitian grass-roots movement was a product of local and transnational forces. From the 1950s, when large-scale Haitian migration to the United States began, to the 1990s, myriads of Haitians have lived within transnational social fields that connect family and friends abroad to those still living in Haiti. Within these social fields, people participated in and learned from transnational social movements, including liberation theology, the international women's movement, the US civil rights movement, immigrants' rights organizations, and community development agencies, as well as from UN discourses on rights. The movement in Haiti was a nationalist movement that demanded political empower-ment for the poor, social justice, solidarity with oppressed peoples around the world, and the liberation of women. In the United States this grass-roots movement has taken up the issue of racial profiling and the murder of black people by the police.

To speak of a *trans-border citizenry* is not to assume that these citizens speak with a single political voice. While such a citizenry is united by a shared identity, as with any other citizenry, a trans-border citizenry will have political divisions based on differ-ences in political party or ideology. In the Haitian case, political repression and assassination, competition for power in Haiti, and continuing intervention in Haitian affairs by the United States and international banking interests, has taken its toll.

Using a concept of trans-border citizenship that draws on notions of social citizen-ship, we can more fully comprehend the behavior of migrants, whether immigrants or refugees, who participate politically in states and make claims upon more than one state as trans-border citizens, even when they are not living within the territory of a state or are not legal citizens of a state. But this use of the term ''citizen'' suffers from the same drawbacks as all concepts of social citizenship. Whatever their claims to membership, people who are substantive but not legal citizens face legal restrictions, lack legal protections, and while their lives may be lived in a transnational space, they have limited access to part of that space when they seek to flee repression or political chaos. The actions of the US government to jail and forcibly deport boatloads of Haitians who fled the collapse of the grass-roots movement in Haiti to seek safety in the United States reminds *us* of the brutal fact of uneven political power within transnational terrains.

## THINKING BEYOND TRANSNATIONAL PROCESSES

While transnational studies has opened new ways of understanding cultural processes and representations, the location and nature of nation-state building, and migrant social practices, transnational research can generate its own blind spots. A focus on the various ways in which nation-state building intersects with transnational processes may distract us from the movements that respond to growing economic disparities and deprivations experienced by most people in the world. Discussion of the balan-cing acts that migrants stage through simultaneous incorporation can deter us from examining the tremendous and growing imbalance between concentrations of wealth and poverty, which make migration strategies and transnational families a necessity. We also may not see the degree to which migrant strategies are being undercut by worldwide economic collapse. Long-distance nationalism and the political agendas, dreams, and aspirations that such nationalist movements sometimes contain can contribute to movements toward globalization from below. In these movements, people are connected through the shared goals of just and more egalitarian societies. However, if we become too entrenched in the way transnational studies frames its problems, we may not be able to make the necessary connections between the transnational processes we are documenting and more global forces. Restrained by our theory, our scholarship will be limited in its contributions.

Movements for social justice need to be built with an understanding of the transnational social fields within which various actors struggle over power, and the images and ideas through which power is legitimated or contested. Particularly missing in the literature on social movements is a consideration of the complex role of migrants and their long-distance nationalism. Migrants' long-distance nationalism, transnational fundamentalist religious movements, and the progressive movements that make up the struggle for globalization from below – all, in their different ways, represent the aspirations of billions of people for a life in which there is respect, dignity, and equality. Transnational studies must not lose sight of the broader global picture in its concentration on the dynamics of specific transnational processes.

Transnational processes are linked to more global phenomena but are not identical to them. It is important to confront the current moment of capitalism and understand what we see and what we miss if we concentrate on the nation-state and its transnational processes. Frequently the literature of transnational studies fails to discuss the contemporary hierarchy of global military and economic power in which the United States dominates political processes throughout the world. Researchers take no notice of the restructuring of states to serve as handmaidens of global corporations and financial interests. Their discourse of "the state" neglects the vast variations among states. Yet variations in states lead to very different futures for populations of poor and rich states, in a world dominated by those who control the accumulation and flow of capital. States that continue to control an impressive military capacity and states that serve as a base of transnational capital differ from most emigrant-sending states.

I suggest that to understand transnational processes and contemporary globalization, we need to revive and revitalize older notions of imperialism. Scholarship that can strengthen transnational studies by placing them within an analysis of global structures of power is emerging in contemporary debates about the past and future of the reemergence of imperialism. This is not the Hardt and Negri vision that heralds an almost mystical emergence of "empire" in a description that is more celebration of power than an analysis of the new forms in which the US as a single power with vast military might is dominating the world.

We must think beyond transnational studies to examine the reconfiguration of power in the world structured by a neoliberal agenda backed by the US military. In this emerging world, few states have a domain of political action that is not directed toward implementing the goals of US power. Transnational studies cannot ignore the tendency in both Europe and the United States to create structures of decision-making which express corporate interests and which lie outside the reach of democratic processes. Nor can we ignore indications that the corporate interests that hold the largest degree of power are the ones linked to the US military. Without continually assessing the global dynamics of capitalism, and the contention between the few states who serve as central base areas for capital and corporate wealth, we miss the dynamics that underlie both the emergence of the transnational paradigm and the movements toward globalization from below. As the US-led war against terror emerges as the new Cold War, it is clear that the new enemy in this war is movements from below, that only the rich and powerful are granted the right to mobility and to networks that span borders. We can respond by remembering that we are participants as well as observers, and that we ourselves live in transnational social fields that connect scholars to people struggling for a more democratic and just future.

## REFERENCES

Ali-Ali, Nadje, Richard Black, and Khalid Koser (2001) The Limits to "Transnationalism:" Bosnian and Eritrean Refugees in Europe as Emerging Transnational Communities. *Ethnic and Racial Studies* 24:601–618.

Anderson, Benedict (1994) Exodus. *Critical Inquiry* 20:314–327.

Basch, Linda, Nina Glick Schiller, and Cristina Szanton Blanc (1994) *Nations Unbound: Transnational Projects, Postcolonial Predicaments, and Deterritorialized Nation-States*. Amsterdam: Gordon and Breach.

Caglar, Ayse (2002) Mediascapes, Advertisement Industries and Cosmopolitan Transformations: Turkish Immigrants in Europe. Electronic document. http://www2.rz.huberlin.de/amerika/projects/newurbanism/nu_pt_caglar_a.html.

Glazer, Nathan (1954) Ethnic Groups in America. From National Culture to Ideology. In *Freedom and Control in Modern Society*, ed. M. Berger, T. Abel, and C. Page, pp. 158–174. New York: Van Nostrand.

Glick Schiller, Nina (1999) Transmigrants and Nation-States: Something Old and Something New in the U.S. Immigrant Experience. In *The Handbook of International Migration: The American Experience*, ed. C. Hirshman, P. Kasinitz, and J. DeWind,. pp. 94–119. New York: Russell Sage.

Glick Schiller, Nina, Linda Basch, and Cristina Blanc Szanton, eds. (1992) *Towards a Transnational Perspective on Migration: Race, Class, Ethnicity, and Nationalism Reconsidered*. New York: New York Academy of Science.

Glick Schiller, Nina, and Georges Fouron (2002) *Georges Woke Up Laughing: Long Distance Nationalism and the Search for Home*. Durham, NC: Duke University Press.

Gluckman, Max (1967) Introduction. In *The Craft of Social Anthropology*, ed. A. L. Epstein, pp. xi–xx. London: Tavistock.

Grahm, Pamela (2002) Political Incorporation and Re-Incorporation: Simultaneity in the Dominican Migrant Experience. In *Transnational Communities and the Political Economy of New York in the 1990s*, ed. H. Cordero-Guzman, R. Grosfoguel, and R. Smith, pp. 87–108. Philadelphia: Temple University Press.

Joseph, Gilbert, and Daniel Nugent, eds. (1994) *Everyday Forms of State Formation: Revolution and the Negotiation of Rule in Modern Mexico*. Durham, NC: Duke University Press.

Lavie, Smadar, and Ted Swedenburg, eds. (1995) Introduction. *In Displacement, Diaspora, and Geographies of Identity*. Durham, NC: Duke University Press.

Østergaard-Nielsen, Eva (2002) Transnational Political Practices and the Receiving State: Turks and Kurds in Germany and the Netherlands. *Global Networks* 1:261–282.

Portes, Alejandro (1997) Immigration Theory for a New Century: Some Problems and Opportunities. *International Migration Review* 31:799–825.

Rouse, Roger (1991) Mexican Migration and the Social Space of Postmodernism. *Diaspora* 1:8–23.

Skrbiš, Zlatko (1999) *Long Distance Nationalism: Diasporas, Homelands, and Identities*. Aldershot: Ashgate.

Stewart, Michael (2002) The Hungarian Status Law: A New European Form of Transnational Politics? Paper presented at the Transnational Communities Conference, Oxford, England.

Suárez-Orozco, Marcelo, and Victor Thomas (in press) Right moves? Immigration, Globalization, Utopia and Dystopia. In *Anthropology and Contemporary Immigration*, ed. N. Foner. Sante Fe, NM: School of American Research.

Tölölayan, Khachig (2001) Transnational Communities. Electronic document. http://www.transcomm.ox.ac.uk/working_papers.htm

Wimmer, Andreas, and Nina Glick Schiller (2002) Methodological Nationalism and Beyond: Nation-State Building, Migration, and the Social Sciences. *Global Networks* 2:301–334.

## SUGGESTED FURTHER READING

Appadurai, Arjun (1990) Disjuncture and Difference in the Global Cultural Economy. *Public Culture* 2:1–24.

Chatterjee, Partha (1986) *Nationalist Thought and the Colonial World: A Derivative Discourse*. London: Zed Books.

Fuglerud, Øivind (1999) *Life on the Outside: The Tamil Diaspora and Long Distance Nationalism*. London: Pluto.

Goldring, Luin (1998) The Power of Status in Transnational Social Fields. In *Transnationalism From Below*, ed. M. P. Smith and L. Guarnizo, pp. 165–195. New Brunswick, NJ: Transaction Publishers.

Handlin, Oscar (1973 [1954]) *The Uprooted*. Boston: Little Brown.

Harvey, David (1989) *The Condition of Postmodernity: An Enquiry into the Conditions of Cultural Change*. Oxford: Blackwell.

Kuper, Adam (1975) *Anthropologists and Anthropology: The British School 1922–1972*. Harmondsworth: Penguin.

Lessinger, Johanna (1995) *From the Ganges to the Hudson: Indian Immigrants in New York City*. Boston: Allyn and Bacon.

Levitt, Peggy (2001) *The Transnational Villagers*. Berkeley: University of California Press.

Ong, Aihwa (1999) *Flexible Citizenship: The Cultural Logic of Transnationality*. Durham, NC: Duke University Press.

Pessar, Patricia (1995) *A Visa for a Dream*. Boston: Allyn and Bacon.

Schermerhorn, Richard A. (1949) *These Our People: Minorities in American Culture*. Boston: D.C. Heath.

Wallerstein, Immanuel (1979) *The Capitalist World Economy*. Cambridge: Cambridge University Press.

Wolf, Eric R. (1982) *Europe and the People Without History*. Berkeley: University of California Press.

# Index